The History of the Congregation of the Mission in China, 1699-1950

The History of the Congregation of the Mission in China, 1699-1950

by

Octave Ferreux, C.M.

Translated by
Hippolyte Henk De Cuijper, C.M.

Edited by
Hugh O'Donnell, C.M.,
John E. Rybolt, C.M.,
Alan Richard Sweeten, Ph.D.

New City Press
Hyde Park, New York

Published in the United States by New City Press
202 Comforter Blvd., Hyde Park, NY 12538
www.newcitypress.com
©2022 by the Congregation of the Mission, Western Province

Translated by Hippolyte Henk De Cuijper, C.M. from the original French edition
Histoire de la Congrégation de la Mission en Chine – (1699-1950), published in
Paris in 1963 by the Congregation of the Mission, in *Annales de la Congrégation de la
Mission (Lazaristes) et de la Compagnie des Filles de la Charité*, 127 (1963): 3–530.
[Available online: https://via.library.depaul.edu/annales/123/]

Cover art: the original, by an anonymous artist, and undated, is in the General Curia
of the Congregation of the Mission, Rome, Italy.

Library of Congress Cataloging Control Number: 2022939153

ISBN: 978-1-56548-545-7 (paperback)
ISBN: 978-1-56548-546-4 (ebook)

Printed in the United States of America

Contents

Part One
Before the Arrival of Vincentians in China

Part Two
Vincentians in China

Fourth Period (1900–1950)
From Boxers to Communists

Appendices

Editorial Acknowledgments

The Congregation of the Mission in the United States is celebrating the one hundredth anniversary of participating in the China Mission. The Eastern Province was first to respond to the invitation of the superior general to send missionaries to Ganzhou, Jiangxi, in 1921. The Western Province committed itself to the China Mission the following year and sent missionaries to northern Jiangxi in early 1923. Daughters of Charity were part of that missioning in both provinces.

Celebrating our centennial has given us an occasion to publish *The History of the Congregation of the Mission in China, 1699-1950*, by Octave Ferreux, C.M., himself a missionary in China from France. Up until now this wonderful account has been available only in the original French and in a Chinese translation.

When he with all the other missionaries left China in the early 1950s, Ferreux took up researching and writing our history. It is a fascinating history describing the joys and sufferings, the devotion and sacrifices, the successes and failures of evangelization in the face of good will and adversity.

I was a teenager in St. Vincent's Parish in Chicago when I got to know some of the returning missionaries after the People's Republic of China was established. Even as a kid, I saw that they had left their hearts in China. The China Mission had for a very long time seized the imagination of the members of the Congregation of the Mission and, I want to affirm equally, of the Daughters of Charity, so it was a great joy for me to be missioned to the Chinese Province in 1993. My twenty-five years in Taiwan and China were an extraordinary blessing. I am happy to be a member of the team that has been given the responsibility of bringing out this English translation of Ferreux's history.

The Chinese Province, and the Western and Eastern Provinces of the Congregation of the Mission are collaborating in publishing this English edition. The provinces together have assumed responsibility for its publication and distribution, because they see telling the story as part of the mission.

Father Henk De Cuijper, after thirty-five years in Zaire (Congo), came to join the China Mission in 1997. He spent the largest part of his time in China and teaching languages was his mission there. To that he joined translating missionary history in China. In the process he translated

Ferreux's history some years ago. Efforts to edit and publish it, though serious, were not successful. Now the time has come with the support of the provinces and the occasion of the centenary to publish Ferreux. Maybe it is providential in the sense that the present climate invites us to remember the mutual love that characterized the China Mission.

In crediting Father Henk for his yeoman's work, it is equally necessary to acknowledge the sustained support Father Kusno Bintoro, former provincial of the Chinese Province, gave to this project as well as Father Aloysius Budianto, who has for many years been developing historical resources on the China Mission. He has constantly supported Father De Cuijper in his translation work. Father Pawel Wierzbicki also devoted much time and energy to advancing the translation and publication of Ferreux, which is soon to see the light of day.

In this final phase, Father John Rybolt gave new life to the project. He did the final editing of the text. His years of writing and publishing on St. Vincent and the Vincentian community has been invaluable. Alan Sweeten, whose many years writing on the Church in China, especially on the Vincentian Mission in China, joined the editorial team and contributed a level of professionalism and attention to details that give a new clarity to our history.

I thank New City Press for welcoming our project. It has become a tradition, dating from *The American Vincentians* of 1988. New City Press published the fourteen volume edition of Saint Vincent's *Correspondence, Conferences and Documents* and recently the multi-volume *Vincentians: A General History of the Congregation of the Mission* by John Rybolt. We thank Gary Brandl and his excellent team for guiding us through the publication process. We deeply appreciate their prompt and empathetic style of communication and their engaged commitment from beginning to end.

I finish also by thanking Fathers Tomaž Mavrič, the superior general, Dandy Labitag, the provincial of the Chinese Province, Patrick McDevitt, provincial of the Western Province and Stephen Grozio, provincial of the Eastern Province, for their decisive commitment to telling the story of the Vincentians in the China Mission.

Hugh F. O'Donnell, C.M.
Chicago, Illinois
July 2022

Editorial Foreword

Chapter numbers: The author divided his work into two parts. The first is the period before the arrival of the Vincentians in China (the Introduction), divided into six chapters. The second part, the majority of the volume, is divided into four periods, but the enumeration of the chapters begins again, running from 1 to 28. To avoid the ambiguity in this dual enumeration, the Introduction has retained the Roman numerals of the original (I-VI), while the rest of the volume uses Arabic numerals.

Chapter titles and headings: The author titled only some of his chapters. Revised titles and sub-headings have been added for ease in reading.

Corrections: Other variants and corrections have been made, generally enclosed in square brackets. Longer comments have been included in the footnotes identifying the source, if available, followed by an editor's initials.

"Ferreux's notes": The author's own notes, in the Archives of the Mission, Paris, correct or update his printed text. These have been included in footnotes. In addition, a Chinese translation of the text: Charles Wu Zongwen, C.M., (1907-1991), *Qianshihui zai Hua chuanjiao shi* (Taipei, 1977), has been consulted for Chinese characters and in cases of questions or variants.

Footnotes: These are numbered in the original work by starting each new chapter with footnote 1; here they are numbered consecutively throughout. All are by Ferreux unless noted otherwise.

Glossary: A glossary of some of the more important terms in this history (personal and place names, religious communities) with their equivalents in Chinese characters inserted by Father Budianto, has been added at the end of the volume, as an aid to Chinese readers.

Imperial names: An emperor of China had several names, including his personal name, his dynastic title (or temple name), and his regnal title (or period name). The imperial names in this text are those the author used, despite the possible confusion of titles or modern standards. The Reign periods given sometimes vary slightly from those used in current scholarly works.[1]

---

1. Index: the editors have followed the practice of Ferreux in keeping his brief introductions to every chapter and not providing an index. This text, set in italics, will help the reader to gain an insight into each section of the book. The main personal and place names occurring in the text appear in each introduction.

Lebbe, Vincent: To balance some of the material presented in chapters 21 and 27, the editors have added at the end of this work as Appendix 5, an article, reprinted with permission: Jean-Paul Wiest, "Vincent Lebbe: The Thunder that Sings in the Distance," in *Western Tides Coming Ashore in a Changing World. Christianity and China's Passage into Modernity*, eds. Timothy M. Wong, Paul W. Cheung, Louis C. Chan, pp. 699–720 (Hong Kong: Alliance Bible Seminary, 2015).

Personal names: Since the French practice is to use the French forms of personal names (Pierre for Peter, Pedro, etc.), the French forms have been retained for the most part in view of the author's inconsistent use of Western names. For dual French names (e.g., Jean-Pierre), the editors have also followed Ferreux's choices in using one or other name. For the names of Chinese priests, the author used a French baptismal name followed by a family name. Some pinyin names for Chinese Vincentians have been added on the basis of Joseph van den Brandt, C.M., *Les Lazaristes en Chine: 1697–1935, notes biographiques* (Pei-p'ing, 1936.)

Place names: For non-Chinese place names, current English names have been preferred. For Chinese place names, most appear in their pinyin form. In some cases, the French names in the original text also appear.

Romanization: The system used here for Chinese names, for persons and places, does not follow the original author's usage of a French romanization form; instead, the names follow the modern pinyin used in the People's Republic of China. There are some exceptions, such as Peking for Beijing, Chala for Zhalan, etc.

Sub-heads: the original publication used these inconsistently, but improvements have been made to help the reader to navigate the text.

Vocabulary choices: The editors have found no easy parallel of the modern term "pagan," (French: *paien*) which Ferreux uses to describe followers of Daoism, Buddhism, or Confucianism. For this reason, we have chosen to keep that term, despite its difficulties.

The editors apologize for any errors of inconsistencies that remain in the text.

Special Terms and Acronymns

Abbreviations for the missionary societies responsible for the various Missions:

C.I.C.M.	Congregation of the Immaculate Heart of Mary, Scheutists
C.M.	Congregation of the Mission, Vincentians
C.M.F.	Congregation of Missionaries, Claretians
C.P.	Congregation of the Passion, Passionists
C.S.S.	Congregation of the Sacred Stigmata, Stigmatines
D.C.	Daughters of Charity of St. Vincent de Paul
M.E.P.	Society of the Foreign Missions of Paris
O.F.M.	Order of Frairs Minor, Franciscans
O.P.	Order of Preachers, Dominicans
O.S.A.	Order of St. Augustine, Augustinians
P.I.M.E.	Pontifical Institute of Foreign Missions (Milan)
S.A.M.	Société des Auxiliaires des Missions
S.F.M.	Scarboro Foreign Mission Society
S.J.	Society of Jesus, Jesuits
S.S.C.M.E.	Missionary Society of St. Columban, Columbans
S.V.D.	Society of the Divine Word (Steyl)

The other societies are listed using their complete names.

P.A.	Apostolic Prefecture
V.A.	Apostolic Vicariate

Maps and Tables

Maps

Tables

About Octave Ferreux (1875–1963)

China was Father Octave Ferreux's passion, and writing *The History of the Congregation of the Mission in China, 1699-1950,* his crowning achievement. He spent forty-nine years in his beloved China, which he served faithfully as an apostle of the Good News. He would have continued in China to the end of his days had he not been expelled in 1951 along with many other missionaries. Nevertheless, his love and memories of China burned steadily in his heart until his death in Paris in 1963.

Missionary work in China particularly the Vincentian mission always was his chief interest. He wrote his account both for his benefit as well as for a wider public. He wished to see it published. Because it was not only a tribute to all the Vincentian missionaries, but also an honest summary and full of interesting details, it was decided to make it available to the general public after Ferreux's death.

Several publications had already been devoted to China, for instance, the *Mémoires de la Congrégation de la Mission en Chine* by Gabriel Perboyre (d. 1880) either in five volumes, published in 1865–66, or in the edited three volume edition of 1911–12, as well as several other studies, mentioned and analyzed in *Bibliotheca Missionum* by [Robert] Streit and [Johannes] Rommerskirchen [et al.] (1960), 14:62–171.

The present work by Ferreux nevertheless presents a valuable overview of early missionary history and brings the story forward to 1950, when the founding of the People's Republic of China put a stop to missionary activity by either imprisoning or expelling all the foreign missionaries. Every thinking Christian feels their sacrifice, but how much more painful was it for those expelled, who would have liked to continue doing good and evangelizing the China they loved and to which they were so devoted. Octave Ferreux was one those apostles.

He was born in Montrond (Jura) on 2 May 1875 into a deeply Christian family. An elder sister became a Daughter of Charity and spent many years on mission in Naples. Octave himself who had artistic gifts, such as design, first took up cabinet making. He also dreamed of spreading the Christian faith in faraway missions from his early days. When he was twenty-five years old, his sister put him in touch with Father Fargues, a Vincentian professor of moral theology in the major seminary of Albi. In order to be near this priest who became his director, Octave went to

Albi, and began to work in the vocational Institute of Saint John, founded by Father Colombier. It turned out to be an important step on the road to realizing his priestly calling. He applied himself with courage and intelligence and showed himself to be a self-motivated student with a capacity for lifelong learning.

At Fargues's urgings, Octave Ferreux was admitted in the Vincentian novitiate in Dax (Landes) on 5 September 1902. A few days later, he boarded a ship for China and arrived in Shanghai on 6 November 1902. In China he continued his formation and his studies together with his young Chinese and foreign Vincentian confreres in the house of Jiaxing. He adapted very well. He pronounced his vows on 8 September 1904 and received priesthood on 9 June 1907 at the hands of Bishop Reynaud. He was thirty-two years old. First stationed in North Zhili as a missionary in North China, Ferreux was sent three years later to the vicariate of Baoding (1910), where he served until 1932. On 8 September 1932 he was called to Peking and in January 1934 became superior of the major seminary of Chala. A confrere wrote of him: "Devout, regular, intelligent, hard-working, he directed the inter-vicariate major seminary with exceptional energy."

In 1946, he was stationed in the Procure of Tianjin under the direction of François-Xavier Desrumaux, who appreciated and valued him greatly. Actually, they esteemed each other very much.

In 1951, when Ferreux was expelled from China with many other missionaries, he returned to Paris. In 1953, he went to Strasbourg where he served in the university seminary, which the Congregation of the Mission founded and directed for the clergy of Central Europe. He dedicated himself quietly to this work for a year. Tired, he went back to Paris and with quiet courage was happy to take up his modest activities of confessions and spiritual direction.

He finished his edifying and generous way of life with an aura of holiness. He died in the infirmary of the motherhouse in Paris on 9 February 1963. He was universally respected and admired. Readers will easily see in the following pages how his own soul shines through in the way he reveals the apostolic personalities of his confreres and friends, the priests and brothers of the Mission, fellow missionaries in China.

[Written by an editor of the *Annales de la Congrégation de la Mission*, 1963]

Part One

Before the Arrival of Vincentians in China

Introduction

Initial attempts at the Evangelization of China

The Congregation of the Mission, which Saint Vincent de Paul founded in France in 1625, had modest beginnings, but developed quickly. Already during its founder's lifetime, it began to put down roots in the principal nations of Europe. Then, after being almost destroyed by the French Revolution, it reconstituted itself and became bigger and more flourishing than it had ever been before the storm. So not only did it resume its interrupted activities, but it expanded beyond the borders of Europe and sent its missionaries to nearly all the countries in the world.

When Saint Vincent's children were spreading in the countries of Europe, they arrived in countries that had been evangelized for centuries. But when they came to China in 1785, whom the Holy See expressly sent to replace the Jesuit Fathers whose Society had just then been suppressed, the evangelization of that immense country had been in progress for less than one hundred fifty years. It is true that the Christian message had been brought to China and the ecclesiastical hierarchy had been established four or five centuries earlier, but it had been so short-lived that the remaining traces were insignificant and hard to detect.

Framework of the History of China

To put the work of the first missionaries into historical context, it is necessary to delve briefly into the history of those early initiatives, which disappeared so quickly. Where did they come from? In which regions of China did they take place? Why did they disappear? The first chapter will give answers to these questions. We will see that before the end of the thirteenth century, i.e., before the Franciscan Jean de Montecorvino arrived in China around 1293, the true Gospel had not yet been announced in the immense Chinese empire.

But because our account will often refer to the authorities of China – a country so different from Western civilizations in its ancient and well-preserved civilization – we have decided to begin with an historical survey of the dynasties relevant to our story. We do not go back to the beginning of the empire, which would be useless for our purpose, but to the seventh century of our era, the time that the Nestorians came from Persia and settled in China.

Readers will see the Tang, Song, Yuan, Ming, and Qing dynasties pass before their eyes; and when in the course of our story a noteworthy event excites the readers' curiosity, it will be easy to refer to this historical summary where one perhaps will find both the date and even the name of the person in question.

Our sources for the dates and names are the Chinese Annals, available in all the manuals of the history of China. For the judgments and characteristics of each of the different dynasties, we could not do better than borrow them from the book *La Chine, passé et présent* by Jean Escarra, who did on-site studies in China. He wrote about it with great breadth of vision. We have copied only a small part of it.

Chinese Dynasties

Tang Dynasty (618–907)

It is the eighth dynasty of our era. It had twenty-two sovereigns, the second of whom, Taizong, was certainly one of the greatest emperors of China. Under his reign and that of his successors, Chinese civilization experienced great development. Literature and arts shone with exceptional brilliance. Administration acquired that majestic order that it was to keep up until our days. Above all, however, Chinese imperialism in Asia reached its apogee and contacts with the outside world increased. During these reigns, Chinese domination spread as far as the Indo-Iranian borders through a series of victorious wars. The Turkish kingdoms of Central Asia were forced into submission. The Tang Empire touched the Arabian Empire, and part of Tibet came under Chinese domination.

After Taizong, the two most outstanding emperors were the third, Gaozong (650–683), and the ninth, Xuanzong (713–756). Under this last emperor, a Chinese general crossed the Pamir passes with an army of ten thousand men and occupied East Pakistan – a feat that amazes historians even today. At that time a part of Korea was also annexed. It was during the Tang dynasty that the Nestorians appeared in China and Taizong himself welcomed them. The eighteenth emperor, Wuzong (841–847), expelled them, but his successors called them back.

These incredible dynastic successes, however, were short-lived. The last one hundred fifty years of the dynasty saw its complete collapse. Little by little China gave back all its conquests, while civil wars desolated the country.

An adventurer, Zhu Wen, deposed and dispossessed Zhaozong (889–907), the last of the Tang dynasty. China was again divided among ten small rival states. During a fifty-year period, five dynasties succeeded one another amid domestic troubles and external attacks. Their capital was generally the capital of the Henan province, Kaifeng. This period of anarchy called in the Annals Wudai, that is, the Five Dynasties (907–960), did not last long. All together there were thirteen minor kings, whose names we will not even bother to give.

Song Dynasty (960–1279)

Thanks to the unrest that followed the fall of the Tang dynasty, the Khitan, a people of Mongolian origin, occupied the northern border provinces of the empire. One of their generals called Zhao Guangyin had his soldiers proclaim him emperor and he inaugurated the Song dynasty. Emperor Taizu (960–976) made Kaifeng the capital.

His reign and the following one of Taizong (976–978) were taken up by wars against the Khitan and a Tangut tribe, both were from the north and had carved out a new State for themselves in the present Gansu province. Under the eighth emperor, Huizong (1101–1126) – this dynasty had eighteen – other barbarians, the Jurchen, who were living in eastern Manchuria, invaded the territory of the Khitan, who had already adapted themselves to the Chinese culture, and established there the Jin dynasty, which waged war on the Song. The latter resisted for fifteen years, had to fall back, left Kaifeng and went and settled first in Nanjing, then, during the reign of Gaozong (1127–1163), in Linnan (today's Hangzhou in Zhejiang province).

Consequently, from 1141 there was a South China, where the Song dynasty lived, and [so-called] Tartar dynasties ruled North China. Inside its reduced domain, the Song dynasty had lengthy periods of relative peace, which allowed literature, philosophy, and the arts (painting, ceramics) to blossom. Two centuries later, the great traveler, Marco Polo, gave us a marvelous description of *Kingsay*, that is, Hangzhou.

The Mongolian Conquest

Around 1160, a Mongolian tribesman was born who at the age of fifty managed through merciless campaigns to unite under his authority all the peoples of Mongolia and Turkistan. In 1206, he was proclaimed "Universal Sovereign" of those peoples.

That was Genghis Khan, whose capital was Karakorum. Under this title he has passed into posterity as the founder of one of the greatest empires the world has ever known. His mounted hordes went and settled next to the Volga and from there penetrated as far as Poland and Hungary making all of eastern Europe tremble. After unifying Mongolia, he undertook the conquest of China. With the help of his lieutenants, he destroyed the Jin dynasty in northwestern China. After his death in 1227, the third of his four sons, Ogedei, finished the conquest of the Jin kingdom, which established itself in the province of Henan after having been chased from Gansu. In 1234, the operations began that brought about the fall of the Song after fifty years of fighting. This was the work of a grandson of Genghis Khan's, Kublai, whose dynastic name was Shizu.

In 1280, he ascended the throne of the "Son of Heaven," established his dynasty under the name of Yuan and made Peking his capital, which at that time was called Yuandadu.

Yuan Dynasty (1279–1368)

The nine Mongolian emperors of this dynasty generally had the policy of distrusting Chinese people. Therefore, the Chinese never stopped loathing their reign.

On the other hand, the first years of the Yuan dynasty were among the most marvelous periods of the history of China. Kublai as ruler of China, theoretical sovereign of Turkistan and of Mongolian Russia, was according to Marco Polo truly the "Great King." He called him "the most powerful warrior and master of territories and treasures that had ever existed in the world since the time of Adam till our days."

Kublai took pride in being a great Chinese emperor and he excelled in this role. He was, however, not very fortunate in his efforts to expand his territory. His expeditions were often failures. Therefore, instead of increasing the possessions acquired by the Tang emperors, China's domain was decreasing.

On the other hand, he made law and order reign inside his immense territory. Concerning trade and communications, the expansive outlook of Kublai and his ministers provided China with unprecedented prosperity. His policy of religious tolerance allowed the Christian religion (Nestorian and Catholic) to develop as well as Buddhism. Marco Polo, Giovanni da Pian del Carpine [Jean de Plan-Carpin], Archbishop Jean de

Montecorvino, Blessed Odoric de Pordenone, all resided in his court by turns. Foreign travelers of every nationality came to China by the roads of Central Asia or by water from the south. It was a great and noble period during which an international mentality blossomed in everything that was most productive and wholesome.

However, this prosperity did not last too long. The last Yuan rulers were inept sovereigns. Rebellions broke out in the south of China. A leader from an ordinary farming family, Zhu Yuanzhang, established his authority and then began taking back the northern provinces from the Mongolians. In 1368, he seized Peking, while the last Yuan emperor fled to the Gobi. Then Zhu Yuanzhang had himself proclaimed emperor and founded the purely Chinese Ming dynasty. His capital was in Nanjing, from where he had come. Consequently, Peking, no longer the capital (*king* or capital) was named Peiping (*ping* or peace), with the sense of "pacification of the north."

Ming Dynasty (1368–1643)

The first and the third of the seventeen emperors of the Ming dynasty: Taizu (1369–1398) and Chengzu (1403–1425) applied themselves – as a reaction against the Mongolians' social laws – to restoring the Chinese national traditions in all spheres. China became again strictly Confucian, withdrawn into itself and hostile to foreign influences. Chengzu (historians generally use the name of his reign, Yongle) was an energetic warrior emperor who re-established Chinese hegemony in Asia. He made Peking the capital once again. The layout of Peking today goes back to his reign: he was responsible for the walls that still enclose the city today, and the wide avenues that cross each other at right angles, as well as the faultless symmetry and orientation of the palaces, which tourists still admire.

The reign of Shenzong (1573–1620), the fourteenth emperor, also called Wanli, was the most magnificent. Yet, the years 1592–1607 witnessed the first Sino-Japanese war because of Korea, which remained an independent kingdom but was a vassal of China, at least in theory, paying the Chinese only a slight tribute. It was Wanli who welcomed Ricci and the first Jesuits.

Towards the end of Wanli's reign, China came into conflict with the Manchus, who had already threatened Peking several times. Rebellions in the provinces also weakened the forces of the empire, so that, undermined by intrigues of eunuchs, whose influence had steadily been increasing, the dynasty was headed towards its downfall.

An adventurer named Li Zicheng, after he established his authority over the provinces of Henan and Shanxi, grabbed the capital from the hands of the last emperor, Chongzhen (1628–1643), who in despair committed suicide by hanging himself from a tree in Mei Shan Park near the imperial palace. Li Zicheng, however, did not succeed the last Ming emperor.

The head of the imperial army, who was in charge of the Manchus in the area around the Great Wall, Wu Sangui, hearing of the downfall of the dynasty that he was serving, offered his enemies peace under the condition that they would help him to take his revenge for Chongzhen's death. The Manchus agreed and, under the leadership of Wu Sangui, re-conquered Peking. The Manchus, however, once they entered the city, refused to leave and return home as they had told the Chinese general they would. They then proclaimed their own ruler, the Shunzhi emperor. A new dynasty in this way took control of China, under the name of Qing.

Qing Dynasty, Manchus (1644–1911)

The first years of this dynasty were used to strengthen their conquests from the north to the south. This was not easy, because Li Zicheng's bands had not been completely subdued, and the remaining princes from the deposed Ming dynasty had supporters in the southern provinces. This continued for a long time. They even had themselves proclaimed emperors several times with Nanjing or Canton (Guangzhou) as capital. The Qing occupied this latter city in 1650, but more time was needed to overcome Wu Sangui's resistance – the general who had blundered so greatly by bringing the Manchus to Peking.

Once the Manchus were masters of China, they wanted to play the role of great Chinese sovereigns – like the Mongolians before them. They honored the immemorial Chinese traditions and preserved the forms of Chinese administration. However, in this latter case, they doubled the administration by adding Manchus to the Chinese civil servants in the military and civilian posts. The only symbol of subjection that they imposed on their subjects was requiring them to wear their hair in pigtails as the Manchus themselves did.

The seventeenth century became famous because of the reigns of Kangxi (1662–1722), the second emperor, and of Qianlong (1736-1795), the fourth emperor.

Under these sovereigns China regained the splendor and the prestige it had known under the Tang and Yuan dynasties: a lavish and refined court life, an abundant literature, albeit not very original, and ceramic art pushed to perfection.

From the Christian point of view, the notorious "Rites Controversy" marked the reign of Kangxi and a violent persecution against the Catholic Church, dictated more by hatred for the religion than by political reasons, marked the reign of his son and successor, Yongzheng (1723-1735).

The Jesuits achieved great influence at the court under Kangxi and Qianlong. Through their positions of trust, they were able to introduce and support many of their confreres both in Peking and in the provinces.

After the suppression of the Society of Jesus in 1773, their successors in the French mission of Peking, the Vincentians, did not have the same influence at court. This did not prevent them, however, from furthering the evangelization in the whole of North China.

Here we end this historical summary of the Chinese dynasties because the splendors of the last dynasty, Qing, will surely be involved in our history of the Vincentian missions in China.

Chapter I

Early Missions, Nestorians, and the Stele of Xi'an

Had God's Word been Announced in China by the Apostles or their Immediate Successors? – The Nestorians in China – The Stele of Xi'an – Expulsion of the Nestorians – The first Catholic Missionaries Sent by Rome to China: Jean de Plan-Carpin, André de Longjumeau, and Guillaume de Rubrouck

Had God's Word been Announced in China by the Apostles or their Immediate Successors?

There are no documents or convincing traditions that indicate that the Apostles or their immediate successors had proclaimed God's Word in China.

The Apostle Saint Thomas is said to have evangelized the Indies. The Roman Martyrology declares that Saint Thomas preached to the Medes, the Persians, the Hircanians and the Bactrians and that he then entered the Indies and was martyred in Calamine. But it is silent about his arrival in China.

The first bishop of Peking, Jean de Montecorvino, at that time named Kambalik, who knew the churches in the Indies founded by Saint Thomas, because he had spent some years there, wrote from China in 1305, "No apostle, no disciple of the apostles ever came to these countries."

Ricci, who tried so hard to find traces of ancient Christians in China, knew absolutely nothing about an apostolic origin. If he had known about it, he would not have omitted mentioning it in his writings. On the other hand, it is not impossible that someday explorers will bring to light ancient, now unknown, documents which could allow us to believe that the Apostle Thomas sowed the seeds of the Gospel in China. For the time being, however, we can stay only with a negative answer to this question.

The Nestorians in China

It seems evangelizing China belonged to the Eastern Church by right. That part of the Church could more naturally reach out towards the regions in the east, whereas this role was less suited to the Church in the west, because of distance.

Unfortunately, the Oriental Church (Byzantium) got bogged down in theological disputes. Heresies and schisms plagued it thanks to the emperors' involvement in church affairs and to the ambition of the patriarchs of Constantinople. Consequently, the Church lost its evangelizing outreach and the heretical Nestorians had the honor to be the first ones to bring the Gospel to China.

It is known that Nestorius, patriarch of Constantinople, was teaching that God's Son and Jesus were two very intimately united persons, but not of the same substance. Consequently, the one who was born of the Virgin Mary was a human being in whom God dwelt, so that in Jesus there are two natures and two persons, each nature keeping its own personality. Mary must therefore not be called Mother of God, but only the mother of the human being in whom divinity dwells. God did not suffer and did not die for us, only the human being did, in whom God was dwelling.

This teaching denying the substantial union of the person of the Word with humanity sapped the dogma of the redeeming value of the Savior's sacrificial death. The Greek emperors, at that time being loyal servants of the Church got together with the bishops to suppress this unfortunate heresy. Nestorius was condemned at the Third Ecumenical Council in 431, was deposed from his see and the members of his sect were dispersed.

The king of Persia, hereditary enemy of the Greeks, welcomed these members with open arms and they founded a flourishing school in his kingdom thanks to Bishop Barsauma of Nisibis (d. 492/495). From there the Nestorian Church penetrated deep into Asia and advanced until the invasion by Tamerlane in the fourteenth century, after which it waned.

Towards the middle of the eighth century, the Nestorians entered China in a caravan of rich Armenian traders, and there they preached the Gospel.

In 635, a group of Nestorians, led by Olopen, arrived in China. Taizong, the second emperor of the Tang dynasty, welcomed them with honor and allowed them to settle in the capital itself, which was Chang'an (today's Xi'an, in the province of Shaanxi). An authentic document gives us exact and certain information on this historical point. It can still be consulted today in Beilin, the temple of Confucius in Xi'an.

The Stele of Xi'an

In March 1625, while excavators were digging foundations for a building in Zhoushi, at about eighty kilometers west of Xi'an and on the river Wei that runs through Xi'an, they found sunk in the ground a large marble paving stone, the kind of stele used to preserve the memory of remarkable events or of famous people for posterity.

This is the opinion of Jesuit Father Havret writing in 1897. Later on, other scientists, like [Paul] Pelliot and [A.C.] Moule put the discovery of the stele in 1623, not in Zhoushi, but in a suburb of Xi'an, located a few kilometers from the city. But, place and date of the discovery are of small importance. The interesting thing is the description that Havret published and that we copy here.[1]

The stele, about two meters high, carries on top the two classic intertwined dragons which surround a small cross, under which have been carved in big Chinese characters the following nine characters, placed on three lines:

ZHONG	JIAO	DA
GUO	LIU	CAI
BEI	XING	JING

It must be read from top to bottom beginning on the right. These nine characters can be translated in this way: "Memorial to the Propagation in the Middle Kingdom of the Luminous Religion from Daqin (the West)."

Then on the whole face is spread a long inscription of 1,780 smaller and finely carved characters; on the lower part, on its base and also on the two edges of the stele, there are ninety lines of foreign characters, which later have been recognized as the Syriac language in its ancient *estrangela* form.

This discovery excited the attention of the mandarins and the intellectuals of the country. The stele was publicly shown and many interested parties went to see it. An intellectual from Fengxiang, named Zhang Gengyu, baptized in Hangzhou (Zhejiang) by Father [Giulio] Aleni, S.J., remarked that the Chinese text had many expressions the meaning of which he did not understand very well, but which he thought alluded to the Christian religion, because he had heard a friend of his speak of it in the old days, Doctor Li Zhizao Léon from the city of Hangzhou.[2] This intellectual

---

1.   Henri Havret, *La Stèle chrétienne de Si-ngan-fou*, 3 vols. (Shanghai, 1895-1902).

2.   He was not a medical doctor, rather a *jinshi*, a metropolitan degree holder, roughly the equivalent of a Ph.D. Hereafter, following Ferreux's usage, the title of doctor

immediately made a copy of these inscriptions on a black background and sent it to his friend Doctor Léon Li, who knew the Christian doctrine that he had received from Ricci very well, and therefore was very pleased to recognize in this text the broad outlines of our religion. Together with Doctor Paul Xu Guangqi he had the inscription printed completely, adding necessary explanations, and they spread it throughout the whole empire as an apologetic writing in favor of the Christian faith. They did not take any interest in the Syriac text, which they could not understand.

Then some Jesuit priests, among others Trigault, a Frenchman, Boym, from Poland, Semedo and Diaz, both Portuguese, took great care to establish the exact meaning of the Chinese text. From then on, many scientists have become interested in this question.

Hearing news of this odd discovery, the government in Peking asked that a copy of the inscription be made and ordered the mandarin of the place to transfer the stele to Xi'an and to place it in a suitable place.[3] It was put in a temple of Confucius, the Beilin, as we said already. It can be visited there nowadays.

The text of the inscription lets us know the circumstances and the date for the erection of the stele. That was under Dezong of the Tang dynasty, who reigned from 780 till 805. Then the text says: "Olopen, a famous man, came from Daqin (Persia) to Chang'an (Xi'an). The emperor at that time, Taizong (627–650) sent officers to the western suburb to meet him, welcomed him to his palace and ordered that the numerous illustrated holy books that he had brought with him be translated."

After examining the books, the emperor decided that the teaching was good and that the books could be published. The decree that he gave to that end is quoted in the inscription.

Here is the summary of these books: short passages on God, on the Holy Trinity, on creation, on humankind tempted by Satan, on sin and its consequences, on the incarnation and the birth of Jesus, on redemption and the Savior's ascension.

It says that Olopen brought the twenty-seven books of the Brilliant Law. Then it tells the history of Nestorianism in China from 635 up until 780. It also mentions that in 638, three years after their arrival, a Nestorian monastery was built by order of Taizong (627–650) in the very city

---

is used in this translation. In some places, Ferreux does refer to those trained in medicine. In other places, it may be taken to mean scholar. (AS)

3. This was under the Ming dynasty, and the emperor was either Xizong (1621–1628) or his successor Chongzhen (1628-1643), the last of the Ming, who committed suicide.

of Xi'an, the capital of the empire. Olopen was promoted to the title of "Defender of the Empire." The religion spread in the then ten provinces, and monasteries sprang up in many towns.

The text says that the Buddhists provoked two persecutions against the monks in 699 and 713. In 742, however, Emperor Xuanzong (713–756) protected them and restored them to imperial favor. Dezong (780–805) also supported them. One can also read poems to praise the emperors, who were favorable to the Faith; and then, the inscription finishes, in the Syriac language, with a long list of seventy names of Nestorian bishops, priests and monks, divided over seven categories or titles.

It can be seen that these Nestorians were not really preachers of the Gospel, but monks who were living in community. According to the testimony of the stele and Marco Polo, Nestorian teaching did indeed spread throughout the different provinces of China at that time, but it is unknown how many converts there were and how many Chinese were admitted to their monasteries.

Shortly after their arrival in China, the Nestorian monks began to translate their books into Chinese. Sinologists say that they probably translated thirty-five of the five hundred thirty books that they brought with them, of which only two are extant.

Expulsion of the Nestorians

Emperor Wuzong (841–847), misled by Daoists, issued a harsh decree ordering the destruction of Buddhism. It said: "We order the destruction of 4,600 temples and the secularization of two hundred thousand bonzes [monks] and nuns." And he added: "Because Buddhism is forbidden, it is not appropriate that the temples of the heretics like Daqinjiao (the religion of the Persians) be tolerated. Their priests must consequently return to secular life and return to their native soil; if they are foreigners they must be sent back to their country." The edict was in 845.

It seems that at that time the number of monks was two or three thousand. The end of the edict, "If they are foreigners. . ." allows us to suppose that among them there must have been quite a number of Chinese.

Probably around that time, the stele was buried in Zhoushi, or according to the other opinion, in the suburb of Xi'an. We do not know the Nestorians' losses, but we know that the successor of Wuzong, Xuanzong (847–860), revoked the proscription and re-established the temples. It is not known, however, whether the Nestorian monasteries benefitted from this favor. Be that as it may, they weathered the storm, because between 1275 and 1292 Marco Polo discovered important Nestorian Christian communities in Mongolia, Gansu, Shanxi, Fujian, Jiangsu, and so on. Besides, it is known that, when the Mongolians came to power again in the twelfth century, the Nestorians returned bringing a still more degenerate doctrine.

Some traces of these Nestorian communities have been found in the course of time. Examples are the iron crosses discovered in the city of Quanzhou in Fujian; other crosses carved on tombstones at Shizhu ziliang in Mongolia; the marble cross at the temple called Shizisi (of the cross), near Liulihe, at sixty kilometers from Peking, a description of which can be read in the *Bulletin Catholique de Pékin* (1923), pp. 218–224.

The first Catholic Missionaries sent to China were the the Franciscans Jean de Plan-Carpin, André de Longjumeau, and Guillaume de Rubrouck.[4]

In 1245, while presiding at the ecumenical council of Lyons, Pope Innocent IV (1243–1254) declared himself to be very anguished when thinking of the sudden advance of the Tartar hordes towards Europe.[5]

Indeed, Genghis Khan's immense conquests, the terrible invasion by his grandson Batu Khan – sent to conquer the West with an army of six hundred thousand men – the invasion of Russia as far as Kiev, the over-running of Poland and Hungary, the Christian armies pushed back by this devastating torrent – all these events plunged Europe into consternation.

Hope of spreading the Faith and stopping the barbarity in the Far East made the pope decide to send missionaries to the Tartars with pontifical letters exhorting them to stop shedding Christian blood and to adopt the Catholic Faith. For this purpose, Innocent IV appealed to the two mendicant orders, the Dominicans and the Franciscans, who, though of recent origin, were already spreading the light of the Gospel far and wide.

He asked the Dominicans' superior to choose four of his members and send them to the Mongolian princes who were in charge in Persia. Then, he himself chose from among the Franciscans the Italian Jean de Plan-Carpin from the region of Perugia, to go as his ambassador to the Great Khan (emperor) of the Tartars.

---

4. It was a habit in the Middle Ages in Europe to designate people who left their country by their first name and add the name of the place of their origin.

5. Tartar hordes consisted of Mongol and allied non-Han peoples of Inner and North-east Asia. (AS)

Jean de Plan-Carpin. He had been Saint Francis of Assisi's companion and disciple. When he received the order from the pope, he was sixty years old and had fulfilled important tasks in his Order. He was given Etienne de Bohême as his companion.

On 16 April they left Lyons, where the Sovereign Pontiff was residing. They crossed Germany, Bohemia, and Poland, where a third Franciscan, Benoît de Pologne, joined them to serve them as interpreter, and they arrived in Kiev, the heart and center of Russia.

The Tartar chieftain who was commanding that city provided them with horses and guides. After six days' travel Etienne de Bohême fell ill and had to stop. The two others, Jean and Benoît, went on with their journey across desolate and uncultivated lands.

After their arrival in Kaniv, the Tartar leader of the place changed their tired horses. On their way, they had been attacked many times by minor Tartar chiefs, who allowed them to pass only after having received money or gifts from them.

On 4 April 1246 they arrived in the camp of Batu, master of the whole region of the Volga River. Batu, Genghis Khan's grandson, was the most powerful prince after the Great Khan. The two friars were led to his quasi-imperial court and Jean, on his knees, presented the papal letter. A few days later, Batu sent people to tell them that they had to travel to the Great Khan. He ordered their guides to make them travel as fast as possible so that they could be present at the election of the new emperor.

Indeed, the throne had been vacant for several years. Genghis Khan died in 1227 and his son, Ogedei succeeded him and died in 1241. Court intrigues delayed the election of his successor till August 1246. The chosen one was Kuyuk (Guyuk), a son of a common-law wife of Ogedei.

After an extremely tiring journey, the friars reached Mongolia and on 22 July 1246 arrived in Karakorum, the Great Khan's capital. While the election was going on, they were given a place to stay and after a few days they had to attend the new emperor's accession to the throne. They were lent a ceremonial costume to wear for the occasion.

Sometime after these festivities, Kuyuk read the Sovereign Pontiff's letters and asked from the friars for the pope's intentions in minute detail. On 12 November an answer for the head of the Church was handed them that the interpreters translated for them word for word. Here is briefly the content of that overbearing answer:

> ... You have the intention of making peace with us. You, pope and all the emperors and kings of the West, you did not delay in coming

to me in order to define the conditions for peace: you will hear our answer and you will know our will. . . . You say that we ought to have ourselves baptized and to have ourselves made Christians. We do not understand why we should do so. Moreover, you are amazed because of the slaughtering of people that we have done, especially of Hungarian, Polish and Moravian Christians. There is more that we do not understand. . . . We shall tell you, however, that those peoples had not obeyed God's and Genghis Khan's will; that is why God ordered us to destroy them. . . . You, inhabitants of the West, you adore God and you believe yourselves to be the only Christians and you look down on other people. . . . We, too, adore God and it is with His help that we ravage the earth from east to west.

The next day, 13 November, Jean de Plan-Carpin had his farewell audience and a few days later he began his journey back with Benoît. After much suffering and extreme fatigue, he reached the Sovereign Pontiff again in Lyons in the autumn of 1247. Named to the archbishopric of Antivari (Albania), Jean de Plan-Carpin died there in 1252.

André de Longjumeau. When Jean de Plan-Carpin was coming back from Tartary, the seventh crusade was going on. Saint Louis, king of France, being in Cyprus on his way to the Holy Land, heard on 20 December 1248 that Kuyuk and his mother had converted. The saint decided to send an ambassador to Kuyuk to congratulate him.

In those days besides Nestorians there were many Western Christians. They were prisoners captured by Genghis Khan's victorious armies. Consequently, there is no reason to be astonished at the rumors that were circulating in Europe about the conversion of Tartar princes.

A French Dominican from Longjumeau, near Corbeil (Seine-et-Oise), was chosen for this mission. Two other Dominicans accompanied him. It was André's task to bring the king's gifts and letters to Kuyuk, and also some relics of the real cross.

The mission left Cyprus on 27 January 1249 and arrived at the Tartar court a year later after a difficult journey. Kuyuk had died in April 1248. His widow, the dowager empress Ogul, received André, who accepted Saint Louis's gifts as a sign of submission (*sic*) to Tartar authority. She wrote the king of France a letter in which she demanded in haughty terms that he pay tribute every year. This letter reached Saint Louis in Caesarea in Palestine in the spring of 1251 through Mongolian ambassadors whom the empress sent with André on his journey back home. The holy king was sorry he sent an ambassador to such an arrogant potentate.

Guillaume de Rubrouck. A few years later, the rumor spread that Sartag Khan, son of Batu and great grandson of Genghis Khan, then governor of an extensive territory in Russia, had converted to the Christian faith. Thus, the king of France decided to send him a congratulatory message. He took advantage of the journey to the east by two Franciscans, Guillaume of Rubrouck, born in the French Flanders, and the Italian Bartolomeo da Cremona, who both were on fire with zeal to convert infidels.

Though they were not the French king's ambassadors, but just missionaries, Saint Louis entrusted them with his letter for Sartag in which he not only congratulated him for having converted to the Faith, as the rumor had it, but moreover, he asked him to allow the missionaries to settle in his country.

The two friars left Constantinople on 16 April 1253 and after a difficult three and a half month journey arrived in Sartag's camp near the Volga River. Sartag, however, did not want to take responsibility for answering Saint Louis' letter and sent them to his father, Batu.

When they arrived in Batu's camp, they were filled with wonder when they saw so many tents lined up in perfect order. The next day they were introduced to Batu. Guillaume, having no letter to give him, said to him simply: "I want to see your son because we have heard that he was a Christian; I brought him letters from the king of France. Your son sent me to you; you must know the reasons." Batu then bade them stand up, questioned them and dismissed them. After some days had passed, Batu had somebody tell Guillaume, "Your king asks that you be allowed to live in this country, but this is impossible without the Great Khan's permission so, you have to go to him with your interpreter."

We already said that Kuyuk had died in 1248. Ogul, his widow, remained empress awaiting the nomination of a successor. This happened on 1 July 1251. His name was Mangu Khan.

After six weeks' stay at Batu's court, a Tartar officer visited the friars. He told them: "I received the task of leading you to Mangu Khan; it is a four months' journey, and it is so cold that stones and trees break; think whether you can make such a journey." "Yes," they answered, "we can with God's help."

They crossed Turkistan, the Uighurs' country, and on 27 December 1253 they arrived in Mangu's camp, located near Karakorum. During this journey, hunger, thirst, cold and fatigue were terrible.

On 4 January 1254 Mangu Khan received the two Franciscans in audience. Having given him some solemn compliments embellished with pious words, Guillaume declared:

> We have heard people say that Sartag was Christian. This had caused much joy for all the Christians and especially the king of France. That is the reason we came to see Sartag and the king sent him a letter filled with peaceful words. Among other things, the king begged him to please allow us to live in his country, because our profession is to teach people how to live according to God's law. Sartag sent us to his father Batu and he sent us to you, to whom God gave a great empire on earth. . . . Consequently, we ask Your Majesty to please allow us to remain in this kingdom so as to serve God while praying for you. We have neither gold nor silver to present to you. . . . We offer you ourselves. . . . At least allow us to wait here till the big cold has gone, because my companion has been so weakened that he would not be able to mount again a horse without danger.

Mangu answered: "As the rising sun spreads its rays everywhere, so my authority and that of Batu spread in all directions!" The next day the friars were informed that they could take a rest for some time or go to the city of Karakorum.

They went there indeed and found quite a few Russian, Hungarian and Armenian Catholics, who had not received the sacraments since their captivity. The friars heard their confessions as they could and gave them Holy Communion. As Bartholomew had not recovered his health, he was allowed to stay on with the Catholics.

On 8 July 1254 the two friars left each other and Guillaume went back to Europe. On his way, he met Sartag, who had come to the Great Khan's court, and he passed again through Batu's camp where he stayed a month. Then he crossed the Caucasus, Armenia and Syria and on 15 August 1255 he arrived in Tripoli. From there he sent the king of France the account of his journey.

One's first impression is that these missions seem hardly to have furthered the evangelization of the nations in the Far East. Jean de Plan-Carpin and Benoît de Pologne only went and came back; André de Longjumeau did the same. Guillaume de Rubrouck, who wanted so much to preach the true faith among those peoples, heard some confessions, conferred five baptisms and converted a Nestorian priest. These painful expeditions seemed to have borne no fruit. It is different, however, when we consider the consequences that followed. These arduous missionaries wrote letters to popes and kings that had a long-term benefit. The accounts they gave of their distant journeys brought Europe and the Church knowledge of countries about which people knew nothing. People did not know where these countries were and they were completely ignorant of their morals and way of life. Those bits of knowledge proved to be very useful later on for diplomatic relations and still more for the future of the Catholic Missions.

To be completely honest, since these first missionaries did not go further than Karakorum, they did not reach China strictly speaking. We are now going to talk about the one who founded the first Catholic Mission in China in the very capital of the great Chinese empire.

Chapter II

Catholic Missionaries during the Yuan Dynasty

Jean de Montecorvino – The First Bishop of Kambalik – An Unexpected Pilgrim in Kambalik: Odoric de Pordenone – Death of Jean de Montecorvino – Guillaume de Prato, Last Archbishop of Kambalik – Extinction of the Church in China

Jean de Montecorvino

We know very little about the circumstances of his birth and youth. Through a letter he wrote in 1305 in which he said he was fifty-eight years old, we can deduce that he was born in 1247. He was successively soldier, lawyer and doctor, entered the Order of Saint Francis, studied philosophy and theology and was ordained priest. Rigid and severe with himself, he could be numbered among the most fervent imitators of Saint Francis, especially in the practice of poverty.

He was hardly forty years old when Nicolas IV charged him with different missions in Asia. This pope, perceiving his qualities and knowing that he had learned eastern languages, accredited him as his ambassador to the princes, the patriarchs, and the nations of all of Asia.

In July 1289, Jean de Montecorvino set off with several companions, armed with letters from the Sovereign Pontiff for the kings and princes of Georgia. A final letter destined for the Great Khan reigning in China made clear the destination of his mission. Actually, this letter was only a belated response of the Sovereign Pontiff to the invitation that Kublai Khan, founder of the Yuan dynasty, sent to his predecessor, Pope Clement IV, through the two Venetian traders and brothers Nicolao and Maffeo Polo.

The khan asked the Holy Father to send him a convoy of at least one hundred well-educated people to teach his subjects religion and the principles of European science.

In 1271, when Clement died, his successor Gregory X entrusted the khan's two messengers with a written answer and appointed two Domini-

22

cans to accompany them. War stopped these Dominicans in Asia Minor, but the two Polo brothers with Nicolao's fifteen-year-old son Marco continued their journey and arrived in Kambalik (Peking) in 1275.

It was not possible to send the scientists that the khan had asked for. Several popes succeeded one another on Peter's throne, but no opportunity presented itself for organizing such an expedition. That had to wait until the year 1289 when Nicolas IV had to send an answer to the king in Armenia and took advantage of the occasion to send Jean de Montecorvino as far as China, as we have already said.

He landed in Antioch, crossed Syria, reached Armenia and set off for Persia, stopping several times in Franciscan or Dominican monasteries, which marked out his way. On his arrival in Tauris, King Argoun of Persia welcomed him with honors worthy of a papal legate. Jean preached there, conferred sacraments and left only in 1291. Of the companions that he started with, not a single one remained with him. Fortunately, the Dominican Nicolas de Pistoie became available to accompany him, and Pierre de Lucalongo a Venetian trader joined them. In their company, Jean reached Ormuz on the Persian Gulf and put out to sea again.

At that moment, a terrible misfortune hit Jean: his companion Nicolas was taken away from him by death. He did not lose courage and continued his journey with his faithful Venetian companion, having the firm intention to reach Cathay (China was then called Cathay).

History is silent about the journey from the Indies to Kambalik. In what year did he arrive? Lacking documents, we can surmise that it was in 1294. The letter that he carried was addressed to Kublai, but it was not he who received it. Kublai had died towards the end of 1293.

His successor was his grandson, Chengzong, whom the khan had chosen and prepared over a long period to continue the empire. Changing the ruler did not change the Mongolians' practical liberalism towards Christianity, or at least towards what looked like it. Nevertheless, that would be one of the factors that increased the difficulties Jean had to overcome. With the Mongolian victory Nestorianism returned, which made its influence felt more and more on Mongolian life and customs. This heresy had a clearly visible life among them and was officially recognized.

Not only were there Nestorian Christians in the new empire, but also whole units of the Mongolian armies were composed of foreign Christians of diverse rites. The Alans who came from southern Russia were the most numerous, and all were of the Greek Rite. The others were Georgians,

Hungarians, and so on, of the Roman Rite. Such was the Christian variety when Kublai was organizing his empire and was settling in at Kambalik.

The Mongolians did not distinguish any differences among the diverse religious groups; for them it was all "Christianity." Understood in this way, the Yuan dynasty gave Christianity official status, similar to what had been given to Buddhism. Regulated and protected in this way, Christianity was transformed into *a function of the state*. The result was that one could see Nestorian priests, Buddhist monks, and shamans at the complete disposition of the khans, to bless them, to guarantee prosperity for them and to interpret the Will of Heaven. The Nestorians ended up performing a purely external cult, where the virtue of religion was completely absent: they allowed gross kinds of licentiousness, like simony, ignorance of the doctrine and even polygamy. These things did not shock the Mongolians.

Such was the situation with which Jean de Montecorvino had to contend. When he arrived in the huge cosmopolitan city of Kambalik, the humble Franciscan had to approach the emperor.

Jean was admitted into sumptuous surroundings to hand the message of the pope to the potentate. Nicolas IV, filled with enthusiasm by the rumors, praised the khan's favorable dispositions towards Christianity and pretended to see in this emperor a new "Constantine." Therefore, he called him "very dear son in Christ," and he encouraged him to become Christian. This was a grand illusion. Nevertheless, Jean was allowed to live in Kambalik. A place was given him and he began to preach the true Faith without delay. Of course, he was the first Catholic priest who appeared in this country. Soon a small group was formed and his residence quickly became too small. It was necessary to think about a bigger place and about building a church. However, he immediately came up against the Nestorians, who, envious of his successes, did not want a new Christian religion established alongside theirs.

They prevented the construction of a church by all means; they did not dare to do it too openly, because they knew that the khan liked the papal legate. Jean, nevertheless, through patience and persistence reached his goal.

Among the first conversions that followed his arrival, the most remarkable one was that of Prince Georges, who was in charge of a camp in Tenduc, west of Kambalik. He was Nestorian, like many of his people. At court he heard about Jean's presence, devotion, and ardent faith, which contrasted with the Nestorian priests' half-heartedness. He wanted to see him and contacted him. As a result of his conversations with the friar, he converted to the Catholic Faith.

Back at his post, Georges encouraged some of his subjects to follow him into the Catholic Church. He had a chapel built, where Jean came from time to time to celebrate the Holy Mysteries. Jean was very happy with these results flowing from his neophyte's fervor, and he took pleasure in harboring great expectations for the future of this young Christian community.[6] These successes, however, riled the Nestorians. They first accused Georges of apostasy, then they soon put the blame on the real person responsible. They resorted to slander.

They had heard, from Jean himself and from Pierre de Lucalongo, of the death of Nicolas de Pistoie in the Indies. So, they spread the rumor that Rome had not sent Jean, and that he had killed Nicolas, the real papal legate, in order to grab the treasure that he brought to the khan, and then had taken his place.

The accusation was serious and the judicial authority took it up. Jean appeared before the judges accused of murder, theft and forgery. The crime, they said, had occurred in the distant Indies, but the accusers asserted this without being able to prove it. Threatened for several years with undergoing the death penalty, Jean de Montecorvino felt the weight of this odious slander. God, however, took care of His servant. Some false witnesses, tortured by remorse, admitted that the Nestorians had given them money to lie. The khan immediately recognized Jean's innocence and the vileness of his slanderers. In this way, the roles were altered: the last mentioned were expelled with their families and Jean was completely exonerated.

Jean did not have to fear the Nestorians anymore, so he could finish his church. This was around the year 1299. Unfortunately, a disaster occurred that overburdened him again. Georges, while fighting against an uprising, was taken prisoner and killed. Jean was very sad because his beautiful expectations for this new Christian community were also dashed by this event. Georges' brothers, who had remained Nestorians, took advantage of this event to force the people to abandon the Catholic Faith and to return to the Nestorian cult.

---

6.   When Ferreux uses the word "chrétienté," as he does many times in the text, it has been translated as "community," that is, a group of ordinary Faithful people (not those of a religious order), that could vary in size from a few individuals or families to hundreds, even thousands. (AS)

Though lacking collaborators, Jean did not get discouraged. He gathered some forty pagan children from seven to eleven years old, taught them the basics of Latin and the catechism, baptized them, and instructed them in the rubrics and ceremonies of the divine office. He made two copies of the breviary and thirty copies of the psalter for them with his own hand. Amazingly, in the center of a town that had never seen a Catholic priest, there rose up something like a monastery of young monks who were singing psalms to praise the Lord at fixed hours of the day announced by bells.

The emperor himself very much liked to hear the children's voices. One day, Providence arranged an unspeakable consolation for our friar. It was the unexpected arrival of a Franciscan, Arnold de Cologne. Finally, Jean could go to confession. He had not done so for eleven years. We have no information on the reasons of this missionary's arrival in Kambalik. According to one of his letters, however, we know that shortly after the passage of the Franciscan, Jean was isolated again. We know also that he wrote a long letter in 1305 to his confreres in Europe, in which he described his situation, his work and his urgent need for collaborators. He asked them to pass his account on to the Roman Curia. In that letter Jean declared that he had baptized six thousand people and that, if the Nestorians had not hindered him he would have baptized thirty thousand.

The First Bishop of Kambalik

Jean de Montecorvino's letter arrived rather quickly at its destination and, according to his wish, was sent on to Rome. Because of the good news from the missionary – about whom no news had been received for twelve years and whom people thought dead – there was great elation both in Rome and in the Franciscan Order. The Sacred College declared itself ready to promote some beautiful projects. Pope Clement V told the Franciscans' master general to choose seven good and virtuous monks and he himself would choose three cardinals to consecrate these friars as bishops before sending them to Tartary. The purpose was to have the three new bishops consecrate Jean de Montecorvino, to whom the pope gave the title of archbishop and patriarch of the whole East.

A large number of Franciscans filled with God's spirit, accompanied those bishops, received Clement V's blessing, and set off. The caravan took the route that Jean had followed. Unfortunately, in that same region of India where Nicolas, Jean's companion had died, death took three bishops and quite a number of priests whose names history has not preserved. The survivors continued their journey and arrived in Kambalik in 1309 or 1310.[7]

What a joy for Jean to receive such helpers. Losing no time, the three bishops, or more exactly one bishop assisted by the two others consecrated Jean bishop. Immediately the new archbishop set about assigning his new personnel to different posts. He kept a group in the capital: Pérégrin de Castello and André de Pérouse with a few priests. He sent priests to Hangzhou in Zhejiang and to Yangzhou in Jiangsu. Finally, he delegated Gérard with some companions to Zaitun (today, Quanzhou in Fujian).

The next year, 1311, the Sovereign Pontiff sent three new bishops to Jean as suffragan bishops, probably to replace the three of whose death the pope had heard. But of these three bishops, only Pierre de Florence reached Kambalik, because the others died on the way. Guillaume de Villeneuve, who had missed departing from Europe with the group, later was sent to China with some companions, but they all disappeared en route.

In 1317, Gérard, the bishop working in Fujian, succumbed to illness. Jean sent Bishop Pérégrin de Castello to take his place.

Though we would like to know what happened in these different missions, there is so much we do not know.

Jean did not write after 1306, or if he did, nothing of it has remained. We have only one letter from each of the two bishops Pérégrin and André, but these letters talk only about the high virtues and ardor of the archbishop of Kambalik and of what he suffered from the Nestorians. Pérégrin wrote in 1317, after having taken possession of his see of Zaitun (Quanzhou). He gave the names of the confreres who were working with him and he expressed the wish to have a hundred more.

André de Pérouse wrote in 1326. He reported that the Franciscans accustomed to convent life built monasteries wherever they lived so as to chant the Divine Office. He said that among the non-believers, many received baptism but very few were living a Christian life. He also remarked that in the first years missionaries did not know the local language well enough, consequently they were obliged to use translators to converse with the people. He reported that Pérégrin de Castello died in 1322.

---

7.   Since one of the chosen seven for some unknown reason did not set out with the others, and three bishops died in India, only three arrived in Peking.

An Unexpected Pilgrim in Kambalik:
Odoric de Pordenone

Having lived as a hermit in a forest in Italy, the Franciscan Odoric left his country in 1314 and with his pilgrim staff in hand set off towards the East, with the sole goal of evangelizing non-believers. In crossing Asia Minor, Armenia, and Persia, he went from monastery to monastery, welcomed sometimes by his Franciscan confreres, sometimes by Dominicans. He worked with them for six years. Then he set out to the Indies, and from there traveled up and down the Sunda islands and finally reached Canton. Not finding Franciscans there, he continued to Fujian and stayed for some time with his confreres in Zaitun. When he resumed his travels, Odoric went to Kambalik, making long detours on the way. He reached Kambalik in 1323 and lived there for about three years.

The tireless pilgrim wrote a long account of his journeys at the request of his superiors. In it he gave interesting details of the geography of the countries across which he traveled and of the habits of the people he had visited. In his account there are many things so marvelous that they seem improbable. He was not himself an eyewitness of these marvels, but he recounted them in the way he had heard people talking about them.

When he spoke about Kambalik, he seemed to have seen only its greatness and the magnificence of the emperor's palace and throne. He noted the prestige with which the archbishop was surrounded and the veneration that the khan had for his person. He almost never talked about the Franciscans' apostolic activities. In a few lines he mentioned the Franciscans' marvelous activity: "Their power over the demons resulted in numerous conversions." To tell the truth he did not say a word about the numerous conversions of non-believers he himself had made, as if in his eyes, doing good was so natural that it was pointless to talk about it.

Odoric, seeing the urgent need that Jean had of receiving new co-workers, decided to go back to Europe to recruit new missionaries for China. He left Kambalik in 1326 and arrived back in Italy in 1330. He immediately began to enlist volunteers. He wanted to go to Avignon to receive the Sovereign Pontiff's blessing, but a serious illness obliged him to stop in Pisa. From there he returned to his monastery in Udine, where he gave his beautiful soul back to God on 14 January 1331.

It is not known whether the volunteers he had gathered went to China. Benedict XIV beatified Odoric in 1755.

The Death of Jean de Montecorvino

In 1328, two years after Blessed Odoric's departure, the founder of the Mission in China died a holy death surrounded by the affection and veneration of Christians and non-believers alike. He was eighty-one years old.

Jean de Cora, one of his colleagues, said that his funeral was very solemn, and people were visiting his tomb with great devotion. How sad that his resting place never has been identified!

In 1333, the pope, after receiving news of Jean's death, named Nicolas de Botras to replace him. He arrived in Kambalik four years later in 1337. It seems that he did not take possession of his see.[8]

After the passage of several years, the pope again asked the Franciscans' master general to choose some friars to send to China. Some of them were to be consecrated bishops. It is probable that the pope's wishes were never carried out. The Yuan dynasty was already in steep decline and fell in 1368. With the advent of the Ming dynasty, the foreign religions that the Mongolians had tolerated and protected – more for reasons of public utility than because of religious convictions – were to disappear.

Guillaume de Prato, the Last Archbishop of Kambalik

It is probable, as we mentioned earlier, that Nicolas de Botras never resided in Kambalik.

Because of the troubles brought on by the imminent fall of the Yuan dynasty, the Christians supporters of the old regime fled from Kambalik. They followed the last emperor, Shunzong (1333–1368), westward across Mongolia. The Franciscans did the same. They went to Sarai (Russia), where the Franciscan, Bishop Cosmas, resided. Urban V had appointed him bishop there in 1362. Then this same pope, who was very poorly informed about what was happening in the Far East, moved Cosmas to the archbishopric of Kambalik in 1370. A few months later he gave him a successor in the person of Guillaume de Prato (Florence), a professor from the University of Paris. Urban V sent twelve companions with him to China, and entrusted him with a letter and gifts for the sovereign of

---

8. For fear of mistakes during this troubled times in the papacy, we omit the papal names.

China, whoever he might be. Nothing is known about these missionaries, not even whether they reached their destination.

Extinction of the Church in China

The new dynasty, being Chinese, applied itself to stopping all communication with the outside world, forbidding entrance to all foreigners, and systematically destroying all that might remind them of the Yuan dynasty. Kambalik became the simple prefecture of Peiping.

The Mongolians' second capital, Karakorum, was razed. Not only the palaces, and the monuments, but also the churches, everything disappeared. Of the twenty or thirty thousand Christians baptized by Jean de Montecorvino, not one single family remained.

Henceforth, for two long centuries (1368-1583), missionaries, who wanted to answer Peter's appeal to go to China and save the pitiful Church there, found the door closed to them.

Chapter III

The Portuguese at Macao and Restoration of the Missions

Portuguese Sailors Near China – The Founding of Macao – Restoration of the Missions in China

Portuguese Sailors Near China

Even approaching the door shut in the face of foreigners had become extremely difficult. The two ways that the Franciscan missionaries had followed: one over land through Russia (which Jean de Plan-Carpin followed to Karakorum), the other over sea and land through Persia and the Indies (which Jean de Montecorvino followed to the heart of China) had become unusable, because once the Muslims had strengthened their hegemony over the Mediterranean countries, they turned their attention to the Orient and kept a close watch over all roads leading to the Far East.

Nobody thought at that time of going around Africa. It was reserved to those burning with youthful energy (Spain and Portugal) to open the first global routes to bring the Gospel to the whole world.

Christopher Columbus, from Genoa, in the service of Spain, went straight westward. The Portuguese were to follow along the coasts of Africa, and gradually they practically encircled this immense continent. These sailors established trading posts all along the coast of Guinea and sailed south along the African coast. In 1486, one of them, Dias, having weathered a terrible storm, was, without knowing it, at the extreme southern tip of Africa. He called it "the Cape of Storms." After he returned to Lisbon, King John II, who hoped to reach the Indies and even Cathay, changed that name to "Cape of Good Hope."

Six years later, in 1492, there was great news that the Indies had been reached, coming in fact from a completely different direction. On 12 October 1492 Christopher Columbus saw land that he thought was the Indies, but it was the New World, which later on received the name of America.

31

The scientists studied their maps, which obviously were incorrect, and swore that the discovered continent was indeed the Indies.

The Portuguese needed ten more years before they discovered the road to the Greater Indies. The Portuguese king sent Vasco de Gama, who left Lisbon on 8 July 1497 with four ships and one hundred seventy crew. He went around the Cape of Good Hope, sailed along the African coast, passed the straits of Mozambique (without ever seeing the island of Madagascar), then turned eastwards, and eventually dropped anchor at Calicut on the Indian coast of Malabar in May 1498.

In the background was the intense rivalry between Spain and Portugal, as to which of these two powers the newly discovered lands belonged.

The Holy See was consulted, because it was considered a tribunal of international peace. In May 1493, Pope Alexander VI fixed a line of demarcation from the South Pole to the North Pole at two hundred miles from Spain: all the lands located east of that line were attributed to Portugal; all the lands located to the west were to belong to Spain. Today we would say: west or east of the thirtieth western meridian. At that epoch the meridians were not yet fixed through international conventions.

That papal judgment has essentially contributed to the solution of many problems about sea and land borders between these two powers. It is a credit to the pope.

A little later, the Portuguese conquered Goa north of Calicut, and finally Malacca, the largest trading center of the Sunda Islands. Goa quickly became a Portuguese colony with civil and ecclesiastical administrations. A church was built. Soon Goa became the ecclesiastical center of the Indies, China and Japan.

We have already seen that the New World, discovered by Christopher Columbus, had fallen to the Spaniards. They rushed towards the continent and soon realized that these lands consisted of two large continents linked to each other by a strip of land (Panama). There was no passage from the Atlantic to the other sea that they had to cross before reaching Cathay and the Greater Indies. Navigators thought to go around South America as the Portuguese had gone around Africa. Again another Portuguese, Magellan, in the service of Spain, worked that miracle. In 1515, he weighed anchor in Buenos Aires, rounded the cape and sailed straight westwards. Soon he reached a group of islands, which later were called the archipelagos of the "Philippines," named after Philip II, king of Spain.

Henceforth, Spain could reach the Indies without going through Portuguese waters.

The Founding of Macao

In 1517, some daring Portuguese seamen setting out from Malacca rounded Indochina and arrived in the delta of the river which waters Canton, harbor of the Guangdong province, and despite the Chinese authorities' protests landed in Canton itself. These sailors were immediately put in prison, but after a short time they were set free and went back to Malacca. After several unsuccessful attempts, they were allowed in 1557 to establish a little colony on Chinese territory on the peninsula of Macao, located at the mouth of the Pearl River. They established a trading post, which became the central depot for European trade with China and flourished until the English foundation of Hong Kong in 1842.

Macao has played a large role in the noteworthy achievements of the Church in China. It was at one and the same time the gateway for those who were preparing to enter China and a refuge for missionaries fleeing persecution. It had moreover a seminary where aspirants could go about their studies in peace and prepare themselves for apostolic life. Besides, the Portuguese traders and officials of Macao, penetrated by the religious mentality of the age, often put their wealth and their credit at the service of the Catholic Missions in China.

Restoration of the Missions in China

The Christian Faithful were extremely interested in these expeditions to faraway places. In the thinking of the popes, they facilitated entrance into the countries of non-believers and enabled the preachers of the Gospel to be heard. The first attempts of establishing the Church in the Far East, however, involved great difficulties.

When the Sovereign Pontiff wanted to send missionaries, he could ask only the religious orders (missionary communities were quite rare at that time), and not the priests of the dioceses in Europe. At the same time, the pope was unable to pay for their journey, which would last at least five or six months, nor could he pay to establish and maintain the new Christian communities. He was still less able to protect the small Christian communities in pagan territories. Consequently, he had to accept the material help and protection of the king of Portugal, who, as a faithful servant of the Catholic Church, was ready to lend efficacious help to the missionaries in order to further God's kingdom among the unbelievers. And because the Portuguese alone were allowed to enter the countries of the Far East, it was fair to grant the Portuguese government certain privileges which could facilitate the task of providing, transporting, and maintaining missionaries in these new lands of unbelievers.

From 1516 Pope Leo X and several of his successors granted and confirmed to the kings of Portugal the right to present candidates for the episcopal sees among many other advantages. This temporary institution was referred to under the name of "Portuguese patronage," in the Portuguese language "Padroado."

The Padroado made it possible for the Church to establish a special hierarchy, the only one possible at that time, in the Indies and China. The king of Portugal had to provide enough clergy to evangelize the conquered countries or the ones that would be conquered. Because the Church was growing all the time, it is easy to understand that a small nation like Portugal could not by itself provide enough missionaries. As a result, the king had to ask for missionaries from other nations and all had first to be accepted by the metropolitan of Lisbon, later by Goa as we shall soon see, and they had to go to the Far East on Portuguese ships.

Later when the Padroado had become inefficacious and even embarrassing, the Church reduced some of the privileges, and then, little by little, dropped an institution that no longer correspond to the needs of the times.

On 5 November 1534 Pope Paul III created the first diocese of these regions, that of Goa, suffragan of Lisbon. The first bishop was the Franciscan Jean de Albuquerque. On 4 February 1558 Paul IV raised Goa to the rank of metropolitan for all the churches located beyond the Cape of Good Hope.

Chapter IV

Returning to Peking —
Ricci's Work and Death There

Missionary Friars Enter China as far as Peking – The Four Stages – First Stage: Zhaoqing – Second Stage: Nanchang – Third Stage: Nanjing – Last Stage: Peking – Ricci's Helpers – Qu Taisu – Li Zhizao – Xu Guangqi – Priests' Daily Tasks in Peking – Ricci's Death

Missionary Friars enter China as far as Peking

The missionaries who came with China in mind steadily increased. Whether they came by the Portuguese route or by the Spanish one by way of the Pacific, all had the same wish of penetrating to the interior of China. The Chinese empire enchanted them. Yet, all the attempts undertaken up till then had ended in failure. The problem of entering China remained.

The Jesuits found a solution. They entered China by the most peaceful means possible. This is the reason for their great glory. Two Italian Jesuits worked together on it: Alessandro Valignani and Matteo Ricci.

In 1573, Valignani's superiors placed him at the head of the missions of the Indies with the title of visitor. He set out from Lisbon in 1574 with forty-one Spanish, Portuguese and Italian Jesuits, and settled in Goa, the ecclesiastical center of the Far East. He first visited Macao, where he had just a few confreres, then Japan, where, more numerous, they were finding it difficult to follow in the footsteps of Saint Francis Xavier. While traveling, he heard many wonderful things about China, and it saddened him that, according to everybody's opinion, it seemed impossible for missionaries ever to enter that empire.

However, he had noticed that missionaries of whatever order did very little to learn the Chinese language. Most of them were traveling from island to island, stuttering some words of the local dialect or they used translators. Thinking about this painful fact, Valignani thought finally that on the contrary, missionaries ought to study the Chinese language, not just local dialects, but the classical language, which was the basis of all Chinese literature. Prepared in this way, missionaries would be able better to understand Chinese thinking, customs, and morals. It was not enough that they enter China, but they had to stay there and adapt themselves to China.

This was his plan. He explained it to his superiors and asked them to send him people able to take up this task.

A thirty-four-year-old Italian priest, [Michele] Ruggieri, was appointed. He arrived in Goa in 1578 with three confreres. Matteo Ricci was among them. He still had to finish his theological studies, which he did in Goa. The following year, Valignani sent Ruggieri to Macao with orders to learn Chinese thoroughly. Ruggieri did not have at his disposal either a dictionary or any other book to initiate him into this study. On the other hand, the priests who knew most about Chinese affairs not only considered Ruggieri's attempt impossible, but they also considered it presumptuous and they tried to turn him away from it. Consequently, the local superior employed him in the ministries of the house in order to keep him from his studies.

At the end of one year, he urgently asked Valignani to let the young student Ricci join him, but Ricci was not allowed to leave Goa before finishing his studies. This did not discourage Ruggieri. Ricci had already learned more than one thousand characters and had begun to speak Chinese. Being a little older, however, Valignani had difficulties in speaking Chinese. He sometimes went to Canton, where he found occasion to talk with Chinese mandarins, among whom he made some friends. One day, he told them about his wish to penetrate deeper into the interior. They made him understand that to get this favor he had to speak to the viceroy[9] of Guangdong province, who lived then in the town of Zhaoqing, about 180 kilometers from Canton, and that, above everything else, it was necessary to offer him gifts.

Ruggieri tried. He had magnifying glasses and other scientific curiosities sent to the viceroy. Then through friends he had himself announced as a Western friar who had come to China not to trade, but to learn Chinese literature, because he was attracted by the fame of that great country. The viceroy showed himself in a good mood and granted him a small temple, located in the suburb of the town, where he could live.

---

9.   More accurately, governor-general of Guangdong and Guangxi. Ferreux uses viceroy to refer to governor-general, sometimes loosely. Hereafter, no clarifying comment will be made. (AS)

At that time, in August 1582, Ricci and another Jesuit named Pasio arrived in Macao. Soon Pasio went to Zhaoqing with Ruggieri, whereas Ricci was to begin his study of the Chinese language immediately. This Jesuit, born in Macerata (Italy) on 6 October 1552 had great qualities. Endowed with a prodigious memory, he was in a short time able to catch up with his precursor Ruggieri in the knowledge of the Chinese language and soon overtake him. From Europe he had brought many objects like clocks, triangular glass prisms, and instruments for mathematics and astronomy. Afterwards he would not stop asking for other items from his confreres in Europe.

While Ricci was studying, Ruggieri continued his dealings with the viceroy. He let the viceroy know that he wanted to offer him an automatic clock that struck the hours. The viceroy was delighted and replied that he wanted to see Ruggieri as soon as possible. Ruggieri decided to have Pasio accompany him. They set off in a small boat on 18 December 1582 and arrived in Zhaoqing on 1 January 1583. The two priests were dressed up like bonzes by order of Valignani, who wanted missionaries to become "all things to all men." That was a serious misjudgment that he corrected without delay.

The viceroy, surrounded by mandarins, welcomed them with great kindness. They were brought to the temple. After a few days, the clock was set up in a sitting room of the viceroy's palace and was admired by everybody. The cultured people and the well-read of the city, seeing the respect that the viceroy had for the bonzes from the West, continued to visit the two priests in the temple admiring pictures and other curious objects that they exhibited there.

The following March, everything changed suddenly. The viceroy was denounced in Peking for misuse of power, so he ordered the priests to leave quickly, for he was afraid that the fact that he had brought foreigners into China without the emperor's permission, at that time Shenzong (1573-1620) known also as Wanli, might bring trouble on himself. Immediately, the priests entrusted their novelties to a friend and returned to Macao. In September of the same year, Ruggieri wrote to the viceroy's successor asking permission to return to Zhaoqing, which was granted. Without delay, Ruggieri returned there, this time with Ricci.

The new viceroy, less informal than the preceding one, did not see the priests and communicated with them only through the intermediary of the prefect. But there was no lack of visits to their home. Ricci, already very well versed in Chinese literature, was able to have interesting conversations with the *literati* [scholars], especially about Confucianism, for he already knew the *Four Books* of Confucius and he quoted passages from them. This astonished his audience.

In August 1585, the Portuguese [Duarte] de Sande joined them. The difficulties they were encountering grew from day to day. They felt that their situation was not secure, because, though sometimes honored, they sometimes were suspected of being spies of Portugal. Moreover, despite the care they took to distinguish their teaching from that of the Buddhists, they were classed as bonzes, naturally, because they were dressed as bonzes and were known as monks. Furthermore, their residence was a temple, so anyone could enter there at any time. Considering all these disadvantages, they thought about settling elsewhere. They were well aware that as long as they had favor only with the mandarins, their safety was precarious. They needed the emperor's permission. But how could they get it if not as ambassadors of the Holy See? They talked about it with Valignani, who agreed. It was decided that Ruggieri was to go to Rome to explain the situation to the Cardinals. He left in 1588, but since he received other kinds of work to do, he did not return to China. Besides, Pope Sixtus V considered the circumstances unfavorable for sending a mission to China.

The Four Stages to Peking

First Stage: Zhaoqing

The two priests Ricci and de Sande were therefore alone to carry on the mission. Their patience was put to a tough test. The viceroy died and was replaced by a third one, who behaved unpleasantly towards the two foreigners. He made them understand that it was not suitable that they live in the same town as the viceroy.

Seeing that he had to leave Zhaoqing – which he actually wanted – Ricci dared to have the question put to the viceroy: would he allow them to live in another town of his jurisdiction? The answer was that they could settle in Shaozhou in the north of Guangdong, at a distance of three hundred kilometers from Canton. Ricci and his companion left Zhaoqing and returned to Macao to prepare what was needed to enter Shaozhou.

The viceroy's plan was to house them again in a temple. Ricci flatly refused, for he no longer wanted to be considered as one of the bonzes. He went and talked to the sub-prefect[10] of the town and found a convenient

---

10.   Sub-prefect refers to the county magistrate. Hereafter, no clarifying comment will

location. The viceroy approved his choice and gave the plot of land without charge. The priests set to work immediately and had a residence built.

Ricci had already explained to Valignani the great disadvantages of wearing the clothes of bonzes and bearing their name. The reasons were these: first, the bonzes were despised by all the people generally speaking and especially by cultured people; second, bonzes were never allowed to be seated in the presence of a mandarin – during official audiences they had to remain on their knees; third, the teaching of the priests wearing bonzes' clothes was considered by the audience as only slightly different from Buddhism. Ricci added that for some time men of letters considered him as a Western doctor, and those who knew him, when talking about him, always called him Doctor Li. Consequently, he could present himself as a doctor [scholar], without taking the required examinations – not a Chinese but a European doctor. For this reason, it would be best to wear the clothes men of letters wore in public as well as when they received cultured people in their residence.

Valignani understood the value of all those reasons and fell in with Ricci's opinion on what to wear. The Italian Jesuit [Lazaro] Cattaneo, to whom Valignani gave a place in their team, brought this good news to them. From that day on in July 1594, the priests no longer shaved their heads, but grew beards and left their bonzes' robes behind. The first visit to the prefect of Shaozhou to introduce Cattaneo to him was done according to the etiquette for men of letters. Henceforth, they were to do the same in their audiences with mandarins.

Ricci introduced himself to all the mandarins of the town. Everywhere the welcome was courteous, likely because he carried out these official receptions quite well. His reputation as a wise man spread more and more and he was already well known in several large cities. Nevertheless, there were fewer visitors than in Zhaoqing, because the town was less populous. They also had to suffer a great deal, above all from the bonzes of a nearby temple, who caused them as much trouble as possible, going so far as to provoke riots against them.

Second Stage: Nanchang

Though the proposal of a papal mission to Peking had failed, Ricci did not lose his hope of going to Peking; he was waiting only for an opportune moment. An opportunity arose. An important mandarin with authority over the viceroys of all the provinces, on his way to Peking by a small

be made. (AS)

boat, came ashore in Shaozhou and visited the priests. Ricci told him of his intention of going to Peking. The mandarin offered to bring him there and Ricci accepted.

He left Cattaneo and the others behind in Shaozhou, and took a small boat on 18 April 1595 and followed the mandarin. On the way, the mandarin, probably fearing the consequences of the step he had taken, told Ricci that it would be very difficult for him to enter Peking and to be accepted there, and that it would be better to go to Nanchang, capital of Jiangxi, where he had been mandarin for ten years and that there he would help him with his influence. Ricci refused and insisted that he wanted to go to the capital. As a result, the mandarin changed his travel plans and said that he would go only to Nanjing, but that to go there he had to go through Nanchang.

Ricci followed him and, having arrived in Nanchang, he stayed there a few days to visit the city. At the end of May he arrived in Nanjing, where he met several mandarins whom he knew and who received him very well. Seeing that he could not continue his journey to Peking, Ricci thought of settling in Nanjing. His friends, however, as soon as they heard about it, were against it out of fear of compromising themselves. Ricci, then, reluctantly retraced his steps to Nanchang. When passing through that city, he had noticed that members of Emperor Wanli's family were numerous there and also that there were many men of letters.

He lived in the home of a bachelor [first-level degree holder], one of his friends. The viceroy of the province of Jiangxi, who was already well disposed towards him without ever having seen him, sent for him and told him that he would be happy to allow him to live in his city. Meanwhile, de Sande sent him help from Shaozhou in the person of Father [João Bruno] Soeiro (Soerio), who arrived in Nanchang on Christmas day 1595.

The viceroy offered them a temple. Ricci refused and bought a house. Men of letters and mandarins flocked to the priests. Up till then, Ricci and his companions taught Catholic doctrine when an occasion came up, but the number of conversions could be numbered on one hand. In Nanchang, Ricci moderated his preaching, for he did not want to preach a new religion before having received permission from the emperor. He introduced himself as a scholar from the West, so he talked only about science. His audience actually liked that very much. For them he constructed spheres and sundials and he drew maps among other things. During the literature examinations, visits were so frequent that they exhausted Ricci.

Third Stage: Nanjing

In 1597, a former president of the Board of Rites in Nanjing, Wang Chongming, visiting Nanchang, went to see Ricci and offered to take him to Peking. That was exactly Ricci's wish. Quickly he prepared many beautiful gifts for the emperor. He took Cattaneo with him and left the two other priests to look after the residence in Nanchang. On 25 June 1598 he boarded a boat and a few days later he arrived in Nanjing, where he saw his old friends again. From there the journey went by way of the imperial canal, which linked Nanjing to Tongzhou, an important city located thirty kilometers east of Peking. On 7 September he disembarked in Tongzhou. Mandarin Wang Chongming went on ahead and was already in the capital, for he was anxious to know whether his nomination to the higher office that he wanted very much had been promulgated.

The next day Ricci arrived in Peking and visited Wang Chongming, who, sadly, was very disappointed. His nomination had not taken place. Unable to do anything to help him, he advised Ricci to turn back; however, Wang Chongming wanted first to see some of his friends who had become mandarins, but they all refused to see him. The situation was dangerous and his failure was complete. Ricci, fearing to be imprisoned, followed the mandarin's advice and immediately went back. Going past Nanjing he stopped at Suzhou, a rich city distinguished by the number of its doctors. In that place he met again Qu Taisu, one of his first friends, who never stopped praising the merits of his teacher, Doctor Li from the West. Ricci made only a short stop there. Wang Chongming had come back to Nanjing. When he heard that Ricci was in Suzhou, he invited him to come and settle in Nanjing. Ricci did not need any coaxing and arrived there in January 1600. He bought a house and pursued his relations with men of letters and the mandarins. This time he freely distributed a booklet that he had written and spread in Shaozhou, "The True Notion of God," which was soon to be printed in Peking in many editions.

Last Stage: Peking

Ricci had just been named superior of the three residences: Shaozhou, Nanchang, and Nanjing. What had to be done was to set up a fourth one in Peking. He prepared a second "attack."

A eunuch, named Ma Tang, a powerful and very sly imperial servant, who had to take to the emperor five or six boats loaded with silk, offered to bring Ricci to the capital for free. Ricci accepted, because of his overriding desire to get to Peking, even though he really distrusted this man.

Cattaneo, who had brought the objects and gifts back from Peking, remained in Nanjing, and another Jesuit, Father [Diego de] Pantoja, a Spaniard, set off with Ricci on 18 May 1600. Trouble soon followed. Ma Tang had heard that the boxes contained precious objects intended for the emperor, so his desires got the best of him. He planned to get part of it for himself and to present the rest to the emperor, while claiming all the credit. The result was all kinds of tricks, lies, and even on occasion violence on the part of Ma Tang against the priests. We are not going to recount this part of the story here.

Suffice it to say that despite all his clever scheming, Ma Tang succeeded in getting a hold of only a few things. Their boat had to stay in Tianjin from July 1600 until the beginning of January 1601. Emperor Wanli, informed of the arrival of the doctors from the West bringing him many gifts and curious objects, gave orders on 8 January 1601 that these foreigners come immediately to Peking. Eight horses and thirty porters were requisitioned and after a journey of four days they arrived in Peking with all their baggage. That was 24 January 1601.

The Board of Rites was put in charge of this case. The gifts were prepared and a list was made. A petition accompanied them. In that document, Ricci explained that he had traveled forty thousand kilometers to come to this country, enticed by its fame. He had lived in Zhaoqing and in Shaozhou for five years. During those years he had learned how to speak and how to write, so as to acquire knowledge of the doctrine and of the books of the wise people of China. He wanted neither offices nor favors in the empire. If his Majesty would be so good as to accept the European objects he offered, that would increase his gratitude for so much kindness.

What kind of person was the sovereign to whom Ricci was writing? Wanli seems to have been endowed with some imperial qualities. After succeeding his father at the age of ten (1573), he maintained the traditions of the ancestors during the first years of his reign. Soon, however, taken to drunkenness and lust, he lived withdrawn at the far end of his palace, allowing the eunuchs to completely dominate him. During his long reign of forty-seven years, people saw him very rarely. He allowed only eunuchs and great ministers to approach him. Living a life of idleness, he seemed to have taken an interest only in his harem and in seeing and collecting rare and curious objects. He never stopped looking for them, not as an artist, but as one who liked to possess curious things.

It did not take Ricci long to understand that such an emperor could not give him the authorization he so urgently desired. Ricci decided to profit from this enormous passion for strange things in order to secure his stay in China, and that was going to be enough for him.

When Wanli saw the paintings, he was very impressed because they represented how people seemed to live. The musical instruments captivated him too; he admired the clock especially, but he was very disappointed that it did not work and did not strike the hours. He was told that it was not yet adjusted and that only the priests were able to turn it on. Then the priests were brought to the hall where the clock had been placed. Ricci explained its mechanism and asked for somebody to whom he would teach in two or three days all what was necessary to make the clock go. On this account the emperor ordered four eunuchs who were good at mathematics to be Ricci's pupils. During that time, the emperor repeatedly sent eunuchs to ask the priests questions.

After the three days passed, the clock was working and the emperor was so pleased that he immediately increased the dignity and the salary of the four eunuchs. Because he did not see the priests in person, he had two of his best artists paint their portraits.

Up till that time it was Ma Tang who arranged living quarters for the priests, but Ricci was anxious to be free of that man, who through his servants kept visitors away from the priests. Besides, Ricci was certain that Ma Tang wanted to have him expelled from China, in order that he himself could receive the reward that – he assumed – the emperor would certainly give the priests to thank them for their gifts.

An unexpected event put an end to their quasi-captivity at the hands of the eunuchs. The president of the Supreme Court [of Judicature and Revision] was angry that the priests had not yet come to visit him. He had them arrested and brought to the tribunal [court]. That was on 4 March.

Ricci, when questioned, told him that he had suffered acts of violence at the hands of Ma Tang. The president, moved by his story, told the priest not to fear anything, that the case would be arranged and that in the meantime he could go and live in the Seu-Yi-Yuan[11] where the priests would be looked after at the expense of the public treasury. They went

---

11. The Seu-Yi-Yuan was a vast space where all the foreigners were lodged who, with a passport, came to Peking either as pseudo-ambassadors or as traders. [Perhaps Ferreux means the (Hui tong) Si yi Guan, where tributary envoys stayed in the Inner City, the place where tributary envoys stayed, located in the Inner City. (AS)]

there and so escaped Ma Tang's clutches; but in turn they fell into those of the mandarins of this Supreme Court.

To become completely free, Ricci rented a small house in the most important area of the city at his own expense. As soon as the priests had settled in this new residence, there was a rush of visitors. So many came that during the day the street was filled with rickshaws and horses belonging to the important people who came to visit the priests.

When the palace clock broke down, the emperor had it carried to the priests' house to be repaired. Then for three days many curious onlookers came to see and admire it. When Wanli heard this, he no longer allowed the clock to be brought outside the palace, but rather he allowed the priests to enter the palace every time the clock needed to be adjusted.

Thus, it can be seen that if the emperor was favorably disposed towards the priests, it was not because of their personalities, still less because of the doctrine they taught, but it was only for the sake of the curious objects that they had brought to him.

After one or two years, Ricci thought about teaching the catechumens who presented themselves. From the first days, his companion, Pantoja, taught catechism to the simple people who approached them and to the servants of the residence. Ricci wrote booklets that contained Christian prayers and explained the great mysteries. For the men of letters, he wrote other books in a more refined style.

Ricci's Helpers

Ricci did not work alone. Among those who listened to him there were men of letters and doctors captivated by his accomplishments, and wanted in the worst way to work with him. Here are the most outstanding ones.

Ignatius Qu Taisu (Kiu Taisou). – Qu Taisu was the first one who offered his services in Shaozhou and who took great pride in being Ricci's pupil. European science appealed to him. He learned geometry and mathematics and did not consider these sciences as intellectual pastimes the way many men of letters did. He learned them for their practical use. He translated or helped Ricci with the translation of several books. At the same time, he applied himself to the study of the Christian religion and quite soon asked for baptism. The priests were in no hurry to give it to him. He received it in Nanjing on 25 March 1606 and went on working with the priests.

Leon Li Zhizao (Li Tche Tsao). – Born in Hangzhou, he became a doctor [*jinshi*] in 1598. He was a talented person. In Peking, he applied himself to the study of the sciences. He wrote several volumes on mathematics and translated Euclid's geometry. After becoming secretary of the Board of Public Works in Nanjing, he nevertheless lived in Peking and took advantage of this situation to continue his intellectual relations with Ricci. He was a great help to Ricci in translating his works on mathematics and astronomy. He too had a great desire to become a Christian, but he had several wives, and his faith was not intense enough to move him to make the necessary sacrifices. When he took sick in 1610, the year of Ricci's death, Ricci comforted him and led him to do what was necessary to enter the Church. He baptized him and gave him the name Léon. He recovered and lived for many more years, during which he put his talents in the service of spreading the gospel, As we have seen at the discovery of the stele of Xi'an in 1625. At that time, he was known as Doctor Léon.

Paul Xu Guangqi (Siu Koangki). – The most famous of Ricci's converts was unquestionably Xu Guangqi, who was born in 1568 in Shanghai to a cultured family. In 1581, he passed the bachelor examination, married and had one child. In 1600, visiting Nanjing, he had a conversation with the priests and held onto this idea, "God is the first principle of everything." This affirmation made him think. He became anxious and in him was born a fierce desire to go deeper into the question. In 1601, he went to Peking to take an examination. He tried to see Ricci, but did not succeed. Besides, he was deeply saddened to have failed the examination. He went away and hid his shame – these were his own words – in Guangdong, where he undertook the direction of a school in Shaozhou.

There he met the priests again. Cattaneo showed him a large image of the Savior, before which Xu kowtowed as before a divinity. Xu was a man of upright judgment. He was passionate about literary studies, but also liked the natural sciences. His ambition at that time was to attain a high office, consequently he did not think of converting. In 1603, he went again to Nanjing and met Father [João da] Rocha, who gave him a beautiful image of the mother of God and some booklets about religion. He did not need more. He passed the whole night reading them and learning the prayers by heart. The next day, he went back to the priest and asked to be baptized. Rocha told him to come and receive instruction every day for a week. He came twice a day and received baptism under the name of Paul with great feelings of faith. Then he returned to Shanghai and a short time later he returned to Peking, where he got his doctoral degree and, moreover, was admitted in the Hanlin Academy. Paul Xu began a frequent and intimate relationship with Ricci and became his right arm.

Later he was to become chancellor of the empire and during several years he would be a great support for the Church in China.

Priests' Daily Tasks in Peking

On 10 May 1605 Ricci wrote that there were more than one hundred Christians in the capital, and he added, "If they did not have several wives, a very common situation among high-ranking gentlemen, a number of them would have entered the Church." During the first four years the priests were in the capital, they were obliged to move several times from one cramped quarter to another. Valignani came to their rescue, and for a reasonable price they were able buy a residence not far from the south gate of Xuanwu. It had forty-five large and small rooms. In August 1605, they settled there and outfitted a very nice chapel. Later on, the Nan-tang [South Church] would be built there, the first and mother of all the churches of Peking. Little by little Ricci's companions began to go to the countryside and talked with the simple people. Sometimes they brought them together and preached the great truths to them. Where they were well received, they returned after some months and baptized those who were best prepared. Their ministry was fruitful, especially in the villages of the region [prefecture] of Baoding, where they baptized about one hundred fifty people. It is a pity that the priests did not give the names of the Christian communities that they founded, but only used names like "Assumption," "Saint Clement," "All Saints," so that it is impossible now to identify those villages with certainty. These relatively numerous conversions were done without fanfare, yet they provoked spiteful remarks from pagans.

In 1607, the priests had to stop their outreach into the countryside. It was only later that they could take it up again.

Every year, Ricci, as superior of all the residences, had to give an account to his visitor of the results of their works. In 1605, he told his superior that the four residences with their outposts had one thousand two hundred Christians. Up till now we spoke only of the activities of the companions of Ricci, who himself could not think of going to visit the villages. Among his activities the most time-consuming one was that of visiting and receiving visits, and also of writing letters to personages spread all over China. Ricci was skilled in the art of talking with visitors. "It is tiring beyond our strength," he admitted, "but we cannot avoid doing it, if we do not want to destroy what we have already built up with so much effort." In this kind of activity, his confreres could offer him very little help.

Convinced that Peking needed missionaries who were also scientists, Ricci continually asked his superior general for them.

Unable to describe here in detail all the activities of this great missionary, we will confine ourselves to telling how his career ended.

Ricci's Death

Ricci's many activities and worries wore his strong body out prematurely. During the first months of 1610, as if he had a premonition of his approaching death, Ricci wrote a report of what he had done during the twenty-five years that he had been in China. As a conclusion, he contended that the "best plan was to win the trust of the Chinese gradually using literature and science; and then when the suspicions had been dispelled, one could begin with the conversions." Some of his companions pressed him to get the permission of staying securely in the empire. Ricci answered: "Do you not see that the emperor talks person-to-person only with the domestic eunuchs of the palace? Only a magistrate's intermediary can hand a petition to him. I know through experience that a petition asking that foreigners may live in China is never going to be presented, because its object is so contrary to the habits and customs of this empire." And he added: "During these last ten years, the priests have been exposed to the danger of being expelled from one town or another, but nevertheless they have remained, because we are here in Peking and because nobody talks about chasing us away. Let us in no way give them grounds to believe that we fear something."

On 3 May 1610 Ricci came back from a visit with a violent headache. When the pain became more acute, six doctors were called but they prescribed medications in vain. On 11 May the patient, in possession of all his faculties, received the last rites and gave his soul back to God.

Shortly before his death, when giving his recommendations to his confreres, he said these words to them: "I leave you in front of an open door of great worth, but not without dangers and labor."

Ricci was really an apostolic man. For twenty times he was frustrated in his daring project to settle in the capital of China, but twenty times he returned to try again till his indomitable energy had merited to see his plan crowned with success. If we spent time recounting his activities,[12] it was to make clear that the one whom God destined to introduce missionaries into a nation opposed to all that comes from abroad had to be wise and prudent, have a wide-open heart, and have the gift of inspiring confidence. His task was to open a hermetically closed door. He opened it, certainly not wide open, but after him the priests could pass. Sometimes the door will only be slightly open, and the missionaries will have to be clever in finding ways to enter and stay; there will be persecutions, but there will also be calm periods. It is an undeniable fact that the Catholic missions secured their foothold in China only through Ricci.

Ricci's Burial

Before Ricci's death in 1610, the number of Jesuits who entered China thanks to their confrere's prestige was not more than fourteen. Some of them died before he did and their bodily remains were buried in the cemetery at Macao.

If the priests were, so to say, established in Peking, they nevertheless still did not have a place to be buried. Doctor Léon Li had the idea of speaking directly to the emperor to ask him to grant the famous deceased a burial place. After many formalities in the presence of high functionaries, the emperor granted the petition and had it sent to the Board of Rites, which judged it favorably.

This favor caused much joy among the missionaries of Peking. Indeed, a burial place for the dead was security for the living.

The priests were offered four equally suitable places and they were invited to choose one. They opted for a large propriety located outside the west gate, six hundred meters from the wall, on which there was a mansion set in a beautiful garden.

In October 1610, the missionaries took possession of the cemetery; they immediately transported the body there, which they had kept in a hall, while waiting for the tomb to be completed. A year later, on All Saints Day 1611, the priests conducted the solemn burial of Father Matteo Ricci.

This cemetery is called by the name of the neighboring village, "Chala [Zhalan]." Later we will see that this property would be the center of very important activities of the Catholic missions of China, among others, the regional seminary of Chala.

---

12. We took the information from Bernard Henri S.J., *Le P. Matthieu Ricci et la société chinoise de son temps* (Tientsin, 1937).

Chapter V

Mission Expansion and Persecution during the Ming Dynasty

Other Missionary Religious of the Era – Macao, a "Holy City" – Foundation of the Christian Communities of Shanghai and Hangzhou – Ricci's Successor – The Persecution by Shen Que from 1616 to 1623 – The Jesuits' Official Return to Peking – Fall of the Ming Dynasty

Other Missionary Religious of the Era

While the Jesuits with difficulty were heading for Peking, the other religious orders were not inactive. We mentioned earlier that Portugal had too small a population to send an adequate number of missionaries to its immense possessions in the Far East.

What Portugal was unable to achieve by itself, Spain was impatient to do and, just as Macao was the staging center for missionaries coming from Goa on their way to China, in the same way the Philippines were to become for a short time another center for missionaries crossing the Pacific coming by way of Mexico or the Straits of Magellan.

From the erection of Macao as a diocese in 1576 until Ricci's death (1610), the Spaniards sent more than two hundred religious to the Philippines, with the express hope of getting a foothold in the Chinese empire. Not one, however, succeeded, even in settling at its doors. The Augustinians confined themselves to the evangelization of the Philippines; the Franciscans dreamed of taking the road to Japan where the Jesuits were inviting them; the Dominicans spent part of their efforts on preaching to the Chinese who were in Manila, hoping that they would be able to enter with them through Fujian. They all went to Macao and there built houses of their respective orders.

For its part, Portugal, snowed under by the immensity of its tasks, could devote little attention to China. Around twenty Portuguese Franciscans went to Goa, but most of them proceeded no further, especially because of the disappointing bits of news that were brought to them from China.

Macao, a "Holy City"

The city of Macao had truly become a Christian city, though quite badly served by its bishops who were too dependent on local politics. Nevertheless, it witnessed an intense religious life within its walls, but not without parochial rivalries, by the way. There was no street without its church: the cathedral, the Church of Saint Paul, the two parishes of Saint Laurent and Saint Anthony, the public chapels of the Jesuits, the Franciscans, the Dominicans, the Augustinians, the Santa Casa, the Senate, not counting the small sanctuaries which the people themselves erected out of private devotion.

In reviewing the different missionary communities in Macao, there was no evidence of progress toward entering China, so we return to our narrative in China.

The Foundation of the Christian Communities of Shanghai and Hangzhou

In 1608, that is two years before Ricci's death, Doctor Paul Xu went to Shanghai to bury his father. There he instructed a catechumen and asked Father Cattaneo, then in Nanjing, to come and baptize the neophyte. Cattaneo went there in September 1608, conferred baptism as requested and then began to catechize those who expressed a desire to listen. In two months, he administered fifty baptisms. That was the first kernel of the Christian community of Shanghai; two years later the Faithful numbered two hundred. After that, Cattaneo went to Hangzhou, Doctor Léon Li's hometown, and opened that town to the Faith. Soon we shall see how this foundation happened.

Ricci's Successor

On his deathbed, Ricci had given his confreres a sealed letter which read, "To Father Nicolas Longobardi, superior of the mission in China, from Matteo Ricci, superior of the same mission."

Longobardi, a Sicilian, had arrived in Macao in 1597 and was assigned to Shaozhou that same year. He had an energetic temperament – he lived to be ninety-eight years old – he was inclined to optimism. He did not understand Ricci's method and did not fail to criticize it: "We have not come to China to teach science, but to instruct the people and save them." In three years, he baptized about three hundred people, but he began to notice that his converts were not very sincere and he began to understand that the approach, undertaken by his superior, was perhaps not completely without merit.

At the time of Ricci's death, Longobardi was local superior in Nanjing. After his nomination as superior of the mission, he did not go to Peking, but chose to live in Nanjing, from where he could tour around and guide his confreres as easily as in Peking. (A new local superior, [Alfonso] Vagnoni, was sent to Nanjing.) As he gradually got to know Ricci's talents and virtues better, Longobardi's respect for his methods increased. Some doubts remained, however, in his mind concerning the legitimacy of certain rites that Ricci had allowed the Christians to practice. Moreover, he had heard that several of his confreres in Japan did not approve of the Chinese rites that the Japanese also were observing. Feeling himself responsible for possible abuses, he began to read attentively the works of Confucius. Other missionaries of China had already discussed the question among themselves and the opinions varied.

From his study, Longobardi concluded that these rites seemed tainted with superstition, if not idolatry. That was the situation when an unexpected storm rose against the missionaries.

The Persecution by Shen Que from 1616 to 1623

A distinguished scholar of Nanjing, the vice-president of the Board of Rites and a fierce Confucian, became annoyed when he saw that the Christian community of Nanjing was making progress under Vagnoni's direction. This person's name was Shen Que.

In May 1616, he presented to the Court a damning accusation against the preachers of the new foreign religion, which was turning the people away from honoring their ancestors. Not having received an answer, he wrote again on 15 August. He said that it was necessary to kill the missionaries and the Christians and not to wait until they had established a foothold in the empire. On 20 August a decree from the Board of Rites ordered the priests to be arrested and exiled. On 31 August Vagnoni and fifteen Christians were imprisoned. Longobardi, warned in time, hastened to Peking hoping to ward off the storm. In Peking he found Pantoja and de Ursis, and they with the three doctors used all their influence to have the unfair sentence revoked. The members of the Board of Rites were hostile to the missionaries and envious of the favor that the Christian doctors had with the Court. These three doctors were Paul Xu, Léon Li and Michel Yang.

Following a new petition by Shen Que, a decree of 1617 sentenced the missionaries to be exiled to Macao. The priests left on 18 March 1617, leaving the cemetery of Chala in the care of two Chinese brothers, not included in the sentence. It took four months to arrive in Canton. Longobardi and another hid in the countryside and were able to exercise a little ministry, helped by the alms and assistance of the Christian doctors. The priests of Nanjing were put into wooden cages and were taken over land to the coast, from where they were carted off to Canton so as to be imprisoned there with their confreres from Peking.

Doctor Michel Yang saved Cattaneo and two other priests, who were in Hangzhou. He lodged them in his house and helped the missionaries so judiciously that during those six years of persecution the residence of Hangzhou was the real center of the mission of China. In 1621, this Christian community numbered one thousand six hundred Faithful.

In 1613, Longobardi sent Nicolas Trigault, a French Jesuit, to Europe with the mission of recruiting missionaries and informing the pope and the Jesuits' superior general about the success and the needs of the work begun in the Celestial Empire. Trigault brought with him Ricci's "Memoirs." Written in Latin they were published in 1615 under the title *De Christiana expeditione apud Sinas* (On Christian travel to China). That book, translated into several European languages, met enormous success.

The Jesuits' Official Return to Peking

For quite some time already, the Manchus had been threatening to invade the north of China. On the other side of the Great Wall, the Chinese armies were suffering defeat after defeat and were looking for some means to block the road against the Tartars.

Emperor Wanli showed little concern and so had done nothing to avoid this rebellion. After his death (1620), his son, Taichang (1621–1628) ascended the throne at the age of fifteen years.

The Christian scholars, during the priests' absence, had tried hard to get a note to the emperor to explain that the Portuguese of Macao had excellent soldiers and that the Jesuit Fathers were skillful scientists, and that both could contribute to the salvation of the empire. The emperor on receiving this suggestion requested a detachment of four hundred soldiers from Macao, but difficulties prevented that detachment from arriving in Peking. Longobardi with some companions hastened to return to Peking. There, they learned that the intention of the Court in calling them back was to have them cast cannons. The priests refused, saying that they were unable to do that. Dr. Léon Li assuaged their scruples by saying, "Just as a tailor uses his needle to make a thread pass, so you will use your title of 'casters.'" His meaning was, "Just come back; the emperor has banished you; come back now that you have an imperial order to do so; later on it will be easy for you to lay down your arms and pick up the pen." Indeed, after having been introduced to the Board of War, they returned to their old residence that a Christian had saved from destruction by buying it with his own money. Then they took up their old works, renewed their old relations and saw their small group of Christians grow, without any one ever talking to them again about casting cannons.

The Christian doctors had in their heads the daring project of introducing some priests into the Bureau of Astronomy to reform the calendar and to guarantee them a more stable situation in Peking. Paul Xu had already introduced the priests to Wanli as well versed in astronomy. The present emperor, responding favorably, charged Fathers de Ursis and Terrenz with the correction of the calendar.

After Taichang's death, his brother Chongzhen (1628–1643) was his successor. Paul Xu had become "Gelao" (State Counselor) and had all the necessary influence to protect the priests.

Fall of the Ming Dynasty

While the Chinese armies, sent into Manchuria to push back the Tartars, were suffering only defeat, the provinces in China were warring with each other. There were at least eight rulers fighting each other, everyone claiming imperial succession. When only two remained, they divided China between themselves: Li Zicheng took the north and Zhang Xianzhong took the south. Li advanced on Peking and had the majority of the imperial family slaughtered. Chongzhen, abandoned by all and desperate, fled from the palace and hanged himself from a tree of the Mei Shan, an artificial hill adjoining the palace. Then Li ordered the Chinese general Wu Sangui, who was fighting against the Tartars in Manchuria, to recognize him as his sovereign. His only answer was to ask his enemies, the Manchus, for help. Only too happy to grasp this occasion to enter Peking, they did not need coaxing. Together, the Chinese and Manchus defeated Li Zicheng in a fierce fight near the Great Wall. Li went back into the capital, grabbed the treasures and fled to Baoding with his bands. Wu Sangui, seeing the rebels outside Peking, thought that the moment had arrived to reinstall the imperial family on the throne. Naively, he tried to convince his helpers, the Manchus, to return home to Manchuria.

They refused, of course. Since their ruler, Taichang, had died recently, they chose his seven-year-old nephew and placed him on the throne of China under the name of Shunzhi. He was the first Tartar emperor of the Qing dynasty.

Shunzhi was to reign over a divided China, but his successor, the great Kangxi, was going to put things back in order.

This dynastic change had no unfortunate disadvantage for religion. The missionaries who had helped the Ming immediately rallied around the cause of the Qing. They were not much bothered, except under the reign of Yongzheng, Kangxi's son, as we shall see later.

Chapter VI

Ecclesiastical Hierarchy and the Issue of Rites

Restoration of the Ecclesiastical Hierarchy – The Chinese Rites

Restoration of the Ecclesiastical Hierarchy

Up to now, the reader may be amazed that in our account there is no mention of bishops. It has been all about evangelization by missionaries almost all of whom belonged to orders or congregations. Actually, the reason is that since 23 January 1576 there was only one bishop, the bishop of Macao, suffragan of the metropolitan of Goa. The first bishop was Leonard de Sâ (1577–1597) of the Society of Jesus. China, Annam, Siam, Cambodia and Japan were under this bishop's jurisdiction.

From time to time, the popes granted broad privileges to the kings of Portugal to thank them for services rendered and to encourage them to render further service. Portugal faithfully fulfilled their responsibilities during the first years of its conquests, but for a long time afterwards it was unable to do so. Short of men and money, it left the churches without missionaries and could not to support the ones it had sent. As a result, one might reasonably consider that Portugal no longer deserved its prerogatives, because it was no longer able to satisfy its pre-conditions. The king, the statesmen, and even the Portuguese clergy did not agree. They wanted to keep all the rights of the Padroado, even if it was impossible for them to fulfill its obligations.

Consequently, hard-working missionaries regularly asked the pope to send pastors for the recently founded churches in the Far East. Innocent X wanted to ordain one of them, the Jesuit, [Alexandre] de Rhodes, but he refused.

Then the pope gave him the task of recruiting missionaries. He found some in Paris among a group of priests who were thinking of founding a society for foreign missions. In France some highly placed religious, worrying very much about the missions, petitioned the Sovereign Pontiff to "create titular bishops and to send them in these regions to represent the Apostolic See, but not with the title of 'ordinary'" (July 1653). Among the signatories of that petition, we find Saint Vincent de Paul's name.

After long hesitation, Rome adopted this plan, which made it possible for the pope to send bishops to the new churches without giving rise to protests from Portugal. The Sovereign Pontiff indeed had the right to evangelize everywhere in the world. By creating apostolic vicars who, though consecrated as bishops, were not Ordinaries but just the pope's delegates, he did not infringe the rights of Portugal. If the pope on the contrary had created Ordinaries for the territories assigned to the metropolitan of Goa, he could have objected that a part of his jurisdiction had been taken away from him.

In 1658, then, Pope Alexander VII initiated this strategy, which became the general rule for all the mission countries. The Holy See promoted three French priests not belonging to religious communities: François Pallu, apostolic vicar of Tonkin, charging him also with the administration of five Chinese provinces; [Pierre} Lambert de la Motte, apostolic vicar of four other Chinese provinces, and [Ignace] Cotolendi, apostolic vicar of Nanjing and administrator of the following provinces: Zhili, Shandong, Shaanxi, Henan; [as well as] Korea and Mongolia.

Soon, thanks to the generous gifts of Louis XIV and to the generosity and devotion of the Duchess of Aiguillon, a Society of Missionaries exclusively destined for the Far East, was born in Paris, under the name of Society of the Foreign Missions of Paris (M.E.P.) which, henceforth, gave an extraordinary number of missionaries to the Church in Asia.

Bishop Cottolendi was consecrated in Paris in 1660, but never reached his destination. Exhausted by fever, he died in the Indies on 18 August 1662 at the age of thirty-three.

His successor was Chinese, Father Grégoire Luo [Wenzao], also known as Lopez (his Portuguese name). Born in Fujian, he was baptized when he was twenty-two years old. He entered the Dominicans and was ordained a priest in 1656. Nominated apostolic vicar in 1674, he could be consecrated only on 8 April 1685. This first Chinese priest and bishop was humble and zealous. He helped the Christians of the southern provinces during the exile of the missionaries in Canton. After his consecration, he lived in Nanjing, where he exercised a very active ministry. He died in Nanjing on 27 February 1691.

This form of hierarchy did not last long. Despite the care that Rome had taken not to insult Portugal, Portugal did not stop its protests against the so-called injury to its rights of patronage through the creation of the apostolic vicars. In order to give the king some satisfaction, Pope Alexander VIII erected on 10 April 1690 the two dioceses of Peking and Nanjing, for which he granted the king of Portugal the right of presentation with the obligation to endow them.

Here is how the territory was divided among these two dioceses and the diocese of Macao:

> For the bishop of Macao: Guangdong and Guangxi.
>
> For the bishop of Peking: Zhili, Shandong, Shanxi, Mongolia, Henan and Sichuan.
>
> For the bishop of Nanjing: Zhejiang, Fujian, Jiangxi, Huguang, Guizhou and Yunnan.

The archbishop of Goa was their metropolitan. Six years after the erection of these three dioceses, Rome took territories from each of them to form eight more apostolic vicariates (in 1696).

This way of proceeding was repeated several times up till 21 January 1856 when the dioceses of Peking and Nanjing were changed into vicariates. The diocese of Macao, whose territory became smaller and smaller, was the only one to continue up to the end

The Chinese Rites

Before we continue our history of the apostolate in China, we have to mention some serious differences among the missionaries about specific practices common in China concerning both the spiritual life of the living and the respect for the dead and for ancestors. First there were the rites practiced by all the public officials and by the students in government schools on certain fixed days and periods to honor the "Sage" Confucius; then, there were the rites that the Chinese practiced privately for the deceased and their ancestors.

The missionaries conceived several ways of proceeding with regard to the newly converted. Some, like Ricci and many of his successors, in order to attract as many proselytes as possible, chose not to touch those customs that were not absolutely against Catholic dogma. They considered that certain exterior ceremonies for dead people, ancestors, Confucius and even for the emperor were not tainted with superstitious beliefs. Consequently they were in favor of tolerating them, thinking to inspire converts little by little with Christian ideas. They thought that sweeping away all the Chinese customs would only provoke systematic opposition from the officials, and among the people a quite natural distrust towards a new religion that did not hesitate to suppress what they valued so much.

This way of proceeding had become the rule, when in turn new missionaries belonging to other religious communities landed in China opened up by their elder brothers. They were upset because of the great freedom with which Catholic dogma was treated. Worrying less than their predecessors about the difficulties of beginnings, they did not understand that it was possible to negotiate the purity of the Catholic teaching. They thought that this purity was much more important, especially in the beginning of preaching the Gospel in China, than the number of neophytes attracted thanks to flexibility granted in relation to existing customs.

The question was taken to Rome, and the Chinese Rites were forbidden through several memorable decrees. A majority of the missionaries who had tolerated the rites did not want to yield, thinking that Rome did not understand the actual situation on the ground.

The others did not surrender either, convinced that they were serving the side of the truth and that they were acting as the "protectors of the Faith." It took many years for the question to become clear and for calm to be restored.

It is beyond our purpose to detail these arguments. It will suffice for us to mention them briefly when the clarity of the account calls for it.[13]

---

13.   Since the names of Western priests are all non-C.M., and it is difficult to know their Chinese names (except for Ricci), they are not listed in the glossary, except for Ricci and his three helpers. (JR)

Part Two

Vincentians in China

Observations. – *We have to divide our account into several distinct periods, because the Vincentian priests and brothers in China ministered in different locations and under varying circumstances.*

Vincentian missionaries arrived in China for the first time as members of a small group sent by the Sacred Congregation of Propaganda Fide[14] *(established in 1622). The superior general did not send them, though he gave his approval. The first two were, Fathers [Louis Antoine] Appiani and [Johannes] Mullener; a little later a third, [Teodorico] Pedrini, followed them.*

The First Period covers the years 1699–1784.

The Second Period covers 1785–1856. In 1783, Rome offered the Congregation of the Mission the direction of the "French mission of Peking," up to then entrusted to the Jesuits, whose Society was being suppressed. It ends with the reorganization of the ecclesiastical jurisdictions in China in 1856.

In 1856, after suppressing the two dioceses of Peking and Nanjing, the Holy See divided the territory of Peking into three apostolic vicariates. With this event the Third Period began and continued to the end of the nineteenth century.

Finally, the rebellion of the "Boxers," which opened the twentieth century, marks the beginning of an era of expansion for the missions of China. That will be the subject of the Fourth Period, which comprises a half-century, and necessarily will be the last period, for we shall have arrived at that ominous moment when Communism, alas, annihilated everything and put an end to the missions in China.

---

14.   The papal office with oversight over the "Propagation of the Faith" (Propaganda Fide), formally called a Sacred Congregation, and commonly called Propaganda. (JR)

First Period
(1699–1784)

Missionaries
and Persecutions

Chapter 1

Appiani and De Tournon

Pope Innocent XII Sent Missionaries to China. – Louis-Antoine Appiani, Vincentian – Bishop de Tournon Exiled from Canton – The Imprisonment and Letters of Appiani and Pedrini – Legation of Charles Mezzabarba (1720-1721) – Appiani's Death – The Persecution by Yongzheng

Pope Innocent XII Sent Missionaries to China

We saw that, through establishing three apostolic vicariates, the Church had removed almost the whole of China from Portuguese influence. On the one hand, however, those three areas, much too vast to be visited efficiently by their chief shepherds, Bishop Pallu, Bishop de la Motte-Lambert, and Bishop Grégoire Lopez [Luo], benefited very little from that innovation. On the other hand, Portugal complained bitterly of being despoiled of its rights in such a callous way.

By erecting the two dioceses of Peking and Nanjing in 1690, Alexander VIII had reserved for himself the right to divide those dioceses and Macao into apostolic vicariates. His successor, Innocent XII, used this power to establish nine new apostolic vicariates. They were the vicariates of:

1* Fujian, entrusted to the Foreign Missions of Paris;

2* Zhejiang, to the Dominicans;

3* Jiangxi, to the Augustinians;

4* Huguang, to the Franciscans;

5* Shanxi, to the Jesuits;

6* Sichuan, also to the Foreign Missions of Paris;

7* Shaanxi, also to the Franciscans;

8* Yunnan, also to the Foreign Missions of Paris;

9* Guizhou, also to the Jesuits.

Note. – When it is said that a vicariate was entrusted to a specific society of missionaries, it does not mean that from that day the missionaries working in that vicariate were all members of the society or the congregation to which the vicariate had been entrusted. The missions of China had only a very basic organization at that time. Propaganda entrusted the administration of the Christian communities to those who had founded them. The first missionaries established Christian communities wherever circumstances allowed and in that way were present in quite a number of the provinces of China. When the dioceses and the vicariates were created, the missionaries continued to manage the Christian communities where they were without any prejudice to the jurisdiction of the local Ordinary, to whom all the missionaries had to submit. It did not matter to which society or congregation the missionaries belonged. This line of conduct was favorable for the neophytes, because in this way they remained under the direction of the priests who had converted them to the Faith, while at the same time falling under the jurisdiction of the bishop or apostolic vicar of that place. This system could not last long, because the scattered missionaries were inclined to go back to the bosom of their spiritual family that was working to support itself in the territory entrusted to it. With this clarification in mind, let us proceed with our account.

In 1597, Pope Innocent XII, after having provided pastors for these apostolic vicariates, thought about giving them good workers. Following his orders, the Sacred Congregation of Propaganda prepared an apostolic expedition to China made up with thirty-two religious priests, among whom were Dominicans, Augustinians and Franciscans as well as an Italian Vincentian, Louis Appiani, spiritual director of the College of Propaganda[15] accompanied by a secular priest, Father Mullener, a German from Saxony by birth, who came from that same college.

The goal of the Sacred Congregation was to establish a seminary in China to form an indigenous clergy. The qualities that Propaganda had seen in Father Appiani gave them great hope that Appiani could accomplish this beautiful work. In order to give him the means to realize this project, he was given the title and the powers of apostolic visitor.

---

15.   This college was built in Genoa in 1626, for the formation of a clergy especially destined for the foreign missions.

Louis-Antoine Appiani, Vincentian

Louis Appiani was born in Dogliani, in Piedmont (Italy) on 22 March 1663. At age twenty-five, already a priest and doctor in theology, he entered the Congregation of the Mission in Genoa and pronounced his vows on 28 May 1689. He taught theology, later philosophy in Rome at the house of Monte Citorio; then he was given the task of doing spiritual direction in the college of Propaganda in Genoa.

Appiani and the young Mullener, twenty-four years old, sailed from Venice on 12 May 1697, landed in Syria, crossed Persia and took another boat as far as Madras, a harbor of the Indies, where they had to wait almost a year for a boat to China. On his way, Mullener was reflecting. Witnessing the virtue and example of his former spiritual director, he determined to lead a more intense religious life, so as not expose himself to the danger of losing his soul while saving others. As a result, he asked Appiani to receive him into the Company of Saint Vincent. Presuming the consent of his superiors, Appiani received him in Madras on 25 January 1699.

They arrived in Canton on 14 August, where they stayed for two years, learning the Chinese language and training themselves to do apostolic ministry.

It was the moment that the "Rites Controversy" was at its height, causing trouble in all the Christian communities of China. Appiani quickly realized that amid such a crisis, he could not have his seminary either in Canton or Macao, nor in Peking; he would have to delay his project till he could find a remote place where Europeans would not go. In Canton he saw Bishop Artus de Lyonne (Lionne), who had just been named apostolic vicar of Sichuan and whom he knew already. He asked him if he could not go and work temporarily in his vicariate with his companion, while waiting for more favorable circumstances. The bishop gladly accepted this proposal.

The two missionaries then left for Sichuan and settled in very poor circumstances near the large city of Chongqing, where they found some Christians. Among great hardships they displayed an ardor that God rewarded with numerous conversions.

As they lacked money for their work and for themselves, Appiani, after hearing that Bishop de Tournon,[16] papal legate, was shortly to arrive in Canton to deal with the Rites question, he left his confrere for Canton to ask the legate for some help for his mission.

---

16.   Charles Thomas Maillard de Tournon. (AS)

On 2 April 1705 de Tournon landed in Macao and from there went to Canton, where Appiani had been waiting for him for two months. The encounter with Appiani, who, like himself, was from Piedmont, gave the legate much pleasure and, because he saw in Appiani a man dedicated to his person and to his mission, already well-versed in the language and in the affairs of China, the legate wanted him as his assistant and asked him to accompany him as his translator. Consequently, instead of going back to his mission in Sichuan as he had planned, Appiani accompanied the delegation to Peking.

The legate, with his entourage, reached the capital on 4 December 1705 and was welcomed in the Beitang, the North Church, by the French Jesuits. The first audience at the imperial court took place on 31 December. There were from both sides compliments and Kangxi bluntly declared that he had prepared a gift for the pope and that it had to be sent to him without delay. The legate, who was very tired because of his long journey, was quite astonished by the emperor's attitude.

The emperor, having heard of the decisions taken by Rome against the Chinese Rites, surely showed his entourage his irritation. Consequently, when the legate appeared again in front him, he had to undergo the repercussions of his bitterness and anger.

In the meantime, Bishop [Charles] Maigrot, apostolic vicar of Fujian, whom the emperor was told was an expert in Roman teachings, was called to Peking. Kangxi asked him if he would agree to abandon his opinions so as to follow those of the throne. He answered boldly: "I would like to do so, but my conscience is against it." This holy stubbornness was to hasten the events. In his indignation, the emperor had the bishop arrested and decreed the banishment of all the missionaries who would refuse to take the *piao*, the safe-conduct and residence certificate delivered by the civil authority in return for the formal approval of the Chinese Rites.

Deeply saddened when he saw the failure of his mission, de Tournon returned to Canton on 18 August 1706. During his stay in Peking at the side of the legate, Appiani was several times subjected to hostile examination by lower-level mandarins. Once he was asked: "Is it true that you had to leave Sichuan because you caused trouble?"

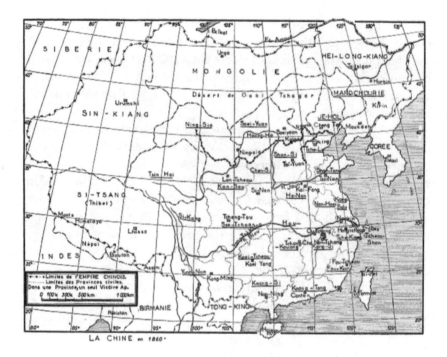

LA CHINE en 1860 ·

Map 1.1 China in 1860

Consequently, Appiani realized that he was under suspicion.

When de Tournon left Peking with his entourage, he took with him as a companion Bishop [Bernardino] della Chiesa.[17] A Franciscan who had become the first bishop of Peking in 1696, but resided in the city of Linqing (Shandong), because he did not like to live in the capital as the only Franciscan. Present in Peking at the time of the mission, he arrived back in his town with the legate on 14 October 1706. The legate stayed there for some days and took advantage of that opportunity to write a comforting and encouraging letter to Bishop Maigrot, who was in police custody.

On 23 November the legate's party was approaching Nanjing when two policemen sent by the emperor entered the small boat, took hold of Appiani and put a chain around his neck. De Tournon was indignant

---

17. On Bishop della Chiesa, O.F.M., see the volumes VI and VII of the *Sinica Franciscana*. These books, edited and annotated by Father Mensaert, contain the correspondence of della Chiesa as well as that of his confreres. Those texts provide the basis for the well-documented biographies of these Franciscan missionaries. Incidentally, Pope Benedict XV (1914–1922) was a member of the della Chiesa family.

and cried out that if Appiani was guilty, he also was and had to wear a chain. The next day, the prisoner's chains were doubled and his hands were bound. He was put in a criminal's chair and in this way was carried back to Peking, where he was imprisoned at the Board of Punishments. So began for this courageous witness of the faith, a Calvary that was to last nineteen years.

After Appiani's return to the capital, Kangxi initiated a series of hostile actions. A downright persecution was unleashed against the adversaries of the rites. A decree of 21 December 1706 said: "Maigrot and Mezzafalce, apostolic vicar of Fujian, are troublemakers. . . . They must be handed over to the Military Tribunal, which will have them sent to Macao. They are never to be allowed to come back. It is reported that Appiani has also caused troubles in Sichuan. . . . The Board of Punishments must be diligent in taking the aforesaid Appiani to the viceroy of Sichuan, who, after inquiry, will report to me."

Maigrot along with his companions were escorted to Canton and expelled from China without delay. Once back in France, he went to Rome, called by the Sovereign Pontiff, who welcomed him with open arms. Maigrot died in Rome in 1730.

The article of the decree aimed at Appiani was also executed strictly. He was transported to Sichuan to have the viceroy conduct the investigation of his case. In chains only when passing through big towns, he covered on horseback the 1800 kilometers that separate Peking and Chengdu, the capital of Sichuan, in thirty-five days. The viceroy, seeing that the court sent him a prisoner with such a large escort, wondered what kind of crime the defendant was guilty of when the emperor himself sent this man to him without any information. Consequently, the viceroy secretly sent a trustworthy person to Peking to ferret out the reasons of his prisoner's arrest. The emissary returned without having found out anything, except there was a rumor saying that Kangxi was angry with the prisoner because he had left the capital without his permission. So as to show his diligence to execute the emperor's orders, the viceroy sentenced Appiani to be struck forty times with a rod and to be exiled forever; then, he sent him back to Peking to get approval of his sentence.

Appiani arrived in Peking on 18 December 1707 and was put in the ordinary jail; afterwards he was taken to the Beitang to live with the Jesuits in an isolated apartment of the priests. There the chains were taken off. The prisoner thought that the tragedy was over. But not so! On the 27th of the same month six soldiers put him into a small cell that had no other opening than a door and there stood guard. Throughout the whole summer of 1708 Appiani suffered from dysentery, and throughout the winter he suffered from the cold. Through the whole time he spent in that cell, he was fed at the expense of the priests.

On 17 May 1710 Appiani was again sent back to Canton. It is not known why. He arrived on 8 August and was imprisoned in a less strict prison. Six soldiers guarded him, but he nevertheless was allowed to receive some visitors.

Bishop de Tournon Exiled from Canton

While Appiani was still being taken to Peking as a criminal, the legate was traveling towards Nanjing. He arrived on 17 December 1706 and took several months' rest. On 7 February 1707 while still in Nanjing, he published a document that repeated the condemnation of Chinese superstitions in the same way as Clement XI had done in 1704. This document, known under the name of the "Decree of Nanjing" was a brave act on de Tournon's part, for he knew very well the danger to which the emperor's anger exposed him. Actually, an order came from Peking ordering the legate to leave Nanjing and to be taken under escort to Canton, making him pass through Jiangxi. The legate arrived there on 24 May 1707 and in the beginning enjoyed some freedom, but on 19 June he was ordered to return to Macao. Ten days later, the legate arrived at the place of his exile. He was accompanied by his entourage and by five priests exiled like himself and for the same reason. In his new prison, de Tournon was deprived of all communication with the outside. They went so far as to forbid this legate *a latere* from exercising any jurisdiction.

They did not manage, however, to stop him from consecrating a religious priest as bishop in his prison cell and in the most complete secrecy. It was Claude de Visdelou, French Jesuit, great sinologist, author of many books which Kangxi himself praised highly saying that their author had shown a great familiarity with and a profound knowledge of the Chinese language. As zealous as he was learned, his work in Peking, Jiangxi and Fujian bore much fruit. In the question of the rites, however, he was against the opinion of the majority of his Jesuit confreres. Knowing his merits, the legate named de Visdelou apostolic vicar of Guizhou and ordered the apostolic vicar of Jiangxi, Bishop Alvares Benavente, to consecrate him bishop, but, this bishop, who was in favor of the Rites, refused. Then de Visdelou went to Macao and succeeded in entering the legate's prison.

The legate consecrated him bishop under cover of darkness (2 February 1709). Bishop de Visdelou could never enter his vicariate, and entrusted its management to Father Mullener. His new dignity brought so many troubles on him that he fled to the Indies, to Pondicherry, where he was welcomed by the Capuchin fathers and worked with them until his death in 1737.

Once Pope Clement XI had word of his legate's activities in China, he made him a cardinal at the consistory of 1 August 1707 in order to demonstrate his approval for the legate's actions. It was only in 1710 that the news reached de Tournon. The bestowal of the biretta took place secretly on 18 January 1710 in the presence of the personnel of the legation and a few missionaries. Shortly after the ceremony, the cardinal felt violent intestinal pains, which obliged him to stay in bed. Day by day the illness became more serious. He suffered all with great calm and perfect resignation to God. On Sunday, 8 June 1710, feast of the Pentecost, after having heard Holy Mass in his private chapel and having received Holy Viaticum, he gave his soul back to God. The cardinal was forty-one years old.

The news of Cardinal de Tournon's death caused great sorrow at the court of Rome. Clement XI eulogized him during a consistory in the following words: "We lost a great and zealous apostle of the Christian religion, a great light of your Order [of the Sacred College]. We have lost our brother, exhausted by the extensive activities he undertook for Jesus Christ, and worn out by the anxieties he had to suffer."

Imprisonment and Letters of Appiani

Let us return to our patient prisoner in Canton: Appiani was no longer in chains. He finally had received permission to say Mass in his cell and to have as jailer his old servant, who in this way was able to serve his Mass and bring his letters out. Actually, Appiani wrote a great deal. His letters, many of which have been preserved, were addressed to the superior general of the congregation, to his brother Jean in Italy, a Vincentian like himself, to Fathers Mullener and Pedrini, and to missionaries and bishops in China.

From the depths of his prison, he never forgot that he was a missionary; he asked for news about events in the missions. Cardinal de Tournon, who could neither write nor visit him, wrote the following to the Cardinal Archbishop de Fermo (Italy), in whose seminary Jean Appiani was teaching: "I recommend him [Jean Appiani] to you especially because of his brother, Louis Appiani, who was taken away from me two years ago. He acted as my interpreter; and during the time of persecution, he suffered most, because he did not want to betray me, but also because he followed the party of truth and the voice of his conscience."

Appiani was treated quite humanely in prison until the arrival of a second apostolic legate in 1721. Afterwards it was not the same anymore. Two bishops, the one of Macao and the apostolic vicar of Jiangxi, had appealed against the Nanjing Decree published by the legate. A decree of 25 September by Clement XI declared that de Tournon's document was in every point in conformity with the pontifical decree of 1704. The cardinal's death, however, gave new impetus to the Rites Controversy. The condemnation of the two dissidents did not bring about their submission. Then Clement XI published the Bull *Ex illa die* (19 March 1715), which renewed all the previous condemnations, added more explicit precisions and finally imposed on all the missionaries – even on those who belonged to the Society of Jesus – an oath of obeying that constitution.

Despite the very strict demands of the constitution *Ex illa die*, the Holy See did not succeed in bringing about obedience. Clement XI thought that a new mission to the emperor of China might convince the emperor to allow one group the peaceful observance of the orders of the Holy See and withdraw his support from the other group. This method was to fail like the others. It became necessary for God to lend a hand by using the rude trial of persecution, a persecution that had absolutely nothing to do with the Rites controversy.

Legation of Charles Mezzabarba (1720–1721)

The pope's choice fell on Bishop Charles Mezzabarba, patriarch of Alexandria, who arrived in Macao on 23 September 1720 and in Peking on the following 26 December. Soon after the meetings began, the legate endured the emperor's sarcasm towards him and towards the pope. He met only with insults.

Convinced of the uselessness of his stay in China, Mezzabarba had no other wish than to leave this wasp's nest as fast as possible, in order to be able to go and inform the pope about the real situation.

On 1 March 1721 he went and took his leave from the emperor in the Summer Palace. On 3 March, despite efforts to make him defer his departure, the legate left Peking. After a six-month stay in Macao, he embarked for Rome on 3 December 1721. He brought with him Cardinal de Tournon's mortal remains, to which the pope wished to grant an honorable burial.

The Imprisonment of Appiani and Pedrini

As long as the legate was present in China, and especially during his stay in Macao, Appiani was under the strictest surveillance by his keepers. No visit, no outing was granted; he was not allowed to write a letter or to receive one.

When Kangxi died on 22 December 1722 his fourth son under the name of Yongzheng succeeded him. According to custom, the new sovereign announced an amnesty, which emptied the prisons. Pedrini, whom Kangxi had imprisoned, was freed. We shall soon talk about this gallant missionary.

Pope Benedict XIII, knowing about Pedrini's release and informed also about the new emperor's feelings, sent him two Briefs (1724). The first one congratulated Yongzheng on his accession to the throne and commended the missionaries to him. The second one asked the monarch for the release of Appiani and [Antoine] Guignes. Guignes, a priest of the Foreign Missions of Paris, had been imprisoned with Appiani for the same reason. After hearing this brief read, the emperor ordered the two imprisoned missionaries to be set free. Appiani was released, but not without difficulties and not without delay. Finally, on 21 August 1726 Appiani and Guignes were freed. Aged, weakened and without money, Appiani went and asked for hospitality at the Procure of Propaganda in Canton. He stayed there for six long years, i.e., until 20 August 1732, the fateful day when an imperial order came and tore him from his residence to expel him from China with all the missionaries (interned) in Canton, because of the persecution initiated by Yongzheng. We shall talk about this persecution later on.

Appiani's Death

Though ill, Appiani had to travel to Macao with other missionaries. Among them was Pierre Sanz, apostolic vicar of Fujian, who became a martyr a little later and was declared blessed. He received hospitality from the Franciscans. His health worsened and he received the last rites five days later. He died on 29 August 1732. He was in his seventieth year, had passed thirty-two of them in China, twenty of which were in prison for defending the Faith. His death, hastened through the brutality of his persecutors, brought him the crown of martyrdom. It crowned a life spent for a large part in chains, which led him to be pleased to sign his letters as Saint Paul had done: L.A. Appiani, *vinctus Christi* [a prisoner for Christ].

The Persecution by Yongzheng

The viceroy of Fujian had launched a violent diatribe on 7 September against the missionaries and against all those who had allowed themselves to be misled by them. He sent his memorandum to the emperor, who handed it to the Board of Rites to get their judgment about it. This board – which had always been against Christianity – unanimously approved the viceroy's conclusions and presented their report to the emperor. It said in substance: "In conformity with what the viceroy of Fujian proposes, it is necessary to leave the Europeans who are useful in the Imperial Court; as for the others, spread over the provinces, they must be taken to Macao, except those who might be useful. No further safe-conducts are to be given. The temples that they have built must be changed into common houses. Let that religion be forbidden strictly. The mandarins who might be little interested in this order must be demoted."

On 11 February 1724 the emperor ratified their decision and annotated it with his red brush. In the decree that he published, he added these clauses: "Because it is to be feared that the people harm them, I order the governors and the viceroys of the provinces to have them accompanied in their journey by a mandarin who takes care of them and prevents every abuse."

Then, the missionaries were pressed to leave on 20 August 1732. Of the fifty-three, twenty-three were allowed to remain in Peking, though their presence was merely tolerated. The other thirty were put in small boats and escorted by four galleys to Macao, which they reached on 24 August.

It is clear that the reasons for expelling the missionaries had no relation to the "Rites" question. They were expelled because they were foreigners, without any distinction between supporters and opponents of the Rites. Nor was there any allusion to that question. This is underlined to answer some badly informed historians who have written that the reason for the persecution was the Rites question. Nothing is further from the truth.

Chapter 2

Mullener

Father Jean Mullener – His Elevation to the Episcopacy – Mullener's Ardor for the Formation of Chinese Clergy – His Death, Arms at the Ready

Father Jean Mullener

Father Mullener pronounced his holy vows in the presence of Appiani on 2 February 1704 before Appiani left for Canton to see the papal legate.

From that moment onward, the two confreres were to see each other only twice and that very briefly. They remained, however, so united in spirit that it is impossible to speak of one without thinking of the other. Moreover, they maintained their friendship through a quite frequent correspondence.

The same will be true when we talk about Pedrini, whose work was quite different from that of his two confreres.

Left alone in Sichuan, Mullener went ahead with his ministry, though he did not have the *piao* required to promote a religion. The immense vicariate had only a few hundred Faithful. Father Basset, M.E.P., as pro-vicar managed the vicariate in the absence of Bishop de Lyonne (who, after his conversation with Appiani, had gone back to Europe and never returned to China). In 1706, Mullener was arrested and was taken to Canton because he had no *piao*. He escaped from his guards and naively thought that he could go to Peking to get a permit to preach. But, once in the capital, he sized up the situation and saw with his own eyes what was the source of so many troubles. He would have liked to see Appiani who was in prison in the Beitang and give him some financial help, but he was told he could not see him and besides the prisoner did not need anything. Having nothing else to do in Peking, Mullener set out to return to Sichuan, a journey full of risks. He was arrested and brought before tribunals several times, and underwent perhaps one hundred cross-examinations, yet he never contradicted himself and never said anything that would compromise the Church.

In 1708, he was again arrested and brought back to Canton, then sent to Macao, from where he was further expelled along with all foreigners living in Macao by a decree of the viceroy of Guangdong in December 1709. He fled to Batavia [Jakarta], but after a few months, he managed to get back to Canton, where he hid so well for a year that nobody was aware of his presence – except Appiani, because the fugitive had sent a reliable Christian to tell Appiani that he was going to visit him soon in prison.

At that moment, the long-expected Pedrini arrived in Canton. Then the memorable meeting took place about which Appiani wrote: "The three of us were able to embrace each other and to have a whole night to talk together."

Eventually, in 1711, always incognito, Mullener went back to Sichuan. When he arrived in Chongqing, he was very sad to find his first chapel occupied by pagans. On his way he had learned that the viceroy of Sichuan at the capital, was looking for him; but he went on with his visits in the disguise sometimes of a porter, sometimes of a travelling merchant, always escaping the pitfalls he encountered.

His Elevation to the Episcopacy

Rome had not yet named a successor for de Lyonne. Basset, his pro-vicar, had taken care of Sichuan since 1705, but he was expelled from Macao in 1709 with all the foreigners. He returned to France and never returned to China.

Pope Clement XI, counting on the probability that Appiani's captivity would soon be finished and wanting to give him a new proof of his esteem, named Appiani bishop of Myriophis and apostolic vicar of Sichuan. Appiani hastened to thank the Holy Father for the honor bestowed on him, but he asked him to pass this dignity to his confrere Mullener, for these reasons: first, his own age and infirmities, and then the uncertainty of his liberation; secondly, the vigorous health of Mullener and his great qualities as a missionary, namely, experience, tireless zeal, kindness, and humility. The pope agreed with these reasons. When sending the Constitution *Ex illa die* of 19 March 1715, the Holy Father had put with it the Pontifical Brief addressed to Mullener by which he raised him to the rank of bishop. The bull ordered the new bishop to have himself consecrated by the nearest bishop. Now, the nearest bishop was the bishop of Peking, della Chiesa, who was living in Linqing (Shandong). Mullener went there immediately and was consecrated bishop on 14 December 1716. On his way back, he passed through Changde (Huguang, which was formed by the two present provinces of Hubei and Hunan), to visit the Christian communities that he himself had founded. He found Thomas [Bottaro], a Dominican from Genoa and missionary in Chongqing, waiting for him for a month to receive episcopal consecration. After the ceremony, probably done very simply, Bishop Thomas returned to his mission and Bishop Mullener continued to his vicariate.

His sphere of activity was immense. We said earlier how de Visdelou, unable to enter his vicariate of Guizhou, had passed its management on to Mullener. Sichuan is almost as big as France, and its population is greater than that of France. As far as Huguang was concerned, Mullener did very little, for in that place there were some Jesuits in favor of the Rites and he did not like being near them. Mullener's apostolic rounds of the vicariate were very exhausting; on the plains or in the valleys he traveled by boat; but most of the villages were in the mountains and then he went on foot over rocky footpaths, crossing rivers barefoot.

For a long time his only collaborators were the Chinese priests he had formed himself, but afterwards he had some others from the seminary of Poulo-Penang erected by the M.E.P. These priests did not work with him; at least he never speaks in his letters about a companion or companions; rather, they preached missions where he sent them.

He had to wait until 1733 to receive a European companion: it was Father Maggi, an Italian Dominican, whom he consecrated coadjutor bishop in 1740. Maggi succeeded Bishop Mullener in 1742, but only for a short time because he died in 1744.

Mullener's Ardor for the Formation of Chinese Clergy

Notwithstanding his long and difficult visits, Mullener founded and maintained a seminary. He wrote in 1721: "I have in my care eight young men in my house, to whom I teach Latin. The oldest one, Paul Su, was twenty-five years old; I gave him minor orders." Mullener, while he himself made his rounds of the missions, placed him in Chengdu to supervise the Christian community and to teach the children to read and write Latin. "All those young people," he wrote, "have been offered to God by their parents. In the province and in our other missions, we have more than fifteen, but they are young. I cannot receive more as long as I am alone and have no other confrere with me."

In a letter to Mezzabarba, the second legate, he said: "While Your Excellency wants me to tell how to make these missions blossom, I shall say that during the twenty-two years that I am here, I never found a more useful and more necessary tool than educating and forming young Christian people for the priesthood." Probably several of his pupils did not arrive at the goal he proposed to them. At least he had the consolation of ordaining three priests: Fathers Paul Su, Etienne Xu – these two were Vincentians – and Father Jean-Baptiste Liu, a diocesan priest, also one deacon and ten with minor orders, who rendered worthwhile service to the mission. Finally, he was able to send four of his students to the Seminary of the Holy Family erected in Naples by Father Ripa in 1732.

His Death, Arms at the Ready

Mullener, as a good soldier of Christ, died when he was still hard at it. He had gone and spent the feast of the Immaculate Conception in a Christian community near Chengdu. He heard many confessions, caught a cold and had to stay in bed for some days. Since his illness seemed serious, he chose to return to his residence to get good care and made the journey on foot. His condition quickly worsened. In the presence of Fathers Martillat and Dartigues, Mullener died on 17 December 1742. He was sixty years old.

Though the vicariate of Sichuan was first entrusted to the M.E.P. Fathers in 1702 with Bishop de Lyonne as apostolic vicar (who appeared there only once) and entrusted to the M.E.P. definitively in 1744 after the death of Mullener's successor, Bishop [Luigi Maria] Maggi, Mullener can for all practical purposes be considered the apostle of Sichuan, which he had served as bishop for twenty-six years.

Chapter 3

Pedrini

Father Teodorico Pedrini – An Adventurous Voyage (1702-1710) – Pedrini at the Imperial Court, Kangxi's Musician – Pedrini's Disgrace – The Missionary of Propaganda – New Afflictions

Father Teodorico Pedrini

Let us turn back a little to 1702 when Pope Clement XI decided to send his legate, de Tournon, to the Indies and China to deal with the Malabar and Chinese rites issues. It was known in Rome that the Kangxi emperor would be very pleased to have an artist sent by the pope in his service. To accomplish this, in addition to the personnel forming the staff of the prelate, Teodorico Pedrini was added to the mission, because he had a reputation as an excellent musician.

Pedrini was born in Fermo (Italy) on 30 June 1670. He studied in Rome and entered the Company of Saint Vincent on 24 February 1698. He was a doctor in civil and canon law.

An Adventurous Voyage (1702–1710)

As the legate had to go to Spain, he told Pedrini to meet him in the Canary Islands in April 1703 so that they could travel together to China. Pedrini wished first to visit the motherhouse, so he went to Paris. When he was ready, however, to embark at Saint Malo for the Canary Islands, he was prevented by circumstances.

At the set date, the legate, though saddened by Pedrini's absence, set out for China without him. Pedrini had to wait till 25 December 1703, when a French ship took him on board at Saint Malo to go to China, not, however, by going east, but by way of South America. They experienced violent storms. On 10 May 1705 they reached Peru, then the boat turned around and went back to its home base. Thus abandoned, Pedrini's best chance was to get to Acapulco in Mexico and from there cross the Pacific to the Philippines. He covered the 1,200 kilometers to Acapulco by land

and by sea, and once there boarded a ship in May 1707 and landed in Manila on the following 9 August.

A voyage from Manila to Macao normally took only fifteen or twenty days. It turned out quite differently for Pedrini. Contrary winds forced the ship back to port three times. Pedrini's wait was prolonged still further, because the Spanish king, Philip V, had just published an edict forbidding Spanish ships from trading with China. After a short time, five missionaries from Propaganda arrived in Macao. They were bringing the cardinal's biretta to the legate, at the time a prisoner in Macao. They were in a hurry to reach China, but they could not find a ship to take them there. Pedrini, thinking that he had received from Providence the responsibility of bringing this papal mission to Macao, conceived a daring project. He went to see the Spanish governor, explained to him why he needed to bring the missionaries to Macao, and proposed to charter a frigate of which he himself was to be the captain.

The proposition was accepted and the frigate was prepared. Pedrini had his beard shaved off and put on a captain's uniform. The priests of Propaganda paid their fare and boarded the vessel. They were warned to keep the captain's identity secret, and consequently, related to him only as the captain of the ship.

On 30 November 1709 they weighed anchor and sailed for Macao. The crossing was a very difficult one. Several times they were pushed back and thrown off course, but they finally landed in Macao on 3 January 1710. Thanks to the audacity and perseverance of the improvised captain, the mission of Propaganda was able to bestow the biretta on Cardinal de Tournon on 17 January. Overcoming all the obstacles that he had met during his long voyage of eight years, Pedrini finally had reached China.

Pedrini at the Imperial Court, Kangxi's Musician

A month after Cardinal de Tournon's death, an order from the emperor called Pedrini to court. First, he had to pass some months in Canton to learn Chinese. There he was overwhelmed with joy to see his two confreres, Appiani and Mullener.

On 27 November 1710, accompanied by Fathers Ripa and [Guillaume] Fabre-Bonjour, priests of Propaganda, he undertook the journey to Peking, where he arrived on 5 February 1711. The three Propaganda priests were introduced to Kangxi, who received them very kindly and assigned each one his function. For Pedrini, it was music, for the two others painting and cartography.

This life of missionaries serving the emperor was not exactly a sinecure. Ripa later wrote: "The emperor's view is that it is both our duty and honor to serve him. Given my experience of thirteen years at court, I can honestly affirm that under this ruler a missionary's life is so exhausting and so hard, that I am accustomed to calling it 'golden slavery.' The fact is that the missionaries employed at the court have only one goal: to make every effort to win the emperor's esteem in order to ensure favorable protection for missionaries evangelizing either in Peking or in the provinces."

Kangxi loved music. Consequently, he gave Pedrini accommodations near his own so that he would be constantly at his disposition sometimes to play some instrument, sometimes to maintain, repair or build new instruments. From the beginning Kangxi showed his favor to him. Kangxi gave him some pupils to whom to teach music. Among them were two of his sons. Every year, during the hot season, Pedrini went with the emperor to his summer palace in Jehol [Chengde].

Pedrini built an organ that played certain Chinese melodies by itself. The emperor was so pleased with it that he had Pedrini called before him to congratulate him. Pedrini also wrote some musical compositions. Some of these have been preserved and, according to connoisseurs, confirm Pedrini's exceptional talent.

Pedrini's Disgrace

We are at the most critical era in the Rites Controversy. The bull *Ex illa die* had already been published. For Pedrini, a true son of Saint Vincent and true missionary of Propaganda, this was not an occasion where he could discuss or hesitate. Since his arrival he had accepted, without any reservation, the orders of Cardinal de Tournon and the oft-repeated directives from Rome. Consequently, he did not enter the controversies of the disputing parties. His task was plain.

But his behavior was bound to irritate those who favored the Rites and felt themselves on the side of the emperor. It was strange indeed that he who openly was against the Rites, nevertheless, retained the emperor's affection.

On the other hand, some mandarins at the court were very jealous of Pedrini's good standing with Kangxi. One of them, Zhao Zhang, whose power was great, denigrated Pedrini in front of the emperor so harshly that Kangxi suddenly turned against his favorite musician. This loss of favor did not last long. Ripa wrote: "one week later, Pedrini was back in Kangxi's favor." This was an early indication of how little imperial favor was to be trusted.

Two years later, in 1718, when Pedrini was seriously ill and almost died, it happened that the empress-mother died. In such situations, missionaries were obliged to go every day to the palace as a symbol of their mourning.

Pedrini, held back because of his illness, was conspicuous by his absence. On 8 February 1720, the first day of Chinese New Year, Pedrini, still sick, did not appear at the palace with the other Europeans to make the nine customary prostrations. In the afternoon he was taken to prison.

He remained there for ten days, then, freed from his chains, he was kept under surveillance in unofficial locations. Zhao Zhang was waiting for him there; having discretionary powers over the jailers who guarded Pedrini, he used them to harass the prisoner in every way.

Kangxi did not change his condemnation, so Pedrini was still prisoner when the emperor died in 1722.

The new emperor, Yongzheng, proclaimed an amnesty that was applied to Pedrini on 27 February 1723. After that, Pedrini retired in the house of the Propaganda priests in Haidian, six kilometers from the capital. He enjoyed peace during the whole reign of Yongzheng, his former pupil, who, by the way, was not at all kind to missionaries in general. His music teacher was among those whom he considered useful for Peking. Pedrini always had free access to the palace.

The Missionary of Propaganda

Though he was the emperor's musician, Pedrini never forgot that it was the Sacred Congregation of Propaganda that sent him.

The missionaries sent by this Congregation did not have their own house in Peking nor did they have a church open to Christians of the capital. So Pedrini decided to buy at his own expense a house that would be theirs where they would also be at liberty to minister to Christians.

Though Ripa already had acquired a small property during Pedrini's imprisonment, it was not enough for the intended purpose. Besides, Ripa was leaving China and going back to Italy in 1723 to organize a seminary for the formation of Chinese priests. He actually did realize this project by establishing the seminary of the Holy Family in Naples in 1732. Over time this seminary gave China quite a number of good missionaries, until the Italian government closed it in 1888.

Shortly after Ripa's departure, Pedrini gathered enough money to buy a large house with seventy rooms. He carefully transformed it and provided it with a chapel. When everything was ready, he invited all the Propaganda priests to come and live in it. Finally, he wrote to the cardinal prefect of Propaganda, asking him to accept the property for the use of the missionaries of the Sacred Congregation. It was on this plot that the Xitang (West Church) was to be built later on.

New Afflictions

His stay in the new residence did not exempt him from new troubles. His property was not officially recognized as a church and did not yet have the name of Xitang. It was still considered a private dwelling. At that time there were only three churches: the Xitang (later renamed Nantang [South Church]) built in 1650 [-1651] by the Jesuit, Father [Johann Adam] Schall [von Bell] and home of the Portuguese Jesuits; the Beitang, built by the French Jesuits in 1700; finally, the Dongtang [East Church], built at the expense of the Portuguese king and dedicated to Saint Joseph.

Yongzheng died in 1736 and was replaced by his son, Qianlong who, misled by the enemies of the Christian religion, published a decree that forbade the missionaries to preach the Faith in Peking and forbade the Tartars to accept it. The result was that the Christians of the capital, unable to visit their own churches, flocked to the chapel of the Xitang [West Church], which was not a church strictly speaking, so not forbidden to Christians. This was a godsend for Pedrini, who with the help of some Propaganda priests was able to take care of the Christians who came to them.

Towards the end of his life, Pedrini had still to suffer. There were those who did not stop creating difficulties for him. They accused him in Rome of letting the goods belonging to the Sacred Congregation of Propaganda become worthless.

Pedrini suffered many other humiliations because of the Rites; but we have hardly mentioned them, since our goal in this book is only to give the most characteristic traits of the persons we are introducing.

Pedrini's health was precarious and he was often enough ill, so that the years weighed heavily on his shoulders. "I live the life of an old man," he wrote to one of his relatives, "with weaknesses and embarrassments of all kinds, because I am in charge of the church and of the house of Propaganda. . . . We have had many conversions."

In 1741, he became seriously ill. "During my illness," he wrote, "the Jesuits have helped me with the greatest charity by day and by night." He recovered and lived a while longer. We have no details, however, about his last days. He died on 10 December 1746 in his seventy-seventh year and his thirty-sixth in China.

Pedrini had suffered a lot, especially morally. If his nature sometimes felt crushed under his afflictions, which paradoxically hardened his spirit, he did not abandon anything that he believed in conscience to be God's will.

Chapter 4

Evangelizing China, 1700–1785

Evangelization in China from 1700 to 1785 – Bernardino della Chiesa, First Bishop of Peking – His Successors in the Diocese of Peking – The Suppression of the Society of Jesus

Evangelization in China from 1700 to 1785

The history of the three first Vincentians in China though very brief, obliged us to anticipate events a little and it has taken our minds off the works of the other missionaries. We shall now give an overview of the progress of evangelization from the arrival of the Vincentians in China, that is, from 1700 until their confreres arrived in 1785 to replace the Jesuits.

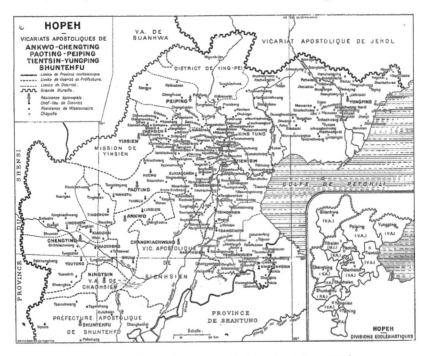

Map 4.1 Hebei and Its Apostolic Vicariates [ca. 1933]

During this period, times of peace were short and infrequent. Afflictions and persecutions were more common. Certainly, the ill-fated Rites Controversy dominated that period, and its unfortunate consequences were still to be felt in the beginning of the following period.

It would be very interesting to know the number of missionaries working in China in 1700. Though reliable documents are lacking, it can be said that the following numbers, coming from different sources, are not far from the truth:

36	Jesuits, 8 or 10 were at court
30	Franciscans
4	Dominicans
10	Diocesan priests (the majority were priests of the Foreign Missions of Paris)
6	Augustinians
3	Vincentians

89	Total

Here is another list for 1723, according to Gubbels, *Trois siècles d'apostolat*, p. 88:

59	Jesuits, of whom nineteen were in Peking (the list includes lay brothers)
32	Franciscans
8	Dominicans
15	Diocesan priests
6	Augustinians
3	Vincentians

123	Total

We do not have reliable statistics about the number of Christians at the time. The missionaries wrote a lot about China because little was known of China in Europe. They described its government, history and customs, but rarely did they give the number of the Faithful, and when they did give numbers, they were always rounded off with a few zeros. For instance, they might write: 600; 3,000; 50,000, which obviously are not exact numbers. They relied on hearsay, did mental calculations, and often had a tendency to swell the numbers. These numbers were thus not reliable. Overall organization of the missions was lacking at the time.

Vicariates and [ecclesiastical] districts were not yet well defined; groups of religious were often mixed together. Moreover, there was no central institution to collect data on what were called the "spiritual fruits" harvested by the various missions during the previous year. Communications and reports by letter took too long and were too difficult. It was only in the nineteenth century that it was possible to get statistics from the whole of China that approximated the actual situation. The first statistics were gathered by the Jesuits and printed in Zikawei [Xujiahui] in Shanghai. Beginning in 1916, Vincentian Father Jean-Marie Planchet began to publish annually in Peking *Les Missions de Chine et du Japon*, thanks to which it became easy to know the spiritual fruits harvested every year, not only in every vicariate, but in every missionary outpost, and, consequently, in the whole of China. The old missionaries were unable to manage this.

However, our minds are not satisfied if we cannot imagine the number of Christians, even though it might be only a very rough estimate. So let us say that at the end of the seventeenth century the number of the Chinese Christians was not more than a hundred fifty thousand.

Someone wrote: "Before the controversy of the Rites there were about three hundred thousand Faithful in China; afterwards, there were only two hundred thousand. The Rites controversy caused the loss of one-third of the Christians."

Obviously, these data are too simplistic to be correct: first, the numbers are not exact, and secondly, even if the numbers were exact, the conclusions drawn would still be false.

To support these two statements, let us examine other numbers given at that time. Luis Gama, a Portuguese from Macao, made a catalog recording the number of the Faithful in the whole of China in 1663. He listed about thirty churches spread over eleven civil provinces and for each church gave the number of Christians in its care. All the numbers, however, ended in two, three or four zeros, which indicates the numbers were rounded off and hence too high. Specifically, we meet for Peking 13,000; for Shanghai 40,000; for Xi'an 20,000; for Zhangzhou 10,000. These numbers clearly are quite exaggerated.

Let us look only at Peking. The Vincentians arrived there in 1785. Their superior, [Nicolas] Raux, made a report in 1788 about the administration of the five districts which made up his mission, of which we will only give two numbers: the one of baptisms of children with Christian parents and the one of yearly confessions: baptisms of children with Christian parents: 465; "not repeated confessions," that is, annual confessions: 2,001.

We know that in those times of frequent persecutions, missionaries would never highlight the number of their Christians in their accounts. To know that number approximately, we must base ourselves on the number of the children of the Faithful baptized during the year, supposing that every birth represents one family and that a family normally was made up of seven persons. The result is that the mission of Peking numbered more or less 3,255 (465 x 7) Christians. We are far from the 13,000 of Gama. What can we say about the 40,000 in Shanghai and the others? It is better not to insist. We can believe, however, that the total of 113,000 is too high for the year 1663, and that thirty-seven years later, that is, in 1700, the number of 300,000 is even farther away from the truth.

If we take as basis the number of "not repeated" confessions, that is, yearly confessions of 2,000, we can suppose that in 465 families of seven persons, there are two or three who do not go to confession, because they have not yet reached the age of reason, or because they are half-hearted. Let us say two abstentions per family. We have 465 x 2 = 930 Faithful to add to the 2,000. 2,000 + 930 = 2,930 Faithful. Let us say there are three abstentions per family, in that case we have 465 x 3 = 1,395 Faithful that have to be added; 2,000 + 1, 395 = 3,395 Faithful. The numbers have spoken.

Table 4.1 Catalogue of Father Gama (1663)

Provinces	Churches	Number of Faithful
Zhili	3 in Peking	13,000
	1 Hejian	2,000
Shandong	1 Ji'nan	3,000
Shanxi	1 Jiangzhou	5,000
Shaanxi	2 Xi'an	20,000
	1 Puzhou	300
	1 Hanzhong	4,000
Sichuan	1 Chengdu	300
Huguang	1 Wuchang	1,000
Jiangnan	2 Nanjing	600
	1 Huainan	600
	1 Yangzhou	800

	1 Songjiang	2,000
	2 Shanghai	40,000
	2 Zhangzhou	10,000
	1 Suzhou	500
	1 Jiading	200
	1 Jiuding	400
	1 Zhenjiang	1,000
Zhejiang	1 Hangzhou	1,000
Jiangxi	1 Nanchang	2,000
	1 Jianchang	200
Fujian	2 Fuzhou	2,000
	1 Yanping	300
	1 Tingzhou	800
	1 Shaowu	400
	1 Jianning	200
Totals	**Churches: 32**	**Faithful: 111,600**

Now that the first statement "the numbers were too high" has been proven, we turn to the second that denies that the Rites Controversy was the only reason for the decline of the missions in China between 1700 and 1800.

Surely, we do not deny that the controversy greatly harmed the Church in China; but to tell the truth, the Christians did not have a big part in it. The trouble existed among the missionaries themselves. They formed two very obstinate parties, but they, nevertheless, did not stop caring for the Christians in their respective groups. Persecutions stopped them from doing their work, not the Rites Controversy. The Rites were never the reason for the persecutions, but rather the hostility of the emperor, who wanted to destroy the foreigners' religion. Remember Yongzheng's red brush. In the emperor's edict no mention was made of the Rites.

The viceroy of Fujian had declared that the *piao* had to be abolished. He did not speak of supporters or of adversaries of the Rites; for him, they were all foreigners who were preaching the same Catholic religion: "That is the only reason we do not want them here, let them go back home!" Yongzheng approved everything, declaring, "We must hold on to what the viceroy of Fujian proposed."

All Yongzheng's successors relied on this edict implicitly or explicitly. Beginning with his son Qianlong and ending with Empress Cixi, all return more or less to this theme: they are foreigners and they bring us a religion that is not Chinese. They will do this indirectly most of the time under the pretext that these foreigners are spies on behalf of their own government. Fortunately, there were calm periods, thanks to which evangelization in China was never completely interrupted.

Now that this has been clarified, we return to our narrative of events.

Bernardino della Chiesa, First Bishop of Peking

He was born in Venice in 1643. He entered the Franciscans in Venice. In 1680, he was named coadjutor to Bishop Pallu, who had just left for the Far East with the title of Administrator General of China. Shortly after his nomination, he was consecrated titular bishop of Argolis in the church of the Propaganda.[18]

Bishop della Chiesa left Rome even before Pallu had reached China. Four Franciscans accompanied him. After their arrival in Siam, they were delayed for a year. Getting free of their confinement, however, they arrived in Canton on 27 August 1684. Their Spanish confreres welcomed them with joy, but they found the situation in Canton very distressing.

Shortly after his arrival, della Chiesa had the honor of consecrating the first Chinese bishop, Grégoire Lopez [Luo], on 8 April 1685. He had been named bishop of Basilinopolis and apostolic vicar of Nanjing on 4 February 1674, but he had been unable up to that time to find a bishop to consecrate him. Then, after the consecration, the two bishops went to Nanjing, where they lived together in a way that it was impossible to distinguish the hierarchical order that united them.

As for Pallu, he arrived in Xiamen [Amoy] (Fujian) on 27 January 1684, where a few months later, feeling that he was going to die, he named Maigrot, M.E.P., to be his pro-vicar for Fujian, Zhejiang, Jiangxi and Huguang, and Pallu died on 29 October 1684.

The episcopal see of Peking was created at the same time as that of Nanjing on 10 April 1690. The king of Portugal, who had the right to present a candidate, proposed della Chiesa who then was named the

---

18. About Bernardino della Chiesa, see the definitive book by Mensaert, mentioned and summarized in the journal *Nouvelle revue de science missionnaire* (1955), pp. 148–150; (1962), pp. 230–235.

first residential bishop of the new diocese of Peking. The official bulls arrived only in 1699.

Because he could not take possession of his see without the bulls, he continued administering the southern provinces. Before going north to Peking, he consecrated Father Maigrot as apostolic vicar of Fujian on 14 March 1700 and at long last went without difficulty to Peking. As there was no Franciscan house or church in Peking, he went to reside in Linqing (Shandong), which was entrusted to the Franciscans.

As the bishop of Peking, della Chiesa was obliged to promulgate the decrees against the Rites. He did so through his vicar general. This caused a lot of difficulties.

Della Chiesa died in Linqing on 20 November 1721. Amid the very delicate situations in which he found himself, della Chiesa was inclined more to patience than to strictness; consequently, his contemporaries sometimes blamed him for treating the supporters of the Rites too gently.

His Successors in the Diocese of Peking

Most of these bishops were Portuguese and several could never occupy their see.

1. François de la Purification, an Italian Augustinian, chosen towards 1725, could not enter Peking because of Yongzheng's persecution. He died in Macao on 31 July 1731.

2. Polycarpe de de Souza (Sousa), S.J., a Portuguese, was born in Coimbra on 26 January 1697. After his arrival in China in 1726 as a missionary in Peking, he was chosen as bishop of Peking on 19 December 1740 and died in 1757.

According to canon law, the administration of the vacant diocese of Peking goes to the nearest bishop, in this case the bishop of Nanjing, Bishop Laimbeckhoven, S.J., who was Austrian. He took possession of the see through a letter of 31 August 1757. But Rome ordered him to name a vicar for Peking in his stead, because he could not leave his own diocese of Nanjing. Great difficulties arose between Rome and Lisbon concerning the choice of this vicar, so that, when finally these two powers agreed on naming a successor for de Souza (Sousa), the see had been vacant for twenty-one years.

This account touched on the disadvantages of the use of the Padroado injected into the affairs of the Church. Here is another one, which is still worse.

3. [Jean] Damascène Salutti (Salustri), Augustinian of the Italian mission in Peking (of Propaganda) was named bishop of Peking on 20 July 1778.

Though duly informed that his bulls had been sent, he waited for them in vain for two years. The bishop-elect wrote to the governor of Macao, asking him if he had received a letter from Rome for him. The answer was negative. [Nathaniel Johann Heinrich] Burger, apostolic vicar of Shanxi, had received orders from Rome to go and consecrate the new bishop of Peking. When he arrived, a serious question arose: was it suitable to do the consecration without waiting for the bulls? There were at that time twenty-six priests in Peking who, consulted about this question, were divided into two camps. Twelve declared that Salutti could be consecrated lawfully. Fourteen opposed the consecration. Burger decided that the moral certainty the bulls had been sent was sufficient to render the consecration lawful under the circumstances and fixed the ceremony for the 2 April 1780. Immediately after the consecration, the missionaries of Peking split into two parties. One party did not want to recognize the new bishop. The question was put to Rome and was decided in favor of the two bishops. But unfortunately, Bishop Salutti had already died from a stroke on 16 September 1781. In fact, the bulls had been held back in Goa.

4. Alexandre de Gouvea, Portuguese; born in 1751, was named bishop of Peking on 12 July 1782. This was a very fortunate choice approved by all parties.

While waiting for him to take possession of the see of Peking, we must interrupt the history of the hierarchy of Peking to tell of an event of the highest seriousness not only for the missions but also for the Church itself.

The Suppression of the Society of Jesus

On 21 July 1773 a brief by Clement XIV suppressed the Society of Jesus. Imagine the emotions of the Jesuit missionaries, when the terrible news arrived in 1774, which brought confusion into their lives, into their house in Peking, and into their work. They could not go back to Europe, for the court in Peking would oppose it, nor could they leave the houses they occupied through the emperor's generosity. Moreover, they did not see anyone who could take their place. Besides the Jesuits there were only Propaganda priests in Peking, whose number was down to four: three Italians and one German, but none of them was able to continue the Jesuits' scientific work. It was necessary obviously to think – and immediately – about finding successors who could continue the scientific work and the apostolate established in Peking.

It was in November 1775 that the brief *Dominus ac Redemptor,* directed against them, was officially communicated to the Jesuits by the vicar of the bishop of Nanjing and administrator of Peking. When they heard the apostolic brief read to them, the religious members of this ancient and venerable company did not utter a word of complaint but proclaimed their respect for the Holy See.

Second Period
(1785–1855)

Vincentians Arrive
and Begin Working

Chapter 5

New Missionaries at Peking, Their Work and Difficulties

Saint Vincent's Policy about New Institutions – The Journey of Three Vincentians to Peking – A Difficult Persecution – The State of the French Mission in Peking – Death of Father Raux – Arrival in Peking of New Missionaries – Appointment of Two Bishops Who Never Could Take Possession of Their See – Death of Bishop Alexandre de Gouvea – The Work of Ghislain: The Indigenous Clergy

Saint Vincent's Policy about New Institutions

Saint Vincent said to his first disciples:

> ... Neither can we make any overture to establish ourselves in a place, if we wish to remain in the ways of God and the customs of the Company. Up to this point, His Providence has called us to the places where we are, without our seeking this either directly or indirectly. Now, this maxim of neither asking nor refusing anything, which keeps us dependent on God and His guidance, can only be pleasing to God, especially because it destroys human sentiments that, under pretext of zeal and of the glory of God, lead us often to undertake works that He neither inspires nor blesses. He knows what is best for us, and He will give it to us at the right time if, like children who have perfect trust in such a good father, we abandon ourselves to Him. Indeed, if we were really convinced of our own uselessness, we would be wary of entering someone else's vineyard before being invited there or of making the first move to have ourselves preferred to other workers, whom God perhaps has chosen for that place. (CCD 6:331; CED 6:308[19])

The priests of the Mission who arrived in Peking at the end of the eighteenth century faithfully followed this policy of their holy founder.

---

19. CCD: Saint Vincent de Paul, *Correspondence, Conferences, Documents* [English]; CED: Saint Vincent de Paul, *Correspondance, Entretiens, Documents* [French].

Indeed, Providence called them there without them seeking it either directly or indirectly, as is evident in the account of the negotiations through which the French Vincentians took the place of the French Jesuits in all their missions in China.

The suppression of the Society of Jesus brought into question the future of the French Mission in Peking as well as the missions that depended on it. The last Jesuit missionaries – their number was not more than twenty – continued to fulfill their responsibilities in the court and to minister to the Christians under the jurisdiction of the bishop of Peking. Father [Jean Joseph Marie] Amiot and Father Bourgeois, the superior, of course, worried about who would take their place. From November 1774, Amiot writing in the superior's name proposed to the king of France, Louis XVI, that the French mission be entrusted to the M.E.P. Fathers. They refused the offer because they had no confreres able to continue the scientific work of the Jesuits in Peking. The French government, then, began negotiations with the Sovereign Pontiff.

Ten years passed after the suppression of the Jesuits and still no decision was taken. Eventually it was agreed that the only possible solution would be to affiliate the French mission to a religious order. The challenge was to find an order or a congregation that had members capable of continuing the scientific work in Peking, while other members were applying themselves to the apostolate.

In a report to the king, the Minister of the Marine said: "In France only the Benedictines and the Oratorians are known as learned societies, however, both congregations must be excluded, the first because it does not devote itself to missions and the second because in the old days the Oratorians and the Jesuits had serious disagreements over the doctrine of Jansenism. These feelings might damage the harmony necessary to live side by side. So consequently, concluded the reporter, "I think that, among all the religious groups known in the kingdom, the one of Saint Lazare is the only one to which the mission of Peking can be entrusted. It is not a learned society, but they have so many members that it must be possible to find among them some priests suitable for the functions in question. For the arts, some of the lay brothers would be excellent."

After this report, the king of France called Antoine Jacquier, the superior general of the Congregation of the Mission. Jacquier refused, saying he was sorry that he could not accept the king's offer because he was not able to provide the necessary people for such important tasks. The king insisted and the superior general answered with a second refusal. Pressing his request, the king sent somebody to tell him that for the present it was only one or two priests that were needed, with a surgeon if possible, and, also this was one of the most interesting missions imaginable. Jacquier then accepted the heavy charge.

The king of France proposed the Congregation of Saint Lazare to the pope to succeed the French Jesuits in Peking. Pius VI granted this proposal of the king of France. The brief of 7 December 1783 from Propaganda stipulated that the Vincentians were charged with all the works that their predecessors had been directing and that they were to receive the same powers and privileges. Concerning material goods, it stipulated "the Most Christian King alone" would be responsible for their disposition. The king indeed did take care of them by the decree of 25 January 1784, which transferred all the possessions belonging to the French Jesuits in China to the Congregation of the Mission.

Having accepted the French Jesuits' mission in Peking, Jacquier gave the minister of France the names of the missionaries he proposed to send to the capital of the Chinese Empire. They were:

1. Father Raux, the future superior, who had already spent a year deepening his knowledge of astronomy and geography, particularly by following the course of Lalande at the Royal College, and who also had been studying botany and natural history.

2. Father Ghislain, who had reviewed the elements of mathematics and done a course in experimental physics by attending the lectures of Macquer at the Jardin du Roi.

3. Brother Paris, who was a watchmaker, mechanic, and carpenter and also had learned about carillons and took harpsichord lessons.

Nicolas-Joseph Raux was born in Ohain in the diocese of Cambrai on 14 April 1754. He was admitted in the internal seminary in Paris on 18 July 1771 and ordained a priest with a dispensation for age on 5 March 1777.

Jean-Joseph Ghislain was born in Salles in the diocese of Cambrai on 5 May 1751. He was admitted to the internal seminary in Saint-Lazare on 4 July 1774 and was ordained on 11 March 1780.

Brother Charles Paris, called Joseph, was born in Verderonne in the diocese of Beauvais on 8 December 1738. He was admitted to the internal seminary in Saint Lazare on 2 June 1783 and pronounced his holy vows in Peking on 14 June 1785.

The Journey of Three Vincentians to Peking

The three missionaries left Brest on 20 March 1784. On 23 August they arrived at Macao, but dared not land because they feared being mistreated by the touchy government of the colony. They proceeded to Canton where they landed on 29 August.

Once there, Father Della Torre, procurator of the Propaganda, welcomed them with a great outpouring of love. In Canton they also met with the new bishop of Peking, Bishop de Gouvea. This prelate was only thirty-three years old, but his qualities of mind and heart made up for his youth. He was affable, prudent and pious, and was to be a blessing for his diocese.

Raux and Ghislain gave him the decrees from Rome. Bishop de Gouvea received these documents with respect and always showed great sympathy for the new missionaries.

Raux had hardly landed in Canton when he wrote the fathers in Peking to announce his arrival. He received a touching reply, which read in part: "We give sincere thanks to divine Providence for having arranged events so well that you and your Brothers from Saint Lazare have been forced, so to speak, to take care of the French missions in our stead. . . . We know also that since the suppression of the Society of Jesus, your confreres have rendered thousands and thousands of services to its dispersed members." This letter was signed by the five priests and one brother, still living in Peking, for death had created many empty places among them since Salutti's consecration.

The viceroy of Canton had received orders from Peking to guide the new "mathematicians" without delay to the capital; however, a persecution made it advisable to postpone this journey through the troubled empire.

Finally, after a stay of five months the travelers left Canton on 7 February 1785 and arrived in Peking on 29 April. They were absolutely welcomed by the missionaries, both Jesuits and the Propaganda priests.

Everyone including the bishop, who had arrived a few weeks before them, came out and congratulated them on their blessed journey. The handing over of the faculties went smoothly thanks to mutual goodwill; the Vincentians were welcomed in the Beitang mission, not as rivals but as brothers. On the other hand, Raux's tact and prudence, his easy and kind character, and even his exterior qualities helped him quickly draw out respect and sympathy. Raux was tall and well proportioned; he spoke easily with grace and majesty. This made his conversation very agreeable.

A Difficult Persecution

Raux had barely been installed as superior of the French mission when he had to use his influence in favor of persecuted missionaries. As was mentioned earlier, Qianlong in the beginning of his reign had issued an edict against the missionaries. The edict mostly affected those in Peking, and even there, those who were working at the court did not suffer from it; moreover, it did not last long. Soon, however, an anti-Manchu rebellion began against the dynasty. It was the White Lotus movement. In response, severe measures were taken against secret societies and almost everywhere the authorities worked hard to classify Catholicism as an anti-dynastic sect. No matter where the missionaries of the provinces hid, they were almost all discovered and brought to the Board of Punishments in Peking. Eighteen Europeans including four bishops were imprisoned in the Xingbu (the Board of Punishments). Chinese priests and many Christians were also captured and condemned to exile. Father della Torre suffered so much that he died after a few weeks. He was not the only one to finish his career in this way. Two Italian Franciscan bishops, Maggi [a Dominican] and Sacconi, two priests of the Foreign Missions of Paris, two Chinese priests, and seven Chinese Christians died because of all kinds of sufferings in the filthy prisons.

Because so many were arrested, the missions in China had almost no apostolic workers. Peking was the one exception. Since the persecution had not touched the churches in Peking, the missionaries ministered freely. When the priests in Peking saw those bishops, priests, and Christians arrive from the provinces in chains, they dared to ask the emperor for permission to care for them. A deaf ear was turned to their requests. Renewed efforts were made by Father [Jean-Matthieu de] Ventavon, a former Jesuit, since he was better known at the court, but this only angered the emperor. He forbade the priest to talk again to him about those prisoners.

Yet, their persistent charity found ways to enter the prisons through daring Christians. As a result, the prisoners received all the consolation that their miserable situation allowed.

It is indeed surprising to see Qianlong's behavior towards the missionaries. He who knew how to make such good use of the talents of the missionaries who served him, this emperor who walked in the footsteps of his grandfather, Kangxi, and knew how to honor the dynasty through his noble views and his wise administration, this emperor who had led his empire in sixty years to the zenith of its power. His harshness towards innocent prisoners could only be explained by blindness caused by the slanders coming from his entourage. In view of such rigorous treatment on behalf of the emperor, no one dared hope that the prisoners would be freed, but, against all expectation, a decree appeared on 9 November 1785 setting them all free immediately.

According to custom, the emperor had passed the summer season in his summer palace in Jehol (Manchuria). "On his return," wrote Raux, "we went and met him; he welcomed us with an appearance of kindness, which gave us hope. It was not in vain."

Father [Louis] Gabriel Taurin Dufresse,[20] wrote, concerning his release from captivity:

> This event was so unexpected that the finger of God appeared clearly in it. It filled the missionaries of Peking with joy, and they immediately sent the good news to us. Then, in the morning of 10 November 1785 we were taken from prison, our shackles were taken off, and we were led to the audience room of the board, where we found that all the priests residing in Peking had come to greet us.
>
> The mandarins handed us over to them and these gentlemen, expressing their greatest joy, took us to the cathedral of the Nantang. Bishop de Gouvea waited for us at the door at the head of his clergy. He gave the pectoral cross and ring to the apostolic vicar of Sichuan, Bishop de Saint-Martin, Bishop Potier's coadjutor. When everyone was in the church, the *Te Deum* was sung.
>
> The imperial edict allowed them either to stay in Peking or to return to Canton. Four missionaries of Propaganda stayed there; the others were taken back to Canton. . . where they waited the opportune moment to return secretly to their missions.

Alas! The Chinese priests and Christians, sent into exile, did not receive any leniency. Let nobody be deluded; the freedom that the emperor granted the European priests was not disinterested, for he hoped to be able to use them further to his advantage. On the other hand, the Chinese priests and Christians had committed the crime of abandoning the Chinese religions in order to take up a foreign religion, which was an unforgivable sin.

---

20. Gabriel Taurin Dufresse was appointed coadjutor apostolic vicar of Sichuan in 1798, and consecrated bishop in 1800. In 1803 he held a Synod in Chongqing. The majority of the members were Chinese, which was an amazing accomplishment. Its decisions, approved by Rome, were authoritative until the plenary Council of Shanghai in 1924. Dufresse suffered martyrdom on 14 December 1815 and was beatified in May 1900, at the same time as Blessed François Régis Clet. [Canonized 1 October 2000, along with Blessed Clet and others. (JR)]

The State of the French Mission in Peking

The account of that brutal persecution of 1785 has made us lose sight of what was the object of this chapter, namely, the apostolate of the newly arrived Vincentians.

Let us first name the different missions or churches of Peking, with the date of their beginning and the year of the construction of the churches:

1. Nantang (South Church), Portuguese mission, established in 1601; Jesuits from Portugal, Italy, or other nations;
date of the construction of the church [1610-1611 and] 1650 [-1651].
2. Dongtang (East Church), Portuguese mission, established in 1657; Jesuits, mostly Portuguese;
the church dates to 1721 [*sic* 1650s].
3. [Beitang (North Church)], French mission, established in 1693; Jesuits, all French up to 1785;
from then on: French Vincentians and former Jesuits;
the church dates from 1703 [*sic* 1702].
4. Xitang (West Church), Mission of Propaganda, or Italian, established in 1711; religious or diocesan priests, almost all of them Italian;
the church was built in 1723.

In the beginning, these different missions were under the jurisdiction of the archbishop of Goa, but more in name than in reality. After the diocese of Peking was erected in 1690, the missionaries worked under the jurisdiction of the bishops of Peking, the first of whom was Bishop della Chiesa.

The Vincentian sphere of activity and responsibility was the Beitang. The former Jesuits who had founded it and wanted to die in it helped them.

Under the terms of the rule laid down long ago by the Sacred Congregation of Propaganda, "the Christian community of a place belongs to those who formed it," the Vincentians, as legitimate successors of the Jesuits, consequently had the pastoral care of the Christian communities formed by their predecessors and belonging to other dioceses or vicariates. There were some in Jiangxi and Zhejiang, under the jurisdiction of the apostolic vicar of Fujian; some in Huguang under the jurisdiction of the apostolic vicar of Shanxi and Shaanxi; and some in Henan, administered by the bishop of Nanjing (diocese).

The lack of workers in such a vast field had worried Raux from the time of his arrival in Peking. In the Christian communities outside Zhili province only two Chinese former Jesuits remained.

That is the reason why one of his first works was the establishment of a seminary, whose direction he entrusted to his confrere Ghislain. Fifteen young men were chosen to form the first group of seminarians.

Raux in all his letters to his superiors repeated the necessity of sending reinforcements. Finally, on 21 September 1788 two young missionaries landed in Macao destined for Peking: Robert Hanna, an Irishman, and Raymond Aubin, a Frenchman, both Vincentians. They had to wait in Macao for a favorable opportunity to go to Peking. After waiting in vain for two years, Aubin managed to enter Huguang incognito; meanwhile, Hanna remained in Macao where he exercised his talents as a professor in Saint Joseph Seminary that Gouvea had erected in 1784. In the region of Gucheng in Huguang, Aubin joined some Chinese priests in charge of that important Christian community with about three thousand Faithful. He was an arduous defender of the bulls that had condemned the Rites, so he worked continually to eradicate the superstitions that had been practiced till then in the province. He was hard working and pious and was accustomed to rigorous penitential practices.

When invited to visit his bishop, Bishop [Jean-Baptiste] de Mandello, O.F.M., apostolic vicar of Shaanxi, he was arrested in An [Ngan] on 27 March 1795. From there he was brought before the courts in Xi'an. He confessed his Faith, but was careful not to reveal the name of any Christian or Christian community. The mandarins, afraid that he would denounce them to the emperor for their excessive rigors, poisoned Aubin in prison on 1 August 1795. This martyr is hidden from popular view, but radiant before God.

While Raux was still waiting for his two helpers, sad news came from Europe adding to his anxiety. On 13 July 1789 a rioting mob looted the motherhouse, so the seminarians had to be sent home to their families and the students to the various houses of the Congregation; before long, all seventy-three Vincentian institutions in France were closed and the confreres scattered.

However – admirable are the ways of Providence – as sad and tragic as these events were, they were the occasion if not the reason that three new missionaries were sent to China.

Francis Regis Clet, who spent eighteen years of fruitful ministry as professor of moral theology in the diocese of Annecy and as the director of the internal seminary in Paris, considered that he could not exercise his zeal in the appalling state France found itself and so conceived an intense desire to dedicate the rest of his life to the work of the foreign missions. He urgently asked his superiors to send him to China.

His repeated request was finally granted. On 10 April 1791 accompanied by deacons Louis Lamiot and Augustin Pesné, he embarked at Lorient to arrive at Macao on the following 15 October. The local bishop, Joseph da Silva, C.M., ordained the two deacons immediately. The ordination took place secretly in order not to disturb the sensitivities of the Portuguese government.

In Macao the three missionaries received a letter from Raux indicating their respective destinations: Lamiot who was good at science was to go to Peking, Pesné to Huguang, and Clet to Jiangxi.

While Fathers Pesné and Clet were able to go to their respective missions, Lamiot had to wait a long time for permission to go to Peking. Clet had hardly arrived in Jiangxi, when Raux, changing his decision, sent him to Huguang (Hunan and Hubei), where the need of missionaries was more urgent than in Jiangxi, and ordered Aubin – unaware of his tragic end – to visit the Christian communities in Jiangxi from time to time. These three confreres along with some Chinese priests formed the entire clergy of Huguang. They worked in the mountains of Gucheng, but did not enjoy community life for very long. While Aubin was killed prematurely in the prison of Peking, Pesné died a month earlier spitting up blood on 29 June 1795. He died in Clet's arms. He was twenty-eight years old.

Because of the death of his two confreres, Clet was alone with three or four Chinese priests at the head of many Christian communities. His stays at the central residence of Gucheng, instead of giving him some rest, added to his extreme fatigue, because when he came back exhausted from his journeys on foot, the Faithful were often waiting to take him some distance to administer the last rites. It was only after some years that the superior of the Beitang was in a position to send him three Chinese priests, students of Ghislain, all Vincentians. They were Father Joseph Li, who later on went to Wuxi in Jiangnan, where he died in 1827, Father Jean Zhang, who died in Wuxi in 1833, and Father Jouventin Zhang, who died in Hubei in 1803.

How clear-sighted and wise had the superior and his right arm, Ghislain, been! As soon as they arrived in China and perhaps conscious that the French Revolution would prevent reinforcements – which they had the right to expect from France – they succeeded in a ten-year period in providing the French missions with enough clergy to pass through their potentially deadly personnel crisis.

We left Fathers Hanna and Lamiot in Macao waiting for a permission the Portuguese refused to grant them. After many diplomatic efforts, Raux finally received the permission for them. Fathers Hanna and Lamiot arrived in Peking on 30 June 1794. The French mission was delighted. It had just lost two of its best workers, Bourgeois, who had been superior for many years, and Amiot, one of the most learned Jesuits ever in Peking, who had done so much to welcome the Vincentians as replacements for the Jesuits.

Hanna, a good astronomer, lent a helping hand to Raux in his role of member of the Bureau of Mathematics [Astronomy], a title conferred on him a few years earlier. Lamiot was a translator at court.

Death of Father Raux

Alas! The French mission was about to lose its principal support. Its superior, Father Raux, after some days of being extremely tired, was taken away by a stroke on 16 November 1801.

From a letter by Ghislain announcing the sad news to his superiors in Paris, we quote these lines, expressing how huge a loss it was for the French mission:

> We miss Father Raux terribly! Indeed, he had all the desirable qualities in a missionary and in a superior: besides order, ardor, precision, which appeared in all he did, he was devout, steady, affable toward everybody, and generous and sympathetic toward the poor; he had unflagging zeal. Oh, if it had only been God's will that he takes better care of himself, we would perhaps still have him among us!

Before his death Raux used the faculties he had received and appointed Ghislain to succeed him as superior of the French mission. This responsibility was burdensome for Ghislain, because he did not enjoy relating with the outside world. Rather, he gave himself completely to his dear seminarians. He kept up relations with the outside and especially with important people only to observe the strictest proprieties.

After Raux's death, the personnel of the house were reduced to Ghislain and Lamiot, three Chinese confreres, the lay brothers Joseph Paris and Paul Wang, and also two former Jesuit priests and one former Jesuit brother.

Brother Paris demonstrated his skills and ability from the beginning. He built a small organ and then a larger one and several clocks and chimes for the emperor Jiaqing (1796–1820). Brother Paris died on 6 September 1804.

Brother Paul Wang, the first Chinese lay brother, was especially useful in caring for the material needs of the house. He had a good grasp of Chinese literature, and accompanied priests on their mission rounds for several years. Whenever someone was needed to be a liaison between the missions in the provinces and the mission in Peking, Paul Wang's devotion was called upon. Consequently, in 1802 he was in Huguang with Clet; in 1805 in Macao; and again, with Clet in 1809, which we learned from a letter written by Clet.

Arrival in Peking of New Missionaries

Above we mentioned briefly that de Gouvea had established a seminary in Macao. He did so after having seen the good qualities of the one that the Portuguese Vincentians were directing in Goa. He modeled his seminary on that of Goa. He invited two Portuguese Vincentians from Goa, Fathers Correa and Villa, to come and join him in Macao. On 1 October 1784 classes with a first group of students began in the old Saint Joseph College of the Jesuits. The queen of Portugal, who had permitted this initiative, took charge of all the expenses of the seminary.[21]

That was the origin of the famous "Saint Joseph Seminary" of Macao, which at first was a diocesan seminary, but later became a center for the whole of China. De Gouvea, in order to strengthen the diocese of Peking, summoned two professors from Saint Joseph Seminary, Fathers Ribeiro and Ferreira, who had taught there for nine years. They were easily approved by the Chinese government and left Canton on 26 February 1801. De Gouvea put them in charge of the Dongtang to replace the former Portuguese Jesuits who were managing that church.

In September 1793, Father Pierre Minguet, C.M., arrived in Macao. He had gone to Portugal to continue his studies, after the sack of Saint Lazare. From there he was sent to China, to be part of the Portuguese mission, though his nationality was French. On 1 March 1800 two other French Vincentians living in England embarked for Peking. They were Fathers [Lazare] Dumazel and [Jean François] Richenet. After many detours they arrived in Macao in February 1801. Raux had a letter waiting for them there by which he ordered them to go immediately to Canton to present themselves to the viceroy as "mathematicians" and "astronomers" of the court. Obeying these orders, these confreres did not land in Macao but

---

21. The queen of Portugal called the Portuguese Vincentians to take over the works of the Portuguese Jesuits expelled by Tombal [Marquis de Pombal, chief minister of Portugal] at the same time that the king of France was substituting the Vincentians for the Jesuits in Peking.

went to Canton. There they met Father Minguet, who was still waiting for a favorable opportunity to advance further into the interior China.

There they also met the two Vincentians, [José Nunes] Ribeiro and [Domingos-Joachim] Ferreira, who already had their passports to go to Peking. The two of them left ten days later and arrived safely in the capital.

Dumazel and Richenet had to wait five years for the promised passports just like Hanna and Lamiot before them. They left Canton on 19 June 1806. On their arrival in Daizhou (Shandong), they received the disheartening order to return to Canton. They immediately sent a courier to Peking to announce the bad news to Ghislain. Without waiting for an answer, they retraced their steps to Canton, where they arrived on 22 December 1806.

This was a rude setback for the French mission. There was no longer any hope of having these two missionaries come to Peking. Then, Ghislain entrusted Richenet with the job of procurator of the missions in Macao. Raux had wanted to fill this post for a long time. Richenet acquitted himself of this responsibility to the greatest satisfaction of his confreres until he returned to France in 1815.

Through Brother Paul Wang, Ghislain ordered Dumazel to go to Huguang province and join Clet. Father Dumazel could not take the road from Canton because of local troubles, so he sailed from Macao to Cochin-china to enter China through that yet unexplored route. Exhausted and with serious health issues, he arrived in Hunan in 1810. For eight years with tireless zeal and dedication he helped Clet in his ministry; but his health eventually gave out. He died on 14 December 1818 comforted in his last moments by his Vincentian confrere Paul Song, who, though living more than sixty kilometers away, rushed to his side to close his eyes in death.

Appointment of Two Bishops Who Never Could Take Possession of Their See

Correa, superior of the Saint Joseph Seminary in Macao, went to Portugal in 1803. He was a missionary who always had a very sincere affection for his French Vincentian confreres. The French confreres took advantage of his return home to ask him to get the Portuguese government, if possible, to extend to French Vincentians the kindness that it bestowed on the Portuguese Vincentians especially, and to remove the obstacles that stopped them at the door of China. Correa managed only to have two of his Portuguese confreres nominated for the dioceses of Peking and Nanjing, nothing else. The Sovereign Pontiff agreed with these nominations.

At first sight, this arrangement seemed to provide a solution for all the difficulties arising from Portugal, because now the three dioceses of Macao, Nanjing, and Peking were each going to have a Portuguese bishop nominated by Portugal. But Peking had already its bishop, de Gouvea, who, though Portuguese, did not belonging to an order or congregation. How could he be replaced? Nothing could be simpler: just give him a coadjutor with the right of succession. That was done when nominating Father de Souza, who was consecrated in Macao on 15 October 1805 as bishop of Tipasa with the right to succeed Bishop de Gouvea.

Since the see of Nanjing had been vacant since 1790, the bishop of Peking was its administrator, and Father Pirès, a Portuguese Vincentian, was named bishop of Nanjing after his arrival in Peking in 1804.

This arrangement, it turned out, did not bring the expected results. The distrust of the Chinese authorities toward the Europeans had grown deeper. From that time on, entering Peking was forbidden to any European priest, whether at the service of the emperor or not. Those who were living in Peking were no longer allowed to leave the capital. That was the reason why de Souza was obliged to remain in Macao, waiting for the opportunity to go to Peking. It never came. He died in Macao on 6 January 1818.

Pirès, on the other hand, received episcopal consecration from de Gouvea in the Nantang in 1806. But he could never take possession of his see in Nanjing because of the prohibition against missionaries in Peking leaving the capital. He died in Peking on 3 November 1838.

Death of Bishop Alexandre de Gouvea

That was the situation at the time Bishop de Gouvea died in his Nantang residence at the age of sixty-seven on 6 July 1808.

Through his kindness he had conquered the heart of all the missionaries in Peking and established concord and peace among them. Violent persecutions overshadowed his whole episcopacy, however, which were for the bishop an uninterrupted source of suffering.

For twenty years de Gouvea had been a member of the Bureau of Astronomy, and towards the end he was its president. Because of this title, the court granted the traditional gift of one hundred fifty taels for his burial.

At de Gouvea's death, de Souza, his coadjutor, who was consecrated three years earlier, became bishop of Peking, but since he could not go there himself, he made Ribeiro vicar general for the administration of

Peking. Ribeiro was superior of the Dongtang, but after de Gouvea's death, he went and settled in the Nantang and managed the diocese, even after de Gouvea's death, not as vicar general, but as apostolic administrator till his death in 1826.

Henceforth, the diocese of Peking would have only administrators till the memorable year of 1856.

Ribeiro was helped greatly by the presence of Pirès, who was very willing to help him by celebrating the liturgical functions reserved to a bishop. But what an anomalous situation it was, caused by the interference of temporal powers in the affairs of the church – the bishop of Peking resided in Macao, while the bishop of Nanjing resided in Peking!

The Work of Ghislain: The Indigenous Clergy

Before continuing this painful account in the next chapter, we pause for a moment to look at Ghislain's fruitful work.

From 1802 onward, he was the superior of the French mission[22] in Peking with the rights and responsibilities of his predecessor, Father Raux.

Though he did not have Raux's renowned gifts, Ghislain by his works proved that he had his own talents and virtues. Being a good physicist, he could have played a role as a member of the Bureau of Mathematics [Astronomy], but when he was offered this honor, he declined it in favor of a Portuguese confrere. What he himself preferred was going on mission to the villages, and especially being involved in the formation of priests.

He visited the Christian communities nearest the capital during the holidays usually for one or two months. The rest of his time was completely dedicated to his dear seminarians. He foresaw that the Chinese priests were going to be the only ones to support the Faith during the bad times. He also had help in this work: he was helped by a Propaganda priest, Father Ferreti; later on by the Vincentian Joseph Han, the assistant director of the novitiate; finally by Father Lamiot towards the end of his life.

All the students who became priests pronounced their holy vows in the Congregation and it can be said generally that they were a credit to their educators.

---

22. This designation "French mission" no longer applies to the reality at the time we are treating here. Indeed, after the Revolution, France stopped taking an official interest in this mission, of which its last king was the principal patron. Henceforth we will call it "The French Vincentians" or "the Beitang," when we are not treating situations prior to 1800.

One of the principal unresolved difficulties that Ghislain encountered was the way the Portuguese created obstacles preventing missionaries from getting to Peking. With young priests languishing for years in Macao or in Canton, the works in Peking stagnated for lack of workers. In addition, he never was without worries as superior, especially when the persecution of 1811 began, which we will mention below.

All these worries ruined Ghislain's health. Feeling that his strength was decreasing, he left his Beitang residence in 1812 and withdrew to Zhengfusi seven kilometers from Peking to take a little rest . . . a very short rest, preparation for his eternal repose.[23]

On 12 August 1812, at ten o'clock in the morning, comforted by Lamiot and surrounded by his novices, Ghislain died at the age of sixty-two, of which twenty-eight years had been spent in China.

Here is a list of the Chinese priests formed by Ghislain with their year of birth, ordination, and death. This does not include the five priests already mentioned above.

Table 5.1 Father Ghislain's List of Chinese Priests and Brothers [ca. 1790–1817]

Names	Birth	Principal activities	Ord.	Death
Han Joseph	1772	Assistant director of the novitiate; mission in Henan and Xuanhua	1798	1844
Cheng Etienne	17??	Mission in the diocese; later he left	?	1826
Deng Paul	1771	Taught in the seminary	1801	1803
Shen Cyrus	1769	Mission in Mongolia and Jiangxi	1800	1827
Song Paul	1774	A companion of Father Clet; arrested with him; confessed his faith in prison	1803	1854

---

23. Zhengfusi was the burial place for the French Jesuits just as Chala was for the Portuguese mission. The first French Jesuits on their arrival in Peking lived in the Nantang with their Portuguese confreres, and so when they died they were buried in Chala. After they established their own residence in the Beitang, they had their own separate cemetery.

Wang Joseph	1777	Replaced Brother Paris as watchmaker; ministry in Peking	1804	1814
He Ignace	1781	Missions in Mongolia and Hunan; exiled in 1829 and died in exile	1808	1844
Xue Matthieu	1780	Ministry in Peking; in 1819 superior of French mission; in 1829 at Xiwanzi	1809	1860
Shen François	1780	Imprisoned with Clet; condemned to be exiled to Yili; ; murdered in 1825	1808	1825
Zheng Antoine	1778	In Hubei and Jiangxi	1809	1835
Yue Jean	1785	In the diocese of Peking	1811	1813
Lin Vincent	1789	In Mongolia	1815	1836
Gao Thomas	1782	In Mongolia	1813	1832
Ai Stanislaus	1785	In Hubei; Henan; Jiang-nan	1817	1849
Kang Jean	1764	In Peking	1811	1814
			Vows	
Yang Antoine	1776	Lay brother in Peking	1796	1817
Wang Paul	1751	Lay brother who rendered valuable service in Peking and elsewhere	1790	1827

Chapter 6

Decline of the Peking Missions

A New Persecution in 1811 – Destruction of the Xitang – Destruction of the Dongtang – Clet's Arrest – Lamiot's Arrest – Condemnation of the Confessors of the Faith – Blessed Clet's Martyrdom – Fate of Clet's Two Companions – Closure and Destruction of the Beitang – Lamiot's Exile to Macao – Gaetano Pirès's Death – New Recruits Arrive in China – John Gabriel Perboyre – Perboyre's Arrest and Martyrdom – Reorganization of the Missions in China – The Clergy, the Seminaries, the Faithful

A New Persecution in 1811

In February 1811, the authorities of Shanghai arrested a Chinese priest whom de Gouvea ordained in Peking. Among this priest's papers was discovered a document mentioning "powers," authorizing him for the *cura animarum,* the care of souls, with faculties for absolving certain sins and giving dispensations. This document intrigued the mandarins very much. They thought that the missionaries were appropriating supreme authority, as well as distributing ranks among themselves and establishing leaders at the head of [ecclesiastical] districts, while keeping in touch with their leaders at all times.

A censor took advantage of the occasion to present the emperor with a hostile report in which the old slanders against Catholicism were repeated. Jiaqing, Qianlong's son, approved of this report and on 19 July 1811 had a decree published in which he declared, "The tree must be cut down at the root." From that time on, no European could remain in Peking except the members of the Bureau of Mathematics [Astronomy] and the French translators, that is, Fathers Ribeiro, Ferreira and Serra as well as Father Lamiot. The others, nevertheless, could stay in Peking and even in the provinces, if they abstained from all apostolic activity on pain of being expelled and sent back to their country. Those who wanted to go back to Europe, however, could leave immediately.

Destruction of the Xitang

On 8 August delegates from the court had all the missionaries with no official position to assemble in a Portuguese residence in order to inform them of the imperial decrees and to ask them what their decisions would be under the circumstances.

The four Italian missionaries of Propaganda expressed their wish to leave China. At that point it was suggested that they sell their residence and take the money with them. The residence in question was the Xitang that Pedrini had bought ninety years earlier and let the Propaganda have. There was also the church that he had built there. The priests were unable to find a buyer, so the emperor gave them its price and immediately had the residence and the church destroyed. The four priests were taken to Canton at government expense.

That is how the mission of Propaganda in Peking ended. The nine hundred Faithful to whom the Propaganda mission had ministered were entrusted to the Vincentians of the Beitang. The Propaganda mission did not have Chinese priests nor did it have a seminary; therefore, they did not have the same strong reasons to stay on in China as the French and Portuguese Vincentians of the Beitang and Dongtang. The Vincentians, in fact, thought that they were duty-bound not to abandon the place, in the hope that they still would be able to take care of their Faithful in some way, despite the fact that it was being forbidden.

Destruction of the Dongtang

A short time after the destruction of the Italian mission, a similar disaster happened to the mission of the Portuguese Vincentians in the Dongtang. Only two confreres were living there at the time, Fathers Serra and Ferreira. After the Xitang affair, some mandarins continually harassed them with visits to their house, visits of a more unnerving than friendly character. They foresaw the day that their church would suffer the same fate as the Xitang, so they decided to prepare for it. One night, however, when they were packing books and other valuable objects, an unattended lamp caused a fire in their library. The flames consumed a large part of their residence. Some days later, wishing to rebuild the ruins at their own expense, they asked the court permission to do so. Not only was the permission refused, but also, they were ordered to go and live in the Nantang. As soon as they left, the imperial authority had the remaining buildings demolished, even the church, which was said to be the most beautiful one of Peking.

Clet's Arrest

Meanwhile the persecution spread to the provinces, sometimes to one, sometimes to another, according to circumstances. The European priests were the principal objects of the searches, but Chinese priests were not spared, if it could be proved that they were spreading the foreign religion. Thus, four Chinese priests of Sichuan were arrested in 1818 and condemned to exile.

Despite his advanced age, Clet continued his journeys by boat and on foot from one Christian community to another in the immense province of Huguang (then made up of the present-day provinces of Hubei and Hunan). His example led his bishop, Bishop Mandello, to say, "May God be pleased to give me just twenty missionaries like Clet!"

In the beginning of 1819, a pagan, for reasons of vengeance against a Christian, set fire to his own house but accused this Christian before the tribunal of having set the fire and that a European was the instigator. As there was no other European in the region but he was clearly the one whom the pagan wanted to designate. The mandarins were happy to find an occasion to show their zeal, so they sent their soldiers into the countryside to arrest Clet and promised one thousand taels to the one who captured him. When the soldiers appeared at his place, Clet had been informed and fled. This seventy-year-old missionary escaped the most detailed searches for four months. Eventually, tired of going from cave to cave and being continuously hunted down, he left the region with hopes of shaking off the police. He went to the province of Hunan, to help the Christians there while waiting for peace.

There, however, he was betrayed by a Christian with scandalous morals, a former schoolteacher, who had already betrayed François Shen, C.M., for the sum of twenty taels. Clet had been the guest of a Christian family in the Jinjiakang village. On 6 June 1819 the feast of the Holy Trinity, he had just celebrated Holy Mass when the house was surrounded by soldiers. Seized and put in irons, he was taken to Kaifeng, the capital of Henan, with some members of the Christian family that had put him up, who were also put under arrest. Judges who wanted to know the names of Christians whom he had evangelized interrogated Clet endlessly. In his papers, three letters were found, which had come from Lamiot, superior of Beitang. Through cunning questions, the mandarins identified the author of those letters. Clet, who did not know how to lie, had stated inadvertently that he had been in correspondence with Lamiot. This had serious consequences, namely, Lamiot's arrest and the closure of the Beitang house, as we shall see.

When Clet heard of the unfortunate consequences of his questioning, he was appalled and till the day of his martyrdom he reproached himself bitterly for having jeopardized Christian communities in China with his statements.

Officials asked Clet about his habitual domicile. Clet answered that he was living in the north of Huguang, that is, Hubei, on the Mopan Mountain. This declaration made the governor of Kaifeng send his prisoners to the viceroy of Huguang, residing in Wuchang. Clet was taken there in a wooden cage, handcuffed and shackled with a chain around his neck, on a twenty days' journey, with prisons along the way as the only lodging. Clet's hard life in the prisons of Henan and the terrible journey that he had just made affected his health. The jailers, seeing him in such a pitiful condition, did not receive him well, thinking that there was probably little money to garner from such a wretched person. He was thrown into a prison where Father François Chen and ten Christians were already incarcerated. Clet, who feared to have only pagans as companions in his prison cell, was overjoyed and grateful to God.

From then on, the prisoners changed their prison into a real *de facto* oratory. Every day they recited together in a loud voice morning and evening prayers. A Chinese priest, Father Jean Zhang, was able to approach them and bring them Communion for a slight bribe to the guards. This was the last of the twenty-seven prisons Clet occupied following his arrest in Henan.

Lamiot's Arrest

The repercussions of these events were felt almost immediately in Peking. At the end of June 1819, Lamiot, superior of the Beitang mission, was in the country house of Zhengfusi together with some priests and seminarians. Suddenly soldiers invaded the property. They announced to the superior that they had a warrant to arrest him and take him to the criminal tribunal. Lamiot was not allowed to return to his house in town and put his affairs in order.

The motive of this arrest remained a real mystery. Only after giving many presents, was Ribeiro, administrator of the diocese, finally informed that this angry outburst was caused by the seizure of some of Lamiot's letters found among Clet's documents.

The next day, during the questioning, the judges, who certainly knew Lamiot as a good man, tried to suppress the affair. They proposed to him to sign a document through which he would declare: that he did not know Clet; or, that the cult that he was spreading was nothing else than the cult of the earth and of heaven, which is the cult of scholars; or that he would promise never to preach again.

Lamiot could not utter such lies, which would have been equivalent to apostasy. He refused absolutely, adding that he would prefer death to signing such a document. One of the judges told him: "You will not die because of it, but it will cost you much!"

After four months of imprisonment, Lamiot was taken to Wuchang to confront Clet. He arrived there towards Christmas 1819. He would have liked very much to see his confrere before appearing, but it was not allowed. He saw him only at the tribunal. Here are Lamiot's words:

> The day after my arrival I was taken to the tribunal where Fathers Clet and Shen were already present. After making us kneel, all three of us, I was asked if I knew Clet. I answered that I knew him though his face was so disfigured that I could not recognize any of his features. I knew that it was he, but I did not recognize him. (The two men had not seen each other for twenty-five years.)
>
> The wisdom of his answers and of his presence of mind moved me. I admired his extreme sensitivity for Father Shen and for me. When they had me kneel down, he began to weep. As they wanted to beat Shen, he cried out: "Why beat him? I alone am guilty." – "Old engine" (coarse insult), the mandarin said to him, "You corrupted too many people. The emperor wants your life." – "Thank you, with pleasure," Clet answered him.
>
> At the time of leaving the tribunal, a Tartar mandarin came and greeted me. During the conversation with him, I saw Fathers Clet and Shen near me. I said to the first one, "Keep up your courage!" He answered me, "I cannot speak French anymore, or Latin, or Chinese." As he said this, he was laughing and Father Shen was laughing, too. We were seen and immediately separated. These were the last words that we were able say to each other.

Condemnation of the Confessors of the Faith

Clet, Lamiot and Shen were definitively judged on 1 January 1820. But twenty-three faithful Christians had to be judged first. They persevered in witnessing to their faith and therefore they were condemned to be exiled.

A separated group of Christians who had renounced their faith were ordered to repudiate their faith publicly by eating meat that had been brought to them. They all ate it, though it was a Saturday, a day of abstinence. This was the sign of apostasy. They were immediately released.

Lastly, the three confreres appeared remaining on their knees. After two or three questions, the governor declared Lamiot discharged of every accusation and ordered him to stand up, the two others remaining on their knees. The judge urged them to repudiate their faith. On their refusal, Shen was condemned to follow the Christians into exile. Clet was declared guilty of "having lived in China." This meant that he was sentenced to death.

Lamiot, having been discharged, expected to be taken back to Peking and to be reinstated in the Beitang. Though not guilty he had to be sent back to Europe without delay. The order was executed so punctually that he was already in Canton on the following 30 March. He, however, avoided returning to Europe.

Blessed Clet's Martyrdom

While waiting for the ratification of the judgment given by the viceroy against him, Clet, was aware that his last hour would soon arrive and so prepared himself more diligently than ever for the final journey to eternity. He went to confession every day and often received Holy Communion, for he knew that the emperor's decree would be executed as soon as it was made known. In this way he received Communion the very morning of his death.

Finally, the day arrived: it was 18 February 1820. Soldiers entered the prison in which Clet was imprisoned. After he heard the decree, he knelt before Shen and asked him for absolution, which his confrere gave him with tears in his eyes. One last time Clet blessed the Christians who surrounded him and after having said words of consolation, he left full of joy and went to the place of execution.

Lamiot had bought new clothes for him, but he refused to accept them. On the contrary, he wore his oldest and most worn-out clothes, saying he went to his death not as a martyr but as a penitent. The execution took place west of the walls of Wuchang. Clet was tied to a pole that had the form of a cross, with a cord around his neck that could be pulled from behind to strangle him. The executioner drew the cord three times and the martyrdom was completed.

The Christians buried his body on the slopes of Hong Shan (Red Mountain) to the west of the city. Leo XIII beatified Clet on 27 May 1900.

Fate of Clet's Two Companions

François Shen, Clet's confrere, was taken to a town in Turkistan, where it is known that the whole population was slaughtered during a Muslim uprising in 1825. Because nothing was ever heard again about Shen, we conclude that he was among those killed in the uprising.

Another mission companion of Clet's is worth mentioning beside his superior: Father [Ignace] He, C.M. He too came from Ghislain's seminary (he is mentioned on the list given earlier). He was working with Clet during the persecution, but thanks to a hasty flight he had not been arrested at the same time as Fathers Clet and Shen. He went back to Peking and was sent to Xiwanzi in Mongolia. But Clet's martyrdom and Fathers Shen's and Lamiot's exile touched He so much, that his mind was affected. Serra, the temporary administrator of the Beitang, sent him to Macao for a rest in the company of Lamiot. Indeed, the rest and the change of environment hastened his healing, and Lamiot was able to send him to Henan, where the persecution was still raging.

In this way he could fulfill his ministry for five or six years, but in 1830, under Daoguang (1821–1850), he was arrested and had the honor of confessing his faith publicly. The judge, wanting to do him a favor, advised him to pass himself off as a simple Christian. "No", answered He, "I am a priest and one of the leaders of the Christian religion." He was condemned to be exiled. Later it was heard from a Christian exiled with him that he had died in 1844.

Closure and Destruction of the Beitang

On 2 September 1820, that is, six months after Clet's martyrdom, the Jiaqing emperor, who had condemned him to undergo the execution reserved for criminals, died and so the martyr's prophecy was realized. He had said to a catechist who was visiting him in his prison in Wuchang: "I have been judged, but the emperor who has condemned me will soon die, for the measure of his sins is overflowing." His successor, Daoguang, when mounting the throne, indicated that he would follow the same policy as his father. At his accession, he granted the customary amnesty to all prisoners, but he made sure that the Christians condemned by Jiaqing were not included.

Lamiot's expulsion had deprived the French Vincentians of their superior in Peking. As soon as he arrived in Canton, Lamiot protested energetically against his expulsion. He succeeded in having a petition given into the emperor's hands in Peking in which he said that he was needed in Peking to take care of the goods of the mission of which he alone was responsible.

The government answered Lamiot that if he had goods to take care of in Peking, the only thing to do was to give his power of attorney to one of the Europeans still in Peking. Lamiot was obliged to do exactly that. He nominated Father [Verissimo Monteiro da] Serra, a Portuguese Vincentian of the Nantang, and the Chinese government accepted the nomination.

Before his official nomination, Serra had already settled in the Beitang together with Bishop Pirès to prevent the Chinese authorities from taking it in the absence of Lamiot. Lamiot had already by letter made Father Matthieu Xue, C.M., superior of the house so that he could go on directing the seminary and the Christians. In the eyes of the civil authorities, however, only Serra was considered as superior of the establishment.

By way of precaution, the library of the Beitang was transferred to Zhengfusi and the precious vestments were sent to Xiwanzi in Mongolia, a small but excellent Christian community located two hundred kilometers from Peking. Events soon justified these precautions.

At that time only three European priests remained in Peking: Bishop Pirès, who had gone back to the Nantang; Ribeiro, administrator of the diocese of Peking after Bishop de Sousa's death; and Serra, temporary superior of the Beitang; all three of them were Portuguese.

Monteiro da Serra grew tired of waiting for the arrival of the several missionaries who for many years had been waiting in Macao for passports to the capital. He dreamed up a means to make the emperor authorize their arrival in Peking. He presented a petition asking the emperor for a holiday to go and visit his old mother, thinking that his departure would oblige the government to call for new missionaries to replace him at least for the Bureau of Mathematics [Astronomy]. To everyone's surprise, however, the emperor took him at his word, allowed him to leave and did not even mention a replacement for him. Serra understood and with an aching heart left China in October 1826. A few weeks after Serra's departure, a serious illness took Ribeiro away. Thus, the only European remaining in Peking was Bishop Pirès, who therefore became the administrator of the diocese of Peking.

With Serra gone, the Chinese government seized the buildings at the Beitang and forced the mission (that is, Xue and his confreres who were left alone to represent the mission) to give the Chinese government the property for the price fixed by the Chinese government itself, that is to say eight thousand taels, though the buildings and the plot of land were appraised at eighty thousand taels. Xue and Han with no place to live went and asked Bishop Pirès to welcome them and their students to the Nantang, while they were waiting for Lamiot whose return they were still hoping for.

The following year, 1827, the church was razed to the ground by imperial order. The emperor gave the houses to a grand Tartar mandarin named Yu who did not enjoy this windfall for long, because there within a few years all the members of his family died and he himself died too without any children. After his death, these buildings became the property of a favorite of the emperor's, who did not take care of them and let them fall into ruin.

Fathers Xue and Han remained in the Nantang for two years. In 1829, an apostate Christian accused Xue before the tribunals of Peking of appropriating goods of the mission outside the Beitang. Warned in time, Xue hid first around Peking; then he went to Xuanhua finally, thinking that it was not safe enough to settle in that town, he went outside the Great Wall to Xiwanzi. It was there that he established the seat for the administration of the Beitang – of which he was alone responsible – and there the eight seminarians that he had taken with him from Peking settled.

Lamiot's Exile to Macao

In distant Macao, Lamiot held on to the illusory hope of going back to Peking to the very end. When he learned the sad events of the Beitang, he was dismayed, but did not become discouraged, because he could not imagine that the scientific work, which had opened the doors of China for the preaching of the Gospel, could possibly disappear.

There is no question that the scientific mission begun by the Jesuit Fathers has been of immense service to the Church in China. This approach, however, was effective for a limited time. Already in Lamiot's lifetime – one wonders how he himself could not see it – astronomy, painting, mechanical engineering, and so on, no longer enjoyed the same respect at court as in the time of Ricci, Schall, and Verbiest. The Chinese in the Bureau of Astronomy, once initiated into the routine of the imperial calendar, were able to make do without the Europeans.

Lamiot consoled himself for his separation from his Christians in the Beitang by trying to be useful for them through the good priests he was forming for them. Xue whose time was taken up with ministry had sent him his eight students. At the same time, Lamiot was able to use his literary talents. In Peking or in Macao he wrote several books about the geography of China; he prepared a dictionary; he also wrote an account about the martyrs of Korea.

Feeling that death was near, he continued his request that a French confrere be sent to take his place. Finally, in October 1829, [Jean-Baptiste] Torrette arrived in Macao. He would render immense service to all the missions entrusted to the French Vincentians in China.

Lamiot died on 5 June 1831. Torrette was his successor as superior of the house of Macao, and at the same time he was appointed as visitor of the missions in China. He died on 12 September 1840.

Gaetano Pirès's Death

In his last days, Pirès, sick and weak, had to resign from his duties in the Bureau of Astronomy. The continual snubbing that he suffered forced him to place himself under the protection of the Orthodox Russians, who had set up house in Peking about forty years earlier. Moreover, the Jesuits had always had respectful relations with that Muscovite mission, which included an archimandrite, three or four monks and some young people studying the Tartar and Chinese languages. The archimandrite, who had offered to help the mission in these difficult times, came in person to the Nantang to free the old bishop from many humiliations.

Pirès died on 2 November 1838, seventy-one years old. After his burial, the Chinese government appropriated the property of the Nantang as it had done to the Beitang, but with this difference that it had the doors of the church sealed and all the doors of the residence closed; then, they gave the Russians the keys. In order to avoid all disorder, the Russians had all the buildings destroyed, sold all the material with the intention of giving the price to Pirès's possible successors. In this way, they showed an obvious kindness for the Catholic Church. The Russians completely justified the confidence that the worthy bishop had put in them. Indeed, as soon as circumstances allowed, they gave back to the Catholic mission of Peking all the deposits, whose guardians they had been appointed.

The administration of the diocese of Peking went to Father João Castro e Moura, a Portuguese Vincentian, who resided in Shandong without the knowledge of the Chinese government, making it dangerous for him to go to the capital. This confrere had arrived in Macao in 1825 not yet a priest. He was ordained in Manila in 1829. A year later, Pirès appointed him as his vicar general for his diocese of Nanjing, and, following the custom established in mission countries, Father João Castro became naturally the administrator of the Peking diocese.

Of the four churches of Peking, only the Nantang cathedral remained, and it was no longer open for worship. The church of Peking seemed therefore to be capsizing. But that did not happen. We shall soon see that it rose up from its ruins, but under another form and more prosperous than before.

While waiting for this revival, let us greet some apostolic workers coming to China.

New Recruits Arrive in China

Up until this point in our narrative, a good number of Portuguese Vincentians had come to China, enabled by the Padroado. Most of them remained in Macao. That is why we have mentioned the names only of those who took part in other missions of China. Henceforth, though, we shall see that very few missionaries were to come from Portugal, because an anti-religious revolution was raging in that nation. One of the most serious consequences of that revolution was that religious vocations dried up. In France, the revolution had almost annihilated our Congregation, but thanks be to God, it rose from its ruins, and beginning in 1830, it could again send missionaries to China.

On 2 November 1830 Jean-Louis Perboyre, who was born in Montgesty (Lot) on 23 November 1807, admitted to Saint Lazare on 9 September 1825, and ordained priest in 1830, embarked for China. Sadly, however, he did not have the joy of landing there. He died at sea not far from Java on 2 May 1831.

After him eight French Vincentians who played an important role in the missions of China arrived. They were: Fathers Bernard Laribe and Alexis Rameaux, who landed in Macao on 3 March 1832; Fathers Joseph-Martial Mouly and François-Xavier Danicourt, who arrived in Macao on 14 June 1834, then Henri Baldus on 25 September 1834; and Fathers Joseph Gabet, Joseph Perry and John Gabriel Perboyre, Jean-Louis Perboyre's brother, on 29 August 1835.

Because the last named achieved the glorious crown of martyrdom after only five years in the apostolate and also because the others had much longer missionary careers than his and will be part of the ongoing story, we shall here give a short biography of John Gabriel Perboyre, who with his great virtues and his long and heroic martyrdom, is justifiably considered one of the purest glories of the missionary apostolate in China.

John Gabriel Perboyre

Born in Montgesty (Lot) on 5 January 1802, he entered the Congregation in December 1818, pronounced his vows on 28 December 1820, and was ordained priest on 23 September 1826.

Though still very young, he was first assigned to the Major Seminary of Saint Flour as professor of dogmatic theology because of his intellectual and moral qualities. Two years later, he became in that same city superior of an ecclesiastical boarding school that was later to become a minor seminary. He had hardly entered the place when a remarkable transformation took place: undisciplined pupils quickly became driven by the best intentions, due to the superior's gentle and firm approach. The school, which had only thirty pupils the first year, enrolled more than a hundred the second year.

When John Gabriel heard the news of his brother Louis's death in the beginning of 1832, he felt an immense sadness. He too had desired for a long time to dedicate himself to the missions in China. He said that it was the principal reason he entered Saint Lazare. His superiors had refused to grant his desire up to that time on the grounds of his frail health.

During the holiday that followed his brother's death, Perboyre went and stayed with his parents for ten days to comfort them. Before leaving them, he informed them that it was his intention to go to China to take the place his deceased brother. They tried to dissuade him by having him think of the dangers, the privations, and the persecutions that would be waiting for him there, but he smiled at these objections and answered that they were exactly what he desired. On his return to the boarding school, he received a letter calling him back to Paris to be assistant director of the internal seminary. That was not what he wanted; he would have preferred to be granted the permission to leave for China. Faithful to his vow of obedience, however, he dedicated himself wholeheartedly to his new task, meanwhile keeping in his heart the conviction that God was calling him to China.

Besides, he was often heard saying that Blessed Clet had died an enviable death and that he wanted the same. His superiors always told him, however, to put it out of his mind. He obeyed; he humbled himself and went on hoping.

One day he heard that missionaries were going to be sent to China but that he was not one of them. Driven by an interior inspiration, he went to the superior general, fell at his feet and tearfully begged him not to oppose his vocation any longer. The superior, moved, promised to talk about it with his councilors. They were against it because of his frail health; one of the councilors, however, suggested that they seek a doctor's opinion. The doctor first declared that it could easily happen that Perboyre would die during the journey. Then, the same day, fearing that he might have made a mistake, he changed his mind and announced that, in conscience, he had no right to forbid a journey that instead of making his health worse might actually improve it. The members of the council fell in with the doctor's opinion and decided that Perboyre could leave for China. Having received all he had wished for, Perboyre thanked God profusely.

Accompanied by his two confreres, Fathers Gabet and Perry, he set off for Le Havre. They embarked on 20 March 1835 and landed after a safe journey in Macao on the following 29 August. After a few days rest among his confreres, he began to study the language, first under the direction of Father Torrette, his old schoolmate, then two months later under [Joaquim Alfonso] Gonçalves, a Portuguese Vincentian and a learned sinologist.

Torrette, who already knew Perboyre's virtue and high intelligence, hoped to see him in the near future at the head of the China mission, or at least as an apostolic vicar. Consequently, he did not wait long to send Perboyre into the mission.

The confreres who had arrived in China two or three years earlier had already been missioned. Fathers Rameaux and Baldus were sent to Hubei. Laribe was working in Jiangxi, while Danicourt remained in Macao to help Torrette in the formation of the seminarians. Mouly, sent northward, arrived in Mongolia on 12 February 1835.

Torrette appointed Perboyre to work with Rameaux, while he made his two companions, Gabet and Perry, continue studying the language in Macao.

To go to Hubei, Perboyre had to pass through Fujian and Jiangxi where Laribe was working. He left Macao on 21 December 1835 with Father [Louis-Charles] Delamarre, M.E.P., who was going to Sichuan, and landed in Fujian not far from Funing on 22 February 1836. After three weeks he continued his journey toward Jiangxi, travelling on foot with his companion. When he was near Jiangxi on 29 March he left Delamarre, who continued on, and he himself made a detour to see Laribe, who was preaching a mission in a Christian community in Jiangxi. One can imagine with how much joy he had in seeing his schoolmate taking care of his Faithful. He celebrated Easter with Laribe, who then took him to Jianchang, where his fellow traveler who had walked on ahead was waiting for him. From this town the two traveled by boat to Wuchang, the capital of Hubei.

Perboyre would have liked it very much to make a pilgrimage to Clet's tomb, but he was told that the missionaries there were absent. So, after crossing the Yangtze River (Blue River), they landed in Hankou, which was in the care of Vincentians. It was 25 April 1836. The next day, Delamarre set off for Sichuan, while Perboyre continued his journey upstream to Hanyang. While going through the town of Shayang, he heard that Fathers Rameaux and Baldus were preaching the yearly mission in the seven villages of that region, so he decided to join them. On 7 May he had the joy of embracing Baldus and on 8 May Rameaux.

"I sometimes stayed with one," he wrote, "sometimes with the other, as a witness to their ardor and their occupations. It was for me like a novitiate in an art at which they were already very good." He remained two weeks with them. Then Rameaux went off alone to the Gucheng Mountains, as if paving the way for Perboyre, while Baldus continued to minister in the area. After that, guided by Christians, Perboyre set out, climbed up exhausting mountains and finally joined Rameaux and a Chinese confrere in the residence of Chayuangou.

Towards mid-July 1836, Rameaux sent him to Henan where he had to continue his language studies with two Chinese confreres and be initiated little by little into evangelizing. Travelling on horseback, he went to Jinjiakang, the very residence where Clet had been arrested seventeen years earlier. From this center Perboyre toured around the province in all directions for a year and a half. We shall not follow him on his journeys; we shall only quote his letters sometimes when we can.

For instance, a letter of his informs us that he gave his first missions with a Chinese confrere whose ardor and know-how he praised highly. In another one, he expressed his gratitude that he was working in the same part of the Lord's vineyard that Clet had cultivated with his sweat and blood. He promised himself to continue the work that had been begun so well. He had about fifteen hundred Faithful spread over some twenty villages. Visiting them required six months and obliged him to cross the whole length and breadth of the province.

He wrote a cousin of his in a letter dated September 1838, "Last January, I was called back to Hubei by my superior, Father Rameaux. The district where I am is in the mountains; in its center we have a residence in Chayuangou. From there a missionary is easily in contact with the Faithful of the whole district." Then he gave a detailed account of how the exercises of the missions were carried out. The short time Perboyre lived in Hubei was reported to have been full of success. His virtue impressed the Faithful, who considered him to be a saint. His continuous occupation was visiting the Christian communities. "Since I have been here," he said, "I have given seventeen missions, and I can say that I have not had a moment of vacation."

Perboyre's Arrest and Martyrdom

Hubei was experiencing a time of relative peace, and nothing foretold the imminent persecution. Yet a storm was to sweep down on this province.

On Sunday 15 September 1839 Fathers Perboyre and Baldus were at their residence of Chayuangou. The Christians had come to hear Holy Mass and to assist at the Sunday ceremonies. After Holy Mass the two confreres had their lunch together with Father Rizzolati, a visiting Franciscan, and with Father Wang, a Chinese Vincentian.

Suddenly some Christians rushed in and told them to seek safety without delay, for soldiers, led by mandarins, were approaching the church. The missionaries fled immediately in different directions so as not to fall into the hands of the soldiers together. Perboyre, convinced that the danger was not imminent, was the last to leave and fled into a little bamboo grove not far from the residence. Hardly had he taken shelter when the mandarins arrived with their troops and surrounded the house.

Angry to see that their prey had escaped them, they grabbed whatever they could find that was precious in the house and burned the papers and most of the books. They seized several Christians, put them in chains and took them to Gucheng.

During the night, Perboyre left his hiding place and went to the catechist's house to have something to eat. The catechist cut off Perboyre's beard so that he would be harder to recognize as a European. Not to jeopardize his host, Perboyre left his home before sunrise and hid in a nearby forest. He had with him only his servant and two Christians.

During that time the other priests were wandering aimlessly, not knowing where to find shelter. Perboyre's hiding place was safe and would have shielded him from all searches if there had not been a traitor as in the case of Clet. A neophyte, because he was afraid or greedy, told the soldiers for thirty taels where the missionary was hiding. The soldiers came immediately and picked up Perboyre and demanded he reveal the place where the other Europeans were hiding. When he answered them that he had no knowledge about that whatsoever, they beat him so ferociously that his whole body was black and blue. Three Christians fell also into the hands of the soldiers.

The soldiers dragged their prisoner to the top of the mountain, took away his clothes, bound his hands behind his back and took him to the market of Guanyintang, where the sub-prefect of Gucheng was living. This man asked him if he was a European and a preacher of the Christian religion. The prisoner answered positively and asked him to give him back his clothes. His request was granted. After he had put on his clothes, he was hung from a pole so that his feet could not touch the ground; then he was put on a bench to which his legs were fastened solidly to make it impossible to flee. In this position he spent the night, meanwhile praising God for being treated as badly as his Divine Master.

The next day, 17 September, very early in the morning, the soldiers were ordered to take the prisoner in chains like a criminal to the town of Gucheng, to undergo civil and military questioning. He had little strength left after the cruel way he had been treated the previous day, so he had to do his utmost to follow the soldiers. On arrival in Gucheng, the prisoner was taken straight to the military tribunal. To the question, "Are you a priest?" he answered positively. "Do you want to repudiate your faith?" – "Never." Then he had to appear at the civil tribunal where he was asked many questions about where he had preached, the number of people he had brought to the Faith, and the other priests. Perboyre gave only vague and inaccurate answers; often he remained silent. He was imprisoned for a month where he was treated quite humanely.

From Gucheng, he was taken to Xiangyang at a distance of fifty kilometers; the prefect asked him more or less the same questions as his previous judges but did not get any of the information he wanted.

Among the objects taken from the missionary, there was a box that contained what was needed for sacramental ministry. The judge had the box brought to the tribunal and the container with the holy oils was taken from it. The judge asked if that was not the container with the water that the priests were squeezing from sick people's eyes. The prisoner answered that priests never did such things. Then the judge presented him with the missal and obliged him to read it aloud. Perboyre obeyed. This provoked the mandarin's laughter. He also had Perboyre put on the sacred vestments and asked him why he used them. "To offer sacrifice to Almighty God." Then the judge laughed at this cult worshipping a God who was not able to save the prisoner from the circumstances in which he found himself. Then he said, "If you do not change your sentiments, I will make you endure serious punishment." Perboyre responded, "I pay no attention to bodily suffering, because I am thinking only of eternal salvation."

At the session the following day, the judge asked Perboyre if he was indeed the priest named Dong. "Yes, I am." The judge told him that Europeans entered China to enjoy a nice soft life, but that he would treat them in a way that would take away any desire of coming back to China. Consequently, he made the prisoner kneel on iron chains with bare knees and he left him in this position for four hours. After that he was brought back to prison.

Some days later, Perboyre appeared at the highest tribunal of the prefecture. He was asked questions similar to those previously asked; then, the judge asked him about the three European priests whom he knew were present in the province. The prisoner kept silent; he knew about the anxieties in which the late Clet had been plunged for having perhaps talked too much – at least in his own opinion – when answering.

The judge was angry, so he made him kneel on iron chains and ordered that he be hung from his thumbs and from the braid of his hair, so that his body could not bow down. In this position, it is impossible to make any move without feeling great pain.

He remained suspended in this way for four hours and meanwhile the judge insulted him and was asking the Christians who were present if their chief was in a comfortable position; then, in ridicule he congratulated them on having believed the fables that this man had taught them.

During another interrogation, the judge tried again to make him repudiate his faith. It was in vain. Outraged, he had him given forty blows on his face with a leather strap with so much force that his face was completely swollen and no longer looked human.

Amidst these terrible tortures, the prisoner never uttered a cry. He showed so much steadfastness that the bystanders were perplexed by it.

The suffering and the torture that Clet endured after his arrest cannot be compared with the ones that were inflicted on Perboyre. Clet had been able to make a little chapel of his cell where he prayed regularly aloud with his companions. On the other hand, the prisons which Perboyre occupied were most of the time filthy dungeons housing the worst villains, who were unrestrained in word and action, opening their mouths only to spit out the most obscene words, curses, and imprecations. The tortures that Perboyre endured exceed all imagining. We do not want to describe them here; it would make the account too long. These things can be read in *Vie du Bienheureux Perboyre*. Clet did not suffer a fraction of what Perboyre suffered. Perhaps his old age and the veneration he inspired because of his humility and his artless sincerity caused his torturers to lessen their fury. Be that as it may, let us continue with the account of the events.

We left Perboyre at the tribunal of Xiangyang. He had to go through the channels of the tribunals of the empire. The investigation for the criminal case had already been conducted at the sub-prefecture[24] of Gucheng, now it had to go to Wuchang, capital of Hubei province, at a distance of about two hundred kilometers. That is where Clet had been condemned.

Perboyre was taken there with ten Christians, who had showed themselves firm in their confession of the faith. All had chains around their necks, hands and feet. It can be imagined how painful the journey must have been for him, who had already endured so much.

Wuchang was to be the theatre of still harsher combat for God's servant. He underwent twenty interrogations, all accompanied by whipping. They lasted for long hours and sometimes for a whole day; he was often beaten with a hundred blows.

During the last session, according to the soldiers' admission, he was given two hundred blows with a leather strap. For four months, every means cruelty could invent was used against him. Several times, the soldiers carried him back half-dead into his cell.

Finally, towards mid-January 1840, the viceroy sentenced him to be strangled. As the sentence could be executed only after being ratified by the emperor, Perboyre had still to wait another eight months in prison. One can imagine what condition he was in at that time. People were amazed that he had overcome so much punishment.

As long as the judicial process was going on, no Christian could reach him. Once the sentence was pronounced, however, some visits were allowed. One of the first persons admitted to see Perboyre was the Vincentian Father André Yang. When this confrere saw Perboyre lying on the ground, his limbs

---

24. A sub-prefecture generally refers to a civil county; Ferreux does not always make clear distinctions about civil administrative units. (AS)

furrowed, his body covered with wounds and his face swollen, he began to weep. Perboyre wanted to go to confession, but two soldiers, who were always at his side because they feared someone might try to poison him, prevented him from doing so. A Christian who accompanied the priest invited the soldiers to step back a little. They did so and the missionary made his confession. From that day on, Christians often visited Perboyre, among them a catechist named Fong, who was very helpful to him. The prisoner's fondest wish was to receive Holy Communion; but it was not possible to give it to him, because his guards had explicit orders to taste everything that was offered him from outside because of the fear of poisoning. Hence, he was never able to receive Holy Communion.

Finally, on 11 September 1840 an express imperial courier delivered Daoguang's edict that ratified the sentence. According to custom, it was carried out immediately. Perboyre was taken from his prison without warning and taken to the place of execution with some thieves who were to be executed that same day. He walked bare-footed; his hands bound behind his back held a long rod at the end of which was fixed a notice with the death sentence pronounced against him. He had recovered his strength and amazingly his wounds did not show anymore, his face was beautiful, his flesh peach-colored like a baby's. Everyone who saw him in this condition called it a miracle.

They began with the seven prisoners, and during their execution John Gabriel was on his knees praying. At the end he was bound to gallows in the form of a cross. His death was more painful than that of the others who had been beheaded swiftly. The viceroy had stipulated for the Catholic priest an execution that made him suffer more: he had to be strangled by pulling the cord tight around his neck three successive times, with an interval between each. The third time, the tightening of the cord was final, but he seemed to be still alive, so one of the executioners gave him a violent kick in the stomach. Perboyre gave his soul back to his Creator. It was Friday noon.

The body remained attached to the instrument of his torture for a day and a night. The next day, on 12 September, the soldiers took him down, put him in a coffin and transported him to Hong Shan. Some Christians, however, decided to give Father Perboyre a more honorable burial and developed their own plan. They gave some money (to the soldiers) and had the coffin containing the precious remains delivered to them. Then they gave the soldiers another coffin filled with sand. While the soldiers appeared to be burying Perboyre, the Christians took him to a chapel that was not far away. They put on him the beautiful clothes that had been made during the previous night, they prayed the usual prayers for the dead, and then they went and buried him on the slope of Red Mountain near the tomb of Blessed Clet martyred twenty years earlier.

Leo XIII enrolled the heroic missionary in the rank of the Blessed on 9 November 1889.

Reorganization of the Missions in China

We end this chapter with an overview of the situation of the missions in China up that time.

After the death of Pirès in 1838, a transformation, first almost invisible, began taking place. Soon this transformation became widespread. The missionaries were changing their methods little by little. Three causes played a part:

1. The end of the missionary presence at the court of Peking freed those who were working there from the kind of slavery life at court imposed on them. In the future they had to rely on their own initiative to remain in the country in the same way the missionaries in the provinces were already doing.

2. The number of European ships in Chinese waters steadily increased. This eventually obliged China's supreme authority not only to show greater flexibility towards foreign residents and gradually stop the bloody persecutions, but also to tolerate the unfettered preaching of the Gospel throughout China.

3. The Holy See changed its old and established pattern of Church organization. The rule had been that every Christian community was entrusted to the religious congregation that had founded it. This rule caused a lot of friction. Serious change had been sought for many years. Soon there would be only one religious community in each vicariate responsible for supplying the apostolic vicar and the necessary material means and personnel. This would happen through the Holy See's plan to suppress the dioceses and replace them with apostolic vicariates. In that process some Christian communities located outside the diocese of Peking and in the care of the Vincentians were organized into three vicariates: that of Jiangxi and Zhejiang in 1838; that of Hubei and Henan in 1839; and that of Mongolia in 1840.

The Clergy, the Seminaries, the Faithful

At that time there were in China about one hundred twenty priests, forty of whom were Europeans. Among the eighty Chinese priests, fifty were Vincentians.

There were three seminaries preparing Chinese clergy, namely:

- Holy Family College established in Naples by Father Ripa in 1732 and under the direction of the Sacred Congregation of Propaganda.

- Saint Joseph Seminary established in Macao by Bishop de Gouvea in 1784 under the direction of the Portuguese Vincentians. It was first a diocesan seminary, later the seminary for the Vincentians in China. We saw that Matthieu Xue of Xiwanzi sent his eight seminarians to Macao, so that all the seminarians from the North were sent to Macao until 1842, when Mouly opened a seminary in Mongolia. This seminary would first be transferred to Anjiazhuang and later on definitively to Peking.

- The Poulo-Penang Seminary (Malacca), which was founded by [Claude-François] Létondal, M.E.P., in 1812 for Society of the Foreign Missions of Paris.

  In 1838, the number of Christians in the three dioceses entrusted to the care of the Portuguese Vincentians, who were assisted by the French Vincentians, were approximately as follows (there are no exact numbers):

- In the diocese of Macao: 15,000 Faithful.
- In the diocese of Peking: 34,000 Faithful.
- In the diocese of Nanjing: 40,000 Faithful.

The French Vincentians of Peking had about forty thousand Faithful spread over the provinces of Zhili, Mongolia, Zhejiang, Jiangxi, and Hubei.

Chapter 7

Mouly and Mission Work in Mongolia

The Arrival of Father Mouly in Mongolia – Mouly in Xiwanzi – Inventory of the Clergy and of the Christians in Mongolia – The Vicariate of Korea – Erection of the Apostolic Vicariate of Mongolia – The Difficulty of Converting the Mongols – The Journey to Tibet by Fathers Gabet and Huc

The Arrival of Father Mouly in Mongolia

Mouly's arrival to China marked a turning point in the history of the mission of Peking. During the thirty years of his administration, a series of events occurred that would mark an epoch.

A whole volume would be needed to recount Mouly's priestly virtues, his activities as head of the mission, and the immense services he rendered to the Church of China. No one has yet written Mouly's definitive biography. We can give here only a summary.

Joseph-Martial Mouly, like Blessed Perboyre, came from the diocese of Cahors. Born on 2 August 1807 in Figeac, he entered the internal seminary in Paris on 18 October 1825. After finishing his studies, he taught for three years in the ecclesiastical college of Roye in Picardie, and was ordained priest in Amiens on 2 April 1831. On 30 September 1833 he and Father Danicourt embarked for China, and after a long voyage they arrived in Macao on 14 June 1834.

The day after their arrival, Torrette told them that the mission of Peking needed a missionary to manage it and that the seminary in Macao needed another, because he was unable to provide the whole education of the seminarians by himself. Torrette, however, struggled to decide which priest to keep with him and which to send north.

What did he do? Just what Saint Peter and the ten apostles did in the Cenacle when they chose Mathias. With the two candidates, he invoked the Holy Spirit, put their names into an urn and drew lots. Providence indicated Father Mouly for Peking and Father Danicourt for the seminary, and that is what was done. Mouly made his preparations for the journey along with studying the language.

Since he wanted to see Father Rameaux, his old superior at Roye and then superior of the Hubei mission, he had to go through Hubei and cross the whole of China. This was a dangerous route; therefore, he had to make the journey incognito, as all the missionaries of that era had done since Jiaqing's edict of 1811.

Mouly disguised himself as an invalid. Whether in a boat or a wagon, he pretended to be unable to get up; in inns he laid down facing the wall to hide his face from the curious. Thanks to these precautions, he was able to visit his confrere in Hubei, remain with him a few days, and in time arrive at the gates of Peking at the beginning of the summer without any problem. He set off on 12 February 1835. When Pirès learned of his arrival, he did not allow Mouly to enter the city, because he feared his arrival might seriously compromise the interests of the faith. He feared it would give the government a pretext to make the measures against the Christians in the capital worse and perhaps to expel the only missionary still tolerated in the capital (he himself). The Beitang was gone. As we saw above the church had been demolished in 1827 and the houses sold or parceled out. Obliged to postpone his conversation with the bishop, Mouly went to Zhengfusi, the French cemetery. He was welcomed there by Father Joseph Han, C.M., who received him as his superior. After three days' rest, he continued his journey to Xiwanzi, where he arrived on 2 July 1835.

Mouly in Xiwanzi

Since 1829 this village had been the headquarters of the French mission with Father Xue as its temporary superior, appointed in 1820 by Lamiot. The remarkable Father Xue at the head of his Chinese confreres welcomed the young superior as sent by God. Xue immediately handed his office over without any hesitation, and wrote the superior general: "I greatly thank the Lord for having inspired you with the good idea of sending us the revered Father Mouly! We need him so much not only to reform us and renew us in the spirit of our state, but also to teach and manage the Faithful entrusted to our care!"

For his part, Mouly wrote, when talking about those who had welcomed him in such a sympathetic way, "They are all worthy of the teachers who taught them. . . . Xue, who was the superior, has more than ordinary virtue united with a great talent for both spiritual and temporal admin-istration. With a great ability, what simplicity! . . . what humility! . . . what punctuality! – I do not say for the rules – but even for the smallest customs of the Congregation!"

The village of Xiwanzi, an important religious center that soon was to become the see of a new diocese, was at that time only a hamlet occu-pied by emigrants from Zhili province, who were clearing the fields the Mongols gave to those willing to cultivate them.

The importance of the hamlet dated exactly from the closure of the Beitang and the transfer there of the French mission by Xue in 1829. When Xue arrived there, there were slightly more than one hundred Faithful; in 1835 there were 676. Before the destruction of this Christian community by the communists, there were more than three thousand Christians.

Despite their poverty, the Christians of Xiwanzi found their chapel too small, demolished it and had begun to build a larger one at the time Mouly arrived. It was begun in 1835 and finished in 1838. It cost one thousand taels, a tenth of which Mouly had given. The village and the neighboring Christian communities supplied all the rest. This church served as a cathedral until 1920.

Inventory of the Clergy and the Christian Communities in Mongolia

The arrival of Mouly had an immediate positive impact. People very soon began to feel new life in this mission that seemed sleepy for lack of an enterprising authority. His clergy was not numerous, only five Chinese priests in all, all Vincentians. From the first days, Mouly wanted to know and respond to the spiritual needs of his flock. He began with his clergy.

Two months after his arrival in Mongolia, he invited his collaborators to meet in Xiwanzi to make their annual retreat. It was on this occasion that the devout Xue asked for pardon in front of the whole community for the faults he committed during the exercise of his leadership. He solemnly recognized his young confrere as the legitimate superior and he promised him obedience. It is known that he kept his word.

After the missionaries, he turned to the Christians. How many were there? According to Mouly's statistics in 1838, there were for Mongolia alone about two thousand Faithful.

Mouly introduced retreats for men and women, and took up again the liturgical practice of Gregorian chant forbidden by Pirès during the persecution. He allowed Christian women to enter the church. That had never happened before. Only men had been admitted there; women had been meeting in a private room arranged as an oratory, where a priest would go and celebrate Holy Mass on Sundays and feast days. So as not to offend their accustomed way of doing things, he arranged an entrance different from the one for men. Moreover, every church with a mixed congregation consisted of two buildings in the form of a right angle, and in that angle the altar was placed, so that men and women could participate in the same ceremonies, everyone able to see the altar without seeing each other. This custom was widespread in the north of China, but disappeared in the beginning of the twentieth century. Today, the church generally is only one building, longer than it is wide. Men attend on one side, women on the other with a common entrance for both sexes.

In order to bring back the observance of Sundays and feast days, Mouly instituted the "Stations of the Cross" on Sunday afternoons, and made it the rule for all the Faithful. From then on this devout practice continued everywhere in the Christian communities, even in those without a priest.

Mouly was also interested in the question of education. The need of religious schools was felt everywhere. But where could teachers be found? Remembering the successful efforts of the old Beitang missionaries, he founded a school for teachers.

During the winter he brought together some good Christians who had time to study; he took care of their upkeep, gave them instructions and formed them for preaching. Later on, he sent these Christians to the villages to run winter schools. Every Sunday they gave the people instructions. He also created traveling catechists, who lived in small Christian communities for a shorter or longer time according to the number of children and the needs of the Faithful.

Establishing schools for girls was much more difficult. On one hand, the customs of the country were against doing so, indeed, study for girls especially those of the countryside was unheard of. On the other hand, the process he had used to teach the teachers could not be used for schoolmistresses. His administrative sense and his perseverance overcame the difficulties. Two virgins and the wives of the two catechists of the village managed the school in Xiwanzi, which had sixty girls from eight to sixteen years of age. Because the mistresses were unable to explain certain passages of the religion books, the first catechist, a sixty-year-old man of proven virtue, stepped in three times a week. This kind of girls' schools was imitated in other places as circumstances allowed.

It is good to remember that the people at that time had catechisms and prayer books, which the first Jesuits who came to China – the majority were Portuguese – composed and printed.

The great task and the one closest to Mouly's heart was the seminary. After arriving in Xiwanzi years earlier, Xue had sent his seminarians to Lamiot in Macao for their formation. He kept only a preparatory school in Xiwanzi. Mouly did the same. The young people who were considered seriously open to a vocation studied the basics of Latin in the preparatory school and then were sent to Macao. Mouly followed this pattern for five or six years. As soon as the apostolic vicariate of Mongolia was established, however, he stopped doing so. In 1842, he transferred his minor seminary to Xiaotonggou, one hundred twenty kilometers to the west of Xiwanzi, and kept the major seminary in his episcopal residence.

Although he was settled in Mongolia, Mouly also cared for the Faithful entrusted to the French Vincentians, even those of the Zhili province. This gave him responsibility for about nine thousand Christians in more than two hundred communities. At the same time, approximately twenty-five thousand Christians remained in the care of the Portuguese mission for whom Pirès was responsible as administrator of the diocese of Peking. Father Castro followed him in this responsibility.

At this point in our account, we will treat the establishment of the vicariate of Mongolia, but to make this event more comprehensible, we are obliged first to talk about the fledgling church in Korea.

The Vicariate of Korea

We mentioned earlier that Mouly arrived in Xiwanzi on 12 July 1835. There he met a bishop who was on his way to take possession of the vicariate of Korea. He was Bishop [Barthélemy] Bruguière, M.E.P., accompanied by his confrere, Father Maubant. These two dauntless missionaries left Siam in September 1832 and arrived in Xiwanzi on 11 May 1835 after having endured unimaginable sufferings and run incredible risks. Bruguière, impatient to reach his final destination, left his companion in Xiwanzi and on 8 August left for Korea with a priest whom Mouly lent him, Jean Qiu, C.M. On 1 November, however, courier-guides came back and announced to Maubant the sad news of the bishop's sudden death on 24 October 1835 after having received the last rites from Qiu's hand. Maubant, overcome with grief, left immediately for Korea and on 21 November celebrated the funeral of Bruguière.

Rome hastened to give him a successor. It was Bishop Imbert, M.E.P., missionary in Sichuan. Like his predecessor, he travelled through Mongolia and Manchuria to reach Korea in 1837.

We will see again the many disadvantages and blunders that were caused partly by the extreme slowness of communications and partly by ignorance, the ignorance of geography, morals and customs of the new mission countries both on the part of Rome and the missionaries.

Erection of the Apostolic Vicariate of Mongolia

When Imbert arrived in Korea, he began to execute the plan Bruguière had already developed, namely, to ask Rome to erect the civil province of Liaodong as an apostolic vicariate, covering Manchuria and Mongolia, with a residence in Xiwanzi as pied-à-terre and asylum near Korea, which was at the time disturbed by persecution. Imbert made this proposal without Mouly's knowledge.

Rome, without seeking more information, shared these views, and, without defining clearly the boundaries of this new vicariate, named Father [Emmanuel-Jean-François] Vérolles (Verrolles), M.E.P., missionary in Sichuan, first apostolic vicar of the region. Vérolles had himself consecrated by the Franciscan, Bishop Salvetti, apostolic vicar in Shanxi. Without delay he set out for Mongolia, and on 2 December 1839 reached Xiwanzi.

As Mouly knew nothing about these events, which nevertheless touched him intimately, it is no surprise that Mouly was dismayed when Vérolles told him the story and showed him the bulls.

He was astonished. This decision of the Holy See took away an immense part of the diocese of Peking, and the so-called "vestibule" that the bishop of Peking gave up as an entrance to Korea was ten times bigger than the "palace" to which it gave access. Moreover, Xiwanzi was the principal and only residence of the missionaries of Peking.

Thanks to his attitude of faith, Mouly accepted the decision by Rome without procrastination and put Vérolles up with the greatest kindness during the three months that he remained in Xiwanzi before setting off for his vicariate.

Torrette, visitor of the Vincentians in China, wrote his superiors and at the same time he sent Propaganda a letter in which he suggested to take away from the new vicariate of Liaodong the whole of Mongolia and to entrust it to the Vincentians, who already had the center of their charitable works there. Several of their missionaries who were about to go there were put on hold. He supported his petition with both just and relevant reasons.

Torrette's petition was too well founded for Rome to reject it. Consequently, on 31 August 1840 the Sacred Congregation sent Torrette the following letter, which arrived only after the addressee's death:

"Very Reverend Father Torrette, the Sacred Congregation has received with the greatest pleasure your report about the missions in China entrusted to your Society in China. . . . Taking into consideration your reasons as well as the huge surface of the Liaodong vicariate, it has approved your petition. Thus, it intends to separate Mongolia from Liaodong and to erect it as a separate vicariate and to give it to the priests of Saint Lazare."

On 15 April 1841 a letter from the superior general informed Mouly that the Holy See had appointed him as bishop of Fussala and apostolic vicar of Mongolia. The bulls arrived only in July 1842.

Meanwhile, Mouly tried to avoid this honor and responsibility; he suggested the nomination of his confrere, Father Gabet, saying that he was better endowed than he himself, especially for administration. Rome with the agreement of Paris had another idea. Mouly, consequently, had to go and look for a bishop to consecrate him. The nearest bishop was Bishop Salvetti, apostolic vicar of Shanxi, though a journey of twenty-five days. On 25 July 1842 he received episcopal consecration in Hongkouzi (a Christian community of the Yangqu sub-prefecture), not far from Taiyuan, capital of Shanxi.

Mouly remained the ecclesiastical and religious superior of the mission of Peking under the visitor in Macao, who at that time was Father Faivre, successor of Torrette. He died on 12 September 1840, age thirty-nine.

The Difficulty of Converting the Mongols

There were no Mongols, strictly speaking, among the Christians in Mouly's care. The Mongol population was resistant to evangelization, because of their nomadic habits. These cowherds moved according to the needs of their herds and lived a tribal way of life in which the chief was master of the people and their goods. Consequently, abandoning the prince's religion meant escaping his authority, and this meant giving up the tribe's pastures and fields. Moreover, the lamas (bonzes) had a very tight hold on these simple and ignorant people firmly rooted in their Buddhist ways.

In 1837, the first European collaborator Mouly received arrived in Xiwanzi. He was Father Gabet, who, as you remember, landed in Macao with Perboyre in 1835. His early apostolic successes caused Mouly to have great hope along with intense joy. Two unexpected conversions by Gabet strengthened him in his projects, because these two neophytes were lamas, monks of the Buddhist religion.

Here is in a few words the story of how these conversions came about. Gabet, who already knew the Chinese language quite well, had a great desire to study the Mongol language. Soon after he arrived, he began to minister to the Faithful. Called to give a dying person the last rites in a Christian community of Jehol, one hundred twenty kilometers away, he learned from the Christians that some Mongols, friends of the mission, were living in the neighborhood. He went and visited with them. Those people spoke Chinese, though purebred Mongols. While talking with them, Gabet expressed his desire to learn the Mongol language and asked them if they could send him a man of good will to teach him Mongolian. They promised him that they would. Sometime later, two catechists from that place arrived in Xiwanzi, bringing with them a young lama, twenty-five years old, named Ji, to teach Gabet the Mongol language. He immediately became the pupil of this new teacher, while teaching the lama, nearly unawares, the science of salvation. When the lama heard in his own language the exposition of the doctrine, he understood its beauty, and renounced his errors. He threw away his Buddhist clothing and entered the ranks of the catechumens in the house under the name of Paul.

The second conversion of a lama followed the first one closely and seemed to prove that Mouly's judgment that his confrere had a special vocation to convert Mongols was correct.

Gabet made the rounds of the Christian communities with Paul whom he taught during the journeys. One day, getting near Gubeikou, a pass of the Great Wall, they met a penitent lama on the way. It is well known that penitent lamas sometimes make long and painful journeys to famous temples, prostrating themselves on the road at every step. Gabet, observing this lama taking a step, then falling down at full length in the dust his forehead against the earth, then getting up, taking another step and again falling down, and so on for whole days, was so moved to pity by this spectacle, that in the early morning of the following day he sent Paul to meet this poor misled person, who he supposed was continuing his pilgrimage on the road. It did not take long for Paul to reach him. "Stop," he said to him, "I want to talk with you. What was your crime that you imposed such a penance on yourself?" "I did not commit any serious crime, but I want to secure paradise for my soul." – "Oh! This is not the best method: I have believed in Buddha too; like you, I have been a lama; well, I have discovered that it was all untrue." Paul talked to him about Gabet and induced him to follow him and talk with Gabet.

Both reached the missionary. "Who imposed on you such a penance?" Gabet asked him. The lama answered again that he had imposed it himself so as to save his soul; that he was on his way to Peking and from there to Wutaishan (Five Mountains) with its numerous temples and famous pilgrimage sites. After many explanations, the young lama thought a moment and said, "I want to save my soul; what must I do?" – "It is not the work of one moment; come with me and every day you will learn something of the knowledge of salvation. Take a rest today."

The lama decided to abandon the two little wooden pads he was wearing on his hands so as not to wound himself in his prostrations and, the next day, he set off with Gabet and Paul. After entering the catechumenate, he was given the name Peter. In Xiwanzi an effort was made to push the two neophytes towards the priesthood, because nobody would be more acceptable to their compatriots than they themselves. Peter indeed followed this vocation – as we shall see – till the end; but Paul remained a layperson and devoted his whole life to missionary activities. Peter, whose Mongol name was "Gardi," which means "phoenix," was given the Chinese family name of Feng, which has the same meaning.

The Journey to Tibet by Fathers Gabet and Huc

Encouraged by the initial successes of Gabet, Mouly toyed with the idea of asking him to make a journey of exploration and evangelization among the nomads. But he needed a companion capable of going with him. Mouly waited some time before carrying out his project.

Evariste Huc, who had been in Macao for two years, arrived in Xiwanzi on 17 June 1841. He was Gabet's confrere and friend. He seemed to have all the qualities required to accompany Gabet in his excursions according to Mouly. And what about the two neophyte lamas? Peter Feng, since he showed himself well-disposed for study and piety, was sent to the seminary in Macao, and Paul Ji continued helping the missionaries in their numerous journeys.

After becoming a bishop, Mouly wanted to push ahead with his project. He had plans involving Peter Feng, the former lama, who had become a seminarian. He thought about having him interrupt his studies, so he could give him to the explorers as the best guide available. The directors of the seminary in Macao did not think it was a good idea and did not grant this wish.

During the summer of 1842, Mouly sent Gabet together with Paul Ji to exercise their apostolate among the lamas. The travelers made a stop at "Blue Town," called at that time Guihuacheng, nowadays Sui-yuancheng. Gabet arrived there with the set purpose of preaching directly to the lamas. He intended to enter the lamasery and had not given up his hope of winning a good number of lamas to Christianity, even perhaps a complete lamasery. Despite all his efforts, the undertaking produced no results whatever.

During that time, Huc gone into the Heishuihe (Black Water River) area where he combined exercising his ministry with the study of the Mongolian and Manchurian languages, at which he was very able. He too made a conquest. At Majiasi he found somebody called Sandatchiemba, born in Gansu, who had been living in the big lamasery of Peking. With Paul's help he brought him to the faith and baptized him under the name of John Baptist. Soon this former lama will appear again on stage.

In 1844, Gabet asked Bishop Mouly to take responsibility for the Jehol district from him, so that he could dedicate himself exclusively to the conversion of the Mongols. At the same time, Huc asked to go with Gabet on his journey of exploration. Mouly, who was very interested in the apos-tolates of these two confreres, granted their requests. The two discussed at length the method they would adopt. They thought that, in order to live among Mongols, it would be proper to gain their trust by adopting their customs. When their plan had matured and a decision taken, they received the blessing of their apostolic vicar and set off in September 1844.

The small caravan was made up of Gabet sitting on a big she-camel, Huc on a white horse, and Sandatchiemba, who, sitting on a black he-mule, was going as their guide. He led the way, pulling behind him two camels loaded with luggage. From the second day of their journey, they took off their Chinese clothes and put on a yellow garment, which was the common dress for lamas and which the guide Sandatchiemba was already wearing.

We shall not follow them on this long and colorful journey. This report has no place here. Moreover, Huc's publications on this subject are well known and still very much appreciated. Let us only call to mind *L'Empire chinois*,[25] which was honored by the Académie Française, *Le Christianisme en Chine* and *Souvenirs d'un voyage dans la Tartarie et le Thibet*, volumes

---

25. *L'Empire chinois*, 2 vols. (Paris, 1854).

which have filled their young readers with so much enthusiasm for voyages of discovery.

We shall say only that when the two missionaries had arrived in Lhasa, the capital of Tibet, at the beginning of 1846, they were welcomed courteously by the regent who governed during the Dalai Lama's minority. They were allowed to enter freely into the lamaseries and expound the great truths to the lamas. They met, however, with a total lack of understanding. Besides, their stay in that strange country was cut short, because the Amban, a kind of Chinese ambassador, made it clear to the regent that the presence of these foreigners could not be tolerated and that they had to be sent on their way to Macao as soon as possible. They departed from Lhasa on 26 February 1846 and after a journey of seven months they arrived in Macao at the beginning of October. Gabet returned to Europe and, in 1849, was missioned to Brazil, where he died in Rio de Janeiro on 3 March 1853. Huc stayed on in China for some years. Summoned back to France, he died in Paris on 25 March 1860.

Chapter 8

New Apostolic Vicars and Catholic Expansion

Nominations of New Apostolic Vicars – François-Alexis Rameaux – Bernard Laribe – Jean-Henri Baldus – Pierre Lavaissière – François Danicourt – Louis-Gabriel Delaplace – The Diocese of Peking – Mouly Settles in Anjiazhuang – Vincentian Missionaries in China (1835-1850) – Mouly's Coadjutor Bishops – Organization of the Missions (Visitors and Vicariates) – Two Successive Meetings of Bishops with Different Goals: The Assembly of Ningbo and the Assembly of Shanghai – End of the "Schism" in the Diocese of Peking – Edicts of Toleration – The Murder of Father Ferdinand-Felix Montels – Mouly Surrendered to the Authorities to Save His Christians – Bishop Mouly's Expulsion

Nominations of New Apostolic Vicars

Amid persecutions – violent here, mitigated there, everywhere possible or imminent – the missionaries were working their way, as it were, through the meshes of a net: good was being done and the missions were growing.

After speaking of Blessed Perboyre above, we promised to retrace our steps in order to relate the activities of the missionaries who had preceded him in China two or three years earlier.

After the first two, Fathers Rameaux and Laribe, landed in Macao on 3 March 1832 they were ready to get to work the following year, one in Hubei, and the other in Jiangxi. We met them in 1835, when we were following Perboyre on his journey to Hubei. The same was true of Baldus, whom we saw fleeing through fields and scrubs, at the time of Perboyre's arrest on 15 September 1839. These three confreres were soon to become leaders of missions.

François-Alexis Rameaux

He was born in Desne (Jura) on 24 May 1802 and was ordained in 1826. He was a professor in the major seminary of Montauban and then superior of the Roye College before his departure for China. As a missionary in

Hubei, he eventually became superior of the Vincentians of that region. He found it difficult to get used to seeing the extreme destitution from which the habitants suffered in that region, which floods had devastated three years in a row resulting in widespread starvation. So much misery and his inability to relieve it pierced his heart with sorrow. Then there was the persecution resulting from Perboyre's arrest. Rameaux fled to the more peaceful province of Jiangxi like a fugitive. He endured a thousand deprivations and inconveniences, while all the time being hunted down by soldiers. He evaded all pursuit.

At the very moment he received the news of Perboyre's capture, he also received the news of his nomination as bishop with the title of bishop of Myra. Rome assigned to him the two civil provinces of Zhejiang and Jiangxi as a single apostolic vicariate. These two provinces were taken from the vicariate of Fujian, under José Carpena Diaz, a Spanish Dominican. He desired this division and had suggested it to Rome for several years because he had no priests to send there.

Rameaux received episcopal consecration in Qitian (Fujian) from the hands of Bishop Carpena on 1 March 1840. This venerable bishop was held in high esteem because of his gentleness and kindness which touched the hearts of the people. "After being a bishop for forty-six years, he was the dean of all the bishops in the world," said his contemporaries.

Rameaux without delay visited all the Christian communities of the two provinces entrusted to him. In Jiangxi he met again with his confrere Laribe, who was Carpena's pro-vicar. He wanted to see the needs of the different communities with his own eyes. Establishing schools was his principal strategy. Rameaux visited the Zhoushan Islands, which were under his jurisdiction. A year earlier, Danicourt had visited there and founded a Christian community on the island of Dinghai. The bishop visited the neighboring islands, where the gospel had not yet been preached. It was a journey of exploration. At that time the British occupied the islands. They welcomed him very kindly.

Rameaux's field of activity was too vast for him alone. He suggested to the Holy See to give him Father Laribe as his coadjutor, and on 2 March 1844 he was appointed bishop of Sozopolis and coadjutor of Jiangxi-Zhejiang. Rameaux consecrated him at Sanqiao in Jiangxi on 13 May 1845.

After the ceremonies, Rameaux heard that an envoy sent by France to China was to arrive in Macao. It was [Théodose] Lagrené, who came to negotiate the treaty between France and China that was to bear the name "Whampoa," similar to what the United Kingdom had done two years earlier in concluding the commercial treaty of "Nanjing." Rameaux decided to take advantage of the occasion to go and discuss the problems of the missions in China with Lagrené. He arrived a few days before the envoy. On 14 July, at about nine o'clock in the evening, the bishop asked his confrere to accompany him to the sea. He wanted to swim there. While swimming, however, he suffered a violent stroke and drowned. All efforts to revive him were in vain. Rameaux's sudden death – he was forty-five years old – was a great loss to the mission in China.

With the death of the apostolic vicar, his coadjutor, Laribe, automatically became his successor.

Bernard Laribe

Laribe was born in Sousceyrac (Lot) on 12 May 1802. He was admitted to the Congregation in Saint Lazare on 31 October 1823 and went to China together with Rameaux. As soon as he arrived at his assigned destination, namely Jiangxi, Carpena appointed him as his pro-vicar for that province. In 1842, the Holy See named him to proceed with the canonical inquiries concerning Perboyre's martyrdom. In order to do so, he made a long and difficult journey in Hubei, which lasted eight months. Because of the persecution that was still raging in that region he could visit the venerable martyr's tomb only secretly and returned without being able to bring his inquiries to a successful conclusion. After his consecration (1845), he took this work up again with renewed energy.

The following year, he received a document from Propaganda, notifying him of the separation of the two provinces of Zhejiang and Jiangxi into two distinct vicariates. He was given the opportunity to choose one. He chose Jiangxi, with which he was more familiar. At the same time, Propaganda appointed Lavaissière as apostolic vicar of Zhejiang, who, named bishop of Myra, received episcopal consecration from Laribe on 27 March 1846.

Laribe served his vicariate through the books he composed and especially through his large catechism, which was a very much appreciated compendium of theology.

His health eventually was undermined by his zealous and active life. In 1850, when Zhejiang lost its bishop through the death of Lavaissière, Laribe who was already ill went to Zhejiang to confer Holy Orders on two young priests. On his return, he made a long detour to give the last rites to some sick people. Traveling on a little boat, he felt his illness worsen. When he arrived in the Christian community, he wanted to celebrate Holy Mass in spite of his illness. Two men had to support him so he could finish the Mass. Then he gave last rites twice before going to bed. Joseph Li rushed to comfort the dying bishop and to give him the last rites. Laribe died on 20 July 1850, forty-eight years old, eighteen of which he spent in China.

Jean-Henri Baldus

Born in Ally (Cantal) on 26 January 1811 and admitted to the Congregation in Saint Lazare on 11 June 1829, Father Baldus was destined for China. He arrived in Macao on 25 September 1834 and went to Hubei where he worked three years. Caught unawares in Chayuangou at the time of Perboyre's arrest, he wandered aimlessly together with Rizzolati, without knowing where to find shelter that would safeguard themselves from their persecutors. They marched day and night, hiding in Christians' houses, which they entered shaking and soon left not to compromise them. Finally, Rizzolati managed to get back to his vicariate of Shanxi, and Baldus on the other hand settled in Henan and stayed there for good.

The Christian communities in Henan depended on the diocese of Peking, because Henan had been entrusted to the Vincentians. Only in 1844 did the Holy See erect Henan as an apostolic vicariate by a decree of 2 March, appointing Baldus as bishop of Zoara and first apostolic vicar of Henan. Laribe consecrated Baldus in Jiangxi on 10 October 1845. On that date, the new Bishop Baldus had only two collaborators, both Vincentians, Fathers Paul Song, seventy-one, and Stanislas Ai, in his sixties and disabled. There was, however, much to be done in these Christian communities that saw a priest only once every five or six years. In the following years some workers were given to this mission, but it was still not enough. That was the reason why the superior general of the Congregation asked the Sacred Congregation of Propaganda to entrust others with the vicariate of Henan, so that he could call back missionaries from there and send them where the needs were more urgent. This took place in 1865. The vicariate of Henan was entrusted to the Society of the Missionaries of Milan, and Baldus was transferred to Jiangxi. Later we shall see later the circumstances of this transfer, and we shall follow Baldus till the end of his career.

Pierre Lavaissière

Born in Grandel (Cantal) on 25 October 1813, Lavaissière entered the Congregation in Paris on 4 October 1835 and landed in Macao on 2 January 1839. At that time the Portuguese confreres in the Nanjing diocese asked for reinforcements but scarcely received any help. Lavaissière was sent there towards the end of 1839.

Let us listen to him talking about his beginnings in Jiangnan. First, he says that this mission, because of the lack of European priests was in a sorry state. "The last one to give a mission here was Bishop Laimbeck-hoven, who died fifty years ago. Portuguese confreres came here but only contracted illnesses and heard some confessions. The Chinese priests were not numerous enough to visit all the Christian communities even once every year."

Setting aside Lavaissière's report, we can say in a few words what the situation of the Nanjing diocese was like. Since its establishment in 1696, this diocese had only two effective bishops. They were Bishop Ciceri, S.J., an Italian (1696–1704), and Bishop Laimbeckhoven, S.J., an Austrian (1752–1787). Of the six others appointed, some resigned immediately, while the others occupied the see only briefly. Finally, the last bishop, Bishop Pirès (1804–1838), never arrived. After him, three administrators succeeded each other until the suppression of the diocese.

In the absence of the Jesuits, some Vincentians were attached to that mission, first some Portuguese, then some French, namely, Fathers Faivre and Lavaissière. The main works of the missions were carried out by the Chinese Vincentians and the Chinese diocesan priests.

A young clergyman became mixed up in the affairs of the dioceses of Peking and Nanjing. He lacked prudence and caused the missionaries a lot of trouble. He was the Count de Besi. A compatriot of Gregory XVI, he knew the pope who favored him. The day after his ordination, he conceived the desire to dedicate himself to the China missions. Peking was his goal. He offered himself to the prefect of Propaganda and put himself completely to his disposal. This young priest was intelligent. He had the noble intention of restoring the scientific prestige of the old missionaries of China and thus win back the favors of the court and of the emperor. Consequently, he took along a chest full of materials for physics and astronomy.

This was de Besi's frame of mind when he arrived in China in 1834. At that time, however, non-Portuguese foreigners were forbidden to enter Macao, so he was obliged to go and look for shelter in Canton.

Very dissatisfied, he attributed this obstruction to the Vincentians and wrote to Propaganda to complain. The cardinal prefect expressed his displeasure to the superior general. Without delay, Torrette sent Paris an authoritative report that made short work of the accusations made against him and his Portuguese and French confreres.

In short, the affair went nowhere.

Since it did not take long for de Besi to recognize that the situation in China was not as he had assumed, he decided not to go to Peking but to enter the missions of Huguang incognito, where Salvetti had jurisdiction as apostolic vicar of Shanxi. In 1838, some Chinese priests of Nanjing heard of de Besi's presence in Huguang and invited him to come and lead them in the absence of Pirès who was near death. De Besi accepted this proposition and went and settled in Nanjing. On 2 November 1838 Pirès departed this world. Three months later, letters from Rome conferred the title of administrator of the Peking diocese on the Portuguese Vincentian Father [Domingos-José de Santo Estêvam] Henriques. Disappointed, de Besi left Nanjing and returned to Huguang, where Salvetti made him his vicar general.

On 3 September 1839 a decree from Rome detached Shandong province from the Peking diocese and erected this province as a vicariate, and named de Besi as the first apostolic vicar of Shandong. He had himself consecrated by Salvetti in Shanxi on 14 March 1841.

Immediately, de Besi went and took possession of his see and named Father Moccagatta, an Italian Franciscan, as his pro-vicar there. He gave him every spiritual faculty, and then returned to Nanjing, which was his responsibility to administer since he was the nearest neighboring bishop.

At that time, in 1842, the Society of Jesus, suppressed by Clement XIV in 1773, and restored by Pius VII in 1814, sent missionaries to China. They made straight for Jiangnan (that is, Jiangsu and Anhui, two civil provinces) and without delay took up their works in the Nanjing diocese.

From that day, de Besi, seeing his vineyard well equipped with workers, and because he had never got on well with the Vincentians, wanted to get rid of them. When the superior general became aware of the situation in 1844, he ordered all the Chinese and European confreres working in the Nanjing sector to give up their places. Faivre went to Mongolia and in 1846 returned to France (He died in Paris on 2 May 1864.[26]) Lavaissière went to Henan, and Henriques, who was sick, had in 1837 already gone back to Macao and was in Portugal after 1841. Among the six Chinese priests, four went north, and the two others, already old, preferred to die where they had been working for so many years.

De Besi also did not get on well with the Jesuits in the end. He returned to Europe in 1847 with no intention of returning, [resigning in 1848] and died in Italy in 1871.

---

26.   Ferreux's notes: Faivre had gone to Macao as an informal visitor.

Let us return to Lavaissière whom we find now in Henan, keeping Baldus company. He did not work there for long, because, in 1846, he became apostolic vicar of Zhejiang.

As soon as he was consecrated, he went and took possession of his vicariate in Ningbo. That city had only a few Christian families, but because it had just been opened up for European trade, the hope was that practicing religion there would be freer.

The bishop dreamed of establishing the Association of the Holy Childhood,[27] for he hoped that the Daughters of Charity would soon come and establish their works, and he wanted there to be the beginning of an orphanage at their arrival. He rented a house, accepted some abandoned children and had them taken care of by somewhat elderly Christian ladies. His dream came true some little time later, but Lavaissière was not around to enjoy it.

In the meantime, the bishop was busy establishing a residence in Chefupang, in the Jiaxing sub-prefecture. On the Zhoushan Islands Danicourt was working at rekindling the fervor of the neophytes whom he had formed there, if they had not yet gone back to their superstitions.

The Jesuits had long ago opened Hangzhou, the capital of the province, for Christianity. They built quite a big church, but the government had confiscated it and it was still in their hands. The time had not yet come to reclaim it. Danicourt was to do so later on. That repaired church still exists today.

Lavaissière contracted a serious disease, which immobilized him for two months. He never got rid of it completely. He had chronic dysentery, which finally carried him off. On 19 December 1849, only in his thirty-seventh year, he finished his far too brief career in Ningbo.

François Danicourt

Lavaissière had hardly closed his eyes, when his activities were to bear fruit in the most admirable way.

Through a decree of 22 December 1850 the Holy See nominated Father Danicourt as bishop of Antiphellus and apostolic vicar of Zhejiang.

Danicourt was born in Anthies (Somme) on 18 March 1806. After being admitted to the Congregation in Saint Lazare on 8 September 1828, he was ordained on 24 September 1831. After three-year's training in the college of

---

27. Now a pontifical association, originally established in 1843 to support the work of caring for abandoned Chinese children. (JR)

Montdidier, he embarked for China with Mouly and landed in Macao in 1834. We have seen how he was appointed professor of Saint Joseph Seminary, where he taught for seven years with unbelievable ardor and success.

Danicourt, who was Lavaissière's vicar general, as he had been Rameaux's, worked on several occasions in Zhejiang, especially on the Zhoushan Islands. He was in Ningbo when he received his nomination. His consecration was done with extreme solemnity in Ningbo itself – we shall mention the reason later – on 7 September 1851. The charities were going well. The seminary established in Ningbo already had twelve students under the direction of the young Father André Li, C.M., who in 1862 was to be a victim of the Taiping (Chang Mao) rebels.

Danicourt immediately began the construction of a part of the buildings destined for the Daughters of Charity. These sisters had been in Macao since June 1848, ready to fly away, so as to land somewhere in China where they were in demand. On 21 June 1852 Danicourt had the consolation of welcoming them. They began their work right away, and the bishop was happy to see how the works that his predecessor had wanted so much were springing up.

Unexpectedly word came from Rome that deeply grieved the bishop: a decree from Propaganda transferred him to Jiangxi. The apostolic vicar of that province, Bishop Delaplace, was to replace him in Zhejiang.

Despite the very noticeable pain he felt, Danicourt obeyed without any hesitation and went courageously to his new mission. He found this province to be given over to all the horrors of civil war. It was the Taiping rebellion by the Chang Mao rebels, "the long-haired." The imperial troops fought for several years without real success against those rebels, who were ruining the south of China. We shall talk about this again when we see the damage they caused in Zhejiang.

For six years Danicourt witnessed those sad events. His chapels were looted, demolished and burned; numerous Christians died of hunger, distress and misery; others were beheaded. He himself was seized at the time of the ransacking of his seminary, he was stripped of his clothes, chained up, taken before a military tribunal, where he bore witness to his faith, and from which he escaped only by a stroke of Providence.

So many troubles over time impaired his health. In 1859, he was ordered by Rome to accompany the precious remains of Venerable John Gabriel Perboyre. He arrived in Paris on 6 January 1860. There he was hit by one of those fevers he suffered from in China, which led him in a few days to the tomb. He died on 2 February 1860, age fifty-three, twenty-five years as bishop. The reader will probably have noticed that in those days the leaders of the missions often died prematurely. Long and difficult journeys needed for their frequent pastoral visits explain the brevity of the lives of numerous apostolic vicars.

Louis-Gabriel Delaplace

Father Delaplace was born on 21 January 1820 in Auxerre (Yonne). He studied in the minor seminary of that city and made his theological studies in the major seminary of Sens, which was directed by Vincentians. He was still in that seminary when the news of Perboyre's martyrdom arrived in Europe. It would produce an immense emotion in France. This for the young man signaled his missionary vocation: it seemed to him that God called him to take John Gabriel's place on Chinese soil.

After his diaconate ordination in 1842, he secretly left his parents to enter Saint Lazare on 9 August 1842. He was ordained priest a year later and sent to Fontevrault. Two years later, his superiors granted his wishes and entreaties by missioning him to China. Delaplace arrived in Macao on 13 March 1846, stayed there for one year and was sent to Henan to work under Baldus's direction. In that mission he showed that his ardor and high intelligence measured up to the task. For three years he traveled the roads previously trod by Blessed Clet and Blessed Perboyre. The Jiangxi vicariate had been vacant since Laribe's death in 1850. To take his place, the Holy See appointed [André] Jandard, Baldus's pro-vicar in Henan. Jandard in his humility refused that dignity, so the name of Delaplace was suggested to Rome. By decree of 27 February 1852 Delaplace was appointed bishop of Andrinople and apostolic vicar of Jiangxi. He received episcopal consecration on 25 July 1852 in Fengqiao, a Christian community in Henan, in a small thatched chapel, from the hands of Bishop Baldus, who was assisted by Fathers Jandard and Jacques Zhou, C.M.

As soon as he took the administration of Jiangxi in hand, the bishop gave it enlightened and strong direction. Deploring that the adversities of the times had not made it possible to give the priests a complete formation, he decided to do something about it. He organized a residence in Jiudu and settled there with the ten Chinese priests who made up the personnel of the mission. He made them go through a second seminary so to speak. Every day he gave them a conference on moral theology, the administration of sacraments, the rules of the Congregation and the virtues of priests.

Since Delaplace lived in Jiangxi for only two years, it seems that there would be little to say about the work he did in this vicariate so damaged by the war. The time was certainly not favorable for making conversions. The new bishop did not want to stay inactive, however, and so he tirelessly focused his energies onto what he called the Charity of the "Good Angels," that is the baptism of abandoned Chinese children and the founding of orphanages. "The Holy Childhood," he said, "is always the highest source of our joy. Look, our baptisms have increased. In 1852, there were 1,500; this year there are 2,245!" It can be said that this was the favorite charity of his whole episcopal life.

To his great surprise, however, a decree of Propaganda came and transferred him to Zhejiang, where he succeeded Danicourt. From a certain point of view, it can be said that Delaplace had jumped out of the frying pan into the fire. If Jiangxi suffered greatly from the rebels, the province of Zhejiang suffered even more because of them, due to their prolonged stay there. Ningbo, Shaoxing, Jiaxing and other important towns came under their yoke. This rebellion of the Chang Mao, which historians call Taiping, put the reigning dynasty to a rude test. It began in 1850 after the death of Daoguang, who was succeeded by his son Xianfeng (1851-1861). It broke out in Guangxi. Southern China had never been favorable to the Qing dynasty, so all the provinces in the south fell easily into the hands of the rebels. Afterwards, their triumphant gangs went north and even entered the Zhili province, without, however, tackling the capital, Peking. Several imperial generals distinguished themselves in this fight, which lasted almost fifteen years. The person who succeeded best was Li Hongzhang, who, however, was not a general, but the civil governor of Anhui. His endeavors drew the attention of the imperial authorities and made him an important statesman.

Convinced that it would be unable to suppress the rebellion, the government suggested that the Europeans should help the government by marshaling troops under the command of the Europeans themselves. The English happily lent themselves to it, later on the French a little less. Peace was established in 1865, but in the majority of the provinces the damage was immense.

We have seen earlier how much Delaplace valued the Holy Childhood; so it can be understood that, when he had taken possession of the vicariate of Zhejiang, where thanks to the Daughters of Charity this charity was already established, the work of the Holy Childhood blossomed.

In 1855, one year after his arrival, the bishop wrote: "While waiting for the Day of the Lord for the adults, we are developing the work of the Holy

Childhood. My plan is an attack by our baptizers of all the Zhoushan Islands, seventy-two in all." He set up the Saint Joseph farm with acres of rice paddies to accommodate the boys twelve or thirteen years old admitted to and educated by the orphanage. He created kindergartens and dispensaries, and he founded a technical school, which he put under the direction of Father [François] Guierry.

The vicariate numbered at that time twenty-six widely dispersed Christian communities, with five chapels and six missionaries. The city of Ningbo had a core of two hundred fervent Christians. They were peacefully hoping that conversions would increase gradually, when the eighty thousand rebels who had brought fire and death to Jiangxi in the previous years, came and surrounded Ningbo and seized it on 9 December 1861. The missionaries and the Sisters sought refuge at the port in the vicinity of a French steamer that had dropped anchor in the harbor. They did not have to suffer too much, thanks to the protection of the courageous Admiral Protet. But for the rest of the province, it was not the same.

Delaplace went from one region to the next to console the Christians and to confer on them the sacraments, or to impress the rebels by his presence. Sometimes he had to face serious dangers.

We have been studying the birth of our missions in the south. Their birth was painful, to be sure, but this is for us a sure sign that the time of their development would come. The calm that will make it possible was already visible on the horizon. Let us give them time to seal the gaps caused by the rebels. Now let us go north to have a look at what has happened since the death of Nanjing's bishop, Bishop Pirès, in 1838.

The Diocese of Peking

In 1841, the court of Portugal, still insisting on using its rights of presentation, appointed the Portuguese Vincentian Father Castro to the diocese of Peking, whose administrator he had been since Pirès's death. The Holy See, however, following a new policy of apostolic vicars, refused his canonical status, and gave him only the title of bishop *in partibus infidelium* [in infidel areas] and administrator of the diocese of Peking, which allowed the Portuguese appointment to stand at least *in name*.

João de França Castro e Moura, born in 1804, arrived in China in 1825. In 1830, he went to Nanjing as Pirès' vicar general. In 1838, he went to Peking as administrator of the diocese, but he could not enter the city because of the imperial prohibition against foreigners entering the capital.

In the face of the conflict between his appointment as bishop of Peking by Portugal and Rome's insistence that he be only an apostolic vicar, Castro found himself in an impossible situation. On one side, he did not want to oppose the measures of the Holy See to gradually suppress the diocese of Peking; on the other, his patriotism loathed being part of a decision that would strip his country of a very ancient and especially a much-appreciated privilege. In other words, Castro, being Portuguese did not want his name to be linked to a Roman measure, which, though legitimate, took away from his country a right it persisted in considering unalienable.

Castro's refusal and the entreaties from Rome were exchanged for about six years. Finally, Rome tired of this abnormal situation and imposed an end to all these procrastinations with an authoritative note. On 28 April 1846 Cardinal Franzoni, prefect of Propaganda, wrote to Castro and gave him notice to accept being a bishop under the conditions laid down by the Holy See, or to hand over the administration of the Peking diocese to Mouly. At the same time, he ordered Mouly to execute this order with all possible consideration and leniency. After receiving these instructions, Mouly hastened to write Castro beseeching him insistently to accept the task offered by the Holy See.

Castro thanked him for his great kindness toward him, then he said: "According to the Gospel I must give Cesar what is Caesar's and God what is God's." The quote was not to the point, because Caesar actually did not have that right anymore. Mouly, not put off by this answer, which was a bit sharp, tried again and wrote a second letter. He met with insurmountable stubbornness. "The sole cause of my departure," answered Castro, "is that I will not accept episcopal consecration in the way the Sacred Congregation wants me to. . . I am submitting my resignation and departing for Macao."

After receiving this irrevocable decision, Mouly came down from the mountains and met Castro in his small residence of Hulinxian, sixty kilometers to the south of Peking. New urgent encouragements were met with new refusals. "I lost my Greek and my Latin there," wrote Mouly, "his mind is made up." And he added, "Finally, I gave him the bull of Propaganda and he retired to his room. After a few minutes, at my request, he handed me three letters, a Latin one for the priests, a Chinese one for the Christians and a third one for me, in which he testified that I was not at all the reason for his departure."

On 15 June 1847 Castro set off for Macao. With him the Portuguese mission in Peking came to an end. Out of consideration for the Padroado, however, the Holy See allowed the diocese to exist – in name it least – for another nine years. Mouly would be only the administrator. In 1856, Rome believed it had waited long enough. It suppressed the diocese of Peking and replaced it with three apostolic vicariates, as we shall soon see.

Castro, after behaving till the end as a loyal Portuguese subject, wanted also to behave as a good missionary. He had always indeed been one. After a short stay in Macao, he went to the island of Timor as a missionary. In 1858, he became a Vincentian again, for the Congregation was just then restored in Lisbon (though the members were soon again to be scattered in 1862). That same year he was appointed bishop of Porto [in Portugal]. Castro refused, but the Holy See persuaded him to accept the responsibility. Castro brought to the episcopal throne the same energy and the same ardor he exhibited in the missions of China. He died in Porto on 14 October 1868.

His behavior in China from 1841 on might seem odd. But Rome had not ordered him to receive episcopal consecration – Rome actually never does so. Rome gave him the choice between two things: either to have himself consecrated in the way Rome proposed, namely, as administrator of Peking, not as its bishop; or refuse it, but in that case he had to leave the place to somebody else.

Castro chose the second alternative. Consequently, Rome did not impose any sanction or blame him. Indeed, he had not disobeyed. It may be said that it would have been better if he had accepted the burden, which is what Rome wished. Mouly encouraged him in every way he knew to do so. Anyhow his contemporaries had only praise for him, and the Christians respected him very much and were deeply attached to him. The small schism that followed his departure proved so.

Mouly Settles in Anjiazhuang

After Castro's departure for Macao, Mouly immediately published Castro's circular letter to the Christians of the diocese to get from them a good reception for his successor; then he sent the Latin letter written by Castro to all the priests.

Mouly had to choose a place in the diocese to settle, more central than faraway Mongolia. He could not reside in the capital, where all Europeans were forbidden to enter; only Chinese priests, Vincentian and diocesan, ministered to the Christians there. He took the advice Castro had given him to establish his residence in Anjiazhuang, a Christian community located thirty-five kilometers from Baoding and one hundred kilometers from Peking. Remember that the Jesuits had opened that region to the faith in the years 1605–1610.

Towards the end of August 1847, Mouly, accompanied by the Vincentian Father Jean Zheng, left for Anjiazhuang. The welcome was not enthusiastic. Castro was esteemed and loved by the Faithful. How would the new master be?

They were not without distrust. The neighboring Christian communities came and offered small gifts. In brief, it was a respectful but cold welcome.

As the bishop could not enter Peking, he had the diocesan priest Matthieu Chen, who was exercising ministry in the capital, represent him and take possession of the see in his name. All went well, thanks to the know-how of this priest.

It was not the same everywhere. In the region of Zhengding the rumor had it that two European Vincentians, Fathers Simiand and Privas, had laid a plot to get rid of Castro and to have Mouly installed instead. Two Chinese priests confirmed this opinion and sent couriers to Macao, in the hope of bringing Castro back with them.

In the beginning Mouly thought that this agitation would quickly disappear, but it lasted. A year later, he wrote these melancholy words: "Actually I am in quite a painful position. The Portuguese in Macao, like most of the new Christians and the priests themselves, see me as the one who chased Castro away. Those who are not against me still view me unfavorably. I am considered as coming from the enemy's side."

The journey to Macao obviously did not produce any results, but the opponents continued to be active. They went as far as open rebellion, by acting as if Castro were their legitimate superior and Portugal their protector. They refused to obey Mouly and brought along into their group the principal Christian communities in the prefectures of Zhengding and Hejian. After taking up a huge collection, they sent several catechists to Rome to complain against Mouly's intrusion and to ask for Castro back. Of the six or seven who set off, some came back to Macao, others died on the way, and only one, Wu Laoyang, from Li village, made it to Rome. Pope Gregory XVI received this messenger with kindness and told him to tell his compatriots that the pope encouraged them to make peace and obey. This was the entire outcome of their mission.

There is no doubt that the principal motivation for this rebellion was Mouly's well-known "poverty." The Portuguese missionaries received from the king abundant financial support, which, it was well known, would not be given to their successors.

Indeed, Propaganda had given Mouly spiritual authority to administer the diocese of Peking, but it had not given him the necessary funds to meet his expenses. The goods of Peking's former bishop still existed, but they were in Macao in the hands of the Portuguese government. Mouly claimed his rights many times. It was in vain.

Vincentian Missionaries in China (1835–1850)

The Congregation of the Mission, which was almost wiped out by the French Revolution, rose from its ruins, gathered its scattered members and resumed its activities. It was able again to send new missionaries to China. That is the reason why, before following Mouly in his new task as administrator of Peking, we will introduce the new workers who arrived in China in the fifteen years following Blessed Perboyre's arrival in Macao in 1835 up until 1850. Below is the list with the dates of their arrival in Macao:

Table 8.1 Names of Vincentians Arriving at Macao [1836–1850]

Name	Date of Arrival
Faivre, Ferdinand	14 October 1836
Guillet, Claude	14 October 1836
Peschaud, Pierre	29 August 1837
Lavaissière, Pierre	3 January 1839
Simiand, Antoine	3 January 1839
Privas, Vincent	31 July 1839
Vautrin, Louis	31 July 1839
Huc, Evariste	31 July 1839
Daguin, Florent	31 July 1839
Carayon, Laurent	16 October 1841
Combelles, Antoine	16 October 1841
Anot, Antoine	24 August 1843
Jandard, André	September 1844
Peschaud, Bernard	12 March 1846
Delaplace, L. Gabriel	12 March 1846

Allara, Jean	21 June 1848
Aymeri, Michel	21 June 1848
Anouilh, Jean. B.	21 June 1848
Talmier, Vincent	28 June 1849
Goettlicher, Victor	28 June 1849
Dowling, Michael	18 November 1850
Montels, Félix	18 November 1850

Mouly's Coadjutor Bishops

After organizing his new mission of Zhili, Mouly returned to Mongolia, which he had left in May 1847 for his eventually fruitless discussions with Castro.

He arrived in Xiwanzi on 1 July 1848. Before leaving Mongolia, he made Father Daguin his pro-vicar to govern in his absence. Daguin had served as a professor in the seminary of Macao for three years before arriving in Mongolia in March 1843.

In accordance with a brief of Gregory XVI, Mouly was authorized to choose and consecrate a coadjutor bishop, who would manage the vicariate of Mongolia in his name while he was administrating the diocese of Peking. Mouly settled on Daguin. But he had to talk it over with the person who was concerned, who had not received orders from the superior general and so did not want to act outside the ordinary channels of obedience. It took a whole night to discuss the matter with him. Finally, Daguin bowed to the reason that the Holy See is a higher authority than his religious community.

The consecration took place in Xiwanzi on 25 July 1848. The ceremony took place in front of five Chinese priests and a crowd of Christians who had come from all directions. Fathers Xue and Guo acted as assistants. Daguin was appointed bishop of Troade and coadjutor for Mongolia.

Organization of the Missions (Visitors and Vicariates)

Here we must introduce an innovation in our missions in China. Up till that time, the visitor of all the Vincentians in China lived in Macao. However, when Vincentians were appointed as bishops, the superior general gave each of them the title and the powers of "visitor" for all the confreres in their vicariate. Henceforth, every Vincentian apostolic vicar became a visitor and every apostolic vicariate was considered as a small province. In this way, the office of visitor in Macao disappeared.

This organization was to last till 1899, when the procurator of the Vincentians in Shanghai received the authority and position formerly held by the visitor of Macao. Then there would again be only one visitor for the whole of China and consequently only one province. The apostolic vicariates would be considered as houses whose local superior would be the apostolic vicar. Later, we shall see still further developments.

For this purpose, the superior general, Father Jean-Baptiste Etienne, appointed Mouly visitor of Mongolia on 4 October 1844. Then, after Mouly became apostolic vicar of Peking, Daguin was appointed visitor of Mongolia.

Because we are talking about Mouly's coadjutors, we must now mention a second coadjutor bishop, whom Mouly as the administrator of Peking chose for himself. This somewhat anticipates events to which we will return later.

On 24 December 1850 the superior general sent a letter to all the leaders of the missions entrusted to the Vincentians, in which he summoned them to go to Ningbo in order to discuss various questions related to their missions. The date set for the meeting was 4 August 1851.

Mouly did not want to embark on such a long and time-consuming journey without leaving somebody in Peking to take his place during his absence. Besides, his field of activity was vast, so there was work for two people. In addition, the Portuguese schism was still going on in some regions, so it was necessary that there be no lack of authority. Mouly had already asked Rome for permission to take a confrere as his coadjutor. Pius IX had given him that power by the brief of 28 March 1848 and had put the title of Abydos at his disposal.

The choice was difficult. Mouly thought of a Chinese Vincentian, Father Jean Chrysostome He. He asked the advice of his superiors, then the advice of Propaganda. But the answer would take a year or more, and the bishop was in hurry. He settled on his vicar general, Father Simiand, most senior of the missionaries of the Peking diocese, having arrived in China in 1840, and whose name the superior general had put forward. Agreement was reached over his name. The whole community of Anjiazhuang was invited to the chapel; the bull of Pius IX was read including Simiand's appointment to the diocese of Abydos. Mouly had forgotten only one thing: to ask if Simiand agreed. He had assumed that Simiand, being vicar general, would surely take up this new responsibility, but he adamantly refused.

His resistance could not be broken. Everybody tried, not only European but also Chinese priests. They all without exception redoubled their entreaties, but to no avail. The modest Simiand absolutely refused the dignity that he was being offered.

Seeing that Simiand would not do it, everyone said they wanted Delaplace, missionary in Henan, to be chosen as coadjutor. Mouly took his time and thought it over. The date of the Assembly was coming closer and closer. He certainly was not going to leave unless he had consecrated a coadjutor. He set his heart on the youngest of his collaborators, Anouilh, who joined fierce ardor to sincere piety and also was a man of energy and drive, which had made him very popular in the region of Zhengding, where he had already preached the Gospel. The choice could not have been better, as events would prove.

After reaching his decision, Mouly set out for Ningbo passing through Zhaozhou, where Anouilh was busy giving missions. He announced to him that after mature reflection in view of Simiand's resistance, he decided to make him his coadjutor.

An appointment so unexpected and so little desired seemed to Anouilh a decree from Providence. Consequently, he answered in the simplicity of his heart, like Isaiah: "*Ecce ego, mitte me!* (Here I am, send me!) You are my father, bishop, do with me what you want."

Rejoicing in this filial agreement, Mouly did not want to waste any time and so decided to consecrate the new bishop at the place where he found him among the four or five hundred Christians who made up the small Christian community of Xiaoyingli.

The consecration took place on 22 June 1851 in a poor chapel with nothing to distinguish it from ordinary houses. A Chinese priest and Father Simiand, who would accompany Mouly to Ningbo, assisted the bishop. Armed Christians stood guard at the entrance to the village for fear that the schismatic members of the neighboring Christian community might interrupt the ceremony. All went well.

Henceforth free to leave his mission and completely at ease now, Mouly went on light-heartedly to Ningbo with Simiand. Though he was one of those farthest away, he was the first to arrive at the site of the meeting.

Two Successive Meetings of Bishops with Different Goals

The Assembly of Ningbo

Father Etienne, the superior general, seeing the growing importance of the missions in China and reassured by the edicts of toleration given to the Catholic religion (though often not carried out), turned his attention to their future. That was the motive for the meeting in Ningbo.

Father Marc Antoine Poussou, the superior general's first assistant, was to preside at the meeting. The specific agenda of the meeting was Vincentian. It had to do with the Congregation as a missionary society, not with the Catholic missions in China, in which case the invitation would have come from the Holy See. That happened that same year in Shanghai, as we shall see.

The meeting opened on 8 September 1851 after all the leaders had arrived. There were eight members:

1. Antoine Poussou, extraordinary representative of the superior general, presiding;

2. Joseph Martial Mouly, apostolic vicar of Mongolia, administrator of the diocese of Peking, visitor of the province of Zhili;

3. François Xavier Danicourt, apostolic vicar of Zhejiang, visitor of the province;

4. Henri Baldus, apostolic vicar of Henan, visitor of the province;

5. Florent Daguin, coadjutor bishop of Mongolia, visitor of the province;

6. Claude Guillet, procurator of the assembly;

7. Antoine Anot, pro-vicar of the Jiangxi vicariate (*sede vacante*, 1850–1852) and visitor of the province;

8. Antoine Simiand, vicar general to Bishop Mouly.

The meeting had twelve sessions. We shall only give the summary of the decisions taken. The assembly approved the transfer of the Vincentian procure from Macao to Ningbo; also, the transfer of the Daughters of Charity (from Macao). The assembly determined in what measure the Congregation would come to the aid of the missions concerning personnel and resources. It recognized that having only one common internal seminary, like the one in Macao, was not practical. It approved using silk for those who were wearing Chinese clothes and it decided nothing about wearing the cassock.

Opinions were divided about Vincentians accepting episcopal dignity: some saw it as a state irreconcilable with our vocation; others saw it as a necessary thing in China in order to avoid authority conflicts in the same field of action. The latter opinion carried the day.

Up to that time, almost all the Chinese priests became members of the Congregation of the Mission. The assembly decided to leave them more freedom and consequently to accept for ordination those otherwise well-disposed who did not want to become Vincentians.

The transfers of the Vincentian procure and of the house of the Daughters of Charity to China were carried out beginning in 1852. The Daughters of Charity left Macao definitively. Later the Vincentian procure would settle in Shanghai when it became the largest port of China. The Sisters would soon establish their central house in Shanghai, too.

The Assembly of Shanghai

In 1848, the Sacred Congregation of Propaganda planned a national synod for China and suggested the island of Hong Kong as the meeting place. All the apostolic vicars received notification of it with a questionnaire covering thirty-four points that would be the basis for the discussions. But some bishops found it impossible to get there, and others were astonished at the choice of the meeting place, which had just been ceded to the English.

The synod did not happen. Special meetings of bishops, however, were less disadvantageous and could produce the same advantages. Several were held in 1851. The one that took place in Shanghai was especially important, because of the presence of several apostolic vicars who had met in Ningbo, which is not very far from Shanghai. Bishop Maresca, administrator of Nanjing, took advantage of the proximity of the two cities and called a meeting, which, without any official character, would examine the points of Propaganda's questionnaire and send Rome the result of its deliberations.

Thus, he invited the four apostolic vicars who had taken part in the meeting of Ningbo to come to Shanghai. All accepted the invitation, except Danicourt, who remained in Ningbo because of important business. The discussions began on 7 November 1851 and ended on 3 December after twelve sessions.

We shall not give the minutes of this meeting, which was only consultative, not legislative. The Sacred Congregation was seeking information; the final decisions belonged to it. Moreover, things in China were evolving quite rapidly and the subjects discussed then are scarcely interesting now.

End of the "Schism" in the Diocese of Peking

Let us say again that this schism was limited to some Christian communities in the neighborhood of the civil sub-prefecture of Zhaozhou (today Zhaoxian) and to some people in the prefecture of Hejian. Judging from experience, when priests enter the schismatic party, the situation becomes more serious and can become a disaster. In the diocese there was a priest who led the dissidents: that was Father Joseph Xu (Ruowang), called Alves according to Portuguese custom. He was from Jiangxi; he studied in Saint Joseph Seminary, Macao, and Bishop Rameaux had ordained him in 1845 to work with the Portuguese missionaries in Peking.

As soon as Mouly returned from his journey to the south, he hastened to put an end to this abnormal situation. In 1852, he visited the center of resistance. He visited thirty communities in the Zhaozhou district. Everywhere he was well received and well treated, except for one community of two hundred Christians that did not want to receive him.

A year later in 1853, wishing to make a final effort, he sent the schismatic group Bishop Anouilh and Father Talmier. In the beginning both had to suffer a lot in that same region of Zhaozhou. People threatened to kill them. Many nevertheless were responsive and submitted to legitimate authority. At the end of the year 1853, there still remained about six hundred Christians who followed Alves Joseph Xu (Ruose).

The principal leaders however, gradually abandoned not only by their compatriots but also by their friends in Macao, eventually came around. On 21 March 1856, Mouly wrote to Propaganda: "It is a pleasure for me to announce to the Sacred Congregation the end, as it were, of our little schism in Peking. The two leaders of the schism indeed and the priest Alves Xu, whom they had carried along, asked for, received and carried out a suitable penance, and thus repaired their scandal. They were received back into the bosom of the apostolic and Roman Church.

That was indeed the end. From then on, any trace of this schism disappeared. People who still remembered it were rare. This rebellion had lasted for nine years.

Edicts of Toleration

Up till now we have only alluded to a certain liberty of the Catholic religion granted by Daoguang. This event had too many repercussions in the Catholic missions, however, not to give some consideration to it.

Several nations were already in touch with China because of commercial interests. When the French government also thought about making contact with this huge country, Mr. Lagrené was the person chosen to fulfill the role of special envoy. This choice could not have been more fortunate, for, being a convinced Catholic, Lagrené made it part of his task to do all in his power to obtain justice and tolerance for Catholicism. He believed it was proper for his government to establish not only purely commercial relations with China, but to aim for a higher goal, namely, to use the prestige of France to serve the missionaries, so often pestered by civil authorities, as if they were not the best civilizers of this large country.

In 1842, the English concluded the Nanjing Treaty with China, which opened to European trade the five harbors of Canton, Amoy, Fuzhou, Shanghai and Ningbo. This event provided the missionaries with five secure places to live, where they would be able to stay in freedom and with five ports of entry to the interior of China; it was true that these ports would be guarded, but it is more difficult to guard five ports than just one. They would pass unrecognized more easily.

Lagrené began negotiations with the viceroy at Canton, Qiying, acting in the name of the emperor. The two representatives signed on board a ship the so-called Treaty of Whampoa, the name of the mouth of the river in Canton. This treaty contained an article which stipulated that, if French people ventured out of specified boundaries, or entered deep into the heart of the country, they could be arrested by the Chinese authorities, which, in this case, would be obliged to have them taken to the consulate in the nearest harbor; it was, however, positively forbidden to harm or mistreat French people arrested in this way, in order not to disturb the harmony which must reign between the two empires. The two parties signed the treaty of Whampoa on 24 October 1844. Actually, it was of little benefit to the Catholic missions.

Lagrené wished to obtain more. Through delicate negotiations with Qiying, he obtained that the Chinese government would issue an edict in favor of the Christian religion. The emperor approved the request and, on 20 February 1846, he published a decree in which this was said in substance:

Qiying and his colleagues have sent us a memorial requesting immunity from punishment for those who profess the religion of the Lord of Heaven and live well; requesting also that they can build places of prayer in order to gather there, recite prayers and preach sermons without experiencing in all these activities the least obstacle. We have given our imperial assent to these different points for the whole territory of China. . . .

Consequently, let all the Christian churches built under the reign of Kangxi in the different provinces of China and which still exist, be given back to the Christians of the respective localities . . . and should it happen that after receiving this edict, local authorities persecute those who profess the Christian religion without committing any crime, then they must be given the punishment which their culpable behavior deserves. . . . Those who falsely borrow the name of Christians, however, and use it with the goal of creating disorder, must be considered criminals and they must be punished according to the laws of the empire. Respect this.

This edict of tolerance, obtained through the viceroy whom Lagrené had skillfully led to his cause, caused great rejoicing in Christian China. Indeed, if it had come into force – though still comprising many loopholes – it would have been for the missions a real boon. Unfortunately, its publication was very limited; the mandarins in the hinterland did not know of it or if they knew, they took care not to promulgate it. Moreover, the notorious decree of Jiaqing of 1805 was not abolished and remained part of the penal code.

The new treaty therefore had only limited effect; nevertheless, it was not useless, for it prepared the way for two other treaties: the Treaty of Tianjin in 1858 and the Peking Convention in 1860, which opened wide the door for the missionaries so that the Church could make magnificent progress during more than fifty years. This was obtained thanks to the emerging French [Religious] Protectorate, which was established without benefit of any official document or contract. It came into being almost spontaneously, by force of circumstances. France never wanted or desired it, but accepted it, because the Chinese government wanted to deal only with the French government about contentious matters with Europeans. France accepted this difficult task in regard to the missions of all the nations and missionary societies in China, though there had never been a written document that obliged France to do so. Despite the treaties, there still were local persecutions.

The Murder of Father Ferdinand-Felix Montels

Born in Castres (Tarn) on 23 March 1823, he was admitted to the Congregation in Paris on 12 June 1844 and ordained on 29 May 1847. He first taught for two years in the Major Seminary of Châlons-sur-Marne, then left for China and landed on 18 November 1850 in Macao, from where he was sent after a short time to Jiangxi, a province at the time suffering from the horrors of the civil conflict between rebels and imperial troops. The latter were not less to be feared than the Chang Mao.

On 25 June 1857 Montels and two Christians went to the large village of Fuwangzhou to administer the last rites to a sick person. Along the way, Father Montels went ahead of his two companions to avoid enquiries by soldiers if he happened to meet them. That is what happened. The soldiers did not pay attention to him. But when the Christians came along carrying the priest's things, the soldiers searched them, opened the parcel and asked them to whom the contents belonged. The Christians answered simply that they were the clothes of Father Zeng, a French missionary, who was ahead of them on the road. The soldiers then berated them, called them thieves and took them to their leader who was stationed in Xifulin village. The officer asked them many questions and then put them in jail. The next day, this officer sent five soldiers to look for Father Montels. They found him quickly. The missionary, indeed, hearing in the inn where he had spent the night that two Christians had been arrested and imprisoned in Xifulin, understood immediately that his two companions were the people in question. Instead of trying to escape, he retraced his steps, and when he was approaching the village, met the five soldiers who were looking for him. They grabbed him and took him to their chief. This man, irritated by Montels's answers to his questions, made him kneel down and ordered him to be beaten with fifty blows on his shoulders. The missionary, unable to bear the violence of such a cruel treatment, got up in wrath and, beating with his fist on the officer's table, he said: "You have no right to kill me! I appeal to your superior." The officer had him beaten again, and then he handed him over to ten soldiers to take him to the camp of the imperial soldiers, about thirty kilometers away.

They had gone just a few kilometers when they met the mandarin of the region. This magistrate asked the soldiers who these three men were whom they were leading in this manner. For an answer they gave him the letter destined for the general, which the officer in Xifulin had entrusted to them. After reading the letter and asking Montels some questions, the mandarin cried out: "Behead him, and his two companions too!" It was carried out immediately. Three days later, Christians of a neighboring village went at night and removed the massacred bodies for burial near their village. Montels was thirty-four years old.

When the imperial general heard that a mandarin had put a French missionary to death, he cursed that civil servant and sent people to him to tell him, "By killing a European you have brought misfortune to China." That was the way of justice at that time.

Mouly Surrendered to the Authorities to Save His Christians

During Holy Week 1854, Mouly consecrated the Holy Oils in Anjiazhuang, and sent a courier to bring the new Oils to the priests in Peking. The courier's name was Fu Jiang. On 15 April imperial soldiers arrested him and dealt with him as a rebel. Questioned by them and unwilling to jeopardize his bishop, he contented himself with saying that he was bringing these objects to someone called Pao, a catechist in Hulindian a village that he indeed had to pass through to go to Peking. This admission immediately jeopardized the whole Christian community of Hulindian (Father Castro's habitual residence). Five Christians were arrested and taken to Peking before the war tribunal, which was given special powers against the rebellion. During these activities an officer ran off with all the liturgical objects of the chapel and took all the books he could find in the residence.

Two Christians hurriedly brought this bad news to Mouly in Anjiazhuang, adding that they had heard that the general had given orders to his troops to be ready to go to Anjiazhuang the next day. In this situation, Mouly thought that it was his duty to save his poor Christians' lives, to save his residence from pilfering and destruction, and all his Christians from persecutions carried out under the pretext of searching for evidence. Spontaneously he decided to give himself up to the authorities. His confreres approved of this project. The bishop did so immediately.

Before dawn on Easter Monday, he sent Brother Jean-Baptiste Zhu, C.M., to inform the sub-prefect of Nansu [*sic* Xushui] that he would put himself in his hands. Brother Zhu first spoke to the chief of police, an old friend of the missionaries' named Zhang Laonian.

Zhang was in a very awkward position because of such a compromise so he ran and informed the sub-prefect, who was appalled by it and did not know what to decide. At Commander Zhang's advice, it was decided by the mandarin that the next day Zhang would go and politely invite Mouly to come to his own family and to give himself up there till this business could be managed as well as possible.

The next day then, Zhang and two scholars appeared at the residence of Anjiazhuang as agreed. Mouly followed them to the town of Nansu [*sic* Xushui], located about twenty kilometers further on. During the two months that he was to stay in that honorable man's home, Mouly could only applaud the consideration he received, and the commander would not accept any compensation for the expenditure caused by the prolonged stay of the bishop and his staff.

The sub-prefect, happy that the chief of the police had taken care of this unusual prisoner, was just waiting for the end of the affair of the Christians of Hulindian to allow Mouly to go back quietly to his apostolic work. The Xianfeng emperor, however, Daoguang's son, who knew about the arrest of the courier and the Christians, had already given orders to arrest the bishop, but to treat him with much consideration. A few days later, when he heard that Mouly had given himself up, the emperor was absolutely happy and again recommended honorable treatment.

The lawsuit against the Christians on the other hand went on. Kept in solitary confinement, they could not communicate with each other and were ignorant of the fact that the bishop had given himself up for their sake. Hence their declarations did not tally. Their judges for their part were very well aware of the noble act of dedication performed by Mouly, and were no longer able to assume that the prisoners had taken any part in the rebellion. Consequently, they changed tactics and directed their questioning to the topic of religion, but they did it in a particularly hateful and hypocritical way. "We do not ask you to tread on a crucifix with your feet, because it carries the image of your God, but what is wrong in just treading upon a simple cross? If you do not, we shall arrest your religious leader and your parents, and in that way by refusing you will act against the filial piety that you owe them."

Among the prisoners there was an old man who absolutely refused to apostatize and tread upon the cross. Consequently, they told him that he had already trampled on it, for, when entering, he had walked on a little cross that had been secretly drawn on the doorstep. The Christian countered that, not knowing this to be the case, he had not committed any act of apostasy; but three of them including the courier Fu Jiang were weak enough to agree with it. The judges went ahead (they wanted to finish this business) and all were freed. They did not know, even in the end, to what they owed their release.

A few days later, when Fu Jiang appeared in Nansu [*sic* Xushui], Mouly severely rebuked him for his apostasy and told him that he had brought an excommunication upon himself. Then Zhang Laonian and his friends, though all pagans, came and interceded for the guilty man, excusing him because he had sinned only by ignorance and weakness. The bishop let himself be moved and shortened the penance. Fifteen days later, on the feast of Pentecost, Fujiang humbled himself publicly in front of the assembled Faithful, accepted a penance and made a three-day retreat, then was absolved and reconciled according to the rules of the ritual.

Bishop Mouly's Expulsion

The Xianfeng emperor, in accordance with his father's decree (the Lagrené treaty, whose letter but not the spirit he was observing), ordered that the bishop had to be given over to the French authorities. It meant he had to be taken to Shanghai where the consul of France resided.

The viceroy permitted Mouly to return to Anjiazhuang and to set the date for his own departure. Mouly solemnly returned to his episcopal residence on the eve of Trinity Sunday. He chose to go in mid-September, not only to have time to finish taking care of his affairs, but also to avoid the heat of the summer.

Mouly set off on his journey to exile on 8 November 1854. Instead of giving him guards unknown to him the viceroy obligingly gave him his two friends, Zhang Laonian and Dai Laozi, the commander and the captain of the police in Nansu [*sic* Xushui] respectively.

The bishop took the overland route and reached Shanghai on 2 January 1855. The guides having fulfilled their mission went back alone. Bishop Mouly remained profoundly grateful for the thoughtfulness with which they had accomplished the role entrusted to them. Through the intermediary of the French consul, he begged the viceroy of Zhili to give them a promotion, which he did.

For their part, they retained an indelible memory of their venerable prisoner. Back home, Zhang Laonian wrote a detailed account of his mission. He added drawings representing the principal scenes of the journey: Mouly's arrest, his departure and his farewell to the Christians, a session at the French consulate in Shanghai, and so on. This manuscript still exists in the Zhang family, where it is guarded as a precious treasure.

The mission in Peking wanted to buy it, but the family was unwilling to part with a relic that made their family famous. However, they permitted pictures to be taken of the six drawings, which are preserved in the Catholic mission of Peking. The drawings are quite expressive, though they are slightly primitive and breach the rules of perspective. The bishop is always portrayed wearing a miter, whether eating, climbing into a cart or walking in the courtyard – always with his miter. The good Zhang was honoring his distinguished friend to the best of his ability.

In the Lagrené treaty, Daoguang committed himself to giving back the churches that had been built in the time of Kangxi. Mouly several times tried to reclaim the institutions in Peking, namely, the two churches of the Nantang and the Beitang and the two cemeteries of Zhengfusi and Chala. He even prepared a petition destined to come under Xianfeng's eyes, but, because he could not present it himself, he tried to have it presented by some high official; but it was impossible for him to find a person who dared commit himself to this task.

We know that Mouly did not have an official title, a *piao*, or any public standing. He never did. He entered China illicitly, as did almost all the missionaries of that era. Only the missionaries called to the Mathematics [Astronomy] Bureau had the right to reside in Peking; all the others were residing there only as a favor in view of the services rendered by the members of the Tribunal. The last missionary member of it was Pirès, who died in 1838. After him, no missionary had been invited. Consequently, those who wanted to enter China did so secretly at their own risk. We can point out, however, that in these cases the law was not rigorously applied, for the missionaries traveling up and down the provinces were rarely bothered. Ordinarily, the mandarins knew where they resided, but as long there was no problem, they did nothing. We say "ordinarily," for there were those who because of personal hatred or ambition did initiate fierce persecutions against them.

Mouly did all in his power (to reclaim church properties), but given his position (rather, lack of an official public position), his efforts were fruitless. In view of this, he admitted defeat, joyfully accepted this lack of success, and went on with his ministry with the same calm and patience as before. A day will come, as we shall see, that he would receive much more than he had asked for.

Third Period
(1856–1900)

Dividing the Peking
Diocese and Changes

Chapter 9

From Mongolia to Peking, 1850s–1860s

The Threefold Division of the Diocese of Peking – Mouly Lays Aside His Resignation as Apostolic Vicar of Mongolia – Reforms Carried Out in Mongolia – Daguin's Death – Transfer of the Mission of Mongolia – Anouilh Was Remanded to the French Consul in Shanghai, and Qiu (Anyu) Exiled to Canton – Reopening of Worship in the Capital – The Treaties – Mouly's Journey to Europe – Restoration of the Churches in Peking – Mouly Receives a Coadjutor – Transfer of the Vicariate of Henan – Mouly's Death

The Threefold Division of the Diocese of Peking

Among the questions to be discussed in the two assemblies of Ningbo and Shanghai, there was the creation in China of new apostolic vicars, though already almost every civil province had its own apostolic vicar. The problem was therefore how to divide civil provinces in order to create new vicariates. For some this seemed unthinkable.

Naturally opinions were divided. In Ningbo, Mouly protested against a possible break-up of his mission of Peking because Zhili was among the smallest in surface area. Despite his early protests, the majority of the members were in favor of the break-up of Zhili because of the relatively high number of Faithful of this mission.

The same question came up in the meeting in Shanghai. The apostolic vicar once more thought it expedient to establish titular bishops and to multiply them in the regions where the number of the Faithful permitted it. But they did not indicate which provinces were likely to be divided.

Touched by this consensus, Mouly saw that it would not take Rome long to carve up the Peking diocese, where according to the last census there were about thirty-six thousand Christians, which was a high number for that time.

Intending only the general well-being, Mouly abandoned his personal opinion, gave up his opposition to the plan, and in December of that same year even sent Propaganda a proposal for the division of his diocese by showing which boundaries he preferred for each part.

Several years passed. Mouly was amazed to see no action on his proposal. Then, in August 1856, the Jesuits of Shanghai informed him by letter that the Holy See, responding to his petition, gave them the southern part of the Zhili province and had nominated Father [Adrien-Hyppolyte] Languillat, one of theirs, first apostolic vicar of that mission.

Mouly, probably somewhat disgruntled because he himself had not received word of this decision from Rome, first excused himself from all official acts concerning this topic. Later on, when he had received the copy of the text of Languillat's nomination, he pulled himself together and wrote the bishop:

> ... But, because Peter has spoken through Pius IX, if Your Excellency feels obliged to go ahead and to come and take possession of his apostolic vicariate, I can assure him, in my own name and in the name all of my confreres, that he will be well received, as it suits a vicar of the Holy See, and that we all will do whatever depends on us to put him duly in peaceful possession of his new vicariate. Take the road to our residence in Anjiazhuang, from where I am writing you, and there we shall welcome you with open arms.

Mouly consecrated Languillat bishop on 22 March 1857. He wrote to the Faithful and encouraged them to accept their new pastor. Moreover, he let the incipient mission have several of his priests: a loan of four Vincentian priests and a transfer of three diocesan priests. The students in the seminary who were born in the new mission would continue their studies with those from Peking.

Actually, Rome had decided to divide the diocese of Peking into three vicariates, namely:

– The vicariate of North Zhili, principal city Peking;

– The vicariate of Southeast Zhili, principal city Guangping;

– The vicariate of Southwest Zhili, principal city Zhengding.

North Zhili remained entrusted to Mouly; Peking would become the episcopal residence as soon as events permitted. It was hoped that this would happen in the near future.

About the vicariate of Southwest Zhili with the city of Zhengding as episcopal residence, Rome had first contemplated its transfer to the

Society of the Foreign Missions of Paris, but that society did not think it was advisable to accept it. So Mouly was asked temporarily to take the administration of that territory, while waiting for the nomination of a titular bishop. To execute this order, Mouly could not find anything better to do than to send his coadjutor, Bishop Anouilh, to take possession of it. A year later, on 14 December 1858, a brief from Rome appointed Anouilh as the first apostolic vicar of Southwest Zhili.

Let us now present an inventory of the mission of Peking as it was divided into three vicariates in 1856. As these vicariates quickly became known by the names of the towns where the episcopal residence was, we will do the same.

Table 9.1 Inventory of the Peking Mission, 1856

District[28]	Personnel	Local Communities	Chris-tians
I. Vicariate of Peking			
1. Episcopal residence of Anjiazhuang – Seminary	Administrator: Mouly, also Coadjutor, Professor of Theology: Anouilh Director of the internal seminary, procurator: Aymeri Pastor: François Liu, C.M.		400
2. Peking	Director of the district: Chrysostome He, C.M. Assistant: André Yang, C.M. One diocesan priest	30	3,000
3. Xuanhua	Director of the district: Paul Zhang, C.M. Assistant: Matthieu Xue, C.M., and two diocesan priests.	80	4,500

---

28. Within vicariates bishops established districts, and these in turn were under the guidance of directors. Many developed further into prefectures or vicariates. The term "district" is also applied loosely in this volume to generic civil areas or neighborhoods. (JR)

4. Jingdong[29]	Director of the district: Jean Zhang, C.M. Assistant: Antoine Everard Smorenburg	100	5,600
5. Baoding		40	3,000
II. Vicariate of Xianxian			
6. Guangping		40	4,000
7. Hejian	Director of the district: Simiand, C.M. Three European non-Vincentian priests	54	6,000
III. Vicariate of Zhengding			
8. Zhengding	Director of the district: Talmier, C.M. Two European diocesan priests.	72	6,000
9. Zhaozhou	Pierre Cai, C.M. and one European priest.	50	6,000
TOTAL	Priest – C.M.: 13; Diocesan: 9	466	38,500

---

29.   An area east of Peking. (AS)

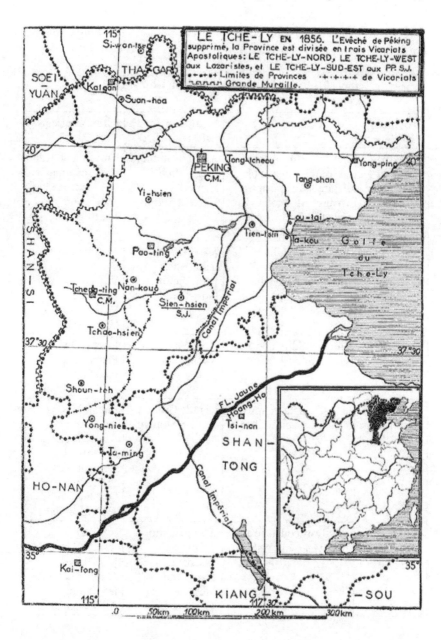

Map 9.1 Zhili in 1856

Here we give also the list of the Vincentian personnel spread over the whole of China.

Table 9.2 Inventory of Vincentians in China, 1852

Province / Vicariate	Governance	European priests	Chinese priests
1. Peking / Apostolic Administration	Mouly: administrator of the diocese of Peking and apostolic vicar of Mongolia visitor of Zhili. Anouilh, Coadjutor	Antoine Simiand Ange-Michel Aymeri Vincent Talmier	Paul Zhang, Jean Chrysostome He, Maurus Liu Jean Zheng Matthieu Xue All Vincentians
2. Mongolia / Apostolic Vicariate	Daguin: Coadjutor Bishop for Mongolia visitor of Mongolia	Jean-Antoine Combelles Jean-Victor Goettlicher	Matthieu Zhou diocesan Vincent Wu Paul Zheng Vincent Fan Vincentians
3. Henan / Apostolic Vicariate [30]	Henri Baldus: apostolic vicar and visitor	André Jandard Michel Dowling	Joseph Qiu Pierre Feng Paul Song All Vincentians
4. Zhejiang / Apostolic Vicariate	L.G. Delaplace: apostolic vicar and visitor	Claude Guillet Protais Montagneux	François Feng André Yang André Li Matthieu Li Vincent Fu Pierre Yuan One lay brother All Vincentians
5. Jiangxi / Apostolic Vicariate	F.X. Danicourt, apostolic vicar and visitor	Antoine Anot Bernard Peschaud Ferdinand Montels	Jean Bai Joseph You Jean Tan Matthieu Lü Jean Wang All Vincentians

---

30. Note that the map of Jiangxi in 1950 was misplaced here in the original text as part of Chapter 9. It has been moved to Chapter 22, as Map 22.1. (AS)

Mouly Lays Aside his Title of Apostolic Vicar of Mongolia

Before the division of Zhili into three vicariates (1856), Mouly combined in his person three different offices, namely, superior of the Vincentian mission in Peking, apostolic vicar of Mongolia, and finally administrator of the diocese of Peking. The decree of 1856, in suppressing the diocese of Peking, named him simply as apostolic vicar of North Zhili or Peking and let him keep the title of apostolic vicar of Mongolia.

From that moment, Mouly was of the opinion that there was no longer any reason for him to retain the latter title, because for several years already that vicariate was in the hands of Bishop Daguin. That is the reason why he submitted this business to the Holy See supported by the above-mentioned reasons. A few months later in 1857, Rome granted his petition.

Some Reforms Carried out in Mongolia

The first Jesuit missionaries noticed that according to Chinese civilization it is indecent for men to be bareheaded. Catholic liturgy, however, expressly demands that every priest who celebrates the Holy Sacrifice be bareheaded. In view of this, they petitioned Rome for the priest to cover, his head during the celebration of Holy Mass. Paul V granted this permission to the Jesuits as well as to all the missionaries working in China until further notice, stating, however, that the authorized headdress be not the ordinary biretta, but some headdress specifically made for divine worship.

To accommodate this, the missionaries had the jijin [tsi-kin] made, a kind of square hat, whose four sides linked only on top and formed four mobile wings. It had two long ribbons that fell at the back like the ones of a bishop's miter. It was decorated to some degree with gold or silver embroideries on a black background. People said it looked very much like the official headdress in the time of the Ming dynasty.

Mouly suppressed the use of the *jijin* in the vicariate of Mongolia, in his desire to conform to the laws and customs of the Church and knowing that Rome only tolerated the practice. He changed nothing, however, in the diocese of Peking after he became its administrator. To those who asked him the reason for this, he answered: "I know that several apostolic vicars do not want to use this privilege; I believe that the Sacred Congregation of Propaganda will soon rule on this question and I shall conform to its

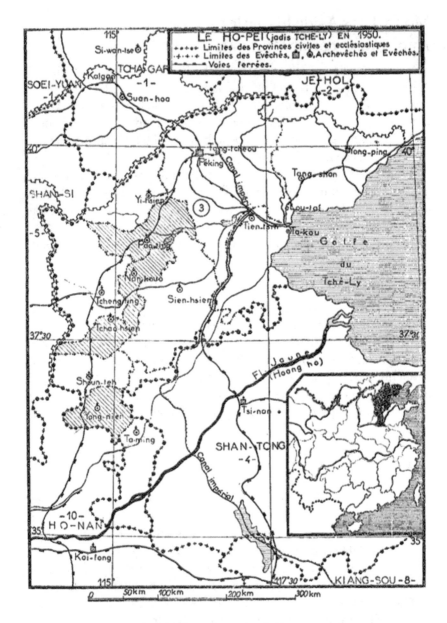

Map 9.2 Hebei (formerly Zhili) in 1950

decisions." It waited till 1883 to decree that the habit in China of wearing the *jijin* should be abolished gradually as circumstances permitted. Actually, the custom was completely abolished only at the time of the Revolution of 1912.

A much more important change was carried out by Daguin. From the first years of his episcopate, he thought about eradicating in Mongolia the senseless absurd custom of condemning Chinese women to deform their feet from their earliest years. He suffered because of the numerous disadvantages that resulted from that strange abuse. Most missionaries were of the same opinion. In order to tackle such a universal custom, one needed to be daring. In March 1850, Daguin had an instruction distributed to his Christians against the custom, in which he maintained this custom constituted an insult to the Creator's honor, and also it caused the women numerous disadvantages for both soul and body. Then, the bishop refuted the alleged reasons for the practice. He ended by exhorting the Christians: a) not to bind the feet of their young daughters; b) to untie the feet of those who were younger than ten years old; and finally, c) he advised the same thing to virgins who did not have husbands to please and even to young women who could do so without any risk.

Notice that Daguin did not impose a precept; he just encouraged his Faithful to abolish an abusive custom. Nevertheless, he was heard and understood. Besides, both European and Chinese priests concurred absolutely with the ideas of their leader.

The Belgian missionaries who came after Daguin maintained this bishop's line of conduct and, since then, the Christian women of Mongolia were as proud of their natural feet as their pagan compatriots were of their 'deformed small feet.' Let us add that it was once again the Revolution of 1912 that put an absolute end to this old custom in the whole of China.

Daguin's death

Daguin had been alone for three months, busy preaching a mission in the east of his vicariate at the beginning of Lent 1859. Feeling that he was seriously ill, he wrote his pro-vicar, Father Taglione, a diocesan priest in Xiwanzi, which was a fifteen days' journey away, "Quickly send me a confrere so that I can go to confession and entrust to him the mission that I have begun. Then I will go back to take care of my health."

Taglione immediately called Father Pierre Feng, the former lama and sent him to help the dear sick bishop. This priest, on his way, was called here and there to confer the last rites on dying people and so took forty days to arrive at the side of his bishop. Having hugged his confrere, Daguin questioned him about current affairs. Actually, Feng had quite bad news to tell him, but fearing to upset him, he answered with reservations and did not tell all he knew. The bishop noticed it and believed that something extremely serious was being hidden from him, like a confrere's arrest. Be that as it may, he gradually worsened. He asked for the last rites and the third day after Feng's arrival, on 9 May 1859, Daguin passed away, age forty-four.

Here are some testimonies about this good missionary's virtues.

Tagliabue: "... Daguin was a tall, well-built person. His kindly way of looking at people won all hearts. We could read on his face the calmness, the seriousness and the gentleness which made up the solid foundation of his character."

One of his confreres said about him: "Daguin was the most innocent, the most upright and the most unaffected persons I have ever known."

Mesnard, M.E.P., missionary of the neighboring vicariate of Manchuria, said:

> The greatest praise I could give him is summed up in what the Christians who knew him used to say about him: Bishop Daguin was a living saint. In all the time I have had the good fortune to know him, I was unable to discover in him the slightest chink in his armor. With his tender and sensitive nature no one could ever empathize more than he with the needs and miseries of his neophytes.

At this point, though Mongolia still would remain for several more years under the Vincentians, we shall recount here the history of the transfer of this vicariate to the hands of Belgian priests, so that we need not come back to this mission.

Transfer of the Mission of Mongolia

After Daguin's death, his pro-vicar Father Tagliabue, who later on would become apostolic vicar of Peking, was the administrator of Mongolia. The superior general, Etienne, was reluctant to fill the vacant see for two reasons. First, throughout Europe the proclamation of religious freedom in China was awaking vocations as well as new religious orders for the foreign missions. Second, he was afraid that he would not be able to satisfy the needs of the many provinces for which his Congregation was responsible.

He begged the Holy See to entrust part of this heavy burden to other societies of missionaries. At that very moment in Belgium, a saintly Belgian priest, Father Theophile Verbist, was founding a society of missionaries, exclusively destined to evangelize the Far East. Its name was "Congregation of the Immaculate Heart of Mary." The founder asked Propaganda to assign him a territory in the Chinese empire. The Sacred Congregation sent him word to work out an understanding with the Vincentians.

The superior general of the Vincentians and the founder met. Then, taking advantage of Mouly's presence in Paris in 1861, Father Verbist had a meeting in the motherhouse of Saint Lazare with him and said: "Our fledgling congregation wants to have a vicariate in the Far East and we asked especially for Mongolia. The Sovereign Pontiff granted it wholeheartedly and the superior general, Etienne, did not have any objection. I shall, however, accept it only with Your Excellency's approval. I have come to ask you for the favor of your approval."

Mouly could have to agree with an affair that was already as good as concluded, but the idea of giving away this field of his initial missionary labors moved him so deeply that he shed tears.

When everything was arranged between the Congregation of the Mission and the new Belgian Congregation (called Congregation of the Immaculate Heart of Mary, from Scheut) the prefect of Propaganda ruled that the Vincentians should stay at their post till the new missionaries arrived and became able, in regard to their number and their experience of the missions, to take possession of the vicariate. Also, a superior had to be chosen from among them, who would have the title and authority of a pro-vicar.

The Belgian missionaries arrived in China only at the end of 1865, because it was necessary to give the first members of the new society time to pronounce vows in their congregation, which happened on 24 August 1864.

The first Belgian missionaries who came to succeed the Vincentians were Father Verbist, superior and founder, Father [Ferdinand] Hamer (the future martyr) and two others. As soon as they were sufficiently accustomed to the Chinese language and customs and were able to take the Vincentians' place, the Vincentians prepared to leave Mongolia. On 24 September 1866 some more Belgian priests added to the number of those who arrived first. When everything was settled to everybody's satisfaction, the Vincentians set off for the posts that had been indicated to them. They went to the two vicariates of Peking and Zhengding.

Fathers Claude-Marie Chevrier, Matthieu Zhao, Paul Zheng, Vincent Wu, Pierre Feng (former lama) and Brother Louis Chevrier, brother of Father Chevrier, were assigned to Peking. Fathers Gérard Bray, Vincent Fan, Quintus Hu, Pierre Guo, Jean Zhang, Paul Zhang and Laurent Zhang went to Zhengding.

There were at that time between seven and eight thousand Faithful in Mongolia.

Anouilh was Remanded to the French Consul in Shanghai, and Qiu Exiled to Canton

We saw that Bishop Anouilh was Mouly's coadjutor in Zhengding, then, he was made administrator of the same vicariate, which did not yet have a titular bishop, at the time of the division of the Peking diocese in 1856.

It was December of the year 1856. The bishop wanted to celebrate Christmas in the small Christian community of Baishikou village. All was going along fine during the visit, when on the night of 1 January 1857 the prefect of Dingzhou with three hundred militia and soldiers, invaded the village, crying out: "Do not be afraid, I do not want to harm anybody, I only want to see the bishop." Since the Faithful clearly understood the prefect's intentions, they rushed to the side of the bishop and begged him to flee under cover of darkness. This was done quickly thanks to the dedication of the Christians. Then the prefect helped himself to everything that was in the bishop's room: crucifix, crozier, the box with the Holy Oils and so on. Next, he asked the Christians where the bishop was. Using a reprehensible mental reservation, they answered that he was in Anjiazhuang. They were sure that the prefect would not go and look for him in a sub-prefecture that did not belong to his jurisdiction. Then he had two catechists and some Christians seized and went back to his residence in Dingzhou.

Why was the mandarin of Dingzhou looking for Bishop Anouilh? The reason was that at that time some contentious cases concerning religion were being dealt with in the tribunals.

Some Christians of the large village of Xujiazhuang had been arrested and been terribly treated by the sub-prefect of Quyang, because they had refused to contribute money for the performance of a superstitious comedy. Anouilh, relying on the Lagrené treaty, undertook the defense of his Christians before the tribunal.

Besides, Mouly had ordered Father Joseph Qiu (Anyu) to open a small pharmacy in Tianjin with a view to establishing a future residence, because Tianjin was an important commercial center which up to that moment had not yet been evangelized, at least, it never had a permanent priest.

By order of the mandarin, the pharmacy was robbed and Qiu was arrested and accused of betraying his homeland because of his relations with Europeans. Put in irons he was taken to the tribunal of Baoding, the seat of the viceroy in Zhili. The judge examined Qiu in this way: "Your religion is false because it is contrary to our holy books. Confucius was a great wise man and nevertheless he was not Christian. Chinese people must not take up foreign religions. . . ." He continued in this vein.

Qiu answered boldly: "My religion is not false; it is not at variance with our books, on the contrary, it is absolutely in keeping with their teaching and with common sense. Confucius was not Christian because he was living 500 years before Jesus. The Catholic religion is not a foreign religion; God is not a foreigner for Chinese people." In short, he answered with such self confidence that the judge did not know what else to accuse him of. This did not prevent Qiu from receiving harsh treatment in Baoding, where he was interrogated more than a hundred times.

The emperor was informed of these dismal affairs. But being inclined to believe the calumnies he had been fed against Christianity and Europeans, he ordered Anouilh to be taken to Shanghai and Qiu to be banished to Canton.

They left together in March 1860 and were well treated on the way thanks to the bishop's *savoir-faire*. After a four-month's journey, they reached Shanghai. Anouilh saw the French-English fleet that the Allied nations sent to China to enforce the treaties in the harbor.

Qiu was taken to Canton, but it did not take him long to go back secretly to his house in Tianjin, where he died a year later.

Anouilh's return was even faster. Admiral Protet offered to take the bishop on board ship. The offer was accepted without hesitation.

On 1 August 1860 the two Allied fleets appeared at the mouth of the river of Tianjin. On 12 August the forts of Dagu were attacked, and on 26 August, the expeditionary brigade entered Tianjin. On 21 September the capture of Bailiqiao left Peking defenseless. On 18 October the Summer Palace was destroyed by fire. The French soldiers did not have any part in that incident.

The emperor had fled to Jehol, leaving his younger brother, Prince Gong, behind with plenipotentiary powers to negotiate. The prince gave orders to find Bishop Mouly to intervene with the foreigners, because he heard people say that Mouly was an excellent man with good advice. The notables in Tianjin had the same feelings about Anouilh whom they had noticed in their city.

Despite the danger and the risks involved passing through areas occupied by the Chinese army, Mouly approached the capital, where he had never been. A mandarin, by the name of Zhang, prepared the meeting of Prince Gong with the two bishops. They first saw the general in charge, Chengpao, who told them: "I called up many soldiers to continue the war: what is your opinion?" Mouly answered: "Excellency, it is difficult to continue the war in the actual situation." Anouilh added: "If all the officers had Your Excellency's courage, it would be possible, but very few are able to die for their homeland." The answer pleased the general, who said again: "Europeans are clever, we cannot resist them." Then he gave the bishops gifts.

On 22 October the bishops arrived at the camp of the Allied Forces; but the suspension of fighting and the opening of the gates of Peking had already been decided. The two bishops were very happy that it was not necessary for them to intervene. Prince Gong wanted to see them nevertheless in a meeting on 28 October for he had doubts about the intentions of the Allied Forces. Mouly put the prince's mind at ease by saying that if the conditions of the treaty were observed on the Chinese side, the Allied Forces would certainly keep their promises. The prince was very much impressed by this conversation and told later to whoever wanted to hear it: "Bishop Meng (Mouly) is a fair, just and virtuous person."

Reopening of Worship in the Capital

Though both sides had not yet signed the treaties, Mouly could finally take possession of his cathedral, where he had never set a foot.

Thanks to the Russian archimandrite, who had been made its guardian since 1838, the Nantang church had not been destroyed. Its walls and the roof were intact, but the interior was in a sorry state: there were neither altars nor windows. French sailors put the cross back on its summit and made the most urgent interior repairs. On 29 October a funeral service was held for those who had died during the war and the service was closed by singing the *Te Deum* to thank God for being able to worship there again.

The Treaties

Prince Gong, in the name of the emperor, signed the treaty with the Allied Forces called "The Treaty of Tianjin," a double treaty, one concerning England, the other concerning France. The two documents made rules about trade and maritime traffic; the French treaty, however, contained one additional point of extreme importance for the missions of China. It was equivalent to an edict of religious freedom. This is the text:

> The Christian religion having as its essential goal to bring people to virtue, the members of all the Christian communities will enjoy complete security for their persons, their properties and the free practice of their religious ceremonies. Effective protection will be given to the missionaries who enter the interior of the country in a peaceful way and also in possession of the passport that is mentioned in article 8.

> The authorities of the Chinese empire will hinder in no way the right, which is recognized, of accepting Christianity and following its practices, without being punishable in any way for this fact. All that had been written, proclaimed, published in China against the Christian religion by order of the government, is completely abrogated and remains without value in the provinces of the empire.

To these already very important advantages for the missionaries, some more were soon to be added, which were no less important.

The Conventions of 1860 had decided the establishment of "foreign legations." Up to that time, China had admitted only chargés d'affaires who could negotiate with China about this or that particular litigious question, but did not represent their own country officially. France and England set up the first legations, that is to say that each sent a plenipotentiary minister. The other nations did not wait long to imitate them and have their own minister recognized and accepted by the emperor.

On 20 February 1865 the minister who represented France, [Jules] Berthemy, received from the Zongli Yamen (Office of Foreign Affairs) the following declaration:

> In the future, if French missionaries buy properties and houses in the interior of the country, the seller (his/her name) will be obliged to specify when drawing up the bill of sale, that his/her property has been sold so as to become part of the collective goods of the Catholic mission in the locality. Consequently, it will be pointless to mention the names of the missionaries or of the Christians.

Therefore, the missionaries' names would no longer appear on the purchase deeds. The purchase of properties would be done *in the name of the Christian Community* of the place where the property, the land or the houses were located. These conventions allowed a development of evangelization in China up till then unknown. There were breaches of these rules, some very serious; but their basis remained a solid support for the missions.

Mouly's Journey to Europe

Bishop Mouly had scarcely taken possession of the institutions of Peking when he had to leave the management of his vicariate in the hands of his pro-vicar Father Smorenburg, in order to travel to France to take part in a general assembly of the Congregation of the Mission.

On his return to Europe this bishop who had lived in China for twenty-five years made a great impression. He was invited everywhere to speak and to preside at conferences, not only in Italy, Belgium, and the Netherlands, but even in France.

He went and greeted the emperor, Napoleon III, and thanked him for his good deeds for China. The emperor welcomed him very graciously and asked him what kind favor he could grant him. Mouly, who had pushed his gentleness and disinterestedness as far as giving to the Charity of the Holy Childhood all the gifts received during his stay in Europe instead of keeping them for his own mission, answered the emperor: "Sire, what I would like most would be to be escorted back to Tianjin, and not only me but also missionaries and Sisters whom I will take there with me." The emperor granted it on the spot.

On 20 February 1862 Mouly embarked on a government ship and reached Tianjin four months later. The following day, 14 July, he went to Peking.

The welcome, organized for the bishop, was enthusiastic. The Christians went and waited for him in groups several kilometers from the capital. Numerous catechists, who had come on horseback or by cart, and eight priests, wearing surplices, escorted him through the streets of the city.

Mouly was carried in a green sedan chair (official color). He went to the Nantang, where the pro-vicar was waiting for him and received him according to the rubrics of the ritual. From the Nantang, the procession went to the Beitang, where the catechists of the four parishes of Peking and the personnel of the French Legation were waiting for him.

Restoration of the Churches in Peking

Once in Peking, an immense task awaited him. Mouly found he had to rebuild the ruined institutions that flourished in the old days. He began with repairing the cathedral. The reader has not forgotten that the residence of the Nantang and all the buildings surrounding it had been razed to the ground and the materiel sold. The bishop first built several rooms that would serve as a residence. In the Beitang, where the church no longer existed, he made do with restoring the old and now dilapidated Chinese houses on the property. It was necessary to work fast, for the seminary of Anjiazhuang had already arrived in Peking. It is well known that the church had been razed, after it had been set on fire in 1827 by government order. The same is true about the Xitang and the Dongtang in 1811. An oratory for men was built, which was also to be a chapel for the seminarians.

In the Xitang and the Dongtang temporary lodging was arranged for one or two priests as well as a prayer hall to be used while they were waiting for a church. All those activities took place at the same time.

In the Beitang, despite a serious fire in January 1864 because of a faulty chimney, a European one-story house with a double veranda in arches was built as the priests' residence. Its style seemed to the people of Peking so strange that it drew the curiosity of the whole of Peking.

What did a residence of missionaries mean, however, without a church? The essential element was lacking. In this immense city of Peking there was only a single church, the cathedral of the Nantang. So, Mouly had a cathedral. But there were many reasons to make the bishop decide to choose another place for his episcopal residence. To begin with, the Nantang was very far from the center of the Tatar [Inner] city where the Beitang property was located. The Nantang property touched the south wall. Moreover, the property was too small to build a seminary and the other charitable centers Mouly had in mind. On the other hand, the memories that the Beitang called up as the cradle of the Congregation of the Vincentians in China, was enough to convince the bishop that choosing to keep the bishop's residence at the Nantang was no longer reasonable.

Once it was decided, the execution was not long in coming. Mouly had a plan for a cathedral drawn by a French architect and had it executed by Brother Joseph Marty, who had just finished other projects. The Zongli Yamen approved the plan, and work began immediately, and as soon as the foundations were just above the ground, the ceremony of laying the first stone took place. This happened on 1 May 1865. Present at the ceremony were: Berthemy, minister of France; the whole Chinese diplomatic corps; three representatives sent by Prince Gong; four bishops and all the clergy.

The work under Brother Marty's skillful management moved forward quickly. The solemn blessing took place on 1 January 1867. For the first time in the Beitang, women were admitted in the same church as men, but the two sexes were separated in the large nave.

The church was in the style of fourteenth century Gothic. Its base, up till a height of a meter and a half was in carved stones, the walls in large bricks, the use of which was usually reserved for imperial constructions. Three altars were built inside the church: the main altar was dedicated to the Holy Redeemer; the two other ones were dedicated to the Blessed Virgin and to Saint Joseph.

The original plan had a steeple, whose spire was to reach to the height of fifty meters. Mouly decided not to build the spire. The emperor would certainly have disliked it, for one of his palaces was adjacent to the Beitang. Instead of the sole steeple, two square clock towers were built, topped by small pinnacles. High, narrow windows and three big rose windows pierced the walls. For reasons of economy, colored glass windows were used in place of stained-glass windows, the price of which would have been out of proportion to the means of the mission. Stained-glass windows came later.

The large yellow glazed tiles used on the roof came from ruined temples and, parenthetically, their use was forbidden to private individuals. In spite of the bishop's efforts to avoid trouble by decreasing the height of the building, it remained an issue. The building was still thought to be too high, too massive. It seemed out of place, an eyesore. They measured the building in the presence of mandarins, who confirmed that its dimensions corresponded to the measurements in the plan approved of by the authorities. Nevertheless, this affair of the towers aroused complaints from the court of Peking for all Mouly's successors, until the day the government bid to buy the residence and the church of the Beitang.

Mouly Receives a Coadjutor

One day during recreation, Mouly opened the newspaper *L'univers*, and read of the appointment of Father Guierry as coadjutor of Peking. He was amazed to receive news that touched him so closely in this way. The slowness of postal communications was the sole cause of this embarrassment. Mouly knew Father Guierry, for he himself, after Daguin's death, had proposed him to Propaganda and to Etienne as capable of filling the vacant see in Mongolia. He congratulated himself on this appointment.

François Guierry, born in Magny (diocese of Sens) on 4 July 1825, entered the community in Saint Lazare on 8 October 1848 and was ordained in 1851; he arrived in Ningbo in May 1853 and carried out the functions of procurator for Vincentian missions and director of the Daughters of Charity in Ningbo. He was in that city when he received Propaganda's decree dated 22 September 1864 appointing him as bishop of Danaba and coadjutor with right of succession to Mouly.

Guierry reached Peking on 17 March 1865 and his consecration took place in the Nantang cathedral on 30 April. That morning, Mouly left the Beitang in a green sedan chair and went to the Nantang together with his coadjutor, plus Bishop Vérolles from Manchuria, Bishop Dubar from Xianxian, and Bishop Anouilh from Zhengding. Numerous priests and catechists escorted them.

The consecrator was Mouly, assisted by Bishops Vérolles and Dubar. Thanks to this markedly episcopal event, the laying of the first stone for the new Beitang cathedral could take place the next day, the first of·May, with great solemnly, graced by the presence of the four above-mentioned prelates.

The Transfer of the Vicariate of Henan

The Vincentians, who already made way for a new missionary society in China by giving Mongolia to the Belgian priests of Scheut, made way for another one, by offering the vicariate of Henan to the recently founded Society of the Foreign Missions of Milan.

The transfer happened at the same time as that of Mongolia, and the two decrees of Propaganda were made the same day, 1 September 1864.

Bishop Baldus, not without regrets, left his dear Henan, which he had been managing since 1839 as director and since 1844 as apostolic vicar. In the beginning of 1865, he went to Jiangxi where the same decree had transferred him. Father Anot as pro-vicar had been in charge of Jiangxi, without a bishop since the death of Danicourt in 1860. A pro-vicar was put in charge of Henan, until the new Italian missionaries would arrive. It was Father Jandard, about whom we have spoken several times but without introducing him.

André Jandard, born in Ardillats (Rhône) on 21 March 1809, was ordained priest in Lyons on 20 May 1837. Admitted in Saint Lazare on 12 November 1841, he pronounced vows on 13 November 1843 and reached Macao towards the end of September 1844. First, he taught in Saint Joseph Seminary. In 1849, as a result of the difficulties with de Besi, and by order of the superior general, Jandard left Macao with his French confreres and went to Henan, and there he worked under the leadership and authority of Baldus.

On 27 August 1850 he was chosen as bishop of Andrinople and apostolic vicar of Jiangxi to replace Bishop Danicourt, who had died. Jandard refused this appointment absolutely. Two years later Delaplace was named for Jiangxi, while Jandard went on exercising his ministry in Henan. But he did not have the consolation of seeing his successors take his place in Henan. In 1867, he journeyed to Peking in order to seek justice for his people, who were being harassed and humiliated by the civil authorities. He died there prematurely on 16 November 1867.

When the first three Italian missionaries arrived in 1869, there remained in Henan only two priests, one French and the other Chinese. At that time, this small vicariate numbered only about three thousand Faithful. On 22 July 1873 Father Siméon Volonteri, P.I.M.E., was appointed its apostolic vicar.

On arrival in Jiangxi, Baldus took his residence in Jiujiang, a major commercial city [and treaty port] on the Yangtze River. This part of the vineyard was too vast for the few missionaries there. Rome was already aware of it. By decree of 25 September 1868 the Holy See appointed Tagliabue as bishop of Pompeiopolis and coadjutor to Baldus.

The superior general had appointed Tagliabue, upon leaving Mongolia, as director of the Daughters of Charity of Ningbo and Shanghai. While still in Shanghai, Baldus invited him to preach a retreat for the priests of Jiangxi, in the community of Jianchang. Tagliabue then set off to Jiujiang, met with the bishop and left to preach the spiritual exercises in Jianchang, where he heard the sad and surprising news of Baldus' death. Only a few days before, he had seen him in good health. Baldus had died on 29 September 1869 after a short illness. He was fifty-eight years old.

As soon as he had finished the retreat, Tagliabue hurried to Jiujiang. On his way, he received from Shanghai a decree made by Rome dated 22 June 1869 which, reversing his earlier appointment as coadjutor of Jiangxi, named him apostolic vicar of Zhengding to succeed Anouilh. Tagliabue left Jiangxi in March 1870 to go to the place that Providence entrusted to him. There Delaplace consecrated him bishop on the following 11 November.

As a result, then the see of Jiangxi was again vacant; but the people did not need to wait long. On 15 March 1870 Father Bray was appointed apostolic vicar of Jiangxi with the title of [the titular diocese of] Legio.

Mouly's Death

Till the end of his long career, Mouly never stopped busying himself with his usual occupations. He never stopped his apostolic rounds of visiting the Christian Faithful among whom he was popular, and deservedly so. However, he felt his strength ebbing, and also suffered frequently from rheumatism. On 30 November 1868 he had to take to his bed, though he did not feel anything other than a sense of unusual weakness. The next day, his state was recognized as very serious, and he received the last rites at his request.

The sacrament provided the venerable sick man with the occasion to show one last time the depth of his spiritual life. At the point of receiving Holy Viaticum he gathered all his strength and asked his confreres to forgive him all the pain he might have caused them during his life, then he asked those present to pray for him and he asked the Christians of the vicariate to pray for him as well. All were moved to tears.

Mouly passed away on 4 December 1868 at seven o'clock in the evening. When the funeral knell was being rung to announce his death, one could feel the universal attachment to this saintly bishop. For three days and nights prayers continued around his mortal remains.

His funeral was a real triumph. The day before the solemn service took place in the Beitang cathedral, the new apostolic vicar, Guierry, did the five absolutions of the dead and a Chinese priest pronounced the funeral oration. The next day, 11 December, the funeral took place. In the church with black drapery, the highest-ranking personalities of Peking were present: ministers of the legations of six foreign nations, the Russian archimandrite, and the highest officials of the Chinese government. After the pontifical Holy Mass, celebrated by Guierry, the procession took the direction of the Fucheng gate, in order to go to the French cemetery of Zhengfusi, at a distance of twelve kilometers from the capital.

Behind the clergy, the coffin with a high catafalque was advancing, carried in turn by two teams of thirty-two men. The procession stretched out for more than a kilometer. Starting at the Beitang, it reached the suburb of Chala at one o'clock in the afternoon. There the crowd of curious onlookers stopped; the procession continued along the road to the burial site, followed by almost four hundred carts with Christian women who wanted to present the last honors to their late lamented shepherd.

This same ceremonial with slight differences was to be observed for the funerals of all the bishops of Peking. Bishop Jarlin was the last of them to die in Peking.

Mouly was a remarkable administrator; he united the most sincere humility with steadfastness, politeness with firmness, uprightness with simplicity, prudence with finesse.

As a bishop, the amount of work he did was considerable. Always on pastoral rounds or on mission, there was not one single Christian community, even the smallest that he had not visited once or several times. People there would still remember his holy examples, his long sermons and his pontifical liturgies, which he did not hesitate to celebrate even in hovels so as to give pleasure to his dear flock who were eager to see the great pomp of divine worship.

All this did not prevent him from keeping up a voluminous correspondence with his superiors, his confreres, bishops and other personalities.

About his place in the history of the development of the mission of Peking, we can say that Mouly was the bridge between the time of the persecutions and that of religious freedom, granted freedom was still relative. Let us recall that the Portuguese mission had left him just one chapel, the one in Anjiazhuang. He bequeathed some thirty of them to his successor. At the time of the division of the diocese in 1856, his vicariate of Peking had about seventeen thousand Faithful; at the time of his death, twelve years later, it numbered twenty-four thousand.

Under Guierry's leadership, the charitable works continued to progress and several churches were built: one called Saint Peter's in the Christian community of Gaojiazhuang, ninety kilometers to the south of Peking; another in Xuanhua under the name of the Holy Cross; another, a very large one, begun by Mouly in Tianjin, at the place called Wanghailou.

Chapter 10

Vincentian Missions in North and Central China, 1860s-1870s

Anouilh and his Method of Preaching to Pagans – Anouilh's Death – Tagliabue Succeeds Anouilh – Bray Succeeds Baldus in Jiangxi – Adrien Rouger, Pro-vicar of South Jiangxi – Rouger's Episcopacy – Second Division of Jiangxi: Casimir Vic – The Young Christian Community in Tianjin – Forebodings of the Massacre – The Massacre of Two Priests, Ten Daughters of Charity, Nine European Civilians, Four Chinese and Twelve Children – Delaplace, Apostolic Vicar of Peking – Evangelization Activities in Peking

Anouilh and his Method of Preaching to Pagans

Towards the end of 1860, Anouilh returned to Zhengding filled with hope. He was fortified by the promises the grand mandarins in Peking made to him, and he was in a hurry to have them fulfill their promises. He had been promised a suitable property for the works of mercy. First, he rented an inn near the yamen (the prefect's [office and] residence) and settled there temporarily with his missionaries. Then he went and saw the prefect and the mandarins of the city, and asked them for a suitable building there according to the promise that he had been made in Peking.

The mandarins suggested – while awaiting an order from Peking – the Zhongyin temple. Though this building did not delight him much, Anouilh, who had been lodged so badly at the inn, went and settled there with his confreres. Finally, in 1863 an order came from Peking that gave the mission of Zhengding an immense piece of ground with some old houses on it. The houses were quickly restored to provide living quarters. Many buildings were going to be built there, both for the missionaries and for the Daughters of Charity.

On one of his pastoral tours in the region of Zhaozhou, the bishop noticed the many obstacles placed to the conversion of the pagans and to the perseverance of the Christians. Even mandarins forced the Christians to contribute to the cost of superstitious comedies, to the construction or repair of temples, and generally to pagan festivals. In practice the freedom promised in the treaties did not exist. Therefore, he had several copies printed of the treaties and he always took one with him in order to show it when an occasion arose.

In a report to the director of the Society of the Propagation of the Faith, the bishop described his way of preaching thus:

> For several months, I have been traveling not only through the old Christian communities, but also the villages where the Lord's name is completely unknown. I preach not only in the houses, but also in public. A table is prepared and a chair, and there I preach as much as I can. Nine villages declared that they are Christians; in twenty others, many families have given up their idols and want to honor the "Lord of Heaven" – in Jiazhuang, seventy families; in Longzhong, fifty.

He preached for hours during the day and often till midnight. Sometimes a Chinese priest took over from him as well as three or four catechists. Addressing the pagans, he began, "I have here with me the emperor's order – he then showed the imperial edict and placed it on the table. Everybody can embrace this religion; nobody can prevent you from doing it, not even the emperor, still less the mandarins." Then he explained the doctrine.

Sometimes he was asked questions, among which this one was frequently asked, "Distinguished person, will you take care of our lawsuits against the pagans?" He would answer, "If the actions are just and reasonable and if you observe the rules of the Catholic religion, do not worry, I will help you." The result was that the bishop was often dragged into lawsuits that hardly touched the Catholic religion.

Wherever he was, there were a lot of people coming and going; after saying goodbye to some, others would arrive and request his help in all kinds of different matters. There were even Christians who had no qualms about exaggerating or misrepresenting the facts and actions of pagans, in order to get the bishop's help against mandarins. What then can we say about pagans who would promise him the conversion of their family or even the conversion of a whole village, should the bishop successfully handle their lawsuit?

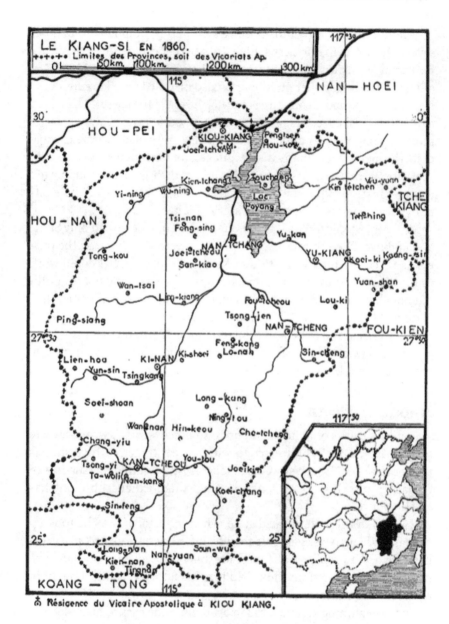

Map 10.1 Jiangxi in 1860
(Showing the Residence of the Apostolic Vicar at Jiujiang)

Anouilh unwittingly introduced a system that would be imitated in several vicariates in northern China. Father Leboucq, S.J., used it openly in the northern part of the vicariate of Xianxian, as François Liu, C.M., did in in Baoding. Other missionaries also meddled with lawsuits occasionally; this period is sometimes called "the era of the lawsuits." It began at the time of the treaties of religious liberty, and lasted thirty years at most. The method was difficult to use and few missionaries were capable of it. The method had many disadvantages, for it happened that, despite precautions, missionaries were misled and in their good faith supported injustice instead of the law. Anouilh himself was able to avoid these pitfalls, because of his prudence and spirit of faith.

Actually, Mouly did not have enough help. Till 1866 he had only Simiand and five Chinese priests, two of whom were Vincentians. The others had received their formation in Macao. Chinese priests could work immediately after their ordination. European priests could not. Anouilh did not allow them to work at the conversion of the pagans before they had spent five or six years in China, so as to have a thorough knowledge of the language and to be well informed about Chinese customs.

At the time of the transfer of Mongolia to the Scheut missionaries, he received Father Bray and five Chinese confreres.

Anouilh's Death

Anouilh's health could not stand up to so much work. A witness wrote to a confrere, "We are threatened with a great tragedy. The bishop is really exhausted. He never wants to take a rest; we cannot persuade him to slacken off a little. A dry, unrelenting cough exhausts him, he has lost his appetite."

He was in this deteriorated state, when in October 1868 he took up his pastoral journeys again. He then heard of Mouly's death (4 December). He had a profound affection for this bishop, whose coadjutor he had been for a long time. He called him his father and still thought of himself as his deacon.

In the beginning of January 1869, Anouilh came back to his residence, where two priests, Fathers Raphael Moscarella and Benoît Jiang, were suffering from typhoid fever. The bishop in his turn got the same disease, but according to the doctors it was not serious. Indeed, a few days later, he wrote to a confrere, "I have caught typhoid fever, but I am getting better." Actually, his illness got worse and he knew it. On 9 February he wrote, "*Jam delibor.* . . I must definitely prepare myself to go and meet Mouly." The following day, Ash Wednesday, he wanted to preside over the ceremony; a relapse was the consequence of this imprudence. On 17 February he received the last rites in complete lucidity of mind and the following day, at nine o'clock he passed away.

Table 10.1 Vicariate of Zhengding, Concise Statistics, 1870

Prefectures	Sub-prefectures	Christian Communities	Faithful
Zhengding	14	145	8,960
Dingzhou	3	15	794
Zhaozhou	6	129	9,729
Shunde	9	50	2,132
Totals	32	339	21,615

We have seen above that in 1856 the mission of Zhengding had about twelve thousand Faithful spread over one hundred twenty-two localities.

Tagliabue Succeeds Anouilh

François Tagliabue was born in Coincy-l'Abbaye on 29 November 1822; he was ordained priest on 17 June 1848. He entered Saint Lazare in 1852, was appointed to China where he arrived on 17 June 1854 and was sent to Mongolia where we saw him working. Then he was sent to Jiangxi where he became on 25 September 1868 Baldus's coadjutor. He had scarcely assumed this function, when, before his consecration, he was already transferred to the vacant siege of Zhengding through the decree of 22 June 1869.

Not yet consecrated, Father Tagliabue arrived in Zhengding in April 1870. The following 11 December Delaplace came from Peking to confer on him the episcopal consecration.

The succession was hard. Tagliabue's facility for speaking in public was not as developed as his predecessor's. He was not as well known among the civil authorities either. He was charged moreover with another task: the organization and formation of the neophytes. He dedicated himself to it completely.

The results of Anouilh's preaching were more apparent than real. The number of Christian communities had more than doubled, but the number of baptized people had not. The bishop added numbers, written on long lists that were presented to him, saying, "That village has this number of converts," but actually quite a number of the inscribed people had not even become catechumens.

Anouilh's merit was not so much to have put thirty thousand names of catechumens on the lists as to have launched the conversion movement by proclaiming that a religion had the right to exist and to be practiced openly, as well as to have settled among new Christians and to have put priests there in order to take his place. What harmed the success of his initiative was that he had not looked sufficiently into the intentions of the people who asked to be admitted to the catechumenate. The majority had heard people speak of the temporal advantages they could get when they became Christians. Anouilh did not spend time on this type of research. According to the occasion, he would spread his net.

As a result, after his death, the conversion movement stopped cold; the number of baptized did not increase for ten years. Therefore, it was necessary at least to maintain the achieved positions and in order to do so, it was absolutely necessary to bring the neophytes to maturity.

This was the task that Tagliabue took up, and we will see that he fulfilled it marvelously. He began by multiplying the missionaries' locations. "Let us go forth," he said, "to Christianize our newly baptized people," and that is what happened. Only a few confreres remained in town; all the others spread out over the countryside.

The main means that he used and which gave the best results was the one of the closed retreats, first given in the central residence, later on in the most important Christian communities. The graces of conversions or improvements in Christian life were numerous. To allow a bigger number of Faithful to take part in these retreats, the bishop himself went to five of the biggest Christian communities of the vicariate. There he gave nine retreats for the men and for the women. One thousand nine hundred twelve people made a retreat. It was an excellent method, which afterwards became a regular institution in this vicariate, until the Chinese-Japanese war (1937).[31]

In 1880, the superior general appointed Tagliabue his extraordinary representative to visit the vicariates entrusted to the Congregation of the

---

31.   Alphonse-Marie Morelli, C.M., *Notes d'histoire sur le vicariat de Tcheng-ting-fou, 1858–1933* (Pei-p'ing, 1934).

Mission. He began in the south. He went to Shanghai. Then he visited Peking and soon after that he went to Europe to give an account of his journey. In November 1882, in response to his insistent demand, he finally obtained Daughters of Charity. Their first superior, Sister Guerlain, was to direct amazing works of Charity for many years.

From this period on, the number of catechumen schools increased steadily. And every year the number of Faithful increased; there were 25,035 in 1884.

Soon, however, Tagliabue had to use his zeal in another mission, a larger one. A decree from Rome, dated 5 August 1884, ordered him to go to Peking to direct the destinies of that vicariate. The bishop left Zhengding at the end of the year. We will meet him again in the capital a little further on.

Bray Succeeds Baldus in Jiangxi

Géraud Bray, already mentioned several times in our history when the vicariates of Mongolia and of Zhengding were being talked about, was born in Syran (Cantal) on 4 December 1825. He entered the community in Paris on 12 December 1848, and was ordained priest on 21 May 1853. On 23 December 1858 he landed in Shanghai and a little later he was in Mongolia, where we have seen him at work till 1866. On 16 October of that same year he was in Zhengding helping Anouilh.

On 15 March 1870 a decree from Rome appointed Bray apostolic vicar of Jiangxi to succeed Baldus who died in 1869. After receiving this news, Bray traveled to Shanghai, where he met Guierry the apostolic vicar of Peking, who had just been transferred to Zhejiang. He asked him to consecrate him bishop and they agreed on 20 November 1870 in Jiujiang.

Bray arrived in Jiujiang on 12 November and, the next day, he announced to the few Christians who came to Mass that the day of his consecration was near. The ceremony was performed without pomp, because there were only a few Christians in that city at the time. Only three confreres were present. The other priests, all invited, could not come because the province had been in turmoil since the Tianjin Massacre, which took place some months before. The horrible tragedy of Tianjin, which will be talked about below, had its repercussion on the whole empire. Scarcely fifty Faithful, among whom twenty orphaned girls, were present at the ceremony. Two of the three priests – with papal dispensation – assisted the consecrating bishop, Bishop Guierry. These were the humble beginnings of Bray's assuming the office of governing Jiangxi; he was to fulfill this office for thirty-five years.

Immediately after beginning his task, Bray drew up the balance sheet of the spiritual fruits for the year that had just ended. This is his summary:

Table 10.2 Catholic Numbers for Jiangxi, 1870

Number of the Faithful		7,288
Baptisms	Adults	159
	Children of Christian parents	365
	Children of pagans at the point of death	4,282
Catechumens		1.058
Priests	European Vincentians	4
	Chinese Vincentians	6
	Chinese Diocesans	4

Several disasters had just swept down on this vicariate. The church in Wucheng, only just finished, had been ransacked from top to bottom by a mob. The orphanage in Fuzhou had been burned down and its personnel scattered. The missionaries, gathered for the annual spiritual exercises, were obliged to stop their retreat and to flee and hide as in the time of persecution. The seminary was closed; some of the students returned home or hid in the mountains.

At that time, the war between Germany and France was at its height, and France suffered terrible defeats that gave cause to fear that the Holy Childhood might collapse. The new bishop anxiously wondered who was going to teach the thousand registered catechumens. Who would evangelize the twenty million inhabitants of his vicariate? Lack of workers, lack of means: those were the two specters that were haunting hm.

Therefore, he was very happy to learn in August 1871 that the charitable organization of the Holy Childhood not only had not perished but also was able to grant him a sizeable sum of money to support his six hundred orphaned girls.

When order had been restored, the missionaries of Jiangxi took up their work again with enthusiasm. There was some discussion whether the Daughters of Charity might be called to take the direction of the orphanages and to establish a hospital, but the disaster of Tianjin made this plan impossible for the time being.

Bray wrote later on: "The Sisters came to Jiujiang only in 1882. As for the missionaries, I had the consolation every year of welcoming some from France as well as adding some new Chinese priests. From 1870 until now, our superiors in Paris have sent twenty priests to Jiangxi and I have ordained ten of our seminarians." As the number of the mission-aries increased, the fruits of their apostolate did too. We may appreciate this by looking at the summary of the spiritual fruits in 1886, compared to those of 1870:

In 1870: Christians and catechumens	8,346
In 1886: Christians and catechumens	19,587
Increase	11,241

We add to this the fruits of the Holy Childhood. In 1870, this organiza-tion supported in Jiangxi 612 orphaned girls; in 1886, they numbered 2,298; even more by means of the monthly "penny" of the Childhood. In 1878, he requested from Rome the division between the dying and the pagan [babies].

Very early on Bray planned to divide his vast corner of the vineyard. In 1878, he asked Rome for the division of his civil province into two vicari-ates. On 19 August 1879 Pope Leo XIII decreed the division of the Jiangxi province into two distinct vicariates, which would take the names of North Jiangxi and South Jiangxi and he drew their respective boundaries. The following September a decree of Propaganda declared that North Jiangxi would remain under Bray's administration and appointed Adrien Rouger to administer the new vicariate of South Jiangxi with the title of pro-vicar, without becoming a bishop, however, for the time being. A letter from the Cardinal Prefect addressed to Father Rouger accompanied the decree.

Adrien Rouger, Pro-vicar of South Jiangxi

Born in Pourrain (Yonne) on 21 September 1828, admitted to the Con-gregation in Paris on 1 October 1851, he was ordained priest on 5 June 1852, [took his vows in Alexandria, Egypt, 2 October 1853] and arrived in Ningbo on 16 December 1855. After studying Chinese for a few months, Rouger left Ningbo and went to Jiangxi to work there under the leader-ship of Danicourt. Immediately the bishop entrusted him with direct-ing what was called the minor seminary located in the mission station of Jiudu. He had as students eight students of Latin, four students of philosophy and two newly ordained priests who had to be taught how to confer the sacraments.

Rouger had to do this work in difficult circumstances. It was the period when rebels were threatening the whole empire. That year, Montels was murdered and a great number of Jiangxi's Christian communities were destroyed or damaged. On one occasion rebels invaded the village and odiously mistreated both teachers and students.

The students scattered for some days, and after the mob had dispersed, returned to their studies. Soon the word went around that a peace treaty supported freedom of religion. Even if the rebels had not yet put down their arms, Danicourt believed that the time had come to aid the Christians. It was decided that Rouger should move from the seminary to the missions. He was assigned the southern part of the vicariate.

The treaty would be promulgated only in 1858, but Rouger did not want to wait for that date. Urged by his zeal, he left immediately and, for almost two years, he went all over the region visiting many small Christian communities which had not seen a priest for five or six years. When he came back to Jiudu to take a little rest, he found that his confrere, Father Jean-Baptiste Glau, who had substituted for him in the seminary, was ill. Rouger had to take up his functions as a teacher again and kept them until 1879 when he was named pro-vicar of South Jiangxi.

In the course of 1860 and 1862, which were the last years of the rebellion, Rouger had to flee four times to save his life and that of his beloved students, seeking often uncertain shelter in the mountains. We will not digress on the risks he ran, or on episodes of his escapes at the head of his flock.

When peace had returned in 1862, the village of Jiudu was only a heap of ruins. The seminary was therefore brought over to Jiujiang, close to the European ships protecting the trade of their compatriots. In 1868, once again a change of residence: the seminary came back from Jiujiang and settled in Qidu, near Jiudu. Now, every change of residence required new constructions. Teacher and parish priest, Rouger was also occasionally architect and bricklayer. But he knew how to get help from the Faithful. Church, oratory, residence, and orphanage sprang out of the ground. The number of students increased rapidly; in the beginning there were twelve, soon he had thirty them, then forty. The students of Latin, of philosophy and theology made up five divisions, which all had daily lessons there. The one teacher taught in turns Latin grammar, philosophy, theology, liturgy and plainchant. He did alone the work of three or four people. If we add the worries that the Faithful and the Holy Childhood gave him, we can understand that there must have been gaps in the formation of the seminarians. Actually, it was not a real seminary; however, nine priests exclusively formed by him came from it. He established a real seminary with the necessary personnel 1886 in Ji'an after he became a bishop.

Above we have seen that the brief of 19 August 1879, by dividing Jiangxi, entrusted the administration of the whole south of the province to Rouger as Bray's pro-vicar. In the course of January 1880, Rouger went to his station and established his residence in Ji'an. His territory consisted of four prefectures: Ji'an, Ningdu, Ganzhou and Nancheng. They were divided into twenty-six sub-prefectures.

South Jiangxi was the unhealthiest and also the most abandoned part of the entire province. No priest was there permanently; the three thousand Faithful who lived there had no other spiritual help than what the missionaries brought on their yearly mission rounds

Rouger brought along only two young French confreres without any experience, and a Chinese confrere, Father Laurent Yuan. There was a lot to do and that with very meager means. He was himself not very healthy. He was only a few months in Ji'an, when he became seriously ill because of the unhealthy shack that he used as lodging. When he recovered his health, he began to travel all over his missionary field. As early as the middle of 1881, he had already set eighty Christian communities back on their feet, but not without many humiliations coming from mandarins. Then an inundation flooded three sub-prefectures. Rouger had to supply food for thousands of hungry Faithful and pagans. Soon he began to build a church and of a residence in the city of Ji'an. This took him two years.

In order to give a new impetus to what was going forward, Bray and Delaplace together proposed Rouger for the episcopacy. The decree of 7 September 1883 appointed Rouger the bishop of Cisame and apostolic vicar of South Jiangxi. On 27 April 1884 Bray consecrated him bishop in his new cathedral, which he had dedicated to Our Lady of Victories. For lack of other bishops, Fathers Jean-Marie Pérès and Boscat filled the role of assistants.

Rouger's Episcopacy

Now began a period of significant ordeals for the new bishop. The circumstances in which he found himself seemed to dictate a certain prudence. Indeed, it was easy to foresee that the mandarins would not pardon him for having defied their influence and authority by founding religious institutes in the middle of completely pagan communities. Rouger could have confined himself, at least for some time, to past achievements acquired with so much difficulty, limiting his activities to the established locations. But his fiery faith pushed him to act; fear of danger did not influence his decisions.

He had the delusion of some missionaries who think that they honor God by building expensive edifices in not yet evangelized regions. "This will impress the pagans!" they would say. What an error!

He had his sights on Ganzhou, the most important one of the four prefectures, which was bounded by the province of Guangdong. In the village of Lan-Tang, there was a little oratory and a hovel that gave shelter to a few children, who had been taken in. This village was part of the sub-prefecture Lan-Tang.[32] Rouger wanted the prefecture of Ganzhou to have the same institutions as Ji'an. How much more reasonable it would have been if he had first intensified the evangelization of Ji'an before establishing charitable organizations in an environment that had been touched so little by the Gospel.

A few days after his consecration, the bishop went with a Chinese priest to Lan-Tang in order to oversee the construction of a chapel and an orphanage. The work had already begun.

But at the same time the workers were busy in Lan-Tang, the intellectuals were plotting in the nearby market town. The sub-prefect of Lan-Tang urged them on. Several times in those days, people were seen prowling around the building site and uttering threats. Finally on 20 May in the afternoon, an angry crowd invaded the building site. In two hours' time, the walls, already two meters high, were knocked down; the old house, which was sheltering the orphans, was likewise demolished.

But that was not the saddest outcome of the riot. That day, the bishop had gone to a place three kilometers away in order to check some stones to be transported to the building site. Some angry people followed him. They caught up with him, insulted him, and beat him. His companion, the Chinese priest, tried to defend him at the risk of his life. In the meantime, a decent pagan from the neighborhood pleaded in favor of the distinguished victim. The priest pleaded also and because the best argument under the circumstances was a bribe, he promised money. Meanwhile the bishop succeeded in fleeing and entered the kind pagan's house. Though given a thrashing, the bishop miraculously had no broken limbs or serious wounds. He accepted a bowl of rice; he seemed to have forgotten all his bruises; moreover, he had

---

32. Ferreux writes "Lan-Tang" village and sub-prefecture but neither the locations nor characters can be determined from the materials at hand. (AS)

not uttered one word of complaint. He had to flee. Then he left the house with the priest and some Faithful who had come to help him. At that point he learned of the disaster in Lan-Tang for the first time. The bishop did not want to flee anymore. He wanted to see his Lan-Tang, and so, he returned there despite all opposition. He saw only a heap of bricks... Christians? Not one single Faithful; they were hiding; the rioters themselves had dispersed. In short, Rouger was able to pass through Lan-Tang almost unnoticed... but it had become a far too dangerous place for him to remain.

Therefore, he had to leave, walking the whole night of 20–21 May and return to his residence in Ji'an. Rouger never recovered completely from this terrible shock. From that day onward, his health was much weakened because of it. He became so ill that the superior general decided to recall him to France. He made do with going to Shanghai in October 1885 for some treatment.

If the persecution had broken his strength, it had not weakened his courage. He sent Father Pérès to Pinglu, a mission post situated not far from Ganzhou, with orders to build there everything that could not have been built in Lan-Tang. Thanks to Pérès's clever direction, work proceeded quickly.

In the meantime, the seminary was progressing well. Its buildings, begun in 1883, were being enlarged and it became a real major seminary, distinct from the minor seminary where the students were being taught Latin. In June 1886, the buildings in Pinglu were almost finished, so Rouger set out for Ganzhou to inaugurate and bless the new buildings. He traveled on the boat belonging to the mission. The day following his arrival, as if obeying a command, the population went to the residence, pilfered the boat, which held the episcopal insignia and important amounts of money to pay the workers, tore it to pieces and sank it in the river; then the mob rushed towards the new buildings and sacked, demolished and burned everything. Pérès was beaten, tied up and left almost naked under a burning sun for three days. They sought a ransom.

Rouger was not harmed. A confrere rescued him, took him away half-clothed under cover of darkness, despite his disabilities, for about thirty kilometers to a place less troubled. Another confrere freed Pérès for a large ransom. The bishop was accompanied to Guangdong province. He walked across this whole province in twenty days and twenty nights, a painful journey. He arrived in Canton at the house of the apostolic vicar, Bishop Chausse, M.E.P, who received him as a brother.

After a few days of rest, he put out to sea and arrived in Shanghai at the end of July 1886. Though he personally suffered much, he worried equally about his Christians and in Shanghai lobbied for just treatment for them. Unfortunately, he would never see them again.

A letter from Paris ordered him to return to France to recover his health. On 23 December he embarked together with Reynaud and arrived in Marseilles on 20 January 1887. He was so weak that he had to rest in that port for a week before going to Paris, where he arrived on 28 January still so weak that he was unable to celebrate Holy Mass. Despite the treatments lavished on him, his illness got worse. On 20 March Reynaud anointed him. On 31 March his sister, a Daughter of Charity, told to come quickly, came to see her dying brother. He recognized her and said only these words to her, "Our poor mother." That was his last word. At three o'clock, he gave his soul back to God. He was fifty-nine years old. He had been bishop for only three years.

The Rouger family expressed a strong desire to have his remains buried in the cemetery of their native place, and Father Antoine Fiat, the superior general, granted their desire. After the solemn funeral celebrated in Saint Lazare, the coffin was put temporarily in the Montparnasse cemetery; then on 25 April it was transferred to Pourrain, where it was opened at a ninety-year-old mother's request. Think of this mother's sorrow.

The number of the Christians of South Jiangxi had grown by about a thousand since its creation. This number is included in the account of the mission of Jiangxi presented by Bray in 1886. Later we will say who Rouger's successor was.

Second Division of Jiangxi: Casimir Vic

The field to be cultivated by Bray was too vast for the means at his disposal. In 1884, he asked Rome to carve up his vicariate of North Jiangxi again. Propaganda approved this project and on its recommendation Pope Leo XIII erected a new vicariate, named East Jiangxi. By decree of 11 July 1885 Casimir Vic was the first apostolic vicar to be appointed for this vicariate, which consisted of four prefectures: Raozhou, Guangxin, Fuzhou and Jianchang, divided into twenty-five sub-prefectures.

The Christian population consisted of about ten thousand Faithful, also included in the above-mentioned account. Vic's title was bishop of Metellopolis.

Father Casimir Vic, born in Mourmentres (Aveyron) on 29 September 1852, did his literary and philosophical studies in Rodez. He entered the community at Saint Lazare on 14 May 1873 and he was ordained priest on 26 May 1877. He arrived in Shanghai on the following 5 October with Father Bruguière and Father Dominique Procacci. Destined for Jiangxi, he was welcomed a short time later with particular joy by Bray.

Vic had to organize all the works that were essential for a new vicariate. For this task he had fourteen missionaries, half of whom because of age or health needed almost complete rest. His four European priests were soon housebound in their residences: they were put to work managing the seminary, the orphanages and the schools. Vic, as a good, calm, prudent and tenacious administrator transmitted a new impetus to his mission. We will see later what fruits were harvested during the twenty-six years of his episcopacy.

We must now return to continue the history of Delaplace's episcopacy. On 21 January 1870 he received in Rome orders to leave Zhejiang and take in hand the administration of the vicariate of Peking, while Guierry, Mouly's successor, was to succeed Delaplace in Zhejiang. Guierry, who had gone to Rome for the Vatican Council, received this new appointment also in the Eternal City.

Because Delaplace took up his new responsibility within a few months of the Tianjin Massacre, we will give a short account of that horrible tragedy here.

The Young Christian Community in Tianjin

We say "young" because the evangelization of that large city had hardly begun.

When Mouly sent Father Joseph Qiu to Tianjin in 1858 to establish a small pharmacy, he found only a few dozen Christians who had probably come from the countryside to earn a living in this commercial environment. After Qiu's death (1861), Talmier took his place and moved temporarily into the small pharmacy. His confrere, by order of the bishop of Peking, had already acquired the property of Wanghailou with a view to building a missionary residence. Talmier also had to prepare for the arrival of the Daughters of Charity.

On his return journey from Europe, Mouly entered Peking solemnly on 14 July 1862. He had brought along with him some Sisters and had left five of them in Tianjin. Talmier received them on 2 July and brought them to the humble residence left by Qiu, which he had arranged as well as he could for that purpose. The house was poorly furnished, and the Sisters could hardly find in it bare necessities. They needed at least three different rooms: chapel, dormitory and refectory. Since furniture was lacking, the five chairs in the house had to be taken from one room to the other according to the time of the day. The small community was well disposed to bear the absence of every comfort willingly; but after two weeks, they were saddened by the fact that they had no task to handle.

In his desire to help them, Talmier told some Christian women to find pagan families who wanted to get rid of some of their numerous children. They found some and a few babies were brought in. Then, little by little they began caring for sick people. A man with cholera was brought to them. They took care of him throughout a whole night. The next day, the man, seeing that he was healed, returned home telling the world and his wife how the Sisters had taken care of him. From that moment, some sick people were brought to them, yet the rhythm was very slow. The dispensary succeeded better because people were happy to receive free medicines for their illnesses. However, distrust hovered around their cornettes.

Soon deep grief seized and saddened the Sisters: an untimely death took from them their mainstay, the good Father Talmier. On 10 August 1862 this worker of the first hour died. Mouly immediately sent [Jean-Baptiste] Thierry to take the deceased's place as procurator, and he entrusted him also with the responsibility of director of the prefecture of Tianjin.

One or two years after the Sisters' arrival, their work had already become substantial. Lack of space, however, hindered their expansion. A new house was purchased. It had a better location on the bank of the river two or three kilometers away from Wanghailou. In the future a residence would be erected there.

Public opinion seemed less suspicious. The Sisters began to appear in town, always accompanied by a laywoman. They even ventured to go to nearby villages. A servant preceded them, telling people that the Sisters were arriving bringing medicine to heal sick children. Then the women would present their babies; the Sisters would treat them, and every time they saw that a child had a mortal illness, they would baptize it in such a way that nobody could see that the child was getting a ticket to enter heaven.

The Sisters, however, were greatly astonished that the orphanage progressed so slowly. The pagans did not understand the motives that pushed these foreign women to receive children, especially girls and to spend money to keep them. Moreover, all over the empire, stupid slanderous remarks were made. "Missionaries," it was said, "extract children's eyes and hearts in order to produce magical remedies." These perverse rumors were being spread all over Tianjin. Some people believed them, while others, without completely believing them, still suspected the intentions of the foreigners.

At the end of 1866, Thierry was called to Peking and was replaced by Chevrier, who had come from Mongolia, and whom we must introduce because of the role he was to play.

Claude Chevrier had had an eventful youth. Born in Saint-Godard (Loire) on 13 August 1821 he felt called to the priesthood. His uncle, parish priest in Marcoux, became his teacher. Young Claude began his studies seriously, but because of his vivacious nature, sedentary life did not agree with him. He abandoned his studies and became a clerk in a warehouse. On reaching the age of military service, he was appointed to the marines. He left happily for Toulon in 1842 and thought that his real way was a military career. On the other hand, being an excellent Christian, he soon disliked the lax life in those camps. After becoming a sergeant, he left for Guyana, where occasionally he had conversations with missionaries. Those conversations made him think of his lost call; and the more he thought about it, the better he understood that "among all the vocations, a priest's life is the most beautiful and for society the most useful."

Back in France and having finished his military service, he went to the minor seminary in Largentière to finish his humanities. Then he began his ecclesiastical studies in Lyons. In the first days there he had occasion to visit Bishop Pavie (Pavy), bishop of Algiers, who had come to France to attract vocations for his diocese.

Claude Chevrier, intrepid and generous, went to the bishop and offered to follow him. He was accepted immediately. The seminary in Algiers was just beginning, consequently it lacked comfort and many things necessary in a house of studies. Nevertheless, this life, hard and full of surprises, pleased the new student. He finished all his studies there and was ordained a priest in 1854. Then, he was put to work taking pastoral care of the people in the countryside of Algiers. Chevrier had found the active life that he had been looking for.

Still, his humble nature was not satisfied because he had too much independence. He dreamed of giving up more, so as to offer himself to God and souls more completely. One day he heard about the Vincentians and their work in Persia and in China and so on. He sent the superior general a request to be allowed to enter the Congregation. After inquiries had been made, he was accepted.

On 22 November 1858 Chevrier entered the internal seminary in Paris. Destined for China, he arrived there on 17 February 1860. A few months later, he was in Mongolia where he was under Mouly's authority. Though forty years old he worked with the enthusiasm of the youngest, yet with gifts honed by experience. Heartbroken, he abandoned his "dear Mongolia," as all his colleagues who had worked there called it. But the apostolate that was opening up before him had works in store for him that were no less important and would have the most glorious outcome a missionary could wish for.

Besides the direction of the Sisters and their works, which he did with the greatest dedication, he undertook the care of the European and Chinese Faithful in Tianjin. As director of the district, he had the oversight of several sub-prefectures, the immediate care of which had been assigned to Father Vincent Wu, who had been his friend in Mongolia, and to Pierre Feng, the former lama. Moreover, he was procurator for all the Vincentian missions in the north of China.

He resided in Wanghailou, not far from the French embassy [*sic,* consulate]. Thierry had set up a small chapel there. But from the first months of his stay in Tianjin, Chevrier wanted to build a big church. In his imagination he saw it already rising in the middle of the property, at the meeting point of the river and the canal, a magnificent site, where the building would rise and be seen from all sides. The new director succeeded in realizing his dream. The first stone was blessed and laid by Guierry on 16 May 1869.

Chevrier started working with all his energy; he was an entrepreneur and was unafraid of risk taking. Under his prudent direction, the Sisters' works were thriving and at the same time catechumens became more numerous in spite of many difficulties. How many times he had to intervene in order to protect his neophytes from vexations by pagans or mandarins! He went and met the latter at their tribunal; he explained the facts, he argued, and often he succeeded in having justice done to his Christians.

The Sisters, for their part, continued to open their doors to all kinds of miseries without fearing the distrust or suspicions of the crowd. Their community doubled; there were ten of them in the beginning of 1870.

Chevrier, overburdened with occupations, overwhelmed with worries, asked insistently and was granted that his friend Vincent Wu come to help him in Tianjin. From that time on he could give himself more to the instruction of his dear catechumens. In 1869, his district numbered two thousand catechumens spread out over sixty localities. The future therefore seemed full of promise.

Forebodings of the Massacre

In May 1870, accusations again circulated among the people about stealing children and killing them then in order to produce magical remedies with their eyes and their hearts. The accusations became unusually fierce. This time not only the common people were taken in by these hateful libelous remarks, even respectable people were influenced by this nonsense. The Sisters, who had succeeded in being well received everywhere because of their disinterested beneficence, now met only angry and cold looks. They were even insulted.

To be on the safe side, they stopped their visits to people's homes. The accusations increased. Facts were mentioned. People believed. People even went to search the cemetery where the people who died in the hospital or the orphanage were buried; they examined the excavated corpses and published that they had neither hearts nor eyes.

All this happened openly and publicly before the civil authorities, who, instead of making some small gesture to calm the rumors, seemed to encourage them through their passivity.

The French consul, [Henri] Fontanier, who could have influenced the Chinese authorities to oblige them to protect all the foreigners in Tianjin, as the treaties demanded, lacked foresight. He did not believe the danger to be immediate and thought that the storm would dissipate, as had happened several times already. Despite Chevrier's and the Russian consul's repeated warnings, Fontanier persisted stubbornly in not perceiving the danger. Seeing the danger increasing, the missionary returned to the consul begging him to intercede with the authorities. The French consul persisted and, irritated, forbade the missionary entrance to the consulate.

The Sisters themselves wanted to try a last effort to enlighten Fontanier and secure his protection; it was in vain; the consul was convinced that the moment had not yet come.

On 20 June in the evening, Mr. Thomassin, interpreter for the French Legation, and his wife disembarked in Tianjin. They had come from Europe and were in a hurry to arrive in Peking. Invited to stay for the night in the foreign concessions, they had preferred to go the French consulate[33] and there they spent the night.

---

33.   The French consulate was near Wanghailou, where the Church of Our Lady of Victories built by Chevrier was located. The foreign concessions were in the southeast part of the city about two kilometers from Wanghailou and were on the right bank of the river. The palace of the Military Governor [*sic* Superintendent] Chonghou was also near Wanghailou, but opposite the French consulate. Chonghou was not

A decision was taken to burn down the Catholic mission and kill the missionaries the next day. The one who, while staying in the shadows, pushed the agitated crowd with all his might, was Chen Guorui, a former leader of the bandits. He had betrayed the partners of his robberies and, in return for his apparent submission, had been put in charge of a militia unit.

He had already distinguished himself in the south of China by his acts of violence and his hatred of Europeans. On his way from Nanjing, he had published tracts in the regions that he passed through announcing the fight against the foreigners, particularly those in Tianjin. After arriving in Tianjin, he managed to worm his way into the community of the mandarins in order to stimulate their hatred and control the fanaticism of the working-class. He suddenly was the master of the hour.

The Deaths of Two Priests, Ten Daughters of Charity, Nine Europeans Civilians, Four Chinese and Twelve Children

On Tuesday morning 21 June 1870 at nine o'clock one could hear the bell ringing in the streets. It was the signal for the gathering. The crowd of troublemakers went towards the Church of Our Lady of Victories. The prefect and the sub-prefect presented themselves in order to search the mission. Chevrier put himself at their disposition to show them all the nooks and crannies of the house and the church. But the search revealed nothing, so the two mandarins left without saying a word to calm the crowd and put the mind of the crowd at ease. At this point, the assembled crowd on both banks of the river was waiting for a signal to rush the mission.

Chevrier, who had always maintained good relations with Governor[34] Chonghou, took Vincent Wu with him and went to the high mandarin's house to ask for protection and to beg him to publish without delay the results of the local authorities' search that had just taken place and also to publish measures necessary for general security. He went home peacefully

---

xenophobic like the other mandarins in Tianjin and did not believe the unfounded accusations against the sisters. But afraid to compromise himself in the eyes of the crowd, he did not dare to act.

34. In fact, Chonghou was the superintendent of trade for the northern ports, that is, the three northern treaty ports. (AS)

without being disturbed by the crowd. Taking advantage of this lull, he began to pray his breviary.

Hearing the rioting crowd's cries of rage, the consul finally thought that he had to leave aside his passive stance and take immediate action. Hastily he sent his chancellor Mr. Simon and a Chinese scholar to Chonghou to ask him for armed protection. The latter sent him just three insignificant police officers with some men. When he saw this, the consul screamed, "What! I asked him for soldiers and he sends me policemen!" Very angry, he sent them away. It was after twelve; Chevrier was eating with Vincent Wu when, suddenly in five different places of the city, the bell was heard as a general call. Firefighters and professional troublemakers armed with swords and spears rushed towards the church. A cavalryman, surrounded by a huge following, appeared in the middle of the crowd and was greeted by frenzied acclamations. He pointed with his finger at the consulate and the mission. It was General Chen Guorui.

Finally aware of the danger, the French consul took an energetic decision to ward off the disaster. Armed and followed by his chancellor also in uniform and armed, he left the consulate through a secret door in order to go to the governor, whose palace was not far, and to demand the immediate intervention of the army. Chonghou declared himself unable to calm the stirred-up crowd; he was already unable to save the missionaries, but he strongly urged Fontanier not to leave his residence, saying, "Here I vouch for your life; you will be killed only after me!" The consul, worrying more about his guests, Mr. and Mrs. Thomassin, and the institutions entrusted to his protection than about himself, became indignant at the governor's advice. He left with Mr. Simon. Almost immediately they met the sub-prefect. Fontanier asked him to calm the crowd down. The mandarin answered, "It is none of my business." Then the consul fired his revolver, but missed him and hit his servant, who fell down fatally injured. The crowd screamed, "He killed one of us! Kill him!"

Back-to-back the two men, using their swords, were soon pierced through with spears; they still had the strength to inch their way through the crowd and arrive at the consulate, where they fell down bathed in their own blood. It was almost two o'clock.

The crowd was in front of the residence; at that moment, the gang of more than two hundred official rioters forced their way through the crowd; having arrived before the closed gates, they banged on them very loudly and forcefully. When the doors were about to give way, Chevrier decided to go and open them himself so as to harangue the attackers.

Seeing the priest so calm and dignified, they had a moment of hesitation; but as soon he had said his first words, the rabble rushed into the yard screaming fiercely. Chevrier and Wu, who remained at Chevrier's side, scarcely had time to flee into the church and close all its doors. The two priests gave each other absolution. One of the doors having broken down under the violence of the blows, both fled to the sacristy and escaped through a window which faced the garden of the consulate, and then they hid behind some rocks near where Thomassin and his wife were already lying on the ground. The rioters immediately attacked the two priests and killed them in a horrible way. After that, the rabble began to ransack the buildings, both of the consulate and the mission, taking all that could be carried away, and then setting fire to the buildings.

The killers, whose program seemed to have been very precise, did not waste any time. They crossed the Grand Canal on the bridge made with ships guarded by General Chen Guorui himself, and then they went to the Sisters' place (Renzitang or House of Mercy) located about five or six hundred meters to the south of the residence.

In a minute, they broke the doors down. They killed the ten Sisters and set fire to the building. Some twelve children died of suffocation from the flames; the others, older, were brought to the sub-prefect on the pretense of saving them.

Some corpses were cut up, supposedly to uncover proof of the crimes. The tragedy of the orphanage ended at three o'clock.

Other victims succumbed. Mr. de Chalmaison, a French businessman, informed about the Sisters' danger, hastened to go and save them, but he was intercepted on his way and was torn to pieces. His wife, dressed as a Chinese woman, ventured to find her husband and was also killed by the rioters in the street. Among Europeans, soldiers or policemen on their way back from the concessions killed three Russians. Among the Chinese people, three or four lost their lives; many more were wounded.

The day following this atrocious crime, the civil authorities began to fear its consequences. The governor went to offer the Europeans of the concessions the protection of his army. It was a little late. The English consul took it upon himself to have the victims' corpses collected and put into coffins and he had them buried temporarily in the English cemetery. Days of anxiety for the mission in Peking: the apostolic vicar, Bishop Guierry, was at the Vatican Council, and the only European priest in Tianjin had succumbed. Who was going to take care of this appalling mess?

Finally, on 15 July two missionaries from Peking, Father [Alphonse] Favier and [Pascal] D'Addosio, were permitted to come to Tianjin with the French chargé d'affaires, to discuss with the local authorities this sad problem of necessary reparations. The difficulties were extraordinary; the massacre coincided with the disastrous war between France and Germany, which made it impossible for France to demand reparations proportionate to the enormity of the crime. First, it was agreed that the victims be buried in the former French consulate. This happened on 3 August. The day before, the coffins were transported from the English cemetery to the Church of Our Lady of Victories, which the fire had not completely destroyed.[35] On 3 August all the French people of the concessions came and attended the funeral. The two banks of the river were filled with spectators. Thierry gave the last absolution and some words were spoken.

Then the settling of the case began, while awaiting the arrival of the new head of the mission in Peking.

Delaplace, Apostolic Vicar of Peking

We saw that Delaplace learned of his transfer from Zhejiang to Peking at the Vatican Council. Immediately after the promulgation of the pope's infallibility, the bishop, aware of the sad events in Tianjin, lost no time in sailing back to China. On 1 November 1870 he entered Peking.

The first thing that he had to settle was the delicate question of indemnities. The governmental authorities already paid some money to the chargé d'affaires as compensation for the material damage suffered by the mission. Another sum of money had also been offered for the victims. Delaplace, who had to express his opinion on the negotiations that had taken place during his absence, wrote a letter to the French chargé d'affaires that showed his noble feelings.

He said that in the tragedy of Tianjin, he saw three things:

> 1. An atrocious crime; 2. a cruel insult carried out against all the Europeans generally and particularly against the French people and against the Catholic missionaries; 3. ruinous damages to our properties in Tianjin. The crime must be punished, the insult repaired, the damages compensated. The punishment of the crime does not concern me: it is a task for the Chinese plenipotentiaries and mandarins. As for the reparation of the insult, I have both the right and the task of demanding a solemn and lasting measure, which guarantees the future peacefulness of our institutions. I would like to see a monument

---

35.   The Our Lady of Victories Church was located at Wanghailou and commonly known as the church of that location. (AS)

erected by imperial decree with inscriptions that stigmatize and disgrace the troublemakers responsible for the massacres.

As for the paid indemnities, we accept the sum granted as compensation for the destruction of our buildings, if the conditions we demanded are met. That is to say that we will not rebuild so long as the situation has no better guarantees.

As for the moneys granted to compensate for the human lives, we refuse them with disdain. We are repelled to accept this payment for blood, because of this principle that when missionaries or Daughters of Charity give themselves for the missions, they do so in order to give their work, their sweat, their life; in order to give them, not to sell them!

The negotiations dragged on because of the obstinacy of the Chinese authorities who refused to make amends. Some notable mandarins were removed or simply given another place. Some twenty rioters, who were taken instead of the real villains, were executed.

Delaplace therefore refused to rebuild the church. But because it was necessary to provide worship and ministry to the European and Chinese Christians of Tianjin, he used the money for the material damage to build a church in the French Concession.

The church was finished before the end of 1872 and was dedicated to Saint Louis, king of France.

It did not take the Sisters long, after having somewhat overcome their intense anxiety, to come and take back the place and role of their ten martyred colleagues. But, because the Chinese would have been suspicious of an orphanage, they preferred to open a hospital open to everyone. On 27 September 1874 Delaplace settled them in the hospital that had just been built.

As to the missionaries, they did not back away from any difficulty facing them. As soon as they could, they gathered the Christians who were dispersed in the storm, restored their hope and strengthened their faith. Father Pierre Feng distinguished himself in this arduous task.

The year 1895 marked the twenty-fifth anniversary of the massacre in Tianjin, but Our Lady of Victories had not yet risen from its ruins. This saddened the missionaries and the Christians very much. The condition laid down by the bishop long before had not been met. China continually refused to make amends for the crime of 1870. The minister of France of that same period used all his talents as a diplomat to arrive, if not at true moral reparation, at least at a symbolic gesture which could be considered as such. Indeed, the passage of time had already blurred the memories of the events. The gesture consisted in the permission granted by the government to erect near the church a stele on which would be engraved the 1870 decree of Emperor Tongzhi (1862-1874) to assess blame for the massacres of June 1870 and to order punishment of the guilty parties. It was a little thing if one remembers Delaplace's demands. But was it not asking too much from a pagan government that it beat its breast before the whole world? According to Chinese tradition, an adversary must never be cornered without a way out, even if he is evidently wrong, but always some way out must be left for him, even if only a fiction.

In any event, if Delaplace (died in 1884) had been present, he would surely have accepted this arrangement. It was possible now without any problem to return to work and rebuild the church. A year later in 1896, the church was finished according to the initial plan. The remains of Chevrier and his companions in martyrdom were buried in its foundations.

Let us now leave Tianjin and go to Peking to see the works realized in the capital under the leadership of the new apostolic vicar.

Evangelization Activities in Peking

Orphanages

One of the first institutions that Delaplace founded in Peking was at Chala (Zhalan) for orphaned boys. There, under the direction of a priest, he gathered the children weaned from the wet-nurses in order to form them little by little for gardening jobs and for ordinary professions, so as to enable the boys, once they were adults, to earn a living.

The property of Zhalan (Chala, the former cemetery of the Jesuits), less than a kilometer from the gates of Peking, was used as a country house for the missionaries of the Beitang.

The Daughters of Charity, after arriving in Peking in 1862, had set up works of the Holy Childhood in the Beitang, but nothing had been done for the sick. The bishop took care of this need by founding Saint Vincent's hospital in the shadow of the (former) cathedral of the Nantang. This institution, destroyed during the tragic events of 1900, was afterwards transferred to the Beitang.

The Indigenous Religious Sisters, Called Sisters of Saint Joseph

Delaplace's most important work was the founding of a community of Chinese religious Sisters under the patronage of Saint Joseph, who therefore were called "Josephines." Their task was the Christian education of female children and catechumens. He began to think of founding it when he was at the Vatican Council, where several apostolic vicars of China were debating this idea. No one had ever tested this idea and several people foretold a sure collapse. Others, on the contrary, and Tagliabue from Zhengding was among them, urged Delaplace to try. Delaplace hesitated and thought about it for two years. The community was born in 1872 in the Nantang, with the help of the Daughters of Charity serving in Saint Vincent hospital. These Sisters were the educators of the first young girls who were to form the new community.

Hospital

It is easy to guess that the Daughters of Charity shared with them the mentality that was driving their own community. The new Sisters' motherhouse was built near Saint Vincent's hospital and was transferred in 1900 to the southern part of the Beitang.

The goal aimed at by Delaplace, when creating this modest institution, was fully attained. In all the parishes that had some importance, the principal occupation of the Sisters was to teach little girls and women catechumens, whom the missionaries sent to them. Later on, the Sisters would establish dispensaries in places that were far from big towns.

The Josephines spread out not only in all the Vincentian vicariates which had been formed by successive divisions of the mission of Peking, but many other Chinese missions adopted the rules made up by Delaplace in order to create similar communities. As a result, quite a few small communities known under other names were only extensions of the institution founded by Delaplace.

The Printing Press of the Beitang

Delaplace was not the first one to have the idea of founding a printing press at the Beitang. It had existed since the Jesuits' former Peking mission. They had some works of piety engraved on plates. It was a very primitive system, convenient only for printing Chinese characters carved in wood.

There is quite a difference with the letters of the European alphabet, for which loose metal characters are used to set type.

Mouly had already thought of it, though he lacked the means to do it. When he came back from Europe in 1862, he brought along a small hand-operated printing machine, with which only a few books were printed, among them a *Grammatica Latina* and a *Vocabularium sinicum*, and that with great difficulty.

Delaplace found the printing shop in such an underdeveloped state and he in turn devoted so much energy to it, that in justice it can be said that his episcopacy has the honor of giving birth to the Beitang printing press.

A printing press was needed all the more because neither Peking nor Tianjin had one. Delaplace asked Paris for two lay brothers to work fulltime at the printing press and he got them. Brother Auguste Maes, as soon as his appointment was known, went and prepared himself for his new job by working in the printing house of Chamerol in Paris.

This brother arrived in Peking on 14 March 1878. He was really the founder of the printing press, which he would manage for more than fifty years. The start was quite difficult, but by dint of hard work he completed what was mechanically most urgent. The first masterpiece that was produced on the new printing equipment that he had brought along with him was a brochure in Latin: *The acts of the diocesan synod held in 1878*. The missionaries received this book of forty pages with a feeling of relief: "Finally we can print!"

In 1885, Maes got a mechanical printing machine that took up all the space allotted to the printing house. They had therefore to expand. During the first years, the bishop himself became the supplier of the printing house with more than fourteen books that his apostolic zeal inspired him to write in order to spread faith and piety among the people.

After 1900, the printing press became huge. Some fifty workers were put to work every day as smelters, mechanics, bookbinders, book sewers, book stitchers and so on. This printing press for a long time was at the service of the Europeans, and more specifically the foreign legations. Later the large number of printing houses set up in Peking and Tianjin by Europeans, decreased the number of customers. But because the first goal of the printing house was to work for the spreading of the Faith, it went on being of service to the missions that requested its help.

Chapter 11

Vincentian Missions in North and Central China, 1870s-1880s

The Five Ecclesiastical Regions – The First Regional Synod of Peking – Foundation of the Trappist Monastery of Yangjiaping – Rebuilding the Dongtang – Delaplace's Death and Funeral – Tagliabue, Apostolic Vicar of Peking – The Transfer of the Beitang to Xishiku – The Saint Louis College in Tianjin – Coqset Appointed Apostolic Vicar of Jiangxi – Tagliabue's Death – The Scientist Armand David – Guierry, Apostolic Vicar of Zhejiang – The First Regional Synod of Hankou – Guierry's Death – Paul-Marie Reynaud, Apostolic Vicar – Reynaud's Episcopacy – The Second Regional Synod of Hankou – Philippe Meugniot, First Visitor of the Province of the Vincentians in China – The Beatification of Blessed Perboyre – The Virgins of Purgatory in Zhejiang – The Vicariate of Zhengding (Southwest Zhili) After Tagliabue's Departure for Peking – Sarthou and Afterward – The Society of Saint Paul

The Five Ecclesiastical Regions

At the Vatican Council, the Holy See had contemplated establishing the ecclesiastical hierarchy in China, and the question was submitted for study to the apostolic vicars of China present at the council. There was no result, however, probably because of lack of time. In 1874, the Sacred Congregation of Propaganda again examined the possibility of resolving the question, but decided against it because the time was not right. It proposed, however, a resolution for approval by Pope Pius IX that would little by little achieve that goal: it was the temporary division of the countries in the Far East into ecclesiastical regions.

On 23 June 1879 this plan was executed by a decree of the Cardinal Prefect of Propaganda, dividing China in the following way:

First region: Zhili (North, Southeast, Southwest), Manchuria and Mongolia.

Second region: Shandong, Shanxi, Henan, Shaanxi and Gansu.

Third region: Hunan, Hubei (East, Northwest, Southwest), Zhe-jiang, Jiangxi, Jiangnan.

Fourth Region: Sichuan (Northeast, Southeast), Yunnan, Guizhou, Tibet.

Fifth Region: Guangdong, Guangxi, Hong Kong and Fujian.

In total: 27 apostolic vicariates.

The decree ended with an order of the reigning pope, Leo XIII, by which he required the apostolic vicars of each region to meet the following year, when summoned by the dean of the bishops, in order to have a synod under the presidency of that same dean. Moreover, this first synod would have to decide on the place and time for subsequent synods.

The First Regional Synod of Peking

Therefore, as dean of the bishops of the first region, Bishop Delaplace summoned all the apostolic vicars of the region to gather on 18 April 1880. He sent them a questionnaire in which he mentioned the principal points that he intended to propose for the deliberations of the synod.

On the set day, the apostolic vicars: Bishop Tagliabue, C.M., of Southwest Zhili (Zhengding); Bishop Bax, C.I.C.M., of Mongolia; Bishop Dubail, M.E.P., of Manchuria; Bishop Gonnet, S.J., pro-vicar of Southeast Zhili, *sede vacante*, each bringing with them two priests of their own vicariate, gathered in the Beitang.

The opening of the synod was done very solemnly, because Delaplace wanted to give this assembly all possible brilliance. The different decrees produced by the synod related to three principal themes, which are mentioned here without going into details:

First Theme: The local clergy – there were five decrees.

Second Theme: Ministering to the Faithful – there were two decrees and a proposal regarding the foundation of a monastery of monks dedicated to prayer and penance.

Third Theme: Standardizing the ways of spreading the faith – there were two decrees.

The synod lasted for three weeks from 18 April to 9 May 1880.

Foundation of the Trappist Monastery at Yangjiaping

Another initiative of Delaplace's was the introduction of the first Trappists in China. For a long time, he had been dreaming of establishing in his mission a monastery of monks or nuns devoted to prayer and works of penance, so as to give an idea of monastic life in contrast to the austerities of bonzes and lamas. Actually, it was under his inspiration that the first synod expressed the wish for such an institute.

In 1872, the offer by a distinguished benefactress gave substance to the bishop's dream: the daughter of Count de Stolberg, Miss Sophie Stolberg, whose conversion to Catholicism had stirred a much comment, offered Delaplace part of her inheritance for the foundation of a monastery of monks or nuns in China, whichever would be the bishop's choice.

The bishop began to look for the necessary personnel to fulfill the wish of the generous donor. In June 1878, he talked to several Carmelite monasteries in France and he thought that it was so certain that he was going to succeed that he had the foundations of their future lodging laid in Tianjin, behind the newly erected hospital of Saint Louis. To his great surprise, his initiative failed.

Because of this failure he halted the work in Tianjin. Then, thinking things over, he thought that a Cistercian convent resembled the Carmelites most. First, he consulted the Cardinal Prefect of Propaganda about the appropriateness of such an undertaking, and he received from him not only permission but also encouragement. His request to the abbey at Staouëli, in Algiers, met with a refusal.

Consequently, Delaplace ordered Favier, who was in France at that time, to continue approaching monasteries to that end. Having knocked at doors of several monasteries without success, Favier went to the Abbey of Sept-Fons, where he finally won the day. On 21 February 1883 he signed a temporary contract with the abbot determining the principal conditions of the foundation. The result was not long coming. Dom Ephrem, with a brother, arrived in Peking on the following 11 June. The place chosen to build the monastery was the hamlet Yangjiaping, located in a valley two days to the northwest of Peking. A few priests and Brothers came and joined the first two. The beginning was very tough, because of how hard it was for the monastery to be self-sufficient and to create for themselves the necessary resources for their life there. That is why during the first twenty years the vicariate of Peking supported the monastery. Later on, a mountain covered with apricot trees was added to this property and also a narrow valley that could be cleared and cultivated.

As for vocations, from the beginning, the Cistercians' only problem was that there were too many candidates to choose from. Having lived modestly as an experiment under the direction of Ephrem, the monastery was erected into a priory in 1886 with Dom Marie-Bernard as prior. Later on in 1891, this priest was appointed abbot and the monastery took the name of Our Lady of Consolation. The small mustard seed had become a big tree. It would spread out first to Japan, where it was to give birth to the monastery Our Lady of the Lighthouse; then later, to a priory in Zhengding, under the name of Our Lady of Joy.

Rebuilding the Dongtang

In 1879, Delaplace decided to build a church before his death to honor Saint Joseph, which, though the last to be erected, would nevertheless be the most beautiful church in Peking. The procurator of the vicariate, Favier, drew up the plans. The first stone was laid on 20 July 1879 but work was interrupted for some time because of the lack of resources. The building was finished only in 1884.

In the course of the construction, the authorities saw that the church would have towers like the Beitang, and that there would be a stairway to the top. Some mandarins climbed to the top and noticed that from there, as from a mountain top, one could see far into the distance to the West and South. They wanted the bishop to modify the plans. Delaplace did not want to yield on this point. According to him, any concession on this point would have given the authorities a pretext to raise questions again concerning the towers of the Beitang.

Delaplace's Death and Funeral

Delaplace's last public action was the blessing of the Dongtang church. The date chosen was 5 May 1884, Saint Joseph's patronage day, and it was done very solemnly. The chargés d'affaires of France, Spain and Belgium had already taken their places in the nave, and the Faithful packed the church. The brass band of the minor seminary welcomed the bishop at the doorway of the residence.

His face radiant with joy, the prelate, in a loud voice, preached, sang the Pontifical Mass, gave the papal blessing, and presided over the banquet that followed, drank to the health of the important persons who had come to enhance the glamour of the festivity through their presence and moreover led evening prayers. One would have said that he had come back to the days of his youth. Alas! This was only the last glow of a torch near extinction.

At about four o'clock in the afternoon, immediately after the evening prayers that he had just led in the new church, he was worrying about the critical state of a sick Sister in the hospital of the Nantang and wanted to visit her before going back home, though perspiring profusely and tired after the long ceremonies of the day. He shivered through the night, the next day he felt dizzy. Strict with himself and used to suffering, he dragged himself around the whole week to attend to the activities of the community; he went about his ordinary business and did not want to go and see a doctor.

On Monday 12 May it was with much difficulty that he wrote a letter to the Christians as their bishop, regarding an encyclical from the pope. On 14 May all were amazed that he did not celebrate Holy Mass, but assisted at one in the chapel of the seminary. His entourage became alarmed. The sick man lay down in bed, never to get up again. Despite the doctor's care, the illness became worse. On 19 May seeing that some confreres were whispering with the doctor, he asked, "Are you thinking of giving me the last rites? Please don't wait till I have lost consciousness." Then the confreres suggested giving them immediately. He said, "I'm ready, thanks be to God!" Then he asked for a quarter of an hour to prepare himself and received the last rites with much devotion from the hands of the priest he had appointed.

On May 24 1884 Delaplace died at ten o'clock in the morning. He was sixty-four, had been living in China for thirty-eight years, six of which as a missionary in Jiangxi, and also in Jiangxi two years as its apostolic vicar, then sixteen in Zhejiang and fourteen in Peking.

This magnificent bishop's burial was no less solemn than the one of his predecessors, Mouly, near whom a tomb had been prepared in the cemetery of Zhengfusi.

With Delaplace a personality of the first order had disappeared. His episcopacy had been outstanding because of the wonderful organization he had introduced into the mission of Peking. His word was rich with meaning, brilliant in form and always full of spiritual originality. A tireless worker, austere religious person, man of duty and punctuality, he did not waste the grand gifts he received from God. But there is no perfection in this world. We must recognize indeed that Delaplace had been, in several instances, a little too rigid when asserting some rights of the Church. A more supple attitude might have made some negotiations easier.

Table 11.1 Inventory of Vicariate of Peking, 1884

Catholic population	32,044
Baptisms	
Children of Christians	1,746
Children of pagans at point of death	8,715
Adults	770
Catechumens with a good intention	1,011
Places of worship	
Churches with a residence	25
Public chapels	128
Oratories	132
Priests	
European Vincentians	15
Chinese Vincentians	12
Chinese diocesan priests	12
Lay brothers	4
Sisters	
Daughters of Charity	32
Sisters of Saint Joseph	31
Hospitals	3

Tagliabue, Apostolic Vicar of Peking

On his deathbed, Delaplace appointed Father Coqset pro-vicar during the vacancy of the see; therefore, it was he who managed the vicariate of Peking until the nomination and installation of the long-awaited new incumbent.

On 5 August 1884 a pontifical decree moved Tagliabue from Zhengding to Peking. He left Zhengding on 5 December of the same year, without noise or pomp. At the moment indeed that he took possession of his see, the war between France and China had just broken out, because the

French armies had occupied Tonkin. From then on, relations between the two countries were severed. This state of war boiled down to a dispute of little importance, though it made many people at the mission of Peking apprehensive. But in fact the Chinese government and the people did not cause the mission any trouble.

The Transfer of the Beitang to Xishiku

The question of the transfer of the institutions of the Beitang to another place had already been discussed several times during Delaplace's episcopacy. When the young Tongzhi had reached his majority in 1872, the regent Cixi, his mother, had to think about leaving the imperial palace. Because she she did not want to lose her dominating influence at the court, she wanted a residence that was not too far away. She had set her heart on the Nanhai Park, near the Beitang, and therefore she worked to acquire this property.

Proposals were therefore made to the finance minister, who refused to go to the mission of Peking and intervene. Then the bishop of Peking was invited very politely by the Office of Foreign Affairs to discuss some important business. Delaplace went there and was received by three high officials, one of whom was Chonghou, whom we know already. These mandarins expounded to the prelate that the emperor had plans to build in the Nanhai Park that were going to include the Beitang. That such was the reason why the Chinese government asked the mission to please give that institution up in return for some compensation or indemnity. The bishop answered that for a question of that importance, he needed some days to think it over and that he would send them his answer by letter.

Three days later, the bishop sent the Zongli Yamen a polite, but negative answer. In that letter he said, "I cannot convince myself that, in peacetime, we will be expelled from the Beitang, where long ago the hand of Emperor Kangxi has placed us. . . . Soon I have to leave for Europe; there I will deliberate with my ecclesiastical superiors and with the French government. . . . Finally, in no case will we ever agree to any indemnity, any exchange."

A few days later, on 10 October, two members of the Yamen in person brought a reply to the bishop's answer. It said in substance, "The point is not to expel the missionaries, as you seem to suspect." Then there were words of praise for the emperors who had been the benefactors of the mission and compliments to the missionaries whose behavior always had been impeccable towards the court. "As for the costs of moving and building, of course the emperor will take care of them. There is no doubt that you could settle this business."

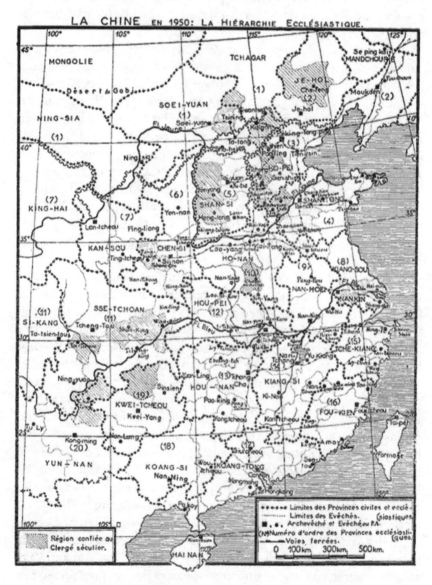

Map 11.1 China's Ecclesiastical Divisions, 1950

After having read this document, Delaplace denied that he alone could take care of this thing and renewed his assurance that once he had arrived in Europe, he would do his utmost so that the problem would be settled to everybody's satisfaction, "so long as, during my absence, you touch nothing and keep the status quo until my return." The mandarins consented to this condition.

But when Delaplace was in Europe, Tongzhi died prematurely on 13 January 1875. A new regency began immediately for the Guangxu emperor (1875-1908), Tongzhi's successor, who was underage. Therefore, it was no longer necessary to build a palace for Cixi, regent again. Thereupon, the discussions were stopped for the moment and the question of a transfer seemed buried for good. We are going to see that ten years had not yet passed, when, in similar circumstances to the previous ones, the question was raised again, this time with a result that in no way displeased the missionaries.

This digression took us away from our topic, which was Tagliabue's episcopacy in Peking. It was necessary in order to explain the bishop's own steps in the question of the transfer.

During the few months that the war lasted, Tagliabue, confined to Peking, decided to offer the Faithful of the city the blessing of a retreat, which had been remarkably effective in Zhengding. During the winter of 1884–1885 until Easter, more than five hundred Christians of both sexes took part in this retreat. When peace was once again established, the missionaries were able to busy themselves with their habitual ministry.

Here we will consider the appointment and the consecration of a new bishop, chosen from among the missionaries of Peking, Father Sarthou.

Hippolyte Sarthou, born in Doazit (Landes) on 22 April 1840 was admitted to the Congregation in Paris on 1 July 1861 and was ordained on 27 May 1866. After teaching in the major seminary of La Rochelle for four years, he was assigned to China, where he arrived on 16 November 1870. Having fulfilled several important assignments in the vicariate of Peking, he was the pastor of the Nantang when he received his nomination as bishop of Myriophis and apostolic vicar of Zhengding and successor to Tagliabue by decree of 16 January 1885. Tagliabue himself consecrated him in Zhengding on 26 April 1885. Later we will follow Sarthou's activities in his new diocese.

In that year 1885, it was the young Guangxu emperor's turn to reach his majority. Obviously, the regency was to come to an end and Cixi found herself in conditions similar to the ones that, in 1872, forced her to look for a residence near the court. It is recorded that, one day, she got angry over the question of the Beitang and said, "Finally, will it ever be possible to settle this problem? I charged several mandarins with it and they have done nothing. Now I will give the task to Li Hongzhang. We will see what he is able to do."

The skilled viceroy, once he had received this task, put his heart into succeeding. In order to succeed, he first wanted to know Rome's opinion. To do that, he sent a foreigner to Rome, an English resident of Tianjin, [John] Dunn, to inquire into this question.

The result of this survey by the delegate was that the pope was not opposed to the transfer of the Beitang, but that he would do nothing by himself without the agreement of the bishop in Peking.

Tagliabue, knowing the pope's opinion indirectly, adopted in the end an attitude quite different from his predecessor. The question of the Beitang seemed already settled in principle, when the negotiations were started. If Delaplace had known all this, he would probably have been less rigid in his refusal to negotiate.

By the way, the bishop did not handle this matter directly. He entrusted it to his right-hand man, Father Favier, who had the gift of dealing with the "high and mighty" and who, moreover, had a good relationship with Li Hongzhang. He traveled to Rome to settle all the details and was back in the capital on 10 November 1886. When all the difficulties had been overcome, the *Journal Officiel* [36] in Peking published an imperial decree about the transfer of the Beitang to the imperial court by the Catholic mission of Peking on 3 December. In this decree, which we will not quote, all the reasons of the transfer were given and there was an explanation of how it would be executed in harmonious agreement between the two parties. In this way the public was completely informed about this event, which was of extreme interest to the people of Peking.

It was even said that the indemnity would be paid in several installments, so that it would be possible to begin the construction immediately. "Bishop Tagliabue has shown great zeal. That is the reason why he will receive the 'distinguished medal second class' (a kind of decoration). Favier and Dunn will receive one of the third class, and they will also receive a gift of two thousand taels, which is to be given them by the viceroy. As for the others who have helped, they will also be rewarded." Then came the closing formula, "Have respect for this."

The location for the new Catholic mission was in the Xishiku quarter, six or seven hundred meters from the old Beitang. It was almost double the previous property at seven and a half hectares.

---

36.   Usually known as the Peking Gazette. (AS)

It was agreed that the emperor would take possession of the old Beitang in two years. It was necessary to wait for the thaw in order to dig the foundations. In March 1887, the first blow with the pickaxe was struck, and the work began enthusiastically. Thanks to the leadership of Favier, who directed the work, the ceremony of laying the first stone took place on 30 May.

It was not long before the government found itself in a difficult position. On the one hand, Guangxu wanted to assume power as soon as possible and the empress wanted to live in her new palace, but, on the other hand, they were restrained by the two years granted to the missionaries, who were asked several times to work faster. Finally, the minister of France promised that the old Beitang would be evacuated in February 1888. The government was pleased and granted additional money, because the quickened pace required it.

The work did progress quickly. Favier, both architect and director of the building sites, made it possible for many teams to work at the same time (fourteen hundred workers). Asked again to push the final February date forward, he speeded up the work so that the keys of the old Beitang were given to the Zongli Yamen in December 1887.

The new cathedral was finished ten months later, and the solemn blessing took place on 9 December 1888. The cathedral in Peking was at that time the biggest church in China. Its total length was eighty-four meters, the width of the transept thirty-three meters, the width of the nave twenty meters and the height under the keystone twenty-two meters.

The main door has on its gable the inscription "cijian" meaning "built by the emperor." On the esplanade in front of the façade two distinctive imperial yellow-colored pavilions were erected, sheltering two white marble steles, which carried the complete imperial decree mentioned above to memorialize the transfer.

The Saint Louis College in Tianjin

In the year 1887 in Tianjin, Tagliabue began a day school for the children in the European concessions, who were becoming more and more numerous. This school took the name Saint Louis College, which it retained till the day we write these lines, though the school changed hands. In the beginning, two priests were appointed for it: Father Claude-Marie Guilloux, later on visitor of the Vincentians, and Father Geurts, the future apostolic vicar of East Zhili. The subjects that were taught were French,

English, and all the subjects of commercial education, the only useful and practical formation for the kind of students attending that school.

The Marist Brothers, called in by the Vincentians of Peking, took over Saint Louis College after their arrival in China in 1891. Under their leadership it was to become very famous throughout North China.

Coqset Appointed Apostolic Vicar of Jiangxi

The province of Jiangxi asked a new sacrifice from the mission in Peking. On 29 June 1887 a decree from Rome appointed Father Coqset bishop of Cardica and apostolic vicar of South Jiangxi to replace Rouger, who died earlier in Paris on 31 March.

Auguste Coqset, born in Ambleny (Aisne) on 28 June 1847, entered the Congregation in Paris on 1 October 1866, and was ordained in Dax on 8 June 1871. First, he was placed in the diocese of Algiers and taught in the "Lavigerie" seminary in Kouba for four years; then, at his request, he was sent to China. He arrived in Shanghai on 21 March and went immediately to Peking, where he held several posts, the last of which was as pastor of the Nantang.

Coqset wished to be consecrated in the church whose pastor he had been for two years. So it was in the old church of the Nantang that on 16 October 1887 Tagliabue, assisted by Bishop Sarthou of Zhengding and Bishop Reynaud of Zhejiang, consecrated him bishop.

Coqset went to his post without delay. On the following 5 December he was in Ji'an taking possession of the vicariate of South Jiangxi. Soon we will meet him there again.

Tagliabue's Death

The Sisters in Chala asked the bishop to give the children of their institution a retreat. He was always ready to minister to souls and especially to the most humble, so, he offered to hear confessions. By fulfilling this act of charity in a cold and humid sacristy, he got the illness that led him to his grave eight days later. He had contracted typhoid fever complicated by pneumonia. He died on 13 March 1890 surrounded by his confreres and strengthened by the last rites, received in perfect lucidity. His funeral was similar in everything to the ones of his predecessors in the see of Peking.

A faithful imitator of Saint Vincent, Tagliabue did his best his whole life to keep in the background and to pass unnoticed. He succeeded partially. The exceptionally brilliant role played by Favier, his right-hand man in all important matters, masked, we might say, the bishop's role. In fact, Tagliabue was really the head who guided all the difficult negotiations; his ardent pro-vicar was only his strong right hand. But the bishop, instead of taking offence at Favier's popularity, supported his confrere in all the difficulties he met. Further, he was his defender against the malevolent accusations occasionally directed at Favier.

Let us leave the Vincentian missionaries' field of work in China for a moment and pay attention to a Vincentian who – a rare exception – was a true scholar and sage in his knowledge of the natural sciences while remaining all his life an authentic son of Saint Vincent.

The Scientist Armand David

Among the missionaries of that time there was one who, because of the number and the value of his scientific works, acquired universal fame and became one of the celebrities of the missions of China. Father Armand David is that man.

Armand David was born in Espelette, near Bayonne (Basses-Pyrénées), on 7 September 1826. His father was justice of the peace. He loved natural history and his conversations aroused in his son a decided taste for the study of animals, plants and flowers. The child loved thinking about the beauties of nature and, because he had faith, admired their Creator.

After his first Communion, his parents sent him to the minor seminary in his diocese. Wishing to devote himself to the foreign missions, he left his home in 1848 and entered the Congregation at Saint Lazare on 4 November, where he pronounced his vows on 5 November 1850.

He had not yet finished his theological studies, when need obliged his superiors to send him as a teacher of natural science to the College of Savona (Italy) under the direction of our confreres. In order to make his classes more interesting, he created a natural history exhibit, the prototype of those he would design later on. Several of the students who were taught by him in this college made a name for themselves as scientists and explorers. One of them, the Marquess Doria, became a famous scientific illustrator in Italy and founded the marvelous Museo Civico of Genoa, so admired by connoisseurs.

David was ordained in Savona in March 1853. After several years Etienne remembered that David had asked for the foreign missions, so he called him back from Italy to send him to China.

Back in Paris he began to prepare himself for his departure for China. One day Mouly, with whom he was to leave, took him to visit a great Sinologist, Stanislas Julien, who had the practice of going to the missionaries to get Chinese books. During the conversation, the bishop told the scientist that his colleague liked natural history. Immediately, Julien, who was interested in everything related to China, told the young priest, "I am going to use your abilities to the advantage of the French scientific community." Consequently he introduced him to several of his famous confreres, so that they could give him tasks. These scientists were all members of the Academy of Sciences. David promised them that he would do his utmost to satisfy their wishes.

After his arrival in Peking on 5 July 1862 David immediately began to explore the vicinity of the capital, as well as to prepare an exhibition room for physics and the natural sciences, which would be useful in the college he was sent to found in the Nantang. It was the way to keep his word to the members of the Muséum of Paris. His first shipments to Paris attracted much attention and his finds caused great surprise. The administrators of the Muséum sent him warm encouragement together with a financial subsidy to help him in his research.

Then the Muséum persuaded the minister of public instruction to ask the superior general of the Vincentians to permit David to postpone the establishment of the college of the Nantang and to make exploratory journeys into the less known provinces of China. Etienne granted permission and the minister honored the enterprise with the title "Scientific Mission" and sent the money necessary to cover expenses.

In 1866, David made his first journey, always on foot, followed by the famous Sandatchiemba, the Christian lama who had guided Fathers Huc and Gabet to Tibet. This journey in western Mongolia from March to October 1866 was used to study the flora, the wildlife and the geology of the High Plateaus. The numerous collections, brought back from this expedition, were sent to the Muséum, accompanied by notices and a travel journal with a geological itinerary, which was published in the *Nouvelles Archives*.

Back in Peking, David worked on his own museum, which became one of the marvels of the capital. It contained more than eight hundred birds, several beautiful mammals, some three thousand insects and butterflies, a herbarium and many mineralogical samples.

In 1868, David left Peking once more and went and explored Jiangxi for four months; then he went to Sichuan and to Tibet. The strain and the hardships during his journeys soon undermined his health so that he had to return to Europe in 1870. An unexpected improvement in his health allowed him to return to China in 1872 and to visit still some other provinces. But his health deteriorated to the point that it did not permit this kind of work anymore. He had to return to France in April 1874.

David recovered his health enough to live another twenty-six years in Saint Lazare, where he used his renewed energies to found a new exhibition hall of natural history, which, thanks to the numerous relations he had formed, achieved notable importance. He liked to bring to his museum the visitors who sometimes came from far away, or the students of Saint Lazare. It was a great pleasure for him to share with them his scientific knowledge. When viewing these superb collections, David gave free reign to his admiration for the God's Creative Power and he drew the visitors' attention to the richness of God's gifts.

If some people wondered why a missionary had devoted almost all his life to scientific matters, when there were all around him so many souls to be saved, they should have gone to the information desk. They would have been informed that his superiors had appointed David to this kind of work. They had understood that God had given him special talents and that it was their task to have those bear fruit for His greater glory. Consequently, David had undertaken nothing that had not been with the blessing of obedience. God called his scientist missionary back to heaven on 10 November 1900 in Paris, where he had been living humbly and normally as a faithful son of Saint Vincent after his return from China.

Let us return to the South, where we will meet again Mouly's former coadjutor, appointed apostolic vicar of Zhejiang.

Guierry, Apostolic Vicar of Zhejiang

We have seen that the two bishops, Delaplace and Guierry, had to go to the Vatican Council and that they received there on 28 June 1870 the decree that made them exchange vicariates. Guierry was back in Shanghai on 1 November 1870 and on the following 8 November took possession of Ningbo (Zhejiang), his new vicariate. When Delaplace was leaving China to go to Rome, he handed the administration of the vicariate to his pro-vicar, Father Montagneux. His successor's first act was to give the powers of pro-vicar to the same man. The choice was excellent, for Montagneux was a trustworthy man and a zealous missionary who had fulfilled important functions for two bishops.

Let us give here an example of this missionary's know-how in the face of unexpected difficulties. It was known that the horrible massacre of 21 June 1870 in Tianjin had provoked throughout the whole of the empire a violent current of hatred against foreigners. On 1 July 1870 ten days after the event, Montagneux wrote to Delaplace in Rome:

> The news from the North of China is disquieting. You have learned through my telegram the horrible tragedy in Tianjin. Though all seems quiet here in Zhejiang, if unmistakable punishment for the abominable crimes is not meted out, we might well feel the repercussions. I tremble for the Sisters in Hangzhou.

The expected repercussions were not long in coming. Alarming rumors were circulating among the people against the Europeans and became more serious day by day; soon they was abusing and threatening. Because there was no French consul in Ningbo, Montagneux went to the English consul and explained to him the seriousness of the situation, and proved to him that danger threatened not only the missionaries and the Sisters, but also all the Europeans whoever they may be. He begged the consul to please inform the governor so as to make him responsible for the mishaps that might happen.

The consul absolutely agreed with him and wrote to the mandarin along the lines indicated by the missionary. The governor, called Wen, had already handled several cases in favor of the mission. He took the matter in hand, drew up a proclamation for the people and sent the draft to the English consul in order to check if it was all right. The latter called in the pro-vicar and together they agreed to make some slight corrections in it, then they sent it back to the governor, who forcefully defended the Europeans and threatened with the most terrible punishments whomever would dare to disturb the public order and harm the Europeans in any way. As soon as this proclamation was known, all the rumors stopped.

That is what this modest missionary achieved; a person who said of himself that he was likely to spoil everything in the mission. The danger found him at his post and duty made him dare everything, in order to protect the people entrusted to his care as well as many other people from certain calamity.

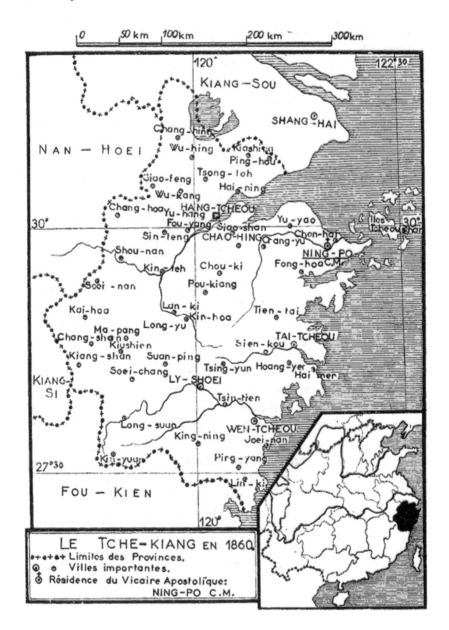

Map 11.2 Zhejiang in 1860

Guierry's first outing was a trip to Jiangxi to consecrate Bray in Jiujiang on 20 November 1870. Immediately after returning, he took up visiting Christian communities in his vicariate. He ministered first to the Zhoushan Islands. He landed in the small port of Dinghai where there was the residence of the priests and he was received solemnly in the minor seminary, located at one kilometer from the town. Its director was Father Jean-Henri Salvan, C.M.

In March 1871, the bishop was in Hangzhou, capital of Zhejiang, where a hospital was already being built to be opened on the following 24 April. He went to Jiaxing and to Chefubang, two Christian communities that were already quite prosperous. The Christians there begged him to build a church for them. Because they were rather comfortably well off, the bishop told them that it was their task to work together to collect the amount necessary for the construction and that he would help with a small part.

In 1872, Guierry realized a project that his predecessor already had in his head, namely, to separate the seminarians of the major seminary from those of the minor seminary. The point was not yet to erect a major seminary; but only to allow the students of philosophy and theology to study in a residence where there were at least two priests, one of whom could teach their classes. The chosen site was Hangzhou, the capital, where the Christians were few. The pastor was Father Pang, a diocesan priest, and the assistant was Father [Jean-Baptiste] Barbier, a young confrere. Barbier was given the task of teaching sixteen or seventeen classes every week to two students of philosophy and two students of theology.

Later on, when their studies in theology were almost finished, the students would have a trial period of one year before being ordained; this probationary stage could consist of fulfilling the task of schoolteacher or catechist in designated residences. Sometimes they might even follow the missionary on his mission tours. This kind of formation would go on until the opening of a major seminary in Ningbo.

During 1872, Guierry made a second pastoral tour of the local communities, as he would continue to do every year till his death. He visited some districts twice a year. He went to Chefubang, with the intention of deciding on the location of the church discussed the year before. We remember that the bishop had encouraged the Faithful to share in the construction costs. Now the pastor, [André-René] Guillot, announced to the bishop that the Christians had given him 1,214 Chinese [*sic*, silver] dollars. In the light of their generosity, it was impossible to delay the construction any longer. During the bishop's stay, the plans were decided upon and on 1 June they began to destroy some buildings that were in the way. At the beginning of the following year the foundations were laid. The Faithful devoted themselves to transporting materials and to helping the bricklayers and the carpenters. By the autumn of 1873, one more church had been erected in the diocese of Zhejiang. It was opened and Guierry blessed it on 14 June 1875.

In June 1874, Guierry was called to Paris to attend the general assembly, which was to elect a successor for Etienne, superior general, who died on 12 March 1874. On 30 June the bishop, accompanied by Bishop Bray, sailed for France. They returned together too and arrived in Ningbo on 29 December 1874. They brought along two confreres, [Jean] Coursière for Jiangxi and [Claude-Maurice] Gontharet for Zhejiang.

Without delay, Guierry took up his pastoral visits again. In January 1875, he was in the Zhoushan Islands, where he had to meditate disputes that had arisen between Christians and pagans and also among Christians themselves. Going into these disputes would lead us too far afield. It is enough to say that he always tried to settle the disagreements out of court.

While the bishop was traveling through his vicariate, the pro-vicar remained in Ningbo, where the missionaries continually provided him with cases to solve. During the summer of 1875, Montagneux contracted a serious case of dysentery, of which he was never completely healed. Very much weakened and almost always suffering he had to slow down a great deal. Finally, on 20 February 1877 a violent attack carried him off. Montagneux was only fifty-two years old. He had spent twenty-six years in China in the midst of worries and activities of all kinds.

Here are the testimonies of his coworkers. Vincent Fu, C.M.: "What amazed me most in him was the strength of his character, amidst the innumerable difficulties and dangers he had to deal with. When every-thing around him was in turmoil, he was remarkably calm; he kept an eye on everything that concerned him; he gave courage and trust to all those around him."

Another one said, "How amiable he was toward everyone! Seeing him, you would not have believed that he was suffering and if his features had not betrayed the pain, you would have thought that his heart and body were free of any difficulty."

Delaplace wrote about him, "Obedience was for him the first virtue among all the others. I declare that for fifteen years; he has always exem-plified for me the saying of Saint [John] Climacus *"qui Christi imaginem superiori suo imposuerat* (he saw the image of Christ in his superior)."

His will was absolutely one with his superiors; with Montagneux it was unnecessary to give orders or even to express a wish; he intuited it and he offered himself. Maybe some rule displeased him, who would have imagined that? He executed it, he defended it, and he showed its advantages. Was there a dangerous post? It was for him."

The First Regional Synod of Hankou

The civil province of Zhejiang belonged to the third ecclesiastical region of China. Because Bishop [Eustachio] Zanoli, an Italian Franciscan, apostolic vicar of East Hubei, was the oldest consecrated bishop of the region, it was his task to convoke the regional synod, which, according to the decree of 1879, had to meet during the following year. Zanoli announced therefore by letter to all the apostolic vicars of the third region that the synod was to open on 8 April 1880 in Hankou.

Guierry went to the synod with his two theologians and with Bray from Northern Jiangxi. They were the only Vincentian bishops; the others were Franciscans and Jesuits. Here we will pass over the synodal decisions, all but one that is special to this region: "The missionaries will do their utmost to dissuade the Christians from cultivating poppies, from selling opium, and still more severely from using opium."

The synod held seven sessions. At the end it was agreed that the next synod would meet in five years again in Hankou.

Back home on 24 May Guierry wrote to Father Fiat, superior general, successor of Father Eugene Boré, "We were seven vicars apostolic, assisted by fourteen theologians. Though we were from four different orders or congregations, all was done as in a family and in the most cordial and edifying way. Therefore, everybody seemed delighted by the decisions which were taken and the decrees that were made."

Guierry's Death

His long and fatiguing travels wore the bishop out. It was the fate of all the bishops of that time: enormous territory to cover and the means of locomotion both slow and painful; that is the reason we see almost of all them die when they were not very old.

At the end of his episcopal journey of 1882, Guierry felt that he had developed edema; his strength was decreasing, he had lost appetite and could not sleep. The doctor ordered a month's rest, at the end of which he felt a little better, but he did not recover his full strength. He thought that he was no longer able to carry the load of his apostolic responsibilities so he asked to be relieved of them.

He presented his case to the Cardinal Prefect of Propaganda. He did not ask for a coadjutor but as if he had a premonition of his approaching end, he asked for a successor. To the superior general he wrote the same.

During the summer of 1883, he did not travel because of the swelling in his legs, but he exercised his ordinary ministry in the residence.

During the first days of August, a typhoon was blowing furiously and the high tide driven by the wind flooded the residence. Two feet of water covered the ground floor. The bishop, alone in his room, threw himself on his bed and waited till five o'clock in the morning, the time the tide was to recede. Despite the swellings in his legs, he had to go on foot. It was Sunday; he wanted to celebrate the Holy Sacrifice. During the day severe diarrhea came on and weakened him greatly. Nevertheless, he followed all the exercises of the day, presided over the meals, and prayed the breviary. At night, his room on the ground floor being uninhabitable, he had to go upstairs. His companions would have liked to call a doctor, but the streets were impassable.

During the night, the bishop was in very bad shape. On Monday, the doctor finally arrived; he noticed that the disease was very serious and wanted to call another doctor. At five in the morning his voice changed, he could not speak clearly anymore, words did not come and his faculties seemed to be lulled.

Then the last rites were given. At 6:30, he died peacefully. He passed away in the easy chair, where he had spent many nights, unable to stay in bed because of the heat. It was 8 August 1883. Guierry was fifty-eight years old. He had spent thirty years in China.

Before his consecration, Guierry had little knowledge of the life of a missionary in the countryside; he nevertheless understood the difficulties linked to the ministry of priests working among pagans; and when one of them asked his advice, he would give an answer as valid as the most experienced missionary might have given.

That he was hard on himself was clear from the continuous journeys he forced himself to take to know the needs of his vicariate; they were not pleasure trips. He was a man of the rule; he made people obey the rule by persuasion more than by force. He advised his missionaries to take good care of themselves when they were sick. He sent them what they wished for or what others had asked on their behalf.

Though he was a little shy and his natural talents were not like those of Delaplace, his zeal to spread the faith in his vicariate was not less than his predecessor. He had the merit to have opened the southern part of his vicariate. Actually, the inventory that follows gives proof that his zeal had been fruitful. All the works were quite developed, though the number of workers had not increased: new priests had arrived, but they only took the place of those who had died.

Table 11.2 State of Vicariate of Zhejiang, 1871 and 1883

Categories	Up to April 15, 1871	30 June 1872 - 30 June 1883
Christians	2,834	5,191
Children of the Holy Childhood	708	892
Totals	3,542	6,083
Adult baptisms	130	318
Catechumens	110	439
Localities served by missionaries	55	80
Churches	3	8
Chapels	23	35
Boys' schools		
Number of schools	18	33
Number of pupils	217	381
Girls' schools		
Number of schools	5	10
Number of pupils	33	256
Priests		
European Vincentians	9	9
Chinese Vincentians	2	3
Diocesan priests	3	3
Seminarians	5	

Latinists	12	
Daughters of Charity		
Europeans		27
Chinese		2
Postulants		3
Orphanages	3	3
Hospitals		
For men		3
For women		3

Paul-Marie Reynaud, Apostolic Vicar

After Guierry's death, his councilors opened his private papers among which they found an envelope sealed with red wax with this Latin inscription: Nomination of the pro-vicar of Zhejiang, to be opened only after my death before witnesses. When opened, the name of Father Paul-Marie Reynaud was read aloud.

What did the other missionaries think of the nomination of the youngest among them, someone who had not yet spent four years in the vicariate? We do not know. But the widespread sympathy he enjoyed among his confreres and the letters written to him by several European and Chinese confreres when they in no way foresaw that he would one day be placed at their head, convinces us that this nomination was received favorably.

Who was this young pro-vicar? Paul-Marie Reynaud, born in Sainte-Croix-en-Jarez (Rhône) on 12 April 1854, entered the Congregation in Paris on 19 May 1873, was ordained on 7 June 1879 and arrived in China on 24 September 1879. He remained in Ningbo more than two years both studying the language and learning how to minister in the parish. Young and full of fervor, he began to find this sedentary life boring.

On 7 July 1882 he was sent to Dinghai (the residence in the Zhoushan Islands) in order to substitute for Father Jean-Joseph Vaissière, director of the minor seminary, who was ill. But Vaissière was at the same time director of the district, in which two or three priests were working. For this reason, Reynaud also had to take an interest in the Christians. During the holidays he visited the three chapels on the island to meet the Christians. On his return from this excursion, which had lasted only a few days, he heard of Vaissière's death. This missionary's death was to change Reynaud's situation in Zhoushan from temporary to definitive.

A little later indeed, Guierry made him director of pastoral ministry on Zhoushan and its neighborhood, which included the minor seminary, the parish of Dinghai, and ministry to the Sisters. He neither coveted this position nor thought that he would be entrusted with its direction. Thus, when he heard the news, his surprise was huge and he was very displeased. He talked with his bishop about the resistance he felt toward taking on such a large responsibility. The latter understood him and promised him some quick help as soon as he had the possibility to do so.

A new missionary reached him on 2 October 1882. It was Father Bernard Ibarruthy, born in Bayonne (Basses-Pyrénées) on 7 March 1859, accepted in Saint Lazare on 26 September 1876 and ordained on 3 June 1882. In the following month of December, he was sent to Zhoushan with the duty of managing the minor seminary. This allowed the director to meet the Christians more easily. But this situation was to change completely after a few months.

Immediately after Guierry's death, Reynaud became pro-vicar, and his new functions required his presence in Ningbo. Consequently, it was necessary to name someone to replace him in Zhoushan.

Reynaud chose Father Antoine Heckman, from Alsace, who had been in China since 1876, and then called Father Ibarruthy from Zhoushan and entrusted him with the work of the procure of the vicariate.

Around the middle of March 1884, Reynaud, who thought that the interior walls of the Cathedral of the Assumption[37] were too bare, called some painters to decorate them with various shapes and colors.

He was busy with this work, when he received a letter from Father Meugniot dated 16 March, inside which there was a telegram that read, "Paul Reynaud appointed bishop, apostolic vicar of Zhejiang." This news spread quickly to the furthest parts of the vicariate. If Reynaud felt afraid to take up such a heavy load, the spontaneous explosion of sympathy and warm feelings from his missionaries must have been a powerful encouragement to accept these new responsibilities.

The two decrees by Propaganda appointing Reynaud bishop of Fussula and apostolic vicar of Zhejiang were dated 7 March 1884. These documents arrived in Ningbo on 11 May.

---

37. There were two churches and two residences in Ningbo, one in town where the cathedral was, the other one in the small harbor by the river. The apostolic vicars lived sometimes in one, sometimes in the other.

As soon as he had received the bulls, he fixed the date of the ceremony of consecration on 29 June, feast of his patron Saint Paul. The Cathedral of the Assumption was beautifully decorated with curtains and garlands. Eight days before the consecration, he left the residence in town for the one in Jiangbei where, through meditation and prayer, he prepared himself to receive the sacrament that was going to give him the dignity of a pontiff.

The consecrating bishop was Bishop Bray assisted by Bishop Garnier, S.J., from Jiangnan and Bishop Vos, C.I.C.M., from Mongolia.

The next day, another ceremony, less triumphant but no less touching, took place in Ningbo. Guierry had been buried in the cemetery of the mission. The wish of the pro-vicar, which was also the wish of the missionaries, was that the bishop's remains should rest near the church of Jiangbei. As soon as Reynaud received news of his nomination, he had the tomb prepared which would receive his predecessor's remains. He set the date for the interment on 30 June, the day after the consecration.

The four prelates went to the cemetery. Reynaud conducted the removal of the corpse; Garnier, who had been consecrated by Guierry, celebrated the High Mass. After the absolutions performed by the prelates, the coffin was lowered into the vault prepared for it.

Reynaud's Episcopacy

Less than three weeks after the ceremony, Reynaud went to Zhoushan to ordain two young Chinese priests. He invited three guests who were staying in Ningbo to accompany him, namely, Bishop Rouger, who had endured mistreatment as we mentioned above and had gone to Shanghai to take a rest, Father Anot, his companion, and Father Meugniot, the general procurator in Shanghai. On 18 July the ordination took place in the Church of Saint Michael in Dinghai and the following day, 19 July, the feast of Saint Vincent, Bishop Rouger pontificated.

The following 12 August, three confreres landed in Shanghai, Fathers Antoine Ganduglia [*sic* Canduglia], an Italian destined for Jiangxi, Paul Ferrant and Charles Mustel, both destined for Zhejiang.

On 6 October 1885 Reynaud lost one of his best Chinese priests. It was Father Vincent Fu, whom we have often mentioned. He was the first Chinese priest from the Zhejiang province. Born in Mapeng in April 1825, he was admitted to the Congregation in the seminary of Macao on 1 September 1843 and was ordained a priest in 1849 by Bishop Lavaissière. From that day until the last hour of his life, he showed himself worthy of his vocation.

He was trusted by Lavaissière who, when Fu was only a deacon, put him in charge of the seminary. Danicourt turned to him too, with a view to managing Zhoushan in the midst of troubles caused by the pagans. With Montagneux, he was the much-appreciated councilor of bishops Delaplace and Guierry; after the death of Montagneux, Fu became Guierry's right-hand man.

Fu, however, was no genius. When he was ordained a priest, he was weak in Chinese literature, but by dint of persevering study of the language, he managed to have such a thorough knowledge of it that the above-named bishops trusted him with writing their letters to the Chinese authorities, and they gave him several books to translate from Latin into Chinese.

The missionaries who lived with him said that they never found Fu idle; as soon as he had a free moment, you could see him with a book in his hands. His Chinese confreres trusted him completely and asked him for advice; all the European priests appreciated him just as much.[38]

Towards the end of 1885, Reynaud was invited to help with the consecration of Father Vic, first apostolic vicar of East Jiangxi. The ceremony took place in Fuzhou on 24 January 1886.

The bishops, present at the ordination, had examined together, during the days after the ceremony, some questions relating to the best means to further the Kingdom of God in their respective vicariates. One of the obstacles for the expansion of the gospel was of course the lack of missionaries, for which some remedy had to be found. After studying all the angles of the problem, the bishops conceived this plan: one of them would go to France to try to recruit personnel in the seminaries. The four bishops signed the plan, but it remained only on paper since the bishops feared that such a step could displease the superior general.

But if the plan was sleeping in some drawer, it became more precise and better thought out in the head of the bishop of Zhejiang, and when he thought that the time had come, he submitted it – as a personal idea – to Fiat.

The superior general answered him, "I am not convinced about the efficiency of the means you would like to use. Nevertheless, I would not think it bad that one of you come to France, after receiving permission from Rome." Reynaud told his fellow bishops of Fiat's answer, which if

---

38.   I point out, once and for all, that the main source of our history about the vicariate of Zhejiang is the monthly review *Le Messager de Ning-Po*, whose long-time editor was Father Boucherie, a diocesan priest of the vicariate.

not in favor of their plan, at least did not refuse to allow a trip by one of them, on condition of having Rome's permission.

On 19 October 1886 Meugniot informed Reynaud of Rouger's arrival in Shanghai, sick and in need of returning to France to care for his health. "But," he wrote, "I would not dare to leave him alone in the state he is in . . . would you be willing to go to France?" Obviously, Reynaud, the youngest of the bishops, would not have dared to propose himself as Rouger's companion. From that day on, there was an exchange of letters between Ningbo and Shanghai and between Shanghai and Paris. Finally, a telegram came and gave Reynaud the authorization to accompany Rouger to France. They left Shanghai on 23 December 1886 and arrived in Marseilles on 31 January.

From Reynaud's first days in Paris, his good will was put to good use. For that matter, it was to be made use of constantly during his stay in France. He gave conferences about the missions or about the Work of the Holy Childhood first in the churches of Paris, then in the dioceses where he went to visit the parents of his confreres working in Zhejiang.

On 15 July 1887 Reynaud returned to Ningbo bringing along two Vincentians, Joseph Donjoux for Jiangxi and Emile Barberet for Zhejiang.

But what happened the plan to recruit seminarians, which was the principal reason for this journey? Let us listen to the bishop himself explaining it to the superior general: "I have been criticized a great deal on my return in that I did not pursue my plan of recruiting seminarians in France for our missions. To do it with authority, I felt that I was too young and too alone. . . . Nevertheless, I have tested the waters . . . I have seen some young people, about whom I have gathered good information." One of these young people arrived indeed the following year.

The Second Regional Synod of Hankou

On 6 May 1880 at the time of leaving each other, the apostolic vicars who had participated in the first Synod of Hankou had decided that the following synod should meet in the same city after five years. Zanoli, who had presided over the Synod in 1880, died in 1883. In 1885, Propaganda gave Father Philippi, a Franciscan, the responsibility for convoking the second Synod. In March 1886, he informed his colleagues of the third region that the Synod would open on 8 May 1887 in Hankou. Reynaud, who was to be absent, nominated Father Heckman to take his place, without naming any theologians. Since Rouger had died at the beginning of 1887, it was Pérès who represented South Jiangxi.

The first session was held on 8 May and the last one on 17 May. On 12 May in the Church of Saint Joseph, a pontifical Requiem Mass was celebrated for the eternal rest of those who, present at the first synod, had died since then: Bishops Zanoli, Guierry, and Rouger; Fathers de Carli, O.F.M., Suarez, O.S.A., Villanova, O.S.A., and Vincent Fu, C.M.

There were twelve sessions. The decrees were arranged according to three titles: 1. The Clergy; 2. The Christians; 3. The Non-believers. There is no point in detailing here the chapters that came with these titles.

Everything was sent to Rome. The cardinals of Propaganda decreed on 19 December 1888 that the acts of the second Synod of Hankou were to be approved. Pope Leo XIII confirmed this recommendation.

In their last session, the members of the synod approved a motion that their next meeting would be held in 1892. It turned out, however, that the third synod would take place in Hankou twenty-three years later than originally planned. Reynaud himself was to preside over it. But before we can arrive at that date (1910), many events remain to be reported.

On 6 October 1888 a new recruit arrived in Ningbo. It was Pierre Louat, one of the young people the bishop had in mind at the time of his journey in France. Born in Givors (Rhône) on 2 February 1865, Louat was studying in the minor seminary of Verrière, when the bishop was there for some days, during which he gave several conferences to the students.

The result was that eight students asked for admission to Saint Lazare, in order to be sent to China. But, when they had heard that as members of the Congregation, it might happen that they would be sent elsewhere, they withdrew their applications. Pierre Louat, who had a family link with the bishop, arranged with the bishop that he could come to Zhejiang without passing through Saint Lazare.

That is what happened the following year. He made his internal seminary with the Chinese seminarians and continued his studies with them. He pronounced his vows on 28 November 1890 and was ordained priest on 21 June 1891.

Philippe Meugniot, First Visitor of the Province of Vincentians in China

At that time an important change took place in the Vincentian missions in China.

We saw earlier that every time a Vincentian missionary was appointed apostolic vicar by Rome, he became by that very fact the religious superior of all the confreres who were working under his jurisdiction in his vicariate. Moreover, the superior general gave him at the same time the powers of a visitor (or provincial); so, every Vincentian vicariate was a small province of the Congregation of the Mission. Consequently, the superior general appointed all the Vincentian predecessors of Bishops Lavaissière, Danicourt, Delaplace, and Guierry, visitors. It was the same in the vicariates of Jiangxi and Zhili. Only Reynaud, though religious superior of his confreres, was not named visitor. The superior general had another plan in mind.

His plan was to unite all these small provinces into one province. This plan was carried out when, in 1890, the superior general named Meugniot visitor of all the Vincentians in China, forming henceforth one single province called the Province of China. Meugniot kept his title and job as Procurator of the Vincentian Missions in China.

Philippe Meugniot was born in Viserny (Côte-d'Or) on 15 May 1844. His mother was the youngest Sister of the one who became Saint Catherine Labouré. Admitted in Paris on 9 August 1863, ordained a priest on 22 May 1869, he was a pastor in France for several years, notably in Saint Pons. He arrived in Shanghai on 16 September 1880 as procurator of the Vincentians in China. Then, ten years later, Meugniot, in addition to his role as procurator, became visitor of the Vincentians in China until June 1899, when he was recalled to France as assistant of the superior general.

The Beatification of Blessed Perboyre

During the year 1890, in Zhejiang like in all the other vicariates entrusted to Vincentians, great celebrations were held on the occasion of the beatification of Blessed John Gabriel Perboyre. A triduum was celebrated in the most important Christian communities of the vicariate. In Hangzhou, particularly, a touching circumstance reminded the missionaries and the Christians of the one who was being honored: it was the presence of the blessed martyr's sister. For many years Sister Gabrielle Perboyre devoted herself to the service of the poor and the sick in the hospital there. She had belonged to the first contingent of Daughters of Charity who arrived in Macao in 1847. Reynaud himself presided at the triduum celebrated in the city of Hangzhou.

The Virgins of Purgatory in Zhejiang

Both in the south and the north, there were many young women who wished to remain celibate and give themselves to works of charity. Not all could meet the necessary conditions for admittance to the Company of the Daughters of Charity. Some instruction or formation was required, but, in those times, only rich families indulged in the luxury of allowing their daughters to study. Aspirants would also have to learn some French. For people who could not read in their own language, or only with difficulty, the prospect of having to learn a strange language was enough to put an end to any thought of entering the community of the Daughters of Saint Vincent. Moreover, the internal seminary was in Shanghai; the candidate had to leave her province and might never come back.

All these reasons worked in favor of beginning a society of local religious women in the different vicariates. Just as Delaplace had been thinking a long time before founding the Josephines, so Reynaud's plan took time to mature.

Finally, on 25 January 1892 the new society was officially erected. Like every religious institution, the first goal the Society of the Virgins of Purgatory aimed at was the personal sanctification of its members. The society offered them as general means to reach this goal the three ordinary, simple, and temporary vows that were renewable on 25 January, the day of the foundation. Before being allowed to pronounce them, the candidates would have to undergo the test of three years of internal seminary (novitiate). To this general goal was added one that was special to the society itself: that was, as indicated by the name of the society, relieving the souls in purgatory. Pious activities, especially for this task, were: praying the divine office for the dead (translated into Chinese) and special Masses to be celebrated for the eternal rest of the souls of the dead. The second goal of the society was the apostolate suitable for their sex: schools, catechumenates and orphanages. The authority of the society was vested in the person of the apostolic vicar, who was its true superior. He would exercise his authority through a director and a vice-director, his spokesmen. The Sisters would have at the head of their society a Sister who would be the superior general, elected by the Sisters themselves, and confirmed by the bishop.

When Father Ibarruthy was assigned to the task and received the first candidates, there were only seven. Two months later, twelve more candidates for the religious life were admitted into the internal seminary.

We will not follow the development of the society. It will be enough here to relate what is in the inventory of 1911: "Up till now, eighty-five young women have entered the community. At this moment their number is sixty." Five years after their foundation, the society began to undertake the charitable works it had been set up for. In 1897, six Sisters left for Haimen; six others to Wenzhou; afterwards to Mapeng, to Shaoxing, and so on.

The foundation of the Sisters of Saint Joseph (Josephines) twenty years earlier by Delaplace and later of the Virgins of Purgatory by Reynaud gave to the cause of the formation of Christian girls and women a signal service. At the same time this initiative gave the missionaries precious coworkers, through whom evangelization could penetrate much more easily into the interior of families. Soon, one saw similar institutions springing up in the various missions of China.

On the occasion of the tenth anniversary of his consecration, Reynaud had a chart drawn up comparing the situation of the mission of Zhejiang in 1884 with that in 1894. We cite here only the most important figures.

Table 11.3. Comparative Inventory of Vicariate of Zhejiang, 1884 and 1894

Categories	1884	1894
Catholics	6,339	9,419
Vincentian missionaries		
European priests	11	12
Chinese priests	4	6
Lay brothers	3	2
Chinese diocesan priests	3	2
Religious women		
Daughters of Charity	30	32
Virgins of Purgatory	0	25
Localities with an annual mission	84	133
Catechumens with a serious disposition	615	2,500
Baptisms of adults	129	477
Residences for missionaries	8	9

Seminaries		
1 Major seminary	7	9
1 Minor seminary	13	19
Schools		
Primary schools for boys	38	35
Number of pupils	400	810
Primary schools for girls	8	15
Number of pupils	188	471

Three years had passed. The spiritual inventories of the year 1897–1898 of the Vincentian vicariates had been published. Reynaud had compared those of the vicariate of Zhejiang with those of Jiangxi and of the North. In a circular letter to his missionaries, he shared with them the reflections that this examination had suggested to him. "Generally," he said, "our results are inferior to those of our confreres of the other vicariates." The bishop seemed to ascribe that inferiority to the fact that certain missionaries had been inclined to shut themselves up at home. (The same remark would be made later by Father de Guébriant, apostolic visitor of the missions in China in 1920) The bishop explained:

> Residences favor regular lives; they are a necessary base for Christianizing the catechumens. . . . But on the other hand, these residences make us lose a lot of precious time. Two missionaries in one residence have not enough to do; one is enough. What can we say if they are three!

> This has been understood in several places, where several missionaries share a district. They cover all directions even several times . . . they take turns at living in the residence when the others are working in the countryside. . . . For them the residence is not the barracks where they pass their time training without ever fighting; it is a cenacle where they come and shake off the dust from the fight, where they replenish their strength for new conquests.

Table 11.4 Catholics in Vicariate of Zhejiang, 1899–1900

Categories	Totals
Catholics	12,597
Catechumens	5,481
Foreign priests	12
Chinese priests	11
Students in the minor seminary	43

As we are arriving at the end of the third period of our history, we will leave Zhejiang to move to the other vicariates to see briefly the progress made there up until 1900. Afterwards we will resume our narration of the fourth and last period, which goes from 1900 until the irruption of communism in China in 1950.

Map 11.3 Zhejiang in 1950

The Vicariate of Zhengding (Southwest Zhili) After Tagliabue's Departure for Peking

After having announced Sarthou's consecration, we said that later we would follow his activities in the vicariate of Zhengding. We know already that his former bishop, Tagliabue, consecrated him there on 26 April 1885. During the vacancy Father Moscarella administered the vicariate as pro-vicar.

To begin with, Sarthou carefully checked out the situation of the mission he was now in charge of. Informed in minute detail of all the existing charitable works and of the plans his predecessor had in view, he decided to go on with the work without making any changes. He confirmed Moscarella in all the duties of vicar general, procurator, director of the seminarians and of the Society of Saint Joseph, which the previous bishop had founded after the model of the one Delaplace began in Peking, with this difference that the Josephines of Zhengding remained under the guidance of the Daughters of Charity for a longer time.

The bishop approved the decision that Tagliabue had taken of separating the whole southern part of the vicariate from Jiazhuang, making it a new district, whose center would be Shunde. The bishop ordered Bruguière, director of Jiazhuang, to buy in the town of Shunde the land necessary to build a residence and a church. Bruguière met with very strong resistance from the scholars and the notables in his efforts to acquire the land. But the matter was brought to a satisfactory conclusion thanks to the existing treaties.

Every year, Sarthou made regular pastoral visits during which he noted the situation of the districts and their needs. We now know the characteristics of each of the five districts because his notes have been preserved. For example, let us look at his thoughts about two districts that later on became prosperous vicariates.

District of Zhaozhou (1886–1887)

This district is completely made up of old Christians. Consequently, the Faith has deep roots; nevertheless, apart from some really fervent Christian communities, quite a few of the others leave a lot to be desired because of their earthly mentality.

District of Shunde (1887–1888)

The impression was generally good. The observance of these twenty-year-old Christian communities is quite good. On Sundays they pray, they stop their work, even though they are poor. The Julu region, despite being a little wild, is very edifying. If well taken care of, this district has excellent prospects. The missionaries will have to be generous and mortified there.

Sarthou and Afterward

Hardly five years had passed when Sarthou received the brief from Rome dated 6 June 1890, which moved him to Peking left vacant by the death of Tagliabue. He left for Peking the following September with regret for he had become attached to the vicariate of Zhengding where he had many consolations in his five years there. "It fitted me like a glove," he said.

After Sarthou's departure, Moscarella again directed the mission during the vacancy. The following year on 28 July 1891 a decree from Rome appointed Bruguière bishop of Cina [Cinna] and apostolic vicar of Zhengding. Like his predecessor, he wanted to be consecrated in his cathedral and in the presence of his Christians. On 13 December 1891 Sarthou came down from Peking and consecrated him bishop.

Jules Bruguière, born in Nant (Aveyron) on 12 August 1851, admitted to the Congregation in Paris on 16 December 1872, was ordained on 26 May 1877. The following 5 October he arrived in China and went directly to Zhengding.

With his keen and cheerful nature, Bruguière learned the spoken language and the habits and customs of the Chinese quickly, so that, when he took the reins of government in his hands, he was able to unravel the most complicated matters. Like Anouilh, he liked to talk with the local people, becoming very popular among Christians and pagans alike.

His first act was to give Anouilh, the founder of the vicariate, a more dignified burial. He had a funeral chapel built in the cemetery located in Baitang several kilometers away from the city. There the first bishop's remains were buried solemnly. In 1892, Bruguière went to the second regional synod in Peking. We will talk about that meeting again when we follow Sarthou to Peking.

After he had returned from Peking, Bruguière set to work on the project that preoccupied him most: the formation of the clergy. Up to that time, the lack of personnel and resources had not permitted the separation of the major from the minor seminary.

Young and adult students were studying together in a hall of the episcopal residence. In 1887, thought was given to doing the formation of the theology students in the seminary of Peking. Coursière, who was in charge, took eight of his students to Peking. But out of their natural environment the students could not get used to the climate in Peking, and the following year not feeling well they went back. The number of vocations, however, kept increasing, so the moment to make the necessary sacrifices had come.

In 1893, the bishop built a number of buildings next to the cemetery of Baitang and moved the minor seminary there, which he entrusted to Father Jean Meineri, while the students of philosophy and theology continued to study in the city. In his account to Propaganda in 1896, Bruguière wrote:

> The vicariate has twenty-seven priests, thirteen are European and fourteen are Chinese. In the major seminary, seven students are studying theology. In the minor seminary, forty-five pupils apply themselves to studying Chinese and Latin and are preparing to enter the major seminary. We easily get students, when they are twelve, thirteen, and fourteen years old; but several leave the minor seminary, some overwhelmed by the difficulties of the studies, others because they lack ability . . . briefly, a small number reach ordination.

Despite this slightly timorous appreciation, the two seminaries gave good results, and Bruguière was able to ordain many Chinese priests, who soon became more numerous than the European priests and allowed them – without neglecting the care of the Christians – to devote themselves more fully to the conversion of pagans.

The great obstacle to conversions was the lack of able catechists. Those good Christians who in the old days fulfilled this task through pure dedication and without a salary were hardly to be found anymore. As conversions were becoming more numerous, a larger number of teachers was needed; but on the one hand the poverty of most of the Faithful did not allow them to be absent for any length of time because they had to take care of their family; on the other hand, the mission also being poor, the salaries that it could offer were inadequate. The Society of Saint Paul tried to respond to this situation.

The Society of Saint Paul

In 1895, a missionary with fifteen years' experience evangelizing in the vicariate, Father Morelli, suggested that a society for religious men should be established whose goal would be to help the missionaries in all their undertakings, and especially in the evangelizing of the pagans and in the formation of the new Christians. Bruguière was immediately won over by this idea and wanted the new association to be put under Saint Paul's protection and have his name.

Some well-disposed men were brought together under a rule that Morelli had drawn up. Father Vincent Chen was put in charge of this charitable work. The beginnings were slow and tedious.

Few similar organizations existed in the other vicariates. The rule of the Paulists – that was the name they were called – was modified several times. In the beginning they had only two vows of chastity and obedience. Later on, the vow of poverty was added. The vows were annual. Their clothes were the normal Chinese clothes, very modest and black. Their main devotional practice was the recitation of the rosary with meditation.

The Paulists' services for the mission were greatly appreciated by the missionaries and foremost by the Christians, who saw them as selfless and as good examples. Their main activities were with catechumenates, prayer schools, and primary schools.

After the publication [1917] of the new canon law, church law governed the society. At that time, it had about fifty members with vows.

Other charitable organizations also received new energy through the efforts of Bruguière. The mission was poor and living from hand to mouth. This made foundations very shaky. The bishop found some money to meet urgent expenditures without touching the annual budget.

During the fifteen years of his administration, he gave the vicariate of Zhengding its organization. It was divided into eight districts, each having a director assisted by two or three missionaries.

Missions were preached in 440 villages. Only the larger Christian communities had a church. In 1900, there were eight of them and 240 oratories. Many villages did not even have a common meeting place to recite their prayers.

Chapter 12

Vicariate of Peking, 1890s

The Apostolic Vicariate of Peking (North Zhili) – The Marist Brothers in Peking – The Orphanage of Chala – The French-Chinese College of Tianjin – The Second Regional Synod in Peking – Favier is Consecrated Bishop – Sarthou's Death – The Palace Revolution of 1898 – The Baoding Incident – Moving the Residence to Baoding City – The Favier Decree – Reception of the Favier Decree – Two Episcopal Promotions for the Vicariate of Peking

The Apostolic Vicariate of Peking (North Zhili)

We said some pages earlier that we were soon to follow Sarthou's activities in his new post in Peking. When he entered the cathedral of the Beitang on 8 October 1890 he met Father Favier in the corridor and hugged him in tears, saying, "Not I, but you ought to have been appointed bishop of Peking."

The truth is that Favier's name, already popular, had been proposed; and as he had been the right-hand man of the two previous bishops for all important matters concerning the mission, he would be so again for the new bishop, who, from the beginning, trusted him completely and gave him complete power without any restrictions.

If on the one hand, Sarthou was happy to be back with his former fellow workers, and especially to have charge again of the same flock for whose salvation he had devoted fifteen years, on the other hand, he regretted leaving his dear vicariate of Zhengding, which for five years had conquered his heart. Certainly, he was not ignorant of the fact that his new responsibilities would bring him heavier crosses than he would have had in his peaceful vicariate of Zhengding. But having the sense of discipline in the highest degree, he accepted without the least ambition troubling his soul.

The Marist Brothers in Peking

The College of the Nantang, established by Delaplace, had begun very modestly, but it strengthened with time. In order to develop further it needed to increase its teaching personnel. At the same time, the increasing number of Christians in the vicariate required more workers. Unable to satisfy these continuous demands for reinforcements, the superiors in Paris began negotiations with the Brothers of the Christian Schools and proposed to them to replace the missionaries and take charge of the College of the Nantang in Peking. Tagliabue did not favor this plan. He would have preferred some priests to be sent or even some lay brothers. But in the face of the serious need of personnel, it was prudent to accept the dedication of another religious society.

Moreover, it was clearly necessary to face the facts as they were: on the one hand, reinforcements from France were inadequate; on the other, missionaries hated leaving mission life to be shut up in a classroom and dedicated to teaching, whose results did not seem to justify the required sacrifices. That is why Peking asked Paris to continue negotiations with the Brothers of the Christian Schools. In the end, the Brothers declined to take charge of such a distant institution.

After this failure, the idea came up of asking the Little Brothers of Mary (Marists), who already were working as Vincentians' coworkers in the College Saint-Benoît of Constantinople and were giving satisfaction. The Marist Brothers accepted, and an agreement was reached almost immediately, so that six Brothers arrived in Shanghai on 12 April 1891, and a few weeks later they were settled in the College of the Nantang. Soon, they would take charge of the College in Tianjin, replacing Fathers Guilloux and Geurts.

The Orphanage of Chala

Hardly a year had passed since the arrival of the Marist Brothers when the mission in Peking offered them the orphanage of Chala. In November 1892, Favier wrote to the Marist Brothers' superior general (in France):

> At the West gate of Peking, we have an agricultural orphanage, with small workshops that could be developed, with more than two hundred fifty children from eight to eighteen years old. These poor children study in the morning and do manual work in the afternoon beginning at a certain age. . . . We beg you to send us four Brothers for this institution. . . . If you want to plant your institution in China, I think that vocations would not be lacking, and we would approve with joy the creation of a novitiate in that vast property of Chala.

That is what happened even before the beginning of the twentieth century. The Brothers accepted the direction of the institution of Chala

(1893), and built their central house there with a novitiate that prospered until the Boxer Rebellion. Later on, it recovered and prospered again.

As for the organization of the orphanage, it did not produce brilliant results. An account of the brother director of that house informs us that in 1898 the institution had 106 children received by the mission, of whom 18 were from poor Christian families. There were a carpenter's workshop and a tailor's workshop; they made sieves there that were sold outside; some ten children learned to produce cloisonné (a specialty of Peking). The other healthy children were employed in the vegetable garden, whose produce was easily sold in the markets of Peking.

After trying for five years, the brother ended his account with this melancholy remark, "The results are in no way proportionate to the sacrifices, trouble, and money that are made for this charitable work." This confirms the opinion expressed earlier, that orphanages for boys rarely succeeded in China. Soon, however, institutions of great importance were to be established in Chala.

The French-Chinese College in Tianjin

The fourth institution entrusted by the mission of Peking to the Marist Brothers was the parochial school in Tianjin. Saint Louis College was exclusively reserved for European children. There was no school where Chinese children could learn European languages and – for many – enable themselves to take up some position with the foreign traders, increasingly more numerous in the open ports. This last consideration was the reason why Sarthou added the study of the French language to the program of the parochial school, founded several years earlier.

This innovation had great success among the Christians, for it opened a path to a career. It also pleased the French Concession authorities, which, after making an agreement with the Brothers, paid for the maintenance costs of the school. It was called the "Municipal School." In 1917, it found its home in the shadow of the cathedral of Tianjin, built in the concession.

It was to function with always more than a hundred students, all Christians, until the Communist takeover.

The Second Regional Synod in Peking

On 13 December 1891 the most senior member of the apostolic vicars of the first region of China, Bishop Bax, apostolic vicar of Mongolia, invited his colleagues to a synod, which was to be held in Peking on the third Sunday after Easter the following year.

On the agreed day, 9 May 1892, all the bishops of the first region and the abbot of the Trappist monastery of Our Lady of Consolation came together in the Beitang. In the opening session Sarthou was elected president.

The task of the synod was divided into seven parts, according to the seven sacraments, studied less from a speculative point of view than from the practical point of view of how to administer them. The acts of the synod were sent to Rome for approval and correction. According to our usual pattern, we do not give the acts in detail. We will refer to only one question that proved difficult to solve.

It was about administering baptism to adults. The synod reiterated the conditions adults must fulfill and pointed out the most ordinary abuses concerning this sacrament. The fourth paragraph was made up in this way: "It is not permitted to baptize the pagans' babies, even presented by their parents, if after baptism they remain under the authority of the parents, unless in danger of death." Propaganda proposed the following text: "Pagans' babies presented spontaneously by their parents must be baptized, even if, after baptism, they must remain under the parents' authority."

This radical change in the discipline for baptism, which the whole Church followed till then, provoked widespread astonishment. Four years later, Propaganda felt it necessary to return to the question and, in a letter addressed to Sarthou, ordered the adoption of a new draft. The new article was word for word identical with the one that had been proposed by the synod.

The synod ended on 26 May. During the last session, it was indicated that the next meeting of the synod would be in Peking on the third Sunday after Easter in 1900. The synod charged Sarthou with calling the synod, and, if he could not do it, it was up to the senior bishop among the apostolic vicars of the first region. But because of the events of 1900, it was only in 1906 that this synod met.

Favier is Consecrated Bishop

Sarthou's health began to decline. It was easy to foresee that in this important mission he soon would need a coadjutor.

But an incident happened which, had it been brought to a good end, would have certainly changed the outlook of things in the vicariate of Peking.

Bishop Crouzet, the Vincentian apostolic vicar in Abyssinia, became available after he was obliged to leave his vicariate along with all his French missionaries following the Italian expedition in Eritrea. Then, the superior general, Fiat, aware of Sarthou's declining health and his need for help, thought that he had the solution for the needs of the mission of Peking. He asked Sarthou if he would agree to have Bishop Crouzet as his coadjutor.

The bishop of Peking immediately agreed. Everything seemed arranged and definitively settled, including the ship on which Crouzet would travel to China, when news arrived that all had been canceled and that Crouzet would not come to China, because he had received another appointment.

What happened? General Duchesne had conquered Madagascar. At that time the only ones asked to evangelize this large island were the Jesuits, but they wanted to share this huge and difficult mission with another society of French missionaries. They offered the southern part of it to the Vincentians.

Recalling that Saint Vincent sent their first confreres sent there, they did not hesitate again to evangelize in Fort Dauphin. Crouzet agreed to be the first apostolic vicar of this mission in need of being brought back to life. So, he went there with his former Abyssinian missionaries.

In 1897, feeling his health incurably compromised and his physical forces depleted, especially after his most recent pastoral rounds, Sarthou begged the Holy See to grant him a coadjutor. The pope chose Favier, who also was everyone's choice.

By the brief of 12 November 1897 Favier was appointed the bishop of Pentacomia and Sarthou's coadjutor with the right of succession.

Born in Marsannay (Côte-d'Or) on 22 September 1837, admitted to the Congregation in Paris on 5 October 1858, and ordained in Paris on 18 October 1861, Alphonse Favier arrived in Peking on 14 July 1862.

His consecration, which took place on 20 February 1898 showed the immense popularity that the new bishop enjoyed both among all the Chinese and all the Europeans. Not only the twelve ministers who represented their respective nations, but also the governor of Peking, the famous Ronglu, representing the Chinese government, the members of the Office of Foreign Affairs and twelve Manchu princes of the imperial family showed by their presence the respect they had for Favier.

Sarthou's physical weakness did not allow him to consecrate his coadjutor. Bruguière, apostolic vicar of Zhengding, aided by Bishops Bulté and Abels, apostolic vicars of South Zhili and East Mongolia, consecrated Favier in the cathedral, the Beitang, that he himself had built.

On that occasion, the emperor gave him the red globe,[39] a distinction given on account of the way Favier had handled religious matters for many years to widespread satisfaction everywhere in the north of China.

Sarthou's Death

On 13 April 1899 this holy bishop passed away peacefully in the Beitang. Painful infirmities that condemned him to inevitable rest made his last years a continuous martyrdom. He suffered all this without ever one word of complaint.

In the meantime, the mission was practically speaking administered by Favier. Even when Sarthou was in Peking, he voluntarily deferred to his brilliant coworker; nevertheless, he kept abreast of all temporal and spiritual matters and continued to guide his confreres. His voluminous directive and administrative correspondence give abundant proof of it. His tact, affability and piety gave all his activities a kind and religious radiance. Sarthou in death was remembered as dear to all; they considered his life as extremely edifying.

The Palace Revolution of 1898

For some twenty years the influential persons in China formed two separate groups. In the south, which had never had much sympathy for the reigning dynasty, there were many who attributed the setbacks suffered by the empire to the narrow-minded Manchu mentality. China must, they said, implement a policy of reform modeled on European methods.

In the north there were also some progressive people, but the great majority of the politicians was conservative and did not want to change anything in the old traditions. The purely Chinese Ming dynasty did not allow any foreigner in the empire, and the Manchu Qing dynasty followed that example. The latter dynasty demanded that the Europeans be forced out. Hence two groups: reformers and traditionalists. In both camps there were pure Chinese and people who were Manchu by birth. It is well known that the officials were chosen almost equally from the two races.

The reformers from the south, however, succeeded in introducing into the court of Peking one of their leaders, Kang Youwei, a very famous intellectual. He was admitted to several private audiences with the young Guangxu emperor and he spoke so eloquently that he led the sovereign to

---

39.   A red globe or transparent ruby was the finial jewel worn on officials' hats, the highest distinction among Qing dynasty officials, here given as a special honor to Favier. (AS)

adopting his reform ideas. The emperor was so convinced of the necessity of these reforms that he wanted to carry them out immediately. The reform measures followed one another quickly. It began with the abolition of the old system of literary examinations. Then there was the project of establishing universities and colleges where all the sciences would be taught as they were in Europe. Military reforms came next, and finally reforms within the government itself. The last edict ended like this, "The deposed mandarins are allowed to leave the capital so as to earn their living in the provinces." The interval between one edict and the next was only a few days. Cixi, who legally had not been regent since 1887, clearly felt that reforms were necessary and did not oppose publishing these edicts; she bided her time, keeping her "veto" in reserve for when matters threatened to get nasty.

Kang Youwei, who feared this veto, pushed the emperor to free himself from his aunt's guardianship and advised him to surround her residence, to overpower her and to relegate her for the rest of her life to the winter palace, which was located among the imperial palaces.

Guangxu was weak enough or thoughtless enough to approve this plot. On the night of 20 September 1898 Cixi got wind of the whole business. Immediately, a real palace revolution took place. High officials were seized and judged. Guangxu was imprisoned and Cixi again took the reins of government. The next day, she published a decree drawn up in such a way that the emperor admitted that he was not able to carry on his shoulders the heavy burdens of government, so he had begged Cixi to take up the regency again and so on. Next, other decrees appeared that annulled all the reform decrees.

So ended what some French people called "the hundred days of reform." This event echoed throughout China, all the more because hatred for foreigners had been one of the motives of reform. It also had brought about increased activity among the secret societies, which were always latent in this country. The Chinese government then, fearing trouble in Peking, called upon Gansu's soldiers. These troops, which numbered twenty-five thousand, trained in Baoding before taking up a position in front of the capital. They, however, caused a serious incident that had extensive consequences for the vicariate of Peking.

The Baoding Incident

On 6 July 1898 two of the officers forcefully entered the residence of the missionaries, which was located at that time in Beiguan, a suburb in the north of the city. The staff of the residence in attempting to oppose the invaders was harshly mistreated and, before anyone could alert the authorities, two hundred soldiers commanded by a captain invaded the residence and beat the servants and the missionaries. Father Dumond, the director, and Father Paul Wang, a Chinese curate, were tied up and brought to headquarters. Uncertain of the fate awaiting them, the two Vincentians gave each other absolution, which seemed to be their last. The sub-prefect, however, as soon as he was informed of what had happened, ran to headquarters where he negotiated with the officers and succeeded in getting the two prisoners into his palanquin. He took them to his place. The next day, he brought them back to their residence. Dumond immediately gave his superiors in Peking a full account of the incident.

Moving the Residence to Baoding City

Ronglu, viceroy of the province, immediately wrote to Favier to beg him to please treat this matter out of court. The bishop agreed and sent him the conditions for an agreement, which consisted of this: if the Beiguan residence were exchanged for a suitable property within the city, the mission would ask no indemnity for the badly mistreated persons or for the damaged furnishings.

A telegram from Ronglu the next day accepted the conditions of Favier's proposal. The only thing that had to be done was to send a missionary there to reach a settlement with the urban authorities and execute the terms of the agreement. Father Jarlin, who had managed the district of Donglü for nine years, was appointed.

In three days, all was finished to the satisfaction of both parties: the property was a yamen (tribunal), long abandoned because it had the reputation of being haunted. It was situated in the middle of town. So the mission at last had what it had been longing for, namely a building inside the city walls, where up until then no foreigner was allowed even to enter. On the other hand, the Chinese government got off lightly for this incident without "losing face."

The Chinese press highlighted the moderate nature of the demands by the Catholic mission in order to arrange the incident, and brought out the advantages of this direct way of managing religious matters. Favier had indeed a direct and loyal way of managing matters. The important mandarins liked this way very much. Ronglu was one of them.

Shortly after the Baoding affair, he visited the bishop and said that it was the sincere desire of the Chinese government to find a *modus vivendi* that could make it easier in the future to solve religious lawsuits out of court. Favier applauded this project – which actually was his – and after conferring with {Etienne] Pichon, minister of France, began to prepare the clauses of that protocol.

The Favier Decree

Obviously, Favier never published a decree.

It was an imperial decree about the official status of the Catholic missions, drawn up at the suggestion of Favier, hence, the name "Favier Decree." The Empress Cixi cunningly published it in order to pull the wool over the eyes of Europeans and Christians.[40]

Here are the essential elements of this decree of 15 March 1899:

> Since the imperial government authorized the propagation of the Catholic religion, churches have been constructed in all the provinces of China. We now want to see the Chinese people and the Christians live in peace. So, it has been agreed that local authorities exchange visits with the missionaries under the following conditions:
>
> 1. A) In the Church hierarchy, bishops being equal to viceroys and governors in rank and dignity, it will be agreed to authorize them to visit with viceroys and governors;
>
> B) Vicars general will be authorized to visit provincial treasurers and judges;
>
> C) Other priests will be authorized to meet with prefects and their inferiors.
>
> 2. When a problem arises in a mission, the bishop and the missionaries can go and see the local authorities, with whom they will negotiate and settle the problem.
>
> When there is a serious and important problem, the bishop and the missionaries of the place must ask the minister or the consuls of the Power[41] entrusted by the pope as the religious protectorate, to intervene.

---

40. The Guangxu emperor published this before Cixi limited his governing powers. (AS)

41. International power, referring to France, because it was to France alone that the pope had confided the responsibility of protecting the Christians in China.

Reception of the Favier Decree

It was received enthusiastically. The Cardinal Prefect of Propaganda immediately sent Favier his warm congratulations in a letter that ended with these words, "And I nourish the hope that it (the decree) will be of much profit for the increase of the Catholic religion in those lands."

As for the bishops and the missionaries, who hardly could believe their eyes and ears, many joyfully thanked the bishop. Alas! The decree was stillborn and was never implemented. It would have taken several years to be known throughout the immense empire for it to become effective. Actually it was promulgated at a very bad moment, on the brink of the Boxer movement, whose rumbling could already be heard. As a result, the decree was just a pipe dream and produced only a brief moment of joy for the missionaries, and for the bishop of Peking a whiff of glory more harmful than useful. If we mention it, it is just to be objective and impartial.

Two Episcopal Promotions for the Vicariate of Peking

In October 1899, Favier went to Rome, then to Paris. He presented to His Holiness Leo XIII the situation of his mission and his project of cutting off the east part of his vicariate, which numbered enough Christians to form a new vicariate.

The pope approved of the idea, divided the North Zhili vicariate to form the East Zhili vicariate and he appointed Father François Geurts its first apostolic vicar.

Moreover, Favier, sixty-two years old, sensing that his energies were decreasing, asked the help of a coadjutor bishop. This was equally granted through the nomination of Stanislas Jarlin. Thus, at the end of the year, the bishop, traveling in France and the Netherlands, could say that he had two bulls in his pocket.

Bishop François Geurts

Born in Maashees (the Netherlands) on 9 December 1862, admitted into Saint Lazare on 8 October 1882, François Geurts arrived in China on 19 September 1886 and was ordained priest in Zhengding on 1 May 1887. Appointed bishop of Rhinocolure [Rhinocorura] and apostolic vicar of East Zhili through the brief of 24 December 1899, he was consecrated in Bois-le-Duc ['s-Hertogenbosch] on 4 February 1900 but he could only take possession of his post on 30 March 1901 because of the troubles that were raging in China.

Table 12.1 Overview of Personnel in the Vincentian
Missions in China, 1898–1899

Designation	Shanghai	Zhili North	Zhili West	Zhejiang	Jiangxi North	Jiangxi East	Jiangxi South	Totals
Catholics		46,894	32,263	12,397	5,071	13,038	5,229	115,091
Bishops, V.A.		1	1	1	2	1	1	7
C.M. European	2	23	10	14	9	13	10	81
C.M. Chinese		16	9	11	2	3		41
Diocesan P.		20	10	3	2	6	5	46
Major Sem.		23	9	3	4	4	7	50
Minor Sem.		88	47	43	17	19	20	234
Lay Brothers	2	2	2	2				8
Paulists			9					9
D.C.	31	36	8	38	14	6		133
Josephines		63	52					115
Virgins of Purgatory				37				37
Daughters of Saint Anne							7	7
Baptisms		1,711	447	739	335	398	198	3,828

[Note] In this overview only these items are given: the situation of the personnel in each of the six apostolic vicariates entrusted to the Vincentians; the number of Catholics; of European Vincentian priests; of Chinese Vincentian priests; of Chinese diocesan priests; of the students in major seminaries; of the students in the minor seminaries; of the lay brothers; of the Paulist Brothers; of the Daughters of Charity; of the Chinese religious women and of the adults that were baptized that year.

Bishop Stanislas Jarlin

Born in Sète (Hérault) on 20 January 1856, accepted in Paris on 7 May 1884, he arrived in China on 4 November 1886 and was ordained priest in Peking on 20 January 1889. Through the brief of 28 December 1899, he was appointed bishop of Pharbaetus and coadjutor of Favier with the right of succession. Favier consecrated him on 29 April 1900 one month after his arrival back from Europe, where he had received the alarming news from Peking and decided to return in haste to China.

As we have arrived at the eve of the storm of 1900, we must finish here, according to our plan, the third period of our account by giving a general chart of all the Vincentian missions at that date. Then we will resume our account with the fourth and last period, which goes from 1900 to 1950.

Fourth Period
(1900–1950)

From Boxers
to Communists

Chapter 13

Boxers and the Siege of the North Church

The Boxer Movement – The Events Leading up to the Boxer Rebellion – The Attack – The Siege of the Beitang – During the Siege (Journal of Favier) – The Victims of the Siege of the Beitang – The Rescue Army – The March to Peking – The French Army Chaplain's Notes

The Boxer Movement

Despite our intention of confining ourselves to recounting the apostolic activities of the missionaries and disregarding as much as possible the political struggles and periodic uprisings among which they worked, we cannot pass over in silence the events that took place in China in the beginning of the twentieth century. The Boxer movement marked a real turning point in the history of the missions. Since then, progress in evangelizing this great country has been, one might say, astonishing, particularly in northern China where the persecution was heaviest.

In the first months of 1899, a sect that began very secretly started to attract attention in several provinces, notably in Shandong and Fujian. This society was not new; it was the old society called Dadaohui (Big Sword Society), which merely changed its name. Secret societies often do so. It was composed of fanatic and violent people, mostly young. Many bonzes were members. These gangs were called Yihetuan, "Righteous Militia [or Fists]," hence the name Boxers.

The Boxers' goal was not easy to pin down because it evolved. In the beginning, it seemed to have been opposed to the Manchu dynasty, which had been unable to prevent foreigners from invading China, becoming deep-rooted in the country and acquiring enormous privileges. They intended to throw out the foreigners because the government was unable to do it. There was a strong superstitious element; the preparatory exercises did not consist in handling weapons, but in learning incantations, which put them in a trance-like state resembling diabolic possession, and which – according to them – gave them supernatural qualities, such as being invulnerable to European bullets.

The Events Leading up to the Boxer Rebellion

We saw how the empress acted after the palace revolution of 1898. Sensing the threat, she avoided the attack destined for her by forcing the emperor to sign something like an act of abdication, through which he put himself back under the guardianship of the terrifying dowager. She was then called regent of the empire.

Once the power was in her hands, she struck the reformers and their accomplices doubly hard and annulled all the decrees of the "hundred days" period (several of which, however, were to be applied a little later). She tolerated troublemakers and honored the governor of Shandong, who had failed to repress the Boxers for the trouble they had caused. She refused the demands of the European plenipotentiary ministers, who insisted on severe repression. All these refusals contributed to the supposition that she was in connivance with this secret society.

This supposition was confirmed when, in June 1899, she ordered that throughout the empire militias be organized in conjunction with the Boxers, whom she called, "patriots who can be found in all the provinces."

In the first days of 1900, the number of Boxers present in the province of Zhili was estimated at one hundred thousand. The ministers of the [Foreign] Powers protested and even threatened; the court, in order to allay suspicion, feigned regrets, apologized, even repaired some of the damage caused in Shandong and promised indemnities. In April, security seemed to have returned. Actually, the worst uprising against the foreigners was about to begin.

The Attack

Suddenly, in the second half of May, gangs of Boxers invaded the villages around Baoding, a hundred kilometers south of the capital, on the route of the Peking-Hankou railway line. Christians were killed and villages were burned.

The [European] ministers thought it was urgent to bring the marines ashore from the ships that were in the China Sea. There was no agreement among them, however. For that matter, most of them did not believe there was a present danger, though they agreed that there was the possibility of a religious persecution. At the same time, they were convinced that the government would never allow the rebels to attack foreign ministers to whom it had given official recognition.

The minister of France, on the contrary, was pessimistic. Pichon, in charge of Catholic interests, had many contacts with the missionaries throughout the provinces and received information from them that the other ministers did not have.

Favier, who had returned from France a few months earlier and who habitually was confident about the future, changed from the most enthusiastic optimism to the darkest pessimism because he received alarming news from all sides and shared it with Pichon.

On 21 May it was clear that there were many Boxers in Peking. The walls were being covered with posters in red characters announcing the destruction of all religious institutions and the massacre of all foreigners.

On 25 May it was announced that several railway stations on the Peking-Hankou line had been burned and destroyed. The diplomatic corps sent a new protest to the Zongli Yamen. The reply was evasive.

On the morning of 31 May detachments of the military disembarked in Dagu. They arrived the same day in Peking by train on tracks that were only slightly damaged. There were seventy Frenchmen, as many Englishmen, fifty Americans, forty Italians and twenty-two Japanese. The defense of the legations was the first order of business, and then thirty French marines and ten Italians were sent to the Beitang, five kilometers from the legations.

On 9 June the ministers asked that all the available sailors come ashore, in order to form a rescue party, while waiting for more troops. Without delay a group of about two thousand was assembled. The English admiral, [Edward] Seymour, was quite confident that he could lead this party to Peking, at a distance of one hundred fifty kilometers. The group started without sufficient preparation. It arrived in Luofa, one third of the way to Peking. There it turned out that the rails were in very bad shape and repairs were delayed by repeated attacks. On 14 June they arrived in the Langfang railway station halfway to Peking, but further repairs turned out to be impossible. Then they went on foot, fighting continuously. The losses were heavy. On 18 June the admiral decided to go back to Tianjin. Finally, the group arrived in Tianjin, exhausted. The marching, fighting, and deprivations, particularly the lack of drinking water, as well as having to transport a large number of wounded personnel took a heavy toll. Forty were dead and 206 had been wounded.

This first expedition was a complete failure. A still more important second expedition was far from being ready. In the meantime, what was happening in Peking? As we saw, about 350 marines of various nationalities had been sent to Peking on 31 May. This handful had to withstand two sieges, the siege of the legations and the siege of the Beitang until the capture of Peking by the Allied Forces on 14 August.

The Siege of the Beitang

Table 13.1 Refugees and Personnel, North Church Enclosure, 1900

Refugees	Number
Christian men and boys	900
Christian women and children	1,800
Young Christian girls	450
Babies in cribs	51
Habitual personnel:	
Major and minor seminarians	111
Daughters of Charity	20
Bishops	2
Vincentian priests	12
Chinese diocesan priests	2
Marist Brothers	7
TOTAL	3,300
Plus, the military defenders	40

On the day following the arrival of the troops, the Beitang was put in a state of readiness to defend itself. There was time to do it, for there were no serious attacks before 15 June. But on 17 June the Boxers and the imperial soldiers did not allow refugees to enter the Beitang. The refugees had come not only from the city of Peking, but also from neighboring villages, from where the fires and the massacre of Christians had forced them to flee. Food for all these people was a great challenge.

Lieutenant Paul Henry, a first-class Christian from Brittany, commanded the thirty French sailors. The ten Italians had Lieutenant Olivieri as chief.

The Beitang was composed of two large rectangular properties, separated by an alley; high brick walls surrounded both. The biggest one in the south was cut down the middle by two paths east and west of the cathedral. To the west of the cathedral there were the caretaker's house, the servants' houses, the bishop's residence, the missionaries' lodgings, two libraries (one Chinese, the other European), and a community chapel. East of the cathedral were the stables and outbuildings and the two courts of the seminary; to the north there was a big vegetable garden.[42]

The northern rectangle contained the works of the Daughters of Charity: the orphanage, schools, dispensary, workshop, infirmary and chapel, everything going under the name Renzitang.

After Commander Henry had examined the premises, he did not hide from Favier that it seemed to him impossible to protect the Beitang against a serious attack with so few personnel. The perimeter to be defended was 1360 meters in length. The available arms were the forty rifles of the sailors, seven or eight rifles of different kinds, some swords and five hundred Chinese spears.

There was neither a cannon nor a machine gun. There was no doctor, and the amount of the most necessary medicines was minimal. Nevertheless, work was begun with passion. In agreement with Henry, Favier decided that in case of a serious and violent attack, everybody would be gathered in the church.

The siege of the Beitang is written up in all its details in the "Journal of Bishop Favier," which we cannot copy here [because of its length]. It began on 8 June and ended on 16 August. We will quote only some of the most moving passages. (Note: sometimes we give explanations in parentheses.)

During the Siege (Journal of Favier)

13 June. – We heard from the legations that Admiral Seymour with his troops arrived in Langfang... Bad night: fires, cries of death on all sides. The women fled towards the church. At nine o'clock in the evening we could see from the top of the tower that the beautiful church of the Dongtang was burning.

14 June. – The Dongtang is still burning. We cannot communicate with the legations anymore or with the parishes, unless by courageous couri-

---

42. To understand easily this position and this situation of the Beitang in 1900, it is enough to have the plan, published in Favier's *Péking: histoire et description* (Péking, 1897), pp. 318–319.

ers who risk their lives on the way. At eleven o'clock in the morning, the ancient cathedral of the Nantang with all its buildings fell prey to the flames.

15 June. – A Christian who escaped from that parish told us that the Missioners, Marist Brothers, and Sisters of Saint Joseph were safe in the legations: audacious French volunteers had gone in the middle of the night and saved them. Late in the evening, we saw the church of the Xitang in flames. Christians came and told us that Father Pascal Doré, the parish priest of the Xitang had been burned to death with his Christians in his church. A letter from Father d'Addosio, pastor of the Nantang and a refugee at the legations, told us that Father Jules Garrigues, pastor of the Dongtang had certainly been killed with numerous Christians. (Obviously, the three churches were burned at the same time.)

17 June. – A courier from the legations reported that there was no news from the Seymour rescue party. More than two thousand houses had been burned close to the immense Qianmen gate, among them twenty-five Chinese banks.

21 June. – From a letter by Mr. Pichon: All the legations [personnel] are gathered in the English Legation, the only one capable of being defended. (Previously, every one defended its own Legation with its own soldiers).

22 June. – Cannons fired on the church; we immediately made people evacuate it. Fourteen Krupp cannons continuously fired the latest model shrapnel shells. Doubled windows were shattered. The cross on the top fell to the ground. At about three o'clock in the afternoon, the attack was so violent that we thought our last hour had arrived. At five o'clock a shell broke one side of our door. Overexcited, Commander Henry and Bishop Jarlin took four sailors and thirty Christians, and they rushed outside [the walls] and seized a cannon, which they brought inside under intense fire. Two Christians were killed and two wounded. Little by little the bombardment eased off. That day alone we received five hundred thirty cannon shots.

24 June. – Severe attack on the Renzitang. Henry sent ten French sailors to lend the Italians a helping hand.

25 and 26 June. – We were fired on with infantry rifles, but the damage was minimal. May God grant that we have enough food and that the rescue party does not keep us waiting too long.

25 June. – The Boxers attacked in tight formations, but firing salvoes routed them. Joannic, the second master was badly wounded. At about eleven o'clock in the evening, the Boxers threw incendiary bombs. Our sailors have magnificent courage; they all wear a scapular and crucifix; they feel protected by the good Lord.

29 June. – Relative calm. We were saddened this morning by Joannic's death. Gangrene got in his wound and took him away in a few hours.

1 July. – We heard many cannons firing far away in the south. Would that be the rescue party? Smallpox has broken out among the children; every day seven or eight are dying.

2 July. – Attacks less fierce. Food diminishing. Everybody's share was decreased. Donkey meat is being eaten; the mules and horses will come next. We have eighteen of them. (The following days: regular bombings of one or two hundred rounds a day.)

9 July. – Intense shooting all day long and one hundred seven cannon shots. In the evening towards midnight, we heard the sounds of a terrible fight coming from the direction of the legations. We know nothing of what is going on.

10 July. – Sailor David died from a bullet to his head. More than a hundred cannonballs have been fired; one of them smashed to pieces the glass of our window and it fell on the bed that I had just left. A Mauser bullet pierced Bishop Jarlin's hat taking away a strip of his scalp. A few millimeters lower and I would have lost my coadjutor.

15 July. – Heavy bombings that caused much damage to the church and the main gate; one hundred forty shots during the day. Two mines were discovered and destroyed on the spot.

16 July. – Several hundred cannonballs have been shot at us. One sailor and one Christian were killed.

18 July. – We have speeded up the work of a counter-mine in the last few days. West of the Renzitang, muffled noises are heard. At five o'clock in the morning, a terrible explosion of a mine. The whole western part of the Renzitang has fallen in ruins: twenty-five people have died and twenty-eight were wounded. Among the deceased was Marist Brother Joseph, who was leading the work on the counter-mine. Women and children in panic are running in all directions.

19 July. – Feast of Saint Vincent. Burial of Brother Joseph. Sailor Frank took a bullet in the head and died on the spot. There was time only to give him absolution.

21 July. – Food is becoming scare; eating very sparingly we will be able to last fifteen more days. Attention is still given to mining activities, but it is difficult to make our Christians work, because they are still frightened by the disaster of the 18th.

26 July. – At 3:00 in the afternoon, Chavanne died suddenly. When on duty, he had been slightly wounded, perhaps with a poisoned bullet, for it caused black smallpox, of which he died.

28 July. – We are worrying very much about the food. We put the share at eight ounces a day per person, in order to be able to keep going eight more days.

29 July. – Ongoing shelling; we counted one hundred fifteen volleys.

30 July. – The cannonade began again with a heavy barrage. The commander went into the breach. A bullet that passed through his neck wounded two sailors. He himself got off the scaffolding and took another bullet in the side. In spite of his wounds, he remained standing for a while but in the end slumped to the ground under the veranda in the arms of a Chinese Vincentian priest, Father Augustin Zou, who administered the last rites to him. After twenty minutes Commander Henry expired, a truly courageous man. Quartermaster Elias immediately assumed command. The Britons mourned their commander's death like children. Bishop Jarlin tried to help them keep up their spirits. Today one hundred fifty volleys. We still have hope, for Commander Henry had said, "I'll disappear only when you do not need me anymore."

4 August. – In the last four days, the attacks during the day have been fewer and less violent, whereas at night the firing hardly ever stops. Probably it is aimed at keeping us from going out to look for food.

5 August. – The problem of food is the only one that bothers us. People stand up to bullets, not so easily to hunger. We have every edible thing weighed; altogether, we have seven thousand pounds of food. We decided each day to give one thousand pounds for the three thousand people.

7 August. – We can hear distant cannon volleys, and because there are practically no attacks, we entertain the hope that the rescue party is near.

10 August. – We are aware that in two days we will have nothing to eat.

12 August. – At six o'clock in the morning, a terrible explosion. A mine, stronger than all the others, exploded in the Renzitang and made a crater seven meters deep and forty meters in diameter. Buried under the rubble there are five Italian sailors and eighty Christians, among whom there are fifty-one babies. Brother Jules-André, visitor of the Marists, was beaten to death when helping a partially buried woman. He was a man of great worth, outstanding intelligence, dedication and rare courage. Some French sailors rushed to the place of the disaster and killed some fifty Boxers who tried to enter.

13 August. – Despondency is general, but the distant sounds of cannons give us hope. At eleven o'clock another mine exploded, but the damage was slight. In the streets we heard the Boxers crying to us, "The European devils are approaching, we will die, if necessary, but you will die before us!"

14 August. – Fight in the south and the east of the capital. We heard cannons, machine guns, and salvoes. From the top of the church, we observed the disappearance of the Chinese flag on the walls. They were shooting at us from all sides. It is clear the rescue party was attacking Peking. At five o'clock in the evening we could see with a spyglass that there were five foreign officers on the walls.

15 August. – Feast of the Assumption. Before the break of day, the East Gate of the city was on fire. From 7:00 to 9:00, the noise of the battle was continuous.

16 August. – From seven o'clock in the morning, the sound of shooting could be heard and it seemed to come from the south. At eight o'clock it was not more than three hundred meters away at the other side of the Zijing city gate (of the Forbidden City), which was closed and occupied by the imperial soldiers who had been continually assisting the Boxers.

We had already hoisted the French flag on the top of the church. Then Bishop Jarlin blew a bugle. A sole officer approached us. A ladder was lowered for him, which he climbed up on and jumped to our side. He was a Japanese captain. He shook hands with Bishop Jarlin and asked, "Can you open the Xihua gate?" "No, it is protected too well and there are not enough of us." "Very well," he said, "I'm going to try to have it blown up." He returned to the other side of the wall. At that moment we saw a small detachment in blue uniforms – they were Frenchmen. They ran straight to the flag, put some ladders up on their side and we did the same on ours. In a few minutes, the fifty men of the Marty Company and their leader were with us. Meanwhile, the Japanese soldiers had broken down one side of the Xihua gate; the French artillery finished the job and despite intense fire, all rushed on to the barricades.

The battle was over. The ground was strewn with the bodies of more than 800 Boxers and Chinese soldiers. We had to lament those two men were lost and three wounded. Captain Marty was one of them.

It was around ten o'clock. Monsieur Pichon and General Frey had been in the Beitang for a quarter of an hour. We hugged each other heartily and congratulated each other.

Signed A. Favier, Apostolic Vicar

The stop at the Beitang lasted only a little moment. The troops marched on to the Imperial Palace. Each of the French, Russian, English and Japanese contingents was assigned a different quarter of the capital to occupy temporarily for the purpose of restoring order. But what the foreign ministers did not know at all was that Guangxu and Cixi had fled.

During the night of 15 to 16 August, the emperor and the regent, disguised as farmers, sitting on two ordinary Chinese two-wheeled carts, followed by three grand councilors and more than a thousand regular soldiers, who had come directly from the siege of the legations, went to the Summer Palace twenty-five kilometers from Peking, where they arrived at eight o'clock in the morning. The empress's intention was to go to the large Summer Palace in Jehol 180 kilometers from the capital. But considering that this place was still too near Peking, she changed her idea went to Xi'an, capital of Shaanxi 1,200 kilometers from Peking. The Imperial Court would settle there and would come back only on 6 January 1902.

The Victims of the Siege of the Beitang

Deceased:

1	Vincentian: Claude Chavanne
2	Marist Brothers: Jules-André, Visitor; Joseph Félicité, Superior
6	French sailors, including Lieutenant Henry
5	Italian sailors
38	Christian spear-carrying fighters
120	Children, starved to death or dead from illness
51	Babies buried in the mine accident of 12 August
80	Women dead from disease and hardship
100	Christian men (approximately)

403 total

Wounded:

9	French sailors
3	Italian sailors

There was no information on how many refugees were wounded.

The reader might wonder why the rescue party of the foreign nations, expected from the first days of June 1900, arrived in Peking only on 15 August, especially considering that the distance was just one hundred fifty kilometers. The following brief account is an attempt to answer that question.

The Rescue Army

We saw that the Seymour rescue party, after it left Tianjin on 10 June had to go back. It was decimated. But when it arrived in Tianjin on 26 June the situation had changed completely.

Houses had been set on fire around the city. Christians were murdered in the streets. Christians and pagans recognized as serving Europeans were beaten or murdered. The Boxers entered shops where imported goods were sold and ransacked everything. On 15 June the Church of Our Lady of Victories in Wanghailou was burned along with the surrounding area. Only the tower of the church remained standing, as it had in 1870. Setting fire to the church took place the same day that the churches in Peking were set on fire. Clearly, the Boxers had a well-devised plan. So the Allied Forces had to gain control of Tianjin before going to Peking. On 17 June all the foreign concessions underwent an intense shelling from the imperial troops, who were shooting from the fortress of Dagu. The admirals decided to capture this fortress. Since the warships were lying at anchor very far from the coast because of their draught, the attack had to be done by smaller cannon boats. For more than four hours they resisted the shelling from the ninety cannons on the forts. The shells from the boats eventually blew up the powder magazine in the fort. All of a sudden firing from the cannons stopped and the Allied troops immediately attacked and soon the foreign flags fluttered over the forts.

There remained still another important goal: taking the walled and fortified Chinese City from where much of the shelling came. It was surrounded on three sides by the extensive territory of the concessions. Its capture cost dear.

On 14 July the French flag was hoisted on the walls. A little later the Japanese blew up a gate, and French and Japanese soldiers rushed in through the opening. That was the end of the shelling.

The losses were divided more or less like this: there were twenty-two Frenchmen, and approximately four hundred Japanese, two hundred Americans and fifty Englishmen killed in battle.

The heavy losses among the Japanese were due to their despising all danger; they were walking during the shelling as calmly as in an exercise.

The French troops were few, but troops from Indochina under the command of General de Pélacot came and were added to the contingent that had recently arrived.

From 10 June onwards, the consuls and admirals constantly received distress calls from Peking. But the international army could begin marching to Peking only on 4 August. It consisted, in round numbers of seventeen thousand men: four thousand five hundred Russians; six thousand Japanese; three thousand Englishmen (most of them Indian soldiers); two thousand five hundred Americans; and one thousand Frenchmen.

The March to Peking

The Allied troops did not have a supreme commander; the generals of each nation agreed among themselves according to the situation. It was agreed that the main body of the Allied Forces would march in front, taking the right bank of the river Baihe. The French and Russians, staying a little behind, would take the left bank. The first meeting with the enemy was in Beicang, an important village where the Chinese army was entrenched. The Japanese, who were always ready to go in front, took their place in front. Fifty of them were killed and two hundred seventy were wounded.

On 9 August the leading contingent of the Allied Forces was in Hexiwu, where the French arrived only the next day. Marching in the torrid heat was slow and exhausting; there were many stragglers in all groups. The escort on the river consisted of small boats of all shapes and sizes, and on land of wagons drawn by skeletal horses hitched up with ropes as well as rickshaws and porters. After having passed this village, they heard a violent cannon barrage in the distance. The Japanese at the head of the party had run into the Chinese army entrenched in the large village of Zhangjiazhuang, located ten kilometers from Tongzhou, a harbor on the imperial canal. Through a fierce attack, the Japanese pushed the Chinese forces back so that the troops in the rear could pass through the village without incident.

On 12 August the admirals decided to allow twenty-four hours' rest to their soldiers when they arrived in Tongzhou, which was twenty-five kilometers from Peking; and to start marching again during the night of 13–14 August. The troops were worn out. The heat had caused many cases of sunstroke. The Japanese in particular had many sick and injured men.

The next day, very early in the morning, the Japanese broke camp and approached the city walls. As they drew near, the five hundred Chinese regulars who were to protect the town fled. Thereupon, the Japanese entered Tongzhou without a blow, and the inhabitants flew flags with the Japanese colors to show their submission. But towards evening, when the Japanese had crossed through the town, the inhabitants became panic-stricken seeing so many foreign troops in town. They immediately deserted their homes, took a few belongings, and went to the countryside. The steady stream of those fleeing lasted the whole night. The French camped west of Tongzhou and the others in the open countryside.

Several roads lead to the capital. According to the plan of attack, all the Allied Forces would approach the capital from the east, where there were four gates. The Japanese were to enter through the gate of the Tartar[43] town; the Russians through the second gate on the left and the French were to follow them; finally, the Americans and the English were to pass through the last one.

During the night of 13–14 August, the troops were to set up camp four or five kilometers from the walls. It was noticed at that time that the forced marches, the fights, the heat and the hardships had reduced the numbers by one fourth. General Frey especially had at his disposal only six hundred able-bodied men and three batteries.

The plan was not executed as intended. The Japanese, always in a hurry, took the lead and tried to blow up a gate, but they were pushed back with heavy losses. Later they tried again and eventually entered.

The Russian vanguard attacked the middle gate and tried to breach the wall, but the enemy fired a murderous barrage from the top of the walls. The Russians suffered this terrible firestorm and lost many men.

Nevertheless, they succeeded in breaking a gate down and in entering the city. The regulars immediately fled as fast as their legs could carry them. At about ten o'clock in the evening the French followed the Russians into the Chinese town. There was silence. The houses were practically empty. A whole Russian battalion slept in the houses or collapsed on the ground, exhausted. Finally, in the morning of 15 August all the troops reached the legations. The minister of France wanted the Allied Forces to go to the Beitang to deliver the besieged people. General Frey could not do it alone with the few troops he had at his disposal. The other troops were ready the next morning, 16 August (see p. 282 above).

---

43.   The Tartar City and the Chinese CIty were side by side, the latter to the south of the other. A solid wall fifteen meters high and fifteen meters wide surrounded them. The walls had thirteen monumental gates and the wall that separated the two cities had three gates.

The French Army Chaplain's Notes

Here we take a passage from the notes by the chaplain of the rescue party, François-Xavier Desrumaux:

> With a view to a military expedition to deliver the legations and the Catholic mission of Peking, Colonel Jean-Baptiste Marchand – the one of Fashoda[44] – French chief-of-staff, asked Father Guilloux, the director of the Tianjin district subject to the bishop of Peking, for a missionary as chaplain-interpreter and for some Christians as stretcher-bearers. I was appointed. The departure of the rescue party was fixed for 4 August 1900 at 4:00 in the afternoon. At the agreed time, I went with some twenty Christians to the gathering point. Because it had been impossible to find a horse for me, though I had been promised one, I had to follow the party on foot. Under Colonel de Pélacot's command (for our Indochinese soldiers) we set off directly northwards on the left bank of the Baihe. We marched until midnight and camped for the night in the open. A Russian column was marching with us. It was bivouacking not far from us, whereas the French gunners had taken another route. That first evening we were edified hearing the Russian soldiers reciting and singing evening prayer; it was really beautiful.
>
> Sunday 5 August, at reveille, we were informed that the Chinese soldiers had broken the dike and that the countryside was being flooded, so we had to go back and take the right bank. Those two nights were spent out in the open. On arriving in Yangcun, I was given a mule.
>
> Wednesday 8 August, we left very early and that night we stopped in Hexiwu where we slept. On Thursday 9 August, we covered quite a distance and arrived in the evening in Zhangjiacun, from where the Japanese had just dislodged the imperial troops. We slept there. The next day we reached Tongzhou; we crossed the town and stopped in the western suburb on the banks of the Baihe.
>
> We stayed there till Wednesday 14 August. Then the party began again its march toward Peking, having the long east wall of the

---

44. The Fashoda (Fachoda) Incident of 1898, pitting Great Britain against France in Sudan. (JR)

capital before us. Suddenly, cannon could be heard: the Japanese were bombarding the Xihua gate, the Americans were bombarding the town, and the Russians, more towards the south, had passed with more difficulties than we experienced. We entered the street where the present Hôtel de Pékin is located, and spent the rest of the night there.

On 15 August at around 5:00 in the morning, I went to the chapel in the French Legation and I arrived at the moment that Father d'Addosio was vesting for Mass. I celebrated Mass after him, and then we had breakfast at the Hôtel de Pékin, which Monsieur Chamot directed. There we talked together for a long time and after that I went back to my post among the troops. At about nine or ten o'clock the Allied Forces put cannons on the wall and bombarded the imperial palaces for some time.

After that, I imagined that I could arrive at the Beitang by passing through a side street. On my way, I met Baron d'Anthouard, who had the same idea, but the Americans did not allow us to pass. Then, I returned to my troops, and stayed there the whole day. There I heard the unfortunate news that Father d'Addosio, also thinking that the Beitang was free, had gone there on a donkey, and he had been killed on the way.

On 16 August in the morning, I went with the French troops. We passed by the Nantang, which was completely ruined. We entered the long street that traverses the whole city. Fathers Bantignie and Gaston Bafcop, who with d'Addosio had remained at the legations during the whole time of the siege, were with us. I crossed through the west wall of the Beitang, destroyed at that place, and had the pleasure of immediately seeing Bishop Favier and Bishop Jarlin safe and sound and also several confreres and we hugged effusively.

It was 10:00. I celebrated my Mass in the house chapel and afterwards, completely exhausted, I threw myself on the bed, the very bed of Jarlin, who had brought me there.

I remained some days in Peking but was in a hurry to return to my post in Tianjin, so as to allow Father Guilloux to go to Peking and see the bishops and the confreres. . . . After going to greet General Frey and to tell him that I was on my way, he answered me that I could not leave Peking because I was appointed chaplain. I told him then that he could find all the chaplains he needed in the Beitang. Finally, Bishop Favier intervened and, on the agreed day, I left for Tongzhou with the Christians who had accompanied me. They had not had the occasion to render the service that had been expected of them, for our small party had not had to fight on our way and, once in Peking, the Sisters immediately took care of the sick.

Signed: Desrumaux

Once the allied armies had freed Peking, it was their task to pacify at least the province of Zhili, to purge it from the Boxers with whom it was still infested. General [Maurice] Bailloud and his troops in the regions of Baoding and Zhengding played this role superbly. The presence of French soldiers was enough on the one hand to convince the local authorities to begin negotiations with the Catholic mission, and on the other to reduce the demands of certain Christians, who, taking advantage of the armed forces, demanded very exaggerated compensations.

Second, the presence of the troops supported the diplomatic action, which had to get from the Chinese government both compensations and guarantees for the future.

The commander of all the non-French occupation troops was Marshal Waldersee, a German. The fifteen thousand French troops, strengthened by recently arrived new contingents, were under the command of General Voyron.

The negotiations begun on 26 October 1900 were concluded on the following 24 December. On that date a memorandum was presented to China containing the twelve conditions required by the Powers for restoring normal relations. On 7 September 1901 the final protocol was signed, which solemnly established the results achieved and the commitments of China.

The emperor, or rather Cixi, still in voluntary exile, approved of everything that her authorized representatives had signed. At the end of October 1901, Their Majesties started their return trip and arrived in the capital on 6 January 1902.

Chapter 14

Boxer Storm in Zhili Province

Burning of the Nantang – Burning of the Dongtang – The Murder of Josephines at the Dongtang – Burning of the Xitang – Murders at Chala – Desecration of the Cemetery at Chala – The Storm Outside Peking: At the Tianjin District – At Baoding District – At Xuanhua District – The Attack on Yongning – The Siege of the Cave of the Goats

We have briefly related what had happened in the Beitang, the largest parish in Peking. There were, however, at that time three other important parishes: the Nantang, the Dongtang and the Xitang, all named after the cardinal points of the compass.

Burning of the Nantang

The Nantang church, quite near the south gate of the Tartar city, was the old cathedral, which the Jesuits built around 1706 on the site of the second church of Peking, built in 1650 by Father Adam Schall, thanks to a generous gift from the Shunzhi emperor, the first of the Qing dynasty.[45] His successor Kangxi granted ten thousand taels for the construction of that cathedral.

In 1775, however, fire destroyed this large building. Then Qianlong on hearing of his ancestor Kangxi's generous gesture in favor of this church, gave orders to do the same, provide the same amount, which at that time was worth seventy-five thousand livres; and imitating his grandfather, he also placed on it inscriptions written with a red brush.

In 1900, the spacious property of the Nantang contained four institutions: the presbytery, Saint Vincent Hospital in the hands of the Daughters of Charity, the motherhouse of the Chinese Sisters of Saint Joseph (Josephines), and the College entrusted to the Marist Brothers in 1891.

When the French sailors arrived, ten of them were placed at the Nantang. But because of the intensity of the Boxer movement, which the

---

45. The Nantang, located near the southwestern gate of the Tartar City, was the site of Ricci's first formal church, built in 1610-1611, but replaced by Father Adam Schall in 1650-1651 thanks to a generous donation from the Shunzhi emperor. [See Alan Richard Sweeten, *China's Old Churches* (Leiden: Brill, 2020), 73-75. (AS)

government evidently supported, the troop commander considered this mission doomed to certain defeat. It was obvious that the fires and murders in the capital were planned and ordered: first the churches were to be set on fire on 14 June and the murders were to begin the next day. There was only one exception, the Dongtang, which was set on fire a day earlier, 13 June; it is not known why.

As soon as the legations were informed, they rushed to the assistance of the parish priest, Father Garrigues, but he had already disappeared. Then they thought of preventing the catastrophe that threatened the institutions of the Nantang. Therefore, on the evening of 13 June the Europeans went to bring the missionaries and the Sisters to the legations. This was not without its difficulties, because d'Addosio did not want to leave his Christians in danger and promised them that he would come back the next day to collect them.

On the following morning, the Christians who went to church for Mass were very surprised to hear that the missionaries had abandoned the residence during the night. The following days, the Europeans worked wonders of courage to save the Christians.

That day, around ten o'clock in the morning, cries were heard at the Shunzhi [*sic* Xuanwu] gate, located about a hundred meters from the Nantang. It was the local gang of Boxers. The attack on the residence began immediately. The Boxers had no soldiers with them and were armed only with swords and axes. After breaking down the double gate with axes, the aggressors entered cautiously into the outer courtyard and after breaking the windows of the apartments located on the left and on the right of the gate, they saw that there was nobody to defend the property and they set it on fire. From there they went to the church and tried to break down the doors, but in vain.

Then they poured paraffin oil on the doors and set them ablaze. At that moment there were some Christians in the tower. They began to ring the bells, but soon they died from asphyxiation.

During the time the fire was enveloping the church, gangs of looters in search of spoils went to the institutions. They evicted the women who had fled there some days before, then took everything that they could carry. These Christian women, who did not know where to go, went to the house of the Josephines, evacuated the night before, but the Boxers followed them there. We do not know what happened then. It is very probable that many of these women who could have fled because of the disorder preferred to die in the enclosure of the church to dying in the city streets, where they could have met a worse fate. The College of the Marist Brothers, which also had been evacuated, was destroyed and set on fire.

The residence of the missionaries and the sacristy next to the church were all that remained. The Boxers did not dare to attack them, fearing a trap. No one in the whole quarter knew of the evacuation of the missionaries, Brothers, Sisters and Josephines the previous night. Therefore, the aggressors, not seeing them anywhere, were convinced that they were hiding either in the residence, or in the sacristy. Seeing nobody coming out, however, the Boxers decided to continue looting and to set fire to the residence.

Finally, they attacked the sacristy. It had a solid terrace roof, to which some fifty Christians had fled. It is difficult to describe the misery endured by these people packed on that terrace roof, up against the church on fire. Their suffering became more terrible when the sacristy was set on fire. The roof heated from below began to burn. Those poor Christians did not stop praying out loud, singing their prayers and their litanies imploring God's help.

Around five o'clock in the evening, the fire had devoured everything; only smoking ruins remained. The stream of curious people and of looters had drifted away, for there was nothing more to steal. At this moment the Chinese Marist Brother Joseph Fan, judging the situation on the sacristy untenable, with ten orphans whom he had brought there a few days earlier, took advantage of this occasion to flee.

Burning of the Dongtang

At that time there was in the Dongtang quite a large residence next to the beautiful church which Bishop Delaplace built in 1884; moreover, there was a girls' school managed by the Josephines. Next to those and separated by an alley, a refuge had been opened for the numerous Christian women who had come from everywhere in the hope of escaping death.

Two priests served this parish of about one thousand Faithful; these two priests, both Vincentians, were Fathers Garrigues, director, and Barthélémy Li. That day, there was in the Dongtang Father André Li, pastor of Jiatuan, who had come to take refuge.

Garrigues did not delude himself about the gravity of the events. He looked at the situation with eyes of faith. His confrere was worrying about the future and looked for information every day about what was happening. Garrigues listened silently to the alarming accounts of the Christians and contented himself with exhorting them to prepare themselves for martyrdom by quoting these words from the Gospel [Mt. 10:28]: "They can kill your bodies but they cannot kill your souls."

As we mentioned above, the church of the Dongtang was the first to be attacked. On 13 June, around seven o'clock in the evening, a hostile crowd suddenly invaded the residence. The refugees who were packed in the residence became panic-stricken; there was a general stampede, every one fleeing wherever possible. While the Boxers were entering by the doors, the refugees were jumping over the walls. Some made it; others fell into the hands of the aggressors and were killed. Immediately the houses were looted and set on fire along with the church. Amid the confusion that followed the looting of the institutions and under cover of darkness, the three missionaries were able to flee individually without each other knowing. André Li left without anybody ever being able to know his whereabouts. The Christian Thomas Lan met Barthélémy Li and led him to the Xihua gate, not far from the Beitang, but the soldiers who guarded it did not let him pass. Repulsed on this side, they tried to get out of the city. Li succeeded alone and went to the west. Despite his age he continued his march and went to Sangyu, a hospitable Christian community at more than sixty kilometers, where he arrived safe and sound.

About Garrigues, there was no information. It was said that a police officer seemed to have seen him on the street, fleeing, with his head enveloped in a handkerchief probably to hide his long beard. Alone, or guided by a Christian, he fled, people said, into an abandoned yard. He was said to have stayed there that night and the whole of the next day, 14 June.

It was eight o'clock in the evening of 13 June, when people in the legations caught sight of the fire in the Dongtang. Pichon, minister of France, wanted to save Garrigues. Taking with him four sailors and three other European civilians, he advanced toward the Dongtang. In an alley they surprised some thirty Boxers holding torches, who were on the point of setting fire to houses. They shot and killed some ten of them. But they could not get any news about the missionary.

On the evening of 14 June Garrigues must have left his hideout to try to escape. Around ten o'clock, as he went along the temple called Longfusi somebody screamed, "A Western devil! Kill him!" Hearing this cry, the people who lived there came out of their houses and arming themselves with whatever they could grasp, they pounced on him and killed him. It was reported that the body of the victim was burned not far from that place with the wood of a house under construction.

More precise information on the martyrdom of this holy priest could never be found.

The Murder of Josephines at the Dongtang

On the east side of the missionaries' residence there was a parochial school, managed by three Josephine Sisters. On 13 June the school, just like all the communities in Peking, was packed with people who had hurried there from everywhere in town and even from out of town. There were also many people in the space separated from the school by an alley. Yet, help came from the Nantang. The superior of the Josephines in the Nantang, knowing that her three Sisters in the Dongtang were indeed overwhelmed with the influx of refugees, sent them help. On 13 June she ordered four of her Sisters to go to the Dongtang to help their companions.

Led by a domestic, they traveled the more than two kilometers on foot without mishap, for on that day the streets were quite calm; the fires and killings had not yet begun. Arriving at the Dongtang, they were immediately charged with the care of about one hundred eighty women lodging in the separated refuge. It turned out that it was the very day the church was set on fire. Thus, on one side there were three Sisters with their pupils and many refugees; on the other side, four Sisters with refugees. Though near each other, they were not to see each other again.

As soon as the flames began to rise from the church, the poor women in the school thought that their last hour had arrived – this was true for many of them. In the school the heat had become unbearable. Believing that they had still just a few minutes to live, the Sisters, instead of fruitless lamentations, showed that they were equal to their task. Forgetting themselves they only thought to save these women who had come to take refuge at their place.

After gathering all the people together in the chapel, they encouraged the Christian women to prepare themselves to die and recited the act of contrition out loud. They told the women to offer their lives to God, receiving martyrdom out of love for Him. Everyone responded to this faith-filled exhortation. Then the superior, Sister Philomena Wang, opened the door of the tabernacle containing the Sacred Species and she and her two companions consumed them to avoid profanation.

That night passed without any further distress other than fear. The next day, 14 June, before daybreak, a large crowd rushed into the schoolyard. These looters broke down doors and windows and began to take everything the refugees had brought: money, clothes, bedding, etc., the candlesticks from the altar, and all the linen that was there. These poor women, stripped naked, did not know what to do. A sympathetic-looking farmer said to one of them, the virgin Marie Chen, "Aren't you going to leave?" "Is it still possible to flee?" she asked. "Certainly, hurry!"

Then she took her place at the head of the fleeing party and left at the same time as the Josephine Sister, Anna Zhang, whom many women and children followed. They went towards the Beitang. The women, in small groups, followed Marie Chen and could go quite far. But Anna Zhang was unable to divide the children into small groups and had to walk slowly. So, she was quickly noticed and killed. It is not known what happened to her followers. Marie Chen, on looking back, saw the turmoil that took place behind her. Frightened, she went faster and succeeded in getting away with some of those who were following her. The two other Josephines must certainly have been killed with many of the refugees.

In the refuge, at about eight o'clock in the evening, the women heard the crackling of the fire that was devouring the church. The superior, Françoise Wu and her companions began to sprinkle the Christians with Holy Water, to encourage them to put their trust in the Lord and if necessary to die for Him. Coming together in the yard for lack of other space, they prayed silently, some standing, some kneeling and spent the whole night with no idea of what was happening at the other side of the street in the girls' school.

The next day at eight o'clock in the morning, screams were heard in the street. Immediately the rabble climbed the wall and rushed into the yard, breaking doors and windows crying to those terrified women, "What! You have not left yet? What are you doing here? Flee!" Pulling and pushing and cursing them, the invaders threw them into the street on the north side of the institution. Only the novice Agnes Ma was still there. She was already half dead of fright and could not flee, so she was killed in the hideout where she had curled up. The other Josephines, followed by the women and the children, whose number was decreasing at every step, some fleeing, some losing their way, went to the girls' school, thinking that it was still there, but they found only smoking ruins. Consequently, they decided to go to the Nantang, but on their way gangs of Boxers followed them. Four Josephines were butchered in the street and thrown into the smoking ashes. Only the superior died; the others pretended to be dead and got away from there, but they probably were killed a little later, except Philomène Zhang, who was to experience the sufferings of a long agony.

A Christian Tartar soldier, Shi Luyi, decided to save her, when he found her lying near the church, wounded, almost naked. But being a soldier and, what was worse, being Christian did not make it easier. The story that he recounted to Father Planchet is so long and so extraordinary, including the steadfastness of the woman, that it is hardly believable. That is the reason why we do not reproduce it here. The end of the story is that the Boxers finally discovered this heroic young woman on 24 June and killed her. She must have suffered greatly in her final ten days.

The other refugees were probably killed alone, out of sight of any witness. At least if some of these fleeing women succeeded in avoiding death, we have no knowledge of it.

Burning of the Xitang

We have told how Father Pedrini, an Italian Vincentian, had founded this church. He built it in 1723, when he was the music teacher for Kangxi's sons, and he gave it to the Sacred Congregation of Propaganda. That is why the priests who served there were all Italian priests, sent by Propaganda, like Pedrini himself. In Peking, they were always called "Propagandists."

The special mission of Propaganda did not last long. It was extinguished through persecution of the Jiaqing emperor in 1811. Its missionaries were repatriated and the church was completely destroyed. The French Vincentians of the Beitang, who succeeded the French Jesuits, looked after the few Christians of that parish.

When, in 1860, the religious properties were given back to Bishop Mouly, the Xitang was just a plot of wasted ground.

In 1867, a church was built under the direction of Brother Marty. When Father Provost was at the head of the parish, he installed a pipe organ that he himself had built. Garrigues was its parish priest for a short time, but this short time was enough to leave a reputation for holiness with the Christians.

In 1900, Father Doré was in charge of that parish for a year and six months. Maurice Doré, born in Paris in the Poissy suburb on 15 May 1862, was admitted in Dax on 26 September 1880 and ordained priest on 17 April 1887. He arrived in Peking on 16 October 1888. Like all the young arrivals from Europe, he was charged with several jobs, first in the districts of Baoding, Yongping, and Tianjin and lastly, on 28 December 1898 he was appointed pastor of the Xitang.

Doré had an artistic character and a lively and generous disposition. He knew how to be informed about the daily news in that troublesome period, and he often informed Favier by letter on the course of events in the capital. By the way, he was not fooling himself about the gravity of the danger that threatened the missionaries and the Christians.

On 3 June, Pentecost, he gave Benediction with the Blessed Sacrament, not in the evening as usual, but in the morning after High Mass, because of the troubles that the Boxers had begun to create. He told the Faithful not to come to the church during the day, but only in the morning, because of the increasing danger. The Christians then asked him his opinion on the actual events; he answered, "For the church, this will certainly turn out badly."

On 8 June, seeing that the situation was getting worse and that his presence at his residence was useless, Doré figured he could leave his church and flee to the Beitang. He stayed there only one night, and the following morning he went back to the Xitang. Favier made it clear to him that abandoning the churches would have the effect of provoking fires and killings in Peking. When the Boxers saw the buildings abandoned, they would destroy them without meeting the least resistance.

Back in the Xitang, he called his most important Christians and catechists, so as to agree with them on what arrangements to make. He suggested that they would put the different altar ornaments, chalices and all that had value in big boxes and bury them.

The Christians answered that those objects would spoil quickly in the ground and that it would be difficult to do this work without being seen and finally that there was no time left to do all this. Doré fell in with their opinion, but a few days later, he alone with his servant, Jean Yang, hid some important objects in the garden: papers, registers, and so on. So as to avoid all profanation, from Sunday 10 June on, the parish priest did not keep the Blessed Sacrament in the church, but he went on celebrating Holy Mass every day. One of his catechists, Gabriel Zhang, one day asked him a little while before the disaster, "If the Boxers come, are you going to use your weapons?" Doré indeed had three shotguns and a six-shot revolver. "What is the use," he answered, "sending some Boxers to hell would be of no avail." In the presence of the catechist, Doré took all the arms and put them in a cupboard under lock and key saying, "Even if I killed some, it would be useless and I would not have any merit dying in this way; in both cases I must die."

The next day, 14 June, Doré had just celebrated his six o'clock Mass, when the outer door, opening onto the street, was banged on very loudly. The people inside the church thought that Boxers were invading the residence.

Then a loud voice from the street screamed, "These are Christians who come from the Dongtang, which was set on fire last night!" Immediately Doré had the door opened. On hearing this bad news, his first worry was the fate of his people. He sent Jean Yang to bring Sister Jaurias a letter to ask her if she could please take in several Christian women. Jean had to retrace his steps. It was too late, because the gate of the Beitang was under guard from the previous evening. The siege of the Beitang had begun. Seeing his servant coming back he cried out, "What is to be done?"

There were many Christians in the yard and the church, both men and women. From that moment on, Doré did not stop going between his room and the church, where there were some fifty people. He exhorted them to accept death from God's hand. Here our documents are sketchy for lack of witnesses.

At about nine or ten o'clock that evening, people in the street cried out, "Fire!" The main gate was burning. A little later the church bell rang a few times, and then the church was in flames. In the church the Christians were praying out loud. It is probable that when the mob was entering the yard, Doré rushed to the bell to ring out a warning, rather than to call for help, which he knew did not exist. It was not to alarm his Christians but to warn them that it was time to seek a secure place.

According to one account, when Doré was ringing the bell, the Boxers had already entered the residence; they rushed towards him and hit him on the head with a sword. The blow knocked him out cold under the church tower. In another account he is supposed to have been burned to death in his church with his beloved Christians.

Murders at Chala

Chala was a suburb to the west of the capital, inhabited under the last dynasty mostly by people of Tartar-Manchu origin. The alignment of houses, all similar, which can still be seen today, reminds a passer-by of a military camp.

The religious institution we are talking about was located at the edge of this village on the north side and had taken the very name of the village itself. Emperor Wanli around 1611 had graciously given this property to bury Matteo Ricci. After the bishops of Peking acquired adjacent properties, an important number of works of mercy came to be established around the graves of the Jesuits.

In 1871, Bishop Delaplace created a parish and an agricultural institution in aid of orphans who were able to work. In 1887, Bishop Tagliabue, his successor, added a hospital and a new orphanage for very young boys. These two institutions were entrusted to the Daughters of Charity.

In 1893, Bishop Sarthou entrusted the agricultural orphanage to the Marist Brothers. The priest living there was in charge of the religious services of the parish and of the Sisters' two institutions.

The martyrs of Chala therefore were to come from the numerous personnel that inhabited these institutions.

In 1900, the priest in charge of that parish was Augustin Zou, a Vincentian. Sister Fraisse managed the hospital and the orphanage, and Brother Jules-André directed the agricultural orphanage.

Near the end of May, Sister Fraisse, seeing the danger that threatened her works, wrote to Favier to ask him to approach the Chinese government in order to get Chinese soldiers to guard the institution. At that time, many Europeans still counted on the promised protection of the Chinese government. Brother Jules-André, deluding himself in the same way, was convinced that military forces would come to protect Chala, when the time had come. In the meantime, Father Zou informed the bishop in a completely different way. He was fifty years old and knew the mandarins' deceitfulness. "Do not count on them," he told Favier, "but you had better choose young and strong men among the many refugees that you have in the Beitang. Send them here to protect us."

The bishop, fearing the worst, ordered the Sisters to come to the Beitang. On 1 June, they left Chala, entrusting their seventy children to Brother Jules-André's care. On 8 June, having discussed it with Favier, the Brother had one hundred twenty children brought to the Nantang. Since that day, the European and Chinese Brothers commuted between Chala, the Beitang, and the Nantang in order to keep the children occupied and to watch over them.

On 14 June, however, the Brothers who were in the Beitang could no longer leave. It was impossible for the people in the Beitang to go and save the Christians of Chala, refugees or others. Father Zou had returned to the Beitang at the same time as the Brothers. From 13 June on, there were no Europeans in Chala. They were not harassed seriously until 17 June. That day, some Boxers climbed the walls of the property, which were barely two meters high. The few orphans that Brother Adon had brought back from the Nantang, the old servants, and the Christian refugees made a good guard. The first Boxer – a leader – who dared to go over the wall was welcomed with gunshot. He was put out of action. This frightened the attackers, who drew back carrying their dead commander. They laid him down under a tree and were advised not to touch him until nightfall, expecting that he would rise again. A short time later, a new group of Boxers arrived from the south and then still another. Soon the property was completely surrounded.

The only gun that Adon's companions had could not withstand such an invasion. The Boxers entered from every side at the same time. For some minutes one could hear nothing but the invaders' cries, ordering each victim to kneel down, then the blows of swords hitting the heads. Some hours later the church and the buildings were burned to ashes.

How had this short and savage tragedy happened? At what time had the fires been set? It is not known. No one among the besieged escaped death. Information could have been had only from the neighbors, actually not very numerous, who lived between the village itself and the institutions of Chala. They saw the flames going up from the church and the houses, but they could not see what was happening inside the property. Their opinion was that the majority of the victims had been murdered in the church before the fire.

After the liberation of the Beitang (16 August), that is, two months after the disaster, when the Marist Brothers, who had lost their two superiors, were able to go back to Chala, they found a heap of corpses in a corner of the west yard quite far from the church. They discovered that the three wells were more than halfway filled with corpses. These wells had a diameter of 1.5 meters, a depth of fifteen meters, holding ordinarily only two or three meters of water. Other corpses were still lying in the garden.

In any case, the number of corpses, found in Chala, certainly was greater than the number of the besieged people. Therefore, corpses of Christians or even of pagans – indeed it is known that the Boxers murdered many non-Christians either by mistake or because of suspicion of connivance with foreigners – had been brought there by people who wanted to get rid of burdensome objects. In their account to Favier, the Brothers wrote:

> We were really led to believe that the majority of the children died in the church with Brother Adon. It was something he expressed several times in his conversations: If I see myself without hope of escaping, I want to die in the church. Already in the Nantang he wanted to bring the children into the church, instead of making them climb on the terrace of the sacristy. Moreover, the charred bones and the remains of clothes that we have found, when rummaging in the rubble of the church, confirm our opinion.

As a result, we can believe that the besieged people of Chala were all martyrs. They had done what depended on them to save the holy place from profanation and the lives of their younger Brothers, and also to wait for the expected help. When God asked them the sacrifice of their lives, they did not weaken.

When order had returned in the country some months after the troubles, Boxers who had participated in the killings of Chala said, "In Chala, no one begged for mercy, no one offered to *beijiao* (renounce their faith)."

Desecration of the Cemetery at Chala

The Boxers did not stop at killing so many innocent defenseless victims. In the cemetery of Chala, there stood almost two hundred marble steles, many magnificently sculpted according to the Chinese style. On their pediment the two symbolic dragons were hugging each other. All the steles carried a long inscription in Latin and Chinese, occasionally also in Manchu, which gave the name of the missionary, his birth and death, and the highlights of his missionary life. The tombs presented these vandals with a unique occasion to satisfy their hatred for Christians and foreigners as well as their cruelty and cupidity. We say cupidity, for they thought the tombs were filled with treasures, like the royal tombs of old that were profaned in the course of history for the sake of profit.

During the two long months before the arrival of the Allied Forces, they had plenty of time to perpetrate their infamies. First, they looted what had not fallen prey to the flames. They left only the walls in the Sisters' residence, in the hospital, and in the orphanage. Afterwards they also destroyed these in order to sell the bricks.

Having finished with the living, they tackled the dead. Using pickaxes, they pulled down the steles. They destroyed the vaults of the tombs and the stone and brickwork, in order to take the usable materials. They broke up the coffins if they still existed, and finding only bones and no gold or silver, they, in their disappointment, broke up and scattered these venerable remains.

They had no tools to break up the steles, so they defaced some of them, and because they were too heavy to be taken away, they left them lying around the empty graves. It was a hideous spectacle: this chaos of maimed symbols, of upended steles, of human remains scattered among the rubble. Everything just laid there spread out for more than two years, waiting for the day of reparations, which began in September 1901.

The eighty-two steles that had decorated the Jesuit Fathers' tombs can be seen now, placed against the base of the wall on the two sides of the nave in the new church built by Bishop Jarlin not far from the old one in 1903–1904. The whole constitutes a moving cenotaph (empty tomb monument). (See Jean-Marie Planchet, *Le Cimetière et les oeuvres Catholiques de Chala 1610–1927*, Pékin: Imprimerie des Lazaristes, 1928, from which we have taken this account.)

The Storm Outside Peking: at Tianjin District

In the district of Tianjin, the ruins were without number. There was the awful siege of Tianjin, especially of the French Concession, which was the one most exposed. In 1900, there were only three concessions: French, English, and German (a short time after the liberation of Tianjin, the American, Russian, Japanese, Italian and Austrian concessions came into existence). They were located on the right bank of the Baihe [*sic* Haihe]. It is obvious that in these concessions the majority of the inhabitants were Chinese, mostly traders. A wall surrounded the city[46] and its forts were located on the right bank. The large Church of Our Lady of Victories was located in the northeast of the Chinese town in a place called Wanghailou. Father Chevrier had built it in 1869 but it burned down the following year at the time of the murders of 1870. Instead of rebuilding that church, Bishop Delaplace preferred to build another one in the French Concession, the Church of Saint Louis, built in 1871–1872. The church still exists today.

At the time of the terrible siege of Tianjin, enormous mountains of salt blocked the left bank of the Baihe. From behind these mounds and without danger to themselves Boxers and regular soldiers fired on the concessions, especially on the Church of Saint Louis filled with refugees and on the nearby hospital, overflowing with wounded civilians and soldiers. The procure and the house of the Sisters were also filled with the wounded and with Christian refugees.

How could the city of Tianjin, so exposed and so poorly protected, resist until 14 July? And how did the Allied Forces, exhausted and almost without ammunition, reduce to silence the Chinese forts located near and behind Our Lady of Victories, which had been spewing out ammunition

---

46. The walls were razed and the city completely dismantled by the Allied Powers after the Boxer rebellion.

on the Europeans for twenty days? It is not easy to explain to people who cannot see in events the effects of a Superior Cause.

Though there were not many missionaries in this district, two Chinese priests, Fathers Pierre Nie, a Vincentian, and Thomas Bao, a diocesan priest, were murdered and burned by the Boxers in Yanshan, the first Christian community formed by Chevrier; three Josephines also shed their blood. Regarding the victims among the Faithful, we will speak of them below.

At Baoding District

In this district, the Boxers were stronger than anywhere else. The leading Boxers from Shandong set up camp there and recruited followers before going up to Peking. During the months of March and April 1900, they met in temples, where they trained their followers, who wore a red turban and a belt of the same color.

On 20 April the first warning was given. Ten thousand Boxers besieged Zhangjiacun thirty kilometers south of Baoding, but with more losses than successes. Furious they returned to the attack, and on 13 May, Father Dumond, the director of the district, wrote, "we received the sorrowful news that in the village of Xuge (fifty kilometers from Baoding), the Boxers murdered and burned fifty or sixty Christians with exceptional cruelty; three villages have been set on fire."

In the first days of June, some fifty other Christians were also murdered in their respective villages in the neighborhood of Donglü. In the meantime and at different places ill treatment continued: villages were set on fire and Christians were murdered. The Christians feeling threatened and persecuted on all sides had the idea of gathering together to resist attacks better and to defend themselves more efficiently. Some of them, the ones from the north of Baoding hastened to take refuge in Peking; others, from the south, went to the large village of Donglü. They dug a wide ditch around the village. The earth from the ditch was used to make a protective surrounding wall. Still others went to Anjiazhuang, the oldest Christian community of the district, and barricaded themselves in as the people of Donglü had done.

The missionaries remained with their Christians and locked themselves in these two villages. But as soon as the residences were vacated, they were set aflame.

Dumond's hope was that the Boxers would not dare attack the charitable works in Peking. But when he heard on 15 June that the Beitang was besieged, he hurried to reach Anjiazhuang. His presence in the walled city of Baoding, from where the Christians had already fled several days before, was perfectly useless.

The attacks were mostly against Donglü and Anjiazhuang. This last-named village was seriously attacked twice, on 24 July and 4 September. The Christians (about five thousand) were very poorly armed. With God's special help, however, behind earthen defenses they withstood a cannon barrage of several hours; then they rose and put the aggressors to flight killing five or six hundred of them. The aggressors' cannons, rampart guns, small weapons and carts fell into the hands of the besieged Christians.

The honor of resisting is rightly due to Donglü. The four thousand Christians gathered there showed extraordinary courage. In the beginning of the siege they had only two small cast-iron cannons, five or six rapid-fire guns and some fifty pistols. On 16 August, the period of the last attacks, they had eighty cannons, fifty rapid-fire guns and innumerable swords and pikes. All this was the result of their audacious sorties when they noticed that the enemy had yielded or hesitated.

They had to face forty attacks of the regular soldiers and the Boxers together. More than two thousand men died in front of the earthen levees of Donglü. The Boxers had to establish a hospital in Baoding to take care of the wounded brought in from Donglü. At the same time during the siege of Donglü only twenty-two Christians were killed. These brave defenders drew their courage from their faith. "During this period of persecution and amid our anxieties," wrote Dumond, "our consolation was our Christians' spirit of faith, courage and steadfastness. Apostasies were very rare, even among the newly baptized; all those who were killed publicly confessed their faith; even several Christians, who practiced little, were happy to find this occasion to go to heaven. From the beginning of the difficulties, the Faithful had taken the decision to die defending the missionaries. Many catechumens asked to be baptized in this time of danger." Dumond finished his account declaring, "Our Christians were Vendée people in miniature." [47]

---

47. The inhabitants of the Vendée region of France, who remained staunchly Catholic at the time of the Revolution and battled the revolutionary troops. (JR)

At Xuanhua District

This large district, located to the northwest of Peking was made up of six beautiful parishes. Father Gustave Vanhersecke was their director and lived in the town of Xuanhua. When going to Peking for Bishop Jarlin's consecration (29 April 1900), he learned that a large movement was forming against foreigners and Christians. Back home, he heard that even in his own town the agitation had begun and that Christians, who were suffering insults and threats, were already becoming alarmed.

The director went to the sub-prefect of the town and asked him to have these provocations stopped, because they could degenerate into murders. The mandarin immediately proclaimed that all activities of the Boxer movement were forbidden. But the rumors were already drowning out the voice of the local authorities. The proclamation had no effect; authority was passing into other hands. On 10 June all communication with the capital was cut off. Then the director decided to gather the Christians to defend the church and the residence of Xuanhua. He called thirty young men, but he quickly understood that it would be impossible to fortify these buildings right in the middle of the town. He sent them away and consulted his two companions, Vincentian Fathers Emmanuel-Joseph Catheline and André Zhang. It was decided that Father Catheline would go to Xiwanzi, where already a great number of Christians of the Xuanhua district were gathered, though this large Christian community no longer depended on the Vincentians but on the Scheut Fathers.

Father André Zhang would stay in town to guard the church and the residence as long as prudence permitted; Dumond would go to Zhang-zhuang, where he might be able to organize the resistance.

That same evening, they set out together, but since the route was not very safe, Father Vanhersecke did not want to be separated from his young confrere, and took him to Xiwanzi. The Belgian priests received them very well, and they took several days' rest there. On 25 June the director set out for Zhangzhuang. In town, André Zhang thought it prudent to flee and after he left, the mob together with the garrison soldiers rushed to the church and the Christians' homes, looted them and set fire to them. It was 5 July. Next, the Boxers and regulars began to attack almost all the Christian communities of the district.

Recounting all those attacks would make our story too long, so we will give an account of two of the most devastating, and that will give an idea of what was happening in the other towns and villages.

The Attack on Yongning

Yongning was the center of a parish located more than a hundred kilometers from Xuanhua. It had seventeen hundred Christians spread over three sub-prefectures. Because this parish was so near the capital, it was the first one to feel the shocks that were rumbling through the north of China.

At the end April 1900, some Boxers from Shandong entered this mountainous region and began to recruit followers, hold meetings, and train new members to fight while crying, "Kill the Christians! Out with the Foreigners!"

One of them named Mazi [Ma Zi?], a carpenter by trade, soon began to lead the movement. He went to Peking, and saw prince Duan, officially in charge of the Boxers of Peking and received from him authorization to train gangs of "celestial soldiers" and to require local authorities to provide for the living expenses of these new troops.

News of this development sent terror coursing through all the Christian communities. The parish priest of Yongning, Vincentian Father Martin Zhou, closed his schools and sent the students back to their families. At the same time, he called the Christians who knew how to shoot a gun to come and guard the church as well as the refugees assembled there. There were many refugees looking for both shelter in the shadow of the church tower and the priest's help to die well.

The Christians were determined to defend themselves, but they were convinced that the town could not be defended because it was too large to fortify adequately. On 16 June, after discussing it with the Christians, Zhou decided to leave the town and to join the Christians of Kongjian, a village located at one or two kilometers from there. They thought the defense would be easier in a small village at the foot of a mountain.

From the following day on, the refugees, women and children and the Christians of the town, all emigrated to Kongjian, following their missionary.

On 21 June, market day in Yongning, the Boxers went to the abandoned church and set fire to it. After this easy victory, they did the same to all the Christians' houses. Two lame elderly folks, who had been unable to follow the others, had their throats cut in the hovel where they had taken refuge; their corpses were burned in the street. This act had a painful repercussion in the whole region: the Christians began to desert their own houses en masse. They scattered, some hiding at the bottom of gorges or withdrawing into the numerous mountain caves in the region.

As soon as they arrived in Kongjian they joined the Christians of the village, around six hundred of them. Aware that the enemy was at the door, they feverishly prepared themselves for the fight. On one hand, the women and elderly stayed in the chapel praying for help and strength. On the other hand, the able-bodied men prepared their quite rudimentary arms. One of them even produced cannons with wood strengthened with ropes, which they put on the roofs more to frighten the enemy than to kill them. They had begun to build an earthen wall, but they did not have time to finish it. So, the defenders crammed into the apartments of a rich family named Wei as their bastion.

On 22 June Mazi, after gathering his gangs, attacked the village on three sides, the fourth being the slope of the mountain. From the rooftops, the Christians could see the plain covered with red turbans, which, when the signal was given, bowed three times, then after straightening up, the "celestial soldiers" flourished their swords, and screamed "*Sha! Sha!*" (Kill! Kill!), which the mountains echoed back.

They rushed towards the village. The first shock was not in their favor. They had counted on the magic power of their incantations and on their invulnerability. The bullets of the Christians, however, killed some ten men and wounded thirty. They withdrew after an hour's battle.

A few hours later, Mazi's gangs returned to the attack, this time helped by the policemen of the sub-prefecture, reinforcements that were to decide the fate of the battle. Thanks to their long-range guns, these new aggressors, despite their small number, were killing the defenders, who, badly armed, could not even look over their roofs without being exposed to gunfire. With the advantage in their favor, the Boxers proceeded without fear to make the circle around the besieged smaller and smaller, murdering all those who tried to escape.

They arrived near the houses of the Wei family and near the chapel, last refuge of the besieged. To cap the misery, Father Zhou, seeing that all was lost, advised those who were around him to flee as fast as possible. The village, resting on the slope of the mountain could not be attacked from that side. The missionary with some Christians escaped by that way. As soon as that news was known, the guns fell from the hands of the bravest defenders. Then the collapse and the butchering of the Christians began: some were killed in their houses, some in the street, those who tried to leave the village were killed immediately, many were blocked in their burning houses and died of asphyxiation, and others, half-dead, were thrown into wells.

During the whole time of the battle, the women did not leave the chapel, which they had made their asylum. When they saw the flames coming to the church, they decided to save the holy images and liturgical objects, and to use them as a palladium (or protective images). They unhooked the images of the way of the cross, divided them among themselves, and also the crucifix and the chalices and went out, taking with them these relics and singing together the litany of the Blessed Virgin.

In a few minutes all these Christian women were murdered one after the other. None of those who fled up the mountain was followed; they were able to escape without crossing enemy lines. So, they were safe . . . that day, but we will see that very few avoided death.

The following day, the Boxers went from top to bottom through the Christians' houses that the flames had more or less spared and found there several survivors, who had hidden as best they could during the fire; they murdered them mercilessly.

The Siege of the Cave of the Goats

Many Christians fleeing the persecutions, had taken refuge in caverns, a kind of natural series of caves more or less spacious, quite numerous in those regions.

One, called "Cave of the Goats," was about forty meters long and eighteen meters wide. At its entrance there was a plateau, which was to be very disastrous for them. Several hundred Christians with women and children had settled there. Some among them had fled from Kongjian. From 25 June on, the Boxers began to go through the neighboring mountains and there murdered eighty Christians.

On 9 July, having killed all the Christians they discovered in the neighborhood, Mazi gathered a great number of fighters in the valley that faced the Cave of the Goats in order to besiege it. He began by securing the well where the refugees came for water, for the top of the mountain had no water at all. The Christians had only some muskets, which were given to the best shots; the others prepared stones they were going to throw at the attackers.

The next day, 10 July, Mazi wanted to try to take the stronghold by force; but the avalanche of stones and the gunshots that the defenders fired wounded a number of attackers. That was reason enough to abandon the enterprise that day.

On 11 July, the Boxers tried to bomb the entrance of the cave with a small cannon; but the gunner had not reckoned with its recoil and the first shot crushed him. Then Mazi commandeered a huge number of bundles of firewood from the villages. He had them carried to the top of the mountain to a place over the entrance of the cavern, and from there he had the burning bundles thrown down in front of the entrance of the cavern, so as to smoke out and burn the besieged alive. The Christians tried to push away the inferno that was suffocating them, hampered by the continuous gunfire from below. Eventually the burning bundles blocked the entrance, and the heat and the smoke became unbearable for the Christians.

The next day, the Boxers redoubled their efforts in this unequal battle; but in the evening, torrential rain forced them to take shelter. Some hundred refugees took advantage of the weather to flee under the cover of night, but they were all murdered in the following days.

On 13 July the Boxers renewed their tactic of dropping burning bundles of firewood in front of the entrance of the cavern with renewed deliberateness during the whole day. The next night, a devout virgin, forty years old, said to the Christian women, "For us, dying is nothing, but the worst evil would be to fall into their hands and to be taken away by them. On the other hand, if God takes our souls, well, we all will meet again in Paradise." They all agreed, weeping, Marie Wang, talking then to everybody said, "The time has come; let us leave the cave and let us be martyrs."

Of course, the misery endured by the besieged was such that death seemed for them sweeter than continuing such a horrible experience. All found this option very reasonable. So, all the hobbling survivors abandoned this place of sorrow. When they covered three hundred meters, they met the Boxers' vanguard. Seeing them surrendering without conditions, the Boxers were very happy. They began to offer to let them go in peace, if they agreed to apostatize. Supported by the virgin Marie Wang, all refused this offer. Then the Boxers began to kill them without distinction. The siege of the Cave of the Goats lasted five days.

Here we will bring to a close the account of the tragic events that happened in this unfortunate district of Xuanhua. The defense of the Christians there had been neither prepared for nor directed. The defenders had great courage, but they lacked organization from the beginning.

Jean-Marie Planchet, a Vincentian missionary of Peking, who lived through the Boxers' persecution, published the documents that he has collected about these sorrowful incidents: *Documents sur les martyrs de Pékin pendant la période des Boxeurs.* 2 vols. Pékin: Imprimerie des Lazaristes, 1922 and 1923.

The author wrote in his foreword, "Despite its length, this book just scratches the surface. Of the more than six thousand victims for the vicariate of Peking alone, hardly a hundred names have been studied in detail. More extended research would not have given more insight; moreover, it would have been boring because of the repetition of identical incidents."

Let us not forget there were six thousand victims. This number has been confirmed by the document that can be seen in the church of Chala (atonement monument, built in 1903–1904 and paid for by the Chinese government).

Table 14.1 Victims of the Boxers, North Zhili Vicariates, 1900.[48]

Places	Totals
Peking, city and suburb	2,700
Tianjin District, city	150
Yanshan Parish	200
Xuanhua District, city	170
Yongning Parish	1,400
Nantun Parish	122
Xiaozuang Parish	300
Nihewan Parish	34
Xiheying Parish	118
Baoding District	800
Totals of the victims	**5,994**

In the church the nave is covered all around to a height of two meters with slabs of black marble on which the names of the martyrs can be read, grouped according to districts, parishes and families: altogether five thousand eight hundred names. This list, despite all the care, is not rigorously exact. Indeed, there are names of Christians who did not die

---

48. This heading and the table are not found in the original text, but the translator apparently inserted the information taken from J. M. Planchet, *Documents sur les Martyrs de Pékin pendant la persécution des Boxeurs*, vol. 2. Peking, 1923. (JR)

at that time, but had not yet re-emerged when this list was being made up. On the other hand, there are lacunae: it has been discovered that several Christians who gave up their lives were not mentioned on this list of martyrs, and this only for the vicariate of Peking.

Around 1920, the bishop of Peking initiated a canonical investigation with the view of presenting to Rome the case of the martyrs. But since 1900, several circumscriptions had been cut off from this vicariate in order to become new vicariates. Bishop Jarlin had to be concerned only with the martyrs whose place of residence had been within the boundaries of his vicariate, leaving it to his colleagues of Baoding, Tianjin and Yongping to gather information in their own vicariates.

In the case of Peking, according to Father Planchet whose responsibility it was, about a hundred names have been studied in detail. Of the six or seven hundred other names, the information was more or less synopsized because the circumstances of their martyrdom were so similar to one another that it would be boring to repeat the same details every time.

The file of this case was sent to Rome in 1937.

Chapter 15

After the Storm

Hierarchical Status of the Seven Vicariates Entrusted to the Vincentians at the Beginning of the Twentieth Century

Before proceeding with our history of the Vincentian missions in China, we will sum up the situation by giving a list of the apostolic vicariates of the Vincentians, with the name of the ordinary at that time and the date he took up his position.

We still use the official name of each vicariate, but soon we will abandon this practice in order to use names that are easier on the memory and in the first place more logical.

From the time of the institution of apostolic vicariates in China, the Church followed, when possible, the administrative divisions of the Chinese territory, which was divided in provinces and these in districts, similar to French departments (*préfectures*) and boroughs (*sous-préfectures*), to mark off the jurisdiction of each of the vicariates. It is true that the first vicariates included several provinces, but soon there was an apostolic vicar in every province and his see was called after the name of the province; for instance, our three vicariates were called vicariate of Zhili, vicariate of Jiangxi, vicariate of Zhejiang and the same for the other fifteen provinces of China.

The successes of the evangelization caused the Congregation of Propaganda to create new vicariates in the provinces; these new vicariates were named after the geographical position they occupied in the province.

Therefore, the vicariates, created in the Zhili, were called North Zhili, Southeast Zhili and Southwest Zhili.

After 1900, because of the growing number of the Faithful, the Church had to multiply the vicariates by again dividing the existing vicariates.

The four cardinal points of the compass, however, even when adding the central point, were not enough to distinguish the new vicariates. The missionaries already were calling the vicariates by the name of the city where the bishop resided. It was only in 1922 that Rome ordered that, from then on, the official name of every vicariate was to be the name of the town or city where the bishop had his habitual residence.

This measure, arriving too late, was all the more necessary and timely because several provinces had received another name. So Zhili had been called Hebei for some thirty years.

Table 15.1 Vincentian Apostolic Vicars in China, 1884–1901

Vicariate	Position	Name	Appointment
North Zhili	Apostolic Vicar	Favier	12 Nov. 1897
	Coadjutor	Jarlin	23 Dec. 1899
Southwest Zhili	Apostolic Vicar	Bruguière	29 July 1891
Southeast Zhili	Apostolic Vicar	Geurts	25 Dec. 1899
North Jiangxi	Apostolic Vicar	Bray	15 March 1870
	Coadjutor	Ferrant	27 June 1898
South Jiangxi	Apostolic Vicar	Coqset	29 June 1887
East Jiangxi	Apostolic Vicar	Vic	11 Sept. 1885
Zhejiang	Apostolic Vicar	Reynaud	7 March 1884

Resumption of the Charitable Works in Peking

No sooner had calm been reestablished in Peking than the charitable works returned to action. One of the first was the French-Chinese College, not far from the Beitang, which the Marist Brothers directed. It was reorganized temporarily in a rented house with two hundred Christian and pagan students, while waiting for a more stable institution, that would receive the officials' sons, who were preparing for the famous schools.

At the same time, the two seminaries were up and running again. Seminary life had hardly been interrupted during the siege. The Beitang indeed had been besieged during the summer of 1900, but the students had lost only the end of the second semester 1899–1900 and the beginning of the first semester of 1900–1901.

Guilloux, superior of the seminary since its liberation, wrote to the superior general in 1903, "The Boxers did not succeed in wiping us out: on the contrary, we never had so many seminarians. The minor seminary had seventy-eight students to start the new school year in September 1902. Last year we had nine new priests."

In the Legation Quarter

The three destroyed churches, Nantang, Dongtang and Xitang, had to wait some time before they were rebuilt. But in each residence a decent lodging for the missionary was prepared, and there were vast halls for the catechumenates and the children's schools, and finally a long shed which would be used as a temporary church while waiting for the rebuilding of the churches.

Favier took care of the most urgent needs first. The small chapel of the French Legation had become completely inadequate for the Europeans, who obviously were going to become more numerous; moreover, a lot of Catholic Chinese were already working in the various European legations. A real church was therefore needed. Favier had a fine Gothic church built dedicated to Saint Michael, the bishop's patron saint. Near this church a residence was built with places for catechumenates and children's schools. Father Jean Capy was the first pastor of this parish called "of the legations."

After taking care of the needs of the souls, the bishop wanted also to provide for physical needs. At five hundred steps from the Church of Saint Michael on the same street of the legations, which went along the south wall of the capital, he built a modern international hospital, destined for the personnel of the legations, for the foreign officers and soldiers, for the railway employees, and finally for all the foreigners who were to come and settle down in Peking. This hospital was immediately equipped with a real pharmacy, which from then on would provide medicine not only to Europeans but also to Chinese.

Consideration, moreover, was given not only to the Europeans. The eight Daughters of Charity who came and took care of the hospital, right away installed a dispensary-hospital for the poor next door, where every day a doctor from the hospital went to see the sick local people.

In a letter addressed to Paris on 23 September 1903 Father Boscat, visitor of the Vincentians in China, wrote:

> ... I have just returned from the north: all our missions there are enjoying great prosperity. The ruins in Peking have mostly disappeared. On the right side of the street that goes to the Beitang, the motherhouse of the Josephines has been rebuilt. Those good young women are already a big credit for our mission in Peking. On the left side of the street, Saint Vincent Hospital has been reconstructed, big, airy, divided into pavilions separated from each other through wide courtyards, everything is well ordered.
>
> Beyond the Beitang, separated from it by a street, comes the Renzitang, just as alive as the Beitang and more animated still: our Sisters of Charity are running around in all directions. The house is filled with children of the Holy Childhood and with women catechumens. Everywhere else Christian life bubbles up: people are praying, studying and singing.
>
> In the district of Baoding, the catechumens are arriving in great numbers, but they lack catechist-teachers. Therefore, Father Dumond, the director, has re-opened a school for catechists in a new style with twenty-four students, who after a course of two or three years will be precious helpers for the missionaries. In 1902, there were one thousand three hundred seventy baptisms of adults.

The Vicariate of Yongping

This vicariate, erected on 24 December 1899, received Bishop Geurts only in March 1901. Consecrated in the Netherlands on 4 February 1900, he had to postpone his return to China because of the troubles that were distressing the country. During his absence, the missionaries of Peking, namely, Fathers Capy, Fabrègues and a Chinese confrere, managed the district of Yongping. Their residence was located in the largest Christian community, Huanghuagang. Bishop Geurts brought with him three Dutch confreres, and took possession of this vicariate; their total of the Faithful was not more than three thousand. A few months later, the two above-mentioned missionaries went back to the mission in Peking.

Because there were few Christians in this vicariate, the persecution had relatively few victims.

The Vicariate of West Zhili[49]

This vicariate was developing peacefully and nothing announced the terrible persecution that was going to swoop down on it. There were, it is true, some vague rumors coming from Shandong in the beginning of 1900. There was talk about a sect hostile to Christians, from which the Boxers would have come.[50] The rumor was being spread that the European Powers intended to divide China into "spheres of influence." The people, however, accustomed for centuries to hear about these kinds of sects, did not seem to attach much importance to these rumors.

From the month of May onwards, the news suddenly became alarming. In a lot of temples boxing exercises were being held. Soon it was said that in the northeast, in the vicariate of Peking, chapels had been burned and a lot of Christians had been murdered. Moreover, the new sect spread quickly. The mandarins of the region, knowing that the Boxers had adopted the slogan, "Protect the Qing dynasty and finish off the foreigners," seemed eager to scatter them, for they feared serious difficulties. The prefect of Zhengding sent imperial troops into one of the Boxers' most important centers, that is, Mengjiazhuang; but there were already too numerous Boxers; the soldiers did not dare to deal ruthlessly with them. Also, they had no orders from the imperial authority.

The cruelties began in Shunde. When the pastor, Louis Zhang, C.M., was absent to give the last rites to a dying person, his residence was completely looted during the night (29 June). The Boxers also looted the Protestant mission of that same town and killed the minister and his wife and child.

Since Louis Zhang could not go back home to Shunde, he fled to Bei-Zhang, one of his Christian communities, where many Faithful from neighboring vicariates had already gathered. These Christians defended themselves bravely and repulsed the attacks. In July, the regular troops

---

49. That is, Southwest Zhili. Excerpts taken from A. Morelli, *Notes d'histoire sur le vicariat de Tcheng-ting-fou, 1858-1933* (Pei-p'ing, 1934).

50. Three years earlier, in 1897, emissaries of some sect that was not yet well known had murdered two German missionaries from Shandong during the night. Germany used it as a pretext to occupy the harbor of Jiaozhou. This daring gesture irritated the Chinese population very much and contributed not just a little to the rebellion that is treated here.

began to help the Boxers and the attacks became widespread. In the beginning of that month Empress Cixi published her famous edict enjoining the Europeans to leave China and the Christians to become apostates if they wanted to save their lives.

The text of the edict: "I, the Government, have always treated the Europeans well, both the businessmen and the Christians. Now they abuse my clemency: they are uncompromising and demand harbors and land. The Christians of the countryside are one with those foreigners who make war with us." And the edict added, "I take it upon myself to finish the Europeans, you, Yihetuan (Boxers), finish off their affiliated members in the countryside!"

It did not take all that much to bring the hatred and audacity of these rowdy characters to an explosion.

The railway engineers, who took refuge there, brought the residence in Zhengding to a state of defense. The mandarins of the city behaved kindly. They proposed to give Bishop Bruguière an escort for him and his missionaries if they wanted to leave the city. Though not doubting their good will, the bishop did not accept their offer. He knew that Protestant ministers had been escorted in this way and it had been impossible to protect them. Moreover, the missionaries did not want to abandon their Christians.

Bruguière's tactics turned out to be very wise. Understanding that it was impossible to save everything, he ordered the Christians to defend themselves only in the big centers. He pointed out eight centers in the different districts. That is the reason that in all the attacks the Christians were victorious. Even when the soldiers joined the party, they repulsed their attacks. Isolated Christians, unable or unwilling to go to one of the centers, were tracked down and sacrificed as soon as they had been taken. Bruguière estimated the number of victims to be one hundred fifty persons. This was not many compared to Peking. The reason is that the Boxers in that region were incomparably less numerous than in the north, and that the imperial army had helped them only haphazardly. It must also be said that the resisting centers of the Christians were numerous, and for the most part quite well organized: the Christians had defended themselves well.

Marvelous Events

Now is the time to mention some marvelous events that happened both in the vicariates of Zhengding and Peking, at the occasion of the Boxers' attacks.

Morelli reports that in many places, when the fights were hottest, the pagans often saw above the churches that a "white lady" or even a small gentleman in white clothes (maybe angels) helped the defense. Now, the same happened in Peking and Donglü.

Concerning Peking, this is what Father Planchet wrote in *Les Martyrs de Pékin* (p. 103): "There has often been talk of apparitions, seen only by pagans, during the siege of the Beitang. As documentary evidence, I will present two accounts, leaving it up to the reader to draw conclusions." We quote only the first one:

> A Tartar Christian woman, called Du, belonging to the parish of the Beitang, claimed to have known through a neighbor, a pagan woman, an extraordinary fact that took place during the siege of the Beitang. On 30 July 1900, the day that Commander Henry was killed, this neighbor, named Zhang, told Mrs. Du that during the day she had seen and heard the Boxers of the quarter go en masse toward the Beitang saying that this time they were determined to absolutely finish it with a fierce attack led by a boxer chief who had promised certain success.
>
> When they came back late at night, this woman stopped near them and asked them what had been the result of the attack. Showing their dead and wounded whom they were carrying on doors transformed into stretchers, they said, "During the attack small gentlemen wearing white attacked us. They killed and wounded many among us. Moreover, the Beitang seemed surrounded by water everywhere and was absolutely inaccessible."

In Donglü, located thirty kilometers from Baoding, the author, who has given missions in this region in 1910, has heard many times Christians among the besieged people of Donglü recalling the different incidents of that terrible siege and relating that when calm had been reestablished, the attackers maintained to have often seen, when the fight was strongest, a majestic, "white lady" standing above the roof of the church, a vision that froze them with horror and took all their courage away. The Faithful never saw anything.

French Troops Restore Order

In October 1900, General Baillou, having the responsibility of pacifying the region, arrived with his troops in Zhengding, where the civil authorities welcomed him as a savior. Up to that moment, Christians could not leave the centers where they had taken refuge, and go back home without putting their lives in danger. Moreover, during their absence, everything had been looted and their houses burned or destroyed. In addition, no harvest had been gathered and winter was approaching.

The presence of the soldiers was enough to make the authorities decide to enter into negotiations with the mission. Bruguière did not want to receive any indemnity from the government; he preferred to negotiate directly with the mandarins, so as to get reparations from the very people who had caused the destruction and the damage. As in Peking, the bishop requested only reparation for the material losses suffered by the Christian community and by the Christians personally. He did not want to receive anything for the victims as victims. He sent the missionaries to the different districts in order to negotiate every case locally: evaluation of the losses suffered, establishing the sums that every village had to pay.

This was not an easy job. The Christians, who had proved courageous during the persecution, often became uncompromising in matters of reparation. Their demands and their evaluations of the losses were often exaggerated. More than once the missionary, charged to negotiate these cases, had to intervene to soften the hatreds and spare the pagans. It is true that they were partly excusable, for while discussions were lasting long, they suffered from hunger.

They had to wait one year before receiving something, and two years before they were completely compensated. It also took a lot to persuade the pagans to settle on the price of this senseless persecution.

Now we will move to our southern vicariates, Jiangxi and Zhejiang, to see what were the effects of the Boxer Uprising on these two provinces. But according to the chronological order that we have adopted in this account, we must here talk about a new institution that will concern both the missions in the north and the ones in the south.

Establishment of a Provincial House in Zhoushan (Zhejiang)

Louis Boscat had been working in Jiangxi since 1880, when on 6 February 1900 he was appointed as visitor of the one Vincentian province in China, as substitute for Father Meugniot, who had been fulfilling this task since 1890 and was recalled to Paris in 1899 to be assistant general of the Congregation of the Mission.

The experience that Boscat had acquired while forming seminarians, either in Kouba (Algiers) or in Jiangxi, had strongly convinced him of the necessity of giving Chinese priests a solid basis of spirituality and of ecclesiastical knowledge and consequently to make it easy for them to enter a religious community. However, to achieve this goal it was indispensable to found in his province a formation house including an internal seminary (novitiate) with a house of studies.

Being at the general assembly of 1902, Boscat pleaded his cause with Fiat, and won. So, he could himself, the following October, return to China with a group of seven clerics, who were to constitute the first members of this work.

On his arrival in Shanghai with his troop, he was quite annoyed not finding the house ready that was to receive these young people, though from Paris he had given orders to Brother Barrière to make the necessary preparations. The latter had to apologize for his being late. It was due to the difficulty of finding a suitable place in such a short time.

Bishop Reynaud, passing through Shanghai and seeing Boscat's difficult position, helped him out by offering him immediate occupancy of his minor seminary on the island of Zhoushan, assuring him that he would easily find another place for his own students at the minor seminary.

With both joy and gratitude, the visitor accepted this very generous offer. A few days later, the clerics landed in Dinghai, a small harbor on that island, and settled down in a house quite well equipped for such a work. This building was located at a kilometer from the harbor. The students had to work there till 21 January1904. Then they were taken to Jiaxing, where a real seminary had been built on a vast plot of land located outside the walls of the important prefecture of Jiaxing, located in the very northern part of Zhejiang.

On 25 January 1904, the feast of the conversion of Saint Paul, Boscat went from Shanghai to bless the new building that already had some twenty students and seminarians.

Chapter 16

Boxer Incidents in North Jiangxi

The Vicariate of North Jiangxi – Armed Robbery in Jiangxi in 1891 – Bishop Bray Receives a Coadjutor – The Boxers in Jiangxi – The Death of Bishop Bray – Persecution in Tangpu – Intervention by Jiang Zhaotang – Lacruche's Complaints – The Attack on the Mission – Burning the Buildings at Machang – Lacruche's Murder – Five Marist Brothers Died – The Sisters Escaped Death – Conclusions

The Vicariate of North Jiangxi

We left this enormous vicariate, under Bishop Bray's jurisdiction since 1870, and we talked also about the two subsequent territorial divisions: the first in 1879, which created the vicariate of South Jiangxi with Bishop Rouger as its first apostolic vicar; the second in 1885, under the name of East Jiangxi, of which Bishop Vic was the first apostolic vicar.

A description of this large province in China involving both its geography and administration seems necessary to understand the history of the missions which developed in these regions according to the plan we have suggested. Bishop Bray himself sent a letter on 20 April 1887 to Father Terrasson, secretary general of the Congregation. From the bishop's letter this might be remembered:

> The province of Jiangxi forms a rectangle with a length of about six hundred kilometers from north to south and of five hundred kilometers from east to west. This makes a surface of about three hundred thousand square kilometers: a little more than half the surface of France. The population is thought to be about twenty-five million inhabitants.

> The province of Jiangxi is bounded in the north by Hubei, evangelized by the Franciscans, and by Anhui, where the Jesuits are; in the east, by Zhejiang, where our confreres are, and by Fujian staffed by Dominicans from Manila; in the south, by Guangdong are the Fathers of the Foreign Missions of Paris; finally, in the west, by Hunan, where there are Franciscans once again.

Administrative Division

> Like other provinces, Jiangxi is divided into prefectures or *fu* of
> which there are thirteen, divided into sub-prefectures. There are
> seventy-three of those. Every province has a civil governor, who
> resides in [a principal] county seat of the province – for Jiangxi it
> is Nanchang – and has under him the thirteen prefects who have
> under their jurisdiction the seventy-three sub-prefects. High and
> wide walls, built with big bricks of baked clay, surround all these
> towns, and only these towns.
>
> Thus, there are in Jiangxi more than eighty walled towns, a big
> number of which have only administrative importance. There are
> indeed many more populated towns, which have never had any
> ramparts: for their importance is only industrial or commercial.
> For instance, the town of Jingdezhen, where exceptionally beautiful
> chinaware is produced, has a million inhabitants.
>
> Jiangxi is a mountainous country, with big plateaus here and there,
> separated by deep valleys carefully cultivated and covered by a very
> dense population. These valleys are crossed with watercourses that
> are the highways of Jiangxi. In them thousands of boats of every
> shape and size come and go, loaded with merchandise, progress-
> ing more or less quickly depending on the shifting winds, unless
> coolies tow the boat.
>
> In Jiangxi, the boat is the principal means of locomotion at least
> for part of a trip. Where there is no water, a missionary travels in a
> wheelbarrow or a sedan chair and, if the path is too steep, he travels
> on foot. Anyway, it is always slow and tedious. Sometimes he will
> have to stop for one or more days in an inn where the only food
> that can be found is what he has brought along.

After these preliminaries, Bray looked in a general way at the work achieved
in the sixteen years from 1870 to 1886 in this province and noted an increase
of eleven thousand Christians. He added this melancholy conclusion:

> These successes compared with the results achieved in other vicari-
> ates in China will seem of little importance to some people; but those
> who know the special obstacles met with in Jiangxi concerning the
> propagation of the Gospel will understand our joy when we see that
> the number of our Christians has been more than doubled through
> God's grace. There are in China three provinces each of which has

more than a hundred thousand Christians, five or six times more than we have in Jiangxi. They are Sichuan, Zhili, and Jiangnan.

In these provinces he saw means of propagation and elements of success that did not exist in Jiangxi and he added, "We, the little gleaners, are already very happy to have put some ears into the granary of the Father of the family, next to the numerous sheaves brought by the big harvesters."

Then he expounded on the fruits of the Holy Childhood. In 1870, in this work of mercy six hundred orphaned girls were cared for. In 1886, their number had increased to twenty-three hundred, thanks to the presence of the Daughters of Charity, who arrived in Jiujiang in 1882.

To be brief, the bishop talked much about the Holy Childhood, begun already before him. It might seem that the missionaries of that region considered this work as their principal work. At that time, they did not yet have religious women to help them. Those, naturally, would have been more capable of caring for the orphan girls than the priests. Also, since there were only few Christians, the missionaries were almost always forced to entrust the babies to pagan wet nurses. In other missions, the missionaries who were too busy with evangelizing pagans and catechizing the baptized, founded, little by little, institutions of Chinese religious women, and then opened orphanages. Bray finished his report with optimistic views:

> In just a few years, the presence of the Daughters of Charity has changed the people's feelings towards us more than all the other Catholic works done for half a century, especially through the care that they give to the sick. In the old days, the population in Jiujiang did not like us very much: we could not cross the town without hearing curses hurled at us. Since the opening of our small hospital, we have not heard any insulting words, and the Sisters themselves can go without risk to any place where they have something to do.

Armed Robbery in Jiangxi in 1891

One of Bray's colleagues, Father Joseph Wang, C.M., wrote from Wangjia on 5 July 1891 to his confrere, "I cannot express the sorrow that overwhelms me. The twenty-fourth of the fifth moon (30 June) I was doing a mission in Wangjia two or three kilometers from Jinxian, a sub-prefecture of Nanchang, and that day, after my Mass, Christians arrived announcing the capture and destruction of Xiebu and four other villages. A few minutes later, other people came and told us, 'In Qianfa the shops of the Christians were looted and destroyed on 29 June.' Then a rich Christian from Xiebu came and said, 'All my possessions were taken from me on 29 June; of my house, only the roof tiles remain; they wanted to burn our houses but did not do so because they feared burning the houses of our pagan neighbors. . . .' Then I was told that robbers had burned the whole Christian village of Xupi." (When reading this letter, we think involuntarily of the disasters announced to the holy man Job one after the other.)

It is very fortunate that we have before us another account of these tragic events. It settles all the details and informs us more clearly. It is the letter that Bray sent to the Prefect of the Congregation of Propaganda, Cardinal Simeoni on 3 September 1891:

> Surely, the newspapers in Europe have informed Your Eminence about the disasters that last June distressed some of our missions and particularly the vicariate of North Jiangxi. . . . For several months rumors had circulated that hostile elements were going to vex and even persecute Christians. So, quite a few chapels and residences of our neighbors the Jesuits were destroyed. Then on 23 June the rabble, whom some gangsters stirred up, ransacked our residence from top to bottom, built last year at great expense in the village of Xiebu, not far from the city of Nanchang, capital of our province. On the same day the chapel in Longjia that we had built only last year was also destroyed. On 27 June the one in Nangong was torn down.
>
> Not only were the chapels of this region demolished, but also all the houses, where, for lack of chapels, masses were celebrated at the time of a mission. Moreover, more than sixty families have been so stripped that they lost their houses with everything in them and that they have nothing else other than the clothes they were wearing at the time the troubles broke out. On the other hand, nobody was killed or wounded. The persecutors merely stole, looted, destroyed and burned down houses; they spared the lives of the Christians.
>
> On 29 June the bandits went to the sub-prefecture of Jinxian, to the village Xupi where there was a chapel and forty-six houses of Christians. All these buildings were set on fire. In the neighboring villages many Christian families underwent the same losses.
>
> While these atrocities were being perpetrated, the mandarins of Nanchang, informed of the danger we were facing, did not take any precautions to prevent the disaster. Fortunately, some mandarins of other districts behaved quite differently, especially the prefect of

Ruizhou, who at my request, sent soldiers to protect our residence, our orphanage and the other charitable works in Sanqiao, such that we had nothing to suffer there. In the town Jiujiang *extra muros* [outside the city walls] the mandarins decisively protected all our charitable works and they put soldiers at our doors, who till today do not stop guarding and defending us kindly.

G. Bray

As can been seen, this persecution against the Christians was not an act of some secret society, as it so often happened in China; this was a rebellion of the rabble stirred up by the intellectuals against all that came from abroad. Badly informed, they saw in Christendom a scheme by the foreign powers to conquer the empire. And because they sought out poor and ignorant people, they gave them the hope of becoming rich by looting the chapels and taking the possessions of the Christians; but they did not go as far as attacking the people.

Bishop Bray Receives a Coadjutor

Responding to Bray's wish for a coadjutor (he was seventy-two years old), the Holy See on 28 June 1898 appointed Bishop Ferrant, the bishop of Barbalissus, as Bray's coadjutor with the right of succession.

Paul Ferrant, born in Wervicq (Nord) on 2 July 1859, admitted in Paris on 7 June 1880, ordained priest on 7 June 1884 arrived in China the following 12 August. Placed in Zhejiang, he fulfilled there some important posts, the last of which was as Reynaud's pro-vicar. Consecrated on 2 October by Reynaud, he left Ningbo on the following 6 December and went to North Jiangxi.

Immediately after his arrival, he showed that he was astonished that the bishop of the place had not yet visited the civil governor of the province, as was done in Zhejiang where he came from. Missionaries and Christians wished whole-heartedly that their bishop be on good terms with the highest authority of the province, like the missionaries were with the prefects and sub-prefects. In Jiangxi, the reason for the bishops' abstention was this: the governor's seat was in Nanchang; this city, however, had always shown itself particularly hostile both to foreigners and to all innovation, even to any improvement authorized or imposed by the imperial government itself. On the other hand, the governor at the time was personally quite well disposed towards the mission.

Ferrant, understanding that any attempt to introduce himself directly as bishop was useless, used a roundabout way. He talked to the consul general of France in Shanghai and asked him to be delegated to go to the governor to sort out an old persecution case. The governor understood the subterfuge but could not refuse the visit.

It took place in the beginning of January 1899 and was very friendly. When he went back, however, rebels, stirred up by lower mandarins, aroused the population and threatened the mission. An immediate and personal intervention by the governor put an end to these threats. This insult towards a bishop gave the occasion to obtain from the imperial government a decree (already in existence, that is, Favier's decree, mentioned earlier), recognizing the bishops' right to deal directly with governors and viceroys, and urging these high officials to maintain good relationships with missionaries in general.

Ferrant had much zeal for proper formation of the clergy; the seminary had changed place several times. First placed in Sanqiao, it was moved to Jianchang, and when this city came under the jurisdiction of East Jiangxi, it was moved back to Sanqiao. Ferrant brought it to Jiujiang, where it would go on growing.

Another goal of the young coadjutor was to bring charitable works to the city of Nanchang *intra muros* [inside the city walls]. Up till that time this had been considered impossible, because of the mentality of the mandarins and the intellectuals, who were always against religion in that capital. The missionaries were hardly tolerated in their small residence in the suburb, which was very near to this town so obstinately closed for religion.

According to the treaties, missionaries had the right to acquire lands both in the walled city and in the countryside. But the mandarins in Nanchang had threatened secretly to punish severely any person who dared sell to missions, Catholic or Protestant, any house or the least parcel of land *intra muros*. Ferrant, however, succeeded in buying a large property in town, observing literally all the conditions the law required; thus, the mandarins could not refuse to register the contract.

There the bishop built there a church, a residence, and, not far away, a boys' school and a catechetical center; the charitable works for women were outside the walls. In 1902, he added a *probatorium* [a pre-seminary program] to recruit and prepare students destined to become seminarians.

The Boxers in Jiangxi

The persecution by the Boxers in the south of China was incomparably less devastating than in the north. Why? The missionaries of the whole province have no doubt about the reason. They say that Jiangxi is far from Peking. It is obvious that the rebellion of the Boxers had its origin in Shandong. If, however, the imperial army had not helped the rebels, they would never have been able to commit such crimes, for the Chinese troops would easily have gotten the better of them. The imperial authority, that is, Cixi, was convinced that – in her desire definitively to get rid of the foreigners – the rebels gave her a unique means of bringing this about. Consequently, she did nothing to stop their acts of violence, but, on the contrary, she gave clear orders to the generals to make common cause with the Boxers.

In the north, it was easy, but in the faraway provinces orders given by Peking took time to arrive. Moreover, under the empire, viceroys and governors were never in a hurry to obey orders from people in high places and they often behaved in quite an independent way.

As a result, the viceroy in Nanjing openly resisted Cixi's orders, when she told him to integrate the rebels with his troops. Those in Wuchang (Hubei) and Canton (Guangdong) acted almost in the same way. These highly placed persons thought about the consequences of a possible victory by the Allied Forces. Because of their uncertainty, however, they took a decision that put the bishops and the missionaries into a very difficult spot: they ordered their subordinates to make the foreigners go to the harbor which was their home base, that is, to Shanghai, and they had the possessions of the missions destroyed, or they had them sealed off with the view of seizing them after the foreigners' defeat, which they still dared to hope for.

These orders explained why the missionaries went from Jiangxi to Shanghai. Some forty of them, among whom were the four bishops, participated in this exodus; two priests fled to the English Concession in Jiujiang. This surely spared the majority of the larger centers from destruction, but it did not prevent quite a number of Christian communities from undergoing the horrors of persecution. From Ferrant's notes we quote the following lines:

> The persecution was perfectly organized. It was not a rebellion by some rabble that followed an improvised leader blindly. Everywhere there were leaders who were giving orders and people who were obeying.

Actually, the imperial soldiers did not take part in the insurrection, but the viceroys allowed – or ordered – their subordinates to organize local militias, whose apparent goal was to maintain public order. The real goal was to form and gather, under an officially recognized title, a completely new organization with their sights on a general insurrection.

Hierarchical councils were organized and directed by influential intellectuals of the district, of the section and of the village. A complete campaign schedule had been drawn up beforehand, not against the Boxers, but against the Christians, and the punishment that had to be undergone had been decided: a heavy ransom or looting of the goods or of the harvest, or setting fire to houses, or still the massacre of one or more Christians taken hostage. Still, we had no missionaries to mourn. The watchword in Jiangxi seemed to have been: "Loot, burn, kill some Christians, if necessary, but spare the foreigners, unless they refuse to leave."

In these conditions, the presence of the missionaries among their Christians, far from being a guarantee of protection for the Christians, meant for them greater danger.

The Daughters of Charity went to their central house in Shanghai, and their three hundred orphaned girls were placed in good families in the neighborhood.

Our three principal charity centers, Jiujiang, Nanchang and Sanqiao, underwent no material damage. The reason is that Governor Song, though very hostile to Christians, wanted to save appearances and leave for himself a way to exonerate himself if necessary, and so he recommended sparing especially the institutions in Nanchang and Jiujiang. These houses were locked and sealed, so that the missionaries, on their return from exile, took back the buildings of our important centers unharmed. The official seal had guaranteed the buildings and all they contained. Nevertheless, the vicariate lost two churches and some ten oratories had been looted and damaged.

Almost seven hundred families have suffered the total or a partial loss of their possessions, either by paying ransoms or because of looting or fire. For six months, from June to December, many of our Christians were exposed to all kinds of humiliations. Destitute, hunted down like wild animals, they suffered from cold and hunger, and several died on the open roads. In addition to those almost unknown victims, twenty-three people were murdered in our vicariate. (Ferrant gave their names and the details of the torture inflicted on each of them.)

After several months of exile in Shanghai, the missionaries could return to their posts; and when peace had been gradually reestablished, the Sisters returned to Jiujiang too, and, a marvelous thing: the three hundred orphaned girls from seven to eighteen years old, placed in families, the majority of which were pagan, were all there.

In 1903, together with Bishop Vic, Ferrant built a beautiful college in Nanchang, common to the two vicariates, destined for the education of the young people coming from rich families among the people. It was entrusted to the Marist Brothers, who had been in Peking since 1891. The principal subject taught in this college was the French language. English was soon added. Quite quickly there were eighty students.

The Death of Bishop Bray

During the night of 24 September 1905 Bishop Bray died in Jiujiang, eighty years old, after a forty-year apostolate in China, thirty-five of which as bishop of Jiangxi. During the last seven years, he had completely handed on the administration of his vicariate to his young and fearless coadjutor, Bishop Ferrant; he continued, however, being interested in the progress of the mission and encouraging the missionaries who were dedicating themselves to it.

After taking over the reins of government, Ferrant did not need to change his behavior. Alas! Big ordeals were imminent.

Persecution in Tangpu

Tangpu was a very commercial town without walls. It had about twenty thousand inhabitants. In town and in the immediate neighborhood there were only a few Christians.

The mission did not yet have any institutions there; however, it had acquired a house in town, according to the norms of the treaties, but the population's hostility had not made it possible to take possession of it yet. Father Jean-Marie Lacruche, director of the district, relying too much on the letter of the treaties, decided to take possession of this building as property of the mission and to occupy it in the name of the mission and for the use of the mission. Indeed, the mission held the legal titles.

He was leaning, it is true, on the authority of the sub-prefect of Xinchang, of which Tangpu was a part, who, not satisfied with approving his resolution, sent him two police officers to implement it. Here is the plan that the missionary and the mandarin decided on: Lacruche would delegate a group of Christians, who, accompanied by the two policemen, would hang on the door of the house which the priests were forbidden to enter a sign on which the three characters Tian Zhu Tang (Catholic Church) could be read.

As soon as the plan was known, the notables of the region stirred the population up against the mission. The sign, brought by the delegation, had hardly been fixed to the pediment of the mission house when the alarm signal sounded. Soon two catechists, four Christian men and a Christian woman were murdered with swords and spears; the others fled. Then the pursuit of Catholic families began; it was going to be difficult to reach them, because they were hiding. Those poor people ran to the caves in the mountains and arrived there in the most complete destitution, because the imminence of the danger had not allowed them to pick up the most necessary objects. It was 25 May 1904.

The persecutors then, unable to get at the people, pounced on their belongings: houses, stores, harvests, furniture, everything that had belonged to the Christians was looted or set on fire.

These acts of violence went on for more than a year. But the persecution did not spread and raged only in the neighborhood of Tangpu. Lacruche did not lay down his arms. Now he wanted the guilty people to be judged. They had made Tangpu the center of their actions.

To put an stop to it, the governor of Jiangxi gave the army orders to surround the town, to force it to give up the guilty people. They began to be afraid and were getting ready to ask for peace. They had already brought together their most important commanders, that is, the instigators of the rebellion, intellectuals and others, and they kept them in shackles, ready to hand them over to the military chiefs.

Intervention by Jiang Zhaotang

At the time the people were preparing to go to the imperial camp to offer their submission and arrive at some settlement, a mandarin arrived calling himself the governor's delegate. Right away he ordered the besiegers to retreat and offered the beleaguered their freedom without any conditions. This delegate was Jiang Zhaotang, the sub-prefect of Xinchang, an ambitious man, who, discredited with his superiors, dreamed of winning the governor's good graces; so, he offered his services as mediator in the case of the murders in Tangpu, and being sly as a fox he succeeded in getting the job. The governor, hearing this audacious proposition, was fascinated by the promise the sub-prefect of Nanchang made, namely, to bring a peaceful and definitive solution between the two adversaries, the rebels and the Catholic mission, without using the army. He quickly agreed with his subordinate's wish and gave him the complete file of this case, promising him a promotion if he succeeded in bringing it to a good end.

The sub-prefect arrived, as we have already said, at the moment the rebels, frightened, were ready to submit. Instead of exploiting such a favorable situation, the mandarin, who wanted the merit of the pacification to be attributed to him, gave the soldiers the signal to retreat and went and offered the rebels peace without any conditions, even without demanding the reparation of the damages inflicted on the mission and the Christians.

After this feat, Jiang Zhaotang returned to Nanchang to see the governor, very proud of his success in this case and covered with the merits of a shrewd peacemaker.

Lacruche's Complaints

The director of the district obviously could not approve a solution that freed the guilty parties without inflicting on them the smallest sanctions. The case therefore was going to get complicated; we will only touch on the principal phases.

What was the heart of the matter? There was an insurmountable antagonism between the sub-prefect and Lacruche. The latter wanted the rebels to be handed over to ordinary tribunals so as to be judged according to Chinese laws. The mandarin, on the contrary, wanted absolutely to remove the guilty people from the sanctions of the law.

Ferrant wanted justice to be done in the case of Tangpu. Appealing to the Legation of France, defender of the missions, was in order. Monsieur [Georges] Dubail, minister of France, agreed to study the file and concluded that a revision was necessary. As far as the Chinese government was concerned, it agreed to reexamine the question and ordered the governor in Nanchang to study the case. But the latter transferred the governmental order to mandarin Jiang, not having treated the case himself, but through this subordinate.

In mid-February 1906 Lacruche was living in Nanchang. At the sub-prefect's request, there were for several days repeated conversations between him and the missionary. This mandarin used to talk with missionaries in a very familiar way without any politeness. That is the reason why some priests noted with humor incidents due to his boorish ways. Lacruche, on the contrary, was amazed and thought that this man's behavior was too friendly to be honest.

Moreover, Lacruche saw very well from the first conversation that Jiang had only one goal: accepting what was done in Tangpu and consequently giving up any legal action.

Lacruche did not give in; he insisted and demanded an appeal to the courts. He had also noted that every time he wanted to discuss the case in question, the sub-prefect always succeeded in diverting the conversation, especially by bitterly criticizing his own superiors of all levels.

In the last of these conversations with the sub-prefect, the latter, having talked about one thing and another, said to Lacruche, "What about the case of Tangpu?" "It is still in abeyance; it must be finished." "That is true. Well, I'll come back on 22 February." "All right."

Lacruche was amazed that the mandarin came back at noon on 20 February. While entering he said, "It is not for today, but I just came to beg you to write a letter to invite me to handle the Tangpu case, but it must be a hard letter reproaching me to be in favor of the opposition, threatening me with your French consul and warships. With this very severe letter, I will be able to deal with my superiors and get concessions that will be favorable for you." The missionary called his scribe, Liu, who acted as his secretary, to write this letter to the officials. Jiang explained to the secretary the meaning he wanted the letter to have; then having had a cup of tea, he left again repeating, "I shall be here on 22 February."

That very evening, Liu wrote a short, very moderate letter, without reproaches or threats. Lacruche had it taken to the governor by courier.

On Thursday, 22 February, the missionary had a meal prepared to receive the sub-prefect, who kept everyone waiting till four o'clock in the afternoon.

At the residence there were Father Jules Martin, associate, and Father Louis Salavert, who was very ill. Father Jean-Baptiste Rossignol was at the residence of Machang in the suburb. It was agreed that Lacruche was going to receive the mandarin alone. The latter ate almost nothing and seemed very worried. Every time the missionary talked about Tangpu, Jiang diverted the conversation and went on complaining against his superiors. After the meal, Lacruche showed Jiang into his small lounge, offered him coffee and a cigar and tried to talk about the case. "Well", said Jiang, "because I came for that case, let us talk about it." He then suggested to the missionary a series of quite satisfactory conditions. Lacruche asked him to put these conditions in writing. "Very well," he said, "but I prefer to withdraw a moment to scribe Liu's office to think." That happened. The priest returned to his room. Twenty minutes later, Liu, carrying a piece of paper, went and explained to the priest the sub-prefect's conditions.

Some seconds later, a servant of the residence hearing some sighs in Liu's office, tried to open the door so as to see what was going on, but the door was locked from the inside; the servant looked then through the window and saw the mandarin, sprawled out on a sofa and covered with blood gushing from his neck. Having been informed immediately, Lacruche rushed there and broke down the door. "What are you doing now?" he cried out, "Why are you throwing a tantrum? The conditions you wrote are acceptable to me." Jiang looked at him dumbfounded and did not answer. The missionary noticed that he had cut his neck, but death was not imminent; he called his servants to take care of the wounded man, who, however, dismissed all of them. Not knowing what to do, Lacruche went to the governor to report the incident. The governor listened attentively and said, "This does not astonish me on the part of Jiang, but do not worry, I will decide what is to be done."

Back home again, Lacruche sent for Rossignol and asked him to go and talk with the wounded man; but no sooner had he gone out, when he saw that the wounded man was being taken away on a litter. The police commander had convinced him finally to be taken away. This shows clearly his intention of dying on the very mission, so as to make the people believe that the missionary had killed him.

The next day, the high judge came to the residence to carry out a careful investigation. The two priests composed a fully documented report about all that had happened.

February 22 was Thursday; the suicide had happened at around six o'clock P.M. The investigations took place on Friday; on Saturday, 24, some thirty soldiers armed with batons guarded the principal door of the building.

During that time, the magistrates and the notables of the city held a meeting and decided to convoke a general assembly of all the inhabitants of the city, which numbered about two hundred thousand. This meeting had to take place on Sunday 25 February at ten o'clock in the morning on the main square. No sooner had the invitation circulated in town, than Christians and even pagans ran to Lacruche, advising him to do what was necessary for his and the Brothers' security and for that of the Sisters in the suburb. A telegram was sent right away to Ferrant, who, immediately notified Dubail. The latter went to see the Chinese government, which ordered the governor of Jiangxi to take the necessary measures to protect the personnel and the buildings of the mission. The governor answered that he was intent on maintaining order.

We shall see that nothing was done. On Sunday 25 at dawn, the Christians again warned the director about the imminent danger; he showed everybody the telegram coming from Peking and reminded them of the governor's promises. Then he wanted the Christians to come to Sunday Mass as usual: he agreed only not to preach.

The moment of the meeting was going to arrive, when the population in serried ranks ran to the meeting place. "Kill and burn", that was the watchword given to the masses. The servants of the residence begged the director to let them go with their modest luggage. He, keeping his head, or rather his illusion, declared himself convinced that in case of disorder the mandarins would act fast and put an end to it. We are stunned seeing such stubbornness.

The Attack on the Mission

It was still the Chinese New Year holiday, which lasts about a month. Therefore, most of students of the Marist Brothers were with their families. At the Sisters, children were for the same reason not very numerous and, in times of danger, it was easy to entrust them to good families. While the crowd was leaving the public place, quite a number of gangs were going to the missionaries' residence. Leading the group of porters carrying cans of paraffin oil was the son of the sub-prefect, who had died in the night. As they moved forward a brother of his directed the convoy of murderers. Then they were in front of the big gate, which soon was broken down. From that moment all the parts of the residence were invaded at the same time.

The rabble's anger was such that looters had not even time to take away spoils. The church was soon set to fire, then the residence and all the other outbuildings.

After all the buildings had been set on fire, the arsonists went with their paraffin towards the Brothers' college, which was five hundred meters away. Thanks to the paraffin spread on the furniture and the wooden floors, the arsonists quickly finished their sinister business. Of this building only the walls remained. It was noon.

Then the rabble went in the direction of Machang, one kilometer away from the city wall. On their way they passed a Protestant church, near which the minister was living with his wife and daughter. Despite being near the mission, they had convinced themselves that the rebels would attack only French people and Catholics. The minister, seeing the crowd coming, went to them, greeted the rebels and invited them to have some tea. He told them that he was not French and not Catholic. In response, they murdered all three of them.

Burning the Buildings at Machang

In that village there was a chapel, a small residence for one priest, a school, a catechumenate for men, and then all the Sisters' works: a girls' school, a catechumenate for women, an orphanage, and a hospital-dispensary and in the middle the Sisters' lodgings. Father Salavert, who was sick, had been brought there after Thursday's problem.

There too they were hopeful, because Lacruche had told them so. The Sister superior had expressed her fear to him. He answered "Do not be afraid; do your ordinary work."

When the assailants were in front of the door of the hospital, there were so many looters following behind that they could not be held in check or prevented from emptying the houses of everything before they were set ablaze. So, before the fires were set, the thieves removed and looted everything of value. After a few hours, only rubbish and ashes remained of these buildings. This is briefly the story of the destruction of the buildings. Let us move to the people.

Lacruche's Murder

When the crowd was approaching the residence, Lacruche and Martin were each in their own rooms, waiting for dinner to be ready. Martin was the first one to perceive the screams and to hear the knocks on the entrance door. Right away he went and informed his superior, who did not pay attention. Time was short. The noise was coming nearer. Lacruche entrusted a box with documents to a servant who was told to bring the box to some hospitable family. Then taking off some clothes so as to be more agile, he went with Father Martin to the garden. But at one end of the garden the rebels were already rushing in. Martin fled to the other side, and there again there were rebels, who threw bricks and stones at him. They wounded him, threw him down and left him for dead. But then he got up, fled to a corner climbed over the enclosure wall and ran to the town gate, where the policemen received him and hid him in a police station. We shall find him back there.

What happened to the director? He was still in the garden and saw murderers who were looking for him in his room. Suddenly he thought of the Blessed Sacrament. The church was burning already, but there was also the Reserved Sacrament in the house chapel, which was a couple of steps from there. He wanted to enter, but the door was locked. He fled, but the garden door was locked too – he had forgotten that he had all the exits locked. The crowd threw stones at him and wounded him in the head. Then a real melee followed; it is not known if he saved the Sacrament from profanation by consuming it. It is known that he elbowed his way to the street. It was noon. All the personnel of the residence had disappeared. Yelled at and beaten on all sides, he received such a violent kick that he slumped to the ground. He got up and tried to go forward hoping to reach the governor's palace, which was still far away. Soon he entered the house of a pagan family that he knew. The head of the family tried to negotiate with the assailants. It was in vain. The house was invaded, and Lacruche became the prey of a frenzied crowd; he was pulled into the street. Finally, while leaning against a wall he was kicked in his stomach so hard that he could not get up any more. He was still breathing when the murderers pulled him by his leg to the pool in the main square, where he died. In the evening, the missionary's body was carried by the police to a temple from where he was to be moved to Jiujiang.

Five Marist Brothers Died

Lacruche had given the Brothers the same order of quietly staying put lest they draw the public's attention. That is why the Brothers had not foreseen or prepared anything in case that they would have to flee suddenly. In such circumstances, the director's order must have seemed very hard to them. They did not hesitate nevertheless to submit.

In the morning they went to Holy Mass as usual and received Communion. It was their last Communion. When the attack on the residence began, they were on the point of having their lunch. But hearing the screaming, they understood right away the gravity of the situation. They took hats and umbrellas, crossed the garden, went out of their property and walked to the gate of the town. Not knowing where to go, they hesitated a moment and then went in the direction of the suburb of Machang. If they had gone in the opposite direction, they would have been able to escape easily through the fields – but they did not know that Machang was to be the rebels' prey in a few hours' time. There was a small river there, thirty meters wide. They thought that having reached the other bank they could escape from their assailants. They hailed a small boat, but the pilot refused to take them.

Unable to cross the river, they began to walk again through the rebels who were hitting them, jostling them and insulting them; they walked to Machang, but having arrived at a small hill, they saw that the horizon was darkened with thick smoke and that the Sisters' place was in flames. They understood that their last refuge had disappeared. Where to go? The crowds were blocking all the roads.

In the neighborhood there was a plain with four small ponds; they had to die or to throw themselves into one of these ponds to escape the kicks, while waiting for the help they were still hoping for.

In order to give his companions the time to reach a pond, the Brother director sacrificed himself; he surrendered to the executioners, in the meantime asking them grace for the other Brothers. Straight away he was beaten to death and trampled underfoot. The other four Brothers, their cassocks torn, covered with mud, their faces smeared with blood, went down together into the ice-cold water. The crowd stood around the pond, throwing stones and all kinds of projectiles at their victims crying out savagely. This ghastly spectacle lasted for four long hours. The four Brothers fell down one after the other and disappeared into the water.

The Sisters Escaped Death

The Sisters had just had their lunch when the crowd came to their building. Rossignol had kept himself informed about the events in town; therefore, he was not caught unawares when the danger became imminent. That certainly prevented the Sisters from being murdered. At the first alarm he ran to the Sisters and ordered them to follow him. He even had to adopt a commanding tone, for the Sisters, calmed down by their superior, did not believe that the danger was immediate.

The first things that had to be done were to save the Blessed Sacrament, kept in the chapel, and to move the sick Father Salavert to a secure place. While Rossignol was consuming the Sacred Species, the sick priest was being brought down from the second floor of the hospital. The thing to do was to flee to friendly neighbors without using the street. A breach was quickly made in the adjoining wall.

They all went through that hole. But they were still too much in the vicinity of the rebels to be really secure. It was quite easy to move the sick priest to a Christian family, which received him and took care of him till midnight; indeed, there was no street that had to be crossed; it was just a transfer from one house to the next. The big problem was to find a place for the Sisters to live.

The only place that offered some security was an empty jail quite near, if the administrators agreed to open its doors and especially if the Sisters could go there without being seen publicly – there were some little alleyways that had to be gone through. The authorities of the jail gave, not without some good objections, the requested permission and very fortunately a torrential rain began to fall at that moment. The Sisters, having left their headgear behind and protected by a big umbrella, entered the hospitable jail one after the other.

A good deal of uncertain information reached them there. They heard about Lacruche's death and the fire in all the buildings. Actually, from their refuge they could see the flames going up from their own houses and they could hear the screams of the looters and the crackling inferno.

At midnight, the army presented themselves in front of the doors of the jail so as to escort the refugees to the harbor, where a boat was to transfer them to Jiujiang. Martin was brought to the boat, also by the policemen who had protected him at the town gate and he traveled with them, and so did Salavert. But a sick person cannot be moved with impunity in these conditions, exposing him to rain and wind. Fear, anxiety, periods of being tired because of traveling, all that made the state of his illness worse.

No sooner had Salavert disembarked from the ship than he died. A very big loss for the mission the death of this young confrere, a man of great value, who had all the qualities that people hope for in a missionary.

For two years he had brought very valuable help to the institution of the seminary first located in Zhoushan and then in Jiaxing, as teacher and assistant director of the internal seminary. Then for two more years he had adapted himself to missionary life in Nanchang so well that superiors had high hopes for him of very significant achievements.

Conclusions

Reading the report of these sad events, the reader, perhaps unused to Chinese customs, must surely have noticed some rigidity in Lacruche's behavior, which contrasts with the usually more conciliatory customs of the other missionaries, when they negotiate contentious cases with Chinese authorities.

There is no doubt that Lacruche had good faith when treating this case. He was right; the Chinese government admitted it when it signed the agreement proposed by the minister of France on 20 June 1906; but he demanded the exercise of this right with too much inflexibility. Obviously if he had foreseen the consequences of his demands, he would have been more flexible. But in his natural uprightness, he would have considered it a failure in his task if he had not demanded what strict justice owed him. He had not yet adapted himself to the inveterate habits of this country. He had not yet noticed the wisdom of this very Chinese proverb, "Never corner an adversary and bring him to a dead end," to such a point that there is no way out for him to escape, if not for the heart of the matter, at least for the sake of form (for the audience). If this way out is lacking, these pagan people allow for the cornered adversary to take the last door out: vengeance through suicide, and this suicide will be in the house of the opponent or in front of it. This happens frequently everywhere in China. Then the crowd spontaneously rebels though it knows very well that there was no homicide but indeed a suicide.

That is what happened in Nanchang. Sub-prefect Jiang Zhaotang, a deceitful and ambitious man, committed suicide in the Chinese way because he was going to lose face while arranging the Tangpu case. He committed suicide in the residence of the Catholic mission in order to cause as much damage as possible to it; this enters clearly into the framework of the old Chinese customs.

A good lesson for young missionaries comes from these events. Jarlin often repeated to his coworkers, "Never forget that here in China you are just guests, you are not at home." This certainly meant: adapt yourselves to the habits and customs of the country where you live, not to adopt them in your own personal behavior, but to take them into account when you take steps to solve problems.

In the face of these murders of English and French subjects and the actions of looting and destroying, the Chinese government agreed to pay the necessary reparations.

After an inquiry made by the Chinese authorities on the one hand and by the French and English authorities on the other, the Chinese government admitted and declared officially that the sub-prefect of Nan-chang, whose death had caused this rebellion, "had committed suicide in a moment of anger." The principal murderers and arsonists were punished according to the Chinese laws.

Thanks to the indemnities, new establishments rapidly rose from the ruins. Soon we will see how the charitable works blossomed again in Nanchang with new vigor.

In the meantime, we will cross into the two other vicariates in Jiangxi, beginning with South Jiangxi.

Chapter 17

Boxer Incidents in South Jiangxi

The Main Obstacles to Evangelization – Boxers in South Jiangxi – A New Movement of Boxers in South Jiangxi – Canduglia's Murder – Lecaille's Flight – Murders and Destruction – Coqset's Transfer to West Zhili and Ciceri as his Replacement in South Jiangxi

The Main Obstacles to Evangelization

We said in chapter eleven that Bishop Coqset, consecrated in the Nantang on 16 October 1887, had gone to take possession of his vicariate of South Jiangxi on 5 December 1887.

The task of the young bishop was difficult. After the adversities in Lantang, enthusiasm had cooled off in South Jiangxi, and far from making new proselytes, missionaries registered apostasies among the Christians.

All the works were being delayed; only the seminary established in the prefecture of Ji'an showed some progress. It had begun in 1886 with eight students and three years later their number had almost doubled. They were, however, badly lodged, for the seminarians' places were joined to those of the residence. The most advanced ones among the students could have begun the study of philosophy if they had books. It is difficult to imagine what missionaries of that time were living without. Indeed, since his arrival, Coqset understood that he urgently needed to build a seminary separate from the residence, but he did not have the necessary money and thus had to delay the execution of his plan.

Another indirect reason of the difficulties to be overcome was the opening up of several Chinese ports to European trade in 1842.

In the old days, Jiangxi was much better known among the old missionaries. Missionaries used to enter the interior of China through this province. After landing in Macao, they went to Canton, where commercial ships could moor. From there they sailed upstream as far as the Guangdong-Jiangxi border. They then would cross the Meiling Pass and sail again on the river Gan; they would cross the whole province of Jiangxi from the south to the north, and then they would arrive with the rivers (especially the Blue River [Yangtze]) in Peking.

Ricci, leaving Canton in 1595, followed this river network to the Yangtze, from whence he sailed to Nanjing and then took the imperial canal that brought him to Tongzhou and the gates of Peking. But after the opening of the ports, travelers and goods were able to get to the north of China along other roads; hence there was quite a decrease of trade in Jiangxi and, consequently, a drop in the wealth of the region. This resulted in a special hindrance for evangelization. The intellectuals, the rich, and merchants, that is, those with influence over the people, suggested that the Europeans had harmed Chinese business by enabling foreign ships to land in the costal harbors and even inland on the larger rivers. Therefore, the officials of the city of Ganzhou consistently prevented missionaries from entering within its walls.

After visiting the local Christian communities in his vicariate for three or four years in all directions, Coqset wanted to correct the statistics his predecessor had drawn up. He was afraid that the situation of his vicariate would be overrated in the minds of those who had read Bishop Rouger's spiritual accounts. He explained that Rouger's statistics were a plan, a project, which he had hoped to realize in some years and which he, in his optimism, saw as already achieved. Actually, Rouger had not been able to achieve it.

Here is the list of the personnel of South Jiangxi in 1899.

Table 17.1. Concise Church Statistics for South Jiangxi, 1899

Various groups	Totals
Christians	4,215
Catechumens	200
Vincentian priests	8
Diocesan priests	3
Major seminarians	7
Minor seminarians	19
Baptisms	**Totals**
Children of non-Christians	1,538
Children of Catholic parents	155
Adults	17

Boxers in South Jiangxi

The information we have comes from a dry report with few details written by Coqset on 4 October 1900 from Shanghai at the time the bishop was still in exile. We copy it here and complete it through letters from missionaries, written a short time after the events.[51]

> Every one of us stayed at his post as long as we could, despite the storm. In the end we had no other choice than to leave our mission and to take refuge in a port (Shanghai).
>
> We had been threatened for a long time with arson and even murder; mandarins asked us to leave, but because they seemed to protect us by order of the viceroy of Nanjing, we stayed on.
>
> At the end of August, the persecution arrived where we were. In order to make us leave, the mandarins gave the people's violence a free hand. On 17 August the residence in Ganzhou, which, installed in 1898, had a blossoming catechumenate of two hundred catechumens, was given over to looting. The two missionaries of the place went and fled to an important mandarin's home; he kept them for two days and then had them taken to Jiujiang. The church in Pinglu, not far from Ganzhou, was burned almost before the mandarins' eyes.
>
> On 19 August the looters attacked the Christians and the residence in Taiheli, a large Christian community, surrounded by many small villages, almost all Christian. The sub-prefect gathered the missionaries, and he took it upon himself to take them to the port in Jiujiang. After their departure, all the Christian villages and the common chapel were set ablaze. Some sixty Christians were murdered there.
>
> On 31 August it was Ji'an's turn. Our not yet completed episcopal residence, the seminary, the church, the orphanage, a completely new but unoccupied hospital, and several chapels in the vicinity, everything was burned down. A moment before the disaster, when the crowd was already surrounding our houses, the mandarins came to make us leave and to make us embark hurriedly on a small military boat. We could not bring anything.

---

51. Ferreux's notes: Before we begin, we want to point out that it was characteristic of the mandarins' attitude towards the missionaries that they promised their protection against every attack coming from the recruited criminals, but unfortunately the help they sent always arrived too late, after the misdeed had already happened.

I left five Chinese priests in the mission, because it is easier for them than for us to hide. Indeed, after our departure they did have to hide and to move quite often. Everywhere Christians were fleeing, and those who wanted to come back to their villages were forced to commit apostasy. I took with me the eight oldest students of our seminary; for we must provide formation for the local clergy we need so much. A. Coqset

Here is a letter from Father Pérès in Ji'an, dated the end of November, 1903, and written to a confrere who had been his coworker in Jiangxi. In a familiar way the missionary gives his friend reassuring news about the vicariate.

When on 31 August the mandarins hustled the two last missionaries of south Jiangxi, Bishop Coqset and your friend, onto a miserable small boat, and when from our boat we saw the flames destroy our buildings, sadness and discouragement came over me, I admit it to you.

In one day, twenty years of work, of fighting, of money spent, and particularly of patience, were in ruins. It had begun so well, I told myself; and now! I wanted to weep then. I was forgetting that God's works needed trials so as to bear good fruit and not allow human beings to attribute to themselves the successes. They need occasions to admire God's goodness and power. He always draws good things from evil. Look. Besides our beautiful house in Wannan and some small oratories here and there, all the rest has been destroyed. And today, three years later, in Ji'an, our principal residence, our church, our hospital, the dispensary, our dear sisters' house, the two orphanages have sung again a joyous resurrection alleluia, for we have put all these buildings back into better condition than they were before the disaster.

Father Thomas Festa, in the lead, went and opened the district of Ningdu at the risk of his life. . . . The districts of Taiheli and Yonglin have been entrusted to Father Clovis Pruvot; those two completely burned residences and chapels have been re-built like new. Father Henri Lecaille, the happy resident in our beautiful house in Wan'an, hopes to baptize, with Father Xie's help, quite a few adults, while directing the minor seminary.

Father Canduglia, your old pastor, has associates: Fathers Zhou and René de Jenlis. This dear confrere, besides his big parish, is very vigilant in the care and dedication he gives to the local Institute of the Virgins of Saint Anne. They will soon provide him with valuable assistants like teachers or directors of orphanages, works that the Daughters of Charity cannot begin yet. He also is very busy

What about Father Legris, you will ask me? He has become a diocesan architect. After building the church in Ji'an, he went away to dig the foundations of the residence in Ganzhou. Back here, he now is finishing the school for the Marist Brothers, who will come back on Christmas day.

From a letter by Father Boscat, visitor since 1900, we quote also some useful items about the situation of the vicariate. Boscat had been working in Jiangxi for about twenty years. On 1 August 1904 he wrote from Shanghai:

I just returned from visiting Jiangxi. I began in South Jiangxi: I shall tell you about that place now.

In all these regions God's work is progressing slowly but surely. In Ganzhou especially, the mission is settling quite well in the middle of the city. A good residence is being finished. Ganzhou is geographically in the middle of the vicariate, and one day the residence of the apostolic vicar will be there, and the main works will also be established there; Bishop Coqset, probably for that reason, has just moved his minor seminary there.[52] For three years there have already been there an orphanage of the Holy Childhood and catechumenate schools for women, everything managed by the Sisters of Saint Anne.

In the old days, I was never able to enter into the interior of the town of Ganzhou; we hardly dared to approach it. On this occasion, I have not only penetrated, I could, so to say, wander around in the busiest streets without my presence producing the least bit of amazement.

In Ningdu, in the southeast, thanks to the persistence of Father Festa, we have, I would not dare to say an establishment, but at least a foot in the door. Festa stays there stubbornly with two catechumenates; but he is alone near the border with Fujian with a Chinese priest set up one hundred twenty kilometers away.

What else can be said about Ji'an, in the north of the vicariate, than that it continues to prosper. The new church, which has not been

---

52. It would still be more than twenty years before a bishop resided in Ganzhou, but this town will be the see of a new vicariate, stemming from the one in Ji'an.

finished yet, is larger than the old one, destroyed by the Boxers four years ago. Above, I mentioned the Sisters of Saint Anne. It is a little community of virgins destined for the instruction of Christian women or catechumens. They follow the same rules as the Josephines of Peking and differ practically in no way from them. They have only a different name. The need for these virgin teachers is felt everywhere; our apostolic vicars try to secure their collaboration.

Coqset himself wrote from Ji'an on 4 October 1904:

> Here, despite rumors of war, rebellions and the unrest that results from them, the mission carries on and we see the number of our Christians increase. We will have more than five hundred baptisms of adults this year. That number was never reached before. If peace is not disrupted, we shall see still more comforting results.

China is going through a crisis; it looks as though this huge population is going to change its old habits. The men will cut their braided hair; the women will unbind their feet,[53] the scholars will be aware that besides China there are other nations, that besides Confucius there are other wise people and that there are other books than Confucius' *Four Books*.

Table 17.2 Personnel, South Jiangxi, 1900

Various groups	Totals
Christians	5,890
Vincentian priests	8
Diocesan priests	5
Philosophy and theology students	7
Students of Latin	13
Daughters of Charity	3
Daughters of Saint Anne	8

These several letters tell us clearly that not only rising from the ruins happens quickly, but also that the disaster was like a spur impelling missionary vigor forward.

It is evident that the number of Faithful increased by almost two thousand since 1890.

---

53.   This happened in 1912.

A New Movement of Boxers in South Jiangxi

One year after the gruesome murder in Nanchang, a quite similar drama was going to take place in South Jiangxi. The causes, however, were very different. In the north, there was a conflict between the Catholic mission and the civil authority; there was no question of a secret organization. In the south on the other hand, it was the work of a sect that under another name renewed the wretched exploits of the Boxers of 1900.

It had taken the name of Shenda (Fight with the Mind), but actually they were real Boxers. The same superstitious practices, same goals: finishing off foreigners and Christians.

The movement, publicly begun in June 1907, ended with the drama of the following 25 September. According to missionaries' accounts, the whole south of China was under the threat of a revolutionary uprising.[54] It would be difficult for the imperial government, they said, to repress a rebellion against the dynasty.

Some other people thought that the peace they were enjoying was only superficial. They were afraid that the revolution that was working on people's minds would not spare them its path of destruction. The Shenda sect obviously developed only in South Jiangxi. The fanatic gangs' principal target was Taiheli, formed by an agglomeration of nine villages, which, badly damaged in 1900, had risen from the ruins. Father Canduglia had exercised his apostolate there for more than twenty years. He and his vicars were fully aware of the danger both by what they were seeing and hearing and by the reports of the Christians.

Canduglia sent out many calls for help to the sub-prefect of Nankang, on whom he was dependent, but always in vain. The sub-prefect thought there was no danger. Canduglia then appealed to the authorities in Ganzhou through Father Schottey, where this priest was residing as director. On 20 July 1907 Schottey wrote, "I informed the intendant [*daotai?*] of Ganzhou officially; he answered me that he knew this sect and that he was busy destroying it, and he added that there was nothing to be afraid of."

Schottey, however, with the information he had received from Canduglia, sent the intendant the names of the places where the rebels were holding their meetings and even the names of the main leaders. The

---

54. This foreseen general revolution happened four years later and was not as drenched in blood as people thought it would be. We cannot deny, however, that the secret societies participated in it and hastened the fall of the dynasty, which was actually already falling into complete decline.

intendant then had his subordinate, the sub-prefect of Ganzhou, make some enquiries and arrests. There was almost no result.

On 21 September Canduglia informed Schottey that the danger was imminent. Right away he submitted this matter to the intendant, who sent sixty soldiers, forty for Nankang and twenty to a big market town some seven kilometers away from Taiheli, but nobody to the village itself, already surrounded by the Boxers. On 23 and 24 September new appeals by Canduglia and new steps by Schottey to approach the intendant, who this time sent to Taiheli a colonel flanked by ten soldiers. That was the rescue party.

Canduglia's Murder

On 24 September there was a small attack. The village of Taiheli is set among hills. A thousand Boxers were seen coming down from them forming tiers on the slopes. Then they were grouped in two gangs, one stayed where they were, the other went forward resolutely to the village, flags unfurled. The leaders prudently remained behind. The Boxers approached and began running, armed mostly with pikes, very few guns. The Christians shot their guns a few times. A melee followed with mostly cries of rage. On the side of the Christians one man died and another was wounded. On the other side several fell. Their first try had failed, they went back taking with them their dead and wounded.

The mandarins provided no help. The night passed without another attack. The next day, at dawn, the colonel with his ten soldiers arrived. The commander tried to gather the forty soldiers spread over the neighborhood of Nankang, but they refused to march because the sub-prefect claimed that there was no danger and that they did not need to arm themselves, lest they anger the Boxers. The colonel could only add to his group three lower officers and he sent them to reconnoiter. Frightened they came back; "There are too many Boxers," they said, "we cannot do anything against so many."

At noon, a column of Boxers could be seen that covered the hills round about; soon the slopes were teeming with human clusters. There were more than ten thousand. At about four o'clock, they set fire to the nearest villages; at five o'clock they were very near the village; soon the orphanage was burning. Lecaille comforted everybody; three times he cried out to all to run to the church. The soldiers, though well-armed, did not dare to shoot. At that moment, the colonel thought that one way out was still free, so he wanted to flee. He made Canduglia mount a horse of one of his officers and, followed by soldiers and some Christians, moved away. The little troop had hardly done a hundred steps, when a group of Boxers suddenly appeared on the road. Canduglia, who had believed in a possible flight too, realized the danger he was in; he blessed the Christians and shook hands with his Faithful servant who had wanted to follow him. Then the unhappy colonel slid down from his chair, bowed down in front of the fanatics who were running towards him and begged them to become orderly again. The only answer he received was the bullet that brought him dying to the ground. At the same time Canduglia was surrounded, his horse was killed and he was thrown to the ground; right away four lances in the chest, and raising his sword one of the maniacs rushed towards the victim and slashed his head.

Lecaille's Flight

While Canduglia was dying, fright was reigning in the church of Taiheli. All the people were there with Father Lecaille. The men had lost courage, the women were lamenting. Families were praying on their knees or were kneeling at the priest's feet begging him to save them. Lecaille did not let the situation get him down; he had not slept for three days, but his courage did not weaken. He told everybody to pray the act of contrition. An ardent prayer went up to heaven. The priest pronounced the words of absolution. It was five o'clock in the evening, he took his gun and with some willing men he shot from the gallery loft. Others threw stones at the attackers. All checked out the surrounding area and shot at those who were trying to set fire to the outside. The school was on fire and the roof was collapsing.

The church was saved. Night had come. The rebels disbanded, some were looting, others were going back home carrying off their spoils. It was the opportune moment to flee; staying in the church would have meant certain death the next day.

At about seven o'clock, Lecaille went outside; Christians followed him on the way to Pinglu. In all they were about one hundred people. The march was slow; the women and children slowed them up; the thirteen virgins of Saint Anne were there too under the protection of armed men. At about two o'clock in the morning, they arrived in Pinglu. There were no Boxers there; there was nobody in the residence. They could have a little rest; at dawn they resumed the march to Ganzhou, where they arrived at ten o'clock in the morning.

The director, Auguste Schottey, who already knew Canduglia's sad end through a fleeing soldier, was happy to receive the refugees and to hug his confrere, whose fate had made him worry very much up till that moment. With Schottey there was Father Joseph Molinari, who, informed about the disaster in Taiheli, had fled one hour before Lecaille's passage; Father Louis Verrière and Brother Van den Brandt were also there in Ganzhou. But the missionaries' odyssey was not over.

Murders and Destruction

Lecaille had arrived in Ganzhou on 26 September in the morning after experiencing the worst emotions.

Though the Boxers were not in town, the news of the murders in the vicinity had provoked agitation, which the arrival of the refugees had intensified. Seeing this, Schottey judged that it would be prudent to go and see the quartermaster together with the missionaries. The mandarin assured them that he preferred to die than to allow rebels to cut the missionaries' throats. He also offered them to escort them to Ji'an if they so wanted.

At about three o'clock in the afternoon, the mob rushed to the residence, set fire to it, also to the not yet finished church, the seminary and the orphanage. It was impossible for them to stay on in this place. Schottey did not lose his head; he organized their departure. The virgins and the orphans were entrusted to the sub-prefect. At more or less ten o'clock in the evening, the five missionaries left the yamen under escort. Two boats were waiting for them; they got on board and traveled to Ji'an, which was about two hundred kilometers away. They were to arrive there on 30 September.

There, things were calm, and the fugitives could rest in the company of several confreres who had just finished their annual retreat. They were Fathers Pérés, Legris who was director of the major seminary, [Clovis] Pruvot, [Félix] Bonanate, [René] de Jenlis and [Henri-Achille] Watthé.

At the end of a week's rest, Schottey and Lecaille went on alone to Shanghai by boat, in order to give Guilloux, the visitor, the information he might need.

The rebellion, however, had not yet calmed down. We saw that Molinari had fled Pinglu in time. The day after his departure the city was looted and set on fire. Nankang had the same fate despite the pacifist sub-prefect's assurances.

Gruesome things happened to Canduglia's body. Having cut off the head, they put it on a pike and displayed it for three days in the neighboring villages. Then soldiers put the corpse into a coffin, brought it to Ganzhou and took it to the military camp where it had to wait for an official inquiry.

The number of Christians killed in Taiheli and the surrounding villages rose to more than one hundred.

In the whole of this sad affair, not once was the name of the Ordinary of the place mentioned. The reason is that Coqset was absent from his vicariate.

Coqset's Transfer to West Zhili and Ciceri as his Replacement in South Jiangxi

By a brief dated 3 May 1907 Pope Pius X transferred Coqset from the vicariate of South Jiangxi to the vicariate of Southwest Zhili (Zhengding) vacant because of Bruguière's death on 19 October 1906. Two months later, a brief from the same Pius X dated 3 July 1907 appointed Bishop Nicolas Ciceri as the titular bishop of Dausara and the apostolic vicar of South Jiangxi.

As soon as the brief of his transfer to Zhengding was known, Coqset did not hesitate to take measures to go as fast as possible to his new vicariate, much more important than the one he just left, for it numbered thirty-two thousand Christians; moreover, it had remained vacant for more than a year.

Then, when he went to Zhengding in June 1907, the news of the difficulties in the south of Jiangxi had not yet arrived in Ji'an.

On the other hand, his successor hesitated, because of his health, to accept the charge that he had been offered, resulting in negotiations with Rome, for it could be foreseen that the Supreme Pontiff might make another choice. Rome, however, did not alter its decision. This explains the delay in taking possession of the see of Ji'an. As late indeed as 16 February 1908 Ciceri received in Ji'an episcopal consecration at the hands of Coqset, who had to travel back from Zhengding to Ji'an.

Nicolas Ciceri, born in Brusciano (diocese of Naples) on 26 May 1854, admitted in Paris on 5 May 1874, was ordained priest on 15 June 1878. After his arrival in Shanghai on the following 4 October he was placed in Jiangxi. From the establishment of the apostolic vicariate of East Jiangxi in 1885, he remained there till 1900. Then he was appointed as assistant procurator in Shanghai and where he received his appointment as apostolic vicar of South Jiangxi. We shall find him there again after we have gone through the other missions.

Chapter 18

Boxer Incidents Mainly in East Jiangxi

General Situation of this Vicariate – Antoine Anot, a Great Missionary – Boxers in East Jiangxi – Rebuilding the Ruins – Bishop Vic's Episcopal Jubilee (18 May 1911) – Vic's Death – Vicariate of Zhejiang – Bishop Favier – Bishop Bruguière's Death

General Situation of this Vicariate

Created in 1885, the vicariate of East Jiangxi embraced one third of the province of Jiangxi both in size and population. It measured about four hundred kilometers from north to south and three hundred fifty kilometers from east to west. Consequently, it covered an area slightly larger than one fourth of France.

It had about ten million inhabitants. It had four prefectures that embraced twenty-five sub-prefectures.

Table 18.1. Personnel and Spiritual Fruits, East Jiangxi, 1891

Categories	Totals
Christians	10,854
Catechumens	973
Baptisms of infants of Christian parents	320
Baptisms of infants of non-Christians	4,128
Baptisms of adults	176
Churches	4
Chapels	24
Oratories	31
Christian communities to be visited	205

European Vincentian priests	10
Chinese Vincentian priests	3
Chinese diocesan priests	7
Seminarians in major seminary	5
Boys' schools	32
Number of boys	411
Girls' schools	59
Number of girls	760
Orphanages	6
Orphaned girls	602
Infants with wet nurses	725

Note: In this list "students in the minor seminary" or "students of Latin" are not mentioned. For reasons of personnel and money, the three vicariates of the province had agreed to establish a minor seminary first in Sanqiao, later on in Ji'an where all the students of Latin studied together. That turned out to be temporary. Soon they were to have in their own vicariates all that was necessary to succeed in the formation of their clergy.

Antoine Anot, a Great Missionary

East Jiangxi suffered a great loss on 21 November 1893, the day Anot passed away. This great missionary had worked in Jiangxi for fifty years.

Having announced this sorrowful news to the superior general by telegram, Bishop Vic wrote a notice about this confrere. We select here its principal passages.

Father Antoine Anot, born in Menneville (Aisne) on 3 May 1814, accepted in Paris on 5 October 1838, ordained priest on 21 May 1842, was appointed, according to his wish, to the missions in China. He arrived in Macao on 24 August 1843 and was sent to Jiangxi, which at that time was under Bishop Rameaux. He made his debut with this valiant apostle, who, a year later (1845) died in Macao still in the prime of life. Anot then worked under the guidance of Bishop Laribe.

No sooner had he began his apostolate than he was hit by a serious and long-lasting disease. Strangely, he not only became well again, but afterwards he was stronger than he had ever been before.

Then he began to be on campaign, visiting Christian communities abandoned because of lack of personnel; he visited, taught, and encouraged neophytes; he gave himself completely, in spite of weariness, privations, and the deceptions of this difficult occupation. As the priests sent to help him at different periods had died early in their lives or had been missioned elsewhere, Anot for twenty years remained almost the only European still visiting Christians, that is, who was evangelizing. His zeal and his activity were enough for everything and everybody.

We have to acknowledge that his robust constitution, which became proverbial in Jiangxi, helped him immensely. To give people the last rites or to move from one Christian community to another, he covered on foot distances of two or three hundred kilometers. It happened that he had to cross steep mountains, use almost impossible paths, and go unbelievable distances, often far outpacing his guides and the porters of his luggage.

This energy and this capacity for long marches, for which he was grateful to Providence, were a real reserve of strength for carrying out his functions. To all this he knew how to add dedication and piety which increased tenfold the value and the merit of his labor.

The successive changes or death of several apostolic vicars left the direction of the mission in his hands several times and in the most difficult periods. Who would be able to relate the troubles, worries and anxieties of this missionary between 1849 and 1871? On top of the jealousy of the scholars, the bad faith and tricks of the mandarins, and all kinds of slanderous remarks, there were the calamities and horrors of the civil war, which lasted not less than twenty years in the province of Jiangxi. All the time there was some harassment either by rebels or imperial troops. It would have been difficult to say from which side people had to suffer more vexations and cruelties: both sides were looting, setting fire and cutting throats.

Nevertheless, as the number of missionaries increased little by little, the second half of Anot's apostolate was less turbulent. Besides, he was no longer able to move as easily as in former days, and it was for him not a small sacrifice to stop visiting Christian communities. At that time, he silently directed the activities of the residence. When communicating with his confreres he shared with them his spirit and his zeal.

For eight years he had carried the seed of the disease that took him away. Vic ended his notice in this way:

> In my opinion, few apostles have had not only such a long career,[55] but also such a full and fertile one. Obviously, he was not alone,

---

55. He was the first Vincentian missionary to work in China for fifty years. He was the

and we cannot attribute to him all the good done in Jiangxi during those many years; but he laid the foundations of Christian communities that are spread out today over the thirteen prefectures of the province.

He was the first to begin the Holy Childhood, and he gave it such an impetus that neither the civil war nor the vexations of the mandarins and intellectuals were able to stop its rising.

In terms of talent, he had an unhurried and sure intelligence, which continue to develop into his latter years. In no way stubborn, his kindness and openness of mind in receiving judgments and ideas from his younger confreres astonished us and elicited our admiration. He was prejudiced against nothing and no one.

Anot's modesty and humility were even more amazing than his achievements. He was first of all a man of prayer. He prayed while traveling, he prayed in the residence, and when sick he prayed even more than when in good health. That was in his long life the secret of all the great things given him to do.

Boxers in East Jiangxi

In an account that he drew up for Father Boscat, the visitor, on 28 March 1901 Bishop Vic clearly expounded the situation with which the missionaries of Jiangxi had to deal as a consequence of the differences of opinion among the high officials at that time in the provinces of the south.

> The viceroys, in fear of becoming the victims of a possible retaliation by the European powers, decided of one accord to tone down the orders coming from Peking.[56] Jiangxi depended on the viceroy of Nanjing; however, he had authority over our province more in name than in reality. Practically speaking, the governor of Nanchang was independent.
>
> In the hinterland of Jiangxi, the only European elements are the Catholic missionaries and, in still higher number, the Protestant ministers. As soon as the troubles began, our governor sent one of his friends who was keeping him informed about events to

---

125th Vincentian to arrive in China.

56. Remember that the viceroy of Nanjing had openly resisted Cixi's order to enlist the Boxers into the ranks of his army.

Shanghai. This man, with obvious bad faith, wrote to his master that, in Peking, the government was winning all along the line, that all the Western devils had their throats cut, and that even in Shanghai people were going to throw the rest of the foreigners into the sea. The governor was in a puzzling situation. On the one hand he had to show his dedication to the orders of the court; on the other hand, the viceroy of Nanjing gave many pressing orders to protect the foreigners' lives.

Our governor found the middle-of-the-road solution of protecting the lives, but destroying the buildings. Hence there was a well-thought-out plan. First, getting rid of the foreign missionaries, then without pressure looting and destroying both the Catholic and Protestant buildings. They were to begin with the east vicariate, and then continue with the south vicariate, to finish with Nanchang and Jiujiang. Indeed, from the first week of July to 30 August this plan was executed point by point.

First, the missionaries were urged to withdraw. The authorities declared themselves unable to protect them; the presence of a priest, even of a local priest, they said, was a perpetual incitement for the people. The missionaries believed it would be wise to give in to these commands.

Several among us left as late as possible, for example, Father [François] Dauverchain who, after the destruction of the residence of Jingdezhen understood clearly the imminence of the danger. He led the Daughters of Charity to Jiujiang, and five days after their departure from Raozhou, their buildings were ablaze. All left the mission reluctantly to go to Shanghai. If they had obstinately persisted in remaining, the missionaries would have exposed their lives for absolutely nothing, and their presence instead of easing would have worsened the Christians' situation.

The situation of the missionaries in the north of China was completely different. The Christians were much less isolated, were more numerous and better organized. There the orders of the court were executed brutally and cruelly. Armed Boxers surrounded the principal Christian communities. Flight was materially impossible.

Armed defense was for the Christians the only way. It was the missionary's task to encourage them and to help them as best he could with the organization of their defense. The history of the Boxers in Peking tells us eloquently with how much simplicity and courage our confreres in the north, the Sisters and the Christians have done their duty.

We thought these explanations necessary to make it possible to understand generally the missionaries' behavior in Jiangxi during the storm in 1900.

We previously mentioned North Jiangxi and the material losses the three vicariates suffered. East Jiangxi had about fifteen victims.

Rebuilding the Ruins

Almost all the buildings of the vicariate had been demolished except the ones of Fuzhou. This was equally the case for the buildings in Jiujiang that remained untouched thanks to the presence of the European boats.

Thus, all these different ruins had to be rebuilt. That was a rough task for Bishop Vic in a vicariate with so few apostolic workers. One of the first repairs was for the Daughters of Charity's house in Raozhou. They could go back to that village on 25 March 1902 and settle in a building two-thirds bigger than the former one. In Hekou, Father [Frédéric] Sageder built a residence, and the Chinese priests built the chapels. In the years that followed up to the great Revolution of 1911, there was in this vicariate an intensified movement of conversions, thanks to the relative calm atmosphere and particularly thanks to the successive ordinations of local priests and the considerable reinforcements sent by Paris, all of which doubled the number of apostolic workers.

Now, in order to show better the progress of this vicariate under the direction of Vic, we present here the comparative statistics of the personnel and the principal spiritual fruits for the years 1902, 1904, 1908 and 1911.

Table 18.2 Comparative Statistics, East Jiangxi, 1902–1911

Groups	1902	1904	1908	1911
Catholics	13,373	14,380	19,080	21,960
Catechumens	2,000	3,800	3,680	2,000
Priests				
European Vincentians	11	16	21	22
Diocesan	8	8	9	10

Seminarians: major / minor	7	12	24	52
Daughters of Charity	6	6	6	7
Josephines				24
Baptisms				
Adults	265	400	1,266	1,600
Children of Christians	689	668	818	1,680
Dying Infants	2,900	4,248	2,800	2,975

Bishop Vic's Episcopal Jubilee (18 May 1911)

Because he was living in a very cramped situation in the ancient episcopal residence in Fuzhou, Vic chose Jianchang for the celebration of his jubilee, not only in order to be better lodged, but also so as to bless solemnly, on that occasion, the new and beautiful church.

Indeed, on the ruins of 1900, the population, from then on sympathetic, had witnessed for three years the construction of the most beautiful church of the vicariate; it was finished just in time, and the dedicated Father Antoine Tamet could ask his bishop to please solemnly bless it as a monument of thanksgiving.

More than twenty priests, some of whom came from afar. The seminarians of the major and minor seminaries carried out as best they could the chants and ceremonies in the two pontifical Masses that were celebrated, and the Christians filled the church these days of feast and thanksgiving. Dauverchain, who related these celebrations, liked to notice the progress of the vicariate in the course of those twenty-five years. He wrote in 1886:

> We were three European confreres of Bishop Vic; today we are twenty-three. The Chinese priests kept their number of ten, newly ordained priests only compensating for the deceased; but progress is currently seen especially in the work of the seminary, which never before was so prosperous.
>
> In 1886, we had only four residences; now, not counting those with no director yet, we have twenty-five all in full operation.
>
> In 1886, we had barely ten thousand Faithful. Now we have about twenty-one thousand. Last year we had 1,234 baptisms of adults; this time we hope to have about 1,500.

For only a few years we have had the local religious women of Saint Joseph, the Josephines: a work for the future. They still have only five institutions, where they are teaching more than five hundred pupils.

Alas! These celebrations and acts of thanksgiving to God were to be the venerated apostolic vicar's swan song.

Vic's Death

For a couple of months, Vic had been feeling his energies decreasing. Towards the end of May 1912 on advice of those around him, he went to Shanghai to visit his doctors and have a treatment if necessary. The doctor told him to rest, to do some walking and have some distraction. Vic decided to stay some days in our provincial house in Jiaxing. He went there with Father Dauverchain and Brother Barrière.

During the evening recreation, he was joyful, and was interested in the conversation as usual. Therefore, the witnesses had every reason to think that this change of environment was good for him. Alas! God had taken a different decision.

The next morning, 2 June, when his servant entered his room at about 4:30 as usual, he found Vic lying lifeless on his bed, the body still warm. Quickly he called for the director of the house, Father [Paul] Ryckewaert, who hurried to give him conditional absolution; death had already done its work; hemorrhage had struck him down.

God had summoned His good and Faithful servant. Vic had indeed been a real missionary apostolic vicar. During the twenty-six years of his episcopacy, he had never spared himself, working like the least of his confreres, whom he had liked to replace whenever they were tired. Therefore, it could be said that he had died exhausted by his apostolic traveling and as a victim of his zeal for gaining souls

Through His Holiness Pius X's brief of 19 August 1912, Father Clerc-Renaud was appointed as bishop of Elaea and apostolic vicar of East Jiangxi. Jean-Louis Clerc-Renaud, born in Lyons on 18 June 1866, admitted in Paris on 26 September 1885, was ordained a priest on 17 December 1892. After arriving in Shanghai on 14 February 1893 he was placed in East Jiangxi.

He received episcopal consecration on 3 November 1912 in the Sisters' chapel in Raozhou, from Bishop Reynaud's hands, with the assistance of Bishop Fatiguet and Bishop Ciceri.

Vicariate of Zhejiang

Here we interrupt our account of this vicariate to move to Zhejiang, which we left at the moment the Boxer movement was just starting. But first, in order to keep to the chronological order, we must mention here the death of several distinguished personalities, namely Boscat, the visitor; Favier and Bruguière.

Boscat was used up before his time. Work and worry had ruined his health. His thick, snow-white beard, which made him look like an old man, and the pallor of his face, despite his very lively eyes, gave the impression that he was very tired. Several times, in the course of his frequent trips to Jiaxing, he blacked out.

What consternation there was among his confreres and his *"carissimi,"* [very dear] as he had loved to address his clerics in Jiaxing, when on 27 December 1904 a telegram from Shanghai broke the news to them that revered visitor had died! He was only fifty-six years old.

His successor was Claude Guilloux, who had arrived in China in 1886 and was directing the seminary in Peking when, in the beginning of 1905, he was appointed visitor of the province of China and consequently superior of the seminary in Jiaxing.

Later we will talk again about the progress of this seminary.

Bishop Favier

Favier had his first stroke while visiting the international hospital of Peking. It was on 15 August 1902.[57] The head doctor of the hospital and the Sisters gave him immediate attention and kept him in the hospital until the end of October. Favier was partly paralyzed.[58] He had to stop almost all his activities and to give over to Bishop Jarlin the supervision the affairs of the vicariate.

A new crisis happened in March 1905. It was the last one. On the following 4 April, after receiving the last rites, Favier died. He was sixty-eight years old, forty-three years of which he spent in China.

A man of decision and action, he was broad-minded. Favier fulfilled a great role in China, particularly at the time of the Boxer Rebellion. With his experience, his lively intelligence, his kindness for all, he had

---

57. Ferreux's notes: 25 August 1903.

58. Ferreux's notes: patient is said to have been brought back to the Beitang the same day and he seemed to recover quite well after some days. He was partly paralyzed, his left arm and his tongue were lightly affected.

acquired real prestige, not only among the missionaries but also among the Europeans and among the Chinese officials. At the time of his death, the government expressed to Jarlin in a very telling way its condolences and its high esteem for the deceased bishop.

As coadjutor with the right of succession, Stanislas Jarlin, already used to governing the vicariate of Peking, took its administration up officially.

Bishop Bruguière's Death

Bishop Bruguière had been a member of the Synod of Peking (1906). He had gone there with Father Nicolas Baroudi. It was his last public deed. After the closing of the Synod, the bishop wanted to take advantage of his trip to pay a visit to a sick intimate friend of his, [Emmanuel Joseph-Marie] Catheline, chaplain of the French detachment in Tianjin. So, he went there by train and put up at the Procure, directed then by Father Desrumaux.

The next day, this confrere took Bruguière to the place called the "Arsenal," where Catheline was living, at some seven or eight kilometers from the city. The friends, who had not seen each other for a long time, were happy to be together again. After dinner, the bishop felt a strange pain, but he did not mention it. During the trip back, however, he said to his companion, Baroudi, "I do not feel well, . . . I have the impression that Catheline has given me his disease [consumption]". "What are you saying, bishop? No, it is only a passing indisposition certainly caused by being tired." Bruguière did not talk about it anymore and went back to Zhengding without stopping in Peking.

Right away he wanted to begin carrying out the synod resolutions. He planned already the project of building a superior primary school in the principal centers, and then a secondary school at the episcopal residence.

But the fainting feeling that he had had in Tianjin became more serious, and despite his will of showing nothing of it to those around him, who had always seen him excellent health and were amazed at seeing him so tired, soon Bruguière had to admit that he was in pain. An able doctor was called for from Peking. He declared that the patient had consumption and heart trouble. People prayed much for the venerated patient and for a time it was believed that heaven had granted what they had prayed for. The patient's usual appetite, joyfulness and liveliness came back. It was only a passing improvement; the disease progressed and soon became so serious that the doctors urged him to change to another climate and go to Europe. Understanding the gravity of his disease, the bishop agreed to the satisfaction of his entourage who hoped for the good results that a stay in France would produce. On 16 October 1906 Bruguière arrived in Shanghai exhausted, and was taken right away to the International Hospital served by the Daughters of Charity. The next day he was given the last rites and on the 19th in the evening he died murmuring: "The shepherd is giving his life for his sheep."

Chapter 19

The Vicariate of Zhejiang, 1900-1912

Boxers in Zhejiang: Faveau's Account – The Ruins are Rebuilt – Wenzhou, a Beautiful Vineyard – Progress – The Daughters of Charity in Zhejiang – Division of the District of Wenzhou – Establishment of a Second Vicariate in Zhejiang – The Fall of the Qing Dynasty – The Chinese Republic (1912-1927) – The Missions in the South and Center during the Revolution of 1911

Boxers in Zhejiang: Faveau's Account

To give an exact idea of what the storm in Zhejiang was like, we need only to copy in its broad outlines the account written for the superiors in Paris by Father Faveau, one of the most competent among Bishop Reynaud's collaborators.

> Among the nine districts that make up Bishop Reynaud's vicariate, five in particular had to suffer during the months of June, July and August 1900. It very nearly happened that the whole province became the theater of an official, general persecution. It was a close call.
>
> Our governor, Liu Zutang, an enemy of Europeans, had received and was preparing the publication of the famous bloodthirsty decrees of Prince Duan.[59] He had already sent orders throughout his province, and the general consul of France had already warned Reynaud to be on his guard, when through a particular disposition of the Providence the viceroy of Nanjing, Liu Kunyi, told our governor to sign the convention, which had been reached between him and the viceroy of Li Hongzhang on the one hand and the foreign consuls and admirals on the other. Through this convention the provinces in the south of China "separated" themselves from the Boxers in the north, "refused to obey" Prince Duan, and

---

59. Prince Duan was Cixi's most influential counselor.

committed themselves to maintain peace throughout the whole of their territory.[60]

This official protection that our governor was obliged to give us saved us from complete ruin. From that moment the proclamations of the majority of the responsible mandarins made the people return to their duties and calmed down the agitation that they had initiated. Several among them showed a lot of good will and even were energetic. The governor himself was very active in his capital of Hangzhou, and no disorder happened there.

In several big cities like Shaoxing and Ningbo, the civil mandarins were at the head of the troops repressing troublemakers and dispersing turbulent meetings. In Haimen, however, a small military harbor of Taizhou, the military leader absolutely refused to shoot at the rebels who were on the point of attacking our buildings; at that moment the civil mandarin took charge of the regular troops and made a sortie to push the attackers back.

The missionaries could, therefore, continue residing in the principal towns, which are at the same time the centers of our districts. Through their presence and their communication with the authorities, they were able to help safeguard their own interests and those of the Christians. Everywhere our churches remained open and church services were celebrated as usual on Sundays and feast days. This helped put the minds of peaceable people at ease.[61]

The situation of the Protestants was completely different. Their temples were closed and their houses were abandoned.

Here is the account of the situation in the five most harmed districts:

1. District of Quzhou: The disorders that erupted in this prefecture coincided with the rebellion of the Boxers in the north, but had only an indirect relation with it. There was in that region a powerful sect of "fasters" who, for a long time had been conspiring against the Qing dynasty. They are the descendants of the Taiping, who from

---

60. The resistance of this viceroy against the orders of the court annoyed the empress so much that she would certainly have recalled him had he not had as much prestige with the other authorities throughout the south of China. This viceroy's behavior spared Jiangxi greater damages.

61. Contrary to what happened in the three vicariates of Jiangxi, the missionaries of Zhejiang were not ordered to go into exile in Shanghai. We do not know the reason for this variant interpretation of the directives of the viceroy of Nanjing.

1850 to 1860 put to fire and sword the biggest part of China. Last year these rebels wanted to take advantage of the anarchy reigning in the north. Several second-order towns opened their gates to them and the crowd of insurgents, whose number was increasing with every success, advanced on Quzhou, the principal town in the region. The regular troops were searching for those suspected of collaborating with the enemy. Quite a few were arrested; the principal among them, the one who ought to have been at the head of the defenders of the town, the mandarin himself, was convicted of treason. Then horrible crimes were committed. The mandarin chased by a delirious crowd fled to the Protestants; soon discovered, he was lynched by the rabble which then attacked the Protestants and – horrible spectacle – killed the twelve people there mercilessly, among whom there were three women and four children, as if they had been the mandarin's accomplices.

At the time these barbaric executions were taking place, our own residence was being invaded, and fire was set to it after it was looted. No missionary was found there. The one who normally resided there had gone a short while before to a confrere in Mapeng, a fervent Christian community eight kilometers from Quzhou. Blessed be Providence that shielded him in this way from being murdered. Except for the buildings in town, this district lost also three country chapels which were destroyed.

2. In Wenzhou, alas, there was a prefect who, favoring the rebellion, visited several sub-prefectures under his jurisdiction to encourage the troublemakers' boldness and to launch their attacks on the Christians. There was, however, little damage.

3. In Taizhou, in the past an area for armed robbers, the disorder took serious proportions, and not only Christians, but even pagans, particularly the rich ones, were victims of armed destruction. Nothing remains of our chapels, and many of our Christians, after losing their possessions, were forced to leave the region to save their lives.

4–5. In Hangzhou and in Ningbo, the fourth and fifth districts, there have been quite serious material losses: in the first one, a residence and five chapels; in the other one, three chapels. Christians there were beaten and stripped of their possessions and had to flee and to leave their region in order to save their lives and to keep their faith.

The Ruins are Rebuilt

The repression of the Boxer Rebellion by the Allied forces was so quick and complete, that as soon as the troubles finished, the missionaries in all of China devoted themselves to rebuilding the ruins. Once again Faveau will inform us about the new situation in Zhejiang. He wrote in 1902:

> In the province of Zhejiang, as in most of the others, the year just finished has seen how the calm, which had been troubled by the Boxers, has been restored. Our destroyed buildings are rising from their ashes little by little;[62] our Christians dispersed by the storm have returned home. The harvest seems to be more abundant than ever and to gather it in, we will certainly have to increase the workers and the means. The appalling crisis that disturbed China seems to have awakened this great country from its age-old lethargy.

China had already effectively started the reform of the very famous examinations on the basis of studying only the *Four Books* of Confucius, the exclusive mold used to shape the whole class of leaders, which Guangxu also wanted to abolish in 1898. Faveau expressed his hopes on the coming results that such a change should produce: "This old routine will be abandoned. People will no longer look at the school of the old wise men for notions of classical literature and old history drenched in mythology. A good part of the time will be reserved for the study of European languages and sciences." He went on being elated when thinking of the future progress of Chinese civilization and he ends in this way: "If this beautiful zeal stays on and spreads, China will be transformed in a not too distant future."

Wenzhou, a Beautiful Vineyard

The district of Wenzhou is located in the south of the vicariate. Already several missionaries had devoted themselves to clearing the way and not without fruit. When Father Cyprien Aroud took over its direction after Father Louat, his predecessor in this post, he used so much zeal and practical sense in his evangelizing that soon this mission was to become one of the most flourishing and of the best organized of Zhejiang.

He began with the work of the catechists. When he arrived, he found eight of them; the following year he had twenty-two. Once they had been formed, these catechists were sent out. They were living in *gongsuo*,

---

62.   Thanks to the indemnifications paid by the Chinese government.

small chapels fitted with a living room. There they received the catechumens and explained to them the doctrine and there also they held school
for the children.

This young missionary, after arriving in Zhejiang in October 1899,
had devoted himself to the study of the Chinese language with all his
enthusiasm. For his study he used works by Father [Léon] Wieger, S.J., a
great Sinologist, who had studied thoroughly not only the Chinese classics, but also the "mechanism," as he called it, of the spoken language.
His analytic mind and shrewdness had discovered in the Chinese language turns of phrases, methods, finally rules which the finest Chinese
intellectual had never notice. These, written up explicitly and with all
the details, helped the French missionary to acquire the spoken Chinese
language just as he heard the Chinese themselves talking. By practicing
Wieger's phraseology, he successfully acquired a language, which in the
beginning had seemed so difficult for him to learn.

At the same time as the mechanisms, Wieger published in common
but correct language a rich series of sermons that he had written or borrowed from his confreres. Sermons loaded with doctrine, which the still
inexperienced missionary could learn by heart and preach to his audience. The listeners understood this familiar language and were amazed
to hear so many truths from the mouth of a priest whom they knew as
not very good at speaking. They were amazed that they could understand him when he was pouring those truths out to them. Gradually,
the missionary adopted all these expressions that he had learned, and
afterwards he could preach on his own and say by himself all he wanted
to teach his Christians.

Aroud did it this way – he told us so himself – and many missionaries
after him did so, too. Therefore, you can say that Wieger was a great help
to all the missionaries who since 1900 went to China to preach the gospel.

Progress

In 1905, after twenty years as bishop in Zhejiang, Bishop Reynaud had the
wonderful idea of publishing for the "Distant Benefactors of the Missions"
a comparative list of the personnel and of the principal works covering
the twenty years that had passed since the beginning of his episcopacy
till the year 1904.

Thus, so as to give the readers a more exact knowledge of the apostolate, he began by expounding some general notions, some of which we
shall copy when they are suitable for our account.

Zhejiang is the smallest province of China, as for its surface area; it is ninety-two thousand square kilometers and its population is about twenty-three million. Innocent XII erected the vicariate in 1696. The first apostolic vicar was Father Pierre d'Alcala, O.P., but he was not a bishop (1697–1705). Because of persecutions and so much disorder in the missions, the Christians were taken care of in only a sporadic way, either by the Dominicans of Fujian or the Jesuits of Jiangnan. In 1839, at the request of Bishop Carpena Diaz, apostolic vicar of Fujian, who had jurisdiction over Jiangxi and Zhejiang, the two provinces were joined to form one vicariate entrusted to the Vincentians, and Bishop Rameaux, C.M., was appointed its apostolic vicar (1838–1845). His successor was Bishop Laribe, C.M.; in 1846, however, these two provinces were separated into two distinct vicariates. Laribe remained in Jiangxi, and Zhejiang had as its apostolic vicar Bishop Lavaissière (1847–1849). Afterwards came: Bishops Danicourt (1850–1855); Delaplace (1855–1870); Guierry (1870–1883); Reynaud (1884–1926); and finally, Defebvre (from 1926).

The province of Zhejiang consists of eleven prefectures divided into seventy-five sub-prefectures. There are five districts (deaneries): Ningbo, Hangzhou, Quzhou, Wenzhou, and Taizhou.

Table 19.1. Comparative Statistics, Zhejiang, 1884–1904

Groups	1884	1894	1904
Catholic population	6,332	9,912	18,413
Catechumens	615	1,861	8,664
European Vincentians	11	13	16
Chinese Vincentians	4	6	14
Diocesan priests	3	2	5
Daughters of Charity	30	34	42
Marist Brothers			5
Virgins of Purgatory		26	47
Residences for missionaries	9	10	17
Churches	7	8	12
Chapels	24	30	106

Seminarians major seminary	7	8	21
Seminarians minor seminary	13	27	29
Boys' schools	24	26	77
Pupils	400	561	1,269
Girls' schools	8	21	22
Pupils	188	487	833
Colleges		1	3
Students		8	150
Adult baptisms	420	285	1,908

The Daughters of Charity in Zhejiang

The Daughters of Charity strictly speaking had their first house in China in Zhejiang. As we have seen, they arrived in Macao in 1847 [*sic* 1848], and in 1852 started working in Ningbo. In 1950, there were forty Daughters of Charity there, twenty-five European and fifteen Chinese.

In Ningbo, in Hangzhou, in Dinghai in the Zhoushan Archipelago, in Jiaxing, they have five houses, which include four hospitals for men and four for women; two orphanages for eighty-two boys and four for six hundred little girls, hospices, workshops and very busy dispensaries.

In Ningbo, their institution is like a real village, divided into four quarters as lively as it is interesting. In the suburb that serves as harbor for Ningbo, they are managing another institution accommodating about four hundred needy people, who resemble a museum of human suffering. There you could find the elderly, orphans, mentally challenged people, sick people and so on. Pagans themselves have chosen to assist this work of mercy with their own money, and it is principally with their charitable contribution that this huge institution has been set up where every needy person can find a place to sleep as well as receive good care.

Division of the District of Wenzhou

The intensifying rate of progress called for a division of the territory. In order to lighten the load for Wenzhou, Reynaud created a new district, whose residence was placed in Chuzhou (eighty kilometers from Wenzhou). He entrusted its direction to Father Leon Marquès, assistant to Aroud, who remained at the head of Wenzhou with six thousand Christians. That was in 1908. The director wanted very much to have Daughters of Charity. He wrote, "Ah! if we just had Sisters, how fast would we see a dispensary, a hospital, and a hospice rise. With how much pleasure and above all with how much advantage would we give to the people of Wenzhou proof of the Christian charity about which we preach."

Aroud had already made preparations to receive the Sisters: he had acquired a large property fifty steps away from the residence. But he still had to wait some years.

Establishment of a Second Vicariate in Zhejiang

Having gone through these last pages, the reader foresees certainly that an important event is going to take place in this flourishing vicariate. Indeed, because of the increase of the Christian population, Reynaud requested the Supreme Pontiff to please divide his vicariate in two. His request was received favorably and, by a brief of 10 May 1910 a new vicariate was created, which was to have the name West Zhejiang, whereas the old one would be named East Zhejiang.

Faveau, who had been working for many years in Zhejiang, was named at the same time bishop of Tamassa and apostolic vicar of West Zhejiang, with residence in Hangzhou.

The population of Hangzhou was at the time of the division around three hundred thousand. Hangzhou is the capital of the province of Zhejiang; it had been the capital of the empire for five hundred years under the Song dynasty (960–1280), from the reign of Gaozong (1127) till the end of the reign of Bingzong in 1280. Therefore, this city is one of the biggest in China for its territory. Its walls are eighteen kilometers long, but the inside for the most part consists of cultivated fields. Hangzhou is that town that Marco Polo admired so much, which he called "Kinsay," transcription of the name : "Kingsse" [Jingzi]: capital. The glory of the city is long gone.

Paul-Albert Faveau, born in Crochte (Nord) on 7 April 1859, was admitted in Paris on 25 September 1883, arrived in Shanghai on 19 September 1886, and was ordained a priest in Ningbo by Reynaud on 15 August 1887. He fulfilled important tasks and became Reynaud's right hand. Faveau was consecrated in Ningbo on 2 October 1910 by his own bishop.

We compare here the respective lists of the personnel in the two vicariates immediately after their separation. We can see that since 1904 the Christian population has increased by more than ten thousand.

Table 19.2 Personnel, East and West Zhejiang, 1910

Groups	East Zhejiang	West Zhejiang
Catholics	19,422	10,318
European Vincentian priests	15	9
Chinese Vincentian priests	4	8
Diocesan priests	7	5
Seminarians major seminary	5	4
Seminarians minor seminary	27	27
Daughters of Charity	27	17
Virgins of Purgatory	53	5

We have arrived at a decisive era for the future of China. This large country is on the point of getting another regime. Up till now, for thousands of years, emperors had governed it who were emperors not only for life, but normally through hereditary succession by a member of one and the same family called a dynasty. At this time the twenty-fourth dynasty of this empire was to disappear without remedy and to give way to a completely different regime. Because this change covered at the same time the whole of China and consequently interested all the missions, we interrupt our account about the individual missions to insert a short historical report of this important event.

The Fall of the Qing Dynasty

After having returned from her self-willed exile in January 1902, Empress Cixi finally understood that some modernization of the empire had become necessary, because relations with foreign powers were henceforth unavoidable. The problem of the "reforms" therefore arose again, though it had been studied earlier and had brought about the Palace revolution of 1898.

Projects were made and discussed, but nothing definitive had been done when on 15 November 1908 the empress died some hours after Guangxu himself had passed away. As result of intrigues, a nephew of the latter, Prince Puyi, two years old, was placed on the throne under the [regnal] name of Xuantong (1909-1911). His reign, under the regency of his father, Prince Chun, was not to last for long.

Then a revolutionary movement rose up, caused especially by the chaos in the administration. On 10 October 1911 the army rebelled in Wuchang (Hubei). The majority of the provinces in the south broke away from the central government. Their party leader was Sun Wen. Abroad he was called Sun Yat-sen. This was his official name: Sun Yixian. *Yi* becomes *yat* in the Cantonese pronunciation. He set up a republican government in Nanjing. The court asked for help from the clever general Yuan Shikai. Two months passed during which the revolutionary movement was spreading, and Yuan Shikai and Sun Wen were negotiating.

On 12 February 1912 the Qing [emperor] abdicated, and Yuan was promoted to the presidency of the Republic of China

The Chinese Republic (1912–1927)

Was it a republic in the meaning that Europeans give this term? Certainly, it was not. Both during these fifteen years and at the time of the next government, which in 1928 was going to take the same name while adding the adjective "national," there were attempts at parliamentary governments, but actually the population never really used its right of universal suffrage. There was to be a more or less central government and provincial governments, relatively independent of the central power. Chinese people indeed had no idea of what a republic was, because in their age-old traditions they had never seen anything that resembled this kind of government.

During those fifteen years there was no peace in China. The provincial military governors, the *doujun*, were warring with each other, sometimes allying themselves with one another, sometimes betraying one another, always fighting to protect the people and, consequently, demanding from the central government the subsidies necessary to maintain their armies.

Moreover, banditry was widespread. Often demobilized soldiers got together in groups and laid waste to the countryside so that the suffering of the people was continuous.

We now stop this general report. We shall take it up again in detail when going through our different missions. We shall first have a look at our vicariates in Central and South China at the time that the political revolution we have just outlined was happening. Beforehand we shall give here the list of the presidents of the Republic of China who succeeded each other from 1912 to 1927.

Presidents of the Republic of China (1912–1927)[63]

> Yuan Shikai (1912/1913)
>
> Li Yuanhong (1916)
>
> Feng Guozhang (1917)
>
> Xu Shichang (1918)
>
> Li Yuanhong (1921/1922, for the second time)
>
> Cao Kun (1922, period of five years with many difficulties, because of the rivalries among the military governors)
>
> Chiang Kai-shek (1927)[64]

The Missions in the South and Center during the Revolution of 1911

As we have seen, the movement was directed against the Manchu dynasty; it was not caused by foreigners, or by Christians, or by religion. From the beginning, the revolutionaries gave the [foreign] consuls the most formal assurances. In all the centers where the revolt broke out, posters recommending respect for the foreigners' lives and possessions were affixed to the walls.

Here is information missionaries gave about some of the important towns.

On 10 October 1911 the capital of Hubei, Wuchang, went over to the revolutionaries as the result of the rebellion. Sun Wen inspired the revolutionaries. Thus, the party of the revolution settled first in Hubei, a province in the center of China, in its three most important cities, Wuchang, Hankou, and Hanyang.

Hankou, which had a population of eight hundred thousand, was one of the most commercial cities of China. Last station of the Peking-Hankou railway line and harbor on the Changjiang or Yangtze River, navigable as far as Hankou for ships of high tonnage, it was, strictly speaking, the heart of China.

---

63. The list does not distinguish between the presidents of the provisional government (1912–1913) and the presidents of the Beiyang government (1913–1928), nor does it include several acting presidents. (JR)

64. Some sources list 1928 for his chairmanship of the nationalist government. Chiang Kai-shek had other terms of office after the 1947 constitution until his death in 1975. (JR)

Hanyang, which was in some way a suburb, was the industrial center of China. A short time after the Boxer Rebellion, the Chinese government, helped by foreign engineers, installed a steel factory and large metallurgical works, which produced in particular railroad rails. The importance of the fact that the revolutionaries took possession of Hanyang is easily understandable. Hanyang had one hundred thirty thousand inhabitants.

Wuchang with six hundred sixty thousand inhabitants was the center of the civil administrative of the province. On the right bank of the river, opposite Hankou, it contained riches that the future republicans grabbed quickly, thus increasing their war funds.

These three cities together formed a triangle, whose sides measured less than forty kilometers in length. From this lively center the revolutionary movement spread out. Before the end of October, the party of the revolution, already master of a part of Sichuan, extended its power over Hunan and Jiangxi. In November it occupied Shanghai and Nanjing.

On 21 October a missionary wrote from Jiujiang, the harbor on the Yangtze in the north of Jiangxi, about two hundred kilometers away from Wuchang: "The revolution that has just erupted in Hubei threatens Jiangxi. The partisans have taken the towns that are our nearest neighbors. This gives rise to serious rumors. People expect to see the revolutionaries' army any moment. The movement, however, is against the dynasty. The Chinese people want to get rid of the Tartars to whom they have submitted for three hundred years. So up till this moment, there is nothing against foreigners or against Catholics." On 24 October the same missionary wrote: "The revolutionaries seized control of Jiujiang last night. The fire set to the intendant's yamen provided the signal for the revolt. The garrison, after chasing the rebels for a short time, went over to their side. A proclamation has been announced threatening with death anyone who makes an attempt on foreigners' and people's lives and possessions. Therefore, for the time being nothing but peace."

Another confrere wrote from Nanchang on 1 November 1911:

> We have been in the republic since one o'clock this morning. The Guomingdang (Nationalist Party) who were camping out in the suburbs forced open the gates of the city and woke up all with very heavy salvoes. A little later, the governor's palace was on fire and so were the police posts, while the shooting was clattering on all sides. All this noise was only a sham; nobody was killed; they only wanted to frighten robbers who might be tempted to do some looting. At dawn the whole city was bedecked with white flags. Posters

proclaimed that everyone would be protected and that all should engage in their everyday occupations without fear.

In Zhejiang, namely in Ningbo, on 5 November at noon an officer together with some men proclaimed the change of government, without a cry, without any manifestation. All the houses were immediately decked out with white flags. The few imperial troops first remained passive; later on in the day they joined the revolutionaries.

In Shanghai on 4 November the future republicans set fire to the intendant's yamen, and then the city raised white flags. Those were the insurgents' tactics: setting fire to the imperial public buildings to impress the population. In Nanjing on 5 November the city fell into the revolutionaries' power in the same way as in Shanghai.

That was it for the center and the south of China. Soon we shall see that in the north, it was quite something else. The imperial armies resisted vigorously and the missions had to suffer, not because of ever being attacked, but the organized lootings in some towns and the fighting between the two groups caused them many anxieties.

Chapter 20

Zhili Vicariates, 1910s

The Third Synod of the Northern Region – The District of Baoding, Creation of the Apostolic Vicariate of Baoding – Vicariate of Central Zhili – The Rapid Establishment of the Essential Works of Pastoral Care – List of the Personnel in 1910 – The French School in Baoding – A Second Internal Seminary (Novitiate) in the North – Division of China into Two Vincentian Provinces

The Third Synod of the Northern Region

From 5 May to 17 May 1906, the Third Provincial Synod of the Region of the North was held in Peking. This meeting had been planned for 1900, but the terrible events in the war of the Boxers delayed its celebration.

The following apostolic vicars were present in Peking: Bishops Jarlin, Bruguière and Geurts, all Vincentians for North and Southwest Zhili; Abels, Van Aertselaer, both Scheutists, for East and Central Mongolia; Choulet, from Paris, for Manchuria; Bermyn, Scheutist for West Mongolia; Menicatti, from Milan for Henan; Maquet, Jesuit, for Southeast Zhili. Jarlin chaired the Synod.

The most important topic, or to be more exact, the only topic of the synod discussions was education. The bishops studied the developments that the missionaries would give to their teaching, and the methods of coordinating it with the intense impetus given by the Chinese government to the study of science, European languages, and European civilization.

We have arrived at the most fertile era for evangelization in the vicariate of Peking. We have already pointed out the remarkable progress made in the years that immediately followed the rebellion of the Boxers. The years we are entering now will show still greater progress. In 1906, the number of the Catholics in North Zhili was 105,170. Here is now the list of the personnel and of the fruits in this same vicariate for the year 1908–1909.

Table 20.1 Vicariate of North Zhili, Concise Statistics, 1908–1909

Groups	Numbers
Catholics	150,582
Baptisms of adults	15,000
Baptisms of children of Christians	5,570
Baptisms of babies of pagans	9,866
European priests	41
Chinese priests	12
Lay brothers	6
Trappists	75
Marist Brothers	45
Daughters of Charity	51
Sisters of Saint Joseph (Josephines)	115
Seminarians in major seminary	39
Seminarians in minor seminary	182
Teachers in elementary schools	605
Women teachers in elementary schools	385
Churches	84
Chapels and oratories	563
Residences or mission stations	53

Among the districts that made up the vicariate of North Zhili, Baoding was clearly the most fertile for conversions.

The District of Baoding, Creation of the Apostolic Vicariate of Baoding

The city of Baoding was the seat of the prefecture of the same name located one hundred forty-six kilometers southwest of Peking. This prefecture numbered seventeen sub-prefectures, but the ecclesiastical district of this name embraced also Yizhou, a small prefecture of second rank consisting of three sub-prefectures.

With its suburbs, Baoding had about eight thousand inhabitants. Its walls, finished in 1500, were in very good shape. They had a perimeter of only seven kilometers, so the houses were confined and tightly packed and the city overflowed outside the enclosure into four populous suburbs.

In the sixteenth century, Baoding was the capital of Zhili province. Much bigger than today, it was the residence of the viceroy, a governor, an intendant, the prefect and sub-prefect of Qingyuan. (In China, a same town can be a prefecture and at the same time a sub-prefecture, but under another name, like for instance Peking, capital of the empire, was at the same time a prefecture under the name of Shuntian, with two sub-prefectures.)

The evangelization of the Baoding district had probably not begun before the arrival of the Jesuits in Peking in 1600. Father [Diego de] Pantoja and Brother Ferreira, both Portuguese, went and brought the Faith to several villages in the region of Baoding between 1604 and 1610. The colleagues of Ricci – about ten – almost all Portuguese, stayed in town in the beginning and there they converted some individuals, but they longed to go to the countryside to preach the Faith. While Ricci was talking with the intellectuals, some priests gradually and unobtrusively penetrated the countryside and when they saw an occasion, they talked with the village people. When the opportunity presented itself, they taught them the first elements of doctrine. If they perceived that they were listened to favorably, they would stay several days; then they would go somewhere else, after leaving with them some booklets with doctrine and prayers. A long time later they would come back to visit the few kernels they had formed. These small kernels were to become later the first Christian communities of the region, the most important of which was Anjiazhuang, one hundred ten kilometers from Peking. The Jesuits baptized about one hundred fifty people in that region.

A short time after Ricci's death (1610) a period of persecution began against all the missionaries who had entered China, except those considered necessary for the court. The persecution was not continuous, and during lulls, missionaries more or less disguised could visit the Christians.

For this district, however, there was almost no evangelization up till the nineteenth century. It has to be remembered that the last bishop-administrator of Peking, Bishop Pirès, a Portuguese Vincentian, died in Peking in 1838. Peking was at that time still a real diocese. The imperial decree, expelling all the missionaries, had not touched him because he was vice-president of the Bureau of Mathematics [Bureau of Astronomy].

Father Castro, Pirès's vicar general, was named administrator of Peking during the vacancy. Castro's nomination as apostolic vicar of Peking happened at that time. We saw above how he refused, and how Mouly, already apostolic vicar of Mongolia, became Gaetano Pirès's true successor, as administrator. Mouly, no more than Castro, could take possession of the see. They were not allowed to enter Peking. Castro sometimes resided in Houlin, sometimes in Anjiazhuang. Mouly adopted this latter Christian community as his episcopal residence. This small village was to become the administrative center of the whole province of Zhili up till 1860.

That year indeed, Mouly entered Peking for the first time and took possession of his see. From then on, Anjiazhuang ceased to have the honor of serving as the episcopal residence, and it became again the administrative center of the Baoding district. The bishop left three priests there, among whom he appointed appointed François Liu as director. With the ministry of this intelligent and zealous priest, the evangelization of this area began in earnest.

François Liu had done all his studies in the seminary of Anjiazhuang and he was ordained priest there in 1853. Thanks to the liberating treaty of 1860, missionaries gradually acquired more freedom, and the pagans proved less suspicious. Father Liu successfully imitated Anouilh's and Fioritti's method of preaching in public places whenever there was an occasion. This priest had a facility in speaking and pagans loved to hear him speak.

In this way he opened a great many villages for the Christian faith. He did not lack opponents because of his almost audacious zeal. He was not afraid to challenge in court those who were oppressing Christians or catechumens and to have the mandarins judge and condemn them. His successes produced conversions.

But, as we said, the method of lawsuits was not without risks, and definite dangers could come from them. Therefore, Liu was called back to Peking several times to avoid trouble. Thanks to his impulse, though, four thousand more Christians were inscribed in the books. In 1870, Liu built the first chapel of Donglü. Then he went and worked in Liujiazhuang, built a large church and died there in March 1885.

Bishop Delaplace, Bishop Mouly's successor in 1868, moved the administrative center of the district to Beiguan, a suburb of Baoding. In 1895, Father Jarlin was appointed as the director of this district and gave such an impetus to conversions that in one year there were six hundred and sixty baptisms of adults. Dumond, his successor, used the same method, and when in 1898 the incident happened (as reported above [in chapter 12]) there were eleven thousand Christians in the district of Baoding.

The result of that confrontation was the admittance of missionaries inside the walls of the town of Baoding. Dumond left Beiguan, settled in a place formerly known as the daotai's [circuit intendant's] yamen, and built there a residence and a big beautiful church. In 1899, the district comprised six residences with 12,026 Christians.

After the Boxer movement, in less than one year, the church was rebuilt on the same foundations; but the missionaries, still too few, had to work hard as to put back in order what had been destroyed, to preach missions, and to welcome the numerous catechumens who were presenting themselves. In 1902, one thousand three hundred and seventy adults were baptized, then a year later, one thousand four hundred and two. The influx of catechumens continued. They baptized 4,195 in 1904, and 6,610 in 1905.

After Favier's death (1905), Father Dumond was called to Peking in May of the same year to be Bishop Jarlin's vicar general. Fabrègues succeeded him as director of Baoding. The rising tide of conversions needed only to be supported and encouraged. Young French missionaries, who were sent to this district, set to work with zeal, happy to contribute to the extension of the kingdom of God. The year 1906 gave 9,062 new Christians, and the following year 9,173. But the year 1908 was still more fruitful – in the thirteen residences there were 19,519 baptisms of adults.

Here is the report on the growth in the number of Christians in this district; the first numbers are for every ten years; the last ones for shorter periods.

Table 20.2 Christian Numbers, North Zhili, 1874-1909

Year	Number of Christians
1874	4,858
1884	6,529
1894	9,594
1899	12,000
1900	12,000[65]
1902	12,700
1905	26,283
1909	69,863

Such remarkable progress gave the missionaries in Baoding reason to foresee an imminent division of the vicariate of North Zhili. All were expecting that news.

---

65. Minus a thousand more or less as a result of the Boxer movement.

Vicariate of Central Zhili

The Supreme Pontiff, by a brief of 19 February 1910 at the request of Jarlin, the apostolic vicar of North Zhili, erected the district of Baoding as a distinct apostolic vicariate separated from the former one with the name of Central Zhili and entrusted it to the Congregation of the Mission.

Three days later, by brief of 22 February 1910 Rome nominated Father Joseph Fabrègues as bishop of Alali and first apostolic vicar of the vicariate of Central Zhili.

These two documents came to the addressees through the intermediary of the superior general (then Father Fiat). His Eminence, the Cardinal Prefect of Propaganda had joined to them a letter asking the superior general at the same time to express the congratulations of the Sacred Congregation of Propaganda to Bishop Jarlin and to the new bishop, Bishop Fabrègues, for the zeal with which they attained this great number of conversions and for their role leading to the creation of the new vicariate.

Fabrègues was born in Montpellier (Hérault) on 26 November 1872, was admitted in Paris on 6 October 1890 and was ordained priest on 30 May 1896.

After arriving in Shanghai on the following 1 October, he was assigned to Peking. During the Boxer movement, he was in the vicariate of Yongping, taking care of the Christian communities during the absence of Bishop Geurts, who had not yet been able to take possession of his vicariate because of these difficulties.

Bishop Jarlin consecrated Fabrègues very solemnly on 22 May 1910 in the church of Baoding.

The Rapid Establishment of the Essential Works of Pastoral Care

As a matter of urgency, essential institutions had to be set up in this vicariate after it became independent from Peking. At the start of the new school year in September 1910, the seminarians of the major and the minor seminary, who had studied up to then in Peking, had to continue their studies in the new vicariate. The few seminarians of the major seminary were put up temporarily in the episcopal residence in the classrooms of the catechists' school, which was moved to Anjiazhuang.

The sixty students of Latin had to live in the house of the Chinese Sisters of Saint Joseph lodging in the center of the city, not far from the episcopal residence. The Sisters were to occupy rough-and-ready rooms in Xiguan.

They needed to build: a minor seminary; a large residence where about sixty priests could be accommodated for communal meetings; a building for the Chinese Sisters (Josephines), already serving in the principal Christian communities for several years; and a major seminary.

The small property of the episcopal residence could not contain all these buildings, and its situation in the center of the city did not allow any expansion. To facilitate expansion, Fabrègues bought a large piece of land located on the border of the western suburb (Xiguan) to build the minor seminary. Some months before his episcopal consecration, Fabrègues had asked one of his missionaries, whom he considered to be his future architect, to draw a plan for a minor seminary which could accommodate sixty students. No sooner was the plan finished and approved when the bishop changed his mind and asked the same confrere for another plan for up to one hundred twenty students.

The piece of land he bought was a wheat field. Work could begin only after the harvest. A single story building seventy-two meters in length was built. Another construction was added, destined to become, later on, a study hall, but which first served as a chapel until a genuine chapel could be built.

On 8 December 1910, the feast of the Immaculate Conception, the minor seminary opened its doors for the sixty students, all born in the Baoding district. Immediately after their departure for Xiguan, the rooms where they had been living were prepared to become the motherhouse of the Josephines.

Also, in Xiguan, Fabrègues had bought another big piece of land near the railway station and not far from the minor seminary, in order to build an orphanage that was first under the direction of the Josephines, later on in 1912, of the Daughters of Charity, for whom he also established other works: dispensaries, schools, and so on.

The construction of the residence for the bishop and the priests was begun in autumn 1911 and was finished at the end of 1912.

This new vicariate, consisting of young missionaries – the oldest was forty-eight years old – offered the spectacle of intense activity. In the first years, every parish priest had a cart and one or two mules that had hardly any rest. Every week they visited the children in the schools and the catechumens. It was often necessary to go to Baoding, to the administrative center, to receive directions from the bishop, to buy furniture and food, et cetera. The bicycle then made its appearance; this flat land made its use easy and economical.

The movement of the conversions had slowed a little since the arrival of Fabrègues, and that was a good thing. This slowing was unavoidable. The number of workers had not increased at the same speed as the number of converts; moreover, quite a number of them were at work either in administration or in the direction of the works or in the two seminaries as teachers. On the other hand, the constructions had required an enormous expenditure, and the maintenance of the schools absorbed most of the allocations. The missionaries were therefore obliged to slow down admissions to the catechumenate. They took advantage of this to improve the instruction of the thousands of neophytes, often too hastily baptized.

Table 20.3 Vicariate of Baoding Personnel, 1910

Groups	Numbers
Catholics	72,531
European Vincentian priests	14
Chinese Vincentian priests	3
Chinese diocesan priests	23
Priests Total	40
Seminarians in major seminary	8
Seminarians in minor seminary	60
Chinese religious women (Josephines)	34

The French School in Baoding

When Fabrègues arrived in Baoding as director in 1905, he found in the residence a French school working at full capacity. How did this work begin? In 1901, when European troops were occupying the whole of Zhili province for the pacification of the country, a group of about fifteen pagan youngsters, addressing French soldiers, expressed their wish to learn the French language. General Bailloud, who was commanding the troops, was interested in this suggestion and wanted to follow it up. He asked one of the chaplains of the troop, Father Clerc-Renaud, to begin to teach these young people French in a rented house in town.

Favier hearing about this, received this initiative very favorably and, in July 1901, sent Fabrègues a Brother, destined eventually to take the responsibility of this embryonic school. Right away students flowed in and at the end of the first year there were fifty pupils, four of whom were Christians. The following year there were seventy.

In 1903, with the number of students still growing, a second Brother was added, then in 1906 a third one. The students who were Christians or who wanted to become Christians could be boarders. The students came from all kinds of families. A mandarin's child rubbed shoulders with a farmer's son or the son of a small shopkeeper. Baoding being the capital of the province, mandarins waiting for a job were numerous and sometimes remained there for long years with their families. That is the reason why among the students there were sons of intendants, of prefects and sub-prefects.

Besides the hope for the sons of these mandarins to become dignitaries, there was the need of managers for the exploitation of the Peking-Hankou railway, a French-Belgian enterprise. Brother Denis was hardly able to satisfy the demands of the directors of the railway company and the postal services. In 1910, Brother Denis reported that 683 students attended the school.

Later we will report on the changes this French school had to undergo.

A Second Internal Seminary (Novitiate) in the North

We related some time ago how Father Boscat established the internal seminary and the study house in Jiaxing in Zhejiang in 1902. This internal seminary did very well for a few years. But soon it was noticed that the candidates came mostly from the southern vicariates, while the northern ones that nevertheless had more students gradually provided fewer and fewer.

This painfully astonished Guilloux, visitor since 1905, who had been working in the north for many years. Moreover, the apostolic vicars of Zhili were very sad that vocations for religious life were so rare among their students. No one knew the reason. Was it a certain animosity that had always existed between the people of the north against the inhabitants of the south? Was it more a question of climate? The one in the south is swampy, while the one on the north is dry and healthier. Whatever the reasons, they thought to create a second internal seminary. The question when asked of Paris received a favorable answer. In his circular letter of 1909, Father Fiat announced:

> Since the postulants of North China have great difficulty adapting to the climate of South China in Jiaxing, the Holy See has allowed us

to open an internal seminary in Zhili. Indeed, our three vicariates there have now more than two hundred ten thousand Christians, and ecclesiastical vocations rise in proportion to conversions; there is every reason to hope also for a good number of vocations for the family of Saint Vincent, and the situation favored them.

Then it was necessary to find a convenient place for the new formation house. Unanimously, those who had to decide considered Chala as especially suited for this institution. Chala, which we have already described, was located in the countryside, though quite near Peking and was perfect for a formation house because of the great and ancient history linked to that place.

Immediately, important constructions were added to those that existed already and at the beginning of June 1909 the building was ready to receive the novices from Jiaxing and the new candidates who were going to present themselves. We shall not follow in details the history of this internal seminary, or of the one in Jiaxing, except to announce, when the time has come, the transformations that occurred.

The Division of China into Two Vincentian Provinces

The division of the internal seminary of Jiaxing announced another more important division. It was the erection of a second province of the Vincentians in China: the single province of China was divided into two: North China and South China. Here is how the superior general announced the event in his circular letter of 1 January 1911:

> Our missions in China occupy too vast an area for one visitor to be able regularly to make a canonical visit. . . . That is why, having consulted my venerable assistants and having received the permission of the Holy See . . . we have erected one province in the north and another in the south. The first consists of the four vicariates of the north with the house of Chala, the visitor's ordinary residence.

> The second one embraces the two vicariates of Zhejiang, the three of Jiangxi, and the formation house in Jiaxing. Father Guilloux remains the visitor in the southern province and moreover is nominated director of the Daughters of Charity in China, who form only one province. Father Desrumaux is nominated visitor of the northern province.

Chapter 21

New Vicariates for Zhili, 1920s

The New Vicariate of Maritime Zhili (Tianjin) – The Christians of Tianjin in 1912 – The 1911 Revolution in the North – Peking – Baoding – Tianjin – Jarlin Meets the President – Expectations of the Missionaries – Methods of Evangelization – Vicariate of West Zhili (Zhengding) – The Great Flood of 1917 – Kindly Attitude of the Government towards the Catholic Church – A New Hospital in Peking – New Names for the Vicariates – A Very Active Missionary – Letters From Jarlin to Lebbe – At the Beginning of the Revolution of 1911 in Tianjin – The Catholic Press in China – The Laoxikai Affair – Bishop De Guébriant's Apostolic Visit – The "Historical Survey" – The Vicariate of Tianjin – The Vicariate of Yongping – The Minor Seminary – Establishing a New Vincentian Province – The Vicariate of Baoding – The Parishes or Stations of Baoding – A Difficult and Unattractive Operation – Establishment of the Apostolic Prefecture of Lixian – New Activities Start in Baoding – The Vicariate of Zhengding – De Vienne's Successor: Bishop Schraven

The New Vicariate of Maritime Zhili (Tianjin)

By Pius X's brief of 27 April 1912 and following the wish expressed by Bishop Jarlin, the vicariate of North Zhili gave birth to a new vicariate. Through another brief of the same day, Father Paul Dumond was appointed as bishop of Curubis and apostolic vicar of the new vicariate, to be called Maritime Zhili.

Paul Dumond, born in Lyons on 2 April 1864, admitted in Paris on 2 April 1883 was ordained a priest in Paris on 11 August 1888. He arrived in Peking on 16 October 1888. He had been Jarlin's vicar general for seven years when he received his promotion to the episcopacy.

While waiting for the construction of an episcopal residence and cathedral, Dumond had to live temporarily in the Wanghailou parish where the Church of Our Lady of Victories was located, a church so many times burned down and always rebuilt. There were not enough rooms there to accommodate the people invited for the ceremony of the consecration, so it was decided to celebrate the consecration in the Beitang and not in Tianjin.

On 30 June 1912 Bishop Jarlin assisted by Bishop Fabrègues and Bishop Geurts consecrated Dumond bishop. Three other bishops were present and sixty-five priests, Marist Brothers, many seminarians and a crowd of Faithful. The minister of France, Monsieur de Margerie, enhanced the ceremony with his presence.

The ecclesiastical district of Tianjin had the city itself as its administrative center. It had about two million inhabitants, and has grown a great deal since then. This prefecture consisted of seven sub-prefectures. The city itself had seven hundred fifty thousand inhabitants in 1900.

Tianjin was the most commercial and industrial town of the whole of North China. Located at the junction of the Baihe River [*sic* Haihe] River and the Grand Canal, thirty kilometers from the sea, it had become one of the biggest harbors of China. A quay two kilometers long on the bank of the river allowed boats and junks to land, not, however, ships of high tonnage, which had to lie at anchor about ten kilometers from the mouth.

Since 1900 the appearance of the city had changed completely. The old town was about two kilometers square on each side, surrounded with solid brick walls, which were razed in 1905. The city overflowed towards the north and the east in two densely populated suburbs. The south of the town was a marshland with few inhabitants. The foreign concessions allowed by the Chinese government with a lease of ninety-nine years settled exactly there. France, the United Kingdom, Germany, Italy, Austria, Belgium and Japan began enormous projects. The goal was to make the river deeper so that boats with deeper draught could land; on the other hand, it was necessary to heighten the level of the land so as to prevent flooding in the future city. The river was dredged with modern machinery, and the mud from the river was channeled to the marshland. Sunshine did the rest. It made the whole place dry so that buildings of all heights could be built.

The concessions, clearly defined from each other, all faced on the quay, whereas the opposite direction was not clearly delimited. That was what was called for instance the "extra, or outside the concession" destined for possible future construction.

Every concession was divided into more or less large plots that private buyers, foreigners or Chinese, could acquire from the nation whose concession it was. Quite soon these concessions were covered with banks, shops, schools, villas, houses and so on. In 1912, a cosmopolitan town had been raised where, in 1900 there were only marshlands and vaguely uninhabited lands.

It is clear that the new vicariate was located in a commercial environment. The inhabitants, foreigners or Chinese, thought first of profits; therefore, the evangelization of these people was going to be quite difficult and would bring the missionary problems that he would not have met in the countryside.

The population consisted, however, for the most part of farmers, coming there to find a lucrative job. The presence of Europeans surely would not always give them an edifying spectacle, but on the other hand, because of their institutions and their organization, it would give them the sense of order and progress.

The Christians of Tianjin in 1912

The evangelization of this district had been very slow before 1900. We have related its tedious beginnings, and also the tragic massacre of two priests and ten Daughters of Charity in 1870, the result of which was to greatly hold up its progress. The storm of 1900 reduced the slight strength of the Christians in this district still further. In 1903, there were hardly three thousand baptized people there. In 1912, the vicariate consisted of thirty-four thousand Christians. Its clergy was composed of nineteen priests: ten foreigners and nine Chinese. Up to then ecclesiastical vocations were very rare among the neophytes. Therefore, Dumond's first action was the creation of a very modest minor seminary with fifteen students of Latin and theology.

In town there were two churches, one, important, in Wanghailou; the other one, smaller, in the French Concession, the Church of Saint Louis built in 1901 (*sic* 1872); a hospital, managed by the Daughters of Charity; two prosperous schools, directed by the Marist Brothers; finally girls' schools run by the Josephines, who had come from Peking.

The 1911 Revolution in the North

Let us sum up the events. On 29 December 1911 a provisional assembly met in Nanjing and unanimously chose Sun Wen as temporary president of the Republic of China. He accepted, while at the same time promising to step down as soon as the imperial government had abdicated.

On 12 February 1912 Emperor Puyi abdicated. Yuan Shikai immediately sent Sun Wen the following telegram: "The cause for which you have been fighting for long years has now triumphed. It is with great pleasure I pay tribute to the new regime. The monarchy is finished forever. May the Republic live forever!"

As he had promised, Sun Wen handed in his resignation as temporary president and encouraged the national assembly of Nanjing to choose Yuan Shikai as president. The latter was indeed elected unanimously as president of the Republic of China on 15 February 1912.

The republican government had still one difficult hurdle to overcome: it was the opposition of the soldiers. We do not say the opposition of "the army," as if there were two parties in the army: one in favor of the monarchy, the other in favor of the republic. It was much more prosaic.

From the beginning of the revolutionary movement, troops had to be recruited. Without any distinction people of all conditions were enrolled, even adventurers and professional thieves. Being well clothed in winter, being sure of food in all seasons and, having the prospect of acquiring, besides their meager wages, some other accidental profits, from looting for example, all that was not displeasing to these people.

However, after the republic had been proclaimed, people wanted to make the majority of these soldiers, no longer needed, redundant and to send them back to their families. Those soldiers felt this would be to their disadvantage; before leaving they wanted to get some compensation. Hence the looting scenes and fires they started in several centers like Peking, Baoding and Tianjin.

Peking

The capital was celebrating the birth of the republic on 29 February: the noise of the firecrackers sounded continuously in all quarters, when towards the evening the rattle of shooting was added. Troops faithful to the empire were rebelling and leaving their barracks in order to loot in town. Later the rumor had it that they had been given these orders: do not kill anybody; do not touch Europeans or churches.[66]

Shooting in the air, they put to flight the owners of the wealthiest shops, stole money and objects of their choosing, and then set fire to the buildings. The first night they looted in this way the long avenue running north and south on the east side of town, and the following day the one on

---

66. Ferreux's notes: Chinese and Manchu officials fled towards the quarter of the legations. On 1 March 1912 Yuan Shikai addressed a note to the foreigners in Peking to express his regret for the recent events and assured them that it would not happen again. On 2 March these promises were not kept. On 3 March the foreign ministers ordered one thousand men belonging to the detachment of Tianjin to be sent to Peking. The next day, three thousand arrived. The population in Peking was reassured. It was again business as usual.

the west. The next day, General Ma Yukun (summoned by Yuan Shikai), arrived in town with loyal troops and quickly finished the business of chasing these gangs of looters away.

Baoding

The writer of these lines was present when on 29 February the grand parade of the inauguration of the republic took place.

It was clear that the enthusiasm among the crowd was not great. Soon it was known that there was real discontent among the troops who had been parading in the streets. The following day, 1 March, after a dispute between revolutionaries and troops, the troops rebelled.

More and more shooting was heard everywhere. Inhabitants fled with their possessions. At the episcopal residence the only entrance gate was hurriedly barricaded. Sandbags, heaps of bricks that were there for future construction were used to block avenues and passageways inside. Gradually, a relative calm returned. Salvoes had stopped

The mandarins were in hiding; several came and sought refuge in our place. In the afternoon, a low-ranking officer presented himself with a letter which said: "Do not be afraid, if tonight there is some noise in town, do not intervene; your guards must not shoot, then your institution will be protected."

At around seven o'clock in the evening, soldiers burned down the east gate of the city. The policemen who were inside opened the second gate for them. The looting of the town had begun. Immediately, seven or eight thousand soldiers entered the town. Only some hundreds were carrying guns with fixed bayonets and were shooting all the time, while the others were breaking into shops and warehouses and running off with all kinds of goods. Carts prepared beforehand were being filled with booty. When the looting was almost finished, they set fire to the houses. From the top of the church tower, we could see the fires being lighted one after the other along the streets bordered with shops. At dawn, most of the soldiers fled to the countryside with their booty; others, joined by townspeople, entered the shops and the back rooms and grabbed objects of lesser value, which the first ones had not taken.

On 3 March no more soldiers were to be seen and very few policemen, who had remained passive and did nothing to stop the looting. On 4 March the minister of France, worried about the fate of the Catholic mission in Baoding, which had been rumored to have been destroyed, sent his first secretary with forty French soldiers. After their commander reached an agreement with Bishop Fabrègues, the soldiers left the railway station and entered into town to the sound of bugles, had a joyful dinner at the residence and returned to Peking in the evening. Their short appearance gave confidence to the city dwellers and, in the following days the runaways came back and calm was restored.

The mission had certainly been protected by orders from on high. But with what goal had Yuan Shikai allowed or maybe even ordered this organized looting? His policy was so devious that we have not been able to guess at his secret motives.

Tianjin

We shall say almost nothing about it, for everything happened outside the European concessions. There was fighting, looting, but no Christian shop was touched. The Wanghailou church, though far from the concessions in the middle of the Chinese quarter, remained absolutely unharmed.

Jarlin's Meets the President

We cannot pass in silence over the apostolic vicar's meeting with the new president. The president received the bishop with the greatest affability; with interest he asked about Catholic activities, about the number of Christians and declared that under the new regime the greatest religious freedom would be granted, and that all functions both civil and military would be within the reach of all citizens irrespective of the worship they professed.

Expectations of the Missionaries

The transition from the imperial regime to the democratic regime in China, when all is said and done, had cost less blood than in most nations when they threw off the yoke of monarchy. The new regime, however, was not a real republic; it had the name of being one, but in reality, it was not one. The missionaries more or less suspected this to be the case. Yet, they were happy to see in the mind of the Chinese people a true desire to make progress, and a visible tendency toward taking Western civilization as a model, and at the same time a greater broadness of mind in their relations with other nations; a behavior that contrasted strongly with the narrow-mindedness and the distrust that had for so many centuries deprived China of the advantages which wise collaboration could have provided. The missionaries indeed cherished the hope that, beginning then, the spreading of the gospel would become steadier and quicker.

Methods of Evangelization

Missionaries have only one goal: to spread Christ's Message. In order to reach this goal, they must use the fittest means according to circumstances of place and time. On the other hand, in the same country and at the same time, it may happen that not all the evangelizing workers use identical means, for, if they belong to different groups, societies or congregations, the formation and mentality that they have received in the group they belong to will intervene too.

In that area of northern China that witnessed in a very short time – about twenty years – so many conversions to Catholicism, particularly in the vicariate of North Zhili and the two which were born from it, Central Zhili and Maritime Zhili, the method used was a method as luck would have it. It could not last long and it could not be used elsewhere. It was like this. When Jarlin was sent to Baoding as director of that district, he found in Donglü and in the neighborhood a quite clear movement of conversions.

From the beginning he did all he could to support it. With this in view he organized schools for catechumens in the winter, a season when village people are not occupied with their work in their fields. Near the school there was a kitchen where they prepared meals for the catechumens who were studying the catechism, so that they did not have to worry about their food and in this way could study and follow catechism lessons all day long. It was an innovation, an attempt that had never before been tried in such a general way. The expenses required for this method were nevertheless considerable.

The results were immediate: the neophytes, better taught and better formed because they had been praying together became good Christians.

After the storm of 1900, the tendency toward becoming Catholics grew, as we have seen, in unforeseen proportions. Jarlin, Favier's coadjutor and successor, had not forgotten his method used in Donglü. He suggested it to his missionaries. The question of expenses was not an obstacle, for the mission had just received the Boxers' compensation.

"We have not been given this money," Jarlin said, "to build expensive cathedrals, still less to save it. We were granted it to compensate our material losses. This money is not ours; it must return to the Chinese in the most useful way for them; and what is more useful for them than their conversion to the true faith!" Therefore, he told his missionaries: "Buy sacks of millet to feed your catechumens; we shall give you the necessary money." The missionaries did this in the first years after 1900. Soon, however, they were overworked, literally snowed under with very material work. Every residence, every Christian community, needed many workers to provide the schools with fresh supplies and to bring them fuel. Intermediaries were responsible for the purchases and they were not done without petty theft and other abuses. The priest, who barely succeeded in visiting them hurriedly once a week, could not check every school. Examining the candidates for baptism and administering the sacrament already took most of his time.

Jarlin understood very well that this method used on such a big scale exceeded the missionaries' capacities. However, he did not want to slow down the movement. Then he sided, albeit regretfully, with the proposition some priests made: giving all catechumens some money to buy their own food. The Chinese catechism in usage consisted of four parts, catechumens would receive a piaster for each part recited from memory. In this way, the priest would be freed from the worry and burden of preparing food and he could give more time to prepare his candidates for baptism.

This last method soon became general in the vicariate. It had its disadvantages, too. In principle, only those with the necessary moral dispositions knew the four parts of the catechism, at least after a fashion. Practical experience proved that only a very small number succeeded in finishing the program; others finished hardly the second or third part.

Some good missionaries, particularly among the older ones, hesitated to use this incentive, but, they said, though effective, it was dangerous because the distribution of the money could only be done through intermediaries, the priest himself being unable to control matters. Hence, there was a danger of greed on the part of these agents, who sometimes were catechumens good at business. Some were afraid that, above all in villages recently opened to the Faith, the crowds of neophytes without having experienced Christian behavior as practiced by the old Faithful, might never become more than half-Christians. Still others wanted the neophytes to receive a more complete formation in schools organized specifically for this purpose.

Jarlin did not see it like that. "They come to us," he said; "receive them; the first generation may not be fervent, so be it; there will be apostasies, no reason to doubt it; but the second will be worth more." According to the bishop's plan, they had to go to the masses. "Some have the task to lay the foundations, others the roof." The starting point he wanted was a solid mass of people, basically roughed out, but fit to be improved: he wanted to provide the block of stone; it was up to his successors to cut and polish it. Those were the declarations that he put up against the criticisms coming from inside and outside of vicariate.

In order not to return to this question, let us say immediately that Rome never criticized the method of Peking either directly or indirectly.[67]

It is not very easy to tell the story of one particular mission without overlapping on the history of a neighbor or some other one, especially when their leaders are transferred from one to another. Therefore, we leave North Zhili for a moment to talk about West Zhili.

Vicariate of West Zhili (Zhengding)

We saw in the previous chapter how South Jiangxi lost its leader at a difficult time. Coqset was transferred to West Zhili exactly at the time that that crisis began in Jiangxi.

On his arrival in Zhengding, he wanted to visit every place in his new field of endeavor. He had an old missionary to go with him on the pastoral trip that he undertook. It was Father Morelli, who knew the vicariate very well. After visiting the district of Zhaozhou, the best of the good ones, he was led to Shunde, but that was a disappointment. "What a difference," the bishop said to his companion, "with what we have just seen. There it was life; here it is death!"

"No," said his companion, "this district has just been born; besides, the country is very poor. I must say, too, that this district is very far from the administrative center and has been somewhat neglected." The bishop answered, "Well, I am also the apostolic vicar of Shunde. I appoint you its director, and the necessary means will be given to you."

And so, it was done. The district was divided into three mission centers and eighty schools were built in the villages that had asked for them. That was the beginning of a beautiful conversion movement; in 1900 there were two thousand Christians; in 1908 there were five thousand.

---

67. In June 1932, a year before Jarlin's death, Bishop Montaigne, his coadjutor, granted an audience with the Supreme Pontiff, explained to him, at length and as exactly as possible, Jarlin's work. Pius XI listened and having thought it over said: " Jarlin was right to do what he did."

Soon a house of the Daughters of Charity was established. Afterwards it was to have an important development. The Boxer Uprising, instead of making the Christian religion despised, drew the attention of the pagans to it. Besides, the numerous conversions brought about in Peking were not ignored in Zhengding. The neighbors tried to imitate the methods of the missionaries in the north; but they did not go so far as the method of giving money. Coqset advised some missionaries to feed the catechumens during the study time so as to prepare them more quickly for baptism.

It was an intense preparation and so it was possible to baptize, in two or three years, several thousand adults. The finances of this vicariate did not allow feeding the catechumens to continue, so the old way came back.

At the end of 1914, Coqset suffered a violent stroke; healing was slow and incomplete. Fully aware of his situation, he understood that his days were numbered; moreover, he was almost seventy years old. He asked Rome for a coadjutor and he got one. It was Father de Vienne.

Jean de Vienne, born in Douai (Nord) on 2 April 1877, admitted in Paris on 9 March 1895, ordained a priest on 9 June 1900 in Paris, arrived in Shanghai on 16 March 1901 and was placed in North Zhili. After becoming used to the ministry of the missions, he was successively teacher and director of the as yet undivided diocesan seminary. When the seminary separated into major and minor, de Vienne was put at the head of the major seminary. Soon, after a new missionary appointment as director of the district of Jingdong and a recent appointment as director of the internal seminary in Chala, he received the brief from Rome, dated 10 August 1915, naming him bishop of Abrytus and Coqset's coadjutor. Bishop Jarlin consecrated him in Zhengding on 21 November 1915.

From that moment on, Coqset's health declined such that the whole responsibility of leading the vicariate fell on Bishop de Vienne. On 4 February 1917 Coqset died of a last attack.

Bishop de Vienne successfully continued the work that had begun so well. His ardent zeal and his humility won him the sympathy of all hearts. He was an able speaker and had friendly conversations with all those who approached him, particularly those to whom nature had not been too kind.

The Great Flood of 1917

After a very dry season in July 1917, torrential rains began to fall without interruption for several days. Soon streams and rivers overflowed their banks and covered the immense plain of Zhili with water. It was a terrible catastrophe because of its extent. Floods are not rare in China, they are actually annual in the river basin of the Yellow River, which almost every year leaves its shallow bed here and there and floods the countryside. Then the disaster touches only some sub-prefectures. In 1917, not only the big rivers, but the smallest streams, the majority of which are dry almost the whole year, were unable to hold the water of such an abundant and lasting rain; in this way, fields that had never seen a flood were now covered with water. Within living memory such a disaster had never been seen. The missionaries' accounts arriving in the centers of the missions all noted: "Our place is under water and so are the neighboring places." Soon, communications were cut, and all thought that the floods were hurting only their own region. Actually, it was the same even far away.

All our vicariates in the north suffered heavy losses. Peking being in a little higher place was the only one not to be flooded, but all the districts in the south of the capital were more or less under water.

We quote these few lines from an account that de Vienne wrote about the floods in his own vicariate:

> To give an idea of the power of the water, it suffices to say that the railway, which crosses our mission for more than two hundred kilometers, was cut in more than a hundred places and that some magnificent iron bridges were swept away by the waters. Whether by the rain or by the overflow of the streams, I can say that the whole vicariate has been flooded. . . . For many days I could not communicate with the missionaries outside. Finally, little by little, the letters arrived, telling me the same news about all the places of the vicariate.

> This is from a missionary who was caught unawares by rains in the mountains: "Fifteen days of flooding, and rivers had to be crossed more than twenty times. Complete villages were destroyed and many people drowned . . . land taken away and replaced with big rocks that could be heard rolling down noisily." He talks about a village of five hundred families reduced to thirty. . . . The mandarin of Houxi has found in one place seventeen hundred corpses of drowned people. Another Chinese priest, who lives at one hundred twenty kilometers, sent me a letter by messenger: "Unable to feed my mule any longer, I send it to you."

We could quote similar accounts from Baoding and Tianjin, but what we have said is enough to declare that natural disasters in China often take the dimensions of cataclysms. The government borrowed money to meet the people's most urgent needs. Soon in 1920 and 1923 two periods of famine were imminent and we will see then those foreign nations, notably the United States, would set up an agency of permanent help that would save thousands of people. It goes without saying that, at times of such ordeals, our "Houses of Mercy" staffed by the Daughters of Charity had always been the first to relieve the victims of all kind.

De Vienne too left a detailed account on the works of the Daughters of Charity in Zhengding. We are sorry that we cannot copy it here. We would have seen how the brilliant charity of the mother superior, Sister Guerlain, succeeded in relieving so much human suffering for many years and obviously in times of disasters, so frequent in China.

The vicariate of Zhengding, already suffering because of the floods, had to suffer a terrible epidemic the following year: exanthematous typhus, which was probably caused by the unhygienic condition of houses that never dried out after the floods. Four deaths in fifteen days saddened the mission: those of Fathers Ildephonse Lemoine and Constant Fiandin, Brother Jean Pénen, and Sister Fielding. Another ordeal was to hit the vicariate: the imminent departure of its young and dynamic apostolic vicar.

Jarlin needed help in his heavy task. He asked the Sacred Congregation of Propaganda to give him a coadjutor. By the decree of 2 April 1919 Rome named Bishop de Vienne as Jarlin's coadjutor. With great sadness, Christians and missionaries in Zhengding saw him leave, their dear Shepherd, who for his part made the painful sacrifice of leaving them. This see was to remain vacant for two long years.

Table 21.1 Status of the Vicariate of Zhengding, 1919

Categories	Totals
Christian population	70,875
European priests	20
Chinese priests	40
Christian communities	855
Residences of missionaries	19
Churches, properly speaking	86
Chapels and oratories	550
Seminarians in major seminary	17
Seminarians in minor seminary	112

Male school teachers	285
Female school teachers	276
Colleges	22
Students in the colleges	700
Male Catechumens	170
Female Catechumens	144
Adult Baptisms	1,753

Let us now return to North Zhili and follow the progress achieved in this vicariate, which though losing two limbs still remains the biggest, because of the number of Christians.

Let us first give an inventory of this mission immediately after the separation of the two vicariates of Baoding and Tianjin, that is, in 1913.

Table 21.2 Vicariate of North Zhili, Personnel and Statistics, 1913

Categories	Totals
Catholic population	133,515
Baptisms of adults	37,465
European Vincentian priests	23
Chinese Vincentian priests	9
Chinese Diocesan priests	35
Seminarians in major seminary	37
Seminarians in minor seminary	131
European and Chinese Daughters of Charity	40
Chinese Religious Women – Josephines	65
European Marist Brothers	29
Chinese Marist Brothers	17

There were fourteen colleges: four Normal Schools; five schools for European languages and sciences; and five for classical Chinese studies. They taught 970 students of both sexes. In 1,990 primary schools, 48,900 boys and girls were being taught.

The Kindly Attitude of the Government Towards the Catholic Church

The generous declarations made by Yuan Shikai at the time of becoming president, to the bishop of Peking were not loose talk. The government kept its word. It had proclaimed that being Catholic would not be an obstacle anymore to having access to public offices. Now to achieve this, the government necessarily had to give up an age-old custom that had force of law in all the institutions of the State: they were superstitious acts which students of schools and universities had to perform on certain fixed days, as well as all the civil servants several times during the year. Thus, on 3 September 1912 the Minister of Public Instruction published an order that stipulated: "The ceremonies for the anniversary of Confucius's birthday and for the beginning of the school-year will not include adorations, genuflections or other religious rites." In this way, a previously closed door was opened for Christian youth.

A New Hospital in Peking

Several hospitals had opened in Peking since 1900, and we would not have mentioned this one, if there there were no relationship with the mission of Peking. We can read in the *Echo de Tianjin* of that time: "A new hospital, the 'Hôpital Central,' has just been built in Peking on the street which leads to Chala. The expenses of the installation – three hundred thousand dollars – are covered partly by the government, partly by private gifts. Chinese doctors formed according to European methods will provide the health service ; and the various services will be operated under the direction of the Daughters of Charity."

The official inauguration of the hospital took place on 27 January 1917 under the presidency of Cao Rulin, Minister of Communications. Those present were Jarlin, Lu Zhengxiang, Minister of Foreign Affairs – who soon was going to become a Benedictine – and many other personalities. Several speeches were given. Let us record briefly Jarlin's words: "Look and see . . . no need to speak, the things that we witness say enough for themselves. . . . We Europeans may have been thinking that the sentiment of charity did not exist in China . . . look and see what has been achieved through the initiative of some private people so as to relieve those who are suffering. It has been said that China is behind the times when compared with other nations . . . look and see if the work which appears shows this being behind . . . let us greet the New China."

Let us say, so as not to return to it, that the head doctor in the Central Hospital was for a long time Doctor Song from Mongolia, an excellent Catholic, who in 1938 at the time of the Japanese occupation had to leave this hospital like the Daughters of Charity. Afterwards the Central Hospital was joined to the American Rockefeller Institution.

New Names for the Vicariates

A change, wished for by missionaries for a long time, consisted in giving the ecclesial circumscriptions more convenient official names than the ones that were used. We have already mentioned this anomaly and we will not come back to it. It is enough for us to know that the Sacred Congregation of Propaganda ordered in 1929 that from then on ecclesial circumscriptions would carry the name of the city where the ordinary of the place, the apostolic vicar or apostolic prefect was residing.

Here is how, since that date, our vicariates in China have been named. The future divisions would henceforth always be named according to the name of the residential town.

Table 21.3 Names of Vicariates and Changes for
Zhili, Jiangxi, and Zhejiang, 1929

Northern Province of the Vincentians		
Previous Name	**Present Name**	**Civil Province**
Zhili North	Peking	Hebei
Zhili East	Yongping	Hebei
Zhili West	Zhengding	Hebei
Zhili Central	Baoding	Hebei
Zhili Maritime	Tianjin	Hebei
Southern Province of the Vincentians		
Jiangxi North	Jiujiang until 1924; then Nanchang	Jiangxi
Jiangxi East	Yujiang	Jiangxi
Jiangxi South	Ji'an	Jiangxi
Zhejiang East	Ningbo	Zhejiang
Zhejiang West	Hangzhou	Zhejiang

A Very Active Missionary[68]

In the two years following the storm of 1900, namely in 1901 and 1902, Paris sent to the vicariate of Peking eleven missionaries, some of whom had not yet been ordained priests. One of them was Vincent Lebbe, who landed in Shanghai on 16 March 1901 together with Father de Vienne, ordained 9 June 1900, and Reverend Mister Joseph Gâté, a diocesan deacon.

Vincent Lebbe, born in Ghent (Belgium) on 19 August 1877, admitted in Paris on 5 November 1895, pronounced his vows on 7 November 1897 and began his clerical studies at Saint Lazare.

Very talented, a tireless talker, he quickly drew attention to himself among his schoolmates. It was the middle of the crisis of Modernism. There was an uneasy feeling among the students. Rome had not yet spoken. People were discussing; some were in favor of Loisy. Lebbe was one of them, and because he talked much and liked discussions, he caused trouble around him. His superiors thought it a good idea to have him change environments and so they sent him to Dax to finish his studies. There too, however, his progressive ideas and his critical and insinuating mentality were pleasing for some of his schoolmates, and so the "Lebbe Party" was created, which made life difficult for the teachers. Beforehand the clan prepared the questions that everybody took turns to ask the teacher. Once, the latter, irritated and unable to contain himself, invited Lebbe to come and take the teacher's place on the stage. Without hesitation, Lebbe got up there and shared his ideas with self-assurance. That was enough to have him called back to Paris in the beginning of 1900.[69]

Because of these facts, the superior in Dax, [Théodore] Vernière, put the situation under their true light, and explained that it was urgent, for the wellbeing of the community of Dax, that this troublesome student be taken away. This happened, and the incident was closed.

This student seemed, however, to have talents and to be well endowed for studies. In Paris, it was thought that some time in Rome in our inter-

---

68. Contemporary readers have commented on the pro-Western (i.e., French) slant of this critical portrayal of Lebbe. For this reason, the editors have included as an appendix to Ferreux's work a contemporary essay on Lebbe by Jean-Paul Wiest. It presents a more developed picture of Lebbe's life, character, ministry, and spirituality, as it is situated in the history of China and the Church at that period. Wiest's work includes a broad selection of sources concerning his subject. It is hoped that it will add a broader perspective to Lebbe's work. (HOD)

69. Ferreux's notes: There he presented the incidents in Dax in such a clever way to his superiors, that Father Fiat, the superior general, wrote a letter to the superior in Dax criticizing the students' bad attitude towards Lebbe.

national seminary would give a better direction to his ideas. He was sent there for the beginning of the school year in October 1900. Because of illness, it was said, he did not follow the courses of the university.

At that moment, Bishop Favier, as soon as calm had returned in Peking after the Boxer Uprising, traveled to Europe mostly to recruit personnel for his Peking mission. In Paris, Lebbe, who had almost finished his studies, was suggested. The bishop agreed, and the person concerned approved with joy.

No sooner had he arrived in Peking than he began to study the Chinese language with determination, and his success was amazing. Endowed with a remarkable memory, ready to talk with anybody, he absorbed it so well that after a few months of living in Peking he could make conversation in Chinese. Ordained a priest on 27 October 1901 he was given the task to teach in the seminary of the Beitang. In one of his first lessons, he told the seminarians that "Ecclesiology" was a "vicious circle." Father Guilloux, learning this, preferred to get rid of his collaborator. Lebbe was sent as an associate to the district of Jingdong, whose director was Father Pierre Scipione, an Italian confrere. Lebbe worked there with great zeal; he informed himself about habits and customs, talking with all those he met, and happily gave his all to ministering.

His confreres had already noticed in him features that suggest his wish to be popular. Obviously, there were no more discussions about Modernism; missionaries had other worries: evangelizing China was important to them and this topic was enough to sustain the conversations, during which Lebbe expounded strange theories. Because he stayed only a short time in this district, nobody paid any attention to them. Thus, he left the impression of an enthusiastic missionary. He indeed had the makings of a good missionary. His natural talents sheltered his originalities. Jarlin trusted him and, in 1903, he made him director of the district of Zhuozhou, on the railway halfway to Baoding.

Having arrived in this mission post, Lebbe thought he could act more independently than in Jingdong under the eyes of his director. Though he spent only three years in Zhuozhou, he showed there his tendency to become, without his bishop's advice, in matters unrelated to religion. Jarlin therefore blamed him because of a lawsuit. "You did a very wrong thing," he wrote him on 16 August 1905, "sending the mandarin a list of guilty people. You took upon yourself a role, which never must be ours. The best thing was to write nothing at all; but because you wanted to protect this rich person, you could have done so with saying – if you were absolutely sure – that he was innocent. Full stop, that is all. But why did you not write me beforehand? If I had known about these steps, I would have ordered you to stop."

Another time, on 14 December 1905, Jarlin gave him this advice: "Do your utmost when you leave your residence for a long time to inform me … make sure that your people know where they can find you."

He often made trips to Peking, not so much to meet his superior, as to pay visits to Chinese priests or to seminarians during their breaks or outings, talking with them about many things and already stirring them up against all that was not Chinese, he being more Chinese than the Chinese themselves.

He had organized in his residence of Zhuozhou a superior modern primary school, over which the imperial flag fluttered and instead of visiting his Christian communities and his catechumens' schools, he made himself one of the teachers of that completely pagan school, with a hundred pupils wearing a uniform that the director had paid for. Three years later, when he was placed in Tianjin, the school fell through, but the pupils had at least the satisfaction of having had free clothes.

He spent a tremendous amount of money and when giving his annual accounts, he was regularly in deficit. Besides, he often submitted inaccurate accounts. Once, the procurator of the vicariate told him there was an error of three thousand taels to the detriment of the episcopal fund. Lebbe heaved high his arms declaring that he did not understand anything about bookkeeping.

The only solution was to forget about it; afterwards this often happened. He lent money to friends in difficulty; most of the time, the loaned money did not come back.

To sum up, he had not been brilliant in Zhuozhou, and according to his successors, the Christians coming from his badly controlled catechumenates lacked formation. So far there were no big problems. We have noted these few eccentricities, not because of their importance, but to show this missionary's mentality, because afterwards he would get himself much talked about, even after his death.

Jarlin, a missionary at heart, still trusted this enterprising worker, despite some escapades. In autumn 1906, he appointed him director of the district of Tianjin, much more important than Zhuozhou. Lebbe's residence was Our Lady of Victories Church in Wanghailou. He and his nine colleagues, three were Europeans, worked intensely. The method of giving out money was at its height and Lebbe used it to the maximum. Jarlin wrote him frequently to give him advice and directives.

We have in hand about forty very short letters addressed to Lebbe by Jarlin. These letters were spaced out over a period of six years, that is, from 1906 to 1912. From some of them we can conclude what Lebbe's activities were like in Tianjin. On 9 May 1912 Jarlin informed him that Dumond had been nominated apostolic vicar of Tianjin. Consequently, Lebbe was to be under Bishop Dumond's jurisdiction and because of this fact the correspondence with Jarlin stopped.

Letters from Jarlin to Lebbe

13 October 1906. – "I advise you to go to bed at nine o'clock all three of you, when you are in the residence." It was in the beginning of Lebbe's stay in Tianjin. The bishop knew the director's habits: spending the evening in company in long conversations staying up late, he would have a less fresh mind in the morning.

21 January 1907. – "Let us be prudent in baptizing and let us not go too quickly. Having Christians who do not carry out their Easter duties equals having nothing. It is useless to convert them. We do not need *baptisms*, we need *Christians*." It is clear immediately that the director was a little too much in a hurry to pour baptismal water on the foreheads of catechumens.

25 February 1907. – "Yes, one of the main needs, not only for you, but everywhere in the vicariate is in the first place to have catechists for men and for women. That is absolutely necessary. I hope you can convince yourself of this! It is not other people's business to provide for this need; every director has to work on it preferably in geography schools and gymnastics schools. To this need you must add the one to work for recruiting seminarians. That is what has to pass as uppermost in our minds." Some days later, Jarlin returned to this issue.

9 April 1907. – "Have you not yet set up schools for catechists? You have been given money for that. Every director has his own school; you had yours in Zhuozhou. Do you have one in Tianjin?" It is difficult to understand that a director neglects the formation of catechists. Lebbe went and begged for them in other districts, even in the neighboring vicariate of the Jesuits. That is the meaning of the sentence, "It is not other people's business to provide for this need."

As for recruiting for the seminary, Lebbe never bothered. We are sure that during the twenty years he had been working in the missions of the north, he never sent or recommended any single minor seminarian for a seminary of the Northern Province of the Vincentians, let alone a Chinese major seminarian. This is a strange omission on the part of someone who soon was going to proclaim loudly that the missionaries who had been working before him had forgotten the formation of a Chinese clergy.

11 April 1907. – "Form catechists; that is your duty. It is one of our really necessary works. Work at it. I thought you had done so since you were director. In any case, begin now. It is never too late to do well." The good father of the family encouraged his son, without harsh words.

4 May 1907. – "Is it strange that all you do is not perfect? Is it not my duty to draw your attention to it? I add that it is almost a consolation, because I wish so much to see you becoming a perfect missionary. Be afraid of making mistakes, but do not be afraid to be told that you did. Do not think that I get distressed because of a word. If I am distressed it is seeing the bad results of hasty or ill-considered affairs."

27 July 1907. – "You spent four thousand three hundred taels on chapels. Last year, however, there were sixty chapels, this year there are only fifty-five. Answer me as soon as possible." Alas, we do not know the reactions that the bishop's gentle remarks could have caused in his dear missionary. We do not have any of his answers.

12 June 1908. – "Do not be saddened because of what I have to say to you. You have great qualities, but there is one you have not: *character*. There are not only sweet moments in exercising authority; it is necessary to know how to take the responsibility of one's actions."

14 July 1909. – "I am sick and I could only glance at your accounts. I found the big surprises: 1) you have fewer chapels than last year; 2) I wonder how you could have spent so much on your catechumens. Take account of how much you have spent on your catechumens. Surely, it is certainly not that you did not hear me preaching thrift. . . . I want absolutely to know exactly how much money you received, including what you have kept for building chapels."

23 September 1909. – "You have just noticed once again how much has been stolen from us. I hope that you will give much attention to this question of accounts. All those petty thefts are the reason why many souls get lost. Let us often think that some twenty taels can enable us to save a family from paganism. Come down from the clouds, dear friend. It is nice to go to them from time to time, but do not remain there. Remain on the earth and think of the temporal affairs that belong to the Church."

Accounts! They were Lebbe's nightmare. He was always short of money. He borrowed without informing his bishop. He had debts that he would be unable to repay. His employees wasted money.

30 November 1909. – "Keep your accounts well. Pay attention to these *temporal* questions. They are absolutely necessary and, my friend, it is on this point that you need to mend your ways."

6 March 1911. – "If you cannot build what we allowed you to build, please do not spend the funds. I no longer want things that exist only on paper. Let us do what we can do and let us leave the rest without engaging the future." We can guess without difficulty that the director, with the authorization to build, hurried to the procure to receive the allotted sum but . . . would use it for something else.

8 July 1911. – "We are waiting for your accounts, but do not hurry too much, I want them to be accurate and without mistakes."

20 August 1911. – "You tell me that you have debts in the shop; that is a very big fault and it is very imprudent. Is it justified to have debts without knowing if they can be paid back?"

At the Beginning of the Revolution of 1911 in Tianjin

We talked about them earlier. Here, Jarlin gives advice to his subordinate, who panicked too easily and got involved in this exclusively political business.

25 September 1911. – "What can I tell you about the situation? What measures are to be taken? I do not see any. Note that we are not attacked and that we cannot and must not fight against a party. In these conditions there is nothing to be done."

25 November 1911. – "Anyway, let us follow Saint Vincent's advice: *Let us follow the main body of wise people.* Let us never be the first, nor the last. The most common prudence obliges us to follow that rule, both for us and for our Christians."

5 March 1912. – "Let us thank God for the protection granted our Christians. Nowhere are they attacked. The churches are not touched either. I think that the Christians from outside make a mistake when they flee to our places. In the city and the larger villages, rich people run a risk. Our poor Christians are sheltered from looting.

"I do not believe that you have to stand up to a siege, neither have we. People besiege those they attack: nowhere are the Church or the Europeans attacked. They are against the *riches* of the Chinese who have them. Your dear republicans go further than the ones in Europe and the United States, who only ask for their share. They want everything and even burn what they cannot steal."

Lebbe was very adept in his relations with his superiors; he only mentioned catechumens and conversions when visiting his bishop or in his letters. "We can hope for anything," this beautiful sentence was repeated ad nauseam. When caught out by his superiors, he knelt down and recognized that he was at fault . . . and for all that, he did not mend his ways. And then he put on a magnanimous air when intervening for rich pagans who had been more or less robbed by the revolutionaries. Lebbe, who had already said much against the French Legation and who soon was going to campaign against the French [Religious] Protectorate, asked Jarlin to intercede with the minister of France to have these rich pagans compensated whom he pitied; in order to get what he wanted, he held out the false hope of converting them.

Jarlin responded on 25 March 1912: "I certainly would like to help those poor rich people, but alas! You know that Monsieur Picot (chargé d'affaires of the French Legation) went to Baoding, where there also was a robbery (see above). He told those who begged for an intervention by him with the Chinese authorities for compensation for their losses: 'We cannot do anything; it is a general calamity!' So do not count on an intervention by the minister. You are convinced, I think, that I, as much as you, want the conversion of the rich, of the powerful and of the poor, and that I am ready to do all I can; but only what I can."

What these letters show clearly is the behavior of a religious person who acts in complete independence and practices obedience only when it suits him.

From 9 May 1912, Lebbe was under the authority of Bishop Dumond. The district he was in charge of became an apostolic vicariate. The bishop, consecrated in Peking on 30 June 1912 made his solemn entrance in Tianjin the following 4 July. There were in Tianjin only two churches: Our Lady of Victories in Wanghailou near the city, which was the director's residence; and Saint Louis in the concessions, where the procurator of the Northern Province was living, who with a Chinese associate was in charge of the European and Chinese Christians of the concession.

Even before taking possession of his vicariate, Dumond intended to establish his residence more towards the center of town. He had to reside therefore temporarily in Our Lady of Victories.

Dumond, who had been director of Donglü, and since 1905, Jarlin's vicar general, knew very little of his new vicariate. Therefore, from the beginning he needed a vicar general. Consequently, despite Lebbe's misdemeanors and bluster, which he must certainly have known of, he gave him his trust, as Jarlin had done before him, and named him vicar general.

We can be amazed that so much trust was given to a missionary who already had given so many clear signs of a real lack of level-headedness and *character*, in Jarlin's words. To understand this, it is necessary to know the situation facing the bishop at the beginning of his episcopacy in Tianjin.

For six years, the director of the district had clearly been very active, and in the same way as everywhere he had gone, almost all his collaborators, who little by little became his admirers, followed him. He could express himself so well and he was so shrewd in his approaches that people really thought that his superiors, who actually did not spare him warnings, approved everything he did. We saw this in Jarlin's letters. Probably Lebbe was careful not to reveal them to his companions.

Jarlin even then did not know everything. If he had known that Lebbe had opened conference halls since 1910 and especially if he had learned how the orator was behaving, it is quite certain that the bishop would have protested.

Actually, in his conferences to which both Christians and pagans were invited, Lebbe introduced himself as the reformer of evangelization, which up till then had erred in its methods. What arguments did he use?

First came flattery. He admitted it himself. A confrere said to him one day, "Would you be the only one then not to see the damage you inflict on the Church in China by praising the Chinese in every dimension and by denigrating the Europeans?" "I am not more stupid than anybody else," he answered, "but I have a principle: I offer to the Chinese people only what they like." This admission speaks for itself. People must not think that this admission was obtained once by surprise. He replied to others who made the same remark, "I always adapt myself to the audience." Or: "I know what they like." Another confrere one day said to him: "But finally, Father Lebbe, why, before Chinese people, do you accuse missionaries without distinction of not observing the Roman rules, especially the encyclical *Maximum illud*, though you know very well that the neighboring vicariate (Baoding) has a school preparing sixty students for the minor seminary, who after two years of elementary studies will enter the minor seminary, which also averages sixty students, and moreover its major seminary has thirty students?" Instead of answering the question, Lebbe, as he did so often, cleverly side-stepped the question and gave the evasive answer, "I see, you are jealous of my popularity; eh well, if you want the Chinese to love you, do what I do." "That is the last thing I would do," answered the other. "What I want is the conversion of China, by teaching the truth, and not the pursuit of prestige, acquired to the detriment of the truth."

Lebbe's other argument was politics, based on exaggerated nationalism, which could very well be named hyper-nationalism. The encyclical, mentioned above, prohibited exactly this attitude.

In view of such a situation, Dumond quickly understood that it was impossible for him to keep Lebbe out of things, because he would have alienated the majority of the priests, a lot of Christians, and even quite a large part of the pagan population of the city. Given these circumstances it is easier to understand why the bishop gave free reign to the fiery missionary who had everything in hand, meanwhile hoping probably – in his compassionate charity – that Lebbe would not take advantage of the trust that he had been granted, and that he, with his talents and zeal would succeed in realizing many good things in this brand-new vicariate.

The Catholic Press in China

In these years of progress and evolution, that is, of a more enlightened civilization, European missionaries discussed among themselves this saying, whose origin is not well known, "If Saint Paul preached nowadays, he would have become a journalist." They felt that the time had come to spread among the people treatises, magazines, and newspapers, as was being done in Europe, in order to spread good ideas, to proclaim the truth, and to defend it when attacked.

Up until that moment, missionaries had only published thin weekly or monthly periodicals, dealing with doctrine and spirituality, and written only for the Faithful. The Jesuits before 1900 produced this kind of printed matter, both in conversational Mandarin and in French. In 1910, Bishop Reynaud founded *Le Messager de Ning-Po*, a real mission magazine interesting for the missionaries and especially for their foreign benefactors. In 1912, the *Bulletin Catholique de Pékin* was born in Peking, appearing every month with forty pages, and which was to become the tribune of all the missionaries of China. Correspondents of any mission would send the director of the magazine, Father [Philibert] Clément, who was its founder, all kinds of information on their own mission or on local events. In this way the magazine worked as a link among the different vicariates and contributed towards maintaining unity among missionaries as well as at the same time stimulating healthy emulation.

Of course, these publications did not fulfill the missionaries' wish to have a periodical in Chinese so that all the Chinese people could read it.

This idea more than any other one haunted Lebbe, and already before Dumond's arrival, he had in mind his project and he began to realize it in 1912. It was a small weekly periodical that he called *Guangyilu* ([The Public's] General Well-being*)*; a vague title which would not frighten pagan people. Its content was: a leading article on a point of doctrine, news about China and Europe concerning religion, informative items, works and methods, open letters, etc.

This small magazine could not only please the missionaries; it did well for the Faithful. In the beginning it had a circulation of five hundred copies, soon it reached a thousand copies, and then disappeared.

The newspaper was not what its founder dreamed of, nor did it meet the wishes of the missionaries. Lebbe still thought about it, but starting a daily newspaper is no small thing. He submitted his project to Dumond, when asking him the permission to go to Europe to look for the funds necessary for the foundation of a Catholic Chinese newspaper in Tianjin. The bishop agreed all the more willingly because Lebbe had not yet gone back to Europe since his arrival in Peking.

Lebbe therefore returned to Europe. During the summer of 1913, a "Social Week" was held in Versailles under Gibier's presidency. Lebbe went there and he gracefully agreed to be interviewed by Catholic journalists. He told them so many beautiful things that they marveled at them. Let us quote these two texts. The parentheses are ours. In the "Weekly Bulletin" of 13 August 1913 it was written:

> Chinese Catholics love France very much. They consider it to be the first country of the world. I myself am Chinese in the first place, for I have to devote myself before anything else to the nation that I want to win over to the Gospel; but in the second place I am French" (his audience was made up mostly of French people). He continued: "With the love of France, Chinese Catholics carry in their hearts the love of the Republic and the love of liberty. It would be an error to think that they received the new regime, inaugurated in their country, with sorrow and trembling. On the contrary indeed, they were among the first ranks of those who established it."

(The Christians, no more than the pagans, had much enthusiasm for a republic that tried to be born from the confusion of the civil war; as for Christians who were of the first rank, they could be numbered on the fingers of one hand.) "If they progress from the political point of view, they have made still more progress from the social point of view. In China, Catholic and social are almost synonyms" (one more example of his bragging). "Soon they will be able to spread their ideas by way of a daily newspaper which will be published in Tianjin."

In *L'éclair* (Lightning) also, there were also beautiful soliloquies. "In the vicariates of Peking and Tianjin, Catholics are one tenth of the population." (How does he count? We have to go to 1930 to find the moment when the Catholic population reaches 2.7% in the vicariate of Peking, and elsewhere hardly 1%.)

The gifts received by Lebbe amounted to sixty thousand francs, which he brought to Tianjin in the beginning of 1914. This sum was far from enough for the enterprise he had in mind. No sooner had he returned, than he worked to found a company that people could invest in (buy shares). Bishops, missionaries and even some Christians enthusiastically took part, because the desire for the paper was great.

On 1 October 1915 the first copy appeared of *Yishibao* (Social Welfare) like the late *Guangyilu* with a slight nuance.

Now we must talk about an event that was for the new Catholic newspaper the occasion of taking a very unfortunate and disastrous orientation from the first days of its publication.

The Laoxikai Affair

We have seen that Dumond's living arrangements were only temporary, and that the bishop wanted to settle in a better and more spacious location. It did not take him long to decide that the quarter named Laoxikai would be just what he needed. This quarter was one of those extra-concessions we mentioned already, which constituted an extension of the French Concession. He foresaw that sooner or later the property would go up till there. Consequently, he bought a very large piece of property at a very good price. Much work was necessary to fill in, raise and level the parcel of land where they were going to build. Dumond intended to build an imposing cathedral surrounded by all the buildings destined for the episcopal residence and for good works.

The land that was not used would be resold in plots to Christian families, which the bishop wanted to attract to live around the cathedral.

In 1915, an agreement – which was the consequence of a promise made by the Chinese government – was concluded between the minister of France, [Alexandre] Conty and the Chinese authorities, and was on the verge of being inked.

The English Concession had already acquired the same advantage and had extended over a much bigger surface, which even included two villages. The whole procedure was quite normal and had already been practiced a long time ago in the concessions of Shanghai, which had been made quite a bit bigger.

But when the agreement about the extra-concession became known in Tianjin, there was grumbling among the new inhabitants of Laoxikai, who were afraid of the French tax forms; for in the concessions, the whole administration and the police were at the charge of the concessionary nation, considered as an autonomous municipality. It is well known that generally every innovation is distasteful for the population, which only contemplates immediate advantages without thinking about other advantages that will come to them from this or that reform.

In the Laoxikai case, the emotions would have fallen away by themselves if Lebbe had not meddled with it. A small delegation of disgruntled people came and asked Lebbe to intervene in this case on their behalf. That is where the difficulties began; Lebbe intervened in person using his press.

In *Yishibao*, June 1916, the director of the newspaper, a layman, Liu Junqing, drew attention to himself through an insulting attack against the consul of France in Tianjin, [Alexandre-Robert] Bourgeois. The minister of France in Peking, Monsieur Conty, persuaded that the mission had made common cause with the newspaper, wrote Dumond a severe and threatening letter.

The bishop knew about the ongoing agitation, but still ignored the part that Lebbe had taken as well as, in particular, the incriminating article. Dumond had no problem in exonerating himself before the minister and he promised to make Lebbe stop taking an interest in this case. Indeed, he ordered his vicar general to withdraw completely from all participation in this disorder. Lebbe, in a written answer, declared that he could not obey in view of the circumstances.

Then Lebbe wrote against the minister an insulting diatribe in which he blamed him for violating justice and the law in the question of the lands of Laoxikai. Conty, cut to the quick, demanded that he leave.

By telegram he threatened to have the episcopal residence and the other buildings of the mission located in the French Concession evacuated with military force, if Lebbe, who was intervening in a purely political matter, was not rendered harmless.

This gave notice categorically. On 22 June 1916 Dumond assembled his council, of which as vicar general Lebbe was a member. He understood – no other way around it – that he had to leave the place. He was given complete liberty to choose the place to which he would withdraw, for he was not being expelled from China, he was being moved far enough away from Tianjin so that he could not exert his influence on it anymore. Lebbe chose Zhengding, a town quite far away, but easy to reach by train. Bishop de Vienne, Coqset's coadjutor, installed in Zhengding less than a year before, agreed to receive the exile.

Instead of following the counsel given to him of keeping silence about the reasons for his departure and saying to the members of his household that he was going to take some days' rest in Zhengding, he told the whole story, after coming back in his residence, to his co-workers and presented himself as a victim.

The following day, 23 June, Lebbe boarded the train that was going to bring him to Zhengding. No sooner had the traveler left, than a group of agitators gathered in front of the Church of Our Lady of Victories, loudly blaming the undignified behavior of the representative of France and the injustice committed by Dumond, whom they held responsible for Lebbe's exile. They yelled, "Down with the bishop!" The group went to the French Concession, but police had reinforced it and the agitators returned home.

The next day, the *Yishibao* insulted Conty and the bishop in a demeaning way using words too unacceptable for us to copy here.

A series of significant events was to follow. Here we will simply mention them.

Since Bishop de Vienne soon noticed that that the newspaper campaign was going on, and probably wanted to move Lebbe away from the episcopal residence, he sent him to Dingzhou, a Christian community along the railway between Baoding and Zhengding. But there Lebbe often received his friends from Tianjin and gave them his instructions.

On 14 July a letter with the signatures of Chinese priests, Christians and notables, addressed to the Chinese Minister of Foreign Affairs, protesting against the scheme by the French consul in Tianjin.

In August, another petition was sent to Rome. Written by Father Antoine Cotta and signed by Chinese priests and Christians, it asked for Lebbe as bishop in Tianjin.

The Vincentian visitor of the Northern Province, who was aware of the role played by Lebbe and his press, forbade him all collaboration with *Yishibao*. He answered: "All has been done without me; I wrote nothing."

In September, noticing that the subversive campaign was going on more than ever, Dumond considered it advisable to call Lebbe back to Tianjin.

On 17 October 1916 [Henri] Bourgeois, consul of France in Tianjin, published an official notice announcing that an agreement had been concluded and signed between France and China concerning the extra-concession called Laoxikai.

Two days later, [Damien] de Martel, chargé d'affaires during the absence of Conty, minister of France, had the quarter of Laoxikai taken over, which had been ceded by China.

The case took a new turn. Agitators organized a boycott of French products and a strike of Chinese employees in the administration, in the power plant, in commercial and industrial firms as well as among servants.

On 15 November the strike was at its height: sabotage of the power plant, the flight of the Chinese police officers in the service of the French Concession. All the French residents lacked servants for a long month.

On 19 November de Martel asked Paris by telegram for the repatriation of Lebbe and Cotta. Who was Father Cotta?

Cotta, born in Cairo on 7 January 1872 of an Egyptian father and an Austrian mother, admitted into Saint Lazare on 18 July 1891, ordained a priest in Paris on 4 June 1898 was sent to Madagascar, where he worked till 1905. After having difficulties with his bishop, Bishop Crouzet, he was sent to China, where he arrived on 3 May 1906 and was placed in the district of Baoding. In 1910, at the time of the establishment of the vicariate of Baoding, he was sent at his own request to the district of Tianjin so as to be near his friend, Vincent Lebbe. Subtle quibbler, he always got in trouble with his superiors. He was for Lebbe a counselor who, instead of keeping him away from trouble, often pushed him further than his friend wanted.

In February 1917, Father Guilloux, visitor of the Southern Province, arrived in Tianjin as extraordinary representative, his superiors in Paris instructed him to study and sort out the affair from the point of view of the Congregation. Claude Guilloux reminded the gathered confreres of their vow of obedience, of the instructions of Propaganda and of the orders of the popes forbidding missionaries to engage in politics. He implored them to respectfully wait for their superiors' decisions, to avoid in future all collusion with a political party and to avoid even talking about the present case, which only concerned the two governments. All promised one by one, Lebbe included, and they took an oath.

The next day, Lebbe gathered the diocesan priests (over whom the representative had no authority), told them all that had happened the night before in the presence of the representative, and decided with them to appeal to Rome.

On 19 March 1917 a telegram from Paris sent Lebbe to the vicariate of Ningbo, and Cotta to Quito (Central America). Lebbe obeyed immediately. Cotta refused, on the pretense that, being Austrian, he would risk arrest on his way (it was the height of the world war).

Cotta's refusal was met by Rome's prohibition by him of all priestly ministry. He ignored it and appealed to Rome.

Actually, he wrote to Rome in order to exonerate himself and stay in Tianjin. As soon as Lebbe had left for the south, the situation in Tianjin became better, but Cotta's presence prevented calm from being completely restored.

Cotta's letter to Rome was so cleverly written that it almost succeeded in changing people's minds. Lebbe might also have written to Rome from Ningbo. Did he write? We do not know.

On 14 August 1918 Dumond arrived in Peking with an amazing letter. Influenced by the offensive coming from Tianjin, the Sacred Congregation of Propaganda ordered Dumond to take back the exiled missionaries and to forgive Cotta after asking him to apologize.

The bishop thought about resigning and came to take advice from the bishop of Peking. The other Vincentian bishops of the north were brought up to date on all this, and with Bishop Jarlin, Bishops Fabrègues, de Vienne and Geurts each sent a telegram to ask for a reprieve and brought the case before the Sacred Congregation of Bishops and Regulars. The orders of Propaganda were annulled.

Bishop de Guébriant's Apostolic Visit

Bishop de Guébriant, apostolic vicar in Canton (1916–1921), was instructed by Rome, at the end of the year 1918 to hold an apostolic visit of all the missions in China. The bishop began his tour in the south and arrived in Tianjin in October 1919.

He was instructed especially to settle the Cotta case during his visit in the north of China. When de Guébriant still was in Shanghai, Lebbe went to him. He wrote to his friend in Tianjin: "Do not destroy, with your untimely sallies, the results that I have obtained here."

For a month and a half, the discussions between the bishop and Cotta did not come to anything. De Guébriant, however, was reading many accounts by apostolic vicars and missionaries about Lebbe and Cotta.

He received another one by the French Chamber of Commerce in Tianjin, which showed, with proofs, how much damage these two individuals had caused to the French residents of Tianjin. Special emphasis was given to the mentality of xenophobia that these gentlemen had incited among the Chinese employees of the French residents.

Finally, on 18 November 1919 de Guébriant wrote an official instruction in Latin to all the priests of Tianjin that was an official reprobation of Lebbe and of his partisans.

When the apostolic vicar had made it clear to Cotta that he had his excommunication on his person, Cotta gave in. On 23 November Cotta went with de Guébriant to Shanghai. On the following 9 December he left for Europe. Soon he was to leave the Congregation and withdrew to America. (He later joined the Maryknoll Fathers and died 28 April 1957.)

The internship period that Lebbe spent in Zhejiang was not very happy. It is true that the language of this province differs so much in its pronunciation from the one in the north, that he was not able anymore to produce in his speeches the oratorical effects that had captivated his audiences in Tianjin. His influence was almost nil with the priests and non-existent with the Faithful. He dared to try to convert Reynaud to his theories, but it was a dead loss.

Soon Ningbo did not please him, and Tianjin was absolutely forbidden for him. The only route open before him was going back to Europe.

For a number of years there had been many Chinese students in Europe, whom, according to Lebbe, nobody took care of. Consequently, he would go there to convert them. He talked about this idea with de Guébriant, who did not dislike the plan, seeing in it an elegant way for China to get rid of Lebbe forever.

In short, Lebbe, who as a Vincentian was under the jurisdiction of Guilloux, asked his permission to return to Europe. The visitor allowed him wholeheartedly to do so. On 5 March Lebbe embarked for Europe.

The "Historical Survey"

In Belgium and France, Lebbe was to lead just as active a life as he had in China. We will not discuss that. We will only mention a booklet he wrote, which, though printed in a very small number of copies, had a great influence on his friends and supporters in Europe. We think that it was published around 1921–1922. The booklet is rare nowadays (1957).

The copy we have consists of forty-six stenciled pages. Its title is "An Historical Survey." The author tried to make it appear as an account that he had handed to the Supreme Pontiff. This obviously is false. Lebbe was not naïve enough to think that an account for the Holy See could be written in this way. Moreover, several times, when writing, he talked to the reader. It was just an explanation of his activities in Tianjin.

Let us quote two passages taken at random, so as to give the reader at least an overview of what the Survey is.

The author has just claimed that, as punishment for some mistake he had made, the superior had cut off his food (this is obvious not true; Jarlin never stopped giving him a double allocation: one for living expenses, the other for the works) and, he said that "the following year began for the whole district of Tianjin without allocation for the expenditure of the Propagation of the Faith."

> That was beneficial; without money they could not seek to buy catechumens. At the same time, no one could keep missionaries from spreading the good news, so they were quite free then to try other ways. They went to work on it immediately. The following year coincided with the establishment of the republic, which inaugurated a period rich in possibilities; and then the offensive began. The plans were made supple enough to make it possible to adapt them to circumstances, to face the unexpected; and in the name of the Father, of the Son and of the Holy Spirit full steam ahead. . . . After six years of thus moving forward, all the objectives were reached, the positions were consolidated, the situation was clear; hopes for the future were boundless.

> Everything had happened as foreseen, and often reality went beyond expectations.

Here is another sample. He has just talked about the famous Laoxikai case:

> Almost at the same time, the Catholics' growing vigor gave birth to a newspaper, the *Yishibao,* which did not take long to become the most widespread and esteemed paper in the whole of North China, and the most fearsome weapon of a well-coordinated response.

> The leading article of the first issue was an open letter, polite but unbending, to the consul, who wanted to trample underfoot the most sacred rights of the Chinese Motherland. . . . This article was like a thunderclap by artillery announcing a major battle. At this call to action, all the forces of the Catholic body in Tianjin came out of the trenches. It was the beginning of an unforgettable fight, during which this army – determined to go to the end – sacrificed everything for the triumph of the cause. Many Christians sacrificed their jobs without any hesitation; leaders of the movement sacrificed more than their own lives. And after several months of courageous fighting, here again the objective was reached.

There is some truth in these words. There is question here of the Affair, which the author introduces as a triumph. There were indeed demonstrations, noisy and insulting for France and the Protectorate, led by Father Lebbe himself in the streets of Tianjin. A Jesuit father, now in his eighties, told us some time ago: "I saw with my own eyes Lebbe, in flimsy clothes, riding on his bicycle around the big parades of young people in the streets of Tianjin, suggesting the slogans they had to repeat."

The "Survey" has been refuted in a masterly manner by Father François Willemen, a Dutch Vincentian of the vicariate of Yongping, and Lebbe's companion in studies, in a booklet that is of the same dimension as the "Survey" but thicker. It is a pity that this answer is not sufficiently well known.

It is mainly though from the "Survey" that Lebbe's apologists draw their material; with their style, they still go one better than the author's soliloquies, which often are just verbiage and dreams corresponding to no reality.

For instance, the last passage that we have quoted textually finished with these words: "Here again the objective was reached." He did not say how, but we know: the three authorities, the civil one, the ecclesial one, and the religious one agreed to move the agitator away from Tianjin. So, we need not bother anymore with Lebbe's activities outside China. Nevertheless, he was to come back in 1927 and to get himself talked about again. When this account reaches that era, we may have to mention something.

Vicariate of Tianjin

Let us now have a look at what happened in Tianjin after Lebbe's departure. While peace was coming back to Tianjin, Cardinal Gaspari, Secretary of

State, sent a telegram to Dumond on July 1920 relieving him of the vicariate of Tianjin and appointing him the administrator of a new vicariate that was being erected. It was Ganzhou, one of the prefectures that Bishop Ciceri wanted to cut off from his vicariate to make of it a new vicariate together with the seventeen sub-prefectures that depended on Ganzhou.

On the following 12 July a decree from Rome nominated Bishop de Vienne, Jarlin's coadjutor, administrator of the vacant vicariate of Tianjin.

Such a sudden decision by Rome could not allow any delay in its execution. Therefore, Dumond hurriedly left Tianjin for his new post, without even stopping to greet Jarlin in Peking when passing by. This transfer from a vicariate that Dumond had administered for eight years to a vicariate in the process of being erected, and furthermore, to a region very far away from Tianjin where the language was very different, demoting him from apostolic vicar to administrator – this transfer, we say, can only be called in clear language by the name of "disgrace."

Let us not forget that, at the time of the controversy of the Chinese Rites, which lasted more than fifty years, popes judged the question of contention according to the information that bishops and missionaries in China were giving them. Now, among them there were two groups clearly opposed: those in favor of permitting the rites, which were only civil according to them, and the others in favor of condemning the rites for being superstitious. When the first group had submitted a document, the pope would answer: "Because the rites are just civil, they are licit;" but he would always add the caveat: "if things are as presented in X's account." And vice versa, when the information had come from the other party.

In Dumond's case, information came only from one side, from Lebbe's side. Dumond and his Vincentian colleagues kept silent.

We have seen above that the four apostolic vicars of the north asked for a reprieve from the execution of the Roman decree which forgave Lebbe and Cotta. The decree was indeed annulled. But in 1920, no claims were lodged in Dumond's favor.

We are still in the North Province; there are two more vicariates that we must visit: Yongping and Baoding.

The Vicariate of Yongping

Despite the difficulties of the beginning, Bishop Geurts could write in 1903 that his six or seven confreres were preaching missions in fifty localities, that they had already baptized several hundred catechumens, and that a small church had been built as well as ten public chapels. A school for catechists was being operated with ten students of all ages (from sixteen to fifty years old).

Geurts used part of the method of Peking, which consisted of feeding the catechumens during the time of their formation. "It seems to me," he said, "that this method is the most practical, for besides the consideration that the Chinese people who learn the catechism are obliged to abandon for several months either their job, or their trade, it is indisputable that grace always adapts itself with marvelous flexibility to the character and the customs of a nation, of an individual. Saint Paul was converted in the twinkling of an eye. Rare exception. Grace must work slowly on the souls of our Chinese people, while guaranteeing them that their material life would not suffer." Geurts did not go as far as the method called "alms;" he did not have the necessary means.

The Minor Seminary

In 1910, Yongping had ten Dutch confreres, but no other Chinese priests than the two old ones who were there in 1900. Therefore, like everywhere else in our Chinese missions, the bishop, immediately after his arrival in 1901, had looked in his small flock of about three thousand Christians, to see whether among the children there were not some whom he could orientate towards studies preparatory for the minor seminary. He found some and, in 1909, he had a minor seminary, several students of which were sons or relatives of martyrs and confessors.

A specialty of the seminary in Yongping was the study program. The bishop and all his confreres had done their humanities in French and their ecclesiastical studies together with French-speaking students. Geurts had noticed that Chinese students had many difficulties in studying both Chinese literature and the elements of Latin. As a result, he set up the study of French from the first classes of the minor seminary, while teaching at the same time the Chinese language, which takes so much time to be learned. Only when the students were very familiar with written and spoken French, were they given the task to study Latin. It was noticed that they learned much faster this new language, which had no relation with Chinese, whereas French has many relations with Latin. French having become for the students like a second mother tongue, it was much easier for them to understand Latin.

This method was special for Yongping and was not imitated elsewhere, because French missions could hardly adopt such a method without drawing on themselves malevolent suspicions in a country where nationalism and growing xenophobia were becoming operative. The Dutch did not need to fear this kind of suspicion, because French was not their mother tongue. The other missions made do with adding to their program of the minor and major seminary a supplementary course of French, or sometimes even an optional course.

In 1910, the number of Catholics in Yongping was almost ten thousand. About thirty chapels and oratories had been built. The cathedral was raised according to Moerloose's plans, a missionary architect from Mongolia, who had built many beautiful churches in the North of China.

Establishing a New Vincentian Province

On 19 March 1921 the superior general, François Verdier established a new province in the Congregation: the Dutch Province. Up to that time Dutch confreres in China were part of either the Southern Province when they belonged to Zhejiang or to Jiangxi; or to the Northern Province, when they belonged to Zhili (Hebei). From that time on, all those who were in the vicariate of Yongping and only those would belong to the Province of the Netherlands.

It consisted of four houses in the Netherlands, three other houses in Bolivia and finally the vicariate of Yongping. To lead the new province, Verdier named Henri Romans.

Few remarkable events happened in this vicariate before Geurts' episcopal jubilee in 1926.

That day the bishop ordained a martyr's son a priest. He could thank Providence when comparing the humble beginnings of his episcopacy with the results of 1926.

In 1901, there were about three thousand Christians, three missionaries, one of whom was the bishop, two Chinese priests but not a single school. In 1926, there were twenty-six priests including the Chinese priests; thirty seminarians for the major and minor seminary; ten Daughters of Charity, thirty-two Chinese Sisters, called Mariales; a college with a hundred students; a boarding school for girls; boys' schools and girls' schools, altogether eighty; nine parishes and seventeen thousand Faithful.

The Vicariate of Baoding

In 1912, this vicariate received a first group of Daughters of Charity, whom Fabrègues placed immediately in Xiguan to manage the orphanage, up to then managed by the Josephines.

They soon set up a dispensary and a girls' school. The Chinese religious women returned to their ordinary work, which consisted of setting up houses of two or three Sisters to busy themselves with the instruction of women catechumens and Christians' children.

In 1914, Fabrègues published a directory or a manual that rendered an eminent service to the missionaries. It is a well-known fact that Propaganda always granted missionaries a great number of faculties called "extraordinary" for they go much further than the powers of common law which rules the countries with an ecclesiastical hierarchy. This set of faculties is published in a booklet titled: *Elenchus facultatum. . .* [List of faculties].

These faculties are granted to the Ordinary (bishop) who delegates them to his collaborators, all or some of them according to the needs. But being expressed in concise formulas, they often need an explanation.

In the vicariate of Peking, Guilloux had already elaborated notes that answered this need. He gave them to Fabrègues, who completed them and succeeded in making of them a book of six hundred pages containing many pieces of information necessary for all the missionaries in China.

This book, written in Latin, has the title *Adjumenta pro regimine Missionum* [Aids for the government of missions]. Printed in the press of the Beitang, only a limited number of copies were made, which many other missions in China copied. This kind of book indeed cannot have a very long life, for besides the fact that the *Elenchus* coming from Rome sometimes carries changes, special events sometimes push the church to change certain laws, like the publishing of the Code of Canon Law, the first General Council of Shanghai in 1924. Despite all this, the *Adjumenta* (1918) were very useful for the missionaries until 1930.

The Parishes or Stations of Baoding

Fabrègues understood quite quickly that the surest way of promoting and maintaining Christian life among the population was the presence of as many priests as possible.

Indeed, when Faithful were at a distance of twenty to sixty kilometers from their pastor, they could claim that they hardly saw him.

Here is the number of stations founded in the district, later to be the vicariate of Baoding, in succeeding periods:

From 1604 to 1840	1	station: Anjiazhuang
From 1840 to 1900	6	stations or parishes
From 1900 to 1910	10	stations
From 1910 to 1923	22	stations
From 1923 to 1950	6	stations
Total:	45	stations.

In this list it can be seen that the strongest multiplication of stations was during Fabrègues' episcopacy. All those stations had a resident priest, sometimes accompanied by one or two associates. It must be understood that no pastor shut himself up in his residence and did not leave his village. On the contrary, every one of them had the care of more or less numerous Christian communities that made up his parish. Some parishes numbered up to twenty communities, others fifteen and rarely less than ten. Given the number of priests in the vicariate, this method of subdivisions could not be pushed further. Moreover, there were disadvantages. Indeed, only large parishes had one or more associates. Everywhere else, the pastor was alone, and isolation – it has been noticed – especially for young priests, is often a cause for defection from the point of view of spirituality. Therefore, afterwards it could happen that two or even three stations were put together into one in order to stimulate community life, so profitable for missionaries.

A Difficult and Unattractive Operation

The Allied Forces had received from the Chinese government the indemnities necessary for the people and for the institutions. But the sharing and distribution of these indemnities required many surveys and long procedures.

The destitute Christians had begun to help themselves to their indemnities by taking food and lodging from their old adversaries. The latter, fearing vengeance, and to repair losses to the local community, offered houses and property, the revenues from which would be used to maintain the missionaries and the chapel and for the expenses of worship.

When, however, the indemnities of the government were being distributed everywhere, the farmers understood quite quickly that they were duplicating what the Christians had taken on their own initiative from them. It did not take long for complaints to be lodged and lawsuits to begin, rekindling hatred and grudges between the two parties.

Fabrègues, aware of the stubbornness of the vengeance mentality in Chinese souls, decided to cut the evil at the root and he ordered the sale of these community goods. In the beginning his Christians resisted very strongly because these properties were a symbol of their victory over the Boxers. The bishop answered that they were also a symbol of the Boxers' defeat, and therefore a symbol of contradiction and dissension. Gradually, the Christians agreed with their bishop's views; the properties were sold. Peace came back.

Establishment of the Apostolic Prefecture of Lixian

In the same way as he had multiplied places with the presence of missionaries in the regions of his vicariate where the population was dense, Fabrègues would have liked to do the same in other parts that were less evangelized, but the personnel at his disposition did not suffice; he saw only one solution for this problem: the division of his vicariate by creating a new region or even two which could be entrusted to other workers. He talked about this plan with Bishop Costantini, apostolic delegate, who not only approved it, but encouraged him to execute the plan as soon as possible.

By the decree of 15 April 1924 Pope Pius XI declared that the apostolic vicariate of Baoding would be divided into three distinct missions and that from that day a new apostolic prefecture, composed of six sub-prefectures was erected, later to be called Lixian. The decree added that the other division would be forthcoming.

That same day, another decree by Rome named Father Melchior Sun apostolic prefect of Lixian. The next autumn Sun went to Lixian to take possession of his new field of activity.

Melchior Sun, born in Peking on 19 November 1869 was ordained a priest in the capital on 24 January 1897. On 25 January 1901 he entered the Congregation of the Mission and was placed in the minor seminary of Beitang to teach Latin. In 1912, he was appointed pastor of Niufang. It was in this place that he received his nomination as apostolic prefect.

In 1925, the vicariate of Baoding had 100,209 Christians. It ceded 26,179 to the new division. After the European missionaries who were working there, had returned to the vicariate of Baoding, eighteen Chinese priests remained, both Vincentian and diocesan, to manage the thirteen parishes of Lixian.

Two years passed peacefully and the prefecture was erected into an apostolic vicariate on 24 June 1926. Sun was appointed its apostolic vicar with the title of bishop of Hesebon. He was one of the six Chinese bishops consecrated in Rome by Pius XI on 28 October 1926. Though the number of Vincentians among the Chinese priests was very small, this vicariate was entrusted to the Congregation of the Mission.

As the town of Lixian had only very few Christians, Bishop Sun asked Rome and was granted the permission of moving his episcopal residence to the neighboring sub-prefecture of Anguo. This transfer took place on 15 July 1929. From then on, this vicariate was to be called by the name of apostolic vicariate of Anguo.

The other division, which the above decree mentioned, took place in 1929. It concerned Yixian, a civil prefecture of second rank in Yizhou, located in the northwest of Baoding and with jurisdiction over two other sub-prefectures. This area was entrusted to the Italian Stigmatine Fathers with a mission title independent of Baoding. It was a mountainous, scarcely populated region, which owed some celebrity to the presence of the [western] imperial tombs of the Qing dynasty. That was why the majority of the population was Manchu, descending from the soldiers who had had the duty of guarding the imperial tombs. These soldiers were living on their pay as members of the imperial army. But since the collapse of the dynasty, these "Tartars," as they were still being called at that time, had become all the more destitute because for centuries they had been accustomed to doing nothing.

The number of the Christians of Yixian was 2,890. Two Chinese priests helped the six Italian priests in the beginning. It was only in 1936 that this mission became an apostolic prefecture with Father [Tarcisio] Martina as its apostolic prefect. That year the number of Christians was 5,080, taken care of by eight Italian missionaries and three Chinese priests.

New Activities Start in Baoding

In the spring of 1921, Fabrègues came back from a trip to Europe cooking up great projects in his head. He had given many conferences in churches in France and especially in Paris about the missions in China, describing the frequent disasters which struck China. He wanted to move the hearts of the Faithful and make them participate in the activities of the missionaries who often, because of the lack of means, were hindered on one hand from aiding unfortunate Christians, and on the other from developing evangelization. He opened a subscription and he himself collected money in the churches.

The generosity of the Faithful was admirable. Fabrègues brought back quite a large amount of money. After his return, he began to execute his plans. He acquired a vast property, located in the southern suburb of Baoding, called Nanguan. He built a modern hospital with one hundred beds. It contained a special pavilion for the poor that could accommodate thirty sick people who would receive free care. This was a gift of Marshal Cao Kun.

On the other end of the property, he had two similar schools built (one for boys and the other one for girls) separated from each other by a public street. These schools, at first upper primary, became after some years schools of second rank recognized by the government. In 1923, all these works were in operation. The head doctor in the hospital was a Chinese doctor educated in Aurora, the Catholic University of Shanghai founded by the Jesuits. The boys' school was managed by a European missionary, assisted by a Chinese priest as sub-director, by three Brothers teaching French and finally several Chinese teachers. They followed the programs of the public schools, and when it became a school of the second rank, the government registered it.

The girls' school was entrusted to the Franciscan Sisters of Mary. Each of these schools could accommodate forty boarders who were Catholic or catechumens and about a hundred-day school students.

The Vicariate of Zhengding

We are still in the [Vincentian] Northern Province. After de Vienne left Zhengding to go to Peking as Jarlin's coadjutor, the vicariate of Zhengding remained vacant for two years. It was fortunate that in the interim there was a vicar general whose zeal was as great as his talent: Nicolas Baroudi. He was Syrian, born in Bmakinn on 3 December 1868. After entering in Paris in 1866, he pronounced his vows on 28 August 1888 and arrived in Peking in October 1890; ordained priest on 27 May 1893 he was placed in Zhengding.

He worked a few years in the missions; then he was occupied full time in the formation of the seminarians who were studying in the major seminary.

Baroudi was endowed with all the abilities of the ideal missionary, but his kindness surpassed his talents, or rather, it made these fruitful and it made him esteemed and loved by all. His influence as spiritual director was strong among the Chinese priests whom he had formed and who considered him as their father, but it was no less strong among his European confreres, who, too, had put their trust completely in him.

Being prudent and clever, Baroudi changed nothing, but maintained all the works and had them progressing to everybody's satisfaction. Being a practical man too, he was able to find the means to support the works entrusted to his management. He was an excellent gardener and farmer. Such a talent seems superfluous for a missionary. He used this talent, however, in such a way that it produced extremely useful results, though this activity seemed for him to be just a nice pastime.

The property where the episcopal residence was established was immense, and the neighboring property taken for the works of the Daughters of Charity was even larger. Baroudi, always thinking practically, thought that these fields, if cared for properly, could produce a large part of the grains and vegetables necessary for the two communities. The Sisters' community had to feed about two thousand people on average. Next, using orphans and still able-bodied men from the old people's home, he began to cultivate those fields and kept part of it for a vegetable garden. He ordered grains from Vilmorin and after some years of experimenting and of trying, he managed to adapt all kinds of European vegetables unknown in China to the Chinese climate.

Instead of wanting to keep his discoveries for himself, he published them either in the *Bulletin Catholique de Pékin*, or in a small magazine, the *Petit Jardinier* (The Little Gardener) and in this way he made known to missionaries the periods favorable for sowing and the methods for cultivating the different kinds of vegetables; he also gave advice on cultivating grapes and making wine.

De Vienne's Successor: Bishop Schraven

On the occasion of his canonical visit, de Guébriant proposed to Rome that this good missionary take possession of the vacant see.

But Baroudi flatly refused and expressed in a way that it was useless to ask him again. By decree from Rome of 16 December 1920 Father Schraven was named bishop of Amyclae and apostolic vicar of Zhengding.

François-Xavier Schraven was born in Grubbenvorst, in Limburg province (The Netherlands) on 13 October 1873. He was admitted in Paris on 29 September 1894, pronounced holy vows on 1 October 1896 and was ordained a priest there on 27 May 1899. After arriving in China, the following September, he was placed in Zhengding. Having ministered in several Christian communities, he was called to the episcopal residence to take care of the accounts. Then in October 1906, Bruguière died.

As vicar general, he assumed the administration of the vicariate until Bishop Coqset's arrival in 1907. Called to assist in the procure of Shanghai in 1908, he was afterwards transferred to the one in Tianjin in 1911. He returned to Shanghai in 1915, as [Maurice] Bouvier's successor. In Shanghai he received his nomination to be a bishop.

On 10 April 1921 Schraven received the episcopal consecration at the hands of his cousin, Bishop Geurts, in his cathedral of Zhengding.

By nominating de Vienne administrator of the vicariate of Tianjin immediately after Dumond's departure for Ganzhou, Rome had deprived Jarlin of a quite necessary coadjutor in such an important mission.

Hoping that he would be given back his right arm, the bishop of Peking waited for some time; but soon, aware that this hope was illusory, he took the initiative and asked Rome again for a coadjutor, indicating the person he wanted. He had to wait till 1923 to be satisfied.

Two decrees were decided in Rome on the same day, 12 June 1923: one nominated de Vienne as apostolic vicar of Tianjin, the other one made Fabrègues Jarlin's coadjutor with the right of succession.

This last nomination was a very painful surprise for the missionaries of Baoding; they were being deprived of a leader who had suited this young and already blossoming vicariate of Baoding well in such a short time.

After giving the administration of the vicariate over to his pro-vicar, Father Paul Montaigne, Fabrègues left Baoding in September 1923. The see remained vacant for more than a year. Finally, on 18 December 1924 Father Montaigne was named bishop of Sidyma and apostolic vicar of Baoding. Bishop Costantini consecrated him in Baoding on 19 April 1925.

We return now to the [Vincentian] Southern Province to follow the events there.

Chapter 22

New Vicariates for Jiangxi, 1920s

The Vicariate of North Jiangxi (Jiujiang) – Fatiguet's Nomination – A New Vicariate in Jiangxi – The Daughters of Charity Resumed their Works of Mercy in Nanchang – The Vicariate of Yujiang – The Apostolic Delegation in China – Catholics Presented Bishop Costantini with a Residence – A General Synod in China – The Plenary Council of Shanghai – Closure of the Council – The Missionary Exhibition of the Vatican – The Apostolic Vicariate of Ganzhou – Communism in Jiangxi and Elsewhere – Von Arx's Arrest – Capture of the Bishop, Missionaries and Sisters in Ji'an – Various Changes Among the Leaders of the Mission in Jiangxi

The Vicariate of North Jiangxi (Jiujiang)

We have seen that at Bishop Bray's death in 1905, Bishop Ferrant, his coadjutor since 1898, became apostolic vicar of this vicariate. His apostolate differed hardly from what it had been before, for during the seven years he was coadjutor, he took care of all the cases and certainly they were difficult, not only that of the Boxers, but even more that of the murders in Nanchang in 1906. He never became disconcerted and after the storm he took up the work again with the same courage as before.

Working together with Bishop Vic, he had the college of the Marist Brothers built in 1903. Then in 1906 there were the murders, followed by the looting and embezzlement narrated above. In the meantime, Ferrant founded the community of Chinese religious women of "Our Lady of Good Counsel," resembling the "Virgins of Purgatory," who like the Josephines had as their mission teaching children, orphans, and catechumens in the countryside.

In 1909, an accidental fire completely destroyed the college, rebuilt on the ruins of the first one destroyed in 1906. After this new catastrophe, however, the mission was unable to rebuild the institution a third time. Moreover, the Marist Brothers had such sad memories of Nanchang – the murder of their five young confreres – that they wanted to devote themselves to the service of the missions in other, more hospitable regions where their help was being requested.

Meanwhile the residence was rebuilt in 1910, and then the erection of the church that Ferrant planned to build in the town when the events of 1906 happened began.

In the winter 1909–1910, Ferrant made a long pastoral tour and wrote after his return: "How I enjoyed this visit! These missions, most of them young, are full of life and hope. In the old days, we harvested blade by blade. Today it is not rare to see groups of families and sometimes whole villages who ask to embrace the Faith."

Unfortunately, it was his last pastoral visit. Affected by a serious liver disease, he had to go to Shanghai to undergo surgery – perhaps inopportune – following which he died. It was 5 November 1910. Ferrant was only fifty-one years old.

During the twelve years that he governed the destinies of this mission, Ferrant, despite savage persecutions and sorrowful ordeals, had the consolation to see a threefold increase of his Christians and the reorganization and increase in the works of mercy. At his arrival (1898), he found 4,700 Faithful, at his death he left behind 15,060. Moreover, he constantly paid attention to forming a good Chinese clergy and Chinese religious women.

Fatiguet's Nomination

The vacancy did not last long. By apostolic brief of 24 February Father Louis Fatiguet was nominated bishop of Aspendus and apostolic vicar of North Jiangxi.

Louis Fatiguet was born in Bordeaux on 21 December 1855. Ordained a priest in that diocese on 17 December 1881, he practiced ministry there for four years and entered the Congregation of the Mission on 17 September 1885. On his arrival in China on 19 September 1886 he was placed in North Jiangxi.

After having got used to the language and customs, he was called to Jiujiang by Bray to take care of the accounts, restore the residence, and build a cathedral. These material activities did not completely absorb the missionary's zeal. Without interrupting these activities, he applied himself for many years to the evangelization of the pagan population that was living north of the river and succeeded in baptizing some five thousand people.

On 11 June 1911 his episcopal consecration took place in the cathedral of Jiujiang, which he himself had built. The consecrator was Bishop Jarlin. Three Vincentian bishops and one Franciscan bishop assisted. That year, the zeal of the bishop and his missionaries was rewarded through the relatively important harvest of four thousand baptisms of adults.

In 1920, the names of the vicariates were changed. In the previous chapter, we announced the new names of our vicariates in the North and in the South, but it is useful to recall here the ones of the Southern Province:

Table 22.1 Vicariate Names, Jiangxi, 1929

Former name	Current name	Civil province
Jiangxi North	Jiujiang until 1924; then Nanchang	Jiangxi
Jiangxi East	Yujiang	Jiangxi
Jiangxi South	Ji'an	Jiangxi
Jiangxi West	Ganzhou	Jiangxi

A New Vicariate in Jiangxi

It is the last one named on the list. On 15 August 1920 the Holy See decided to form a new vicariate in the southern part of Ji'an whose central residence would be in Ganzhou. This division became effective only after the arrival of the Vincentians from the United States of America. This new vicariate of Ganzhou was to be entrusted to them.

Let us leave this young vicariate just being formed. When it is going well, we shall talk about it again. For the time being let us continue exploring the vicariate of Jiujiang.

In 1918, Fatiguet founded a religious magazine, called *L'Ami des Missionnaires du Kiang-Si Septentrional* (The Friend of The Missionaries of North Jiangxi). This periodical came out twice a year with forty or fifty pages and even more and it has rendered great services not only to the missionaries of those times but also to present day historians.

It contained monographs on old missionaries, on the first Christian communities of these regions, and geographical descriptions, all written by either missionaries or by the bishop himself. This publication stopped in 1931, and despite its short life, its twenty-six installments are a precious source for the history of the missions in China.

The Daughters of Charity Resumed their Works of Mercy in Nanchang

On 25 February 1922, sixteen years after the destruction of the works in Nanchang, the bishop proceeded to inaugurate and bless the new institution of the Daughters of Charity, recently returned to take up their post again in the outskirts of Nanchang. He entrusted them with the hospital dedicated to Saint Louis, king of France. Two doctors, one French, the other Chinese, were engaged in it. The two dispensaries received quite a number of poor sick people every day.

On 3 December 1924 the Holy See changed the name of the vicariate of Jiujiang to the vicariate of Nanchang, the capital of the province, but it was never to be the episcopal residence of the bishops, except for Joseph Zhou after 1949, about whom we will talk later.

During Fatiguet's episcopacy, the vicariate, which had already ten stations or parishes, became enriched with fourteen more stations. The most important of all the parishes was by far the one of Jiujiang, the mother of all the others. Extensions and improvements were realized in the hospital, transforming it into a modern hospital.

Lastly, thanks to the generosity both of Chinese and foreign Catholics, a beautiful chapel was built near the small sanitarium that the mission owned in Guling since 1910, in the mountains near Jiujiang. Every year the freshness of the mountains draws thousands of holidaymakers from many Chinese provinces.

Conforming to Pope Pius XI's wishes to promote the progress of the Faith, especially by the local clergy, Fatiguet created at the end of 1927 a special district that he entrusted exclusively to his local clergy. Foreseeing the possibility that a vicariate for a Chinese bishop might be erected there later, he chose one of his best districts for that goal, the one of Ruizhou, where there was the ancient Christian community of Sanqiao. Regrettably, he could hardly suppose that after a small time Ruizhou would serve as headquarters for the communists formed by Moscow, who would come to make its initial intrusion into China.

The Vicariate of Yujiang

We left this vicariate at the very moment that Bishop Vic's successor had taken in hand the management of the vicariate. It was November 1912.

We have little information about the first ten years of Bishop Clerc-Renaud's episcopacy, because, unlike his predecessor, he did not write much. We have only an inventory of the vicariate dated from 1922. The bishop resided in Yujiang. The major seminary was erected in Jianchang, south of Yujiang with fifteen students. The minor seminary numbered thirty-one students.

The vicariate, which had three civil prefectures, was divided into four ecclesiastical districts:

1. The district of Fuzhou had 11,917 Christians spread over six parishes;

2. The district of Jianchang had 5,889 Christians in four parishes;

3. The district of Guangxin had 8,440 Faithful in seven parishes;

4. The district of Ruizhou numbered 4,309 Christians in four parishes.

The total was 30,555 Christians.

European priests 14; Chinese priests 14, four of whom were Vincentians. There were 9 Daughters of Charity, whose works were: an orphanage with 125 children; a workshop for 42 boarders and 73 workers living outside; and a hospital, where in that year 406 men and 73 women were treated.

The Apostolic Delegation in China

Though we are in the Southern Province, we must report on the institution of a very important organization of the Church in China. This organization does not concern only the two Vincentian provinces, but the whole of Catholic China. Besides we have alluded already several times to the person of the new apostolic delegate.

India and Japan had already been provided with an apostolic delegation; and yet China, so vast with its several hundreds of ecclesiastical entities still had to do without. Pius XI, on taking in hand the rudder of the bark of Peter and taking an anxious look at the entire Church, did not take long to discover this lack and fill it. The establishment of the apostolic delegation in China was one of the first important actions of his pontificate. Pius XI was very well informed about the ongoing progress of the Church in China, particularly through the accounts of the apostolic visitor, Bishop de Guébriant.

Bishop Celso Costantini, archbishop of Theodosia, was named for this important mission. Very approachable, stamped with politeness and candor, Costantini came from the practical world of parochial ministry – not from the Curia – and spent his life in contact with the people. A doctor in theology and philosophy, he was first parish priest of the cathedral in Concordia, his native region near Venice, where he remained for fifteen years. After the World War, during the troubles that distressed the diocese, he was nominated vicar general and led the diocese during the bishop's absence. Then, he performed various difficult missions, notably as administrator of Fiume after the occupation in 1921; he was made bishop of Fiume in 1921. When he had just finished building his episcopal residence there, Pius XI, knowing his eminent capabilities as an organizer, called him to be apostolic delegate in China. Costantini was forty-six years old at the time.

He arrived in Hong Kong on 8 November 1922 and stayed there for about a month; after that he went to Shanghai where he stayed for the Christmas celebrations and was very engaged during his short stay. The place of his residence had not yet been chosen. But a rumor spread that he was to be installed in the center of China, possibly in Hankou.

Costantini arrived in Peking on Thursday 28 December. The Christians of Peking and all the clergy received him in the cathedral of the Beitang. The delegate gave a very warm speech in Latin when addressing the priests and said some friendly words to everybody in French. On Saturday 30 December, he visited the Minister of France and the Minister of Italy, and the first day of the year 1923, together with Bishop de Vienne, went and presented his wishes to the president of the Republic, Li Yuanhong, who received him in a splendid manner, surrounded by his ministers and superior officers. The following days, he visited the most important institutions of Peking, and then he went for a few days and visited Tianjin and Baoding. Back in Peking, he wanted to visit all the Houses of Mercy. He did so with the greatest sympathy.

One of the joys the delegate expressed during these visits was the sight of so many Chinese religious women among the Daughters of Charity and the Franciscan Sisters.

Catholics Presented Bishop Costantini with a Residence

The kindness of the Holy Father, who had given them face by sending them his delegate, had touched the Christians so much that they greatly wished to show him their gratitude with a tangible sign, but they did not know how to tackle this problem. The Christians of Peking had already presented the delegate with a present, consisting of a chalice, a paten, and so on, everything in cloisonné enamel of Peking, but this was only a gift intended for the person of the delegate himself. What they really wanted was to prove their gratitude towards the Supreme Pontiff.

A member of the Catholic Council of Peking had the idea of presenting the apostolic delegation with a residence. The idea gained ground. But they did not know the place that Costantini had chosen or had to choose for his residence. On the other hand, they wanted all the Christians of China to contribute to this gift; they wrote the delegate a letter to ask him for his opinion. The letter ends in this way:

> It is up to you, Excellency, to decide yourself where you want to choose your residence, for the whole of Christian China, proud to have you, offers you, its hospitality. But if we dare to express a wish, it would be that Your Excellency chooses a place in Peking for his residence. Peking is for us as Rome is for the Church: it is not only the metropolis of our motherland, but it is also the place where the first preachers announced the gospel and where the first bishops founded the Church of China.

> Sixteen signatures of the members of the Council of Peking followed at the end.

Here in a few words is the substance of Costantini's answer:

> Hankou, 15 March 1923

> With great satisfaction I received your letter so noble in its form and so elevated in its spiritual meaning. . . . The emperor made the first gift of a piece of propriety to the Catholic Church in 1610 for Father Ricci's funeral monument (Chala). Your offer today has a still higher meaning of life. . . . I do not see any difficulty for settling in Peking. . . . I must, however, give you one recommendation: the house must be worthy of its destination; but please exclude every superfluous expenditure and luxury. If a ready-built house cannot be found, I shall be happy to give instructions for the construction. In that case the house will have a purely Chinese character. . . . (Then an exhortation to pray.)

> (Signed) Celso Costantini, apostolic delegate

The Catholics in Peking therefore did their utmost to find and acquire a property that would suit the apostolic delegation. They chose one that was in good condition. It consisted of numerous pavilions separated by rectangular yards with a few quite large buildings, one of which was fitted out as a chapel; all in Chinese style and a single level. This residence was located in the quarter called Dingfu dajie between the imperial palaces and the north wall of the city.

Costantini came and took possession of his residence on 18 July 1923 and right away His Excellency notified all the bishops of China of his installation.

A General Synod in China

As soon as he arrived in China, Costantini received instructions from Rome about the preparation of a general synod in China to be convened very soon. The delegate hurriedly informed the vicars apostolic and asked them to meet with each other in conferences in the principal centers that he indicated. In view of the coming synod, they were to study a series of questions whose outline he gave them.

These conferences took place from the end of 1922 and the beginning of 1923 in the following cities: Peking, Tianjin, Ji'an, Hankou, Zhifu, Shanghai and Hong Kong.

All these episcopal conferences had to be ratified by a larger conference. This one met on 25 May 1923 in Wuchang, the capital of Hubei, under the presidency of Costantini. This assembly consisted of counselor theologians, charged with uniting in one outline the opinions coming from the seven conferences. The assembly did its utmost to find general formulas that could be accepted in the whole area throughout China. The delegate had wanted the counselors to be chosen in a way that every order, congregation, or society of missionaries and even every nationality be represented in the Commission. Indeed, there were present in Wuchang: seven Chinese counselors, six Frenchmen, three Italians, two Belgians, one Dutchman, one German, one American and one Spaniard.

Under the vigorous leadership of the apostolic delegate, all the points of canon law concerning the future of the Church in China, all the means of religious promotion, all the big questions raised by intellectual developments were studied with great care. The conference lasted a month.

The Plenary Council of Shanghai

On 20 January 1924 through a brief, Pius XI enjoined Costantini to summon the apostolic vicars and prefects as well as the superiors of the different societies of missionaries in China for a general synod, which was to take the name of the Plenary Council of Shanghai, and which was to be opened in the Saint Ignatius church in Zikawei in the city of Shanghai on 15 May 1924.

At the time this council opened, China had thirty-five bishops and two apostolic prefects. The number of the priests was 2,552 among whom 1,071 were Chinese. There were one hundred eight members for the council, including the officers of the synod.

People might wonder why this council had not been given the name "general" instead of "plenary," or better "national," for actually it was indeed national: all the bishops of China took part, except obviously those who were prevented (ten) because of important reasons and who had duly informed the competent authorities. The reason had not been given officially, but it can easily be guessed.

Let us not forget that the Chinese nation was pagan. Once the foreigners who presided at the various missions in this nation had given their seats to Chinese bishops, the meeting of those at a general council would it seems naturally take the name of "national," but at that time, of the forty-seven mission leaders, making up the council, forty-five were foreign bishops; the two Chinese were just apostolic prefects and recently nominated. Let us add that the twenty-four religious superiors were also all foreigners. Consequently, the word "national" was not proper, whereas "plenary" fitted better and would not insult anybody.

Closure of the Council

The last plenary session of the great meeting was held in Saint Joseph of the Yangjingbang on 11 June.[70] The following day, the closing ceremony took place in Zikawei.

After Costantini celebrated the Pontifical Mass, the celebrant came forward to the foot of the altar and read the Latin formula of the consecration of China to the Blessed Virgin; all the bishops repeated it after him. Then the moving rites of closing the council took place. Next, the delegate repeated his feelings of affectionate admiration and wished them an excellent trip back to the communities entrusted to them. After signing the Acts of the Council, the fifty bishops in pairs formed a magnificent procession. The "Pathé" cinema company took pictures and several photographs of groups would remain a superb souvenir of these festivities.

The delegate sent the Acts of the Council to Rome and received from Pope Pius XI a letter dated 12 October 1924 acknowledging their receipt.

In his consistorial speech of 18 December 1924 the pope spoke first about the plenary council of Shanghai.

> We are happy to talk about the first General Council of China, which we announced to you last March and which in that huge country has radiated like a new dawn. In Shanghai, under the presidency

---

70.   The boundary between the British and the French Concessions. (JR)

of our apostolic delegate, all the apostolic vicars of the missions of China were assembled; no difference of race, motherland or religious family gave birth to divergence or division among them; only the charity of Christ, the same respect for the Holy See, and an equal compassion for this people that lacks the light of the gospel, animated all of them. . . . Now already we can foresee the council decisions will result in great steps forward for the Catholic Faith in these regions, and perhaps it will be given us to see them one day ourselves if, in his kindness, the Lord gives us a long enough life.

Finally, the apostolic delegate told all the bishops of China on 12 December 1928 that the decisions of the plenary council of Shanghai were to come into force on 12 June 1929.

The Missionary Exposition at the Vatican

The *Acta Apostolicae Sedis* of 5 May 1923 had a letter by His Holiness Pius XI to His Eminence the Prefect of the Sacred Congregation of Propaganda, Cardinal Van Rossum, about the universal exposition of the missions that was to be organized in the Vatican for the jubilee year of 1925.

The delegate gave instructions to all the leaders of missions in China, enjoining them to nominate a priest who would be especially charged with the preparation of the missionary exposition in the Vatican. All the missions had to participate by sending in objects. Later he sent them particular instructions about the choice of the objects to present.

This exposition was a great success. At the time of its solemn closure on 10 December 1925 the pope made a speech in which he underlined the results of the exposition:

> It has shown first of all the living universality of God's Church, for it was a true triumph of affectionate discipline. On one simple signal of the common father, there was an answer from all over the world with matchless energy, generosity and self-denial. Next, the exposition has been and remains like a huge book, of which every object is a page, a sentence, a phrase or a line demanding profound study in order to be read.

The Holy Father, however, did not want the pages of such a beautiful book to be scattered. He announced that the precious collection of objects brought together in the universal exposition would remain under the form of a Museum of the Missions, which would be located in the Lateran Palace.

Let us now return to the province of Jiangxi to witness the birth of a new apostolic vicariate.

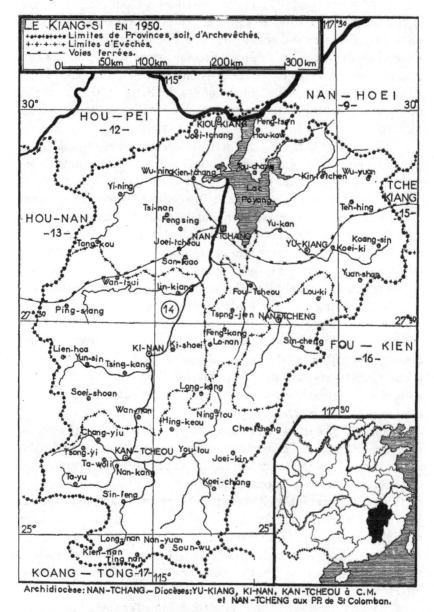

Map 22.1 Jiangxi in 1950 (Archdiocese: Nanchang; Dioceses: Yujiang, Ji'an, Ganzhou to C.M.; and Nancheng to the S.S.C.M.E.)

The Apostolic Vicariate of Ganzhou

We related how Dumond had been moved away from Tianjin in 1920 to be sent as administrator of the new vicariate of Ganzhou. Dumond left without delay, but did not go directly to his episcopal city. He stayed about a year in Jiujiang with Fatiguet because the workers of that mission were not yet in place. Actually, the apostolic document that erected this vicariate entrusted it to the Vincentians of the Eastern Province of the U.S.A. While waiting for their arrival, the previous missionaries of Ji'an continued to manage it.

The first group of the American missionaries arrived in Jiujiang on 24 August 1921. They were five priests, their superior Father John O'Shea was one of them, and four theology students.

The surface area of the vicariate of Ji'an before the division was about ninety thousand square kilometers, and the separated part was more or less fifty thousand. On the contrary, Ji'an had two million more people than Ganzhou. At the time of the separation the number of Catholics was 16,279 in Ji'an and 9,287 in Ganzhou.

These young evangelical workers had no experience of mission life in China. Arriving full of enthusiasm, they were amazed as they gathered their first impressions of the huge field that they had been asked to cultivate. What they were seeing did not correspond with what they had dreamed. But if the ideal that their imagination had formed in their mind about the missions in China was completely different from the reality, it did not diminish their zeal for the salvation of souls; and they began their work with as much courage as generosity.

In a letter, written in 1921 by one of them, we read: "These eight or nine months have been dedicated to a kind of apprenticeship under the direction of our good Bishop Dumond, apostolic administrator, and of three French veteran missionaries."

O'Shea saw that the Gan River (which has given its name to Ganzhou) had many branches in the country and that most of the waterways were navigable; he was astonished to notice that the missionaries were traveling with a mule or sedan, rarely over water, though a quicker means of travel. In order to solve this, therefore, he ordered Shanghai to have a little motorboat built for him.

At another time, an old-fashioned lamp almost caused a fire in their house. The superior immediately asked for the cost of an electrical installation and found in town a Chinese company that would take care of it cheaply. In this way those missionaries from across the Atlantic knew how to improve the comfort, which, we must admit, was at quite a low level when they arrived in this mission.

The first American Daughters of Charity embarked on 1 November 1924 to make the long trip across the Pacific in order to arrive in Ganzhou and set up their works of mercy.

Dumond became apostolic vicar of Ganzhou through a decree by the Holy See on 12 May 1925. The missionaries, most of whom were American, had already done good work, because the number of Christians of this vicariate had grown from 9,287 to 14,892. There were sixteen foreign priests, Vincentians, and as many Chinese priests of whom some were Vincentians.

Two years later, the vicariate had 16,228 Catholics. Then Dumond expressed to Rome his wish to have a coadjutor in the person of O'Shea. He was nominated indeed Dumond's coadjutor on 15 December 1927 and titular bishop of Midila in the consistory of the following 22 December. Dumond consecrated O'Shea on 1 May 1928.

John O'Shea was born on 7 October 1887 in Deep River (Connecticut, U.S.A.). He was admitted in the Congregation in 1908 and did his ecclesiastical studies in Germantown. Ordained on 30 May 1914 in Philadelphia, he was sent to Niagara University as professor. There in 1920 he received his nomination as superior of the missionaries of the future vicariate of Ganzhou.

Communism in Jiangxi and Elsewhere

Now we are at the first meeting point of the missionaries and the nationalist and communist revolution.

The history of this period is so complex that it is impossible to make here even the shortest summary. Let us just take up some markers so as to date and locate the facts that concern the missions.[71]

In 1916, General Zhang Xun's failure to restore the empire gave a new chance to the enemies of the dynasty: the revolutionary Sun Wen and his partisans of the Guomindang. Canton proclaimed its independence and gave itself a constitutional military government with Sun as its generalissimo. A war broke out then against the North Republic, characterized as reactionary and imperialist. Sun achieved easy successes in the south and

---

71. Ferreux's notes: Sun Wen seemed sincerely to long for an amicable reunion of the North and the South.

went as far as Nanjing where he set up his capital. But the reverses that the northern armies inflicted on him forced him to go back to Canton.[72]

In 1923, he called in Soviet councilors. Moscow hastened to send him Borodin and Gallen and a numerous staff. That was the beginning of the red period that saw blossom a military, political, and social organization copied from Moscow's.[73]

---

72. Ferreux's notes: from the beginning, the government in Canton was very well supported by Russia, which considered Sun Wen and his companions to be agents of Bolshevik propaganda able to conquer the whole of China.

73. Ferreux's notes: Those two did their utmost to inspire the Guomindang party's exaltation of nationalism and resistance against the imperialism of the capitalist Powers. Then the national government became aware that the USSR tried to hand China over to the Third International (Communist International), at least to its agents, so it began a fierce fight against Communism. It was a little late. In several provinces of the South, Communism already existed. (See, Escarra, *La Chine, passé et présent*, pp. 151–153.) Let us mention some dates: In 1917, there was still no trace of Communism in China. In 1919, Sun Wen got in touch with Moscow. He admired their methods, not their ideology. Some students of "Young China" knew this and made contact with Russian Soviets who had entered Canton quietly. In 1920, in Shanghai, Canton and Peking, three cells were formed of already about a hundred members. Communism was spreading and followers were quickly multiplying. In 1922, there were enough followers so that their groups could send twenty delegates to a Communist congress in Shanghai. They asked for affiliation to the Third International. In 1924, a nationalist congress was held in Canton summoned by Sun Wen; among the members there were quite a few Communists; Sun Wen, however, declared that he admitted them, not as nationalists, but as helpers to make up the numbers for the war they were preparing to wage against the north. Two parties had formed: the one of Canton or the Southern Party, which was calling itself also "National"; the opposing party, more or less linked to the central government in Peking, called themselves the Northerners and their soldiers called themselves the "Pacification Army." It was an alliance of several generals against the south. Never winners or losers, the southerners, helped by Red Russia from where they got money, arms and guidance, made clever propaganda south of the Yangtze. At the Russian Soviets' instigation a cadets' school was created in Canton. Thousands of young people from the schools came and filled it. Many others went to Russia in order to get a better initiation into Bolshevist theory and the art of spreading it. Beginning in 1926, the Southerners felt able to launch a major offensive under the leadership of the young general Chiang Kai-shek, whom Europeans were to call Chiang Kai-shek according to the Cantonese dialect. Success smiled on them from the beginning, and their enthusiasm was great, when in September the Southerners were resolutely entering Jiangxi. We shall not describe the ups and downs of national events further. We are interested in the Southerners' behavior towards the Catholic Missions. Immediately after the Boxers' Rebellion, from 1901 onwards, the properties of the missions were respected as never before. Disorderly soldiers or bandits invaded them only rarely. Because of such immunity, which they enjoyed during each local war, missionaries' residences would be filled with merchandise and other riches, which the inhabitants, pagan

To achieve his program, and to reestablish the integral sovereignty of China, Sun first had to realize the unification of North and South. He went to Peking in 1924 to meet the important commanders Duan Qirui, Feng Yuxiang and Zhang Zuolin. The conference did not succeed and Sun, leader of the Guomingdang, arriving sick in the capital, died there on 12 March 1925.

On 1 July 1925 Wang Jingwei succeeded him as president of the nationalist south government. The efforts to achieve harmony with the north having failed, it was necessary, in order to reorganize China, to get rid of these reactionary military chiefs. The war began again. The first actions were the conquests of Guangdong and Guangxi, the two first provinces placed under the control of the Guomingdang.

After the second national congress, which took place in the beginning of 1926, General Chiang Kai-shek was nominated commander in chief of the nationalist army. During that year, Fujian, Jiangxi, Hubei and Hunan were taken away from the Northerners one after the other. The presence of these nationalist troops, who were xenophobic and thus the enemies of whatever was foreign, including religion and its members, wreaked havoc in the missions of these provinces.

Let us quote here some witnesses from the Jiangxi province, where we left the reader so as to open this long parenthesis.

On 1 October 1926 Dumond wrote from Ganzhou:

> Here we are again, for the third time since my arrival in Ganzhou, under the rule of the Canton government. Let us hope that our new masters will be pushed back out of our province, as happened the last two times; or else a Soviet regime will be set up. That regime does not recognize any of the privileges agreed upon by the treaties either for the missions or for foreigners.

On 18 November the same bishop wrote:

> This time the situation seems more serious than in the past: the capital Nanchang and the door of Jiangxi, Jiujiang, have just fallen into their hands. The southern troops, composed mostly of minors

or Christian, had hastened to deposit at their own risk as in a sure asylum. Regular troops never thought about setting up their quarters there. Soldiers had orders to respect the compound of the mission. They never entered, except from curiosity and with the priest's permission, in small groups and as well-behaved visitors. For that matter they knew that in times of public disaster, flood or draught, missionaries were the first distributors of help, even when these relief goods did not come from the mission itself but were provided by an exterior organization.

and led by Russians, march for an ideal: to destroy imperialism, expel the foreigners, abolish Christianity and all other religions, and, above all, to replace the others and share the goods in a uniform way. Students are, as always, at the head of the movement.

Bishop Ciceri on 2 November 1926 wrote from Ji'an to the superior general: "Since the Bolshevik troops have taken Jiangxi, we have been living moments of anxiety. . . . After they chased the missionaries away, soldiers occupied many of our churches, oratories and residences."

From Nanchang, Father Monteil announced that the Sisters were taking care of wounded and sick occupying forces to the exclusion of every northern soldier. "Those people," he wrote on 7 December, "are rude. They are anti-Christian and anti-European and would even like to indoctrinate the Chinese Sisters."

From Yujiang, Bishop Clerc-Renaud described similar abuses of power on the part of the southern armies. There were cases, more serious, where people and even their lives were not spared.

Von Arx's Arrest

Father Henri Von Arx, a confrere of Swiss nationality, missionary in the vicariate of Nanchang, prepared himself on 15 October 1930 to leave his residence of Pengze to make his annual visit of Christian communities, when he was told that Communist troops were approaching the city. Believing that Nanchang was well defended by the Northerners, he did not worry much about it and, though he was advised to flee, he did not want to abandon his post. He said only that he was deferring his trip for some days. The next day in the evening, the Reds arrived. Towards nine o'clock in the evening, wild screams and gunshots were heard. The whole town was invaded, even the residence. Von Arx was caught, tied up and locked in the boys' school. A battalion of Reds occupied the church and the schools. The commander settled in the priest's residence. The next two days were days of looting, murdering and the pursuit of rich and influential people.

These gangsters, however, fearing the arrival of the gunboats of the Northerners, left Pengze on 10 October, taking away with them about thirty prisoners, among whom the missionary and his servant Luo. Three days later, news arrived that the prisoners had arrived in the neighborhood of the Christian community of Xiebu, fifty kilometers to the south. On 29 October the servant Luo was freed by the gangsters' boss and ordered to take to the Catholic mission of Jiujiang a letter demanding a ransom. It was said at the end of November that von Arx was kept prisoner in Jingdezhen, a large industrial town (that produced chinaware). After that, despite searching and inquiring, no news about him could ever be garnered. When and how did he die? We may never know. It is quite probable that this innocent victim may not have been able to endure the bad treatment inflicted on him. He might have died during his first year in prison.

Capture of the Bishop, Missionaries and Sisters in Ji'an

Before beginning the report of this sad event, we must introduce the apostolic vicar of Ji'an, the Reds' victim.

Bishop Ciceri, exhausted at age seventy-three, had returned to Italy in August 1927 to take a rest. There, he asked the Holy See for a coadjutor.

He was given satisfaction: one of his missionaries, Father Mignani, was elected as coadjutor with the right of succession, and he was nominated bishop of Cassandria on 16 July 1928.

Gaetano Mignani was born in Castelfranco (Bologna) on 31 August 1882; in October 1904 he was admitted in the Congregation of the Mission in Rome; he was ordained there on 19 March 1905. He practiced his ministry in Italy and was sent to Ji'an in China only in 1923. Dumond consecrated him in that town on 17 February 1929 and took over as apostolic vicar of Ji'an from Ciceri when the latter, still disabled, had submitted his resignation on 15 October 1931.

In these very troubled times, sometimes there were quiet periods. On 17 February the consecration could be celebrated in the cathedral of Ji'an. The consecrating bishop was to be the apostolic delegate, who at that moment was in Shanghai on an apostolic tour. Prevented, however, through some disease, His Excellency telegraphed Ji'an that he was abandoning making this long trip and at the same time he invited Dumond to consecrate the new bishop-elect. That is what was done.

Let us return to our report. For more than a year, the Communists had been occupying almost all the sub-prefectures around. Pushed back from Hunan in September 1930, this Red army was made up of the troops of General Zhu De, but the real chief was Mao Zedong.[74] It came back to Jiangxi in order to attack Ji'an.

74.　Ferreux's notes: These two names should be remembered. These two men have led

General Deng Ying was commanding the thirteenth division of the Northerners charged with the defense of Ji'an. This division had only four thousand soldiers against the thirty thousand Southerners, well-armed with rifles, machine guns and cannons, commanded by good officers of the regular army who had gone over to the Revolution.

A huge group of more than twenty thousand men followed the Red Army: they were farmers and people recruited from everywhere, armed with hunting guns, spears and swords, even with baskets to carry away the fruit of their lootings.

Towards 1 October, the town of Ji'an was surrounded and the defenders, aware of being inferior, thought of fleeing. On the 4th, before dawn, the Reds attacked. The battle lasted until the night. At that moment, General Deng Ying, believing all resistance useless, fled by the river with the remains of his army. When the victorious troops entered, the town was filled with refugees, who had come from the countryside and neighboring towns with a big part of their belongings. Moreover, Ji'an had many well-stocked shops, resulting in fruitful looting.

The Catholic institutions were numerous in city and in the suburbs. There were two parishes, a seminary, a hospital, works of charity of the Daughters of Charity and the formation house of the Daughters of Saint Anne.

On 5 October 1930, the day that the Red Army entered Ji'an, the managing personnel of all those institutions were at their posts. As soon as the Reds entered the city, the missionaries scattered, looking for shelter in the houses of the Christians; but they were discovered very quickly. Bishop Mignani and Father Fernand Thieffry were apprehended, tied up, beaten and then locked up in a jail, together with the notables of the town and some northern officers. They were told: "We know that you are the vanguard of the imperialists; that is the reason why you have to leave the country; for the moment you will only be penalized." Then they were freed and led to the hospital with other missionaries to care for wounded people there.

On 13 October the Red governor released the bishop and Father de Jenlis, on condition that they go to Shanghai to get five hundred thousand dollars ransom for the foreign priests and Sisters. They were given a passport to be able to cross the Reds' lines. From there, they left for Jiujiang and later on for Shanghai. During that time, missionaries and

---

China to the point where it is now today (1963) and have the fate of this big country in their hands.

Sisters were led to an immense temple in order to care for wounded people. Two Chinese priests, Fathers Paul Chen and Matthieu Jin, hidden in Christian families were discovered and sentenced to death because they were guilty of having been "[running] dogs for the foreign imperialists and spreaders of superstition." They were forthwith executed, without any other judgment.

There were nine prisoners, of whom four were priests: Fathers Thieffry, Edouard Barbato, Antoine Capozzi and Octave Purino; and five Daughters of Charity: Sister Leport, superioress, Sister Merle, Sister Larmichant, Sister Rognoni, and Sister Ramos. The Chinese Sisters were kept in their house in Ji'an, whose first floor was occupied by Red officers.

The other European and Chinese priests were able to escape, some to Nanchang, some to other places. The murders of the notables took several days, at the rate of one hundred fifty a day, said a refugee escaped from this hell.

What was going to be the fate of our prisoners? To understand how they were to be saved, we have to reverse course a little and follow the political events.

Having conquered the central provinces, the Nationalist government moved to Hankou on 1 January 1927. They occupied Nanjing on 15 March and Shanghai eight days later.

The influence of Borodin and Soviet councilors dominated the government of Hankou. The differences of opinion that had existed for a long time between the moderates in the party and those with a Communist tendency became so serious that Chiang Kai-shek was deposed as commander by the extremists. This was the rupture. The generalissimo on 18 April 1927 established a new government in Nanjing, which immediately fought the one in Hankou and demanded the ejection of all the Soviet agents.

In autumn 1927, the troops in Jiangxi, having joined the Chiang Kai-shek party, took Hankou. Borodin and his agents had fled. Wang Jingwei, with the extreme left, disappeared from the scene. On the other hand, two northern generals, Yan Xishan and Feng Yuxiang joined the nationalist cause. In March 1928, Chiang Kai-shek took up again the attack against the Northerners and three months later he entered Peking. That was the victory of Nanjing and the Kuomintang. Chiang Kai-shek then undertook a new campaign against his Communist adversaries that would enable the release of our prisoners in Ji'an.

From the beginning of November, many southern troops in Nanjing moved to Jiangxi. In the first days of December, the regulars recaptured

Ji'an. On the 23rd the prisoners were in the Reds' headquarters in the neighborhood of Donggu, eighty kilometers to the south of Ji'an. While drawing back before the regular troops, the Reds concealed the prisoners in a small village hidden in a deep valley and guarded them to prevent them from fleeing, for they certainly hoped to come back and retake their prisoners. But that was not what happened. When the guards heard the gunshots from the enemies' camp, they fled. Then the prisoners left their hiding places and saw some soldiers on the top of a hill. Fathers Thieffry and Purino hurriedly improvised a red cross flag with a Sister's white apron and a piece of red tissue, and waved it for an hour. After long hesitations, two of the regular soldiers came to investigate and were very surprised to face nine prisoners. They took them to their camp, where the officers were equally astonished by their discovery, too.

The prisoners, all in good health were congratulated heartily by the pagan general of the regular troops, who received them in Donggu. He himself told them: "Your Shangdi (God) has delivered you."

On Christmas day, they were brought to Ji'an by three companies and presented to the governor. He had a good meal prepared for them and seeing their miserable clothes, he gave them a thousand dollars to buy something to wear. However, the situation in Jiangxi was still far from secure, because the Reds had only been dislodged but not suppressed. That is why the governor had all the prisoners taken to Shanghai at his expense.

Various Changes among the Leaders of the Missions

Towards the end of 1927, Bishop Clerc-Renaud received considerable reinforcements through the arrival in Yujiang of several groups of American confreres. But broken by illnesses and ordeals, he had begged the Holy See to give him a successor, while expressing his desire to submit his resignation. Rome granted his wish, but delayed the decree till 4 February 1929. With this decree Father Edward Sheehan was nominated bishop of Calydon and apostolic vicar of Yujiang.

Father Sheehan, born in Farm Ridge (Illinois) on 22 May 1888 was admitted in the Congregation on 30 April 1908 in Perryville (Missouri) and was ordained on 7 June 1916. Sent to China, he arrived in Yujiang in February 1923. Clerc-Renaud consecrated him on 14 July 1929.

Since his arrival in China in 1886, Bishop Fatiguet had never returned to Europe. At the period we are talking about now, he liked to speak of an upcoming trip. The continuous troubles made him delay his trip. In October 1930, Von Arx's seizure and mysterious captivity gave him profound pain. Von Arx had been one of his collaborators. Already affected by laryngitis, the bishop's condition quickly worsened. On 11 February 1931 Fatiguet received the last rites completely conscious and died the next afternoon at 2 P.M.

Fatiguet had been a great bishop. His distinguished manners and his enthusiastic ardor inspired trust. He knew how to encourage missionaries and Christians and he could ask much of them because he too exerted himself to the limit.

It did not take the Holy See long to fill the vacancy of this important see; on 3 July 1931 a decree from Rome moved Dumond from Ganzhou to Nanchang. By taking possession of the vicariate of Nanchang, Dumond was put at the head of seventeen European and twenty Chinese priests, with 31,649 Catholics. O'Shea succeeded him as apostolic vicar of Ganzhou.

Let us give peace some time to be established again in Jiangxi and let us go in the meantime to the civil province of Zhejiang.

Chapter 23

New Vicariates for Zhejiang, 1920s

Vicariates of Zhejiang – The Vicariate of Ningbo – Bishop Reynaud's Funeral in Ningbo – Nomination of Six Chinese Bishops – The Consecration of the Six Chinese Bishops by His Holiness Pius XI in Rome – Bishop Joseph Hu Takes Possession of the Vicariate of Taizhou – Bishop Reynaud's Successor – Bishop Defebvre – Adversities: Deaths, Captures and Massacres – A Model Missionary: Claude Guilloux – François Boisard's Premature Death – Ibarruthy's Beautiful Death – Cyprien Aroud's Apostolic Zeal – Three More Victims of the Communists in Ji'an – The Murder of, Giacomo Anselmo, – The Murder of Joseph Hu – Bishop Sheehan's Death – His Successor: Bishop Paul Misner

The Vicariates of Zhejiang

Our account on Zhejiang finished at the erection of the new vicariate of Hangzhou, first under the name of West Zhejiang, later on simply under the name of Hangzhou, with Bishop Faveau as apostolic vicar.

Hangzhou, the capital of Zhejiang, is a very old city. It was the capital of the empire at the end of the Song dynasty from 1140 to 1279. It has a population of about six hundred thousand inhabitants, but the walls stretch out over an immense area, hardly half of which is inhabited; the other half is cultivated.

The only church in Hangzhou was one of the oldest of the missionary era in the Far East opened by the Portuguese with Saint Francis Xavier and the Jesuits, his successors.[75] It was necessary to wait till the time of Father Ricci, who reached Peking in 1601. His immediate suc-

---

75.   Ferreux's notes: Remember that the Nestorians blossomed in China from the sixth till the eighth century. Having been chased out of China by the emperors, they came back in the eleventh and towards 1280 they put up a monastery in Hangzhou, then they left without leaving any traces. . . . In the beginning of the fourteenth century, Rome sent to China Franciscans, who built up in Hangzhou a beautiful Christian community. The town, however, was destroyed through the revolution that in 1368 overthrew the Tartar dynasty of the Yuan and replaced it with the Ming dynasty, this one purely Chinese – which was unfortunate for religion, because those Chinese emperors, tolerated no foreign influence, chased away all the Europeans and hermetically sealed all the entrances of China.

cessor, Father Longobardi, sent Father Cattaneo to Hangzhou together with Doctor Léon Li Zhizao, a native of this city. There they converted Doctor Michael Yang Tingyun, a very famous mandarin of high rank. The latter had a first church and residence built, where Cattaneo spent the his final years. Thirty years later, Father Martini, one of a group of four Jesuit Fathers there, rebuilt the church on a larger scale with decorations in European style: work on it was finished only in 1661 by Father Augery. It was, according to the missionaries of that time, "the most beautiful and the most talked about church in the whole of China." Other Jesuits went to the big town of Shaoxing and made some conversions. Unfortunately, a fire destroyed the church in 1692. Restored or rebuilt, it was confiscated at the time of the persecution of 1730. An edict by the Yongzheng emperor ordered all the churches to be transformed into temples. At the residence of Hangzhou, the stone on which the edict was engraved can still be seen. The building exists also, but on the front, separated from the church by a yard, the pagans had raised a platform, similar to their temples to expose their idols, and a hall to store the decorations and cult objects.

When Bishop Delaplace came in 1854 and took possession of his vicariate of Zhejiang, the idols were still there, though Emperor Daoguang had published an edict of tolerance in 1846, ordering that all the churches changed into temples must be brought back to their first destination. Publishing a decree is one thing, realizing its execution is another, for the mandarins, being very superstitious, needed a lot of persuading to execute them. To sum up, the church was given back, it was restored, but the hall was left as it was, without the statues. Three rooms were made there, one to live in, the others to store decorations.

Bishop Faveau, the new bishop, had a plan to destroy that hall and to use the material to enlarge the church that had become too small. Then, during the night of 21 to 22 November 1912 a fire broke out in the hall. The firefighters were able to keep the church and the residence, but the materials they were counting on were burned to ashes. One had to wait till 1916 to be able finally to enlarge the church.

One of the first of Faveau's achievements was the construction of the minor seminary. In the residence of Hangzhou there were no rooms big enough to receive the eighteen seminarians who up till then had been studying in Ningbo.

The revolution of 1911–1912 took place without harming this vicariate very much. Later on, political convulsions that followed one another from

1926 onwards; one government expelling the other caused troubles and anxieties here and there, but never completely blocked the works of the missionaries. That is the reason why regularly the number of the Faithful grew and the works prospered.

The following comparative list, covering twenty years of Faveau's episcopacy, shows clearly the progress achieved.

Table 23.1 Zhejiang Numbers during Faveau's Episcopacy, 1910–1930

Categories	1910	1930
Christians	10,318	32,100
Foreign priests	8	12
Chinese priests	13	41
Seminarians in major seminary	4	27
Seminarians in minor seminary	15	52
Daughters of Charity – foreign and Chinese	17	31
Chinese religious women	6	37
Residences	15	25
Churches and chapels	170	220
Hospitals	0	2
Homes for the elderly	1	2
Chinese priests ordained	0	36

In 1935, Faveau, aged seventy-six, felt his strength waning, and not wanting the administration of the vicariate to suffer because of it, wished not for a coadjutor, but to hand on the burden entirely to younger shoulders. Rome had no problem with accepting his resignation, but nominated him administrator of the vicariate while awaiting his successor's nomination.

On 18 February 1937 Father Georges Deymier was nominated bishop of Diospolis and apostolic vicar of Hangzhou. Faveau immediately retired in the house of Jiaxing, where he still practiced a fruitful ministry till his death.

Georges Deymier, born in Saint-Michel-Lapujade (Gironde) on 13 February 1886 was admitted in Dax on 4 September 1904, was ordained on 14 July 1912, and arrived in China on the following 7 September. He was first appointed to the minor seminary of Hangzhou, and then became both procurator and the director of the Hangzhou district. Faveau himself consecrated Deymier in the cathedral on 30 May 1937. That year was the beginning of the Sino-Japanese conflict – which was a real war – and which was to cause so many difficulties in all the missions of China and give missionaries hard servitudes for many years. We will come back to this topic.

The Vicariate of Ningbo

A short time before the Council of Shanghai, during which Bishop Reynaud, dean of the bishops in China, was to play an eminent role, the missionaries and Christians of Ningbo wanted to celebrate a threefold anniversary in honor of their revered bishop. That year of 1924 was indeed the seventieth of his age, the fiftieth of his religious life and the fortieth as a bishop.

These were beautiful feasts where Christians and missionaries tried to outdo each other in good taste to decorate cathedral, residence, and reception rooms.

The most important Christian communities sent their delegates bringing gifts and offerings labeled with flattering inscriptions for the benefit of the revered bishop celebrating his jubilee. At the thanksgiving Mass, celebrated by the bishop himself, all were united, praying for the intention of their first shepherd, thanking God for the many and fruitful years granted him for the greatest wellbeing of China. When Father Yin, the preacher of the day, went into the pulpit, his impressive audience listened with profound interest to the dignified exposition he gave of the meaning of this threefold anniversary. He finished his explanations with an exhortation for all to imitate the beautiful examples they all had witnessed.

The year 1925 highlighted the sixteenth centenary of the great council of Nicea and was celebrated in Rome as a jubilee year. For the Congregation, that year was the three hundredth anniversary of its own foundation by Saint Vincent; moreover, the convocation of a general assembly had been decided for that year. His confreres had chosen Reynaud as their delegate to the assembly. So many reasons for the bishop not to hesitate to go to Europe!

The bishop, however, felt his strength leaving him more and more. At the council of Shanghai, he left the impression of a man at the end of his abilities. He would therefore have liked very much to free himself of a long and for him tiring trip. On the other hand, the reasons to go were in his eyes so pressing, that he thought it would be a lack at least of good manners if he stayed away. He embarked in July and having spent some time in France went to Rome. His health was deteriorating rapidly.

Back in Paris in the beginning of January 1926, he had to take to his bed and he would never get up again. Reynaud went to sleep in the Lord on 23 February 1926. The funeral was on the 26th. The superior general began the funeral in the house; Faveau, who was in France for the same reasons as Bishop Reynaud, sang the High Mass. The five final absolutions at the bier were performed by Bishops Chaptal, Faveau, Fabrègues, coadjutor of Peking, de Guébriant, superior of the M.E.P., and Cardinal Dubois. Behind the catafalque there were numerous official personalities. The burial was done temporarily in the Montparnasse cemetery, because of the reasons that follow.

Bishop Reynaud's Funeral in Ningbo

A few days after Reynaud's death, a telegram from China announced that the Christians in Ningbo claimed their venerated bishop's precious remains. In their filial piety, these Faithful had decided on his return and they set about doing it at their own expense. They were answered: "On the first boat, the one on 12 March, Faveau will embark bringing you the precious cargo entrusted to his care." The Christians were happy and the missionaries were proud; and rightly so, this gesture was an honor both for those who made the gesture and for the one who had been able to inspire the gesture.

The maritime freight company for its part, in charge of the transportation, wanted to give the noble dead bishop a witness of high respect by doing the transport free of charge.

On 15 April 1926 the *Angers* docked in Shanghai and Father Jean-Baptiste Lepers, pro-vicar, took delivery of the precious cargo entrusted to Faveau. On Sunday 18 April the venerated shepherd's coffin was received in Ningbo with a religious ceremony. On the following 24th a solemn funeral was celebrated.

According to his wish, several times expressed, Reynaud was to rest among his people in the cathedral, near the residence where he had had lived so many years.

Nomination of Six Chinese Bishops

The choice of six Chinese bishops by Pope Pius XI by a decree of 24 June 1926 was an event of major importance for the missions in China. These are their names:

1. Father Philippe Zhao, a diocesan priest of the vicariate of Peking, appointed bishop of Vaga and apostolic vicar of Xuanhua (Hebei).

2. Bishop Melchior Sun, C.M., apostolic prefect of Lixian, appointed bishop of Esbon and apostolic vicar of Lixian (Hebei).

3. Bishop Odoric Cheng, O.F.M., apostolic prefect of Puqi, appointed bishop of Cottena [Cotenna].

4. Father Louis Chen, O.F.M., appointed apostolic vicar of Fenyang (Shanxi).

5. Father Simon Zhu, S.J., appointed bishop of Lesvi and apostolic vicar of Haimen (Jiangsu).

6. Father Joseph Hu, C.M., appointed bishop of Theodosiopolis and apostolic vicar of Taizhou [Linhai] (Zhejiang).

As can be seen, two Chinese Vincentians, Sun and Hu, became bishops. Moreover, Bishop Zhao, a diocesan priest, did all his studies in the Vincentian seminary of the Beitang. Therefore, it is possible to judge the value of Lebbe's angry declarations, claiming that the Vincentians, his confreres, had forgotten only one thing in their work in China: the formation of a clergy able to assume the episcopacy.

When Rome decided to create a Chinese episcopacy, there was no difficulty in finding the three first clergymen among those who had been formed by Vincentians, while waiting to choose others when as needed, as in:

1928: Bishop Pierre Cheng, diocesan, apostolic vicar of Xuanhua;

1931: Bishop Joseph Zhou, C.M., apostolic vicar of Baoding;

1932: Bishop Jean Zhang, diocesan, apostolic vicar of Zhaoxian;

1936: Bishop Joseph Zhang, apostolic vicar of Xuanhua;

1937: Bishop Jean Baptiste Wang, C.M., apostolic vicar of Anguo;

1939: Bishop Job Chen, C.M., apostolic vicar of Zhengding;

1947: Bishop Peter Wang, diocesan, apostolic vicar of Xuanhua;

1948: Bishop Joseph Fan, diocesan, apostolic vicar of Baoding.

All these diocesan and religious had been formed in the seminaries directed by the Congregation of the Mission.

Consecration of Six Chinese Bishops by Pius XI in Rome

As announced, the six newly nominated bishops went to Rome to receive episcopal consecration from the Supreme Pontiff's very hands. On 10 September 1926 they embarked in Shanghai with the apostolic delegate.

On Thursday 28 October 1926, feast of Saints Simon and Jude, anniversary of his own episcopal consecration in Warsaw, Pope Pius XI consecrated with his own hands the first six Chinese bishops.[76] Here is not the place to describe that beautiful ceremony. The newspapers and other publications of the time filled their columns with the story.

After the consecration, the six new bishops in their answer to the speech the Holy Father insisted with much delicacy on the feelings of gratitude they felt towards the missionaries who had brought them the blessings of the truth at the expense of their lives.

In Rome, the Gregorian University, counting fourteen hundred students of various nationalities, received the Chinese bishops solemnly, greeting them in more than twenty languages. Among the six bishops, only three spoke French fluently; the others understood it just a little.

Leaving Rome, some of them went to Assisi and to other Italian sanctuaries; the others went to Lourdes, and then to Paris, where they all met again. Cardinal Dubois received them in Notre Dame, where one of them spoke in Chinese to his present compatriots. Bishop Hu spoke in French and amazed the audience because of the facility of his diction. He made them smile when expressing his gratitude for the warm reception the French Catholics had given the new Chinese bishops, he repeated several times: "C'est épatant!" (That's terrific!).

Then they were taken to several cities in France and even in Belgium and the Netherlands.

They arrived back in China only in March 1927 and were received with much joy.

---

76. The first Chinese bishop was actually Grégoire Luo, with the Portuguese family name of Lopez. He was a Dominican. He was consecrated in Canton on 8 April 1685. He exercised his episcopal office amid great difficulties until his death, on 27 February 1691. Ordained in Manila in March 1656, he was also the first Chinese priest.

Bishop Joseph Hu Takes Possession of the Vicariate of Taizhou

The evangelization of the region of Taizhou had not yet gone very far. In 1927, the number of Christians was 4,383. There were six Chinese priests and one European, who left after a few years. There were fifteen seminarians in the major seminary and eight in the minor seminary; all in the seminaries of Ningbo. There were also fourteen Virgins of Purgatory.

When the new bishops returned to China, the political and civil situation in Zhejiang was such that prudence advised Hu to defer taking possession of his vicariate. The Christians and missionaries could not do this ceremony decently without some exterior show of joy. It was decided that, when the situation would become better, the feast would be held at the first anniversary of the bishop's consecration, that is, at the end of October 1927. That is what was done and in a satisfying way.

The mission had only one single residence in the town of Taizhou and Hu wanted to settle in Haimen, a small port on the East Sea, where there was a pied-à-terre built by Father Lepers which could be easily changed into a real residence. On the other hand, Hu had very cordial relations with the Taizhou authorities, whereas he had none with the Haimen authorities. The question was then to get acquainted with the latter. The bishop gave it a try. He invited some twenty Taizhou authorities and notables. All without any exception accepted the invitation. This was a good omen. But for the reception at the taking possession ceremony, it was necessary to invite the Haimen authorities, too. Haimen was to be the future episcopal residence. As a result, all those pagan personalities not only accepted the invitation, but several of them offered to work together with the Christians to prepare the festivity with as much dignity as possible.

A few days before Sunday 13 November, the date fixed for the celebration of the feast, gifts and presents of all kinds came showing how people honored Hu and the mission.

On Sunday morning the bishop entered the church solemnly in order to celebrate the Pontifical Mass. After the gospel, a Chinese priest explained the reason of this ceremony to the Christians and to the pagans. After the Mass, Hu had a light meal and clothed in his Roman mantle, he entered the hall and received the homage of all the authorities and notables: everybody in his turn came in front of the bishop, bowed three times and the majority kissed his ring.

Nobody stayed away: bank directors, the Chamber of Commerce director, government chiefs and police chiefs, all paid tribute. Hu, with dignity and affability responded to all those polite compliments. In the evening a dinner took place that seated one hundred seventy guests. This celebration was an excellent occasion for the missionaries to get acquainted with many people whom they had known just a little or not at all. Let us say here some words about Bishop Hu.

Joseph Hu belonged to a line of Christians that numbered already eleven generations born in Ningbo. He was born in Dinghai, a small port of the Zhoushan Archipelago on 22 February 1881. He studied in the seminary of Ningbo, which was located in Dinghai.

When Father Boscat, the visitor, returned from France in November 1902 with ten Vincentian clerics as foundations of the provincial house of China, he brought them temporarily to the minor seminary of Dinghai to continue their studies, while waiting for the construction of the house that was going to be the novitiate and house of studies.

The students of the minor seminary therefore had to move and settle down in another building very near the seminary. Father Barberet, director of the minor seminary, had appointed Joseph Hu, a young student of the rhetoric class, the liaison with the Europeans, among whom was the director, Father Dutilleul, recently arrived from France. In this way, this young, bright, French-speaking student could render many practical services both to the director and to the seminarians and students. The author of these lines saw how this very accommodating young Levite was always ready to give very useful advice and information to Europeans who did not know the habits of this very strange country in which they had just arrived. Hu asked Father Guilloux, Boscat's successor, to be admitted in the Congregation. This was granted on 6 November 1906. Ordained in Jiaxing on 5 June 1909 Reynaud sent him first into the district of Taizhou, where he remained for eighteen months. Then he was called to manage the College of Saint Joseph for three years; next he was appointed professor at the major seminary. In 1922, Reynaud sent Hu as his delegate to the assembly of the missionaries in charge of the preparation of the plenary council of Shanghai. There, from the beginning, he was spotted by the delegate, who was presiding at the sessions, and who chose him as one of the Chinese counselors called to collaborate for the council of 1924. One can say that from that moment he was predestined to be among the six future Chinese bishops who were to be consecrated in Rome.

Bishop Reynaud's Successor

In the consistory of 23 December 1926 Pope Pius XI proclaimed as bishop of Gibba and apostolic vicar of Ningbo Father André Defebvre, missionary in Ningbo.

André Defebvre was born in Tourcoing (Nord) on 24 June 1886. Admitted in Saint Lazare on 5 August 1903, he arrived in China on 17 September 1904 and went immediately to the seminary in Jiaxing to finish his internal seminary and to apply himself to priestly studies. He was ordained on 3 July 1910. Assigned to the vicariate of Ningbo, he was sent as an associate priest to a residence in the countryside. A few years later, he was called as professor for the major seminary, whose director he was soon to become. It is there that for more than ten years he had Father Hu, his schoolmate in Jiaxing to whom he was linked in a frank friendship, as collaborator in the formation of the clergy.

On 1 May 1927 Defebvre's consecration took place in Ningbo. The consecrating prelate was nobody else than Bishop Joseph Hu. It is easy to see in this choice a touching expression of the brotherly affection which, for some twenty years had been uniting in a community of life and work the two students of Saint Vincent Seminary in Jiaxing, now united the two professors of the major seminary of Ningbo. It was at the same time a direct affirmation of the equality before God and before the Church of all races and of all peoples and also an obeying of the pontifical directives about the role given to the local clergy.

Quite some time before his death, Reynaud had taken measures to have in the near future a new division of his vicariate. It affected the civil prefecture of Chuzhou, which later on took the name of Lishui. This district, which was to be the third one taken from the vicariate, had eighteen sub-prefectures. To begin with, the Canadian society of the Scarboro Foreign Mission Society, S.F.M., was invited to send some missionaries to work in this district together with those of Ningbo, till the moment it could become independent from the mission of Ningbo. In 1927, these secular missionaries were six, among whom was the superior, Father [John Mary] Fraser.

Table 23.2. Vicariate of Ningbo Numbers after
Establishment of Taizhou Vicariate, 1926

Categories	Totals
1st District: Ningbo – Catholics	17,100
2nd District: Wenzhou – Catholics	23,718
3rd District: Chuzhou – Catholics	2,300
Total	43,118
Vincentian missionaries	
European	16
Chinese	10
Diocesan priests	
European	7
Chinese	24
Seminarians in major seminary	26
Seminarians in minor seminary	63
Daughters of Charity	
European	23
Chinese	30
Chinese Virgins of Purgatory	55
Homes for elderly men and women	6
Schools for boys, for girls	71
Pupils	3,400
Orphanages	5
Children received	841
College for boys: students	204
Catechumenates for men and women	10
Residences	19
Churches	31
Chapels and oratories	262
Localities with mission activities	297

Adversities: Deaths, Incarcerations, and Massacres.

A Model Missionary: Father Claude Guilloux

Claude Guilloux was born in Trévy (Saône-et-Loire) on 10 January 1856, the twelfth child of a very Catholic family. After finishing his ecclesiastical studies in the major seminary of Autun, he entered the community in Saint Lazare on 9 October 1878 and was ordained on 3 June 1882. After a short training period as the sub-director of the internal seminary in Paris, he was professor for three years in the major seminary of Saint Flour. In 1885, he was called away from there suddenly to be sent to China, where he arrived on the following 6 October and was assigned to Peking.

An assiduous student of the Chinese language, he quickly became able to administer a post outside. Tagliabue placed Guilloux first as an associate in Dakoutun; but a little later he called him back and asked him to go to Tianjin and to found a college destined for the sons of the numerous Europeans living in that city. Father Geurts, future apostolic vicar of Yongping, helped him in this task. When, in 1889, the Marist Brothers took over the direction of this school, Guilloux was appointed as parish priest of the important parish Xiheying, north of Peking. In 1894, he was named director of the Tianjin district and at the same time procurator of the mission in that same town. During the siege of 1900, he spent anxious days with his young associate Desrumaux. No sooner had the storm calmed down than Guilloux was called to Peking as Favier's vicar general, and what is more, he was entrusted with the direction of the seminary, and of the Chinese religious women, the Josephines. The division of the province into two sectors, of the North and of the South, happened in 1910. Guilloux was to be in charge of the one of the South and Desrumaux of the one of the North.

Just citing so many different duties entrusted to him already leads us to suppose that Guilloux had exceptional qualities; but his merit laid in the way he fulfilled his functions. He kept his habitual drive, meanwhile staying calm and jocular. He was preaching, recruiting catechumens, visiting stations, arousing vocations wherever he was and never seemed hurried.

Especially the occasion of his canonical visits made Guilloux known in the best light. With all of his missionaries he avoided all familiarity incompatible with his obligations as a visitor. He did not fear to impose on himself supplementary hardships visiting them when they were far away or difficult to be reached. He wanted to help them keep up the very pure ideal of their vocation. He was gentle with them and encouraging. Never morose, always ready for an amiable joke, he was able to keep his unruffled calm amid the most annoying problems. Always having a simple and supple fidelity to the rules of the Congregation, he had earned respect and affection of all.

In July 1924, a serious cardiac crisis pointed to a fatal end. He recovered, however, quite well for a few months until Christmas and was still teaching the young priests a course in pastoral ministry. Because he was still very weak, the superior agreed that he was not going to be present at the Midnight Mass. Therefore, he went to bed, but sleep did not come, because breathing was difficult. At ten o'clock in the evening, he called for the nurse, Brother Marco, to help him to sit down in a deckchair, in this way looking for a position that ordinarily eased his breathing. Towards midnight, feeling worse, he asked for the superior, who, seeing the danger, gave him the last rites. After some difficulties breathing, Guilloux died peacefully.

A confrere who had known him very well wrote:

> Father Guilloux's dominant characteristic was his priestly dignity. Those who were nearest him could not but have a respectful veneration, seeing him so welcoming and meanwhile so serious and dignified. His face was such that he seemed to be smiling while remaining serious. Especially when he directed the practice of ceremonies, his priestly dignity appeared, or when he explained to us the texts of the Pontifical during the retreats for ordinations. There he was really in his element and he excelled without any difficulty, very naturally. You would have said Christ was educating his apostles. With calm, graceful gestures, he persuaded, he showed … I was going to say, in his person, the greatness of priesthood. He was solemn without suspecting it himself; we said among ourselves that he always seemed to be in a festive mood, always happy.

> How could we, seeing him, not feel a great deal of respect combined with affection and esteem!

François Boisard's Premature Death

Born in Challain (Maine-et-Loire) in 1882, he entered the Congregation in Dax on 2 October 1901; he arrived in China in 1909 and worked from the beginning in the Wenzhou district in collaboration with Father

Aroud, the director. Boisard had some great organizational qualities, but his health left much to be desired. He returned to France in April 1927 to recover his health. This return voyage, however, had been so difficult for him that on his arrival in Paris he entered Saint Joseph Hospital. He died there on the following 11 June. He was forty-five years old. It was a big loss for the vicariate of Ningbo.

Ibarruthy's Beautiful Death.

Bernard Ibarruthy, born in Bayonne (Basses-Pyrénées) on 7 March 1859, admitted in Paris in 1876, was ordained on 3 June 1882 and arrived in Zhejiang the following October. From the first hour he was included in Reynaud's initiatives, in his initial enthusiastic hopes, as well as in the difficulties that were soon to arise. He was the fearless and disinterested worker, ready for whatever task. As a result, he went through almost all the posts of the vicariate successively. In turn missionary, professor, pastor, superior of the major seminary, founder and director of the community of Chinese religious women, the Virgins of Purgatory, up till the day when, more than sixty years old, he became again professor and director of the minor seminary, erected in Ningbo, after having been for many years in Dinghai.

Ibarruthy was always pious, active, charitable and prudent. His native sagacity as a Basque who was moreover from Gascony, still more though, his very lively sense of the supernatural, gave his bits of advice and his behavior that character of moderation, prudent reserve and discretion that were so remarkable in him.

He had only one wish: to work for God and souls till the end. He feared only one thing and he mentioned it often: to become weak, useless, a burden for the mission. He sometimes wept because of it; for him a best way to die was a death with weapons in hand. He asked for this grace and received it.

On Sunday 21 August 1927 he had preached about heaven. On Monday he prepared a conference that was to be given to the seminarians on Tuesday. That Tuesday he did not show up for the meditation or for Mass. People worried about him and soon, opening his room, they found him sitting in his deckchair, fully clothed, the eyes half shut holding against his chest his vow crucifix. He died devoutly, probably while preparing himself for meditation and Mass. It was the worthy crowning, at the age of sixty-nine years, after forty-five years of apostolate in China, the desired reward after a life that had been full of love for God and of zeal for the redemption of souls.

Cyprien Aroud's Apostolic Zeal

Born in Lyons on 15 January 1876, Father Aroud was admitted in the Congregation in Paris on 28 September 1893; he arrived in Zhejiang on 30 September 1899. He was placed in the barely formed district of Wenzhou and he worked there till the end.

Father Louat succeeded Father Procacci, who had opened the mission post, and was given the newcomer. Everything had to be done; people worked hard and with God's help the results were amazing. Aroud became its director. once the mission was founded. Here is in a few words what he achieved.

At that time there was in the whole district only one residence, two or three oratories with two priests to minister to a few hundred Christians. In this same territory four stations were full of activity. Chuzhou, which we mentioned briefly above, was to be entrusted to the young Society of Canadian Missionaries, with 2,300 Christians and six priests; Yunjiachang: 5,780 Christians and four priests; Pingyang: 7,621 Christians and three priests; finally, Wenzhou, which after three important divisions still numbered 10,317 Faithful, to whom the six priests of the central parish can hardly administer. Therefore, this became the respectable total of more than 26,000 Catholics, to whom eighteen priests and more than one hundred fifty catechists devoted their time and energies.

It is easy to understand that managing such an undertaking, founding it, maintaining it and developing it on such a scale, necessarily required time, means and energy. The director, and with him his European and Chinese collaborators, whom Aroud gladly praised, were working hammer and tongs. We must indeed believe this: Aroud's secret was that he knew how to communicate his zeal to his collaborators, priests and Christians. But in this kind of life people exhaust their health. The director maintained an abundant correspondence with his foreign benefactors. During the day he would visit Christian communities and schools; in the evening he often spent a part of his nights writing by candle light. His eyesight could not put up with so much overwork and caused strong worries among the people around him. When he asked doctors for their advice, they did not hesitate to pronounce a formal order to return to Europe as soon as possible, or else he would face after a short time complete blindness. Moreover, his whole body was exhausted and needed a long rest. Consequently, he left for France on 15 January 1928.[77] It was a loss and sadness for the vicariate of Ningbo and for the mission of Wenzhou.

Three More Victims of the Communists in Ji'an

Father Paul Chen, a diocesan priest, was pastor of the cathedral in Ji'an. The Reds arrested him in the first days of October 1930 and jailed him not far from the episcopal residence with a bonze and an opium-smoker, all destined to undergo the same punishment. He was judged very briefly and sentenced to death under the only pretext that he had sent for imperialists, who were molding people according to occidental doctrines and were preparing to invade the country. The execution of the sentence took place on the following 13 October with the blow of a saber.

Some Christians got the victim's corpse for three piasters; they took him away and buried him at the foot of the wall of the orphanage hoping to give him a more honorable burial when the time would allow it. They had to wait for two years. Finally, on 17 October 1932 Father Chen's remains were put in a coffin, which they placed into a mortuary chapel opposite the cathedral, his parish church.

From morning till evening, for three days the Christians came to pray for their dear parish priest's soul. The funeral took place on 20 October. More than six hundred Faithful formed the funeral procession. Father Wang, Father Chen's successor as parish priest presided at the funeral. It was a real triumph for the martyr and for the Catholic faith. Such honors rendered to their pastor were enough to inspire some bit of confidence in these Christians, who had suffered so much for several years.

The Murder of Giacomo Anselmo

The town of Lingjiang, located at more than one hundred kilometers north of Ji'an had been visited in October 1930 only once by the Reds, probably the same ones who had killed Father Chen. At that date, Father Anselmo, pastor of Linjiang, had had time to find a safe place. Afterwards, when the danger had passed, he had come back to his mission and had taken up again the ordinary occupations of his ministry.

---

77. Aroud did not lose his eyesight completely, and he recovered his health, so as to allow him to still fulfill important tasks for many years. He was superior of the House of the Missionary in Vichy when he died on 23 August 1949.

In the beginning of December 1933, on the occasion of a retreat that Anselmo organized and presided over, the Faithful wanted to offer their good wishes to their pastor, who had just turned fifty. This caused a much ado in the region and the Communists, always roving about the countryside looking for some opportunities for raiding, learned that the town garrison had moved elsewhere. On 24 December 1933 in the morning, a strong troop contingent of two or three thousand men approached Linjiang and entered it. In town there were only thirty policemen, who quickly fled.

Anselmo hastened to the church to consume the sacred hosts. This done, he left the residence looking for shelter; but as soon as he was outside, the Reds apprehended him, and led him outside the town. There, Anselmo had to lie down on the ground, just like his escort, because planes had come from Nanchang to chase the audacious Reds. After the danger had passed, they robbed the priest of all he had on him and demanded money. Then he got them to take him to the residence to prove to them that as far as money was concerned, he had none. There the Christians knelt down and begged the kidnappers to leave their benefactor with them. These gangsters answered: "We will not harm your Father; when he has paid the money as agreed, he will come back to Lingjiang to take care of you." On 24 December, late in the evening – as elsewhere Midnight Mass was being sung – the whole gang left Linjiang taking Anselmo to the mountains of the southwest. Two servants followed the priest; but when they arrived at the Xishan mountain, the Reds sent the two Christians back arranging to meet them in the town of Wanzai where they would have to pay twenty thousand dollars as ransom for the captive.

What was Anselmo's fate? Just as for Von Arx, an agonizing mystery floated over this case. Soon different rumors were circulating: according to some, he was murdered already in the first days; according to others, he was seen alive a few months after the kidnapping. His confreres did not stop trying to negotiate the captive's release. Mignani himself addressed the military authorities of the government without positive results. Finally, in July 1935, a high officer of the police forces told Mignani that he had Anselmo's remains and that the mission could come and take them in the town of Jishui. The bishop sent two missionaries to examine if they were really Anselmo's bones. These two confreres judged those certain particularities of the skeleton did not allow them to doubt their authenticity. According to information that they could gather, the gangsters probably beheaded Anselmo in March 1934.

The Murder of Joseph Hu

Joseph Hu, born in 1982, ordained in 1922, was assigned in 1926 in Liangkou, a parish of the Wan'an district.

At that revolutionary era, the students were always heading riots. In Liangkou, they often came to the parish priest's residence in order to insult him and on Sundays they even entered the church yelling all kinds of abuse and invectives against the priest and the Christians. On Easter Sunday 17 April 1927 their challenges were so unbearable that a fierce discussion began at the residence, went on in the street and degenerated into a serious brawl. A student was stabbed. Hu, seeing that the brawl was turning out badly, went to the prefect of the police. He did not know that at that time the police were in connivance with the students. Bands of students chased the priest and caught him in the police station, tied him up and drew him up on a platform, making an spectacle of the priest for the curious audience, which gradually was gathering around the platform. The maniacs were behaving as if they were the masters of the police. The servant of the residence arrived hurriedly to protect the priest, but he was immediately tied up and exhibited on the platform next to Father Hu. This ignominious drama lasted for several hours. In the evening, the church and the residence were looted from top to bottom. During the following night, the two captives were taken in a small boat to Wan'an, the sub-prefecture, in order to be judged. They were accused of having made an attempt on a student's life. Actually, the wound about which they were accused was not serious at all. Because the captives denied that they had taken part in the brawl, they were beaten very cruelly with batons and finally sentenced to death. The execution of the sentence took place on 20 April 1927. When Hu arrived at the place of the execution, he knelt down and cried out: "Jesus, Mary and Joseph, save me!" He was hit with two bullets and died after several hours of agony. The servant was hit only at the shoulder and was still breathing when he was put into the coffin.

The list of the missionaries killed by the Reds or other bandits in that rude era which lasted from 1926 to 1936 is already long. But the vicariate of Ji'an is the one where our people suffered most.

Bishop Sheehan's Death

The vicariate of Yujiang was not able to enjoy its new bishop for very long. We said that Bishop Edward Sheehan had been consecrated in Raozhou on 14 July 1929. On 7 September 1933 he died in the hospital of Nanchang at age forty-five. Young, blooming with health, Sheehan was expected to manage this vicariate for many years. It is true that this province of Jiangxi had been exposed to all kinds of disasters: famine, floods, and, above all, the devastations by the Reds. In the vicariate of Yujiang there was no single sub-prefecture that was spared their visit. Hence the dispersion of the Christians and the insecurity of the roads often prevented the missionaries from visiting their Faithful. Moreover, the soldiers of one or the other side occupied almost all the residences for months.

The schools and the catechumenates no longer functioned. All these miseries caused continuous worries for the bishop. He had to fight, therefore, to keep or reclaim looted or ransacked residences.

In August 1933, Sheehan caught a cold, not usual for that warm season. Because he had a high fever, it was thought prudent to move him to the hospital in Nanchang. The trip was long and tiresome; on the other hand, his constitution was so solid that people around him could not consider this illness as serious. Against all expectation the illness became more serious. It was seen fit to give him the last rites. Father Misner, his confrere, had no sooner finished the ceremony, than the patient fell into a coma. He died during the night. It was 7 September 1933.

Sheehan's death filled with consternation the priests, Christians, and pagans, several of whom had for him a great respect.Before his death, the bishop had expressed the wish to be buried among his people. Therefore, his body was taken from Nanchang to Poyang, where the cemetery of the mission was located. At his arrival, a crowd of more than three thousand people, Christians and pagans, were there to express their respects for the venerated deceased.

His Successor: Bishop Paul Misner

On 10 December 1934 Father Misner, missionary in Yujiang, was chosen as bishop of Myricena and apostolic vicar of Yujiang. Paul Misner was born in Peoria (Illinois, U.S.A.) on 16 January 1891; entered the Congregation in Perryville on 2 November 1911. After studies in the college at Perryville and in the Angelicum in Rome, he became a doctor in theology.

In 1923, he was part of the group of American Vincentians destined for the vicariate of Yujiang, along with Sheehan. But soon he had to leave China for health reasons. He came back in 1928 and was named superior of the mission of Yujiang.

The consecration took place in Yujiang on 25 March 1935, the feast of the Annunciation. The consecrator was Bishop O'Shea, from Ganzhou, assisted by Bishop Dumond from Nanchang and Bishop Defebvre from Ningbo.

There was for this occasion in Jiangxi the biggest assembly of clergy ever seen up till then with three more bishops: Bishop Montaigne from Peking, Bishop Espelage from Wuchang, and Bishop Cleary from Nancheng. Father Emile Moulis, procurator in Shanghai, was there, plus fifty-five priests from ten vicariates, besides the clergy of the vicariate. All that enhanced the solemnity.

Chapter 24

Additional Vicariates for Hebei (Zhili), and War, 1930s

The Vicariate of Zhengding – A Trappist Monastery in Zhengding – First Division: Zhaoxian – Second Division: Shunde – The Vicariate of Xuanhua – Bishop Zhao's Sudden Death – The Successor: Bishop Pierre Chen – The Catholic University of Peking – Founding Two Colleges in Peking – Another Bishop's Sudden Death – The Two Colleges of Wulongding – A Coadjutor Bishop in Yongping – Montaigne Appointed Coadjutor of Peking – Bishop Joseph Zhou, Apostolic Vicar of Baoding – Pilgrimages to Our Lady of Donglü – Philibert Clément's Leaflets – The Sino-Japanese War – The Marist Brothers in Heishanhu – The Horrible Tragedy in Zhengding – Bishop Job Chen's Successor – Bishop Melchior Sun's Resignation – Bishop Jarlin's Death – Bishop Zanin, Apostolic Delegate – Bishop Geurts' Death

The Vicariate of Zhengding

We left Bishop Schraven who was beginning a ministry quite different from the one he had exercised previously.

Before it was temporal affairs and bookkeeping for the Vincentian missions; in the future it would be the spiritual accounts of only one mission that he had to manage, his mission. But to harvest spiritual fruits, it is necessary to use temporal resources. With his practical mind, Schraven saw quite quickly that in Zhengding much money was spent on maintaining the students of the seminary, who were presenting themselves in greater and greater numbers. The reason was that their maintenance had always been completely free. Thus, he tried something new. Understanding was reached that the candidates for the minor seminary had to pay an annual fee of twenty dollars. Then, the following year, the number of candidates did not decrease. The truly Christian parents, fervently wishing to see their sons turn towards the priesthood, willingly made this sacrifice. In the following years the number of students remained on average from one hundred thirty to one hundred forty. Actually, several other vicariates used the same method.

When there were not enough rooms, the bishop had a beautiful one-story building built with spacious study halls and well-aired dormitory. In 1924, Schraven believed the cathedral was too small to receive the crowds of Faithful on the feast days. He had it extended according to de Moerloose's plans.[78] He made it a magnificent church. Thanks to the proximity of a marble quarry, the cost of stone was reasonable, which allowed the architect to build a superb Gothic edifice with all the altars necessary for the community.

A Trappist Monastery in Zhengding

In 1925, Schraven made his *ad limina* [official] visit to Rome. Before meeting the abbot of La Trappe who wanted to found a second monastery in China, he wrote from France and told his pro-vicar, Baroudi, that he intended to offer the abbot the vast area on the banks of the Hutuo River, which had been bought recently at a very good price, to build a monastery if the monks so desired.

The offer being free of charge, an agreement was easily reached. A few Trappist monks from Yangjiaping (Our Lady of Consolation) came and settled temporarily on this land two kilometers from the city of Zhengding in order to prepare the construction of the necessary buildings. They met with great difficulties: when the construction had progressed quite far, an unforeseen flood ruined their work. The monks could begin their work again only after the water receded and dikes were built as to avoid being flooded again. Finally, in 1928, the new monastery was founded under the name Our Lady of Joy. This monastery remained a priory still depending on the monastery of Our Lady of Consolation.

This vicariate had to suffer much because of the comings and goings of troops in North China. Zhengding was on their route and they occupied the episcopal residence for many months. The missionaries in the countryside had to suffer the unavoidable troubles and losses caused by each occupation army. Despite this, the missions made visible progress. In 1928, the vicariate of Zhengding had 87,168 Catholics, eighteen European priests and fifty-seven Chinese priests.

---

78.   De Moerloose was a member of the Belgian missionary society of Scheut (The Congregation of the Immaculate Heart of Mary), in Mongolia. He was an architect by profession. He drew the plans of many beautiful churches in the North of China. He himself often directed the construction.

First Division: Zhaoxian

Seeing the number of his Chinese clergy increasing every year, Schraven proposed to Rome the division of his vicariate in favor of the Chinese clergy. To do so, he had in mind the most beautiful area of his vicariate, the Zhaozhou [ecclesiastical] district, called afterwards Zhaoxian, a civil prefecture of second rank comprising six sub-prefectures. This district had some very well organized Christian communities.

By decree of 9 April 1929 Rome erected the apostolic prefecture of Zhaoxian, and Father Jean Zhang was appointed as its apostolic prefect. On the following 4 June Schraven installed the new prefect in the village of Biancai, chosen as residence and administrative center.

Father Jean Zhang, born in Xiaoyingli, in Ningjin county, one of the six sub-prefectures, on 8 January 1893 was ordained a priest in Zhengding on 22 December 1917. At first, he was professor in the minor seminary, and then he worked in the missions and became director of the district of Baixiang.

At the time of the division, the prefecture of Zhaoxian had 20 priests, all born in this district, and 30,198 Catholics, 303 Christian communities, 36 churches, 198 chapels, 40 oratories and, finally, 9 students in the major seminary of Chala and 60 students in the minor seminary of Zhengding.

It is clear that ecclesiastical vocations in that region were plentiful, because a good number of the Christians were of old stock. The first Jesuits had gone there from Peking at the end of the seventeenth century and had planted the Faith.

By decree of Rome, the prefecture was erected as a apostolic vicariate in December 1931, and a decree of 11 January 1932 appointed Bishop Zhang as the bishop of Antipyrgos and apostolic vicar of Zhaoxian.

On 24 April 1932 the priests and Faithful of Zhaoxian were in a festive mood. On that day in Biancai, their dear bishop was to receive the episcopal consecration from Schraven's hands, with the assistance of Bishop Sun from Anguo and Bishop Joseph Zhou from Baoding, the latter being the chosen one's schoolmate in the minor seminary and the major seminary of Zhengding. Father Antoniutti, auditor, represented the apostolic delegate. A great number of European priests and especially Chinese priests had come from all over to participate in the ceremony. There was no way to tell how many Christians assisted. Hardly one-tenth of them could enter the church; the others had to remain in the yards. It was quite difficult to keep some order in this crowd both inside and outside the church. Priests had received this duty and some police officers helped them. One stand, having too many people, collapsed and luckily crushed no one; only the harmonium suffered from it and also the organist, who had followed the instrument to the ground in front of the church and who had his leg bruised.

Second Division: Shunde

Our Polish confreres also had a great desire to take part in the missions of China. In 1929, the visitor of the Polish province sent some of his missionaries to Ningbo as well as to Zhengding, with the hope that someday some mission field would be entrusted to the province.

That year, Father Ignace Krause, previously at work in the Polish missions of Brazil, arrived in Zhengding with Father Antoni Gorski, a young priest. Two years later, in 1931, five more confreres arrived. And because Schraven had placed Krause in Shunde as director, he also sent the new recruits there with the intention of making this district an "independent mission." During the following years many young Polish confreres came to reinforce the personnel of that mission.

This district of Shunde was far from being as well organized as Zhaoxian. In addition, the Christians of that region were very poor and only recently formed. But the missionaries' zeal and ardor improved the situation very quickly. Among them there was the medical doctor, Wenceslas Szuniewicz, a famous ophthalmologist. It is well known that in China eye diseases were widespread. Szuniewicz first set up a pharmacy and a dispensary at the central residence and immediately began to cure eyes so efficiently that soon he had countless patients. Then he taught Chinese nurses to help him to give treatments to the patients. After sufficient training, they were sent to the countryside to give the more basic treatments in the ordinary cases. He reserved to himself the most complicated and difficult cases. Moreover, some confreres whom the doctor had initiated in the art of healing eyes helped him in his work.

Consequently, with treatment freely given without distinction to Christians and pagans alike, the Polish missionaries gained the population's respect and trust. This was a great help for their apostolic activities.

They had brought in with them Polish Daughters of Charity, who with their works of mercy helped them a great deal. A modern hospital, built in the town of Shunde, was quickly filled with sick people.

The troubles of the civil war, however, put them in danger and caused them a lot of trouble. We said earlier that General Feng Yuxiang, commander in chief of the Guomindang army, had rebelled against Chiang

Kai-shek, but some of his generals, including Shi Yousan, remained faithful to the government. Feng Yuxiang, having fled to Taiyuan, the capital of Shanxi, hastened to gather around him all the enemies of Nanjing and managed to persuade Yan Xishan himself to lead the new coalition. Fearing to be caught in a crossfire, General Shi Yousan rebelled and made an about-face with his army. After capturing Shunde, his troops, as was quite common, made exactions and looted. Only the courage of the missionaries stopped the worst excesses in the hospital. It was full of wounded soldiers belonging to the government army, and they would have been killed without the priests' forceful intervention.

In 1933, Rome promoted the independent mission to the status of apostolic prefecture and appointed Krause as the first apostolic prefect of Shunde.

Ignace Krause, born in Mielno (Poland) on 9 June 1896, admitted in the seminary of Krakow on 18 October 1912, was ordained a priest on 21 June 1919. He went and worked for ten years in Brazil (State of Parana) before coming to China.

At the time of its establishment, the apostolic prefecture of Shunde had 15,240 Catholics, twelve European priests and four Chinese priests.

This civil prefecture had under its jurisdiction nine sub-prefectures. We shall talk about this mission again when it becomes an apostolic vicariate.

The Vicariate of Xuanhua

By decree of 13 May 1926 the Holy See erected the apostolic vicariate of Xuanhua and appointed Father Philippe Zhao as apostolic vicar of this vicariate.

Philippe Zhao, diocesan priest of Peking, was at that time the personal secretary of His Excellency the Apostolic Delegate. Born in the capital on 4 October 1880 he entered the minor seminary of the Beitang in 1893 and was ordained on 24 February 1904. He was successively professor at the minor seminary for four years, associate in Xuanhua for two years, pastor of Xin'an for ten years, and then director of the normal school in the Xitang. From there Costantini took him on 8 January to be his personal secretary.

Zhao, therefore, because of his origin and his priestly career, belonged to the vicariate of Peking. One of his brothers, Venance, also a diocesan priest, was professor in the minor seminary of the Beitang; another one was a Trappist monk in Yangjiaping. His father was a victim of the Boxers in 1900.

Zhao was a good scholar of Chinese and spoke French fluently. On the occasion of his consecration in Rome in 1926 with his five countrymen, he had the occasion several times to speak in public and like Bishop Joseph Hu, C.M., he did so with a tact and even a distinction that pleased the audience very much.

Table 24.1 Vicariate of Xuanhua, Brief Inventory, 1926

Categories	Totals
Catholic population	27,644
Chinese priests, all diocesan	19
Students in major seminary	20
Students in minor seminary	46
Houses of Josephines (Chinese)	7
Churches	21
Chapels and oratories	176

The Trappist monastery of Yangjiaping was located in this new vicariate and numbered at the time forty choir monks and fifty lay monks.

This vicariate was mostly composed of old Christians; consequently, it had provided the mission of Peking with a great number of ecclesiastical vocations.

Bishop Zhao's Sudden Death

Alas! We read in the *Bulletin Catholique de Pékin* of November 1927 the sad news: "The joy that the Church of China felt at the nomination of six Chinese bishops changes today into great sadness. Six months after taking possession of his episcopal see, Bishop Zhao was called back by God on 14 October 1927, at the age of forty-seven!"

Zhao's first preoccupation was in favor of his minor seminarians who up till then had studied in Peking. He wanted to keep them in his sight. That is why he hastily had enough rooms fitted out in his episcopal residence to receive them. The major seminarians, however, would go on studying in the major seminary of Chala.

Next, seeing that the danger of civil war was imminent, he founded, together with the pagans, an aid association for refugees and he gave orders to open shelters to receive them.

Indeed, war did break out. The bishop himself personally took charge of organizing help. While doing so, it sometimes happened that he worked late into the night. On 13 October, having visited the surroundings of the cathedral, he returned to his room and a little later he felt quite a painful attack of dizziness so that he called for his servant. Seeing the danger, the latter warned some priests. One of them, Father Thaddée Wang, without waiting gave the last rites to Bishop Zhao, who did not stop calling out the Holy Names of Jesus and Mary. A little while after midnight he breathed his last.

The Successor: Bishop Pierre Cheng

Pierre Cheng, born in Xuanhua on 6 March 1881, made all his studies in the Beitang and was ordained a priest in Peking in June 1904. He was nominated for the district of Baoding. Endowed with good intelligence, right judgment, and great energy, he very quickly proved able to fill important functions.

He was the pastor successively of two large parishes until 1912, when he became professor in the minor seminary till 1923. Next, while sub-director of the normal school in Nanguan, he was appointed pastor of the cathedral in 1925.

Towards the end of 1926, he was called to Peking to substitute for Zhao in the secretariat of the delegation. At the latter's death, the delegate appointed Cheng pro-vicar of Xuanhua during the vacancy. Cheng left right away to where obedience sent him. He found the town agitated. The priests were overwhelmed by their pastor's sudden disappearance. Soon he restored their courage, and as soon as calm was reestablished, he decided to contact priests and Christians. He spent several months crisscrossing the vicariate – quite well known to him because he was born there. Everywhere he encouraged people of good will.

After seven months of being the *locum tenens*, Cheng was appointed apostolic vicar of Xuanhua in April 1928, and the apostolic delegate consecrated him on the following 1 July.

Cheng went on with more ardor, if that were possible, with the work that he had begun. He had a special solicitude for his seminarians, his future helpers, who appeared to him, reasonably so, the best pledges for the future. His major seminary students were studying in the seminary of Chala, but according to its rules, this seminary ought to receive only students from vicariates entrusted to Vincentians.

That is the reason why, in 1931, at the apostolic delegate's request the Holy See erected a regional seminary in Xuanhua for the neighboring diocesan vicariates.

Not only did Cheng visit the stations of his vicariate, but he also taught and preached everywhere he went. His sermons went straight to the heart of the matter; abuses were attacked head on. He spoke rapidly, even too rapidly for simple people, who did not always manage to follow him, but at the end of the sermon he said so clearly what had to be done or to be avoided that everyone knew his meaning.

This intensive and uninterrupted work bore fruit. His priests and his Faithful loved him. Actually, Christians in China respect and greatly appreciate the priests who give their all.

That is why the 27,644 Christians, whom he had received, had increased by 6,000 in 1935, the year of his death. The report of that year showed 33,200 Faithful.

This energy, this willingness to serve was the reason that he underestimated the seriousness of the illness that hit him in 1932. Despite a seemingly very strong body, Cheng was struck with tuberculosis.

In spite of his intense pain and the extreme weakness, he did not want to declare himself defeated. Confined in the hospital or in his room, he followed what was going on and directed everything. This strength of soul remained visible till his death. In his last moments he called near him his vicar general and the leaders of the Christian communities and gave them his advice. "I am dying. It is up to you to make Catholic Action, the Eucharistic Crusade . . . flourish. Work!'

Those were his last words. He breathed his last on 25 August 1935. A beautiful figure of the Chinese episcopate disappeared.

We shall not mention this vicariate any further, because it was entrusted to the diocesan clergy, and Vincentians had no further part in it. For the history, however, we note that his successor was another diocesan priest of Peking, Father Joseph Zhang, who after teaching in the minor seminary of the Beitang became spiritual director of the Catholic students of Fu Jen University. In 1933, he was called to Rome as professor of the Chinese students of the College of Propaganda. There, in 1936, he received his appointment as apostolic vicar of Xuanhua, and Cardinal Cremonesi consecrated him.

But being sick, he too was forced to resign around 1943 and went to a hospital in Hong Kong where he died in 1946. Bishop Pierre Wang, a native of Xuanhua, replaced him.

The Catholic University of Peking

Many times, have we mentioned Fu Jen, the university set up in Peking. It is time to talk about it more explicitly, though the Congregation of the Mission had no special role in its creation, but because this institution, built in our vicariate of Peking, has had such an influence on our works, it would be a real historical lacuna to say nothing about it.

In November 1917, a Chinese Catholic layman of the vicariate of Peking, Ying Lianzhi, asked Pope Benedict XV for the favor of creating a Catholic university in the north of China. His letter made a deep impression in Rome. The question was studied and the Holy See looked for information. Benedictines in America were sounded out about this important work and without engaging themselves they made it clear that such an endeavor would not displease them.

After long negotiations between the Curia and the Benedictines, the Cardinal Prefect of Propaganda announced in June 1924 that the Order of Saint Benedict had accepted the direction of the future university. The developed project declared: "The new university will contain five faculties: Theology and Philosophy; Chinese and European literatures; Natural Sciences; Social and Historical Sciences; and Mining and Engineering."

In 1925, some Benedictine Fathers, under the direction of Dr. O'Toole, took in hand the beginning of this institution by setting up preparatory courses for the university. They settled in a rented property that sufficed for the moment while awaiting the construction of the university. On 4 November 1927 the Ministry of Education recognized that temporary institution under the name of Fu Jen.

Thanks to the activity of O'Toole and his Chinese, European and American collaborators this work expanded rapidly despite difficulties. At the beginning of the school year of September 1929 students numbered four hundred.

It became necessary to put up a building in the very place where it all had begun; this vast property was bought and the new university was built there, a masterpiece of Chinese art. On 3 November 1929 His Excellency, the delegate, placed its first stone.

Several years passed during which the institution made steady progress. In February 1933, Costantini left China to take care of his health weakened by a recent illness. During his stay in Rome a significant event took place.

The Sacred Congregation of Propaganda in the name of the Holy See entrusted the American Province of the Society of the Missionaries of the Divine Word (Steyl) with Fu Jen University. Next, by decree of the Holy See, Father Grandel, superior general of the aforementioned society, was appointed as the chancellor of the Catholic University of Peking.

These few notes on Fu Jen are sufficient for the time being. We return now to the history of our missions of the Northern Province.

Founding Two Colleges in Peking

Fabrègues, Jarlin's active coadjutor, had already greatly improved the works in Peking: modernizing the cathedral through appropriate paintings, which enhanced the beauty of the interior; renewing the organ; modernizing the Saint Michael Hospital in the legations; extending the Saint Vincent hospital in the Beitang, and so on. He worried still more, however, about progress in education.

On returning from a trip to France where he had collected generous contributions in view of putting up two secondary colleges (boys, girls), he, with the approval of Propaganda, bought a large property, which, though located in the center of the city, was far from the commerce and noise of the town and so offered quiet very commendable for such institutions. He had two beautiful similar buildings built there, separated by a high wall. In the one for the boys, he had a vast conference hall built.

During his stay in France, Fabrègues had asked the Dominican Fathers to take responsibility for the direction of these two colleges: the one for the boys would be directed by the Dominican Fathers and the one for the girls by the Dominican Sisters. The proposal was accepted and from the beginning of 1928, Father Menne, some other priests and Sisters arrived in Peking, led by Father Leroy, their superior, who wanted to check the new foundation on site.

Fabrègues had very carefully prepared the beginning of the courses for the first days of September 1928. Already about four hundred students ages between fifteen and twenty-five had been enrolled, that is, three hundred boys and one hundred girls.

The ceremonious inaugural session took place on 6 September. There were speeches, people listened and applauded, and then these beautiful beginnings almost ended in disorder. The girls, brought there in groups of three, by the Dominican Sisters, listened in silence and behaved very well. The boys, with astonishing lack of consideration, totally free, whispered, went out and came back as it pleased them. In short, they behaved in an uncivilized way. Fabrègues probably had recruited his students without enough care, or at least had not taken enough information on the students' worthiness and their past. Numerous students who had already been in other schools had been dismissed for who knows what reasons. There were also agitators among these young people who wanted more amusement than study. Even politics played a part. Some claimed to belong to one party, others to another party. Hence fights began among the students.

On the other hand, the classes, which ought to have begun a few days after the inauguration, were not yet organized. What is more, the priests recently arrived from Europe had not yet any experience with the behavior of students in China, so the classes began in confusion.

With the girls, however, all went well and the students were studying. Hardly had a month passed when rumors circulated about "Daoming (Dominican)," the boys college; there were murmurs against Europeans and especially against Fabrègues. Students stopped coming to school. The boys' college had to close its doors. Fabrègues, very affected by the events, seemed to think that the Dominican priests had not been equal to the situation and so he dismissed them. The two colleges were closed and the priests as well as the Sisters had to return to Europe.

Another Bishop's Sudden Death

Towards the end of October 1928, a letter from Rome called Fabrègues for urgent business. Despite his health, weakened by a serious crisis in July, the bishop set out on the Trans-Siberian railway with his personal secretary, Father Alphonse Hubrecht. On 26 November in the morning, a telegram, sent from Omsk in Siberia, arrived in Peking, bringing this laconic and sad news: "Fabrègues dead of apoplexy." How surprised and sad people were in the Beitang and in the whole of Peking at the announcement of Jarlin's coadjutor's sudden death. In the Beitang more precise news was anxiously awaited. Finally, on 26 December a letter by Hubrecht, written in Paris on 8 December, said: "In the morning of Saturday 24 November towards seven o'clock, the bishop called me; I found him bathed in sweat, already unable to speak clearly, complaining of violent pain in the neck. Three doctors called in, could only note the progress of the illness. Death happened at seven o'clock in the evening about two hours before arriving in Omsk. Imagine my worry in those sad days. When the train stopped, the railway police were summoned. Telegrams with the French ambassador in Moscow were exchanged. The final decision was for temporary burial of the body in Omsk where there is a Catholic church with a cemetery nearby. After the funeral, I continued my trip and arrived in Paris on 6 December. More news soon."

This stunning death during a trip added further to the sympathy that people had for Fabrègues. A numerous crowd of Chinese and Europeans, among whom the French chargé d'affaires and the personnel of the French Legation, squeezed into the cathedral to participate in the celebration of the funeral office for the eternal rest of his soul.

The absolution at the bier (the commendation of the departed) was performed by His Excellency the apostolic delegate, and then the crowd withdrew, moved by this tragic death in a faraway country of a bishop who had loved China and the Chinese.

The Two Colleges of Wulongting

What happened to the two closed colleges? Jarlin let several weeks go by after the departure of the Dominican Fathers and Sisters, and then he offered the boys' college to the superior of the Marist Brothers. The superior agreed very willingly and placed one of his best Brothers as superior of the college with several others as professors. The students, the majority of whom were Christians, filled up the house quite quickly and soon the school was a success.

Concerning the girls, Jarlin called in the Daughters of Charity and entrusted them with the buildings to start a girls' school. Recruiting students was less easy than for the boys' school. In the beginning they had only students who came from their own various schools in the capital. Gradually others were added, Christians and pagans; from the end of the second year, the school was well attended.

Obviously, from the beginning these colleges had to change their names. They were the Wulongting schools taking the name of the quarter. In 1934, these two colleges were very prosperous. They had reached the number of five hundred students, a number that they were not able exceed for lack of space.

As can be seen, the desire that Fabrègues had conceived to promote the intellectual culture of the Chinese youth had not been idle. One might say that it had been more than fulfilled.

A Coadjutor Bishop in Yongping

As Geurts had aged, he expressed to the Holy See his wish to have a coadjutor. By decree of 16 July 1928 the pope appointed Father Eugene Lebouille as bishop of Conana and Geurts's coadjutor.

Eugene Lebouille, born on 7 February 1878 in the diocese of Roermond (The Netherlands), was admitted in the Congregation in Paris on 6 September 1897 and was ordained on 28 May 1904; he arrived in China on 17 September. He was successively missionary, procurator, director of the minor seminary and finally vicar general.

Lebouille received episcopal consecration in the cathedral of Yongping from the hands of Geurts himself on 18 November 1928.

Montaine Appointed Coadjutor of Peking

In the large vicariate of Peking, Jarlin could not manage without a coadjutor bishop. Fabrègues's tragic death had taken from him an essential helper.

He had to wait, however, a whole year. On 15 January 1930 Montaigne was appointed as coadjutor of Peking with the right of succession, exactly like the late Fabrègues.

Montaigne went to Peking on the following 7 February after having given his instructions and the necessary powers to his vicar general of Baoding, because Montaigne remained apostolic administrator of Baoding, that is to say for one more year.

Bishop Zhou, Apostolic Vicar of Baoding

Joseph Zhou, born in Xiaoguangyang (Zhengding) on 8 November 1891, admitted in the Congregation in Chala on 24 January 1915, was ordained on 29 June 1919. At first a missionary in Zhengding, he returned to Peking as student of the "The Institute of Higher Studies," whose director was [René-Joseph] Flament, and he studied there all the time that this school lasted; then he went back to his mission. In 1929, he was appointed professor of philosophy of Chala. There he received his appointment as bishop of Cratia and as apostolic vicar of Baoding dated 26 March 1931.

On Tuesday 7 July Zhou, together with Montaigne, administrator of Baoding went and took possession of his vicariate.

Zhou's consecration was scheduled for the following 2 August provided that political and military complications, with their poor communications, did not require its postponement. Many invitations were made: the presence of nine mission leaders and of seventy priests was counted on. But events were going to disturb these beautiful projects.

Civil war was indeed going strong. Shi Yousan's troops, which we left in Shunde, had already passed Zhengding. On 29 July 1931 the northern army met the southern army thirty kilometers south of Baoding, which was at risk of being attacked. The noise of the cannons and the airplanes terrified the population. The farmers of the south left their villages and came to the north. The situation was serious. The bishop suggested that the missionaries in this area remain at home; he was even thinking of delaying his consecration, when luckily it was learned in the evening of 30 July that Yan Xishan's troops were falling back.

It was a peaceful and warm day, when on Sunday 2 August at eight o'clock the ceremony of consecration began. The consecrator was Bishop Montaigne, helped by Bishop Pierre Cheng and the Reverend Father Martina, superior of the Stigmatine community. The missionaries who were not in the battle zone were all present; the cathedral was filled with Faithful, but the crowd would have been bigger without the troubles.

Once again, His Holiness Pius XI had realized his plan to equip China with indigenous-led churches. Up till then, however, Rome had entrusted the new bishops with a new territory or one that was not yet opened up for evangelization.

At the time of making the district of Baoding an apostolic vicariate, it was already in a very prosperous situation: it was functioning very well, having already charitable works and well-established institutions essential for a vicariate. In a word, it was a well-equipped vicariate that gave high expectations.

Table 24.2 Vicariate of Baoding, Brief Inventory, 1931

Categories	Totals
Catholics	77,786
European priests, all Vincentians[79]	10

---

79. Since the vicariate of Baoding had been confided to the Chinese secular clergy, although the apostolic vicariate had been Vincentian, the European and Chinese Vincentians who were already there, continued at their post as auxiliaries. One of them, M. [Jean-Marie] Trémorin, was appointed superior of the European and Chinese. Then, little by little, whether through deaths or transfers, the number of Vincentians continued to decline. In 1943, there no more missionaries. There remained only one Chinese Brother.

Chinese priests, among whom were four Vincentians	49
Seminarians in major seminary of Chala	20
Seminarians in minor seminary of Xiguan	80
Probatorium	40
Religious women	
Daughters of Charity, among whom were eight Chinese	15
Franciscan Missionaries of Mary, among whom two were Chinese	5
Josephines, all Chinese	38

Pilgrimages to Our Lady of Donglü

Throughout our account we have often mentioned the large village of forty-five hundred people located twenty-five kilometers to the southwest of the city of Baoding. Father François Liu, a Vincentian, who through his zeal and his eloquence had opened quite a number of villages to the Faith, and planted it in Donglü in 1863. But, ten years later, the Christian community of Donglü still had only two hundred Faithful. Jarlin, then a young missionary went and spent a year there, from 1894 to 1895; he inaugurated the catechumenate-family method, which consisted in feeding the catechumens during all the time they were studying catechism. When he left, six hundred Christians stayed behind in Donglü. He preserved a very good memory of his method.

From that time on, Donglü had its permanent pastor and was to become the most beautiful Christian community of Baoding.

In 1900, in the period of the Boxers' persecution, about nine hundred Christians from the region fled to Donglü. There they withstood a siege of four months, during which they fought forty-eight battles, four of them against Boxers and forty-four against the regular army that supported the rebels. Thanks to the seizure of cannons and other arms, carried out during their sorties, they always won and lost only about twenty people.

We have mentioned the marvelous things that happened during fights of Christians with Boxers in the north of China. During the siege of Donglü, it was a majestic "white lady" seen only by the pagans above the roof of the church, sometimes surrounded by white soldiers (angels?), who were protecting the besieged people. Be these visions as they may, the Christians have always been convinced that the protection they received during those terrible days had been due to the intercession of the Blessed Virgin.

At the time of the siege, the Christians had not had time to build strong fortifications. They had surrounded the village only with an insufficient earthen embankment. When peace had been reestablished the Christians of Donglü and the neighboring villages, while never losing their trust in God's Mother, applied the axiom: "Help yourself, Heaven will help you"; they built high earthen ramparts, while digging a wide ditch around the village. It did them much good, for following the revolution of 1911, Baoding and environs frequently was the scene of civil war, and each time the population rushed to Donglü with all their possessions. To quote just one example, in 1928, when the southerners went to Peking, Donglü received thirty thousand Christians and pagans who thus avoided destructions and lootings.

Let us now return to the story. Immediately after the Boxer Rebellion in 1901, the pastor of Donglü, Father Louis Giron at the time, began the construction of a big church, using mostly materials coming from temples destroyed by the victorious Christians. He had a big painting made on paper by a person of some talent, showing Donglü's pastor in surplice standing before the Blessed Mother and presenting her with an ex-voto, the scale model of the church that he had just built. In 1908, his successor, Father Flament, pleased to notice the fervent devotion with which the Christians were honoring their heavenly guardian, asked and was granted Jarlin's permission to publicly honor Mary with the invocation: "Mother of God, Queen of Donglü, pray for us!" From then on, Christians would repeat three times singing at the top of their voices the invocation in front of the painting, at the end of common prayers recited in the church.

The Christians liked the painting because they had never seen a more beautiful one. Actually, it was quite primitive. Flament had the idea of offering to the Faithful a more artistic painting, representing Mary's beauty in a more dignified way. He went and saw the Jesuit Fathers of Shanghai in their painting workshop, from where beautiful paintings for churches had come. To explain his intentions, Flament gave the director of the workshop as a model for imitation the photography of a well-known painting of the Empress Cixi in her most beautiful imperial finery.

That painting was a real success; it was three meters high and two meters wide. The painting was hung on the wall quite far behind the altar and covering the old picture by Giron. When the Christians saw it, they were filled with amazement and quickly forgot the old one. Its genuine Chinese decor pleased them enormously.

In 1928, Father Clément wrote in his *Bulletin Catholique de Pékin*: "We hear from various sides that many people wonder if the Holy Virgin's extraordinary protection of the Christians and pagans who in time of danger fled towards Our Lady of Donglü with complete trust, might not be a providential indication. Would this not be the moment to direct towards Donglü a pilgrimage movement?"

People were talking about it, and the idea was gaining ground. Trémorin, for fourteen years pastor in Donglü, had wanted it for a long time. The apostolic delegate, several bishops, and many missionaries wished wholeheartedly that Donglü would become a place of pilgrimage.

When everything had been decided, the date of 7 May 1929 was designated for the opening of the pilgrimages. Here is the description:

> The previous evening, on 6 May, Bishop Vienne from Tianjin and Bishop Montaigne from Baoding arrived together in a wagon. Schoolchildren and quite a number of Faithful received the two bishops at the gate of the village.[80] The procession was being formed, while music was being played; the streets resounded with hymns, prayers and invocations to Mary. At two o'clock, the seventy-five seminarians of the minor seminary of Baoding arrived on foot led by Father [Théodore-Antoine] Erkelens, their director, and by the whole staff of professors. Already thirty priests had arrived and half of them took their places in the confessionals. At four o'clock Bishop Sun from Anguo arrived with a delegation of Faithful. From everywhere Christians of the district arrived with their parish priests. There were more than three thousand of them. At six o'clock in the evening, Bishop Montaigne held a solemn Benediction.
>
> On 7 May at half past eight, a High Mass was celebrated by the bishop of Baoding. They entered the church in procession. At the head were the schools (boys and girls: three hundred) with their banners, the seminarians, then the clergy in surplices. The litanies of the Blessed Mother were sung. Everywhere order and silence were kept. Behind the bishops the Faithful entered the church quietly. All were standing since for there were no pews or chairs. There were more than four thousand people. The seminarians sang directed

---

80. High earthen walls surrounded the village of Donglü with four gates in brickwork, each carrying the inscription of one of the titles of the Blessed Mother. One was "Help of Christians"; another was "Tower of David," and so on.

by Erkelens. After the gospel, Vienne preached a beautiful homily about the glories of Mary.

All left the church in the order they entered. Then delegations of Christians gathered in the yard to present their greetings to the bishops and to receive their blessing.

As the residence had no room big enough to serve as a dining hall, the bishops and priests had their meals under the big verandah. A tent had been put up for the Christians to accommodate one thousand persons. In the afternoon, at about three o'clock on a platform built in the open air four priests explained to the crowd the meaning of this uniquely Christian festival. At six o'clock a large procession of the Blessed Sacrament was organized in the streets of the village with exposition on two repository altars.

The crucifix first, then the altar boys, the music band, the students, the two hundred eighty girls of the Josephines' schools and finally the Christian men and women, all proceeded in rows of four. The people who did not take part in the procession formed a line along the streets with calm and admiration.

The next day, 8 May, during the High Mass, offered by de Vienne, the bishop of Anguo, Sun, reminded the Christians of the love they owed Jesus and His Holy Mother strongly stressing faith and piety. After the lunch, bishops and priests signed the register of the pilgrims.

Trémorin added that there were four more pilgrimages that year, less numerous than the first one.

In June 1931, the pastor of Donglü noted: "This year we have had thirteen pilgrimages in which three bishops, sixty-five priests and about twenty-five thousand Faithful took part. People came from the neighboring vicariates of Zhengding, Zhaoxian, Xingtai, and from the vicariate of the Jesuits. While leaving, a French missionary told me: "It is like Lourdes."

On 28 May 1932 he wrote: "We had three bishops and about one hundred priests; forty parishes sent more than twenty thousand Faithful."

In 1933, briefly: "Three bishops and a mitered abbot, eighty priests, eighteen thousand Faithful, sixteen processions of the Blessed Sacrament."

In 1936, twelve pilgrimages, the most devout since the beginning: two bishops, seventy priests, thirty-five thousand Faithful, twelve processions of the Blessed Sacrament.

In 1938, it was the height of the Sino-Japanese war. The pastor of Donglü announced regretfully that pilgrimages that year would not happen. After him we can say: not only "that year," but all the following years. The last pilgrimage took place in 1937 and would not be renewed. After the war with Japan, Communism was to come like a storm that was going to destroy the most beautiful works.

Philibert Clément's Leaflets

The founder of the two monthly magazines, the *Bulletin Catholique de Péking* (*B.C.P.*) and the *Sacerdos in Sinis* (*S. in S.*), Father Clément, pastor of the parish of the legations, and always driven by tireless zeal, sent the readers of the two magazines in 1925 an appeal in aid of a publication work that he intended to set up.

In that appeal, Clément highlighted the immense power that the press had in China, as in the whole world, either to spread the truth or to sow error. He remarked that regretfully false and bad ideas were the ones that were spread most and this to the detriment of the readers. He knew that the Catholic printing shops of China produced quite a few good works, books and brochures. There was place, however, he said, for publications that looked shorter, and would be better suited for a larger diffusion: leaflets. To try the idea out, he proposed the following topic: "The situation of the Church in the world," written in Latin so as to appear in the *S. in S.*, read by many Chinese priests, and he asked them to translate it in current Chinese as used by newspapers. Those who made the translation would send it to the director of *S. in S.* The best translation graded by an ad hoc committee would be published in the *S. in S.*, afterwards a special off-print would be made in the form of a leaflet. Clément added: "We hope in this way to be able to do a popular presentation, as objectively as possible, of all Catholic doctrine."

Clément wished to grant a bonus of ten dollars to the three best translations, so as to encourage the authors. He needed money. He opened a subscription, which right away brought in many and generous offerings from all regions in China. This proved how much this work pleased the vicars apostolic and missionaries.

According to the draft of the rule established by Clément, the leaflets were to appear at the rate of one every week. From the end of the first year, there were thirty-six. The first one appeared at the end April 1925.

In 1926, Clément announced to his collaborators that from then on the leaflets should be written in such a way that pagans can read and understand them; for the goal was not only to enlighten the Faithful, but to teach the truth to all the readers whom we might reach. The copies that had been written in this way were to be indicated with an asterisk.

In 1927, we read in the *B.C.P.*: "The work of the leaflets progresses; ten thousand leaflets have been distributed to regular readers. Number 89, very important these days, gives the documents on which the freedom of the Catholic religion in China is based; number 90 is about angels and demons. It is excellent to refute the pagans' superstition about all kinds of ghosts in creatures. . . . All these leaflets ought to be reprinted."

In April 1927, Clément wrote: "The two million leaflets, which we have sown already for two years to the four winds of China, must sometimes have found some good field. . . . We have no other ambition than sow the good grain of God's word abundantly." In May: "The competitors still come in a great number for the translation that is proposed for a contest every month."

In June 1930, Clément announced: "The publication of the leaflets was finished last April. We give in the general catalog of all the leaflets that have appeared." Then there is a list of one hundred eighty leaflets. Next, he remarks:

"The one hundred eighty leaflets printed have been collected in four volumes of the size of the *B.C.P.*, comprising altogether seven hundred twenty pages. Moreover, the leaflets are not sold out. It will be easy to get them at the printing shop of the Beitang according to needs; we will also be able to reprint some numbers that are more in demand."

Though the work of the leaflets had lasted only five years, it had done a considerable amount of good; but it demanded so much work of the director, that no one, even Clément, could guarantee it for a long time. Let us not forget that Clément considered the leaflets and even the two magazines, of which he was the soul, as extra work. His principal occupation was the service in the parish of the legations, and as if the parish was not big enough for his zeal, he had created a branch of the parish in the middle of the Chinese City, in Nangangzi, two kilometers away, which he actively cared for. Because he had only one associate most of the time, he had often to celebrate Holy Mass twice on Sundays and feast days. Moreover, he regularly distributed the *Bulletin paroissial* (Parish Bulletin) in which he announced the ceremonies and their meaning, recommended works, and gave advice on good articles to read.

After few years, the worker was to receive the wages of his labors which he continued up till the last hour.

In the evening of 16 December 1933 he had a crisis of shortness of breath and could not breathe anymore. He was immediately taken to the Hospital of Saint Michael quite near the residence. The first medication given was effective and the illness seemed to be overcome. Following the doctor's advice, he stayed a few days in the hospital, but not the whole day. Christmas was drawing near and the pastor of Saint Michael felt the need every day to get away for a few hours for ministry. On 22 December he went to his church and sang a Requiem Mass. After that he went back to the hospital saying that he thought about certainly leaving it the next day, Saturday. After a light snack, he began writing his magazines. At noon he had a heart attack and died (23 December 1933).

No sooner had he asked for others eternal rest than he himself was called there. He died in the middle of his work, of his activity. His hands still smelled of the ritual incense that he had spread around the catafalque. His hands, which had taken up the pen again immediately after that to work on his dear *B.C.P.*, had suddenly to stop all work.

Philibert Clément was born in Trivy (Saône-et-Loire) on 31 January 1868. As a bachelor of arts, he acquired the diploma of Bachelor of Theology. After seventeen years of ministry in France, notably as chaplain in Paray-le-Monial, he conceived the idea of devoting himself to the missions and because he was regularly corresponding with his uncle, Father Guilloux, visitor of the Southern Province, he went to China. He arrived there on 25 November 1910 and immediately asked to be admitted to the Congregation and began his internal seminary in Chala on 8 December. After his first year of probation, and in view of the beautiful examples he gave of humility to his young novitiate companions, he was posted to Dakoutun for the works of the missions. In May 1912, he received his appointment as pastor of Saint Michael Church and of the parish of the legations. He fulfilled this function for twenty-three years without flinching for a minute.

He studied both Chinese and English in order to meet more completely his parishioners. He worked so hard on studying Chinese that, despite his age, he became quite familiar with it and could make himself understood easily.

To the parish ministry, we have seen it, he had added the publication of his two magazines, of the leaflets and of the *Echo of Saint Michael*; this did not stop him from being correspondent for two daily newspapers, the *La Croix* from Paris and the *Echo de Chine* to which every month he sent interesting articles about the evolution of ideas in China, in the legations, Clément could indeed easily find bits of information about the public domain.

At any time, Clément was available for the Faithful, receiving their confidences, giving sound advice and words of consolation that went straight to the heart. We cannot elaborate here on the virtues of this great achiever. We would have to mention his uprightness, his loyalty, which was proverbial. He did not like beating about the bush and when he noticed during a conversation some deviousness, his glare alone would show his disapproval and the disdain he had for this kind of cleverness.

Seeing all the work achieved by this tireless worker, people might wonder how many hours of work he imposed on himself every day. He never seemed overburdened, worried, the way it happens to people who are in a hurry. Busy? So he was. Always. Worried? No. He knew how to converse fruitfully with friends. Did he meet a missionary? After the usual greetings, he would ask about his work, congratulate him on his successes and he would ask him information about his methods; he would submit to him this or that idea in view of making that missionary develop his ideas. He was innately a journalist who habitually garnered material for possible articles. The missionary would not realize it, but Clément would have done useful work during that quarter of an hour. Moreover, both would be happy with the interview.

Certainly, the vicariate of Peking had lost an irreplaceable missionary. Several people had to take up the tasks he himself fulfilled. Paul Corset, superior of the Regional Major Seminary of Chala, became pastor of Saint Michael and other confreres of the Beitang took on the publication of *B.C.P.* Because *S. in S.* was less useful, it was suppressed.

The *B.C.P.* continued to appear as its founder had left it at the rate of twelve numbers a year, forming a volume of about five hundred pages every year. It ended publication in 1948. This collection of thirty-three volumes, occupying a whole library shelf, remains a precious mine for the historians of the missions in China.

The Sino-Japanese War

The history of that war cannot be written here; it is enough for us that we briefly draw the framework of the events so that the facts that interest us can find a fitting place in it.

The Communist troops, defeated in Hankou, reassembled and undertook a long and difficult journey that followed the course of the Yangtze, then through the province of Sichuan and the Qinling mountains to the town of Yan'an in the south (*sic* north) of Shaanxi. Settled in that peaceful region, leaders Mao Zedong and Zhu De, assisted by Moscow's advisors and instructors, were to form a strong and disciplined army and the military and civil cadres for the creation of a new China, after the expulsion of the Japanese.

Without a declaration of war, the Japanese occupied Manchuria, but to hide their occupation of it, they put the Manchu prince Puyi at the head of this immense country.

From this base they continued their conquests in Mongolia, in Chahar; they occupied the north and the east of Hebei province and marched towards Peking. It was there that the incident of Lugouqiao happened. On 7 July 1937 a shooting battle broke out between Chinese and Japanese soldiers, near the famous Marco Polo Bridge, about twenty kilometers to the west of Peking. The Japanese claimed that the Chinese troops shot at their troops, which were only doing exercises, which is how the battle began. On 23 July the twenty-ninth army, which defended the capital, was defeated in Nanyuan (the former imperial park south of the town) and the Japanese occupied the city.

In our account we mention only what touched our missions in this war.

The Marist Brothers in Heishanhu

On 31 August a gang of robbers (or fleeing soldiers) hiding in the hills of the west, made a raid on the Marist Brothers' country house in Heishanhu, twenty kilometers north-west of Peking. They arrested the chaplain Father Willems and seven European Brothers, took them as hostages to the mountains. The priest, from whom these robbers demanded a large ransom, was unwilling to cooperate and was set free after eighteen days. The Brothers also refused to pay money; they were released at the end of October 1937 without their abductors treating them too badly.

It seemed that these robbers had no other goal than to get money and that the close presence of Japanese troops had dissuaded them from resorting to violence.

The Horrible Tragedy in Zhengding

On 9 October 1937 in the morning the Japanese took the city of Zhengding and, a little later, soldiers entered the mission compound, attacked and looted the many refugees who were there, Christians and pagans alike.

Japanese officers, however, visited Bishop Schraven and promised and assured him that the mission would be respected. However, towards six or seven o'clock in the evening, ten armed individuals clothed as Japanese soldiers appeared at the main gate and went to the quarter of the Chinese religious women (Josephines).

The mission was composed of a vast compound divided into four quarters of unequal size and well separated from each other, everyone accessible from the outside. The smallest one was the one of the Chinese Sisters, locked like the others. The biggest was the quarter of the Daughters of Charity with all their works of mercy. Then there was the quarter for the bishop and priests. Finally there was the one for the boys' schools, a workshop and a vast garden. The cathedral occupied the center of the entire property.

Notified of the ten soldiers' entering, Fathers Charny and Bertrand wanted to reach them and stop them from entering the Josephines' quarter, but they were apprehended by two soldiers and locked in the guard's place. Two soldiers remained guarding them.

A little after seven o'clock, time for the missionaries' supper, eight people arrived in the dining room, where Bishop Schraven and his priests, more than twenty, had just entered. Right away, the one who seemed to be their chief gave orders – in good northern Chinese – that all were to stand and keep silent, the eight soldiers kept their revolvers pointing at the priests; then some grabbed the bishop and the others laid hands on all the other Europeans, saying loudly that they were only after them. They blindfolded them, tied their hands behind their backs, and with a long rope tied them all together and led them towards the main gate. Arriving there, they tied up Fathers Charny and Bertrand in the same way and added them to the other captives. They had them get on a big coal van, which was all prepared; then they went away.

They were:

> Bishop Schraven, Dutch, sixty-five years old;
>
> Father Lucien Charny, superior, French, fifty-five years old;
>
> Father Thomas Ceska, assistant to the superior, Austrian, sixty-five years old;
>
> Father Eugene Bertrand, procurator, French, thirty-two years old;
>
> Father Gérard Wouters, missionary, Dutch, twenty-eight years old;
>
> Brother Antoine Geerts, painter, Dutch, sixty-two years old;
>
> Brother Wladislas Prinz, Polish, twenty-eight years old;
>
> All Vincentians

Father Emmanuel Robial, Trappist, French, sixty years old;

Mister Biscopich, layman, Czech, who came from Peking to repair the organ.

Note that when Biscopich saw those brutes laying hands on the bishop, he rushed at them screaming: "Stop, do not touch that man, he is a bishop!" He was quickly silenced and treated like the others.

Father Albéric, prior of the nearby Trappist monastery, Our Lady of Joy, was likewise visiting the mission. Because he was old and weak, however, he had not gone to the dining room, which saved his life.

After the departure of the captives, the Chinese priests, who had just witnessed this brutal arrest, were plunged into indescribable shock. They were terrified and did not know what to do. There they were without a leader and no one dared make a decision. Great confusion! Nobody among them dared even to go out of the compound. This made the subsequent inquiry so difficult: they knew nothing about what had happened close by the residence.

Father [Louis] Chanet, pastor and director in Dingzhou, a railway station located halfway between Zhengding and Baoding, was grappling with huge difficulties. The authorities in town had fled, while Christians were arriving in big numbers all at once to find a shelter in the priest's house.

On 17 October Chanet received a courier from Zhengding carrying written on the lining of his clothes some words announcing the tragic arrest. Right away, he sent another courier to Peking to inform Montaigne and the embassy of France and made it his duty to go to Zhengding. Unable to get a pass from the Japanese, Chanet was forced to go there on a bicycle at his own risk. He got there on 22 October. He found that the priests were still terrified, not even daring to get together. encouraged them and began to inquire about the events. Were the confreres still alive? Had they been taken as hostages? If so, where were they? From his own circle, he could not find out anything. The witnesses of the missionaries' arrest had been so terrified that their accounts were imprecise and even contradictory. Moreover, all were ignorant of what the abductors had actually done with their victims. Finally, on 10 November it was learned from beggars that in the evening of 9 October they had seen a big fire near the tower located at some three hundred meters from the bishop's residence and that they had heard cries: "Mong-di! Mong-di!" which they did not understand. Without any doubt these cries were: *"Mon Dieu! Mon Dieu!"* [My God! My God!]

At the foot of that tower, the Japanese, according to their habits, burned the corpses of their soldiers killed during battle. Probably the captives were killed there, it is not known how, and then they were burned too. Indeed, the place indicated was examined and in the mixture of ashes and mud the discovery was made of charred bones, of remnants of rosaries, of medals and of things that only missionaries could have had in their pockets. Everything was collected and kept in the residence.

While Chanet was going to Zhengding, his associate, Father Henri Vonken went by bicycle in the opposite direction to Peking. When he arrived, the sad news of the captives' murder was already known.

Meanwhile, Bishop Zanin, the apostolic delegate, not wishing the vicariate of Zhengding to remain without a leader, appointed Bishop de Vienne the temporary administrator of this vicariate, while waiting for Schraven's return if he was a hostage, or for the nomination of his successor if he were dead.

On 16 November Bishop de Vienne arrived in Zhengding accompanied by a Japanese officer. Right away the latter made a short inquiry and the next day he recognized the Japanese army's guilt and showed himself ready to compensate for the damage. He summoned the Japanese and Chinese authorities of the town to come to the mission so as to clarify the situation and to bring understanding among all of them. It was decided that a solemn funeral service would be celebrated to honor the victims. That celebration took place in the cathedral on 22 November. Another one was held also in Peking, in the Church of Saint Michael of the legations.

Besides, the Japanese army promised to build a monument for the victims near the cathedral of Zhengding and to indemnify the mission for the damages caused by the shells.

Some months after the events, the promised monument was erected. It consists of a marble stele placed on a pedestal and flanked by two small columns on top of which a pediment in the form of a capital, altogether two meters high and one meter wide. The inscription carved on the stele reads: In Memoriam / Victimarum / Diei 9 Octobris 1937. [In Memory of the Victims of 9 October 1937.] This is followed by the names of the nine victims.[81]

That was all. There was not one word of regret on behalf of the culprits. The Japanese army had recognized its guilt in the presence of Bishop de Vienne and the Chinese authorities. This is not mentioned on the stele.

It is a recognized fact that the Japanese army did not make any reparations, moral or material. On the other hand, we must say that around this sad case there has always floated much doubt.

---

81.   The monument still stands (2022). (AS)

Who were the immediate perpetrators of the crime? According to serious indications they were not Japanese, but Manchurians or Koreans, or people from those two countries paid by the Japanese army. We have seen that the chief of the eight intruders was speaking Chinese like a Chinese and not like a Japanese person. Japanese at war, it is said, sometimes would send in a vanguard willing to risk their lives to frighten the populace.

The war was just beginning. Afterwards it was seen that soldiers sometimes acted rigorously and even cruelly against spies, but never against Europeans as such, still less against the Catholic Church and the missionaries.

Be that as it may, if the murderers were not native Japanese, the army was nevertheless responsible for their crimes because they were part of the Japanese army. The army indeed recognized this publicly.

On balance, this implicit avowal by the small stele seems quite weak; it may have been just a compromise.

Bishop Job Chen's Successor

By Pius XI's decree of 26 January 1939 Father Job Chen, director of the district of Gaocheng, was named bishop of Perta and apostolic vicar of Zhengding.

Job Chen, born on 8 November 1891 in Wangjiazhuang, entered the Congregation on 2 September 1911 in Chala, where he was ordained on 6 June 1916. Having fulfilled various posts in the mission and in the minor seminary, he was director of the district of Gaocheng beginning in 1932.

The Faithful would have liked very much that the episcopal consecration would take place in their presence, and it was also the wish of the newly chosen bishop to be ordained in his cathedral, but the troubled times did not allow it. The consecration took place on 21 May 1939 in Tianjin. The consecrator was Bishop de Vienne, administrator of the vicariate for almost two years, assisted by Bishop Joseph Zhou from Baoding and by Bishop Jean Zhang from Zhaoxian.

Table 24.3 Vicariate of Zhengding, Brief inventory, 1939

Categories	Totals
Catholics	51,106
European priests	15
Chinese priests	48

Bishop Melchior Sun's Resignation

In 1936, Bishop Sun, apostolic vicar of Anguo, was brought by circumstances beyond his control to offer his resignation. It was neither his age (he was sixty-seven and healthy) nor his disabilities which forced him to take his retreat; but the situation, created by Lebbe's schemes in his vicariate, had become such that the bishop did not find another solution than asking the Holy See to discharge him from the administration of this vicariate.

Rome granted his wishes and immediately named as temporary administrator of the vicariate of Anguo Father Jean-Baptiste Wang, the then-director of the minor seminary of this vicariate.

By the decree dated 1 July 1937 the Holy See named Wang titular bishop of Lamia and apostolic vicar of Anguo.

Jean-Baptiste Wang, born in Daligezhuang (Baoding) on 6 June 1884, was admitted in the Congregation in Jiaxing on 27 August 1908 and was ordained on 18 March 1911. He exercised his ministry in Baoding for twenty-two years, either in mission work or as professor in the minor seminary. In 1924, Montaigne appointed him as councilor. Finally in 1933, he was moved to Anguo to lead the minor seminary.

The episcopal consecration of the newly appointed bishop took place on 24 February 1938 in the Beitang cathedral. The consecrator was Bishop Sun himself, who had moved outside Peking to a house of the Little Brothers of Saint John the Baptist and still lived there for fifteen years. The two assisting bishops were Bishop Montaigne from Peking and Bishop Zhou from Baoding.

Bishop Jarlin's Death

Jarlin had suffered several serious illnesses in his life, from which he recovered very well every time. As soon as he had turned sixty, however, without being really sick he felt his forces decreasing from one year to the next and he was forced to gradually limit his activities. Traveling especially tired him; soon he had to avoid traveling completely, leaving this kind of ministry to his coadjutor.

During the last four months of the year 1932, Jarlin was so weakened that he could not go to his house chapel to celebrate Holy Mass. He had it celebrated in a room next to his room and he received Holy Communion every day. He even received Communion the day he died. On 15 December 1932 sensing that death was approaching, he himself asked for the last rites, which he received in the presence of the personnel of the Beitang, with a lively faith, a great devotion and evident resignation to God's will. Then the patient became weaker and weaker and his sight declined: the sight of one eye was lost and the other grew dim. On the first of January we went and presented him with our best wishes. Jarlin received us sitting at his desk and always humorous, he said to us showing us his closed eye: "You see! Death is already quite near; it will happen quickly, I will need to close only one eye." He still lived a few weeks, getting up only a few hours every day. On 27 January his situation became worse; his nurse did not leave him. At about eleven o'clock he still had enough strength to announce, from his office to his visitors, the death of Father Verdier, the superior general, while showing the telegram announcing the sad news.

Towards two o'clock in the afternoon, coming back from his closet, he almost collapsed; the nurse held him up immediately and carried him to his bed. Seeing that the patient was suffering much, he suggested some devout thoughts, like putting his trust in the Blessed Mother of God: "Holy Mary, Mother of God, pray for me." The patient repeated this prayer clearly. They were his last words; he died at three o'clock. Montaigne, informed immediately, gave him a final absolution.

A great missionary disappeared. Jarlin had followed to the letter the instruction which, under Pope Leo XIII, the Sacred Congregation of Propaganda gave to the apostolic vicars in 1883: "Because the conversion of the pagans is the main goal of the missions, apostolic vicars must work at that with their whole soul." Indeed, he put the accent on this task, and he did not stop during his whole ministry in China making it his principal duty. He was always obsessed by the word of the Master: "I shall make of you fishers of men." That is why he had put on top of his coat of arms the words: "*Duc in altum*" and "*In verbo tuo laxabo rete*" (Set out into the deep; because of your word I shall let down my nets). He let them down in the person of his missionaries, and he realized an abundant catch. Of course, on arrival on the shore it was necessary to throw away the bad fish. There had been waste, perhaps abuses, but the great work has become efficacious. The statistics that we offer throughout our account are there to prove so.

Bishop Zanin, Apostolic Delegate

Above we have seen that Costantini had traveled to Italy to recover. After a few months, however, though his health had improved, Costantini felt obliged to tell the Holy Father that he was no longer able to face the very tiring effects of traveling in the interior of China.

Indeed, he had spent more than ten years in China and had worked hard, crisscrossing this immense country in all directions. The means of communication then were still very uncomfortable and very tiring.

Pope Pius XI appointed Mario Zanin for this important task, elevating him at the same time to the titular see of Trajanopolis. The same day the pope named Costantini as one of the councilors of the Sacred Congregation of Propaganda. The new delegate received episcopal consecration in Rome from Cardinal Fumasoni's hands on 8 January 1934.

Mario Zanin, born in Feltre (Italy) on 3 April 1890 and ordained a priest in 1913, had fulfilled important functions in Rome since 1926 till this last nomination.

The delegate landed finally in Hong Kong on 31 March 1934. From there he went to Nanjing to present his letters of credence – though he was not apostolic nuncio – to the president of the Republic, who was at that time President Lin Sen. Zanin read his speech in Latin, immediately translated in Chinese by the pastor of Nanjing; then the president read his answer. His speech and the reply were both models of respect, consideration and sympathy.

After a short stay in Shanghai, then in Tianjin, the apostolic delegate arrived on 4 June in the capital, where a relatively triumphal reception was held for him. On 10 June His Excellency went to the regional major seminary in Chala to offer there the first fruits of his episcopacy by ordaining thirty-five clerics prepared to receive Holy Orders. It is noteworthy that from Hong Kong to Peking, going through the three major cities mentioned, everywhere the high officials behaved spontaneously not only correctly and politely, but respectfully and even affectionately towards the Catholic Church.

This kindness was also shown during the many trips that the delegate was to make in the interior of China. The reasons for this progress in the relations of the Church with the public authorities can be discovered easily. First, the honor the pope gave China by sending a permanent representative in the person of the apostolic delegate. Next, China, in former days closed for foreigners, had finally opened its doors and had understood many things in its contact with other nations. The very visible progress of the evangelization in China, and also the missionaries' behavior during the troubled years, all these things had drawn the Chinese officials' attention on the importance of the Catholic Church and its leader, the pope.

All this was a good omen for the progress of religion. The missionaries of that period, seeing these proofs of respect and sympathy, had a right to hope that the Chinese government would one day give legal standing to the Catholic Church.

We, who know the rest of the history, the Japanese war, Communism, are profoundly sad that we have to say: These hopes were never realized.

Bishop Geurts's Death

After a short illness, François Geurts died in the night of 21 July at the age of seventy-eight. In the beginning of his illness, no one worried about his dizziness, neither did he. Every year actually, he had this kind of indisposition for a longer or shorter time. Soon his condition worsened; that is the reason why Bishop Lebouille, his coadjutor, thought it would be prudent to give the venerated patient the last rites. After several seconds of hesitation and reflection, Geurts prepared himself to receive Extreme Unction in possession of all his faculties.

Geurts was one of the first Dutchmen to be received by the Vincentians, who at that time were hardly known in the Netherlands. He left for China in 1882, when he was still just a subdeacon. For this young cleric, tall and quite slender, it seemed he would not have a long career in China. He lived there, however, for fifty-eight years.

Above we noted the various posts that he occupied before his elevation to the episcopacy, and also the very slow progress made in a vicariate where everything still had to be done. Nevertheless, gradually the number of Christians increased from one year to the next, in a more regular way than everywhere else. In certain other vicariates of the north annual progress was sometimes remarkable because of the enormous jumps in numbers, but this certainly was not always indicative of solid and lasting results.

Geurts left to his successor, Lebouille, a vicariate having the essential works and institutions. The Faithful, who in the beginning numbered three thousand, now were thirty-five thousand. The number of priests had grown from three to forty-one, among whom there were fourteen Chinese priests. All was ready for more rapid progress. Unfortunately, we were nearing the end.

Chapter 25

Additional Vicariates for Zhejiang, 1920s-1930s

Condition of the Province in 1925 – Situation in 1941 – Division of the Vicariate of Ningbo: Mission of Lishui – The District of Wenzhou – The "House of the Missionaries" in Vichy – Bishop Misner's Death – His Successor: Bishop Charles Quinn – A Great Christian: Lu Bohong – Lu Bohong Died a Victim of his Charity – Centenary of the Vicariate of Nanchang – Summary List for 1939 – The Missions During the Sino-Japanese War – A Gruesome List by Father d'Elia, S.J. – Sister Gilbert – Bishop Dumond's Death – Father Paul Monteil – The Vicariate of Ningbo and the Japanese War

Condition of the Province in 1925

After Father Guilloux's death on 25 December 1923, the Southern province needed the nomination of a new visitor. On 25 July 1925 the superior general nominated Father Legris as visitor of that province.

Paul Legris, born in Cerci (Somme) on 10 December 1867, admitted in Paris on 27 February 1891, ordained in May 1894, arrived in China in September 1894 and was placed in South Jiangxi under the direction of Bishop Coqset.

This vicariate was to become the Ji'an vicariate, entrusted to the Italian Vincentians.

During the Boxer persecution, while the majority of the Jiangxi missionaries had withdrawn to Shanghai, Legris was available to answer the call from the north for some priests destined to render the service of chaplains for the French occupation troops. Legris followed General Bailloud's troops towards Baoding and Zhengding.

When quiet had been reestablished, he returned to his mission in Jiangxi, where his zeal was applied mostly to the formation of the seminarians. In 1915, Guilloux called him to Jiaxing in order to manage the seminary, whose superior he became in 1920. Since its foundation, this seminary had always had the visitor himself as its superior. But Guilloux, overburdened with business, wanted to entrust an experienced confrere with this function, one who would be able to manage this vital work.

Since the foundation of this seminary in 1902 till Legris's arrival in 1915, forty-one Vincentian priests had been ordained there.

Situation in 1941

That year, Legris had under his jurisdiction, in the four vicariates of the southern province, fifty-six European Vincentians and forty-three Chinese, assisted by one hundred three Chinese diocesan priests.

Designation of the Vicariates in the Southern Province

1. In Zhejiang: the vicariates of Ningbo, Hangzhou, and Taizhou, the bishops of which were at that time Bishop Defebvre, Bishop Deymier and Bishop Hu. Another division of the vicariate of Ningbo, forming the future vicariate of Lishui, will be the topic of the next chapter.
2. In Jiangxi: only the vicariate of Nanchang, with Bishop Dumond as its bishop, remained under Father Legris's jurisdiction. While the Ji'an vicariate, which had been handed over to the Italian Vincentians, depended on the visitor of Turin, the one of Ganzhou depended on the Eastern province of the United States; the one of Yujiang was under the control of the visitor of the Western Province (Saint Louis, Missouri); finally, the vicariate of Nancheng was under the jurisdiction of the Columbans.

In the report on the spiritual fruits of the seminary in Jiaxing it can be noted that the number of the priests ordained between 1915 and 1941 is 113; if the 41, mentioned above for the years between 1902 and 1915, were added, there would have been 160 confreres who had received their formation – if not completely, at least partially – in this institution.

Division of the Vicariate of Ningbo: Mission of Lishui

A diocesan priest, Father Fraser, came in 1902 and exercised his apostolic zeal in the Ningbo vicariate. First, he worked in the district of Ningbo. In 1911, he returned to Canada, his motherland, remaining there for two years. On his return to China, he was placed in Taizhou, later called Lishui.

From that time on, Fraser made several trips to Canada for more or less extended periods. During one of these stays, he laid the foundations of a Society of Overseas Missionaries. Rome approved this Society in 1926 under the name of "Scarboro Foreign Mission Society" or S.F.M.

Meanwhile, Fraser was appointed apostolic protonotary and came back to Zhejiang, in the Hangzhou vicariate under the jurisdiction of Faveau, who placed him in Jinhua. Later, after some confreres of the new society arrived to join their founder, the apostolic vicar of Ningbo entrusted them with the area later called Lishui as a mission dependent on Ningbo.

In 1932, the Holy See declared this mission "independent" and at the same time erected it as an apostolic prefecture comprising ten civil sub-prefectures. The population of that area was estimated at 2.3 million souls and, in 1932, had only 2,580 Faithful. Progress was slow, though many missionaries had arrived.

The first apostolic prefect was Father [William Cecil] McGrath till 1940 and after him Father [Michael Leo] Curtin. In 1941, the personnel consisted of thirty-eight foreign priests and six Chinese priests. Helping them there were nine foreign religious women. The number of Faithful had grown to six thousand two hundred fifty.

In 1946, the prefecture was erected as a vicariate to which eight civil sub-prefectures were added. But the Marxist cataclysm about to sweep through the country in destructive waves was to render this last promotion moot.

The District of Wenzhou

After Father Aroud's definitive departure in 1929, Father Marquès took the direction of the district and Father Joannès Prost replaced him from 1936 to 1939.

Some Polish confreres had come in 1932, and others followed; in 1935, there were ten of them. They hoped that one day their province of Poland would be entrusted with this area or another one, as it had happened for their compatriots in Shunde in the north.

The circumstances, however, did not permit the realization of this hope in Wenzhou, which always remained under the jurisdiction of Ningbo. Afterwards some of those who were in Wenzhou went and joined their confreres in Shunde; the others went somewhere else or returned to Europe.

The "House of the Missionary" in Vichy

After Father Watthé arrived in China in 1903, he was appointed to South Jiangxi, which became later the vicariate of Ganzhou, but the World War obliged him to return to France. In 1916, like several other French mission-

aries, he was assigned to the category of translators for the Chinese workers whom the French government was using for different kinds of work.

After the armistice, Watthé had to think about taking care of his quite
broken health before returning to China. He was advised to take the cure in
Vichy. In the solitude of the sanitarium, Watthé was thinking that his case
was similar to the one of quite a number of tired or sick missionaries for
whom returning to their country was not enough to help them recover. He
was dreaming of an institution that would receive missionaries freely for the
time of a cure in the waters of Vichy. This institution would be the "House
of the Missionary" where a missionary could feel at home, and enjoy the
company of confreres who were living like he did and shared the same ideal.

Gradually this idea took shape in his mind and he became convinced
that he himself could found this work of mercy. He had, however, at his
disposal only his love for his confreres and he had no other means than
his good will; so he needed help.

He talked about it and he talked about it eloquently with conviction.
His principal argument was that such a work would extend the lives of
many missionaries. He even talked to highly placed people like French
President Doumer and General Lyautey and not in vain. He was applauded,
he was approved and, even more, he was helped.

Starting the work demanded backbreaking labor from Watthé: conferences, letters, trips, worrying about the installation and even powerful
oppositions; nothing discouraged this courageous founder.

Needless to say, that in this enterprise Watthé had his superiors' approval.

Gifts made it possible to rent a house in Vichy and to prepare rooms
in it to receive the first missionaries. The municipality in Vichy took an
interest in the case and lent its support. In 1922, a committee was formed
and missionaries began to arrive. As soon as the beneficial results of
the institution were known, the number of lodgers from all nations and
from all congregations increased year after year. In 1930, at the sixth general assembly of the committee, it was noticed that since the foundation
almost one thousand missionaries had come to receive the benefits of
the Celestines and of the "Grande Grille" [in Vichy]. It was fast proven
that the initial installation was not enough. The committee decided to
put up a good-looking building where everything would be organized
without luxury, but with moderate comfort.

On 19 July 1931 the solemn inauguration of the House of the Missionary took place. Even Pope Pius XI deigned to congratulate and to

bless the founder "because he had realized a work which must give back to missionaries, suffering in their health, the strength necessary to face the hard labors of apostolate . . . . The Museum of the Missions and the course of conferences organized for the instruction of those who frequent the thermal spa are also a meritorious apostolate . . . by changing false mentalities, by increasing sympathies in favor of the great work of the salvation of the infidels."

Watthé's health, consumed through so many occupations and worries, declined very fast and soon, after confreres came to help him, he had to stop all activity. Watthé died in Vichy on 19 November 1935 at the age of fifty-eight. Confreres, former missionaries, came and took over and the work continued prospering. It still procures the same benefits to missionaries who want to recover their health, which had been weakened either through the harshness of the climate or through the labor of the ministry.

Bishop Misner's Death

Some pages earlier we said that on 25 March 1935 Bishop Misner's consecration took place in Yujiang. His great health made for the hope of a long episcopate. Alas! This episcopate lasted just three and a half years. God called this good worker back on 1 November 1938. During this short interval, Misner proved to be an excellent administrator: the finances of this vicariate were put in a better shape; four parishes were set up; a new minor seminary was built. He ordained seven Chinese priests, acquired new recruits from the United States and brought back the Daughters of Charity, sent away following the invasion of the Red army.

A sudden death put an end to his activities. At least he died with his weapons in hand. In the last days of October 1938 he was on a confirmations trip, when he became violently ill. On 1 November 1938 he died. The venerated bishop's body was brought back to Yujiang where Bishop O'Shea, apostolic vicar of Ganzhou, came and celebrated the funeral services in the church, where on 25 March 1935, just three years and seven months before, he had consecrated Misner bishop.

His Successor: Bishop Charles Quinn

By decree dated 28 May 1940 Father Charles Quinn was named bishop of Halicarnassus and apostolic vicar of Yujiang. Born in Savannah (California) on 16 December 1905, Charles Quinn did his humanities in Cape Girardeau and entered the Congregation in Perryville in 1923. Ordained a priest in 1931, he was sent, according to the proposal of Bishop Sheehan, the then apostolic vicar in Yujiang, to Rome to continue his studies of canon law at the Angelicum.

Next, after a short stay in the United States, his superiors sent him to the vicariate of Yujiang, where he arrived in 1934.

Initially he was Bishop Sheehan's secretary, then procurator, later on associate in Yujiang. Misner, Sheehan's successor, delegated him as his vicar. At the latter's death, because he was pro-vicar, Quinn took over the temporary administration of the vicariate. Bishop O'Shea from Ganzhou consecrated Quinn in Yujiang 3 October 1940.

Table 25.1 Inventory of Vicariate of Yujiang, 1940

Personnel	Numbers
Catholics	26,826
Foreign priests	24
Chinese priests (among whom were 12 Vincentians)	32

A Great Christian: Lu Bohong

This man was not one of "ours" (Vincentians); he was from the Shanghai vicariate, administered by the Jesuits. So why in our account do we mention this Christian who seems to be an outsider for us? We made a place for notes about bishops, sometimes about priests who had distinguished themselves by their evangelization work, but we never mentioned simple Christians.

There are two reasons for this exception: 1. This man honored the Catholic Church through really admirable works of charity. 2. Among these works, there was one – probably the most important one – with which he entrusted our Sisters, the Daughters of Charity: it was the Saint Joseph home, whose creation in itself would be enough to illustrate the greatness of this Christian. If, as a rule, the Sisters of Saint Vincent de Paul worked in areas entrusted to Vincentians, it must not be forgotten that their Central House was located in Shanghai and that the Jesuits were happy to entrust them with the direction of some of their important works, for instance, the General Hospital and later the Sainte Marie Hospital, among others. Consequently, if Lu Bohong did not strictly belong to the members of the Vincentian family, he became one through his works.

Lu Bohong was director of the biggest electricity company in Shanghai, member of the council of directors of the Water Company in the same city, member of the French local council, director-administrator of the Central Hospital, national president of Catholic Action, permanent member of the Eucharistic Congresses, president of a relief society, and we pass over others.

A Christian, educated and formed by the Jesuits, Lu was a credit to his teachers. Since his youth, he served Mass and received Communion every day. He had received a good literary education and had got the grade of Bachelor under the previous regime. Since his adolescence, he took part in truly Catholic activities. In 1904, he was teaching catechism to poor people whom he gathered together. In 1911, he organized a kind of Catholic Action. Its rules were severe. Every day: meditation and examination of conscience; every Saturday, the president asked about the way every member had fulfilled the task given the previous week. These tasks were: visiting the sick in their homes or in the hospital, teaching Christian doctrine, visiting prisoners, setting up day nurseries, and so on.

Let us now turn to the foundations of his works of mercy. In 1912, he founded in Shanghai's southern suburb the Saint Joseph Center, which he entrusted to the Daughters of Charity. This vast institution would comprise successively a dispensary, a home for elderly people, an orphanage, schools, workshops and an asylum for incurable people. In 1914, he founded another dispensary that grew to become in 1924 the Hospital of the Sacred Heart for four hundred patients.

In 1933, he organized the Hospital of Mercy, destined exclusively for mental patients. It was the only one of its kind in China. He entrusted the care of the male patients to the Brothers of Charity from Trier, while the American Sisters of Saint Dominic (Maryknoll) took charge of the women. This institution received up to five hundred boarders. From its foundation, half of the sick people left healed.

Lu not only provided for the needs of unfortunate people; he wanted to promote progress under all forms. He set up a professional school for young girls. The construction of that school cost four hundred thousand dollars; it could accommodate one thousand students. It was a modern institution built in accordance with the latest requirements of hygiene. The study program was for six years. Physics, chemistry, art, music and painting were taught.

Lu had many works of less importance on his hands. He used his own resources for them, which certainly were extensive, for he was a wise businessman. He used them as far as he could. Having arrived to the point where he could not do any more, he asked for help. He called himself "the first beggar of the world," the "coolie of Saint Joseph," whom he considered as the provider of his needs. He appealed, however, to the generosity of his friends without distinction of religion. Keeping his optimistic trust, he succeeded in multiplying his works of charity.

The provinces devastated by floods or starving through drought received from him prompt and generous assistance. As a result, it is not surprising that such activity and generosity drew to him the attention and respect of the whole world.

The Holy See made him Knight of Saint Gregory and Commander of the Order of Saint Sylvester, then *Camérier de cape et épée* [Chamberlain of Cape and Sword, a further papal honor].

France made him Knight of the Legion of Honor. Belgium decorated him with the Order of Leopold II. Italy conferred on him the distinction of Commander of the Order of the Cross of Italy, and so on.

To give an idea of the importance of the works of Charity set up by Lu Bohong, we show here the details of the population just of the Saint Joseph Home, managed by the Daughters of Charity.

Table 25.2 St. Joseph Center, Shanghai, Patients Treated, 1936

Categories	Totals
Men	
Hospitalized patients	295
Hospitalized elderly	208
Hospitalized prisoners	42
Blind, handicapped, mentally challenged	124
Schoolboys	380
Pre-school boys in the care of the Sisters	38
Teachers and assistants	30
Nurses and servants	70
Elderly able to do some work	26
Administrative personnel	38
TOTAL	1,251

Women	
Hospitalized patients	92
Elderly, blind, mentally challenged	456
Women and girl prisoners	64
Girls	424
Girls in the workshop	113
Girls in classes	279
Very small babies	580
Weaned from wet nurses	644
Infants in the day nursery	97
Patients in isolation	117
Teachers and nurses	98
Small families	298
Sisters of the Home	20
TOTAL	3282
GRAND TOTAL (men and women)	4533

Lu Bohong Died a Victim of his Charity

The Sino-Japanese War caused Lu all kinds of troubles and increased the demands and the expenditures of his works. When in 1937–1938 the Japanese came and occupied Shanghai with its suburbs, Lu worried about his works, which were more necessary than ever among the disorders caused by the war: stoppage of the factories, difficulties with money-changing, and so on. Who could come to the assistance of those who were suffering, if not the very occupying forces? As a result, he went and proposed it to them directly and he got wonderful, completely unexpected results. But right away the dark suspicion of collaboration with the enemy arose.

In February 1938 when Lu left a friend's house and entered the street, a fatal bullet struck him right in the heart.

We do not know the date of Lu Bohong's birth, but having seen him in 1923 in his full maturity, he must have been at least sixty years old on the day of his death. We recounted only his activities that are best known by the public, and we lack the documents to go further. What we do know about him is sufficient for us to be able to express this judgment. This model Christian had as a principle: earn much money so as to help a greater number of needy people. It meant: direct your commercial and industrial businesses so as to produce a maximum of earnings, which can serve the apostolate. This supposed on his part a great understanding of temporal businesses, while relying on an unwavering faith and an unlimited trust in Divine Providence.

Centenary of the Vicariate of Nanchang

Only the war in 1938 prevented the celebration of this anniversary; but the absence of every exterior ceremony did not diminish the importance of this historic fact.

Our intention in reporting it here is in the first place to throw some more light on the account, of which Jiangxi has often been our interest.

Successive divisions, changing names of the vicariates in 1920, giving various vicariates to different congregations: all that elicited more confusion than clarity. Remember that Bishop Carpena Diaz, O.P., apostolic vicar in Fujian (1812–1849) – a vicariate which encompassed in his jurisdiction the two civil provinces of Zhejiang and Jiangxi – asked Rome that those two provinces be taken away from him for he did not have enough missionaries to administer them.

The Holy See granted his wish and in 1838 entrusted the Vincentians with Zhejiang and Jiangxi. The first apostolic vicar of those two provinces was Bishop Alexis Rameaux, C.M., who died in 1845 in Macao and had Bishop Laribe as successor. This vicariate, consisting of two provinces was still too large. In 1846, Rome divided the two provinces to create two vicariates. Bishop Pierre Lavaissière, C.M., was the first apostolic vicar of Zhejiang and Bishop Laribe, who had been given the right to choose, kept Jiangxi, which had at that time seven thousand Christians.

Long ordeals took place: persecutions, rebellion of the Chang Mao, and so on. In 1870, under Bishop Bray's jurisdiction, Jiangxi was divided into north and south. North Jiangxi kept ten thousand Faithful, while south had no more than three thousand three hundred six.

In 1885, a new division of North Jiangxi was made to form the vicariate of East Jiangxi, which had nine thousand eight hundred five Christians and left only three thousand two hundred to North Jiangxi.

In 1920, North Jiangxi underwent a further division. Two civil prefectures that were to join South Jiangxi had two thousand five hundred seventy Faithful. At the same time, however, south Jiangxi was divided in two parts to form the vicariate of Ganzhou. On that date in 1920 names were changed. The north was to be called Jiujiang in the beginning, then after some years it became Nanchang, for the simple reason that Nanchang was the capital of the Jiangxi province.

> Bishop Joseph Zhou was the first bishop to reside in Nanchang, beginning in 1949.

> South Jiangxi was to be called Ji'an.

> East Jiangxi would be Yujiang.

> Ganzhou would stay with the name Ganzhou.

In 1932, Yujiang surrendered five civil sub-prefectures, which became the apostolic prefecture of Nancheng and was then entrusted to the Columbans. It became a vicariate in 1938.

Summary List for 1939

Calling the vicariates by the name used in 1939, we give the date of their establishment, the respective totals of Christians, European priests, Chinese priests, the responsible missionary society and the name of the apostolic vicars.

Table 25.3 Jiangxi, Statistical Summary of Priests and Catholics, 1939

Year Erected	Catholics	European priests	Chinese priests	Missionary society	Apostolic Vicar
1838 Nanchang	34,230	15	25	C.M.: French	Paul Dumond
1879 Ji'an	23,981	12	12	C.M.: Italian	Gaetano Mignani
1885 Yujiang	26,826	24	32	C.M.: American	William Quinn
1920 Ganzhou	17,863	22	15	C.M.: American	John O'Shea
1932 Nancheng	9,093	25	3	S.S.C.M.E.	Patrick Cleary
Totals	111,993	98	87		

Of these five vicariates, the French Vincentian province of Paris directed only Nanchang.

The Missions During the Sino-Japanese War

From 1937 onwards, the war continued its devastating work. China is so huge that, when in some areas there was destruction, in other places, things were peaceful. It was not possible to do for the war in China what is done for other wars, namely, indicating the front on a map with small flags. There was no battlefront, or better, there were scores of them far from one another. The Japanese armies, following the larger communication arteries, were plunging into an immense country and occupying a province here and there, a port, a strategic location. If there had not been warplanes, this immense body of China, which covers almost ten million square kilometers would have ignored the war for a great part; but planes were crossing the Chinese sky in all directions, sowing fear, destruction, and death, so that even in the regions furthest away from the coast, where never a Japanese had been seen, Chinese people knew that their hereditary enemy was waging war on them.

In all the towns that were hit, there were missionaries of different congregations and nationalities. Jesuits in Shanghai and Nanjing, Vincentians in Ningbo, Taizhou, and in the large cities of Jiangxi, Dominicans in Fujian, Italian missionaries in Henan, Franciscans in Hubei, Foreign Missions of Paris in Guangxi and Sichuan. All these missions were bombed more or less heavily and suffered in various ways.

Missionaries were arrested and even murdered, not as direst casualties of the war, but due to robbery born from the disorder caused by the war. The horrible massacre of Zhengding was not repeated. In the area of Baoding, Japanese soldiers in 1941 killed two Chinese [diocesan] priests, Fathers Augustin Chen and Léon Li, but it has never been made clear why; at the same period, however, and in the same vicariate a Communist group killed [two diocesan priests] Fathers Jean-Marie Hu and Paul Liu.

In the same way in Hangzhou: two more diocesan priests and a layman, Father Fabien Wu and his servant, were killed after having been robbed. In Nanchang, Father Jean Fu was murdered during a trip, but there is no way to know by whom and why.

Because we are now recounting incidents of innocent victims sacrificed in troubling times, let us quote the statistics by Father D'Elia, S.J. This Shanghai missionary went to a lot of trouble to make a minute inquiry throughout China on violations of liberty and attempts on the lives of missionaries during the period of twenty-two years, from 1911 to 1933. Now, he was able to make a set of statistics that have surprised even missionaries in China. During that time, fifty-two Catholic missionaries were killed and three hundred thirty-four put into prison for a more or less long time, sometimes even up to three years. The list is introduced by a declaration on reliability of his research, which lets no room for doubt. "All their names," he says, "without a single exception, together with historical data and the photograph of most of them, are in our possession." Note that among the three hundred thirty-four captives, there are about ten who were imprisoned again one or several times after their release, though in the list they have been numbered only once. Three among those prisoners died during their captivity and nevertheless have not been numbered among the fifty-two who were killed. At the end of 1933, five missionaries were still in prison. (See Pascal D'Elia, S.J., *Les Missions catholiques en Chine* [Shanghai, 1934], p. 68.)

Table 25.4 Missionaries Captured and Executed in China, 1912–1933

Year	Capt.	Exec.	Year	Capt.	Exec.	Year	Capt.	Exec.
1912	1	1	1919	1		1926	20	4
1913	1	1	1920	4	1	1927	33	6
1914	4	2	1921	9	1	1928	30	4
1915			1922	12	1	1929	43	8
1916	3		1923	10	2	1930	77	7
1917	1		1924	12	1	1931	36	8
1918	2	1	1925	10		1932	13	2
						1933	12	2
TOTAL							334	52

Table 25.5 Missionaries Captured and Executed by Category

Category	Captured	Executed
Apostolic vicars	6	2
Apostolic prefects	3	
Mission superiors	2	
Religious superiors	5	
Religious priests	126	27
Diocesan priests	93	17
Seminarians	29	4
Lay brothers	10	
Sisters	60	
TOTAL	318	48

Note that these statistics cover only a short period of time (1912–1933); consequently, those we have mentioned ourselves throughout our account from 1933 on have not been listed in it.

Moreover, we are quite sure that from 1933 to 1955 arrests and killings were more numerous; but we do not have the necessary witnesses to give even an approximate number of them.

After this macabre reading, sad readers would probably like to come back to more consoling facts. We will satisfy them by presenting a short note about a religious woman, who certainly has merited it. Up to now we have spoken about Daughters of Charity only to signal their presence in this or that mission, without describing in detail their works, nor mentioning persons. A thick volume would not have been enough.

Among the Daughters of Charity who worked in China, there were two who had a significant place at the head of the auxiliary works of the missions that we cannot keep silent about their well-known names: Sister Gilbert in the Vincentian Southern Province, and Sister Guerlain in the Northern Province.

Sister Gilbert

She was thirty-one years old when she landed in China, after spending twelve years in Biskra (Algiers). First, she busied herself with works in Dinghai, the harbor of Zhoushan Island; then she was placed in the hospital home of Ningbo, whose superior she became and which she developed marvelously till the end.

Sister Gilbert wrote many letters and sent them all over. Her name was well known in the world of the missions. The *Missions Catholiques* in Lyons, the *Annales de la Sainte-Enfance*, and several English magazines made Ningbo and the Maison de Saint Vincent known far and wide, by publishing the good Sister's letters. Her letters contained touching appeals on behalf of the little Chinese children or of the poor elderly people she received. Only God knows how much money she received during her long life. The most miserable poor people were her darlings. The doors of her house were always open and her charity was never called upon in vain.

The institution was often crammed with people. Babies, the elderly, and the sick were always taken in free. When all the places were occupied, she still took people in and when the cashbox was empty, she went on admitting people.

Her colleagues, snowed under with work, protested: "There are no more places." "Come on," she would say, "find a way!" Where else do you think they can go? But I promise you, this is the last one." And another one soon followed this last one. A missionary to whom she expounded both her plans and her difficulties said to her: "If you go on like this, you'll soon be without a penny; what are you going to do then?" "The good Lord will see to it," she answered. Actually though it often happened that there was nothing left in the till, but at the end of the year she was never in debt; Providence had indeed seen to it.

There were painful days, however, sometimes much had to be spent just at the time when there was no money. Employees and workers took advantage of her good faith. There were disappointments. People talked a great deal about Sister Gilbert, judged her methods severely, sometimes condemned them in advance. She had to suffer, but she knew how to keep her mouth shut and always to use exemplary discretion.

She had also her moments of honor. She was decorated with the Legion of Honor on 25 May 1925; she knew very well how to transfer this distinction to the whole mission. When she was eighty-two, her superiors called her back to Shanghai to the rest home for elderly Sisters. She still felt able and strong enough to go on working; so, her colleagues were amazed by this decision. Sister Gilbert, however, accepted the order without complaining. She left and disappeared from public view to bury herself in silence. She unaffectedly went to the kitchen and helped with the cleaning of the vegetables as long as she could do so. She lived six years in retirement, a commendable feat for a person who had the habit of giving orders. After six months' illness, Sister Gilbert gave her soul back to God on 14 February 1936.

We will introduce Sister Guerlain when we have arrived in the North.

Bishop Dumond's Death

Dumond always had quite weak health. He had suffered for years from asthma, which those around him hardly realized. It showed how tough the bishop was, for he never complained. It could be said of him that he had bad health of steel.

Towards the end 1942, the war was raging. American planes were bombing railways and harbors. In Jiujiang, the bishop's residence and the mission procure, being near the river port, were not really threatened, because the planes flying very low, their bombs were on target; but the noise of the explosions was extremely tiring for the residents on the banks of the Yangtze.

To enjoy more tranquility, Dumond withdrew to the seminary located in the countryside not far from town. There he got chronic enteritis that slowly wore him out.

In the beginning of 1944, the patient saw clearly that the sickness was becoming more serious. Nevertheless, he always followed the main exercises of the community. When he himself wanted them, he received the last rites from the hands of Father Rossignol, whom he had appointed for this in advance.

On 17 February, the feast day of Blessed Clet, he took lunch with the professors of the seminary and then withdrew to his room. Several hours later, his nurse saw that the patient was in very bad shape and called the confreres. They arrived just in time to witness a calm and peaceful death. Dumond, born on 2 April 1864, was going to finish his eightieth year, after having spent fifty-six years in China, thirty-two as a bishop.

Dumond had given his confreres a beautiful example of submission, patience and discretion in adversity.

Father Paul Monteil

The vicariate of Nanchang had been mourning its bishop for two years, when it was hit with a new disaster through the death of the pro-vicar, Father Monteil. Leading the vicariate during these especially terrible years in this region suffering from the war, Monteil managed to face up to the biggest difficulties in order to maintain the works of this mission.

Born in Ally (Cantal) on 7 November 1881, Paul Monteil entered in Saint Lazare on 17 March 1901 and arrived in Jiujiang on 14 September 1906. Because this young missionary had remarkable talents for all kinds of construction, Ferrant soon gave him responsibility for rebuilding in Nanchang the works destroyed through the horrible persecution of 1906.

In one year, a vast central residence was built to receive the missionaries of the vicariate; next the foundations of a beautiful church were laid. Ferrant's death did not stop the ongoing construction. The church was finished in 1913.

During the war of 1914–1918, Monteil courageously fulfilled his whole military service as an army chaplain. Back in China in 1919, he continued with the interrupted constructions in Nanchang. Then came the main work of his life, the Saint Louis hospital, so popular in Nanchang. Fatiguet, convinced nobody else could do it better, entrusted Monteil with the construction. Monteil applied himself to it with all his heart and with all his intelligence. In February 1922, the Saint Louis hospital was inaugurated and placed in the hands of the Daughters of Charity.

After that, Monteil directed, from nearby and from afar, the construction of churches and chapels, whose plans he had drawn up. His kindness and zeal had a very beneficial influence in the whole area during the disasters that followed one another from 1926 to 1946: invasions by the southerners, devastations by Communist troops, the Japanese war, and so on.

After Father [Eloi] Domergue's death in 1940, he became Dumond's vicar general and, later on, he became the leader of the vicariate in 1944 at the death of the bishop himself.

At that moment he took up the direction of all business with all his courage and all the experience he gained in the forty years in this vicariate. His main worry was not to develop the works, but only to maintain the lives of his priests and to boost the demoralized courage of some of them. Alas! In June 1945, Monteil felt that he was suffering from a terminal disease. The doctors in the Saint Louis Hospital discovered a cancer in the pancreas that grew very fast. It was an admirable spectacle: the patient, once the truth was known, forgot his suffering so as to think only about the mission that he was responsible for. Before dying he dreamed of putting everything into the hands of the future bishop in perfect order. And he did it. God alone knows at the expense of how much stress he succeeded in this. He was seen sitting for whole days at his worktable in his hospital room, busy with bringing order in his papers and, at the same time taking care of all the matters that were cropping up.

The witnesses of this spectacle understood then what a treasure they were going to lose and what an ideal bishop Monteil could have been at the head of the vicariate. On 12 March 1946 the patient received the last rites at his request and went on working. On 22 March his eyesight became blurred and his tongue confused. On the 23rd he was only praying and in the evening at about five o'clock without any agony he fell asleep in the Lord. This good and faithful servant had gone to enjoy the reward merited through such a full life of service.

The Christians of Nanchang and numerous pagans wanted a very solemn funeral and asked to delay it till 1 April to have the time to prepare it. It was a beautiful manifestation of the Faith in this city, so hostile to Christianity fifty years before.

In the other vicariates of Jiangxi, the situation in those last years of the Japanese war was almost like that in Nanchang. The missionaries' efforts were directed towards the protection and maintenance of existing works, and to providing them with fresh supplies, fortunes having to be paid for foodstuff.

To talk about Zhejiang we turn to Bishop Defebvre, who in *B.C.P.* commented on the situation in his vicariate during that difficult period.

The Vicariate of Ningbo and the Japanese War

He wrote:

> We have undergone the Japanese occupation here in Ningbo and in the north of the vicariate for four and a half years, while in the south, that is, in Wenzhou, the region had to suffer only three occupations, one of them for ten months. During that time, communications between the north and the south of the vicariate were cut; that is the reason why I could visit only the Christian communities in the neighborhood of Ningbo. The missionaries of the different districts had equally large difficulties in visiting their Christian communities wherever the Japanese occupation was raging.

> Because of the impossibility of finding the means necessary for the seminarians' upkeep, I have been obliged grudgingly to send them back to their families for extended holidays. The works of charity were also obliged to slow down their activity, without, however, being abandoned completely. Again, the lack of financial resources forced the missionaries to eliminate a large number of the catechists who were taking care of distant areas; but I hope that soon we will be able to take up again our former apostolate. Here, like in the rest of China, essential foodstuffs are at frightening prices. One hundred fifty pounds of rice are sold today for thirty-one thousand dollars. For several years everybody has been suffering the harshest food restrictions, and we still do not know when they are going to stop. We have confidence nevertheless in God's providence, which has protected us up to now and which will not abandon us.

Chapter 26

Mission Work in Hebei during the War Years, 1930s-1940s

Vitality of the Work of Evangelization – The Chinese Ecclesiastical College – Floods in Hebei in 1939-1940 – Sister Guerlain of Zhengding – Works of Mercy by the Daughters of Charity in China, 1935-1936 – The Many Conversions by Father Etienne Wang, C.M. – Paul Dutilleul – Brother André Denis – Concentration Camps – The Close of the Japanese War

Vitality of the Work of Evangelization

It may seem paradoxical. It was wartime, everything was turned upside down, the sky was full of planes, the countryside was devastated, foreign armies occupied complete provinces, and towns were destroyed. Nevertheless, it was a fact. In the period from 1935 onwards, there was a wave of remarkable efforts by the missionaries in the Missions in the north and the south of China.

Around 1930, the Scheut Fathers had opened a big school in Tianjin to teach the Chinese language to their young missionaries arriving from Europe.

Soon they moved that school to Peking and improved it further in 1935. The Franciscans and the Jesuits set up similar institutes that were no less well organized. Therefore, from the beginning of the Japanese war, the capital was enriched by the presence of more than two hundred clerics. People said that Peking had become a small Rome; young missionaries from other societies flocked to these schools in order to attend the language courses that were taught by expert professors, both priests and laypeople.

Zanin, the apostolic delegate, wishing to contribute to the formation of the future missionaries, had the marvelous idea of organizing in the Catholic University of Fu Jen a series of special conferences called Missionary Academies. We personally attended the majority of those conferences. One day having a seat at the highest point of the amphitheater, we enjoyed with emotion the beautiful spectacle of two hundred missionaries, ready, willing to go in all the directions, and well-trained to spread God's Word. We were thinking in our heart, not with a feeling of fright: "Is this a beginning? Or maybe a climax?" We were already in 1941. The Japanese war was at a critical point in the whole of Asia. The United States had entered the war. At the same time, Communism was building up a strong army in Yan'an (Shaanxi), the center of its operations and of its formation. It was already settling in the north of Mongolia and Manchuria. Already the conferences became more rare and soon stopped completely. Our question got its answer: "It had been a climax."

The Chinese Ecclesiastical College

The University of Peking, Fu Jen, had overcome many obstacles. Moreover, in 1939 it was one the rare survivors among the fifteen universities that Peking took pride in. It came out of the storm as the most seasoned and the strongest. Thanks to its courageous bearing, the Chinese and Japanese authorities respected it. There were more enrollments that year than in all previous years. Conversions to Catholicism by students and professors went at the rate of several dozen a year. But at the end the apostolic delegate wanted fervently that the Chinese clergy take part in university courses so as to acquire more profound and more specialized knowledge of Chinese literature and the different branches of science.

To achieve this desire and to make the possibility of taking part in the courses easier, it was, if not necessary, at least very convenient to gather them in a special seminary built near the university. The apostolic delegate was convinced of this and so decided on its foundation. This study house, this clerical "studium" [house of studies] certainly had to fit naturally into the university complex, which itself was ecclesiastical property, in legal terms, a possession of the Church. Indeed, the Church had founded the university and paid for it, and the Church was paying for its maintenance. Its goal was not only to prepare a clergy able to take responsibility for the management of the Church in China, but also to form for the nation a crack corps of valuable citizens, of able servants, devoted to the common good.

This second goal seems to have been underestimated in the beginning by the persons concerned. The government hesitated a long time before granting permission for the foundation. Moreover, in order that the diplomas of Fu Jen be recognized by the government, the Ministry of Public Instruction insisted on its reserving the leadership of the university by keeping the right to nominate the chancellor. It was hoped that the government, in return for this privilege, would agree to contribute for its part to the expenses of installing and maintaining the school. But nothing was forthcoming. Therefore, the Sacred Congregation of Propaganda every year had to pay a large amount to Fu Jen for the salaries of professors and all the other expenses.

Zanin had many discussions about the future university seminary with the authorities of Fu Jen and finally succeeded in making a contract, according to which the clerics could be admitted to the university courses, and that, after a training of three years, they could be admitted to sit for exams on the same basis as other enrolled students. In this way they would receive a diploma that would entitle them to teach in secondary schools or in equivalent institutions; in practice, to teach in the minor seminaries, which already had to bring their study programs in line with the norms decreed by the state.

This seminary or ecclesiastical college was built in the vicinity of the university, and Zanin appointed a Divine Word Father to take up its direction.

The college was Zanin's pet, on which he lavished his affectionate and paternal concern. Every Sunday – when he was not on an apostolic trip – he came to the college and spent a big part of the day with his beloved students, sometimes giving them a speech or a conference, sometimes having a friendly conversation with them, telling them about his trips throughout China, sometimes giving them advice on their studies or instructions about their future ministry.

Let us say that the college was developing very well when the Communist hurricane rose up. The training time had been extended to a fourth year. In 1949, the college had about sixty priests as students.

Floods in Hebei in 1939–1940

After describing so many calamities, we are sorry to still recall this one. It raged, however, so terribly in the Vincentian Northern Province, whose borders were the same as those of the civil province of Hebei, that we cannot proceed without mentioning it.

An American relief society, established in 1923 with the permission of the Chinese government on the occasion of another disaster, sponsored an inquiry by missionaries in the vicariate of Anguo, the southern part of Hebei. The outcome of this inquiry was that, in a population of 1,330,000 inhabitants, more than four hundred thousand people were reduced to the severest misery and destined to probably die of hunger the next spring, if no solution could be found for the food problem.

The missionaries had already made known that Christians were dying of hunger and that countless groups of hungry people, Christians as well as pagans, were roaming in equally famished regions of the vicariate looking for anything edible: millet, cotton grain, bran, buckwheat, even roots. Help in grain was arriving slowly, for communications were made very difficult because of the war and because of the flood itself. The missionaries volunteered to distribute it.

In Tianjin, there was a real disaster in the low-lying sectors. That was the reason why Bishop de Vienne, in collaboration with the Jesuits, performed miracles to save as many disaster victims from the floods as possible. In the British concession, which was on higher ground, he had one hundred fifty huts made with mud mixed with straw. More or less one thousand people found shelter in them. Half of those people were Christians. In another suburb, the mission alone set up another camp for refugees with equally one hundred fifty shelters only for Catholics. All those refugees received two millet meals a day. Schools were set up for the children.

Sister Guerlain of Zhengding

As we have already mentioned, here we shall give a short note about Sister Guerlain and also about some confreres in the North.

Born in Saint-Omer (Pas-de-Calais) in 1841, Sister Guerlain had received a good education with the Ursulines. At the age of twenty-one she revealed her vocation to her father, who did not want his darling daughter to leave him. The aspirant's energy overcame the difficulties and she entered into the novitiate of the Daughters of Charity in Paris on 23 December 1862. First placed in Fribourg, where she became responsible of the asylum, she was then called to Rome.

Tagliabue, apostolic vicar in Zhengding (1869–1884), had insistently asked Paris for Daughters of Charity for his vicariate. With five companions, Sister Guerlain was part of the first group to arrive in Zhengding. It was 11 November 1882. The missionaries were happy to place into their hands the orphaned girls, who certainly gave them much trouble. In this embryo of an orphanage, where everything still had to be done, Sister Guerlain displayed so much energy that she soon had turned it into a house of mercy, where all the charitable works gradually were begun.

During the Boxer persecution, she was in France busy interesting benefactors in her cause. No sooner had calm been reestablished than she returned to Zhengding. At that time General Bailloud and his troops were pacifying the country, causing the Chinese to like them and so favoring greater progress in the vicariate. After that, some ten years passed in great calm and the works were prospering.

The revolution of 1911 came, however, and floods, famines, and wars by the partisans followed. All this brought in more needy people to the already full house. In this period, without permanent financial resources, living from day to day, strong because of her trust in Saint Joseph, Sister Guerlain, like Sister Gilbert in Ningbo, took in and took in again. Sometimes the people who had to be fed had tripled.

In 1926, eighty-five years old, her infirmities and fatigue forced her to yield the government of her house, but she did not leave it; she remained half-retired, always interested in the way the works were going. In 1930, her strength failed her and even her faculties became weaker. Then came some months of prostration followed by nine days of her final agony. Sister Guerlain passed away on 19 May 1931. The numerous masses that Christians asked for the repose of her soul were a beautiful witness to the respect and the gratefulness they had for this woman who had done so much good for them.

Works of Mercy of the Daughters of Charity in China, 1935-1936

To give an idea of what the works by the Daughters of Charity had been in China, we introduce here a short list of their activities for the year 1935–1936

It is well known that the Daughters of Charity in China never have had more than one Province. Their central House was in Shanghai (vicariate of the Jesuit Fathers) and it was in this city that their visitatrix was living, and also their director, who was the provincial superior of the Vincentian Southern province. The Sisters were spread over the two Vincentian provinces almost equally; their houses and works were scattered over thirteen vicariates. They were:

In the North: Peking, Tianjin, Baoding, Zhengding, Shunde and Yongping.

In the South: Shanghai, Ningbo, Hangzhou, Nanchang, Ji'an, Yujiang and Ganzhou.

Table 26.1 Daughters of Charity's Work in Vincentian
Areas (plus Shanghai), 1935–1936

Categories	Totals
Daughters of Charity: Foreigners	169
Daughters of Charity: Chinese	241
Total	410
Schools: parish, primary, secondary pupils	3,778
Catechumenates: 15 – Female students	713
Workshops: 14 – Female workers	929
Hospitals for men: 20 – Patients	26,930
Hospitals for women: 18 – Patients	9,130
Dispensaries: 61 – Outpatient visits	2,101,900
Visits to sick people at home	47,586
Visits to prisons	1,540
Homes for elderly men: 12 – Men cared for	800
Homes for elderly women: 11 – Women cared for	570
Orphanages for boys: 3	
• Boys in the nursery	100
• Boys in school	103
• Boys in workshops	140
Orphanages for girls: 21	
• Girls with wet nurses	3,400
• Girls in nurseries	738
• Girls in school	1,100
Baptisms of adults in these works	1,040
Baptisms of adults at the moment of death	5,166
Baptisms of the children of Christians	7,247
Baptisms of children at the moment of death	20,568

The Many Conversions by Father Etienne Wang

Father Etienne Wang, born in July 1858 in Lingluo north of Peking, did all his studies in the capital. He was ordained priest in January 1897 and appointed in the district of Baoding, where he has been working all his life. In 1899, he was the curate of Dumond, the director of the district.

When the Boxer movement was already at its height and had wreaked havoc, Dumond and his associate fled to Anjiazhuang, where they remained only four months and, in October 1900, after calm was restored, they returned to rebuild the ruins. While Dumond was busy rebuilding the church, razed to the ground by the Boxers, Wang exerted himself building chapels in the Christian communities in the vicinity. He set up seven or eight of them in good condition and they were very useful for those communities of Christians.

Dumond had discovered great talents in his associate. He was a good speaker, very enterprising, and at the same time very obedient to his superior; besides he was successful in his enterprises. Very devout, he omitted nothing of his exercises of priestly piety, despite his many occupations.

In 1903, Dumond sent Wang toward the south of Baoding with the mission of creating a parish in the very center that the Boxers had most ravaged. The center of the parish would be Xiezhuang, a large village, influential in the whole region; it had been a nest of Boxers. The number of Christians in this village could have been counted on the fingers of one hand, but there were more in the neighboring villages that had suffered very much at the hands of the rebels.

Wang was an achiever. Must there be a parish? There was going to be a parish and a beautiful one! This one, unlike all the other parishes of Baoding, was to be purely Chinese in the sense that no European missionary ever had ministered in Xiezhuang, not at all by exclusion – no one had ever thought of it – but by chance and simple happenstance. He had been given two associates, and in 1905 two more were added, all Chinese. The beginnings were difficult indeed, but quite quickly Wang's convincing words moved the whole neighborhood.

People filled the catechumenates. Josephines were called in for the formation of the women. Wang built a chapel and a residence. The number of Christians increased as if by magic. In 1909, in the village itself, there were nine hundred fifty baptisms and many more in the hamlets that were part of the new parish.

In 1912, Wang entered the Congregation, left his parish and went to Chala to do his novitiate. His temporary replacement in Xiezhuang was one of his associates, Father Pierre Cheng (future bishop of Xuanhua).

The next year, 1913, his probation having been finished in optimum conditions, Wang returned to his post as pastor. Then he built a beautiful big church with a well-arranged residence. Soon, the parish of Xiezhuang prepared other parishes, more than one pastor of which had been his associate. In this way they fathered Jiangjiazhuang, Xiwangli, later on Beiwangli, Duanjiazhuang, and then Beizhuang.

At the time of the World War, 1914–1918, the influx of conversions decreased as they did everywhere in the vicariate; the missionaries had to reign themselves in because they were overburdened with work. It was necessary to take care indeed of a mass of recently converted Christians; they had to maintain and deepen their religious life, educate the youth, build schools, and set up works. All that kept quite a lot of the personnel busy in the mission, so that there were few people who could go out and work with the pagans.

From its creation, the Xiezhuang parish and all those to which it had given birth were part of the Donglü district. This went on till 1931, that is, until Bishop Joseph Zhou took possession of the Baoding vicariate entrusted henceforth to the diocesan clergy. Consequently, the number of European Vincentians had to decrease and eventually disappear completely. Fact is that the district of Donglü consisted at that time of more than thirty-three thousand Christians. The time to divide it had come so as to make of it two districts. Zhou left Donglü with about ten thousand seven hundred ninety Faithful and erected the district of Xiezhuang with a little more than twenty-two thousand Christians. But Wang was not there anymore.

In 1928, the twenty-five years of Wang's presence, the silver anniversary of the parish, had been celebrated with joy. As it happens too frequently, this feast was the swan song for the incumbent. When Wang had passed sixty years of age, he seemed to be worn out: his eyesight was diminishing; his voice – he had talked so much – gave only a hoarse sound. That is why he had to slow down. He went, however, to Baoding with the other confreres to make his annual retreat. The second day of the exercises, Wang had a stroke from which he did not recover. Taken to the hospital of Nanguan, he did not recover the use of his voice, but his mind was lucid.

On 20 September 1930 he gave his soul back to God. This courageous fighter against the devil must have been received well by Saint Michael, whose feast was being celebrated that day.

Etienne Wang left an example of tireless zeal for the conversion of pagans. Certainly, he had natural talents, but he knew how to use them for the salvation of souls. He achieved great influence even over the pagan population. He knew intimately the mind of his fellow Chinese; the pagan's sly tricks and shrewdness had no secret for him; he was not easily taken in. When he was dealing with some complicated marriage or court matter, or any dispute whatsoever, he guessed right about the inner intentions of the partner and he had almost always the last word.

He was sometimes reproached with going a little too fast in his formation of new Christians. "Our Christians," he would answer, "are no present-day saints, they are future saints."

Paul Dutilleul

Though less restless than that of the previous one, Father Dutilleul's life was no less devoted to the salvation of souls. Born in Cambrai on 14 July 1862 he did all his studies in the diocese and was ordained there on 29 June 1886. Professor at the college in Roubaix for eleven years, he felt at thirty-five years of age that he was called for mission life. He was admitted in Paris on 6 November 1897 and made his novitiate in Wernhout (The Netherlands). After he took vows, he asked to be sent to China. He arrived in Shanghai on 25 September at the time Boscat, the visitor, was setting up the seminary and the house of studies in China. Dutilleul was immediately appointed as its first director, in the beginning in Zhoushan, later in Jiaxing in 1904. He remained there till 1909, the year he was called to direct the second novitiate, founded a short time before in Chala.

In 1913, Dutilleul became professor at the major seminary of Peking, then superior in 1916. When the students of this seminary moved to the regional seminary in Chala in 1923, the elderly Dutilleul no longer had any determined occupation. This did not stop him from exercising a fertile ministry for the clergy, especially for the diocesan priests who were members of the Apostolic Union, a world-wide priestly organization, which Fabrègues had instituted together with Dutilleul. The latter was its general director for China and Japan.

Dutilleul was a holy priest and an excellent spiritual counselor. His ministry in France and China was completely devoted to the formation of priests; that is why he had acquired such a great experience of souls.

Since he had arrived late in China, he had much difficulty in learning the language. He tried hard, but his visual memory hardly remembered the complicated strokes of the Chinese characters and on the other hand, his pronunciation was all the more defective because he had never mingled with the Chinese population, like the missionaries did.

Being basically a good and charitable soul revealing with simplicity his true feelings, he harvested the affection that he lavished around him generously. His conferences, seriously prepared, were well appreciated by the audience. He drew them directly from the Gospel and from Saint Vincent's maxims. Full of gentleness and charity, they led people to love God and spread a solid devotion for Saint Vincent. Therefore, he was heard saying: "The Gospel and Saint Vincent have always been enough for me."

After a short illness, Dutilleul died peacefully in Saint Vincent Hospital on 19 December 1929 after having received the last sacraments devoutly. We do not think that we exaggerated by saying that the memory of this man of God was sweet and beneficial for a long time for those who had had the chance to meet and know him.

Because it is impossible to mention all the missionaries who have distinguished themselves in our two provinces through their work and their virtues, we are obliged to make a more or less good choice among them and bring into the limelight only those who, to our mind, deserve it most. Moreover, in any human history it is the same phenomenon: only the names of those who because of their position or the nature of their activities have come to the fore. A great number of other people are passed over in silence.

Brother André Denis

Born in Lyons on 5 December 1858, received in the Congregation in Paris on 26 September 1877, Brother Denis arrived in China on 31 October 1881. Placed as "factotum" in the bishop's residence of Zhengding, he was of much service because of his many skills.

In 1887, Brother Denis was called to Peking to teach French in a school established in Nantang. When the Boxer Rebellion began in 1900, the influx of Christian refugees in the Beitang was such that the brother had to abandon his school and go to the Beitang to care for the refugees. Actually, during the siege, he did all kinds of jobs, but mostly that of a nurse. He distinguished himself through his dedication in looking after the many wounded people, soldiers and refugees.

When calm had resumed, he was sent to Baoding to take charge of the French school that one of the chaplains of the French troops, Father Clerc-Renaud (future bishop of Jiangxi), had just founded.

This school had great success. Brother Denis, assisted by two other brothers, taught French to about a hundred students, among whom forty were Catholic boarders, and the others were almost all pagans. There were also one or two professors to teach Chinese.

It was not enough for Brother Denis to teach French, but, aware that he was a missionary too on his level, he wanted to educate his students. Every year, he converted a number of them and had them baptized by a priest who first tested their intellectual and moral preparation. His former students appreciated him very much, especially those who had benefited from his admonitions and corrections.

When missionaries were traveling on the Peking-Hankou railway line, it often happened to them to be spoken to, either in the train, or in a railway station or an office, by an employee, who in the conversation with the priest asked if he knew Brother Denis, teacher of French in Baoding. If the missionary answered that he did, then he could hear from the young man words of praise, which showed the respect and affection that the employee had for his former teacher.

Thus, for twenty years, administrators of schools asked good Brother Denis to provide them with many of their employees. But the time came that many public schools created by the government were able to take care of their needs for employees. Moreover, the English language, having become the principal commercial language in the whole world, quickly supplanted the French language.

Noting this fact, Fabrègues thought about doing away with the French school so as to make of it a *probatorium* [pre-seminary] for the minor seminary, a work that would be more directly useful for the mission than a school for French.

That is what happened in 1921. Then the Brothers began to teach the basics of Latin for children who felt called to the ecclesiastical life, so that they were able to read it when entering the minor seminary. There were sixty pupils, and they were doing two years' training course; about thirty entered the minor seminary every year.

In 1923, Fabrègues founded in Nanguan (suburb in the south) a secondary college, which had to become a normal school approved by the government. The bishop gave its responsibility to a European confrere and withdrew the three Brothers from the *probatorium* so as to place them in the new college in order to teach the French language again to the students who wanted it. Brother Denis was very happy to be back in his element. From then on Chinese priests always managed the *probatorium*.

When in 1927 it was the fiftieth anniversary of Brother Denis's vocation, the missionaries of Baoding wanted, by organizing a small family feast, to show the good brother how much they respected him. Bishop Fabrègues, who had had Brother Denis under his direction for twenty-five years, came from Peking; Father Desrumaux, the visitor, came from Tianjin, too. All the lay brothers of the province were there and also many priests of the vicariate. Everything went very well indeed. But it was also a swan song. Those who had taken part in this anniversary, those who had seen that day Brother Denis so joyful and so pleasant, were very sad to hear some days later that a facial paralysis had stopped the brother from teaching again. The illness made quick progress. On Sunday 13 November he once again attended Holy Mass and received Holy Communion; but back in his room he felt that the pain was becoming acute and he asked the superior for the last rites before, he said, losing consciousness. Then he was taken to the mission hospital, located on the same property of Nanguan, where he soon lost speech completely. Tuesday 15 November 1927 at ten o'clock in the evening, Brother Denis gave God back his beautiful soul.

The mission of Baoding had lost a precious helper, who, with his specialty had contributed not a little to the progress of the communal work of the missionaries in Baoding.

Concentration Camps

After long negotiations with representatives of the Japanese government, the U.S.A. had not been able to succeed in persuading them to give up their hold on China, already quite strong; so, it felt itself forced to defend China and to declare itself against Japan. Right away, Japan – which only waited for this decision – took action. It was 9 December 1941 and the majority of the American population hardly knew that their country was at war, when a really exceptional news item was broadcast: the Japanese destroyed the American fleet in Honolulu. A few days later it was Great Britain's turn to deplore with stupefaction the loss of two of their strongest warships lying at anchor in Singapore.

It was an inexpressible humiliation for these two powerful nations. Afterwards several countries: the Netherlands, Belgium, and Canada also declared themselves to be at war against Japan. France, crushed, did not even think about it; and this fact was an unexpected chance for the missions in China, as we shall see.

Then Japan began to apply the regime of internments of foreign subjects residing in China and belonging to the nations that had declared war on it. The American residents were the first to be interned; later, in 1942–1943, it was the turn of the others. In order not to shock the residents too much, who were numerous in China, the masters of the day gave the name of "gathering camps" to these true Prisoner of War (POW) camps that were called afterwards concentration camps. France, having made no declaration, was considered by Japan to be a friendly nation. Consequently, all the French missionaries and civilians living in China were unharmed.

Here is an example, taken from Chala, of the way the Japanese proceeded to arrest so-called "hostile" subjects.

On 12 March 1943 towards ten o'clock in the morning, a dozen Chinese policemen, soon followed by the Japanese vice-consul, turned up at the regional major seminary in Chala. They asked the superior to call the three Dutch professors, Fathers Marijnen, Ophey and Herrijgers. In the living room, the vice-consul, through interpreters, questioned them with quite some deference about their nationality and their previous activities in China. Then he told them, that, being members of a hostile nation, to go to town on 15 March to a place that would be indicated to them, and from there, on 24 March they would be taken to a gathering camp in Weixian (Shandong). After that, he gave every one of them his travel warrant with the bits of information necessary both for their departure and for their stay there. At last, he left, leaving twelve policemen to guard the prisoners.

During those three days great confusion reigned in the seminary. The policemen, however, did their service quite decently. The three confreres remained in their room at whose door two guards had taken up their position day and night. Nobody could enter their rooms, but they could go themselves to the dining room, to the chapel, only for celebrating Mass, and to the toilet, always accompanied by one or two guards. During that time their classes and their instruction were interrupted.

On 15 March the three prisoners, despite their sadness, went to the Beitang, which was the designated meeting place; they remained there till 24 March, when with quite a number of Belgian, Dutch and Canadian missionaries they took the train to Weixian. That town is in the northeast of the province of Shandong, at a distance of six hundred kilometers from Peking as the crow flies, and seven hundred by train.

The departure of those three professors left the seminary in an embarrassing situation. The visitor had declared that he was definitely unable to find helpers at that time to replace the missing professors. Therefore, the four remaining professors were forced to distribute among themselves the classes of their three confreres. Consequently, for two and a half months everyone had to double his daily tasks for the seventy students (normally their number reached a hundred, but the war situation had kept some in their families).

The camp of Weixian was at the site of a former American university, located in the middle of the countryside eighty kilometers from town. Among the seventeen hundred internees there were three hundred twenty priests and one hundred sixty religious women.

Though the administration was not troublesome, the missionaries were languishing from having no work. Through long and laborious negotiations, Zanin, the apostolic delegate acquired from the Japanese authorities the transfer of the Catholic missionaries interned in Weixian to the institutions of their respective societies, which were installed in the capital. On 25 August 1943 all the missionaries – except some individuals for every congregation who remained in the camp for the well-being of the interned civilians till the defeat of Japan – returned to Peking, some to the Jesuits, others to the Franciscans, others again to the Belgian Scheutists. The Vincentians were put in an old catechist school in the Beitang. There were forty of them, among whom was Bishop Lebouille, apostolic vicar of Yongping. Though having quite narrow lodgings (they were most of the time in a common hall), they were there infinitely better off than in Weixian, because it was easier to have community and priestly life. They remained there two full years.

In the south, the internment of missionaries was done in almost the same way. The concentration camp was located in the suburb of Shanghai. After some months, thanks to Zanin's negotiations with the Japanese authorities, the missionaries returned to the procures of their respective religious societies.

It was a very lucky circumstance that France had not been included among the nations hostile to Japan; otherwise quite a few vicars in China would have been stripped of their missionaries for more than two years.

The Close of the Japanese War

From 1943 on, the successes of the Japanese armies changed into setbacks; all their conquests of the Pacific and of Asia got away from them one after the other. In August 1945, the Americans dropped the first atomic bomb on Hiroshima, and the Soviet Union declared war on Japan. It was the end. On 15 August Japan surrendered and had to undergo American occupation.

As soon as the emperor of Japan had given to the nation, by radio, the order to surrender, all bowed with profound respect, similar to the one that the ancient Chinese in the old days showed for every declaration of the Son of Heaven.

The officers and soldiers laid down their arms with an almost solemn dignity.

It could be thought that the peace signed with Japan would bring joy to the Chinese population. But no, it was not so. A black cloud hovered on the horizon as a formidable threat: Communism. Everybody knew that there was a real Communist army, well trained and well equipped. It was the one in Yan'an, which had developed itself and made itself strong thanks to the Japanese war. The Communists themselves undertook, without president Chiang Kai-shek's permission, to disarm the Japanese divisions in Manchuria, and in this way they were enriched with extensive armament.

Chapter 27

Changes Affecting Vincentian Mission Work, 1940s

The First Chinese Cardinal – Establishment of the Ecclesiastical Hierarchy in China – Importance of these Events – Appointment of an Internuncio in China – Cardinal Tian's Arrival in Peking – The Minor Seminary of the Beitang – Two New Vincentian Visitors in China – Bishop Zhou's Transfer to Nanchang – China Goes from the Frying Pan into the Fire – A Mission Completely Ruined – The Internuncio's Visit to Tianjin – The Situation in the Diocese of Tianjin – The Monastery of Our Lady of Consolation (Yangjiaping) Burned by the Reds – The Monastery of Our Lady of Joy (Zhengding) Evacuated – Lebbe's Final Activities

The First Chinese Cardinal

Thomas Tian was born on 24 October 1890 of pagan parents in Zhangqiuzhen in the vicariate of Yangguxian (Shandong) entrusted to the German Divine Word Fathers. His father had a bachelor's degree and was a teacher. He was appointed professor of Chinese language in the minor seminary of Polizhuang in 1898; he became Christian the same year and died in 1899. His mother on the other hand received baptism only in 1914 and died in 1922.

The child, received in the primary school of the mission in Polizhuang in 1901, studied the Chinese classics and was baptized in 1902 under the name Thomas. In 1905, he entered the Minor Seminary of Yanzhou and later the major seminary where he was ordained priest on 9 June 1918. He was successively a missionary in Fanxian and Shanxian, and then, on 8 March 1929 he entered the Society of the Divine Word in Taijiazhuang.

In 1932, he was appointed superior of the independent mission of Yanggu xian. By decree of 23 February 1934 that mission became an apostolic prefecture, and Tian was appointed its first apostolic prefect.

This vicariate had at that time 28,980 Catholics with fifteen priests. Three among those Chinese priests along with four Germans were members of the Society of the Divine Word. Tian, called to Rome, received episcopal consecration from the hands of Pope Pius XII on 29 October 1940; afterwards he returned to China to take possession of his vicariate.

In 1942, he was moved to Qingdao, a seaport of Shandong. This vicariate had at that time 21,500 Christians, twenty-eight foreign priests and six Chinese priests.

On Christmas 1945, to his great surprise, Bishop Tian was created a cardinal. His titular church was Sancta Maria in Via. Again, he traveled to Rome, where on 18 February 1946 he received the cardinal's red hat. From Rome, His Eminence undertook a trip during which he had the pleasure of making many visits. After having visited the Netherlands, Germany, Switzerland and France, the cardinal left for the U.S.A.; in New York, he was Cardinal Spellman's guest. From there he went to Boston where on 7 April he celebrated Mass in the Cathedral of the Holy Cross in the presence of a great number of the Chinese of that city.

The archbishop of Boston presented His Eminence with the gift of eleven thousand dollars.

Then Cardinal Tian visited Georgetown University, the oldest Catholic university of the United States, which offered His Eminence two complete scholarships to him to give to two deserving Chinese students.

The cardinal visited several other major cities in the U.S.A.; everywhere he was received enthusiastically.

His Eminence was still in the U.S.A. when a capital event for the missions in China took place.

Establishment of the Ecclesiastical Hierarchy in China

The Sacred Congregation of Propaganda announced to the apostolic delegation that the Holy See by the decree of 11 April 1946 established the Catholic hierarchy in China.

A few days later, on 25 April, the cardinal, who was in San Diego (California), received a direct telegram from the Holy See appointing him as the archbishop of Peking. Because of this news, His Eminence returned home without delay.

From the United States he flew over the Pacific and the Philippines and landed in Shanghai. On his arrival in China, the cardinal was welcomed and greeted by Bishop Zanin, the apostolic delegate, Archbishop Yu Bin, archbishop of Nanjing, and by the bishops of Shanghai, Haimen and Xinyang, while a crowd was kneeling to receive the cardinal's blessing.

The following morning, 2 June His Eminence celebrated a Pontifical Mass in Zikawei and during the next few days visited the different Catholic works of mercy in Shanghai. On 7 June he headed for Nanjing, traveling in a special train which the Chinese government put at his disposal. In Nanjing, he was the guest of Generalissimo Chiang Kai-Shek. On 14 June he left for Qingdao in the generalissimo's personal plane.

Importance of These Events

The Holy See, at the same time that it instituted the hierarchy in China and elevated to the rank of cardinal a Chinese bishop who had done no studies outside China,[82] wanted to show solemnly the great respect and trust that it had for the Chinese nation. It would have been really inelegant to place the first Chinese cardinal in a small vicariate, which was not even the capital of a province, but a simple civil sub-prefecture. It was much more decent that he be made an archbishop, all the more so because from that moment on – because of the hierarchy – every apostolic vicar of a provincial capital would become an archbishop, while all the other apostolic vicars of that same civil province would be his suffragan bishops.

Moreover, it was still much more proper that the cardinal was the archbishop of Peking, which had always been the capital of China, except during short periods of time.

On the other hand, a difficulty seemed to stop this project: Bishop Montaigne, apostolic vicar of Peking, occupied the see in Peking. Faced with this situation, however, Bishop Montaigne generously submitted his resignation.

From that moment, the see of Peking was vacant. Rome could now install the cardinal there. This explains Cardinal Tian's transfer from Qingdao to Peking.

People might wonder what the reasons were which motivated the institution of the ecclesiastical hierarchy in China at a moment that pacifying the country after the Japanese war was far from completed and that the threat of Communism was imminent.

The considerable increase of the number of Catholics during the previous thirty years can be mentioned among the tangible reasons. In 1941, there were 3,313,400. It is true that among the four hundred ninety million inhabitants in China, the ratio of the Catholics was still weak, hardly sixty-seven out of ten thousand. The Church, however, does not just consider

---

82. There were already many Chinese priests who every year went abroad, notably to Rome, to complete their ecclesiastical studies and get their degrees there.

quantity; it envisages first the organization of the Church in a pagan country and the place it occupies in the country from the social point of view, that is, through its influence on minds; from the educational point of view, through its schools; from the moral point of view, through the prestige and respect it draws on itself through its works of charity, and the advantages of the doctrine it is teaching. Indeed, in the situation of the Church in China at that time, the aforementioned principles were magnificently realized and the Church's growing maturity could not be denied. The Holy Father was considering the role assumed by the Chinese episcopate in the management of Chinese Christianity and the rapidly rising number of Chinese priests.

Of the one hundred thirty-eight vicariates and prefectures, twenty-eight were headed by Chinese ordinaries, that is, twenty-one bishops and seven apostolic prefects, who were not bishops.

Of the 5,298 missionary priests, 2,186 were Chinese. Of the 1,358 religious brothers, 750 were Chinese; equally of 6,609 religious women, 4,257 were Chinese.

There were 1,066 seminarians, of course all Chinese, in the major seminaries, and 3,688 in the minor seminaries; this gave hope of numerous new Chinese priests in the future.

The Catholic schools were also visible realizations: the secondary and upper schools numbered 14,094 male students and 9,787 female students, many of whom, in fact, were not Catholics. The same was true for the primary-upper schools with their 28,509 male pupils and 17,674 female pupils, and the primary lower schools, with their 122,553 boys and 68,450 girls.

Though the students of all these schools were for the great majority non-Christian, they were inhaling an atmosphere of discipline and morality that they would generally not find in the public schools. This Christian environment was probably the reason for more or less numerous conversions to Catholicism every year.

The 201,577 students of both sexes in the schools of doctrine and basics were all Catholic.

Note that in the total number of the Faithful mentioned above, we only gave the number of the baptized, without saying anything about the catechumens who numbered five hundred twelve thousand according to the statistics. It could be hoped that soon they would notably increase the number of Christians.

The buildings of worship made an impression on the crowds that had to be reckoned with, too. Of the 2,485 churches on Chinese ground, the smallest ones could seat four hundred people. They were highly visible especially in the countryside, where they stood out above all the buildings. Less conspicuous were the chapels and oratories, but their number, 13,430, could not fail to impress the inhabitants.

Turning to the works of mercy, it was well known that their ordinary customers were pagans; consequently, the influence of the Church entered into the heart of the Chinese population, which unsommoned came freely to the institutions of the Church in order to receive almost always free temporal help.

All these reasons show clearly enough that the time for the creation of the ecclesiastical hierarchy in China was really well chosen.

Appointment of an Internuncio in China

On 7 July 1946 His Holiness Pius XII appointed Bishop Antoine Riberi as internuncio in China. Born in Monte Carlo (Monaco) on 15 June 1897, Riberi fulfilled, from 1925 onwards, different functions in apostolic delegations and, in October 1934, he was appointed apostolic delegate in Liberia (West Africa). It was there that he received his appointment as internuncio. It is well-known that the internuncio's main function is to promote and to maintain friendly relations between the Holy See and the civil government to which he was accredited in a permanent way; the other task for the internuncio is to tell the pope his observations on everything that touches the situation of the Church in that country. This last task was the only one with which the apostolic delegate had been entrusted officially. The two previous apostolic delegates, however, Costantini and Zanin, always maintained the best possible relations with the highly placed people of the government, if not officially, at least practically.

Let us here mention briefly the most important achievements of the apostolic delegation in China.

The first incumbent, appointed in 1921, was Costantini. At the time of his arrival on Chinese soil, there were fifty-six missionary circumscriptions; at the time of his departure in 1933, there were one hundred twenty of them, to which the First Council of Shanghai, that he himself had summoned and presided over in 1921, had assured a solid framework.

On 14 May 1934 the second apostolic delegate was Zanin. He found the Church already well established in China and he had only to continue his predecessor's work. First, he tried to provide a more complete formation for the missionaries and their collaborators, the leaders of the already functioning Catholic Action.

For the missionaries, he favored the organization of various schools in Peking destined for the formation of young foreign priests particularly in language study. That was the reason why more than two hundred fifty priests, brought together, confirmed by their presence the capital's name of "Rome of the East."

For Catholic Action, he organized in various regions religion courses for it and summoned big gatherings, like the ones in Shanghai in 1935 and Canton in 1937.

For the Chinese priests, which we saw personally, it was the fact of establishing up the Chinese Ecclesiastical College in Fu Jen, open exclusively to the priests who were doing academic studies.

Zanin worked in difficult circumstances. The Sino-Japanese War hit his projects and works hard. The situation became still more serious when the war spread to the rest of the world. Then, despite his very delicate health, Zanin began a real pilgrimage throughout China in order to encourage some, comfort others and bring his beneficial help to all. It was to last seven years. In this way he covered thousands of kilometers visiting the missions of the country. During his trips the delegate obtained from the Japanese authorities that they would move to Peking and Shanghai for their own houses the seven hundred missionaries and religious women kept in the concentration camps.

The prisoners knew how to use this forced imprisonment, some by preparing material for the translation of the Bible in Chinese, others by writing up the Index of Forbidden Books, and so on.

Zanin had sections for women students organized in Fu Jen, in Aurore of Shanghai, and in the School of Advanced Studies in Tianjin. He organized the Lumen Agency to publish news about everything that would be of interest for the missions in China. He chaired nineteen episcopal assemblies in various provinces.

Zanin once opened a special meeting of bishops. It was in June 1940; the students of the regional seminary in Chala had just left for their holiday. The delegate invited eleven Chinese apostolic vicars to Chala. The work of this specialized assembly began on 17 June. Under the appearance of a synod, it was a family meeting where people discussed with one another without conferences. Zanin's goal was to make direct contact with the Chinese bishops to know their thoughts and mentality.

The meetings were held in the seminarians' oratory, transformed into a conference hall. Every day two meetings of two hours and a half took place for three days. The topic was the missions. Every bishop could freely ask questions, express doubts, propose methods of evangelization, raise objections, and so on. Among them the secretary, Bishop Joseph Zhou, had to record the result of the discussions.

As these bishops were honored by the trust that Zanin showed them, they were able to talk absolutely freely face to face with the delegate of the head of the Church. Zanin declared afterwards that the goal set for that "episcopal week" had been amply reached. The following apostolic vicars participated in the meeting:

Simon Zhu, from Haimen (Jiangsu);

Jean Zhang, from Zhaoxian (Hebei);

Joseph Fan, from Xining (Mongolia);

Jean-Baptiste Wang, from Anguo (Hebei);

Thomas Tian, from Yangku (Shandong), the future cardinal;

Joseph Zhou, from Baoding (Hebei);

Joseph Cui, from Yongnian (Hebei);

Joseph Zhang, from Xuanhua (Hebei);

François-Xavier Zhao, from Xianxian (Hebei);

Job Chen, from Zhengding (Hebei);

Pierre Cheng, Hongdong (Shanxi).

Zanin had invited only those for whom the trip to Peking was easiest. He avoided obliging the others to undertake a very uncomfortable journey.

After a twelve years' stay, like his predecessor, Zanin left Peking in August 1946, and returned to Rome.

In keeping with the establishment of the hierarchy in China, twenty archdioceses were created corresponding to the twenty capitals of the civil provinces, and also seventy-nine dioceses, whose incumbents were to be the suffragans of the twenty metropolitan archdioceses. On the other hand, thirty-eight apostolic prefectures were still to remain outside the hierarchy and to depend for everything on the Sacred Congregation of Propaganda, until such a time that they would be raised to dioceses to be headed by a bishop. No change was made concerning the titulars of the new archdioceses and dioceses; so, the apostolic vicars who previously managed them could stay on in their places and they received the title of archbishop or bishop according to being in a civil prefecture or sub-prefecture.

It was the role of Riberi, the internuncio, according to canon law, to install every archbishop and bishop in his archdiocese or diocese. A very difficult task in those troubled times. He would be forced to execute this task by a proxy in several places, because practically he could not go there himself.

Cardinal Tian's Arrival in Peking

We have said before that His Eminence the cardinal had left Nanjing by plane on 14 June 1946 for Qingdao. Then he was going to stay a few days in Xi'an, and from there, on 29 June, feast of the Holy Apostles Peter and Paul, again by plane, he was going to land on the airport of Nanyuan, thirty kilometers from Peking.

The Chinese army had kindly put fifty trucks at the disposal of the Catholic authorities, which were used to transport students from schools and colleges as well as complete communities to welcome the cardinal as he disembarked.

Cardinal Tian was welcomed officially by the mayor of Peking, by the military government of the province and by all the authorities of the government of Peking. After that, the religious authorities with Bishop Montaigne leading came and bowed before the first cardinal of China. The entrance into Peking was done in a majestic way amid an astounded crowd. On his arrival at the bishop's palace, the cardinal was led to the living room to vest, and then he entered the cathedral, adored the Blessed Sacrament and took his seat on the throne. His secretary read the enthronement bull in Latin, and after that there was the obedience of the diocesan and religious clergy. Finally to close the ceremony, the cardinal gave an allocution and a blessing.

In the evening, a banquet for about one hundred fifty guests was served in one of the areas of the minor seminary. His Eminence, in a short speech, indicated the action plan he intended to follow in order to spread the Faith, following which numerous ecclesiastical and lay speakers spoke to assure the cardinal of their cordial support.

The Minor Seminary of the Beitang

One of the Cardinal's first undertakings was the reorganization of the minor seminary of Peking. His intention was to put the study program of that institution in line with the rules of the State and to acquire the recognition of the said seminary as a secondary school allowed to confer on its students the regular diplomas.

Several minor seminaries in the north, for example, the one of Baoding, had already received this recognition. They introduced the study material demanded by the government into their programs, while keeping the old discipline. The most important point was to admit to the seminary only those students who intended to enter the clerical state.

His Eminence thought that it would be good to reorganize both the leadership and the discipline in the seminary of Peking. The teaching personnel were changed; only one Vincentian was retained: Father Pierre Sun, the old director of the previous seminary, who became the director of discipline and the procurator of the new seminary. The other professors were Jesuits, Scheutists and priests from the Ecclesiastical College of Fu Jen. The minor seminary lost its name and was called "The Gengxin Middle School.[83]"

Previously the cardinal had had a series of conversations with all his suffragan bishops in the Hebei province. They committed themselves to send all their students to this seminary, which belonged to all of them now, so that in 1949 the number of students of Gengxin was seven hundred. According to the new program, more time had to be given to subjects considered of greater importance for our time, like English and Physics. The opening of the Gengxin School took place on 20 September 1946.

At the same time the "Institute of Saint Thomas" was created in Peking, destined to raise the level of the work of the Catholic Press and to put into the public's hands works coming from various domains and also written in a more sophisticated style than previously. The most important goal of the institute was the production of new books in Chinese and later to translate worthwhile books coming from abroad. Father Maur Fang, a diocesan priest from the Hangzhou diocese, was entrusted with the direction of the institute. He had as his collaborators five or six priests chosen among the most able ones. They began by publishing a magazine called *Saint Thomas* every three months. The inauguration of that institute took place on 19 September 1946. It was housed temporarily in rooms adjoining the property of the Beitang.

This initiative did not have time to grow before the arrival of Communism, which destroyed everything, old and new. Moreover, these two institutions had been organized a little hurriedly. Only by looking at the following dates: 29 June, the cardinal's installation; 19 September, inauguration of the institute; 20 September, opening of the Gengxin Middle School, can it be understood that some maturing had been missing.

---

83.   These two characters *geng* and *xin* are Cardinal Tian Gengxin's Chinese given name. The name *tian*, field or soil, and *gengxin*, grow. The cardinal wanted to give his name to the school he had created.

Two New Vincentian Visitors in China

Father Desrumaux, visitor of the Northern Province for thirty-six years, asked his superiors, towards the end of 1946 to be taken out of this important office. His request was granted by Father Edouard Robert, vicar general of the Congregation since Father Charles Souvay's death (1939). Robert chose Father Hippolyte Tichit to succeed Desrumaux. The latter, seventy-six years old, continued to fulfill his task as procurator of the Vincentians in Tianjin.

Hippolyte Tichit, born in Chabannes (Lozère) on 3 February 1903, admitted in Paris on 13 October 1922, was ordained on 30 June 1930 and arrived in Peking in the following October.

The new visitor took over the leadership of the Vincentian province at a difficult moment. A special *modus vivendi* had to be established for the Vincentians in the archdiocese of Peking, now entrusted to the diocesan clergy. For this goal, Father Moulis, procurator of the Vincentians in Shanghai, had been appointed extraordinary representative of Father Robert. Negotiations had begun, but events overtook them so that nothing definitive could be concluded before the Communist seizure.

At the same time, Legris, visitor of the Southern Province, also asked, forced by his seriously weakened health, for his replacement. Father Deymier replaced him in 1946.

Joseph Deymier, brother of Bishop Deymier, archbishop of Hangzhou, was born in Notre-Dame de Lorette (Gironde), on 26 September 1894; admitted in Dax on 18 September 1911, he was ordained there on 2 September 1923 and arrived in Shanghai on 2 October 1925 after having studied for two years in Rome to get his degree. After being director of the minor seminary of Hangzhou from 1929 to 1936, he was appointed director of the Daughters of Charity in Indochina from July 1936 to October 1938. Back again in China he once more took up the direction of the minor seminary of Hangzhou, which was forced to move to Lingshan (sub-prefecture of Longyou) by the bombings of the city. In October 1943, at Father Michel Bouillet's death, Deymier became director of the district of Quzhou, and then vicar general of the diocese of Hangzhou for the non-occupied part of Zhejiang. In 1946, with the burden of visitor of Southern China, Joseph Deymier eventually was named director general for all the Daughters of Charity in China.

Bishop Joseph Zhou's transfer to Nanchang

By decree of the Sacred Congregation of the Propaganda of 25 July 1947 Bishop Zhou, bishop of Baoding, was transferred to the see of Nanchang vacant since Dumond's death (17 February 1944). As Nanchang was the capital of the Jiangxi province, Zhou became, by that fact, archbishop.

The same day, a second decree of Propaganda appointed Bishop Jean Zhang as administrator of the vacant vicariate of Baoding and titular bishop of Zhaoxian, which he had to abandon because of the Reds' guerrilla warfare.

This vicariate indeed bordered Shunde, already devastated by the guerrillas, as we shall see. Now, the personnel in Zhaoxian were completely Chinese. It shows that the Communists attacked not only foreigners but also Chinese; this proves clearly that they wanted to destroy the Catholic religion.

Moreover, Zhang resided in Baoding only a few months, after which he returned to the safe haven of Peking and never returned to Zhaoxian.

On 6 October 1947 Bishop Zhou arrived in Jiujiang to take possession of his archdiocese. Actually, his official see was in Nanchang, but up till then the bishop's residence had always been Jiujiang, and his itinerary obliged him to pass through this city in order to reach Nanchang.

He was welcomed magnificently in Jiujiang by all the civil and military authorities as he landed. After the presentations, a parade was organized that went all over the suburbs and the city of Jiujiang among a very sympathetic population. For several days, visits made and received made an excellent impression on Zhou, and it could be said that everyone, both Christian and pagan, had been touched by His Excellency's kindness and especially by his presence of mind in his conversations with them.

After checking the situation of the works in Jiujiang, he went to Nanchang on 15 October where the welcome was still more solemn than in Jiujiang, thanks to the provincial authorities' perfect organization and kind sympathy.

After a few days' rest, Zhou left for a long trip throughout the Jiangxi province in order to visit his suffragan bishops.

China Goes from the Frying Pan into the Fire

The war with Japan had hardly finished when the Reds began to infiltrate China from the west and north. During the war their guerillas had already penetrated deeply, but it had not yet been in the nature of an occupation. The complete seizure of China was going to happen only in 1949.

Among the missions that experienced the Communist regime, Shunde, which became a vicariate in 1944 with Bishop Krause as apostolic vicar, was certainly the one that was the first to know what it really meant.

We borrow what follows from the account that one of the missionaries of this unfortunate vicariate gave in 1948, Father Stoja [Wojciech Sojka], who was not there at the time of the collapse, but whom his confreres had informed.

At that time there were sixteen Polish confreres including the bishop, and seven Chinese priests, three of whom were Vincentians.

A Mission Completely Ruined

When the Sino-Japanese war had ended, the Japanese troops began to leave Chinese territory and soon they abandoned the town of Shunde. There remained in the town a small group of the Chinese army who hoped, while waiting for reinforcements, to defend it against the Reds. The whole region was already virtually in their grip. For ten days the town remained closed, and the Nationalist troops did not arrive.

The tenth day, the Reds, who were numerous and well-armed, reached the town and attacked it. After a short fight with much bloodshed, the town was taken. Therefore, from 24 September 1945 on the nine subprefectures were under Communist control.

During that fateful night, as if by a miracle, the bishop's residence suffered no damage, despite the explosion of more than forty grenades in the garden of the minor seminary. Following the Red soldiers' progress, administrators arrived almost immediately, and among them those who were called "political commissars." That very night, one of them assured Bishop Krause and his missionaries that it was a priority of the Red government to protect their lives, their goods and the freedom of religion. A few days later, the military leaders and civil officials, already installed, searched the whole house from top to bottom, and discovering nothing, they left quietly.

Everything was going beautifully, it seemed, and the mission thought that it could go on with its work without any difficulty. In the hospital, Sisters took care of the Red soldiers and little by little all life and activity were being ruled by the new regime's demands, which seemed moderate enough.

However, both in the residence and in the countryside, soldiers or administrators often advised missionaries quietly but insistently "Go back to your country." Soon to this soft approach, they added a more explicit one, declaring openly: "We are going to destroy your institutions, your churches, and your schools, and we shall scatter and expel you." It happened that Red soldiers, coming from the countryside and going through the town cried out in amazement: "What's this? Are there still foreign devils here? They haven't been expelled yet?" Day by day these threats became more numerous.

Towards the end of July 1946, Christians coming from the south warned the missionaries in Shunde, that special agitators, from a politico-military school in Lu'nan, had the task to promote the social revolution, that is, by suppressing the rich, abolishing Catholicism and Protestantism, as being the worst enemies of Communism, and that they were soon to arrive in Shunde.

Indeed, towards the feast of the Assumption, they were seen in two of our parishes, Beizhang and Nandao. Those emissaries spread out in the villages, leaving there one or more spies and still more in those villages where there were missionaries. The pastor in Beizhang fled under cover of darkness, went to Shunde to warn the bishop and then went on to Peking to let them know the situation. The parish priest in Nandao stayed on. Then the emissaries looked for pretexts to accuse the pastor. When interrogated, the people told them that many years previously (more than fifty) a Christian had torn away a tree (a thuya) from the yard of a temple belonging to the district. Punishing the guilty party had solved this case. The emissaries judged that the imposed fine had not been proportional to the crime. They themselves ruled that the mission, responsible for the crime, ought to have paid a certain sum; and because it had paid only a very small part of that sum, it had to pay back now the complete sum and add the compound interest of fifty years. This was, according to them, a sum of 224,549,000 Chinese dollars, at that time the equivalent of two hundred thousand American dollars. The parish priest of Nandao, unable to pay this debt, was incarcerated and appeared twice before the "People's Court."

On 8 September, having been robbed of all he had, he was asked to leave the place, to go to his country, from where he ought to bring back the money necessary to repair the damages inflicted by the mission on the people. The missionary returned to Shunde.

In Beizhang, the young associate, Father Casimir Skowyra, agreed to submit to the judgment of the people in place of the pastor. But because in his naivety he wanted to harangue his judges, they threw him into jail for three months, after which he was sentenced to pay two hundred forty million Chinese dollars, that is, his confrere's debt to which was added his own debt – probably estimated to be twenty-five million. Because this sum could not be paid, all the possessions of these two parishes were confiscated and considered to be a down payment of the reimbursements owed by the mission.

Then it was Shunde's turn. The emissaries knew that a search had been carried out the year before, and that nothing untoward had been discovered; but they wanted to carry out another and they found that the railway administration had entrusted the mission with a deposit of some money at the time of the Japanese invasion. This deposit had been there for seven years, and the Reds had respected it at the time of their first search; but tactics had undergone an evolution. The new emissaries considered this deposit as sure evidence that the Church and all the foreigners were enemies of Communism and hence had to be considered as traitors.

It requires an effort to understand their stupid ways of reasoning. According to them, this was a very important charge.

The storm began when Father Paul Qiao, a diocesan priest who had studied in Rome for two years and who was the director of the school of the mission, was arrested, convicted, and sentenced to life imprisonment. A few days later, eight hundred members of the people's militia invaded the residence, tied up the bishop, the missionaries, some Daughters of Charity, and the Chinese religious women and took them to a town jail. The narrator was unwilling to give more details about their captivity; he mentioned only that all the prisoners appeared four times before the People's Court. These scoundrels were more impudent with the women than with the men.

On 21 December 1946, as a conclusion to the people's judgments, all the captives had to listen on their knees for two hours to the harangue of one of the judges. After that, Bishop Krause, clothed in a pair of trousers and an undershirt, was forced to climb up an elevated platform and make a public confession of his alleged crimes. Photographs were taken, which later on would be posted in the office of the mayor of the town. Finally, a comedic parade was organized: amid the jeering of the rabble, missionaries and Sisters were taken along the main streets of the town; at the head the bishop, wearing as a headdress a tube of white paper with a mocking inscription. After this masquerade, the victims were brought back to jail.

When all were together and it was calm, the bishop said: "Now the mission of Shunde has received its baptism of blood, let us say the *Te Deum*." And it was done.

The sentence was that the mission was condemned to repair all the damages that had been caused by it. The sum was 1.2 billion Chinese dollars, which, having been devaluated once again had about the same worth as 600,000 American dollars. So all the goods of the mission, estimated by the Reds to be worth a third of that sum, belonged to the people, while waiting for the payment by the mission of the other two thirds.

Finally, on 21 January 1947 the servants and four missionaries were released and they returned to the residence. On the following 8 February all were released, except Krause, considered to be the instigator of all the crimes, and [Kazimierz Stanislaw] Skowyra, the procurator.

Missionaries and Sisters, back in the residence, all hoped to resume their activities, but many things had disappeared and all was turned upside down. In the orphanage there remained only some blind or mentally handicapped children, all the others had been scattered. Of the old people there remained only the disabled.

The missionaries claimed the liturgical vestments and got them. Gradually religious life began again. On 19 March, feast of Saint Joseph, there was a solemn Mass. But it was impossible to take up again the works in such a situation.

At the general arrest of the missionaries on 10 December 1946 a few Polish and Chinese missionaries had remained among the Christians, living with them. This was very dangerous for both parties. They were very careful not to be taken prisoner in Shunde. When they heard that their confreres had been released from prison, they went to the bishop's residence, except for two Chinese diocesan priests who wanted to stay on to exercise their ministry among their compatriots. In Shunde, a unanimous decision was taken to flee to Shijiazhuang, a commercial town not yet occupied by the Reds. From there they would go to Peking, if possible.

Equipped with a pass delivered by the Communists, they set off on foot towards the north in small groups to cover the sixty kilometers that separated them from Shijiazhuang. On their arrival there, American cargo-planes took them to Peking, where various communities welcomed them.

We left Krause and his companion, languishing in their prison. What happened after the departure of the people who were released? The high authorities of the Reds did not know what to do with the bishop.

Expelling him from China without his paying his debt would have been ridiculous in the people's eyes. Keeping him in prison was definitely useless, because the bishop had nothing to pay with. How could they get out of this dilemma? A leader went and visited the bishop and asked him this question: "Do you want to pay your debt or not?" "There is nothing I would like to do more, but give me the means to find the necessary funds." "What are these means?" "Going to Peking" "All right. You will go to Peking." They saved face: they had now a reason they could give the public for the prisoner's release. "We allowed him," they would say, "to go and look for the money that he owes us." Yet, they knew very well that the bishop was never going to pay. This procedure is indeed absolutely in the line of the mind of people in the Far East: "Never corner the enemy in a dead end; always leave some way out."

The Reds' indulgence did not go as far as releasing Father Qiao. He was to stay in jail and to die of privations and terrible moral sufferings.

Krause and his companion were led under escort to Gaoyi, a town located at some one hundred kilometers from Shunde, outside the diocese and in a region that was still free from Red domination. From there, they traveled as they could to Peking, where they rented a house that could accommodate all the missionaries.

This beautiful, young mission of Shunde was destroyed in this way. It would be the first in a long series. For the sake of brevity, we omitted several incidents of less importance; this is enough to make the reader aware of the Communists' judicial methods, and at the same time it exempts us from describing in the future "People's Courts" and the hypocrisy of leaders who hide their responsibility behind the fictitious entity of "'the people."

The Situation in the Diocese of Tianjin

This diocese, one of the ten suffragans of Peking, had a great deal of trouble during the Japanese war; with the end of the conflict their troubles increased.

In these regions, the Japanese soldiers had been quite kind to the Catholic missions. In the beginning, they even thought that the clergy and the Christians were going to collaborate with them. They were deceived on this point, because the European missionaries were not political or nationalistic, whereas the Chinese priests were of course on the side of their invaded country.

During that time the Church continued with its beneficial works, helping the more unfortunate people day by day, for example, victims of the war or of Communists, flood victims, and refugees looking for asylum and for the means to make a living. The Catholic schools of Tianjin carried on in full prosperity. In the countryside, on the contrary, most schools had been forced to close their doors and only a few of them were kept open thanks to the generosity and dedication of the local Christians.

With the end of the war in August 1945, the already precarious situation became only worse when the country fell under the domination of the Communist soldiers, the Balu (Ba = 8; lu = army), the Eighth Route Army.

Organized and trained by Russians, they applied the Communist theory to the last detail, and, because they were almighty, nothing or nobody could stop them from doing whatever they wanted to do. Wherever they went, there was the immediate distribution of land, the looting of the houses of the rich, and much more sadly, the disorganization of the family. Children did not owe respect or obedience to their parents, while young boys and girls were forced to become militant Marxists. Wherever they were, the Balu would persecute religion; they tried to force the Christians to apostasy and they would prevent all religious ceremonies and assemblies; they did it brutally, without method; they had not yet been formed. That would come later.

The Internuncio's Visit to Tianjin

Riberi, traveling in the north of China, went to Tianjin on Saturday 30 August 1947. The next day, he officiated at the installation of Bishop de Vienne as bishop of Tianjin, in the Laoxikai Cathedral. In the evening, the internuncio visited the important parish of Our Lady of Victories (Wanghailou) and talked with the Christians in an informal way. The same day, the bishop of Tianjin, happy to make concessions to the new mentality, announced to his diocesans the resignation of the vicar general, Father Molinari, and the appointment of his successor, Father Alphonse Zhao, C.M., and also the appointment of two diocesan priests as members of the episcopal council.

The following day, a reception in honor of Riberi took place in the Jesuits' school of "Higher Studies" in which the municipal authorities participated.

The Monastery of Our Lady of Consolation (Yangjiaping) Burned by the Reds

There were only two Trappist monasteries in China, both located in the province of Hebei. Moreover, Vincentians had called the Trappists to China. It was Bishop Delaplace who called them in 1883. For these reasons, we want to recount here the dire troubles these venerable religious underwent due to the Communists.

Already before the Japanese capitulation, the Reds controlled the whole region surrounding the monastery of Our Lady of Consolation in Yangjiaping, in the most mountainous area of Hebei. In small groups, these Reds had already made several incursions into the monastery, wishing to create difficulties for the monks, who, they said, had collaborated with the Japanese. That was the pretext why, in the beginning of 1946, they abducted the abbot and two monks, took them to a village of the mountains, kept them fastened with chains to the naked ground for a whole night in rigorous cold; after that they jailed them for two months. After their release, Abbot [Alexis] Baillon and his two companions returned to Europe.

Then the Reds occupied the monastery almost completely, leaving very little space to the monks, several of whom, old and weak, passed away during the occupation. In April, all the monks, priests and lay brothers, were submitted to the "People's Court," after which they were taken into the mountains. Meanwhile the village people of the neighborhood of Yangjiaping, urged on by the Reds, completely ransacked the monastery. On 30 August 1946 flames devoured the monastery with all its outbuildings. The pretext of that destruction was, the Reds said, to suppress that position which was going to serve as a stronghold for the Nationalist troops sent to fight with them.

The Monastery of Our Lady of Joy (Zhengding) Evacuated

It has been mentioned that this monastery was only a priory depending on the abbey of Yangjiaping. At the time the Reds were approaching, Father Paulin Li, the prior, having heard about their way of proceeding, began to fear that the youngest ones among the monks might be incorporated by force into the services of the Red army, and so he decided to evacuate the monastery, although he would keep there a dozen elderly priests and lay brothers. He thought of profiting of this forced emigration to begin a new foundation in the neighborhood of Chengdu in the province of Sichuan, because indeed it had already been discussed. Actually, Father [Jean-Marie] Struyven, a Belgian monk of Our Lady of Joy, had been to Sichuan shortly before to study the possibilities of this project.

Therefore, Father Li, with forty of his monks set off for Shanghai to prepare their urgent journey to Sichuan. These brave monks went there indeed, and settled as best they could amid terrible difficulties. The Communist invasion, however, was soon to reach there, too (1949–1950). Then it became evident that Li had to move away. Consequently, he left for Canada, accompanied by some monks, in order to look for resources and help. When he came back in 1950, he founded his monastery on Lantao, one of the small islands in the bay of Hong Kong, under English protection. In the sixties the monks were still there and their novitiate was prosperous.

The Trappists of the north had to suffer much. Several were tortured and murdered. Others were dispersed, some returned to their families, and others went to live with Christian families or with friends. Struyven, back from Sichuan, where he had gone to settle his companions, accomplished the almost impossible feat of bringing to Peking a large number of those roaming monks. He gathered them in a place located in the northwest corner of Peking, not from the large Lama Temple [Yonghegong]. He organized a temporary monastery, of which he made himself the abbot, also temporary.

After their sad isolation, these monks were happy to resume monastery life, a of prayer and work. For quite a long time the temporary abbot resisted the Communists' demands by his quiet and often ironic audaciousness. Finally, he was expelled in 1952 and went back to Europe. After his departure, the Communists grabbed, of course, the monastery and occupied it as its new masters. We do not know what happened later.

Lebbe's Final Activities

We said above that after leaving China together with Father de Guébriant in 1920, Lebbe busied himself with Chinese students in colleges or higher schools in France and Belgium. We added that if he was to come back to China, we might have an occasion of talking again about him.

After the consecration of the six Chinese bishops in Rome on 28 October 1926 Lebbe implored Bishop Melchior Sun to accept him in his vicariate of Anguo. The bishop, surely, did not want this missionary, who had caused so many troubles in the missions of the north, but because of repeated requests by highly placed personalities, Sun yielded. Then, in the spring of 1927, Lebbe returned to China, a few months after Sun's own journey back home.

One of the first of Lebbe's steps was to become naturalized as a Chinese citizen. From then on he enjoyed complete liberty, moving very frequently outside his vicariate with complete independence and without any authorization.

Soon it became clear that his goal was to find and to bring together young people of good will in view of forming a community of men that Lebbe was going to call the Little Brothers of Saint John the Baptist; after that, another one for women, who were to be called the Little Sisters of Saint Therese.

When we were talking about the first institution of Chinese religious women, the Sisters of Saint Joseph or "Josephines," founded by Bishop Delaplace in 1872, we said that was imitated not only by Vincentian bishops, but by a huge number of mission leaders who also founded for their jurisdictions Chinese religious communities with rules almost identical to those of the Josephines. It was therefore proven that religious vocations were numerous among the Faithful, provided they were favored. This is said concerning religious vocations among women.

Was it the same for men? First, it must be said that the apostolic vicars, mostly religious, did not see the usefulness of religious lay brothers other than the ones who helped the missionaries in congregations of priests. And when the foreign brothers whom they had taken with them were not numerous enough, they would form in their provincial novitiate young people who felt that they had been called to that task of dedication, but their number was limited to the needs of their mission. The main worry of bishops was recruiting priestly vocations and simultaneously of making it easy for the seminarians to enter into religious priestly congregations.

Indeed, the monasteries of monks with a contemplative life of Our Lady of Consolation and Our Lady of Joy, the only ones existing in China, had proven also that being a monk was pleasing to Chinese men, and therefore their candidates were numerous.

Lebbe began a very beautiful work, and his enthusiasm and his convincing eloquence made his task easy when in the presence of upright souls. There were certainly among these young men and young women beautiful souls who found in these two institutions the realization of their ideal of perfection and dedication to which their simple devotion had inspired them. Moreover, the founder, who had become Chinese, took pains for their formation with his whole heart. He stopped carrying his long pipe in the way of Chinese intellectuals, and began to practice the rule faithfully that he himself had elaborated.

He asked the appropriate person for the dispensation of his perpetual vows in the Congregation of the Mission. As he had been living for many years definitely outside all control of his superiors, they readily granted him the requested dispensation on 11 July 1934.

If he had stayed with his work, Lebbe could have done a lot of good. But then the Sino-Japanese war came on. As a result, he imagined that he had to get mixed up in it with his whole troupe and to take an active part in the defense of the country, better, of his country. Alas! It is difficult to believe where the person who gives his imagination free reign will wind up; he believed firmly that it was his duty as a priest to lead a patriotic movement, and he did so from the first week of the conflict. On 18 July 1937 he gathered the Brothers and said to them that they had only to think of their country.

All those who were not kept in the monastery because of some indispensable tasks had to go with him to the armies. The novices had to go to Shanxi, away from the front, to continue their formation till they were also ready to reinforce the corps of stretcher-bearers. If he had made do with providing the people wounded in the war with this beautiful service of stretcher-bearers, he could only have been praised; but the next year, in Shanxi, he created among the Christians of that area a body of irregulars of more than five hundred combatants, accompanied by Little Brothers in every group, who attacked the Japanese in the steep mountain passes. Their colonel was a Belgian priest, Raymond de Jaegher, member of the Society of the Missionaries founded by Father Boland to work under the direction of Chinese bishops.

Far be it from us to tell the story of these adventures. It is enough for us to quote only one page from *Vie du Père Lebbe* written by Canon Jacques Leclercq (Chapter 11, "The Great Inferno," p. 319):

> Lebbe was bruised more than once by the behavior of missionaries and even of bishops.

> While he was doing his best to show by all means that Catholicism was the surest rampart of the fatherland and was ordering his people to support the soldiers' morale, to form the people in healthy patriotism, and to comfort the refugees, many missionaries

and even bishops were thinking in the first place of not compromising themselves.

In short, whether the Chinese ruled China or the Japanese did not matter to them. This war was not their war; they had come to China to preach the Gospel and not to be political activists.

Did you read this well, dear reader? Those naïve missionaries and bishops "who had come to China to preach the Gospel, not to be political activists;" while Lebbe, on the contrary, "had come to be a political activist." He had done hardly anything else, against all the popes, who had always rigorously forbidden the missionaries of all the countries to meddle with politics, but had enjoined them to preach only the Gospel.

On the same page, a little further on, we read:

Lebbe wrote to the apostolic delegate, repeating what he had written already twenty years before to Bishop Reynaud. But the delegate also insisted on preparing for the future. He would just recommend that people pray for the salvation of China and that all work together to relieve its misfortunes.

It is always the same question. Lebbe's rage stays as fresh as in his youth. Lebbe's rage, opposed to the behavior of Pope Pius XI's direct envoy! The author of the apology seems completely at home with this genial missionary, whose view of evangelization was more penetrating than that of the pope and all his delegates!

Zanin, indeed, from the beginning of the war, had warned all the missionaries in China not to take sides, not to lean to the right or to the left. Obviously, Lebbe had not complied with this rule. He was far beyond those timorous initiatives.

We quoted only one page of the three hundred forty-seven that the volume contains; it is enough, we think, to show that the great majority of the missionaries in China were not wrong when blaming the schemes of this priest, who despised as much as possible the great work of the missionaries who had preceded him in China or were his contemporaries.

On the other hand, Lebbe suffered a lot during his last years. Once twelve of his Brothers were arrested, tortured and killed (we do not know whether the perpetrators of this massacre were Japanese or Red guerillas). He also was so mistreated that his health was definitely weakened. Thanks to Bishop Yu Bin, apostolic vicar of Nanjing, and to president Chiang Kai-shek, he was transported by plane to Chongqing, seat of the government during the war. Father Lebbe passed away there on 24 June

1940 having received the last rites, according to the writings of the witnesses of his death, who were scarce, for that matter.

An important doubt rises here. A few months after Lebbe's death, a rumor was spread that, before his death, he had backed down, and that he would have declared that he had made a mistake, that he had erred. If it turned out that he had publicly admitted to his faults – even if the number of witnesses was small – then everything would be arranged at best. *To err is human.* There is the main question: did he confess his error? Yes or no? Zanin claimed so for instance when talking to Deymier, archbishop of Hangzhou.[84] Other testimonies go in that direction, too; and they justify two important conclusions: 1. Those who had been reproaching certain of Lebbe's extreme methods and attitudes have been justified. 2. The myth is finished that people had tried to create: Lebbe, a model missionary.

---

84. Ferreux's notes: Biographies of the personage, written by his devoted friends, do not mention this admission. The doubt remains unresolved until there is more information.

Chapter 28

China Under Communist Rule, Early 1950s

Preliminaries - The Beginnings of Communism in China - The Installation - The Three Autonomies - The Attitude of Catholics - Results of Communist Propaganda - Bishop de Vienne's Deportation - Deportation of Bishop Riberi, Apostolic Internuncio - The Evolution of Communist Tactics - The Legion of Mary - Reeducation of the Recalcitrant - Arrest of Father Tichit With Four Chinese Priests - Tichit's Release - Jacques Huysmans's Internment - Tichit's Unfortunate Companions - Internment in and Deportation from the Vincentian Southern Province - Bishops André Defebvre and Others

Preliminaries

We saw earlier that the Japanese attack had begun on 7 August 1937 with the incident of Lugouqiao, near Peking, and how the invaders, equipped with motorized vehicles, easily gained the upper hand over Chiang Kai-Shek's soldiers, less armed and not battle hardened.

The Japanese armies first occupied the big seaports of Tianjin and Shanghai, the big inland port of Hankou on the Yangtze in the heart of China, and after that, the commercial towns located along the railways. But they hardly spread into the interior of the country, for the Chinese armies not anxious to fight face to face against an enemy, who was stronger than they were, though less numerous, preferred to spread out in the countryside and multiply their guerilla activity.

The Beginnings of Communism in China

The Communist movement, which had suddenly appeared in Canton, settled down at first in Fujian at the instigation of two skillful agents from Moscow, Borodin and Galen, and then came and established itself quite solidly in Jiangxi in the years 1926–1930 (see above).

General Zhu De, leader of these Reds, who had done his military studies in Germany, applied the Soviet system: land reform, confiscations, and so on. He recruited followers and made soldiers out of them.

Chiang Kai-Shek, perceiving the imminent danger of China being contaminated by Communism, pushed the Reds rudely towards the northwest, where their numbers and strength grew so that they became a real army.

Then Japan attacked. The president without other alternatives did not hesitate to turn to the Red army to help him in the defense of the soil of the fatherland. The Communists agreed to participate in the protection of the territory, as long as they remained independent and were maintained by the government. Chiang Kai-Shek, driven by need, granted them what they demanded.

The Communists' political leader was Mao Zedong, still very young at that time. He had taken part in the unforgettable retreat from Jiangxi to Gansu and had learned a lot and had matured during that exile of seven or eight years. The military leader was Zhu De.

Strengthened by the president's license, the Reds slipped into the eastern and northern provinces of the Republic of China in small groups recruiting young people and presenting themselves as the real defenders of the fatherland. Indeed, their soldiers, although they had few weapons and almost no military uniforms, were well disciplined and made life difficult for the Japanese through their elusive guerilla tactics. Moreover, not disguising their objective, they told whomever wanted to listen that their first enemy was nobody else but Chiang Kai-Shek, the imperialist, whom they wanted to shoot as he was the biggest obstacle to planting the new Marxist regime in China. They announced also that thirty percent of their work was against the president, twenty percent against Japan and the other fifty percent were dedicated to the formation of cadres of the party.

Not all their words were just bragging. Up till the end of the world war, their formation center was Yan'an, a civil prefecture of Shaanxi. They had invited from Moscow master-professors, able to pour into the minds of their followers the purest sap of Leninist Marxism.

Yan'an had been a apostolic vicariate since 1924. From the time of the Reds' arrival, the seventeen missionaries including Bishop Ibañez, who were Spanish Franciscans, had to flee, leaving behind them a few Chinese priests. This meant that this mission, which had about nine thousand Faithful, was disorganized and has never been able to recover.

At the time of the Japanese capitulation in August 1945, the Communists, exploiting the president's inertia, undertook to disarm the defeated soldiers wherever they met with them, and in this way they acquired an important quantity of war equipment.

Understanding that the end of the war with the Japanese, instead of bringing peace, had on the contrary strengthened the internal enemy, and Chiang Kai-Shek decided to attack this enemy directly. At the end of autumn 1945, his troops attacked the rebels.

At that instant, the American president, Harry Truman, stepped in. He urged the two enemies to reach a settlement before coming to blows, and to meet each other halfway, if necessary, rather than throw the country into the horrors of civil war; then he put forward for them General [George] Marshal as mediator. The two parties agreed with this and began negotiations in Chongqing in Sichuan, where the Chinese government had been sitting during the whole Japanese war. There was deliberation for many months ending only in a ceasefire, which was not observed due to the bad faith of the Communists.

The failure of the mediation had as its result the resumption of hostilities and this was to the advantage of the rebels, for the Nationalist troops were fighting without enthusiasm; quite a few of them refused to kill their compatriots. Soon, the Communists entered Hebei province (we mentioned this when speaking about Shunde), first in the larger villages, and later on in the small towns.

The first important town they occupied was Shijiazhuang, where the Polish missionaries had fled after their expulsion in the first days of November 1947. This victory of the Communists caused real consternation in North China. As long as they were staying in the countryside, people deluded themselves by imagining that they would not dare take a densely populated area or an industrial town, because they would not be able to handle its administration. Nobody suspected that teams, completely prepared in Yan'an according to Marxist theories, were closely following the Red battalions and as soon as a town was captured, these bold men spoke to the authorities who were in control, ordered them to continue directing their district, and to await new orders. If these authorities refused or had fled before the invader as often happened, then the teams took over the direction and, after a few days, a relative calm would be established. That is what happened in Shijiazhuang; they took over the administration and order, with some troubles during a few days, were soon restored.

After that notable success, the Communists went into Manchuria and, in February 1948, they took Anshan where the Japanese had created big metallurgic plants, sixty kilometers south of Mukden [Shenyang], capital of Manchuria. On the following 2 November the Reds entered Mukden, capturing one hundred twenty thousand Nationalist troops, who abandoned to them weapons and ammunition with a huge number of completely new trucks, coming directly from the U.S.A., not counting enormous stocks of supplies. These conquests made them all the more audacious. Two big centers were before them: Peking and Tianjin.

The Reds crossed the Great Wall during the first days of winter 1948 and spread out towards the north and the east of Hebei, advancing up to the surroundings of Peking; then worming their way along the coast, they neared Tianjin. They met little resistance, for the Nationalists were intentionally drawing back as the enemy was approaching. From there, the Reds increasingly infiltrated the population in small groups, especially in the cities of Peking and Tianjin. Almost every night, the railways from Peking to Tianjin and from that town to Tangshan were cut. The saboteurs did not intend to do much damage, but only to create difficulties and hinder the traffic. Their plan was certainly not to destroy lines that were soon to be very useful for them. In Tianjin however, the governor of the place seemed determined to defend the city.

The attack on Tianjin began on 1 January 1949 with violent bombing, directed not towards the city, but towards the troops surrounding it. The cannonade, quite infrequent the first days, became more intense as the attackers were approaching it.

On 14 January the firing of one hundred fifty batteries was extremely violent. On the 15th Lin Biao, the Communist general, sent Governor Chen an ultimatum, ordering him to surrender without conditions, otherwise the city would be bombed intensely. The governor surrendered and the Reds entered Tianjin in triumph.

Two weeks later the capital was taken almost without fighting, but not without negotiating. Under the threat of bombing, Peking had to yield. At that time the personnel of the regional seminary of Chala had gone to Peking to take refuge and they went on with their studies in the buildings of the Scheut Fathers, while the Nationalist troops were occupying the entire property of Chala and had made of it an entrenched camp.

On 26 January 1949 Peking opened its doors and the Communists entered the city without resistance.

These major centers having been conquered, the Reds were able to advance more quickly. In a few months, they arrived at the Yangtze. Surely, it would have been easy for the Nationalist troops, with the artillery they had, to bar the way across the Yangtze; but either because of the failure of leadership, or for some other reason, it was a fact that the Communist armies crossed the Yangtze wherever and whenever they wanted. A few days later, they entered Nanjing, which after the Japanese army had been defeated, had become again the seat of the Chinese government. The latter had withdrawn posthaste to Canton as soon as the Communists camped on the left bank of the Blue River.

Foreseeing that that city would fall also into the hands of the invaders, the president fled by boat with all his ministers to Formosa, where he established his government that was still there in 1963.

It was soon the turn of Shanghai, but conquering that immense and densely populated city took a little more time. They seized it on 25 May 1949.

The Installation

Entering towns with unfurled flags, when there is almost no opposition, is not very difficult. Claiming to be saviors, calling their arrival and their occupation of the land "liberation" does not ask for much effort either. Taking in hand, however, all the public and official administration functions is much more difficult work. Now, that was the task that fell to the new occupying powers from the first day of the "liberation" of every town.

That was why it was not astonishing if the beginning times of the "liberation" were a period of tranquility for the population and for the missions. For about eighteen months the Catholics continued to go to church freely. The police had orders to keep an eye on Christians and sometimes sent police officers to churches, especially to listen to the sermon, but nothing bad ever happened; it is true that the priests had received from their bishop strict orders never to talk about politics when in the pulpit, but to preach only Catholic doctrine.

In the countryside the situation was, however, much different. Twenty kilometers from Tianjin, any practicing of worship was forbidden; Christians could no longer assemble to pray together; priests no longer had the right to celebrate Mass in the churches, which had become meeting halls, destined for the political education of the people. The Christians in Tianjin were well aware of what those outside the city were suffering, and as a reaction, they became more fervent than ever before. It was noticed indeed that the "Legion of Mary," founded a few months before the Reds' arrival, made quick progress. More than forty centers (*praesidia*) were established in Tianjin, and the activity of legionnaires of both sexes proved very beneficial. The fruits of their zeal were seen in the conversions of pagans, the return of lukewarm Catholics to regular practice, and the regularizing of marriages. Police officers themselves kept order at the magnificent ceremony that was celebrated in June 1950, on the occasion of fifty years' priesthood of Bishop de Vienne, bishop of Tianjin. The pontifical Mass, celebrated in open air in the decorated yard of the Laoxikai residence, in front of several thousand people, was followed by songs and compliments offered to the bishop by delegations of all the works of the diocese. All this went on under the eyes of the police, without the least protest on their side.

The missionaries from outside present at the celebration, knowing what was going on in the countryside, were astonished. One could say that, till the end of 1950, the Christians in the major cities were not bothered because they were Christians. Let us not think that this tolerance, which was granted them, was an effect of the Communists' kindness for the Catholic religion. It was far from it. Already during the frequent meetings in which Chinese priests (not the foreigners in the beginning) and Christians had to take part, they were hearing many strange words that threatened the freedom of Christian worship. If they were not yet applied, it was because the attack plan had not yet been elaborated or had not matured enough at the higher levels.

Besides, from the end of 1949, the authorities of Tianjin told all the non-Chinese clergy that they had to get a "residence permit." To acquire this document, they had to answer numerous quite insidious questions, and while granting it, the police officers made it clear that they were undesirables who were allowed to stay temporarily in town, not somewhere else, and moreover that this "permit" had to be renewed at a later unspecified date.

We arrive now at the threshold of the year 1951, a fateful year for the Catholic missions in China. During the year 1950 an intense effort had been made to instill in the educators of all levels a new spirit, so that they could communicate it to their pupils, the younger ones and the older ones. Courses in special pedagogy were taught to them during the summer and winter school vacations in order to study the pure Communist doctrine; there was insistence on the necessity of teaching political science in the classrooms even in the lower grades; for this teaching had to take a dominating place in the school programs beginning with the secondary schools.

The Three Autonomies

From January 1951 on, the Communist newspapers – the only ones in the whole country – began a campaign to enlighten the public about the serious question of religions.

First, they published the conditions to which all the churches established in China had to conform, if they wanted to continue to exist. These conditions, considered as essential, boiled down to three, having some similarity with the "Three Principles of the People" (*sanmin zhuyi*). They were the Three Autonomies: economic, administrative and doctrinal, published in short terms that could be explained in different ways. Here is the literal meaning of the Chinese characters that compose the wording of the three principles: *Zi Yang; Zi Zhi; Zi Chuan.*

The character zi, common to the three principles, is a personal reflexive pronoun: oneself.

- *Yang* = feed, maintain. The first autonomy of the Church is *Zi Yang*. The Church must live and maintain itself without foreign help.

- *Zhi* = govern. The second autonomy is *Zi Zhi*. The Church must rule itself, that is, independently of any other Church, especially foreign to China (Rome).

- *Chuan* = teach or spread a doctrine. The third autonomy is *Zi Chuan*. The Church must teach by itself, without help of teachers foreign to China, its own doctrine, not the doctrine of another Church.

The ecclesial authority, under the direction of the internuncio, Bishop Riberi, was upset and studied the question attentively. It was agreed that these three principles could be understood in a way that their application would not go in any way against natural law, divine law or church law. The bishops signed a declaration with the view of teaching the priests and the Faithful about the way the three autonomies ought to be understood. It enjoined them to accept them only in that sense.

Here is the sense adopted by the bishops:

Zi Yang means "economic" autonomy. – The Christians themselves must take care of the expenditure for the worship and the upkeep of their pastor; they must also contribute in accordance with their ability to the works deemed necessary by the Church authority. On the other hand, nothing forbids them from accepting gifts from private individuals, even if they are foreigners.

Zi Zhi means "administrative" autonomy. This is about the collaboration that the Faithful have to render to the Church authority, in the great work of spreading the Gospel directly or indirectly, through their zeal of helping the missionaries in all kinds of activities, but always under the direction of their bishop. This is what has been called Catholic Action.

Zi Chuan means "doctrinal" autonomy. The doctrine that the Church teaches is nothing else than spreading God's word contained in the Holy Scriptures and the ordinary Teaching of the Church.

The Christians of Tianjin, including the Chinese priests, almost ten thousand people, signed this declaration and transmitted it to the civil authorities. Far from accepting it, the leaders told them that they did not find the Three Autonomies in the bishops' explanation and that the Faithful would have done nothing so long as they had not signed the declaration of the government. That declaration, however, gave a literal and absolute sense to each of the three autonomies, namely:

1. "Economic autonomy" means a total rupture with foreign nations concerning financial matters; suppression of all help with money, including subsidies from the Propagation of the Faith, the Holy Childhood and the work of the Saint Peter the Apostle.

2. "Administrative autonomy" means that Chinese churches must reject all interference of any Western authority in their affairs; they will decide themselves without depending on any other authority besides the Chinese government, so that their laws and their worship can be in all aspects conform to the needs of the Faithful. This was their break with the Vatican.

3. "Doctrinal autonomy" could not be understood if it had not the Gospel as its basis. But up until those days, the formation of the preachers has been purely Western; the books at the Faithful's disposal are mostly translations of European or American books. It is the task of the priests and Catholics in China to explore the treasures of the Gospel by doing away with the fetters of the theology of the West and by creating a theological system belonging exclusively to the Chinese Christians.

For several months, the papers were talking every day about the Catholic Church. Complete columns were dedicated to this question with a variety of titles, which all used these three characters: Tian Zhu Tang, Catholic Church. Unawares these authors made known the existence of the Catholic Church as far as the most remote regions where it had never been mentioned. Yet the total number of Christians still did not amount to four million. Among the five hundred million Chinese, the ratio of Catholics was still far under one percent. Why did they take such great trouble? The answer is that statistics very often are misleading. Influence and prestige cannot be contained in numbers. Why did they take so much trouble to gain the adhesion of such a small minority? The answer to this question is: Catholicism already held an important place in Chinese society; the Communist government would have been happy if it could have attracted to their group this elite community of the society. These enemies of the Church actually spread the knowledge of the existence and importance of the Catholic Church among all the Chinese.

The Attitude of Catholics

Let us return to the facts. We saw the Faithful of Tianjin sign in vain a form that was too mild in the eyes of the Communists. What were the Communists going to do to make the Faithful adopt the official form?

In Tianjin, a quite advanced party had been formed. Several priests, already compromised through a past life that was not edifying, had gotten together with Christians, who in former days had influence because of their connections with the Guomindang (Chiang Kai-Shek's party) at that time in office, but who now, fearing to be suspects in the eyes of the Communists, felt the need to appear zealous in favor of the new party. Both groups, because of their eloquence, their audaciousness and their desire for popularity, drew behind them quite a few Faithful, who were called "progressives" because of their advanced ideas. It was these persons who took upon themselves the task of having the majority of the Christians sign the form.

What did they do? They clouded the issues. The priests talked to the Faithful and told them that they themselves knew canon law very well and assured them that the fact of signing the official form was not a sin. The others, visiting families, were not afraid to tell people that the bishop had recognized the necessity for Christians to sign so as not to lose the jobs they might have in the public service. Therefore, these people ought not to hesitate. They added that Faithful who did not sign would be considered as non-patriotic.

The two entities of "patriotism" and "religion" having been mixed up as much as possible, the poor Christians no longer knew exactly what it all was about; and as they had obediently signed the bishops' form the first time, so equally they signed a second time what they were told was necessary. The following day, their family names and given names appeared in the *Official Journal* as having accepted the Three Autonomies.

Results of Communist Propaganda

As can been seen, the campaign against the Church was done less on a religious level than under the cover of "patriotism." Besides, the tactic was to make the Christians themselves do the work, to use them to destroy the religion. The Chinese Catholics and even priests who wanted to prove their patriotism were ordered to accuse foreign missionaries and bishops. During the many meetings in which they had to take part, they were told:

> Do you not know that it is the 'People's' government? . . . You yourselves are now the people; how is it possible that you were collaborating with your enemies, the foreigners, while you ought to have denounced them, to have accused them of sabotaging the movement of progress, while you ought to have demanded the expulsion of the most guilty among them, like bishops and notably the internuncio, who is the first among the oppressors in China?

Furthermore, the libels repeated in the Communist newspapers, and never refuted, eventually shook the minds and convinced some people that the European or American missionaries were agents of their own nations, sent to China under the cover of preaching the Gospel. This prejudice existed already in the mind of many pagans, but this wretched campaign developed this idea remarkably.

That generalized xenophobia had its influence on Catholics and even on some priests. Among them there were unfortunate failures and apostasies, perhaps more material than formal, we hope. It is certain that for those who had not seen Communism in China, it was not easy to understand these hesitations and compromises. The reason is that Chinese Catholics and priests felt like they were in the jaws of pincers that were closing on them more and more every day. They had no prospect of relief or appeal to a higher authority. They were forced to take part, twice or three times a week, for months, in meetings that lasted three or four hours. During those meetings a party spokesperson in charge of their indoctrination poured out argumentations, promises and threats in an endless stream. When one speaker was tired of talking, another took over, while the audience did not have a break. Paper was put in front of them; they had to write their impressions about what had been said and their opinions and objections about everything. At the end of the session all those papers were gathered and at the next session they were discussed either to prove the contrary or to approve.

If the desired result was not reached, the police would send their officers to the homes of private people, going from one family to the other asking the most unexpected questions, and demanding they sign documents in which were written crimes the signatory had never committed; or they would oblige them to sign petitions or accusations against certain authorities. It could happen that a person, exasperated by the long sessions eventually yielded and signed anything.

The Communist leaders, with perfidious cleverness, did everything to cover themselves by projecting on the Christians what was odious in the deportations of the foreign missionaries. We have a striking example of this in the deportation Bishop de Vienne of Tianjin, and in that of the internuncio, Bishop Riberi, which followed a little later.

We have seen that the Christians in Tianjin were very rebellious. It had been so since the years that followed the First World War, the time that Lebbe had caused much trouble in this beautiful Christian community. Fortunately, the prudent administration by de Vienne came and pacified the minds and made this vicariate one of the most blossoming ones in the north within the space of thirty years. Due to Communism, however, their old rebellious mentality rose up again.

Bishop de Vienne's Deportation

The most influent catechists in town and, among them, Wu Guorui, former director of the newspaper *Yishibao*, who was to become a famous Communist leader in Tianjin, yielding more or less happily to Communist pressure, secretly decided to accuse their bishop of imperialism or something similar to it. But they needed a charge. In the first days of May 1951, the catechists went together to the bishop and asked to show them the previous year's accounts. The bishop told them that he did not have to show them the accounts, for Christians have nothing to do in the management of the goods of the mission. The bishop is accountable to the pope or his delegate, the internuncio in Nanjing. They insisted, but to no avail.

The next days, more of them came and renewed their demand, using words that became more and more arrogant.

The bishop refused again. Once, toward midnight, they came and knocked at his door and obliged him to get up and appear before them; then they ordered the bishop to immediately give them the accounts of the mission, or else they were going to accuse him of wasting the goods of the Church. The bishop did not comply.

The next day, 16 May, forty Christians came and told the bishop that he had become their prisoner and that they would take turns as his guards. They ordered him not to leave his room and assured him that they personally would take pains that he receives no visit, either from outside, or from anybody living in the bishop's residence. Only one servant would be admitted to take care of his room and to bring him his meals; every time he would enter the bishop's room, two guards would accompany him.

These Christians occupied a big part of the ground floor, and some twenty priests, among whom there were two Europeans, all under the control of the Christians, occupied the first floor. They allowed the priests to practice their ministry in the cathedral and those who were chaplains to go and celebrate Holy Mass in the various communities in town.

The first days of his internment, de Vienne did not celebrate Holy Mass, for he did not want to ask his jailers for any favors. The latter, feeling perhaps how odious it was for the bishop to be deprived of Holy Mass, allowed him to celebrate in the community oratory, which was located a few steps from his room. The next day, the bishop went there, but, because he was very shortsighted, he had noticed only at the end of the Mass that his two acolytes were apostates (two of his jailers). He did not go back there and the other days he celebrated Holy Mass alone, without an acolyte, in a small sitting room beside his office.

During his internment, which lasted for twelve days, the bishop was taken twice to the central police to be questioned. The author of these lines does not know what questions were asked.

On 26 May 1951 two police officers came and informed de Vienne that in two days they were going to take him and bring him somewhere else, and that consequently he was to prepare the things he might want to take with him.

The bishop prepared two bags; he thought that he was going to be put into a real jail. On 28 May towards noon, the bags were taken away – probably to inspect their content – and at four o'clock, a car with two police officers came and picked up the bishop and took him to the harbor, without letting him say his farewells to anybody. The police officers invited him to embark on the Hanyang, a freighter of an English company bound for Hong Kong. The police themselves had reserved his place and paid for everything.

The following day, 29 May, some missionaries having heard about this event, went to the quay and greeted the venerated captive and exchanged only a few words, for the two guards never left him by so much as an inch. At nine o'clock the boat weighed anchor.

Later on, we heard that the police officers had treated their worthy and patient prisoner with deference and they had made sure that he had everything he needed. Disembarking on English territory he was left free. Bishop de Vienne boarded a plane and a short time later he was in Rome.

As soon as the police car that took de Vienne away had left the Laoxikai residence, all the Christians who had kept him in custody returned home . . . silently. A few days later, there was an article by Wu Quorui in the *Tianjin Daily*. After congratulating the Tianjin police for deporting the bishop and considering this measure as a first step in the direction of progress, he declared that a second step had to be taken, more important than the first one, namely the deportation of the internuncio.

Deportation of Bishop Riberi, Apostolic Internuncio

At the end of June 1951, four articles were published in the same newspaper signed by four diocesan priests expounding in different ways the necessity of expelling the most important enemy of progress in China: the Internuncio, Bishop Antonio Riberi.

The majority of the Chinese priests had not taken part in deporting their bishop. Certainly, they ought to have protested and they should not have remained passive in the face of the reprehensible behavior of the agitators. They did not dare. But in the face of the new Communist pressure to deport the internuncio from China, they were in anguish. They all met in the bishop's residence to study the question: can we in conscience participate in Bishop Riberi's expulsion? What happened in this discussion? We do not know. We even do not know if there was someone to lead the discussion.

What followed, however, seems to show that the controversy had no positive conclusion and that everybody in the assembly remained free to follow his own opinion.

The question was asked throughout the whole of China, however, and soon local newspapers reported endless lists of signatories who demanded that the government deport the internuncio. Afterwards it was learned that the majority of these signatures were false; names of priests and of Christians that had been on other documents had been transferred to the deportation petition. For instance, in Tianjin, the names of those who had signed the first form presented by the bishops, were copied onto the official form. The goal was reached. The government had clean hands. The Church of China had repudiated its apostolic internuncio, the pope's direct delegate.

In the beginning of 1952, Bishop Riberi was deported by the military from Nanjing and taken to Hong Kong against all diplomatic rights and customs, and in a way that was as rough as it was ludicrous.

Riberi first stayed in Hong Kong, after that, in 1953 he went and established his residence in Taipei, the capital of the island of Formosa and center of the Nationalist Chinese Government, to which the internuncio had been accredited in 1946.

So far, we have reported what happened, so to speak, under our eyes, for we left China in July 1951. We must speak now about the disgusting measures taken later by the Communists against the orphanages managed by our Sisters, and against the Legion of Mary. They are facts that missionaries, having come back to Europe told many times. Our intention has been to write the history of the Vincentian missions up until their "collapse," that is, up until the complete destruction of these missions.

Now, for our confreres, we have arrived there. Moreover, it is too early to write the history of Communism in China, even from the point of view of the Catholic missions, because this history is still unfolding (1962–1963). We shall say a few words about the evolution of Communist tactics, and later on about the Legion of Mary.

The Evolution of Communist Tactics

The rigorous application of the Three Autonomies failed, according even to the Communists. They thought to be clever by insisting more on the notion of "patriotism." They wanted now to establish so-called "patriotic" churches; the only ones viable in a democratic regime. Every priest and every Christian who was not a member of a "patriotic" Church was anti-patriotic because of that very fact. In former days they would have said anti-revolutionary.

The Legion of Mary

About the Legion of Mary [*Legio Mariae*], it may be said that to name this beautiful association and all its parts by using military terms was unfortunate. Indeed: *Legio* = troop, army; *Praesidium* = post, garrison, guard; *Centrum* = headquarters.

It would have been best not to translate these Latin words literally into Chinese according to their meaning. The internuncio, Riberi, who had been at the apostolic delegation in Liberia (Africa) where he busied himself with this work, had noticed these unfortunate names. On his arrival in China, he tried to replace them by others that had no military resonance; but he was too late; the association, though recent, was already so widespread in China that it could not accept these changes.

Then, the Reds wanted to see or rather they pretended to see in these military names the obvious proof that the legionaries were part of a vast plot against the people's government. This was for them clearly just a pretext, for during their enquiries they were never able to find the least trace of a plot. But these exterior and purely verbal signs were enough reason for them to crush this work in a ferocious manner.

Reeducation of the Recalcitrant

Another one of their odious maneuvers was the one they hid under the name of "reeducation" of the criminals who were filling their prisons. It was only putting to forced labor those who were imprisoned as counter-revolutionaries and who more or less resisted the indoctrination that was imposed upon them. All those who were able to do some physical works were employed in huge building sites and were working as slaves. There were hundreds of thousands of them, among whom there were priests and Christians. The Communist newspapers published these bits of information for the glory of the regime, as a work of high human quality, that was trying to lift up the morale of these delinquents through work and to make good citizens out of them eventually. Meanwhile in reality, the government had found a clever way to get cheap labor.

We have recounted the story of the deportation of a bishop who had not officially been incarcerated or ever judged.

Now we will tell of the deportation of another confrere, incarcerated for three years and who eventually was condemned to be deported from China and absolutely forbidden from ever returning to China. We shall limit ourselves to these two examples and we shall cite only these cases without giving a detailed description.

Arrest of Father Tichit with Four Chinese Priests

In June 1951, Hippolyte Tichit, visitor of the Northern Province since March 1947, told the non-Chinese professors of the regional seminary of Chala and two other European confreres in Tianjin that they had to prepare their departure from China, adding that he himself was making his arrangements to get his *exeat* [exit visa] so as to leave, too. These confreres got their authorization to leave after repeated difficulties and delays. They embarked in Tianjin for Hong Kong where they landed in August and September 1951. From there they set out for Europe, some by plane, others by boat. On 25 July 1951 towards four o'clock in the afternoon, armed and helmeted police officers in uniform appeared at the Beitang and summoned Father Tichit and took him to a separate room to give him their summons. Immediately they handcuffed him and had him get into a van, where there were already some Chinese priests; after that the car went to the common prison. On arrival there, some police officers led Tichit to court to question him about his identity; then he was put in a cell where there were some ten other prisoners. He was subjected to frequent and very long cross-examinations. Because most of his answers were negative, he was treated roughly. His fellow prisoners had received order not to spare their new fellow prisoner.

When once the guard of the cell threatened to beat him, the prisoner answered that if he put his hands on him, he would defend himself. That is what happened, but then the whole room rose against Tichit and beat him so hard that he fell down on the ground unconscious. When he came around, he saw that there were handcuffs on his hands and chains on his feet.

After this unforgettable incident, he was forced to remain standing facing the wall during the day, and at night he was brought before the judge to answer questions. After twelve days, he began to talk drivel. After the prison doctor's intervention, chains and handcuffs were taken off him, but his legs were so swollen that they had decided to amputate them. His wounds drained, which lessened the pain and made it bearable. From that moment on, after one month in prison, the captive was made to sleep, though the nightly questioning continued, and his wounds were bandaged every day.

The judge forced him to tell the story of his life beginning from his childhood; he did it three times. Then in November, he had to undergo the famous indoctrination. But Tichit was resistant and so not easy to teach. His teachers, probably losing all hope of converting him to their ideas left him somewhat alone. Almost three years passed in this way.

Tichit's Release

Release came for Tichit as a surprise. It was one of the results of the Geneva Conference. On 17 January 1954 a prison guard entered his cell at two o'clock in the afternoon and said to him: "Let us go out in the yard . . . we are going to release you. What do you think of the generosity of our government?" "It is probably because of the declining health of the prisoners living always within these four walls." "No, it is to show imperialists that we take better care of prisoners than they do." Still three long months passed.

In the end, on 12 April a guard brought him his belongings and told him to follow him. They then went to listen to the judicial sentence passed on him: "Deportation forever from Chinese territory."

After that, accompanied by Monsieur Vetel, a Frenchman interned in 1951, Tichit was taken to Tianjin and interned. On 23 April, he boarded a ship and landed in Hong Kong on the 29th . . . free but sick. Four months of care in the Hospital of Saint Paul were necessary before he could board the steamship that was to bring him back to France in the first days of September 1954.

Jacques Huysmans's Internment

Father Huysmans, a Dutch confrere, was Tichit's assistant. At the time of Tichit's arrest, he was visiting people in town. When he came back a few hours later to the Beitang, a police officer who guarded the entrance barred his way and asked him for his name. "We have been looking for you," he told him, "come, I will go with you to your room." Having entered both, the police officer asked Huysmans for the keys of Tichit's room. "I do not have them," answered Huysmans, "Tichit has probably taken them with him." Another police officer was sent immediately to prison to bring back Tichit's keys. The police officers then began to search Tichit's room and went through the drawers before Huysmans's eyes while asking him many questions. Next came the assistant's room, which they examined in minute detail. Eventually almost all the rooms of the Beitang were searched in this way from top to bottom over several days.

On 29 July Huysmans was incarcerated, too. He changed cells ten times and, during his comings and goings, he met several captives whom he knew, but he could never talk with any of them. Once he saw Tichit but could not say a word to him. Interrogations and indoctrination were his lot for almost three years.

In spring 1954, the Geneva Conference met. Just as France and the U.S.A. had asked for the release of the incarcerated missionaries, so also the Netherlands demanded the release of its missionaries. On 24 May Huysmans was told his release was imminent. Just like Tichit, he was taken to Hong Kong where he arrived on 4 June. How amazed he was when he saw Tichit on the landing, whom he thought still to be in prison in Peking. At the end of July, both boarded the *Cambodge* and arrived in Marseilles on 1 September 1954. Then, on the 6th, a dozen missionaries, who had recently returned from China welcomed the two travelers to the Gare de Lyon [in Paris].

Tichit's Unfortunate Companions

What happened to the four Chinese priests who left the Beitang on 25 July 1951 along with Tichit in a truck escorted by many police officers to the prison destined for them? They were Father Pierre Sun, director of the minor seminary transformed into Gengxin School, and Father Paul Zhang, the parish priest of the cathedral since 1937, both Vincentians. There were also Fathers Ignace Qi and Thomas Bian, two diocesan priests, who were Zhang's associates.

Sun did not live long in prison. Few details are known about his death. His chains, it is said, had been tightened so much that his wounds became gangrenous. He died on the following 16th of September.

Paul Zhang, being Chinese, could not benefit from the release acquired thanks the Geneva Conference. We do not know one single thing about his internment. The fact is that in June 1954 the Beitang was informed that he was dying. Immediately, Chinese confreres hastened to the prison and brought him back to the Beitang. Three hours later, Zhang passed away.

Concerning the two other diocesan priests, Qi and Bian, we have never had any information. Probably they were still in chains in 1963, if they had not died.

Internments in and Deportations from the Vincentian Southern Province

Bishop Georges Deymier

In the province of Zhejiang, the majority of the churches were transformed into meeting halls for indoctrination. In the big towns, the churches were left at the Christians' disposal until noon; the rest of the day they again were used as meeting halls.

Very early on a case against the archbishop was opened and the Christians were urged to formulate accusations against him. As soon as the Three Autonomies were applied, Bishop Deymier explicitly opposed them and gave his priests orders, the most important of which was this: "Neither the Faithful nor the priests have the authority to reform the Church. It is the task for the Church itself." Equally, in 1952 he publicly defended the internuncio when there was question of deporting him. This attitude caused Deymier cruel treatment. He was never incarcerated however, but in his residence he was kept under surveillance. At that time, overburdened with troubles, he became sick. He was allowed to have a few days' rest; a police officer even came several times to inquire about his health. At the end of March, interrogations were begun again. Finally, on 29 May 1952 at four o'clock in the morning, the archbishop was taken to the central station. After the ordinary questions about identity and some insults uttered for his benefit, everyone in the hall rose up and the president read the sentence of perpetual banishment. Here are some passages from that text:

> It is a recognized fact that the Vatican appointed the Frenchman Georges Deymier as archbishop of Hangzhou. . . . He has been in contact with feudal military leaders, the Japanese robbers; he has made friends with American imperialists and with the outlaw Chiang Kai-Shek. . . . After the liberation, this foreigner opposed the government of the Chinese Republic. . . . Following the imperialist Riberi's instructions, he has secretly organized the reactionary society of the Legion of Mary. . . . With false rumors, he has slandered and sabotaged the orders of the government. . . . In the church he has published reactionary pastoral instructions. . . . He has urged the Catholics to oppose the People's government. Of these crimes we have sure proof. That why the people of this city and the patriotic Catholics have insistently begged the government to deport this foreigner from our country. . . .

> That is why our committee, for the security of the state and for the well-being of the people, has pronounced against Deymier the sentence of perpetual banishment and has entrusted the municipal police with the immediate execution of this sentence.

> Signatures of the president and of the vice-president

Immediately, with photographers flashing away, three soldiers took Deymier off. They made him sit among them on an open van with three other police officers. When he arrived at the residence, his luggage was examined. All the books, registers, and pictures relating to China were confiscated.

The trip, by train to Canton, took two days and one night. He arrived in Hong Kong on Pentecost Sunday, June 1952.[85]

Bishops André Defebvre and Others

Bishop Defebvre was caught at his residence in Ningbo on 16 June 1953 and was incarcerated in a prison of that town for three months. On the following eleventh of September, he was moved to a prison in Shanghai. Deported from China on 19 April 1954 – probably thanks to the Geneva Conference – he went to Canton and arrived in Hong Kong on 22 April. On 15 May he set sail accompanied by several missionaries likewise deported and landed in Marseilles on 10 June 1954.

Defebvre had not been mistreated like the others. He had suffered from the regime of the prison, lack of food, isolation and especially from the lack of information about his missionaries, as well as the uncertainty of the future. During his interrogations he had not been insulted or tortured.

The same was true for Father Deymier and his companions. Joseph Deymier, the bishop of Hangzhou's brother and visitor of the Southern Province, was incarcerated in Shanghai on 16 June 1963 in the prison of former Massenet Street. These persons were incarcerated with him: Fathers Prost, procurator of Shanghai, Joseph Lassus, assistant procurator, and Jean-Louis Corcuff, missionary of Ningbo. As always, these prisoners were in different cells.

All were set free at the same time as Defebvre, and they traveled together by train from Shanghai to Canton and by boat from Canton to Hong Kong, except, alas, one. They learned in Hong Kong, indeed, that Lassus had died in prison on 6 January 1954. When they did not see him appear at their release from prison, they thought that he had not yet received his release. The cause of his death is not known, but it is quite probable that he, who had delicate health and never was appointed to do the hard mission work outside, had been unable to stand the privations of Chinese imprisonment.

Bishop O'Shea of Ganzhou (Jiangxi) was interned in autumn 1953 in Ganzhou itself. The prison regime ruined his health. Deported in

---

85.   Deymier died on 2 April 1956 in Le Bouscat (Gironde), near Bordeaux.

March 1954, he was exhausted and had to have medical care for almost five months in Hong Kong before being able to make the trip back to the United States.

Bishop Mignani, bishop of Ji'an, was deported on 11 June 1951.

Bishop Quinn, bishop of Yujiang was also expelled in 1951.

Archbishop Joseph Zhou of Nanchang was arrested in 1951 and sentenced to five years in prison. His judges handled him quite carefully, for they hoped to put him at the head of all the bishops in China. When they proposed this project to the bishop, he bowed deeply before them. He thanked them for the great honor that they wanted to do him by appointing him pope of the whole China. "But if I am to be the pope," he said, "I want to be the pope of the whole Catholic Church, and not only of China." He was released in 1957 after his term. Back in his church, he immediately resumed his apostolic activities. He imposed ecclesiastical penalties on all the priests in his diocese who had taken part in establishing "patriotic" churches and he forbade Christians to go to ceremonies celebrated by priests who were openly adhering to the Communist party. Straight away Zhou was again arrested and put under guard in his episcopal residence, and absolutely forbidden to communicate with his priests or any Christians.

Bishop Joseph Hu of Taizhou was arrested in 1955 and sentenced to ten years in prison. Since then we have received no information about this venerated captive, except that he died in prison on 28 August 1962.

We have now arrived at the critical moment where all missionary activities in China were to stop completely. We must give next the list of the personnel present in our missions immediately after the collapse.

Appendices

General Comments

List of the Personnel of the Vincentian Missions in 1941

The year 1941 is the last in which the general reports of the missions could be published completely. The years that followed were so disturbed by the Sino-Japanese war that it became impossible to gather the annual reports of some vicariates. Partial statistics cannot give the whole picture.

That why we have been obliged to take as basis the last published issue of the yearbook *Les Missions de Chine*, 1942. It took ten more years before China was completely in the power of Communism, during which time missionaries were still working and producing fruits; some of the numbers will be somewhat inexact, especially regarding the numbers of the Faithful.

We shall give three lists. The first list gives the situation of the personnel of every Vincentian vicariate, mentioning for each of them the province to which it belongs. This first list does not include the vicariates or prefectures entrusted to the diocesan clergy or to other missionary societies. Nevertheless, because these missions have been fathered, so to speak, by Vincentians, we give their personnel situation in a second list, with the same details as in the first list. The third list covers all the missions in China.

Notes on These Three Lists

1. The numbers of inhabitants are only approximate. The numerous zeros they contain indicate that the numbers are not exact, and have been rounded off. A serious census had never been attempted in China. The Communist government has the tendency to increase the number of the Chinese population: it mentions 600 million, perhaps including Tibet and the whole of Inner and Outer Mongolia.

2. The number of Catholics has certainly increased since 1941, as we have said. That year the Vincentians had about five thousand adult baptisms and nearly twelve thousand baptisms of infants of Christians. The following years there were fewer. In a word, it is not far from the truth if about forty thousand is added to the total number of the Faithful.

3. The number of foreign priests has remained more or less the same while Chinese priests increased by at least fifty up to 1950.

4. In the first list, which concerns only Vincentians, we see that the number of foreign priests is 223. Now, by the close of 1954, all these missionaries had left China. The number of Chinese priests is 450, among whom there were 120 Vincentians. There were also in the two [Vincentian] provinces, Northern and Southern, ten lay Brothers not mentioned in the list.

During the last years (1953–1960) we have been informed about the death of a dozen Chinese confreres, but about the 108 others we have no precise information. It is quite probable that several of them are in prison; several may have adhered to the movement of the Patriotic Churches. We believe, however, that among the faithful priests there are some who, among a thousand difficulties and with danger for their life, fulfill an efficacious ministry among their Faithful. We would have preferred sure knowledge to all this guesswork.

The bamboo curtain is woven so hermetically that all correspondence with the West is impossible. It is one of the greatest miseries that the old missionaries suffer, that they have been left in ignorance about the real situation in this great country that they had made their country of adoption.

5. In the first list we see: 108 foreign Daughters of Charity and 208 Chinese Daughters. Those in Shanghai need to be added to them. They are not on the list because that city is not in one of our vicariates. The Daughters of Charity had their central house and works in Shanghai. There were forty-three foreign Daughters of Charity there and fifty-one Chinese Daughters. Now, those 151 foreign Sisters had all returned to Europe or the U.S.A. by the end 1954. The 260 Chinese Sisters have remained by and large in the institutions that they were occupying, but they are no longer in charge. Some of them probably returned to their families.

Appendix 1: First List

Vincentian Missions in Hebei, Zhejiang, Jiangxi, 1941

(1) Northern Province, Peking (Civil Province of Hebei)	
Categories	**Totals**
Population	4,000,000
Catholics	245,000
Foreign Priests	31
Chinese Priests	111
Seminarians major seminary	15
Seminarians minor seminary	63
Foreign Daughters of Charity	30
Chinese Daughters of Charity	60
Chinese Religious Women	118
Boys in middle schools	2,272
Girls in middle schools	1,944
Boys in primary-superior schools	496
Girls in primary-superior schools	395

(2) Northern Province, Zhengding	
Categories	**Totals**
Population	4,000,000
Catholics	51,985
Foreign Priests	15
Chinese Priests	47
Seminarians major seminary	15
Seminarians minor seminary	67
Foreign Daughters of Charity	6

Chinese Daughters of Charity	60
Chinese Religious Women	103
Boys in primary-superior schools	672
Girls in primary-superior schools	246

(3) Northern Province, Tianjin	
Categories	**Totals**
Population	2,500,000
Catholics	55,647
Foreign Priests	23
Chinese Priests	34
Seminarians major seminary	6
Seminarians minor seminary	42
Foreign Daughters of Charity	7
Chinese Daughters of Charity	18
Chinese Religious Women	35
Boys in middle schools	1,672
Girls in middle schools	504
Boys in primary-superior schools	458
Girls in primary-superior schools	277

(4) Northern Province, Anguo	
Categories	**Totals**
Population	1,270,000
Catholics	34,388
Foreign Priests	2
Chinese Priests	24
Seminarians major seminary	5
Seminarians minor seminary	38
In primary schools	387
Lower schools	535

(5) Northern Province, Shunde, Polish Vincentian Province	
Categories	**Totals**
Population	1,100,000
Catholics	21,605
Foreign Priests	15
Chinese Priests	7
Seminarians major seminary	2
Seminarians minor seminary	20
Foreign Daughters of Charity	8
Chinese Daughters of Charity	6
Chinese Religious Women	15
Boys middle schools	75
Girls middle schools	12
Primary schools	135
Secondary schools	25

(6) Northern Province, Yongping, Dutch Vincentian Province	
Categories	**Totals**
Population	4,582,000
Catholics	35,965
Foreign Priests	25
Chinese Priests	16
Seminarians major seminary	10
Seminarians minor seminary	25
Foreign Daughters of Charity	6
Chinese Daughters of Charity	13
Girls in middle schools	295
Primary schools	109
Secondary schools	290

(7) Southern Province, Ningbo (Civil Province of Zhejiang)	
Categories	**Totals**
Population	9,200,000
Catholics	52,200
Foreign Priests	28
Chinese Priests	54
Seminarians major seminary	23
Seminarians minor seminary	41
Foreign Daughters of Charity	16
Chinese Daughters of Charity	38
Chinese Religious Women	64
Primary schools	577
Secondary schools	77

(8) Southern Province, Hangzhou	
Categories	**Totals**
Population	6,600,000
Catholics	35,050
Foreign Priests	11
Chinese Priests	45
Seminarians major seminary	9
Seminarians minor seminary	31
Foreign Daughters of Charity	10
Chinese Daughters of Charity	28
Chinese Religious Women	55
Boys middle schools	40
Girls middle schools	80
Primary schools	717
Secondary schools	276

(9) Southern Province, Taizhou	
Categories	**Totals**
Population	2,000,000
Catholics	7,874
Chinese Priests	18
Seminarians major seminary	2
Seminarians minor seminary	6
Chinese Religious Women	11
Primary schools	299
Secondary schools	106

(10) Southern Province, Nanchang (Civil Province of Jiangxi)	
Categories	**Totals**
Population	5,000,000
Catholics	34,230
Foreign Priests	15
Chinese Priests	25
Seminarians major seminary	10
Seminarians minor seminary	24
Foreign Daughters of Charity	12
Chinese Daughters of Charity	23
Chinese Religious Women	39
Boys middle schools	9
Primary schools	32
Secondary schools	15

(11) Southern Province, Yujiang, Vincentian Western Province, U.S.A.	
Categories	**Totals**
Population	4,400,000
Catholics	26,825
Foreign Priests	24

Chinese Priests	15
Seminarians major seminary	7
Seminarians minor seminary	36
Foreign Daughters of Charity	4
Chinese Daughters of Charity	2
Girls middle schools	82
Primary schools	187
Secondary schools	245

(12) Southern Province, Ganzhou, Vincentian Eastern Province, U.S.A.	
Categories	**Totals**
Population	3,000,000
Catholics	17,863
Foreign Priests	22
Chinese Priests	15
Seminarians major seminary	1
Seminarians minor seminary	5
Foreign Daughters of Charity	5
Chinese Religious Women	34
Primary schools	124
Secondary schools	10

(13) Southern Province, Ji'an, Vincentian Province of Turin	
Categories	**Totals**
Population	4,000,000
Catholics	23,980
Foreign Priests	12
Chinese Priests	12
Seminarians major seminary	2
Seminarians minor seminary	21
Primary schools	53
Secondary schools	100

Totals	
Categories	**Totals**
Population	51,652,000
Catholics	643,406
Foreign Priests	223
Chinese Priests	450
Seminarians major seminary	107
Seminarians minor seminary	419
Foreign Daughters of Charity	108
Chinese Daughters of Charity	209
Chinese Religious Women	532
Boys in middle schools	4,068
Girls in middle schools	2,917
Primary schools	3,859
Secondary schools	2,067

Appendix 2: Second List

Vincentian Vicariates Entrusted to Diocesan Clergy or Missionary Societies, and Their Personnel, 1941

| Baoding (Hebei), Diocesan Clergy ||
Categories	Totals
Population	2,100,000
Catholics	79,369
Foreign Priests	7
Chinese Priests	62
Seminarians major seminary	27
Seminarians minor seminary	49
Chinese Religious Women	64
Boys in lower primary schools	293
Girls in lower primary schools	331

| Xuanhua (Hebei), Diocesan Clergy ||
Categories	Totals
Population	1,700,000
Catholics	36,027
Foreign Priests	2
Chinese Priests	43
Seminarians major seminary	11
Seminarians minor seminary	71
Chinese Religious Women	34
Boys in lower primary schools	335
Girls in lower primary schools	343

Zhaoxian (Hebei), Diocesan Clergy	
Categories	**Totals**
Population	930,000
Catholics	45,635
Foreign Priests	0
Chinese Priests	39
Seminarians major seminary	13
Seminarians minor seminary	87
Chinese Religious Women	50
Boys in lower primary schools	500
Girls in lower primary schools	60

Yixian, Apostolic Prefecture (Hebei), Stigmatine Fathers	
Categories	**Totals**
Population	800,000
Catholics	6,490
Foreign Priests	10
Chinese Priests	7
Seminarians major seminary	8
Seminarians minor seminary	32
Chinese Religious Women	12
Boys in lower primary schools	292
Girls in lower primary schools	185

Nancheng (Jiangxi), Missionary Society of Saint Columban	
Categories	**Totals**
Population	480,00
Catholics	9,093
Foreign Priests	25
Chinese Priests	3
Seminarians major seminary	2
Seminarians minor seminary	17

Chinese Religious Women	0
Boys in lower primary schools	44
Girls in lower primary schools	21

Lishui (Zhejiang), Scarboro Fathers	
Categories	**Totals**
Population	2,300,000
Catholics	6,250
Foreign Priests	38
Chinese Priests	16
Seminarians major seminary	5
Seminarians minor seminary	4
Chinese Religious Women	0
Boys in lower primary schools	180
Girls in lower primary schools	254

Totals	
Categories	**Totals**
Population	8,310,000
Catholics	182,864
Foreign Priests	82
Chinese Priests	160
Seminarians major seminary	66
Seminarians minor seminary	260
Chinese Religious Women	160
Boys in lower primary schools	1,643
Girls in lower primary schools	1,194

Note:

Vicariate of Baoding: the seven foreign priests were the last Vincentians to remain there. In 1948, three of them had passed away; the others were transferred to Peking.

Vicariate of Xuanhua: the two foreign priests were two Belgian S.A.M. Fathers, who left in 1948. [Société des Auxiliaires des Missions, founder: Vincent Lebbe]

The Stigmatine Fathers (C.S.S.), Italians, had only this mission in China.

Lishui was still an apostolic prefecture; it became a vicariate in 1946. The Scarboro Foreign Mission Society (S.F.M.) has its headquarters in Canada.

The vicariate of Nancheng was entrusted to the Missionary Society of Saint Columban (S.S.C.M.E.), founded in Ireland.

Appendix 3: Third List

Statistics of all the Missions of China, 1941

Categories	Totals
Approximate Number of Inhabitants	486,000,000
Catholics	3,313,400
Catechumens	512,263
Apostolic Vicariates and Prefectures	138
Churches able to accommodate 400 Christians	2,485
Chapels and Oratories	13,429
Personnel	
Foreign Missionaries	3,112
Chinese Priests	2,186
Foreign Religious Women	2,372
Chinese Religious Women	4,237
Seminarians in major seminary	1,066
Seminarians minor seminary	3,866
Middle and Superior Schools	
• Boys	14,094
• Girls	9,787
Superior Primary Schools	
• Boys	28,509
• Girls	17,674
Lower Primary Schools	
• Boys	122,553
• Girls	68,451
Doctrine and Basics Both Boys and Girls	201,577

Charitable Works and Spiritual Fruits	
Orphaned Boys	3,171
Orphaned Girls	27,514
Baptisms	
• Of Adults	82,338
• Of Adults at the Point of Death	81,019
• Of Children of Christian Parents	90,157
• Of Children of Non-Christians at Point of Death	273,970
Confirmations	104,920
Marriages	25,440

Appendix 4

The Church Hierarchy (Ecclesiastical Missions) Established in China, 1946

The following lists all the missions in China at the time that the Roman decree of 11 April 1946 established the Catholic Hierarchy in China.

For some decades already the Sacred Congregation of Propaganda, with a view to better management, had decided that every civil province would be considered as a Province or better as an Ecclesiastical Region: in this way the five Regions already in existence became twenty Regions, which is the number of the civil provinces.

From 1924 onward, as mentioned above, the ecclesiastical jurisdictions no longer bore the name of the civil province to which some point of the compass was added (e.g., Southwest Zhili), but they took the name of the place that Propaganda indicated as the residence of the bishop, apostolic vicar or head of the mission.

A short time after the promulgation of that decree, the Communist grip gained ascendancy and, like a storm from hell, overturned all the institutions. The Church did not have time to make any changes concerning the incumbents of the new archdioceses and dioceses, so that the apostolic vicars residence in the capital or a principal town of a civil province retained the title of archbishop. The apostolic vicars that had responsibility over a circumscription detached from the principal vicariate retained the title of bishop.

Independent missions and apostolic prefectures were not touched at all by the decree of 1946 and remained outside the hierarchy, that is, they remained under the immediate jurisdiction of the Holy See and their names did not change.

It is probable that they would have acquired a special statute, if peace had persisted.

In the list of the ecclesiastical regions that became ecclesiastical provinces, we have followed the numbering fixed by the Sacred Congregation of Propaganda, and for the jurisdictions created in every province in course of time, we have followed the chronological order of the formation of each jurisdiction.[86]

First Ecclesiastical Region: Mongolia

1. Xiwanzi – It was detached from the diocese of Peking as Apostolic Vicariate [V.A.] of Mongolia in 1840. It became V.A. of Central Mongolia in 1883 and V.A. of Xiwanzi in 1924. It became a diocese in 1946. (C.I.C.M.)

2. Suiyuan – It was detached from the V.A. of Mongolia as V.A. of Southwest Mongolia in 1883 and V.A. of Suiyuan in 1922. It became an archdiocese in 1946. (C.I.C.M.)

3. Ningxia – It was detached from V.A. of West Mongolia in 1922 as V.A. of Ningxia in 1922 and became a diocese in 1946. (C.I.C.M.)

4. Jining – It was detached from V.A. of Xiwanzi, as V.A. of Jining in 1929 and became the diocese of Jining in 1946. (C.I.C.M.)

It covered 845,000 square kilometers and had 3,300,000 inhabitants, of whom 146,359 were Catholics and 22,055 were catechumens.

Second Ecclesiastical Region: Manchuria

1. Mukden [Shenyang] – It was detached from the diocese of Peking as V.A. of Manchuria in 1838, became V.A. of South Manchuria in 1898 and V.A. of Mukden in 1924. It became an archdiocese in 1946. (M.E.P.)

2. Jehol [Rehe] – It was detached from V.A. of Mongolia as V.A. of Eastern Mongolia in 1883 and V.A. of Jehol in 1924. It became the diocese of Jehol in 1946. (C.I.C.M.)

3. Jilin – It was detached from V.A. of Manchuria, as V.A. of Northern Manchuria in 1898. It became V.A. of Jilin in 1924 and a diocese in 1946. (M.E.P.)

4. Jiamusi – It was detached from the V.A. of Hongshan as the independent mission of Yilan in 1928. It became the independent mission of Jiamusi in 1934, then the Apostolic Prefecture [P.A.] of Jiamusi in 1940. It was outside the hierarchy. (Tyrol Capuchins)

---

86. For additional clarification of this list, see "Roman Catholic Jurisdictions, 1924-1946" in *Handbook of Christianity in China, Volume Two: 1800 to the Present*, ed. R. G. Tiedemann, *Handbook of Oriental Studies*, vol. 15/2 (Leiden: Brill, 2010), pp. 971-976. (AS)

5. Qiqiha'er – It was detached from the V.A. of Jilin as the P.A. of Qiqiha'er in 1928. (Missionary Society of Bethlehem)

6. Yanji – It was detached from the V.A. of Hongshan as the V.A. of Yanji in 1928. It became a diocese in 1946. (Benedictines of Saint Odile)

7. Xipingjie – It was detached from the V.A. of Mukden in 1929 as the V.A. of Xipingjie and became a diocese in 1946. (Missionary Society of Quebec)

8. Chifeng – It was detached from the V.A. of Jehol as the P.A. of Chifeng in 1932. (Diocesan Clergy)

9. Fushun – It was detached from the V.A. of Mukden as the P.A. of Fushun in 1932. It became the V.A. of Fushun in 1940 and a diocese in 1946. (Missionary Society of Maryknoll, U.S.A.)

10. Lindong – It was detached from the V.A. of Xipingjie as the P.A. of Lintong in 1937. (Foreign Missions of Quebec, Canada)

It covered 1,304,292 square kilometers and had 32,869,054 inhabitants, of whom193,156 were Catholics and 20,205 were catechumens.

Third Ecclesiastical Region: Hebei (previously Zhili)

1. Peking – It was the archdiocese of Kambalik 1307–1483. It was the diocese of Peking 1690–1856 and became the V.A. of North Zhili in 1856. The name changed to the V.A. of Peking in 1924 and was made the archdiocese of Peking in 1946. (Diocesan Clergy)

2. Zhengding – It was detached from Peking as the V.A. of West Zhili in 1856. It became the V.A. of Zhengding in 1924 and a diocese in 1946. (C.M.)

3. Xianxian – It was detached from the diocese of Peking as the V.A. of Southeast Zhili in 1856. It became the V.A. of Xianxian in 1924 and a diocese in 1946. (S.J.)

4. Yongping – It was detached from North Zhili as the V.A. of East Zhili in 1899. It became the V.A. of Yongping in and a diocese in 1946. (Dutch C.M.)

5. Baoding – It was detached from the V.A. of North Zhili as the V.A. of Central Zhili in 1910 (C.M.). It became the V.A. of Baoding in 1924 (C.M.) and in 1930 (Diocesan Clergy). It became a diocese in 1946. (Diocesan Clergy)

6. Tianjin – It was detached from North Zhili as the V.A. of Maritime Zhili in 1912. It became the V.A. of Tianjin in 1924 and a diocese in 1946. (C.M.).

7. Anguo – It was detached from the V.A. of Baoding as the P.A. of Lixian in 1946. It became the V.A. of Anguo in 1929 and a diocese in 1946. (Diocesan Clergy)

8. Xuanhua – It was detached from the V.A. of Peking as the V.A. of Xuanhua in 1926 and became a diocese in 1946. Diocesan Clergy.

9. Yixian – It was detached from V.A. of Baoding an independent mission in 1929 and became the P.A. of Yixian in 1936. (Italian Stigmatine Fathers)

10. Zhaoxian – It was detached from the V.A. of Zhengding as the P.A. of Zhaoxian in 1929 and became a V.A. in 1932 and a diocese in 1946. (Diocesan Clergy)

11. Yongnian – It was detached from the V.A. of Xianxian as the P.A. of Yongnian in 1929. It became a V.A. in1933 and a diocese in 1946. (Diocesan Clergy)

12. Shunde – It was detached from the V.A. of Zhengding as the P.A. of Shunde in 1933. It became a V.A. in1944 and a diocese in 1946. (Polish C.M.)

13. Daming – It was detached from V.A. of Xianxian as the P.A. of Daming in 1935. (Hungarian S.J.)

14. Jingxian – It was detached from the V.A. of Xianxian in 1939 as the P.A. of Jingxian. It became a V.A. in 1945 and a diocese in 1946. (Austrian S.J.)

It covered 153,600 square kilometers and had 28,644,000 inhabitants, of whom 785,823 were Catholics and 48,441 were catechumens.

Fourth Ecclesiastical Region: Shandong

1. Ji'nan – It was detached from the diocese Peking as the V.A. of Shandong in 1839. It was renamed the V.A. of North Shandong in 1886 and the V.A. of Ji'nan in 1924. It became an archdiocese in 1946. (German Franciscans)

2. Yanzhou – It was detached from the V.A. of Shandong as the V.A. of South Shandong in 1885. It became the V.A. of Yanzhou in 1924 and a diocese in 1946. (German S.V.D.)

3. Zhifu (Yantai) – It was detached from the V.A. of North Shandong as the V.A. of East Shandong in 1894. It became the V.A. of Zhifu in 1924 and a diocese in 1926. (French Franciscans)

4. Qingdao – It was detached from the V.A. of Yanzhou as the P.A. of Qingdao in 1925. It became a V.A. in 1928 and a diocese in 1946. (German S.V.D.)

5. Zhoucun – It was detached from the V.A. of Ji'nan as an independent mission of Zhangdian in 1929 and a P.A. in 1932. It became the V.A. of Zhoucun in 1937 and a diocese in 1946. (Franciscans U.S.A.)

6. Weihaiwei – It was detached from the V.A. of Zhifu, as an independent mission in 1931 and became a P.A. in 1938. (French Franciscans)

7. Yiduxian – It was detached from the V.A. of Zhifu as an independent mission in 1931. (French Franciscans)

8. Linqing – It was detached from the V.A. of Jinan as the P.A. of Linqing in 1931. (Diocesan Clergy)

9. Yanggu – It was detached from the V.A. of Yanzhou as a P.A. in 1933. It became the V.A. of Yanggu in 1939 and a diocese in 1946. (Chinese Clergy)

10. Chaozhou – It was detached from the V.A. of Yanzhou as the V.A. of Chaozhou in 1934 and became a diocese in 1946. (German S.V.D.)

11. Yizhou (Linyi) – It was detached from the V.A. of Jinan as the V.A. of Linyi in 1937 and became a diocese in 1946. (German S.V.D.)

It covered 179,200 square kilometers and had 38,029,000 inhabitants, of whom 785,823 were Catholics and 84,836 were catechumens.

Fifth Ecclesiastical Region: Shanxi

1. Taiyuan – It was detached from the V.A. of Shaanxi-Shanxi, as the V.A. of Shanxi in 1844. It became the V.A. of North Shanxi in 1890 and the V.A. of Taiyuan in 1924. It became an archdiocese in 1946. (Italian Franciscans)

2. Lu'an – It was detached from the V.A. of Shanxi, as V.A. of South Shanxi in 1890 and became the V.A. of Lu'an in 1924. It became the diocese of Changzhi (Lu'an) in 1946. (Dutch Franciscans)

3. Datong – It was detached from North Shanxi, as the P.A. of Datong in 1922. It became the V.A. of Lu'an in 1924 and a diocese in 1946. (C.I.C.M.)

4. Fenyang – It was detached from the V.A. of Taiyuan as the V.A. of Fenyang in 1926 and became a diocese in 1946. (Chinese clergy)

5. Shuoxian – It was detached from the V.A. of Taiyuan as the P.A. of Shuoxian in 1926 and became a V.A. in 1932. It became a diocese in 1946. (Bavarian Franciscans)

6. Yuci – It was detached from the V.A. of Taiyuan as the P.A. of Yuci in 1932 and became a V.A. in 1944. (Italian Franciscans)

7. Hongdong – It was detached from the V.A. of Lu'an as the P.A. of Hongdong in 1932. (Chinese Clergy)

8. Jiangzhou – It was detached from the V.A. of Lu'an as the P.A. of Jiangzhou in 1936. (Dutch Franciscans)

It covered 155,900 square kilometers and had 11,601,000 inhabitants, of whom 131,180 were Catholics and 24,520 were catechumens.

Sixth Ecclesiastical Region: Shaanxi

1. Xi'an – It was detached from the diocese of Peking, as the V.A. of Shaanxi and of Shanxi, in 1696. It became the V.A. of Shaanxi in 1844, the V.A. of North Shaanxi in 1877, the V.A. of Central Shaanxi in 1911, and the V.A. of Xi'an in 1924. It became an archdiocese in 1946. (Italian Franciscans)

2. Hangzhou – It was detached from the V.A. of Shaanxi as the V.A. of South Shaanxi in 1885. It became the V.A. of Hangzhou in 1924 and a diocese in 1946. (Foreign Missions of Milan)

3. Yan'an – It was detached from the V.A. of South Shaanxi as the V.A. of North Shaanxi in 1911. It became the V.A. of Yan'an in 1924 and a diocese in 1946. (Spanish Franciscans)

4. Xing'an – It was detached from the V.A. of Hanzhong, as a P.A. in 1928. (Italian Conventual Franciscans)

5. Sanyuan – It was detached from the V.A. of Xi'an, as the P.A. of Sanyuan, in 1931. It became a V.A. in 1944 and a diocese in 1946. (Italian Franciscans)

6. Tongzhou – It was detached from the V.A. of Xi'an as the P.A. of Tongzhou in 1931. (Italian Franciscans)

7. Zhoushi – It was detached from the V.A. of Xi'an as the P.A. of Zhoushi in 1932. (Chinese Clergy)

8. Fengxiang – It was detached from the V.A. of Xi'an, as the P.A. of Fengxiang in 1932 and became a V.A. in 1946. (Chinese Clergy)

It covered 187,300 square kilometers and had 7,717,000 inhabitants, of whom 83,227 were Catholics and 23,763 were catechumens.

Seventh Ecclesiastical Region:
Gansu, Xinjiang and Qinghai

1. Lanzhou – It was erected in 1878 as the V.A. of Gansu. It became the V.A. of North Gansu in 1905, the V.A. of Lanzhou in 1924, and an archdiocese in 1946. (S.V.D. in Steyl)

2. Qinzhou – It was detached from V.A. of Gansu as the P.A. of South Gansu in 1905. It became the V.A. of East Gansu in 1922, the V.A. of Qinzhou in 1924, and a diocese in 1946. (German Capuchins)

3. Pingliang – It was detached from the V.A. of Qinzhou as the P.A. of Pingliang in 1930. (Spanish Capuchins)

4. Xinjiang – It was detached from the V.A. of Lanzhou as an independent mission in 1930. It became a P.A. in 1938 (S.V.D. in Steyl)

5. Xining – It was detached from the V.A. of Lanzhou as the P.A. of Xining in 1937. (S.V.D. in Steyl)

Note: The civil province of Xinjiang with the P.A. of Xinjiang is joined to the Eighth Ecclesiastical Region; and the province of Qinghai (or Koukounor) to the P.A. of Xining.

It covered 378,000 square kilometers and had 6,705,000 inhabitants, of whom 27,220 were Catholics and 6,022 were catechumens.

Eighth Ecclesiastical Region: Jiangsu

1. Nanjing – It was erected as a V.A. in 1658 and a diocese in 1690. It became the V.A. of Nanjing in 1856, the V.A. of Jiangsu in 1921, the V.A. of Nanjing in 1922 and an archdiocese in 1946. (Chinese Clergy)

2. Haimen – It was detached from the V.A. of Nanjing in 1926 as the V.A. of Haimen. It became a diocese in 1946. (Chinese Clergy)

3. Xuzhou – It was detached from the V.A. of Nanjing as the P.A. of Xuzhou in 1931. It became a V.S. in 1935 and a diocese in 1946. (French-Canadian S.J.)

4. Shanghai – It was detached from the V.A. of Nanjing as the V.A. of Shanghai in 1933. It became a diocese in 1946. (French S.J.)

It covered 108,300 square kilometers and had 36,469,000 inhabitants, of whom 282,108 were Catholics and 51,935 were catechumens.

Ninth Ecclesiastical Region: Anhui

1. Anqing – It was detached from the V.A. of Wuhu in 1929 as the V.A. of Anqing. It became an archdiocese in 1946. (Spanish S.J.)

2. Wuhu – It was detached from the V.A. of Nanjing in 1921 as the V.A. of Anhui. It became the V.A. of Wuhu in 1930 and a diocese in 1946. (Spanish S.J.)

3. Bengbu – It was detached from the V.A. of Wuhu in 1929 as the V.A. of Bengbu. It became a diocese in 1946. (Turin S.J.)

4. Tunxi – It was detached from the V.A. of Wuhu as the P.A. of Tunxi in 1937. (Spanish Claretians, C.M.F.)

It covered 134,400 square kilometers and had 23,265,000 inhabitants, of whom 117,075 were Catholics and 55,802 were catechumens.

Tenth Ecclesiastical Region: Henan

1. Nanyang – It was detached from the diocese of Nanjing as V.A. of Henan in 1844. It became the V.A. of South Henan in 1882, the V.A. of Nanyang in 1924, and a diocese in 1946. (Milan Foreign Missions)

2. Weihui – It was detached from the V.A. of Henan as the V.A. of North Henan in 1882. It became the V.A. of Weihui in 1924 and the diocese of Jixian in 1946. (Milan Foreign Missions)

3. Zhengzhou – It was detached from the V.A. of South Henan as the P.A. of West Henan in 1905. It became the V.A. of West Henan in 1911, the V.A. of Zhengzhou in 1924, and a diocese in 1946. (Parma Foreign Missions)

4. Kaifeng – It was detached from the V.A. of South Henan as the V.A. of East Henan in 1916. It became the V.A. of Kaifeng in 1924, and an archdiocese in 1946. (Milan Foreign Missions)

5. Xinyangzhou – It was detached from the V.A. of Nanyang as the P.A. of Xinyangzhou in 1927. It became the V.A. of Xinyang in 1933 and a diocese in 1946. (S.V.D.)

6. Guide – It was detached from the V.A. of Kaifeng as the P.A. of Guide in 1928. It became the V.A. of Guide in 1937 and the diocese of Shangqiu in 1946. (Spanish Augustinian Recollects)

7. Luoyang – It was detached from Zhengzhou as the P.A. of Luoyang in 1928. It became the V.A. of Luoyang in 1935 and a diocese in 1946. (Parma Foreign Missions)

8. Xinxiang – It was detached from the V.A. of Weihui as the P.A. of Xinxiang in 1936. (American S.V.D.)

9. Zhumadian – It was detached from the V.A. of Nanyang as the P.A. of Zhumadian in 1933. It became a V.A. in 1944 and a diocese in 1946. (Chinese clergy)

It covered 172,700 square kilometers and had 34,282,000 inhabitants, of whom 153,594 were Catholics and 53,750 were catechumens.

Eleventh Ecclesiastical Region: Sichuan

1. Chengdu – It was detached from the diocese of Nanjing as the V.A. of Sichuan in 1696. It became the V.A. of Northwest Sichuan in 1856, the V.A. of Chengdu in 1924, and a diocese in 1946. (M.E.P.)

2. Chongqing – It was detached from the V.A. of Sichuan as the V.A. of East Sichuan in 1856. It became the V.A. of Chongqing in 1924, and an archdiocese in 1946. (M.E.P.)

3. Dajianlu (Xikang) – Erected as the P.A. of Tibet in 1846, it became the V.A. of Tibet in 1857, the V.A. of Dajianlu in 1924, and the diocese of Kangding in 1946. (M.E.P.)

4. Suifu – It was detached from the V.A. of East Sichuan as the V.A. of South Sichuan in 1860. It became the V.A. of Suifu in 1924, and the diocese of Suifu in 1946 (M.E.P.)

5. Ningyuan – It was detached from the V.A. of South Sichuan as the V.A. of Jiannchang (Xichang) in 1910. It became the V.A. of Ningyuan in 1924, and the diocese of Xichang in 1946. (M.E.P.)

6. Jiading – It was detached from the V.A. of Suifu as the P.A. of Yazhou (Yachow) in 1929 and the V.A. of Yazhou in 1933. It became the V.A. of Jiading in 1938, and the diocese of Leshan (Jiading) in 1946. (Chinese Clergy)

7. Xunqing – It was detached from the V.A. of Chengdu as the V.A. of Xunqing in 1929 and became a diocese in 1946. (Chinese Clergy)

8. Wanxian – It was detached from the V.A. of Chengdu as the V.A. of Wanxian in 1929 and became a diocese in 1949. (Chinese Clergy)

It covered 431,300 square kilometers and had 52,963,900 inhabitants, of whom 180,685 were Catholics and 11,635 were catechumens.

Twelfth Ecclesiastical Region: Hubei

1. Hankou – The V.A. of Huguang (i.e., Hubei and Hunan together) was erected in 1696, but was really managed, since its foundation till 1838, by the apostolic vicars of Sichuan and Shaanxi. In 1838, the Italian Franciscans of Venice were entrusted with North Huguang (Hubei). In 1856, this V.A. received the name of Hubei. It became V.A. of East Hubei in 1870, the V.A. of Hankou in 1924, and an archdiocese in 1946, under the same missionary society.

2. Yichang – It was detached from the V.A. of Hubei as Southwest Hubei in 1870. It became the V.A. of Yichang in 1924, and a diocese in 1946. (Belgian Franciscans)

3. Laohekou – It was detached from the V.A. of Hubei as the V.A. of West Hubei in 1870. It became the V.A. of Laohekou in 1924 and a diocese in 1946. (Italian Franciscans)

4. Hanyang – It was detached from the V.A. of East Hubei as the P.A. of Hanyang in 1923. It became the V.A. of Hanyang in 1927 and a diocese in 1946. (S.S.C.M.E.)

5. Qizhou – It was detached from the V.A. of Hankou, as the independent mission of Huangzhou in and became a P.A. in 1932. It became the V.A. of Jizhou in 1936 and a diocese in 1946. (Italian Franciscans)

6. Puqi – It was detached from the V.A. of East Hubei as P.A. of Puqi in 1923. (Chinese Clergy)

7. Shashi – It was detached from the V.A. of Yichang as the P.A. of Shashi in 1936. (U.S.A. Franciscans)

8. Shinan – It was detached from the V.A. of Yichang as the P.A. of Shinan in 1938. (Chinese Clergy)

9. Xiangyang – It was detached from Laohekou as the P.A. of Xiangyang in 1936. (Chinese Clergy)

10. Suixian – It was detached from the V.A. of Hankou as the P.A. of Suixian in 1937. (Irish Franciscans)

11. Wuchang – It was detached from the V.A. of East Hubei[87] as the P.A. of Wuchang in 1923. It became the V.A. of Wuchang in 1930 and a diocese in 1946. (American Franciscans)

It covered 207,600 square kilometers and had 25,541,000 inhabitants, of whom 184,645 were Catholics and 140,494 were catechumens.

Thirteenth Ecclesiastical Region: Hunan

1. Changsha – It was detached from the V.A. of Huguang (currently Hubei and Hunan) as the V.A. of Hunan in 1856. It became the V.A. of South Hunan in 1879, the V.A. of Changsha in 1924 and an archdiocese in 1946. (Italian Franciscans)

2. Changde – It was detached from the V.A. of Hunan as the V.A. of North Hunan in 1879. It became the V.A. of Changde in 1924 and a diocese in 1946. (Spanish Augustinian Hermits)

3. Yuanling – It was detached from the V.A. of Changde as the P.A. of Shenzhou in 1925. It became the V.A. of Shenzhou in 1934, the V.A. of Yuanling in 1938 and a diocese in 1946. (American Passionists – C.P.)

4. Yongzhou – It was detached from the V.A. of Changsha as the V.A. of Yongzhou in 1925. (Austrian Franciscans)

5. Hengyang – It was detached from the V.A. of Changsha as the V.A. of Hengyang in 1930. It became a diocese in 1946. (Italian Franciscans)

6. Lizhou – It was detached from the V.A. of Changsha as the P.A. of Lizhou in 1932. (Spanish Augustinian Hermits)

7. Yuezhou – It was detached of the V.A. of Changsha as the P.A. of Yuezhou in 1931. (Spanish Augustinian Hermits)

8. Xiangtan – It was detached from the V.A. of Changsha the P.A. of Xiangtan in 1938. (Italian Franciscans)

9. Baoqing – It was detached from the P.A. of Yongzhou as the P.A. of Baojing in 1938. (Hungarian Franciscans)

It covered 273,200 square kilometers and had 28,293,000 inhabitants, of whom 71,024 were Catholics and 17,502 were catechumens.

---

87. Hou-Nei-Est, typographical error in the original French publication for Hou-Pei-Est [East Hubei].

Fourteenth Ecclesiastical Region: Jiangxi

1. Nanchang – [It was founded as the diocese of Nanking, 1696.], It was detached from the V.A. of Fujian, Zhejiang and Jiangxi, as the V.A. of Zhejiang and Jiangxi in 1838.[88] It became the V.A. of Jiangxi in 1846 the V.A. of Northern Jiangxi in 1879, the V.A. of Jiujiang in 1920, and the V.A. of Nanchang in 1924, and finally an. archdiocese in 1946. (C.M.)

2. Ji'an – It was detached from the V.A. of Jiangxi as the V.A. of Southern Jiangxi in 1879. It became the V.A. of Ji'an in 1924 and a diocese in 1946. (Italian C.M.)

3. Yujiang – It was detached from V.A. of Northern Jiangxi as the V.A. of Eastern Jiangxi in 1885. It became the V.A. of Yujiang in 1920 and a diocese in 1946. (American [West] C.M.)

4. Ganzhou – It was detached from the V.A. of Ji'an as the V.A. of Ganzhou in 1920. It became a diocese in 1946. (American [East] C.M.)

5. Nancheng – It was detached from the V.A. of Yujiang as the P.A. of Nancheng in 1932. It became the V.A. of Nancheng in 1938 and a diocese in 1946. (S.S.C.M.E.)

It covered 200,200 square kilometers and had 15,820,000 inhabitants, of whom 112,849 were Catholics and 11,282 were catechumens.

Fifteenth Ecclesiastical Region: Zhejiang

1. Ningbo – It was detached from the V.A. of Fujian, Zhejiang and Jiangxi as the V.A. of Zhejiang and Jiangxi in 1838. It became the V.A. of Zhejiang in 1846, the V.A. of Eastern Zhejiang in 1910, the V.A. of Ningbo in 1924, and a diocese in 1946. (C.M.)

2. Hangzhou – It was detached from the V.A. of Zhejiang as the V.A. of Western Zhejiang in 1910. It became the V.A. of Hangzhou in 1924 and an archdiocese in 1946. (C.M.)

3. Taizhou – It was detached from the V.A. of Ningbo as the V.A. of Taizhou in 1926. It became a diocese in 1946. (Chinese Clergy)

4. Lishui – It was detached from the V.A. of Ningbo as the P.A. of Lishui in 1931. It became a diocese in 1946. (Canadian Missionaries of Scarboro)

---

88.   Original French publication has 1938, a typographical error for 1838.

It covered 103,000 square kilometers and had 21,230,000 inhabitants, of whom 104,774 were Catholics and 19,346 were catechumens.

Sixteenth Ecclesiastical Region: Fujian

1. Fuzhou – It was detached from the diocese of Nanjing as the V.A. of Fujian in 1680 or 1696. It became the V.A. of Fuzhou in 1924 and an archdiocese in 1946. (Spanish Dominicans)

2. Xiamen (Amoy) – It was detached from the V.A. of Fujian, as the V.A. of Xiamen in 1883. It became a diocese in 1946. (Spanish Dominicans)

3. Tingzhou – It was detached from the V.A. of Northern Fujian as the P.A. of Tingzhou in 1923. (German Dominicans)

4. Funing – It was detached from the V.A. of Northern Fujian as the V.A. of Funing in 1926. It became a diocese in 1946. (Spanish Dominicans)

5. Shaowu – It was detached from the V.A. of Fuzhou as an independent mission in 1929. It became a P.A. in 1938. (German Salvatorian Fathers)

6. Jian'ou – It was detached from the V.A. of Fuzhou as an independent mission in 1931. It became a P.A. in 1938. (American Dominicans)

It covered 158,700 square kilometers and had 11,755,000 inhabitants, of whom 89,025 were Catholics and 9,939 were catechumens.

Seventeenth Ecclesiastical Region: Guangdong

1. Macao – It was erected as a diocese in 1575 comprising China and Japan, with Goa in the Indies as metropolitan. In 1588, the diocese of Macao administered only China. In 1690, Macao was responsible for only Southern China, and later it was to administrate Timor, Malacca and Singapore. In the nineteen sixties, the diocese of Macao comprised only a small part of Guangdong. (Portuguese Missionaries)

2. Canton [Guangzhou] – It was detached from the diocese of Macao as the P.A. of Guangdong and Guangxi in 1858. It became the P.A. of Guangdong in 1875, the V.A. of Canton in 1924 and an archdiocese in 1946. (M.E.P.)

3. Hong Kong – It was detached from the diocese of Macao as the P.A. of Hong Kong in 1841. It became the V.A. of Hong Kong in 1874 and a diocese in 1946. (Missionaries of Milan)

4. Shantou (Swatow) – It was detached from the V.A. of Canton as the V.A. of Swatow in 1914. It became a diocese in 1946.

5. Beihai – It was detached from V.A. of Canton, as V.A. of Western Guangdong in1920. It became the V.A. of Shanhai in 1924 and the diocese of Beihai in 1946. (Maryknoll Fathers)

6. Shaozhou – It was detached from the V.A. of Canton, as V.A. of Shaozhou in 1920. It became a diocese in 1946. (Salesian Fathers of Don Bosco)

7. Jiangmen – It was detached from the V.A. of Canton as the P.A. of Jiangmen in 1924 and became the V.A. of Jiangmen in 1927. It became the diocese of Jiangmen in 1946. (Maryknoll Fathers)

8. Hainan (Island of) – It was detached from the V.A. of Shanhai (Beihai) as an independent mission in 1929. It became the P.A. of Hainan in 1935. (Picpus Fathers)

9. Jiaying – It was detached from the V.A. of Shantou as the P.A. of Jiaying. It became the V.A. of Jiaying in and a diocese in 1946. (Maryknoll Fathers)

It covered 217,400 square kilometers and had 32,385,000 inhabitants, of whom 146,141 were Catholics and 9,361 were catechumens.

Eighteenth Ecclesiastical Region: Guangxi

1. Nanning – It was detached from V.A. of Guangdong and Guangxi as the P.A. of Guangxi in 1875. It became the V.A. of Guangxi in 1914, the V.A. of Nanning in 1924, and an archdiocese in 1946. (M.E.P.)

2. Wuzhou – It was detached from the V.A. of Nanning as an independent mission in 1930. It became the P.A. of Wuzhou in 1934, a V.A. in 1939, and a diocese in 1946. (Maryknoll Fathers)

3. Guilin – It was detached from the V.A. of Wuzhou as the P.A. of Guilin in 1938. (Maryknoll Fathers)

It covered 217,500 square kilometers and had 15,820,000 inhabitants, of whom 19,181 were Catholics and 3,672 were catechumens.

Nineteenth Ecclesiastical Region: Guizhou

1. Guiyang – It was detached from the diocese of Nanjing and from the V.A. of Sichuan in 1696 and in 1846. It became the V.A. of Guiyang in 1924 and an archdiocese in 1946. (M.E.P.)

2. Anlong – It was detached from the V.A. of Guizhou and from Guangxi as the P.A. of Langlong in 1922. It became the V.A. of Langlong in 1927 and a diocese in 1946. (M.E.P.)

3. Shiqian – It was detached from V.A. of Guiyang as an independent mission in 1937. (Missionaries of the Sacred Heart – Issoudun)

It covered 179,400 square kilometers and had 9,043,000 inhabitants, of whom 37,909 were Catholics and 13,715 were catechumens.

Twentieth Ecclesiastical Region: Yunnan

1. Kunming – It was detached from the V.A. of Sichuan as the V.A. of Yunnan in 1840. It was the V.A. of Yunnan, the capital, in 1930 and became an archdiocese in 1946. (M.E.P.)

2. Dali – Detached from V.A. of Yunnan as the independent mission of Dali, it became the P.A. of Dali in 1935. (Betharram Missionaries of the Sacred Heart)

3. Zhaotong – It was detached from the V.A. of Yunnan as an independent mission of Zhaotong in 1935. (Chinese Clergy)[89]

Statistics

The surface of China, properly speaking, was at that time 5,936,990 square kilometers. By adding the western part of Tibet from the 90th degree of longitude, the whole of Xinjiang and the northern part of Mongolia, the surface would exceed nine million square kilometers.

The population in 1941 was 447,725,000 inhabitants.

Catholics at that same time were 3,282,950.

Catechumens numbered 648,424.

If we take the *Nouvel Atlas des Missions* published in 1951 by J. Despont, we can find several minor differences, though actually not very important ones.

Number of archdioceses was 20, of which 3 were Chinese.

Number of dioceses was 81, of which 20 were Chinese.

89.　In *Qianshihui zai Hua chuanjiao shi*, Charles Wu Zongwen adds information on Taiwan's ecclesiastical status and various divisions after 1946 as well as a very brief history of the Vincentians on the island. See pp. 736-741. (AS) .

Number of apostolic prefectures and independent missions was 37, of which 5 were Chinese.

Total number of Ecclesiastical jurisdictions was 138.

The number of foreign and Chinese missionaries and religious men and women can be found in the general statistics.[90]

---

90.   The editors are unable to determine what source Ferreux used. (AS)

Appendix 5: Vincent Lebbe

"The Thunder that Sings in the Distance"

Jean-Paul Wiest[91]

"I will go to China and die a martyr's death" declared the eleven-year-old Belgian boy upon finishing reading the biography of the missionary martyr Jean-Gabriel Perboyre.[92] When Vincent Lebbe passed away in Chongqing in 1940, he had fulfilled the promise he had made to himself some fifty years earlier. His martyrdom however was not the quick and violent shedding of his blood at the hands of persecutors but the result of the many tribulations he endured over some forty years for courageously denouncing injustice in the church and the civil society of China. Today Vincent Lebbe (pronounced with the final "e" silent) is far from being a household name – even in Roman Catholic circles – and yet he is one of the foremost figures of modern Catholicism. Of all the things that could be said about Vincent Lebbe, his spirituality, his total identification with the Chinese people, his stand for justice, and his creativity in fostering new forms of apostolate constitute the most significant facets of his legacy.

Preparation for China

The future missionary to China was born on August 19, 1877, in Ghent, Belgium, and was baptized under the name of Frédéric. Freddy, as his family members called him, was the first born of seven children. His mother, an English convert of French descent, was a deeply spiritual woman who had considered a religious vocation. His father, a lawyer, possessed a keen sense of justice and integrity. Their generosity to the poor, their stand for justice, their kindness and concern for each other and for their children, and their steady practice of prayer reflected the

---

91. Prepared for the symposium on "Christianity and Modernity in Modern China: Comparative Perspectives," Hong Kong Baptist University, June 14–15, 2013.

92. Dom Beda Lebbe, O.S.B., "My Chinese Brother, A story of Self-immolation", *Good Counsel*, (Dublin: Quarterly Review of the Augustinian Fathers) January-March 1941.

strength of their inner convictions. Lebbe learned well from his parents and never relented. His dedication to the poor and the oppressed, his unflinching stand for justice, his abnegation and submission to God's will, his constant and serene joy that so impressed those who met him, all were strongly anchored in the education he received from his parents.

As already alluded to, the young Freddy Lebbe was impressed by the life of Jean-Gabriel Perboyre. A Vincentian missionary in Hubei, Perboyre was captured in 1838 and tortured for several months in a prison of Wuchang. Finally on Sept. 11, 1840, at the height of the first Opium War, he was strangled to death on a cross.[93] A the age of eleven on the day of his Christian confirmation, the young Lebbe took the name of Vincent to signify his resolution to emulate both St. Vincent de Paul, the seventeenth century Catholic priest who founded the religious congregation of the Vincentians, and Perboyre, the Vincentian missionary he admired so much.[94]

It is not surprising therefore to see him, in November 1895, journeying to Paris to enter St. Lazare, the Vincentian seminary.[95] Upon arriving at the seminary, Lebbe identified himself by his confirmation name. From then on, except to his immediate family, Westerners knew him as Vincent Lebbe. During his first two years of formation, the young novice gained a deep appreciation for the founder of the Vincentians and decided to emulate him. Vincent de Paul (1581–1660) was a priest who dedicated himself to serving the poor. From his namesake who used to say that "charity that does not express itself in action is a sham," Lebbe learned to stay in tune with his time, to identify problems, and to come up with solutions and remedies.[96] While still in the seminary Lebbe wrote:

To be effective, we have to stay in tune with our time, adapt to its customs, ideas and manners of expression.... We must enter in its movement

---

93. In 1996, Jean-Gabriel Perboyre was the first martyr on Chinese soil to be canonized by Pope John Paul II.

94. Beda Lebbe, *ibid.*

95. The official name of this Catholic religious community is La Congrégation de la Mission (The Congregation of the Mission). Founded in 1625 by St Vincent de Paul, it had as its first objective the home mission in the French countryside. Later overseas missionary work became increasingly important until, by the nineteenth century, it was the congregation's chief activity. Because one of their first the motherhouses in Paris was the former priory of Saint Lazare (Lazarus), the Vincentians in France are commonly called Lazarists and their seminary "Saint Lazare."

96. Paul Goffart and Albert Sohier, eds., *Lettres du Père Lebbe* (Tournai, Belgium: Casterman, 1960), February 7, 1900, p. 26.

not as counterforce, but rather to guide this world according to the light of faith and sound reason.[97]

On Chinese soil, Vincent Lebbe was to pay dearly for translating those brave words into brave deeds, which turned his superiors and many foreign missionaries against him.

At St. Lazare, Lebbe found in Anthony Cotta, an Egyptian seminarian a few years his senior, a kindred spirit who shared his ideals. Cotta, who possessed a deep appreciation for the writings of St. Paul, greatly contributed to the laying of a scriptural underpinning to Lebbe's missionary spirituality. The apostolic interests, which Perboyre had been the first to arouse, combined with the fire and zeal of St. Paul and the calm and deliberate dedication of St. Vincent de Paul to shape Lebbe's approach to missionary life. The bonds of friendship between Cotta and Lebbe grew stronger over the years and sustained them through the many tribulations they brought on themselves by their staunch advocacy of the Chinese against the elitist mentality prevailing in the missionary community.

After two years of novitiate, Lebbe began in October 1897 his study of philosophy. In the spring of 1898, Lebbe, then a first-year philosophy student, began his first serious and prolonged encounter with the mystery of the cross when his health started to deteriorate. Within two years, he became almost an invalid, suffering from terrible bouts of headaches and afflicted with an eye illness that rendered him at times unable to read. In September 1900, at the start of his second year of theology, his hopes of going to China seemed crushed when his superiors informed him that his sickly condition disqualified him for the missions. Instead, he had been slated to become a professor in one of their seminaries of Europe and North America and therefore would be sent to Rome to further his studies. Disappointed but abiding by what he considered to be the will of God, Lebbe let go of his original resolve. "Clinging to nothing, nothing, nothing except God," he traveled to the Vincentian College in Rome where he was told to go to lectures whenever he felt well enough. This was just a rehearsal for the many times in his life when he would again be forced to put aside plans or abandon promising missionary activities, for as sincere as they might have been, they were still too much his choice and could not become God's work until he had renounced them. This attitude of total self-denial would remain forever a cornerstone of his spirituality: a complete submission to the will of God like Jesus on the cross.[98]

---

97.   *Ibid.*, May 1, 1900, p. 30.

98.   *Ibid.*, December 25, 1899, pp. 23–24; August 26, 1931, p. 276.

On this first instance, it was indeed as if God took charge when Bishop Alphonse Favier, apostolic vicar of Beijing, and a Vincentian by training, came to Rome to report on the recent tragic events of the Boxer uprising. Lebbe informed the bishop of his desire to be a missioner in China despite his poor health. Favier was so moved by Lebbe's fiery enthusiasm that he convinced the Vincentian authorities in Paris to let the ailing seminarian accompany him to Beijing. In February 1901, only five months after he had been told to renounce his dream, Lebbe sailed together with Bishop Favier out of Marseilles for China on the *Ernest Simons*. Eager to learn Chinese, he spent the next two months learning the language from a missionary returning to China.

Becoming Chinese among the Chinese

The first letter from China we have from the hand of Father Lebbe was addressed to his youngest brother Robert. This letter, written at sea between Hong Kong and Shanghai is quite revealing because Lebbe signed for the first time with his Chinese name in Chinese characters "雷明遠" (Lei Ming Yuan) with following explication: "*Lei* (l'éclair [Lightning]), *Min* (brillant [bright]), *Yuan* (au loin [in the distance]), my Chinese name."[99] It is only some years later that his good friend Ying Lianzhi would give him the more poetical name of 雷鳴遠, (Lei Mingyuan) 'The Thunder That Sings in the Distance', the name by which he would be known for the rest of his life.

When Lebbe arrived in Beijing at the end of March 1901 the missionaries, for the most part, preached the Gospel with great zeal, loved their Christians and contributed to their welfare without much thought of self. Yet the psychological attitude towards the Chinese was radically different from the one displayed a few centuries earlier by Matteo Ricci and his companions. The industrial age had given Europe a sense of superiority and arrogance that most missionaries carried with them unconsciously. They looked down on the Chinese civilization and its people as inferior, odious, and full of corruption; they treated the Christians as children and kept the Chinese clergy in subordinate positions. They also relied heavily on the protection and interventions of the Western Powers, France in particular, to preach their Christian faith. To be fair, some missionaries

---

99. *Ibid.*, no date, p. 35. Most likely Bishop Favier or Father Joseph Ponzi, his language teacher on the ship, gave him the Chinese name of Lei Mingyuan. Lebbe had not yet realized that his name meant "thunder" rather than "lightning."

realized the harm being done but could not see a way out, taking refuge in the belief that God someday would take care of it. Lebbe was among the very few who, by their life-styles, words and deeds, dared to call for and bring about changes.[100]

What Vincent Lebbe saw in the streets of Beijing and experienced while studying at the Beijing seminary raised many questions in his mind as to whether the Church was on the right path and on the side of the Chinese people. He spoke freely of his feelings and ideas to his bishop who believed that these impressions, those of a generous-minded but 'inexperienced and naïve' young man, would become less strong with the passing of time. Lebbe's attitude raised quite a few eyebrows among the missionaries teaching at the seminary. He was accused of purposefully mixing socially with the Chinese students and employees and to prefer their company.[101]

When summer of 1901 arrived, the sickly newcomer had managed to complete his theological studies at the Vincentian seminary in Beijing. Yet he knew that Bishop Favier would not ordain him if his health did not show signs of improvement. The bishop decided to send him for two months to a rural parish to help the local priest. Traveling all over the countryside on foot and on horseback, the young Lebbe found great joy and comfort in his contact with the local Christians. This is precisely when his health began to improve. Realizing what was happening, the bishop decided to call the Belgian seminarian to the priesthood. Lebbe was ordained priest on October 28, 1901, on the feast of St. Jude, the patron saint of lost causes. For the rest of his life, Lebbe suffered occasional headaches but his eyes never bothered him again.[102]

In a letter to his other brother Adrien, Lebbe made it clear that he had cast all his life on the side of the Chinese so as to become one of them: "I am Chinese with all my heart, with all my soul and with all my strength. China is my lot and my country, and the Chinese are my brothers."[103] To signify this transformation, he signed with his Chinese name Lei Ming-yuan, and a thunder he would indeed be to the foreign missionary community of China.

---

100. Jacques Leclercq (George Lamb trans.), *Thunder in the Distance, the Life of Père Lebbe* (New York: Sheed & Ward, 1958), pp. 54–55, 62–63.

101. Goffart, *Lettres*, September 8 and 10, 1917, pp. 43–48. Levaux, *Le Père Lebbe, Apôtre de la Chine modern (1877–1940)* (Bruxelles and Paris: Éditions universitaires, 1948), p. 76.

102. Goffart, *Lettres*, August 31, 1901, p. 42.

103. *Ibid.*, July 13, 1901, p. 39.

Lebbe went on to being "all things to all men," becoming a Chinese among Chinese ("*Chinois avec les Chinois*"). From the time he arrived in China, he set himself apart from most missionaries by donning the cotton dress worn by Chinese priests and seminarians instead of the western style cassock. He even smoked a Chinese pipe, shaved his head, and wore a long Chinese pigtail until the Chinese Republic of 1912 abolished this custom imposed by the Manchu dynasty.[104]

The first five years after his ordination Lebbe was assigned to work in rural parishes. He moved among the ordinary people just like one of them, refusing to travel on horseback, in sedan chair or rickshaw as most other missionaries did. And yet Lebbe was not one to let go a practical means of transportation when he saw one that would greatly facilitate his ministry without appearing ostentatious. Whether it was just for a few minutes' ride in town or a long journey in the countryside, he and his bicycle became a familiar sight at a time when this mode of locomotion was still very rare in China. He was as hardy as could be: the days when he was haunted by fear of illness were long past.

Endowed with good memory and musical sense, he acquired a good command of the spoken language and eventually became one of the best foreign-born Chinese speakers of his time. With his sight restored, he developed the habit of setting time aside to study Chinese classics and to practice writing with a paintbrush.

"The Tientsin Method"

In 1905 Bishop Stanislas-François Jarlin, who upon the death of Bishop Favier had become vicar apostolic of Beijing, assigned Lebbe to the important post of Tianjin. Although he had been instructed to confine himself purely to religious activities, the missionary spent a lot of time befriending the city's Chinese authorities and paying attention to local customs and etiquette. He soon used his mastery of the language not only to perform traditional ministries of instructing catechumens and visiting the poor and the sick, but also to launch new ways of reaching Christians and non-Christians.

Lebbe liked to describe his multiple involvements as the "Tientsin method." It was based on two main principles: 1. Seizing every opportunity of meeting concerned people in every layer of society not just with a view to convert them to Christianity but also to bring about social progress

---

104. Leclercq, *Thunder*, pp. 73–74.

and national cohesion; 2. Enlisting Chinese Christians to become missionaries within their own community and place of work.

He emphasized by his own example the importance of reaching out to the non-Christians. In 1911, thanks to the generosity of a Chinese Christian, he opened a public lecture hall. This became a way of getting into the life of the city and bringing the church before the public. Lebbe teamed with some Chinese priests and educated laypersons, such as the well-known literary figure Ying Lianzhi, to give talks every evening. These halls, soon to number eight in the city, provided a forum for discussing social and moral contemporary issues in the light of the Gospel, and thereby for introducing Christ to the non-Christian Chinese.[105] Conversions, especially among intellectuals, multiplied at the rate of one hundred a month in some halls. Lebbe's popularity was such that, by 1914, he was invited to speak in the largest non-Catholic public hall in front of several thousand Chinese, including the city's high officials. The following year when Japan handed China a note containing twenty-one demands whose effects would have turned the country into a vassal state, Lebbe delivered several addresses on the love of one's own country. One series of lectures in particular was entitled *Jiuguo* 救國 [Save the Country]. The title attracted large audiences. After describing the patriotism that China needed as a country, Lebbe went on to present the Christian teachings about salvation as an affirmation and support for the civic duties of loving and protecting one's country. His message was so well received that some thirty thousand copies were sold on the streets.[106]

Lebbe also utilized his command of the language in pioneering the use of news media by the Catholic Church. In 1912, with the help of his friend and well-known literary figure, Vincent Ying Lianzhi, the editor of *Dagongbao* 大公報 *(Impartial Daily)*, he began publishing *Guang Yi Lu* 廣益錄, the first Chinese Catholic weekly. The paper contained not only news about Christian activities all over China, it also provided articles meant to enlighten Catholics about their duties and responsibilities as citizens of the new Chinese Republic. Its popularity was such that it was soon distributed in almost all the Catholic vicariates. Three years later, encouraged by the success of the *Guang Yi Lu*, Lebbe chose October 10th, the Chinese national

---

105. The missionaries referred to them as *salles de conférences* and in local newspapers they were introduced as 公教宣导所. *Annales de la Mission*, vol. 78, 1913: 279–280. Leclercq, *Thunder*, p. 115.

106. Leclercq, *Thunder*, p. 141. Goffart, *Lettres*, May 25, 1915, p. 99. Levaux, *Le Père Lebbe, Apôtre*, pp. 134–141.

day, to launch the first Chinese Catholic daily, entitled *Yi Shi Bao* 益世報 *(The Social Welfare)*. The newspaper was an instant success among the Chinese, Christians and non-Christians alike, because of the accuracy of its news and its independent outlook. Within three months, it became the leading daily in Northern China. At the end of the first year, the newspaper printed already more than 20,000. By 1916, the daily had not only two editions, one in Tianjin and one in Beijing, but also two versions, one popular and one for a more educated readership. Soon Lebbe added to them two weekly: the *Zhuribao* 主日報 was apologetic in nature; and the *Nübao* 女報 focused on women's issues.[107]

The lecture halls and the Catholic newspapers were only two among the many ways to foster lay apostolate. Lebbe's personal contacts with non-Christians wishing to assist him and the arrival in 1909 of Austrian Father Francis Selinka who organized an *Association for the Propagation of the Faith* were the point of inception for a *Catholic Action* movement. The *Catholic Action,* formally established in 1911, rapidly became a nationwide movement. The first major congress took place in Tianjin in 1914 under the presidency of Father Lebbe.[108]

On the social front, Lebbe played also a key role in the formation of a Red Cross committee for the city of Tianjin. In 1910 he pledged to raise 1,000 Chinese dollars from his friends, which he indeed did successfully. It might well have been the missionary's first stunt that soon turned him into some kind of a celebrity on the city. This particular one got the ball rolling and donations poured in. Subsequently Lebbe was able to enlist wealthy Tianjin Christians and non-Christians in a variety of social action committees for building a hospital, providing relief for victims of a plague and flooding, and resisting Japan's Twenty-One Demands.[109] Through Ying Lianzhi he befriended prominent Catholic educator Ma Xiangbo and supported their drive to launch a Catholic university. Their combined efforts were finally rewarded with the founding of Fujen University in 1925.[110]

---

107. Leclercq, *Thunder,* pp. 116–121 Goffart, *Lettres,* December 22, 1915, p. 100 ; July 19, 1916, p. 108; August 21, 1916, p. 111. Levaux, *Le Père Lebbe, Apôtre,* pp. 141–145.

108. Leclercq, *Thunder,* pp. 112–113. The first national Catholic Action congress was held on October 1914 congress in the Canton Club situated in the heart of the Chinese part of Tianjin. Levaux, *Le Père Lebbe, Apôtre,* pp. 146–147.

109. *Bulletin de la Jeunesse catholique chinoise,* Associatio Catholica Juventutis Sinensis, May 1931: 104–106. Goffart, *Lettres,* 22 December 1915, p. 100.

110. Goffart, *Lettres,* September 1, 1912, p. 92.

Passion for Justice

From childhood, Lebbe strived to live up to the words of the Sermon on the Mount. Among all the beatitudes, *Blessed are those who are persecuted for upholding justice* (Mt. 5,10) is the one that first comes to mind when considering his missionary career:

I would be ready to die rather than go on living simply neutral, not daring to call good and evil what they are, not being able to be wholeheartedly on the side of the oppressed, even if I were the only person of my kind in the world, simply to give an example of Christian indignation.[111]

For denouncing all sorts of injustices, Lebbe endured the pains of isolation and misunderstanding, ostracism and exile. In fact, the word justice and its synonyms are the terms appearing most frequently in his correspondence. He was especially relentless in saying that as long as foreigners remained in control the Catholic Church in China would never prosper. To become Chinese, the Church had to have its own Chinese leadership. "China to the Chinese and the Chinese to Christ" was one of his favorite slogans.

What made his stand for justice especially painful for Lebbe was that, for the most part, it opposed or contradicted the prevalent attitudes of the missionary community concerning Chinese patriotism, the French protectorate, and the native clergy. Lebbe was profoundly influenced by French Canon Léon Joly book's *Le Christianisme et l'Extrême Orient* (Christianity and the Far East).[112] This critical analysis of missionary history denounced the unfortunate collaboration between mission and politics, the inadequate promotion of the Chinese clergy, and the failure to consecrate Chinese bishops. At the time the publication was severely criticized by several Catholic scholars in Europe and bishops and missionaries in China as one-sided and full of exaggerations and generalizations.[113] But for Lebbe the book came as a confirmation. In order to bring about a Chinese episcopacy the Holy See ought to be directly represented in China and no longer represented via the intermediary of the French Protectorate.

During his first sixteen years in China, Lebbe was often reprimanded by his superiors for treating the Chinese clergy as equals and was urged to give up what they called his "utopistic ideas" of a new China and a Chinese

---

111. ·Goffart, *Lettres*, September 20, 1939, p. 307.

112. Léon Joly, *Le Christianisme et l'Extrême-Orient* (Paris: Lethielleux, 1907); see also, Léon Joly, *Tribulation d'un vieux chanoine* (Paris: Lethielleux, 1908).

113. For a study of this polemical exchange see Maurice Cheza " Le Chanoine Joly (1847–1909) et la méthodologie missionnaire", Ph.D diss., Catholic University of Louvain, Faculty of Theology, 1963.

church. They did not like his support of Chinese patriotism, which they considered a dangerous and disruptive movement:

What my superiors cannot forgive me is my belief that if we are to bring salvation to the Chinese we must, especially today, not only love them but love China too, just as anyone loves his or her country – as a Frenchman loves France.... What they find even less forgivable is my belief that the protectorate is harmful to China and the Church and to have said so.... And what perhaps they find most difficult of all to forgive is my belief that the establishment of a complete indigenous clergy is our first duty... and my saying that I would die happy if I could kiss the ring of the second bishop of China.[114]

The "Lao-Si-Kai affair" of 1915–1916 was the event that made the tension between him and his superiors boil over. Briefly said, in April 1912 the Holy See made the eastern section of the huge vicariate of Beijing into a new vicariate under the leadership of Bishop Paul Marie Dumond. The new bishop had constructed his cathedral on a piece of land purchased in a newly developing district of the city known as Lao-Si-Kai 老西開 that was adjacent to but not part of the French Concession. Trouble began in September 1915 when the French consul Henri Bourgeois built a road linking the concession to the cathedral and, with the collusion of church authorities, laid claim to the land along that road by levying taxes on Chinese shops and residences. The Beijing government together with the Tianjin Chinese municipal authorities and the local population protested vehemently against this illegal annexation of Chinese territory. In its first issue on October 1, 1915, the *Yi Shi Bao* issued an open letter to the consul exhorting him to reconsider his decision.[115] Bourgeois, on the contrary, made his intention even more blatant by planting along the road wooden posts affixed with French flags and posters in Chinese reading: French Road *Faguo gongdao* 法國公道. It was meant of course to mean "French Road" but the consul had not realized that it could also be read as "French Justice." What kind, of justice was that, ask sarcastically the Chinese people?

Bishop Dumond, pressured by the consul, summoned the clergy and the Catholic press to maintain strict neutrality in the affair. Meanwhile Chinese Christians kept asking Lebbe what to do, and he could not honestly say that the French consul was in the right. Finally, Lebbe decided to

---

114. Goffart, *Lettres*, September 18, 1917, pp. 153–154. When Lebbe wrote this letter, in 1917, the only Chinese bishop had been Lo Wenzao, ordained in 1685.

115. *Yishibao*, October 1, 1915. The initial editorial was continued in the next two issues of the newspaper, October 2 and 3.

appeal directly to the French Legation in Beijing through a personal letter to the French Minister Alexandre Conty. France, he wrote, is the guardian of justice and inalienable rights and the protector of the underdogs. Why then for the sake of a bit of earth, loose a whole heritage of esteem and affection? For the sake of the honor of France and the Church he begged the minister to intervene.[116]

Unfortunately, the letter backfired. The Minister's response was an angry note to the bishop whom he blamed for allowing such an "insolent and near traitorous" letter to be written by one of his priests. Rather than disobeying his bishop's directive to remain "neutral" in the question Lebbe, in June 1916, requested a new assignment. He was first sent to the neighboring diocese of Zhengding and then to Shaoxing, a mission nine hundred miles away from Tianjin.[117] For the rest of his life, Lebbe was to remain in the eyes of many foreign bishops and clergy a persona non grata.

A Chinese Episcopacy

Even from there Lebbe never stopped promoting what he believed was being of vital importance for Christianity to grow solid roots on Chinese soil. In September 1917, during his annual retreat, he wrote to Bishop Paul-Marie Reynaud, his superior in the diocese of Ningbo, a twenty-five page letter that detailed his ideas on patriotism, the Chinese clergy and the French protectorate.

There was, he wrote, an absolute necessity to acknowledge and encourage Chinese patriotism and to replace the "spiritual colonies" under foreign congregations by "living Churches" administered by a Chinese episcopacy. Stemming from these first two necessities was another urgent one, that of separating the Church from the French protectorate, which constituted "an obstacle to the elite's entering into the bosom of the Church".[118]

He summed up his all argumentation in a very forceful sentence:

> The time has come to found a living, fruitful, national Church, yeast in the dough, flesh of the people's flesh, blood of its blood, sanctified by Christ, the only Church that can endure, the Church with all the promise of the future in its womb.[119]

---

116. Goffart, *Lettres*, June 1916, pp. 101–103.

117. Leclercq, *Thunder*, pp. 152–153, 156, 158, 179.

118. Goffart, *Lettres*, September 18, 1917, pp. 137–158. Levaux, *Le Père Lebbe Apôtre*, pp. 195–209.

119. Leclercq, *Thunder*, p. 202.

In a lengthy postscript, Lebbe begged bishop Reynaud, as the dean of the bishops in China, to remedy the situation by taking action. Until then concluded Lebbe he would never allow himself to become a *canis mutus non valens latrare,* a mute dog unable to bark.[120]

Lebbe's letter remained unanswered. He seemed to have lost but, in fact, the tide had already turned in his favor and the day was approaching when his position would receive the endorsement of the Holy See. It began in the fall of 1916 with a small group of Chinese priests and foreign missionaries writing in support of Lebbe to the Vincentian superiors in Paris and to Cardinal Domenico Serafini, Prefect of Propaganda Fide in Rome. Among them was Anthony Cotta, Lebbe's long-time friend, who all along had sided with him in the Lao-Xi-Kai affair. The two maintained a steady correspondence and continuously exchanged viewpoints. By the end of that year, Cotta send to Serafini a long memorandum expounding the same arguments and reservations toward the state of the Catholic Church in China that Lebbe would develop a few months later in his letter to Bishop Reynaud.[121]

Another influential supporter of Lebbe was Bishop Gaston Vanneufville, a longtime friend and pen pal who was the Roman correspondent of the French Catholic newspaper *La Croix.* Vanneufville often forwarded the content of Lebbe's letters regarding the situation of the Church in China to the authorities of the College of Propaganda in Rome. Toward the end of 1918, Lebbe send him a lengthy document, which not only incorporated lengthy excerpts of Cotta's memorandum and his own letter to Reynaud but also went even further by profiling Chinese priests of great zeal and ability who could assume the new leadership.[122] This document as well as the previous letters from Cotta and like-minded Chinese priests and laymen caught the attention of Pope Benedict XV and Cardinal Willem van Rossum, Serafini's successor at the Propaganda Fide. The apostolic letter *Maximum Illud* released on November 30, 1919, was pregnant with the ideas, and at times, the exact words of Cotta's let-

---

120. Goffart, *Lettres,* September 18, 1917, p. 157.

121. Soetens, Claude, *Recueil des archives Vincent Lebbe: Pour l'Eglise chinoise, I. La visite apostolique des missions de Chine 1919-20* (Louvain-la-Neuve, Publications de la Faculté de Théologie. 1982), pp. 25–70. The front page of the letter is dated December 29, 1916 and the last page February 6, 1917. A typewritten copy in English of Cotta's memorandum to Cardinal Serafini is kept in the archives of the Maryknoll Society in Ossining, New York, U.S.A.

122. Part of the memorandum has been published in Soetens, *La visite* apostolique, pp. 92–140.

ter and Lebbe's memorandum. In addressing missionaries and mission heads, the pope condemned the doings of those who seemed more intent in "increasing the power of their own country rather than the kingdom of God," and deplored the absence of native priests in positions of leadership. Although never mentioned by name, the missionary church in China was the intended primary target of the letter. [123]

Both Cotta and Lebbe had to pay the price for being so outspoken and in 1920 were recalled to France by the Vincentian superior. From there Cotta went on to the United States where he joined the Maryknoll Society. Lebbe worked for seven years among Chinese students in Europe. [124]

The next pope, Pius XI, further disengaged the Catholic Church in China from France's control by creating, in 1922, a permanent apostolic legation in Beijing and sending Archbishop Celso Costantini to fill the position. Four years later, Pius XI decided the time had come for some local churches in mission territories to have their own leadership. This was the main thrust of his February encyclical *Rerum Ecclesiae*, and the June letter *Ab Ipsis Pontificatus Primordiis* made it clear that China was his primary target. [125] On October 28, 1926, the pope took the major step of ordaining six Chinese bishops in St. Peter Basilica in Rome:

> Odoric Cheng Hede for the prefecture apostolic of Puqi in Hubei
>
> Melchior Sun Dezhen for the prefecture apostolic of Lixian in Hebei
>
> Philip Zhao Huaiyi for the vicariate apostolic of Xuanhua in Hebei
>
> Aloysius Chen Guodi for the vicariate apostolic of Fenyang in Shanxi
>
> Joseph Hu Ruoshan for the vicariate apostolic of Taizhou in Zhejiang
>
> Simon Zhu Kaimin for the vicariate apostolic of Haimen in Jiangsu

---

123. *Acta Apostolicae Sedis* (Rome; Typis Polyglottis Vaticanis), December 1, 1919, pp. 445–446. Leclercq, *Thunder*, p. 227.

124. From April 1920 to February 1927, Lebbe devoted himself to serving hundreds of students for whom he found colleges, accommodation, and financial assistance. His actions led in 1922 to the creation of the Young Chinese Catholics Association (*Associatio Catholica Juventutis Sinensis* [A. C. J. S.]). Lebbe also took care to ensure that upon their return to China the Chinese graduates kept up their religious observances and found professional openings: many of his former students in Europe later became influential figures in their own country. This period of Lebbe's life deserves to be thoroughly researched.

125. Levaux, *Le Père Lebbe, Apôtre*, pp. 233–234, 274. *Digest of the Synodal Commission* (Peking), July 1928, p. 205. See also *Collectanea Commissionis Synodalis* (Peking), September-December 1943, p. 726.

Lebbe had on several occasions been asked to provide a list of possible candidates. Three, Zhao, Cheng and Sun, were among the six selected by the Holy See. Lebbe was present at the ceremony, which took place on the twenty-fifth anniversary of his own ordination.[126]

A few months later, Lebbe was on his way back to China to serve under newly ordained Bishop Sun Dezhen in the prefecture apostolic of Lixian (Anguo). His exile in Europe had lasted almost seven years but now Bishop Sun, the only [living] Vincentian among the new bishops, had invited him to work on his prefecture apostolic. Although the "decolonization" of the Chinese church was to remain a slow and difficult process, it had reached the point of no return.

Founder of Chinese Religious Congregations

His return to China gave rise to a campaign of opposition in certain missionary circles. The Vincentian religious authorities ordered him to stay away from Beijing and Tianjin. The Apostolic Delegate Costantini, however, thought otherwise. He allowed Lebbe to come to Beijing for business matters concerning the prefecture apostolic of Lixian. He also let him fulfill his duties in the same city as the newly appointed chaplain and secretary general of the *Catholic Universities Association,* an association created to regroup all Catholic students presently enrolled in Chinese universities as well as those returning from studies abroad. Costantini also sent Lebbe to Tianjin to reorganize the *Yi Shi Bao.* But above all, Lebbe devoted the greater part of his time to improving the methods of evangelizing the rural masses of his prefecture apostolic. With that goal in mind, he founded in 1928 two Chinese religious orders.

Indeed, for Lebbe, the establishment of a native hierarchy was just one of the many steps that needed to be taken to bring about a Catholic Church rooted in the culture and society of China. Responding to the call of *Rerum Ecclesiae* to consider the advantage of founding new religious congregations that would correspond better to the genius, character, and needs of different countries,[127] Lebbe founded the *Little Brothers of St. John the Baptist* in 1928 and the *Little Sisters of St. Theresa of the Child Jesus* in 1929. The first two monasteries were built in the western suburbs of Anguo, the larg-

---

126. Goffart, *Lettres,* September 9, 1920, pp. 182–185; December 20, 1920, p. 190; December 28, 1920, p. 194; May 11 and 21, 1926, pp. 239–240; and November 4, 1926. Levaux, *Le Père Lebbe, Apôtre,* pp. 233–234, 274. Leclercq, *Thunder,* pp. 225–226.

127. Levaux, *Le Père Lebbe, Apôtre,* pp. 344–345.

est city in the prefecture apostolic. These men and women, once trained according to a strict and austere way of life in the Trappist and Carmelite traditions, were sent in small groups to preach the Gospel while at the same time earning a living from the fruit of their hands. Their task and challenge were to contribute to the spiritual and social renovation of China. Lebbe led the way by the example of his own life of prayer and penance. On July 4, 1933, taking one more step toward his total assimilation with the Chinese, he left the Vincentian Congregation to join the Little Brothers of St. John the Baptist. On Christmas Day of the same year, after having received all the necessary dispensations from the Holy See, he took his solemn vows in the presence of Bishop Sun.[128]

Chinese Patriot

When the Japanese troops invaded Manchuria in September 1931, Lebbe led from Anguo a campaign to arouse patriotism.[129] Not only the campaign was successful but many townspeople also became interested in the Catholic faith and converted. As the war against Japanese invaders intensified, Lebbe embraced unreservedly China's cause and did not hesitate to demonstrate in deeds his patriotism as a Catholic Chinese citizen.[130] He and his Brothers began training teams of nurses and stretcher-bearers to be sent out on the battlefields to rescue the wounded. When the Japanese penetrated as far as Jehol, Father Lebbe placed himself at the disposal of the Chinese army together with 20 of his Brothers and 240 hurriedly trained stretcher-bearers, many of whom were Catholics. He also established a hospice in Beijing for recovering soldiers.[131]

This totally disinterested patriotism was the prelude to his final commitment during the Sino-Japanese war declared in July 1937. In September of that year, after having drawn up two spiritual testaments addressed to the Little Brothers and the Little Sisters, Lebbe left Anguo for the last time. Several dozens of Brothers and more than 200 locally recruited first-aid Catholics accompanied him. Under his direction, they assisted

---

128. *Ibid.*, pp. 336–337, 343, 353–354. Leclercq, *Thunder*, pp. 270–271. *En Chine il y a du nouveau—Le Père Lebbe nous parle* (Louvain: Association catholique de la jeunesse chinoise, & Paris: Librairie Peigues, 1930), pp. 175–179.

129. In 1929 Lixian Prefecture Apostolic was renamed Anguo Vicariate Apostolic.

130. In 1928, Lebbe had received the Chinese nationality.

131. Goffart, *Lettres*, 28 June 1933, pp. 283–290. « Le Christ en Chine » *La Revue Catholique des Idées et des Faits* (Bruxelles) March 20, 1934: pp. 6–8. Levaux, *Le Père Lebbe, Apôtre*, pp. 373–377.

the health service attached to the 12th division of the Third Army Corps under the command of General Tang Huaiyuan 唐淮源.[132] The Third Army Corps fought bitterly, but unsuccessfully, to prevent the Japanese army's invasion of Shanxi. Lebbe was responsible for organizing the evacuation of some 20,000 wounded as well as aid relief for countless of refugees. He even wrote that he had become aware of the Japanese offer of a reward to whomever would deliver him dead or alive.[133]

Lebbe suffered greatly from the neutrality of the Holy See, which, under Japanese pressure, forbade its Chinese missions to take sides in the war. This was all the more bitter because some missions made no secret of the fact that their sympathies lay with the invader. In his letter of February 1, 1938, he described the situation to Archbishop Mario Zanin, the apostolic delegate of the Holy See, warning him that if the Church did not change its stands, it could have dire consequences for the future of the Chinese Church.[134] He concluded one of the last letters we have from his hand with these words:

> I will rather die than remain neutral and not daring to call good and evil by their name, shedding all my blood on the side of the oppressed to show, even if I were the only one in this world, the Christian indignation against the devil of imperialism. I will never be a voiceless dog unable to bark! (written in Chinese: 我永遠不會是一直不回叫的啞巴狗!)[135]

During the Sino-Japanese war his motto was "To live and die with the wounded." He and his brothers dedicated themselves with total disregard for their own health and safety to helping others, inspiring much devotion and heroism in those who came into contact with them, so much so that General Tang Huaiyuan, a Buddhist, called Lebbe the "father" of his division and promoted him to the rank of colonel with a gold medal. As

---

132. Guomindang general killed in action in 1941 during the war against Japan.

133. Goffart, *Lettres*, Mai 23, 1938, p. 299; July 3, 1939, p. 301. See also « Nos Cloîtres dans la Tempête, » *SAM Magazine* No. 4, 1939 (III): pp. 8–11. Levaux, *Le Père Lebbe, Apôtre*, pp. 388–389, 394–395.

134. Goffart, *Lettres*, February 1, 1938, pp. 296–298.

135. *Ibid.*, September 20, 1939, p. 307. The quote in Chinese refers to a text in Prophet Isaiah, chapter 56, verse 10. He already used the same quote in a report he sent a year earlier (September 9, 1938) to Bishop Eugenio Massi, vicar apostolic of Hankou: see Levaux, *Le Père Lebbe, Apôtre*, p. 408. See also note 30: letter to Bishop Reynaud.

for his Brothers stretch-bearers he called them the country's best "spiritual column" and rewarded them with an "honor flag."[136]

In September 1938, Chiang Kaishek gave Father Lebbe the task of setting up and directing the Dudaotuan 督導團 or "Unit to Act as a Guide". This was an auxiliary corps whose role was to awaken patriotic awareness in the combat zones of Northern China, Shanxi in particular, and organize resistance behind enemy lines. With that goal in mind, the unit set up a number of social services such as schools and health and food distribution centers among villages affected by the war.[137]

In the fall of 1939, Lebbe moved with some members of his unit to south Hebei to organize the resistance there. The collaborative effort of the Chinese Nationalists and the Communists to fight against the Japanese had become very tenuous. The Communists had become more and more suspicious of people associated with Chiang Kaishek. On March 9, 1940, Lebbe, a number of Brothers, and several members of the Dudaotuan fell victim to these tensions and were taken prisoners by a unit of the Communist army under the command of General Liu Bocheng 劉伯承.[138]

By then, hardships had taken their toll of Lebbe. His body was that of an old man full of arthritis and feverish with malaria. During his six-week detention, his health deteriorated rapidly. As his internal organs began to fail, his face turned yellow and waxy, and he would joke, "Look, I'm finally yellow, I'm absolutely Chinese!"[139] At that point, Chiang Kaishek managed to obtain his liberation. After being initially cared for in Loyang, Father Lebbe was transported to Chongqing, the war capital of Free China, where he died on 24 June 1940, the feast day of St John the Baptist, patron saint of the Little Brothers, which was also the feast day of St Jean-Gabriel Perboyre, who had inspired him with a desire to be a missionary in China and devote his life to the Chinese people. He was buried in a nearby place called Geleshan and his tomb is still there hidden in the woods.

---

136. Goffart, *Lettres*, March 20, 1939, pp. 305–306. The medal is inscribed with the words: "We owe to him the life of our wounded".

137. *Ibid.*, November 19, 1938, p. 303; March 20, 1939, p. 305. Leclercq, *Thunder*, pp. 282–284, 298–299.

138. Leclercq, *Thunder*, pp. 311–314.

139. *Ibid.*, p. 318.

Conclusion

In 1931, a friend asked Lebbe what spiritual program he would recommend for missioners. Lebbe replied that there was only one program, the same for all Christians, and that it consisted in "actualizing the Gospel in one's own life without delay." Drawing on a spiritual experience that had begun long before he set foot on Chinese soil, he then explained that this program could be achieved only through total renunciation, true charity, and constant joy:

Total Renunciation, Caritas non ficta (Authentic Charity), Gaudete semper (Constant Joy).... Note well that all the power of the program resides in the three words underlined.... You will tell me that this is nothing very original, but I believe it is enough to enable you to become a saint.[140]

His distinct spirituality of total renunciation, authentic charity, and constant joy gave him the freedom of being bold and challenging to others while nonetheless remaining humble and obedient. He thereby achieved a high degree of effectiveness and persuasion.

His sensitivity to Chinese culture at least equaled if not surpassed that of Matteo Ricci. He completely identified with his chosen people, becoming one of them, a Chinese among Chinese. "To save the Chinese people, wrote Lebbe to Bishop Reynaud in 1927, we must not just love the Chinese but also China like one loves his country, like a Frenchman loves France."[141] A few months later (August 8, 1927), Lebbe was granted one of his dearest wishes to fully identify with the Chinese people when he received the Chinese nationality.

His stand against injustice and his actions to bring about changes made him, as he wrote, "shed my blood on many bramble bushes."[142] But they were the necessary claps of thunder that trigger the life-giving rain: they shook the foreign missionary community in China and began a process of renewal within the entire Catholic Church.

In the very long run, Lebbe paved the way for the revocation of the condemnation of the Chinese rites in 1939, the full recognition of a Chinese local Catholic church in 1946, and much more. Truly enough, Cardinal Léonard-Joseph Suenens, one of the major figures of the Vatican II coun-

---

140. Goffart, *Lettres*, August 26, 1931 and February 11, 1932, pp. 278–280.

141. *Ibid.*, September 18, 1917, pp. 153–154.

142. *Ibid.*, p. 157.

cil, described Lebbe as "the precursor of what were to become the major orientations of the council."[143]

The legacy of Vincent Lebbe is that of a life uncompromisingly dedicated to the growth of a truly Chinese Church grounded in China's own culture, society, and national institutions. Long before the word "inculturation" (本地化 or 本土化 in Chinese) was coined, his whole missionary life was a testimony to the spirit and the meaning encompassed by that word.

---

143. Vincent Thoreau, *Le tonnerre qui chante au loin* (Brussels, Belgium: Didier Hatier, 1990), p. 161.

Glossary

Archbishops

Tian, Gengxin, Thomas (田耕莘)
Yu, Bin, Paul (于斌)
Zhou, Jishi, Joseph (周濟世)

Bishops

Anouilh, Jean-Baptiste (董若翰)
Baldus, Henri (安若望)
Bray, Géraud (白振鐸)
Bruguière, Jules (包如略)
Chen, Qiming, Job (陳啟明)
Ciceri, Nicolas (徐道麟)
Clerc-Renaud, Jean-Louis (田烈諾)
Costantini, Celso Benigno (剛恒毅)
Danicourt, François-Xavier (達尼古)
Da Silva, Joseph (施利華)
Defebvre, André (戴福瑞)
Delaplace, Louis-Gabriel (田家壁)
Della Chiesa, Antonio (伊大仁)
Deymier, Georges (梅占魁)
Dumond, Paul (杜保祿)
Fabrègues, Joseph (富成功)
Fan, Xue'an, Joseph (范學菴)
Fatiguet, Louis (樊體愛)
Ferrant, Paul (郎守信)
Geurts, François (武志中)
Guébriant, Jean-Baptiste de (光若翰)
Guierry, Edmond (蘇鳳文)
Gouvea, Alexandre de (湯士選)
Hu, Ruoshan, Joseph (胡若山)
Jandard, André (賀安德)
Jarlin, Stanislas (林懋得)

Krause, Ignatius (葛樂才)
La Motte-Lambert, Pierre de (郎)
Laribe, Bernard (和廣德)
Lavaissière, Pierre (石伯祿)
Lebouille, Eugène (劉士杰)
Lyonne, Artus de (梁)
Maillard de Tournon, Charles Thomas (多羅)
Misner, Paul (高其志)
Montaigne, Paul (滿德貽)
Mouly, Joseph-Martial (孟振生)
Mullener, Johannes (穆天尺)
O'Shea, John (和若望)
Quinn, Charles (光一辛)
Rameaux, Alexis (穆導沅)
Reynaud, Paul (趙保祿)
Riberi, Antonio
Rouger, Adrien (王吾伯)
Schraven, François (文致和)
Sheehan, Edward (徐安慶)
Sun, Dezhen, Melchior (孫德楨)
Tagliabue, François (戴濟世)
Vic, Casimir (和安當)
Vienne de Hautefeuille, Jean de (文貴賓)
Wang, Zengyi, Jean-Baptiste (王增義)

Persons

Anot, Antoine (羅安當)
Appiani, Louis-Antoine (畢天祥)
Aroud, Cyprien (馮烈鴻)
Canduglia, Antoine (江都烈)
Chen, Aosi, Augustin (陳奧斯定)
Chen, Madou, Matthieu (陳瑪竇)
Chevrier, Claude-Marie (謝福音)
Chevrier, Louis (謝鳳來),
Clet, François-Régis (劉方濟)
Coqset, Jules-Auguste (顧其衛)

Cotta, Raymond (湯作霖)
David, Armand (譚微道)
Denis, André-Alexandre (狄德緵) Brother
Desrumaux, François-Xavier (羅德芳)
Fan, Joseph (范若瑟) Brother
Faveau, Paul-Albert (田法服),
Ferreira (費奇規) Brother
Fu, Dao'an, Vincent (傅道安)
Gabet, Joseph (秦若瑟)
Geerts, Antoine (艾德思) Brother
Ghislain, Jean-Joseph (吉德明)
Guilloux, Claude (劉克明)
Hanna, Robert (韓納慶)
Herrijgers, Jan (和振華)
Hu, Ruose, Joseph (胡若瑟)
Huysmans, Jacques (于惠民)
Ibarruthy, Bernard (伊伯鐸)
Jin, Madou, Matthieu (金瑪竇)
Jules-André (安德肋) Brother
Lamiot, Louis (南彌得)
Lebbe, Vincent (雷鳴遠)
Li, Ande, André (李安德)
Li, Rulin, Barthélémy (李儒林)
Li, Zhizao, Léon (李之藻)
Liu, Yonghe, François (劉永和)
Luo, Grégoire (羅文藻)
Maes, Auguste (梅士吉) Brother
Marco, Louis (馬類思) Brother
Marty, Joseph (馬若瑟) Brother
Mustel, Charles (方嘉祿)
Paris, Charles (巴茂正) Brother
Pedrini, Teodorico (得理格)
Pénen, Jean-Aristide (裴若望) Brother
Pesné, Augustin (李思定)
Prinz, Wladislas (白來福) Brother
Qiu, Ruose, Joseph (邱若瑟)

Qu Taisu (瞿太素)
Ricci, Matteo (利瑪竇)
Sarthou, Hippolyte (都士良)
Shen, Fangji, François (沈方濟)
Shen, Que (沈㴫)
Song, Baolu, Paul (宋保祿)
Su, Baolu, Paul (蘇保祿)
Szuniewicz, Wenceslas (宣尉仁)
Tichit, Hippolyte (狄俊儀)
Verbist, Theophiel (南懷仁)
Von Arx, Henri (鳳鳴善)
Wang, Baolu, Paul (王保祿) Brother
Wang, Datu, Thaddée (王達徒)
Wang, Renhao, Joseph (王仁浩)
Wang, Wenlu, Philomena (王雯祿) Sister
Wu, Zongwen, Charles (吳宗文)
Xu, Guangqi, Paul (徐光啟)
Xu, Ruowang, Joseph (許若望)
Xu, Side, Etienne (徐德望)
Yang, Ande, André (楊安德)
Yuan, Dao'an, Laurent (遠道安)
Zhang, André (張德安)
Zhang, Runbo, Joseph (張潤波)
Zhang, Ruwen, Jouventin (張儒文)
Zhang, Shushi, Louis (張淑世)
Zhao, Jinhua, Alphonse (趙錦華)
Zhao, Madu, Mathieu (趙瑪竇)
Zhao, Huaiyi, Philippe (趙懷義)
Zhou, Yage, Jacques (周雅各)
Zhu, Shengming, Jean-Baptiste (朱生明) Brother
Zou, Huanzhang, Augustin (鄒煥章)

Religious Communities, Organizations

Augustinians (奧斯定會)
Congregation of the Immaculate Heart of Mary, Scheutists (聖母聖心會)
Congregation of the Mission, Vincentians (遣使會)

Daughters of Charity (仁愛修女會)
Franciscan Sisters of Mary (方濟各傳教修女會)
Franciscans (方濟各會)
Legion of Mary (聖母軍)
Marist Brothers (聖母修士會)
Marist Brothers, Heishanhu (黑山戶聖母昆仲會修士)
Paris, Society of the Foreign Missions of (巴黎外方傳教會)
Sisters of Saint Joseph (Josephines) (若瑟會修女)
Society of Jesus, Jesuits (耶穌會)
Society of Saint Paul (聖保祿修士會)
Society of the Divine Word (Steyl) (聖言會)
Virgins of Purgatory (浙江的拯靈會修女)

Places

Anjiazhuang (安家莊)
Baishikou (白石口)
Beiwangli (北王力)
Beizhuang (北莊)
Chala (Zhalan) (柵欄)
Chayuangou (茶園溝)
Chuzhou (處州)
Donglü (東閭)
Donglü Pilgrimage Site for Our Lady (東閭朝聖地)
Duanjiazhuang (段家莊)
Fuzhou (撫州)
Ganzhou (贛州)
Guanyintang (觀音堂)
Gucheng (谷城)
Hongdong (洪洞)
Jianchang (建昌)
Jiangjiazhuang (姜家莊)
Jiujiang (九江)
Julu (鉅鹿)
Laoxikai (老西開)
Linqing (臨清)
Liujiazhuang (劉家莊)

Quanzhou (泉州)
Quzhou (衢州)
Taizhou (台州)
Wanghailou (望海樓)
Wenzhou (溫州)
Wuchang (武昌)
Xiangyang (襄陽府)
Xiaodonggou (小通溝)
Xiaoguangyang (小廣揚)
Xiaoyingli (小營李)
Xiezhuang (謝莊)
Xiwangli (西王力)
Xiwanzi (西灣子)
Xuanhua (宣化)
Xuanwu Gate (宣武門)
Xujiazhuang (宿家莊)
Yangguxian (陽穀縣)
Yangjiaping, Our Lady of Consolation (楊家坪聖母隱修會)
Yangjiaping, Trappist Monastery (楊家坪苦修院)
Yangguqu (陽穀區)
Yongjiachang (永嘉場)
Yongning (永寧)
Zhangjiakou (張家口)
Zhangjiazhuang (張家莊)
Zhangqiuzhen (張秋鎮)
Zhangzhuang (張莊)
Zhaoqing (肇慶)
Zhaoxian (趙縣)
Zhaozhou (趙州)
Zhengding (正定)
Zhengding Trappist Monastery (正定熙都隱修會)
Zhengfusi (正福寺)
Zhoushan Islands (舟山群島)
Zhoushi (螯室)
Zikawei (徐家匯, Xujiahui)

New City Press

New City Press is one of more than 20 publishing houses sponsored by the Focolare, a movement founded by Chiara Lubich to help bring about the realization of Jesus' prayer: "That all may be one" (John 17:21). In view of that goal, New City Press publishes books and resources that enrich the lives of people and help all to strive toward the unity of the entire human family. We are a member of the Association of Catholic Publishers.

www.newcitypress.com
202 Comforter Blvd.
Hyde Park, New York

Periodicals
Living City Magazine
www.livingcitymagazine.com

Scan to join our mailing list
for discounts and promotions
or go to www.newcitypress.com
and click on "join our email list."